THE COMPLETE

ROCK
CLIMBER

THE COMPLETE
ROCK
CLIMBER

MALCOLM CREASEY

WITH NIGEL SHEPHERD, NICK BANKS,
NEIL GRESHAM AND RAY WOOD

LORENZ BOOKS

CONTENTS

INTRODUCTION   6–7

This edition is published by Lorenz Books

Lorenz Books is an imprint of Anness Publishing Ltd
Hermes House, 88–89 Blackfriars Road,
London SE1 8HA
tel. 020 7401 2077; fax 020 7633 9499
www.lorenzbooks.com; info@anness.com

© Anness Publishing Ltd 1999, 2003

This edition distributed in the UK by Aurum Press
Ltd, 25 Bedford Avenue, London WC1B 3AT;
tel. 020 7637 3225; fax 020 7580 2469

This edition distributed in the USA and Canada by
National Book Network,
4720 Boston Way, Lanham, MD 20706;
tel. 301 459 3366; fax 301 459 1705;
www.nbnbooks.com

This edition distributed in Australia by Pan Macmillan Australia,
Level 18, St Martins Tower, 31 Market St, Sydney, NSW 2000;
tel. 1300 135 113; fax 1300 135 103;
customer.service@macmillan.com.au

This edition distributed in New Zealand by David Bateman
Ltd, 30 Tarndale Grove, Off Bush Road, Albany, Auckland; tel.
(09) 415 7664; fax (09) 415 8892

A CIP catalogue record for this book is available from the
British Library.

Publisher: JOANNA LORENZ
Senior Editorial Manager: JUDITH SIMONS
Consultant and Project Editor: NEIL CHAMPION
US Consultant: BOB DURAND
Designer: LISA TAI
Location Photographer: RAY WOOD
Studio Photographer: MARK DUNCALF
Illustrator: GEORGE MANLEY
Production Controller: ANN CHILDERS
Editorial Reader: RICHARD MCGINLAY

10 9 8 7 6 5 4 3 2 1

The authors and publisher wish to stress that they strongly
advise the use of a helmet in all climbing situations.
However, some of the photographs in this book show
people climbing without one. Similarly, some
photographs show instances of people a long way above
the ground without a rope and harness. There are no laws
or regulations governing the sport (except at indoor walls
and on instructional courses); climbing and
mountaineering are all about self-reliance and taking
responsibility for your own decisions and actions.

INTRODUCTION

Rock climbing today is a complex sport, complete with its own vocabulary and equipment that have come about over decades of experimentation. It has for many years been one of the fastest growing leisure activities, involving millions of people world-wide. From its relatively simple beginnings in Victorian Britain and Europe, it has evolved into a vast game with many facets, defying easy definition and categorization. Around it there has developed a mass of special terms describing particular aspects of the sport (bouldering, soloing, sport climbing, traditional climbing, competition climbing, and so on); pieces of equipment (harness, karabiner, quickdraws, belay devices, rock shoes); moves (dyno, Egyptian, layback, mantleshelf); and particular holds and how to use them (sloper, off-width, crimp, jam). Even the environment in which the sport takes place has changed and developed – from the original mountain gullies and ridges, to the harder rock walls and faces, the smaller outcrops of rock closer to cities, towns and roads, and finally to the totally modern phenomenon of the indoor climbing wall.

Rock climbing has always been a sport with few rules, and this remains the case today. It has also carried with it from its earliest days the element of risk. Personal safety at an indoor climbing wall is one thing, but out on the crags or in the mountains it is certainly

another. Personal judgement when weighing up the degree of risk involved in doing a particular climb is still an important aspect of being a competent rock climber. To some degree, these things set climbing apart from most other sports, which have set rules, generally carry far less objective risk, and do not exact such a high payment for poor judgement and decision making.

There are many skills to be learned before anyone can claim to be a confident and competent all-round rock climber. These encompass the physical, technical and mental strengths that the sport draws on. The process of gaining new skills in each of these areas never stops. That is one of the great things about the climbing game. Even a highly experienced professional mountain guide cannot claim to know it all! But above all, the sport should bring enjoyment and fulfilment to those who practise it. Each day on the rock should bring a little more fun, an opportunity to learn new skills, and a good reason to explore unknown territory, either close at hand or far away. The challenges that you may choose to accept are always personal ones – they relate to your physical ability and to your own level of risk acceptance. At whatever level you choose to climb, this book will provide you with the essential knowledge to apply safe practice and to gain that all-important experience in this multi-faceted sport.

Above and opposite: *These are just two facets of rock climbing today, the indoor environment differing considerably in both physical and mental approach from the outdoor one.*

1

A HISTORY OF CLIMBING

To understand the modern sport of rock climbing, you need first to have some idea of its history and development. Rock climbing has not always existed as an independent pastime – it has grown out of the greater game of mountaineering, which itself has been part of human culture for thousands of years. Early hunters and traders have left evidence of their passage through the mountains and passes all over the world. They developed rudimentary mountaineering skills to cope with the steep ground, the rocky paths and scrambles, and the snow. They even developed special clothing to help them survive the severe cold, wind and rain that are part of mountain travel. A brief history of mountaineering will, therefore, deepen our understanding and appreciation of the sport.

Opposite: *To many rock climbers this is the ultimate challenge, where high alpine terrain has to be climbed quickly before bad weather turns it into a fight for survival. Others, who have no desire for the high mountains, can still enjoy the pleasures that rock climbing brings on less hazardous terrain far from the mountain environment.*

Explorers and scientists

I n recent times, scientists and geographers have scaled some of the easier heights in the world's remote places to help further their knowledge or fill in the blanks on their maps. Throughout the eighteenth and nineteenth centuries these hardy explorer-scientists discovered many of the world's great mountain ranges, passes and glaciers. But neither early hunter nor later scientist went where they did for the sake of climbing.

THE START OF ALPINISM

The shift in attitude to climbing came about through the British middle and upper classes, whose summer vacations in the Alps of Switzerland, Austria, France and Italy led to the development of alpinism, the sport of climbing high mountains. Those with the inclination and physical stamina took to the mountains with local men who acted as hired guides. One significant climb that is usually given as the start of the "golden age" of alpine climbing was the ascent of the Wetterhorn in 1854 by Sir Alfred Wills and his guides. Slowly over the following years all the high mountains

of the Alps were to be climbed. Probably the best known ascent was that of the Matterhorn by Edward Whymper and his party in 1865. Four members were killed while trying to descend the mountain, which instantly made the event infamous.

OPENING UP THE BRITISH HILLS

In Britain, people began to explore the hills of Wales, the Lake District and Scotland. This was initially done to provide training climbs for the more serious business of the alpine season. The Alpine Club had been formed in London in 1857 to cater to the needs of this growing sport and the class of men that enjoyed it. Many of its early members were involved with opening up the hills of Britain.

● CLIMBING NAPES NEEDLE

In 1886 W.P. Haskett Smith climbed the rocky pinnacle called Napes Needle on the flanks of Great Gable in the Lake District. It did not take him to the top of any hill or mountain. It was a pure rock climb, done for no other reason than to test himself against the challenge of climbing 20 m (65 ft) of sheer rock. This is often given as the date on which rock climbing in Britain, as distinct from mountain climbing, was born. The sport was never to look back. It took off throughout Europe and the rest of the world. From now on it could be treated as still part of the greater game of mountaineering, where climbing difficult rock might be included in an ascent of a mountain which also entailed climbing on snow and ice, as well as on gentler rocks. Or it could be carried out as an end in itself.

▽ The North Face of Ben Nevis in Scotland is over 600 m (2,000 ft) high and was the scene for many early developments for climbing in Britain. Ascents of the Northeast Buttress and Tower Ridge were done by the leading British climbers of the day in preparation for alpine vacations.

△ The Tre Cima di Lavarado in northern Italy, where the Italian climbers Comici and Cassin led many daring and innovative attempts in the 1930s. Ascents of the north face of the central tower (Cima Grande) and the left-hand skyline (Spigolo Giallo, Yellow Edge) were led by Eduardo Comici in 1933.

△ 1950s climbing equipment might include a wide-brimmed hat for equal effectiveness against wind and sun, but no harness, special footwear or running belays. In those days the leader didn't fall, at least not very often!

▽ A selection of early climbing equipment: a "rack" from the 1960s (left); some pitons, often referred to as "bongs" because of the sound they made while being driven into cracks (centre); and a pair of nailed boots from the 1950s (right).

PROGRESS AND WAR

By the turn of the century, active and forceful climbers had made increasingly daring ascents, notably in the limestone areas of Austria and northern Italy. Methods of belaying (anchoring the party to the rock face) were developing, which made these leaps forward possible. Progress slowed down significantly during and after World War I. Many of the adventurous spirits who participated in rock climbing were killed in the conflict, but by the late 1920s and early 1930s things had gathered momentum once again. The Italians Eduardo Comici and Ricardo Cassin carried out a string of magnificent ascents in Europe, particularly in the eastern regions of the Alps. Britain lagged behind at this stage but there were still some significant developments, mostly involving Colin Kirkus and John Menlove Edwards, who left a legacy of fine rock climbs in England and Wales. They were both from relatively ordinary backgrounds, as were many of the new breed of climber throughout Europe.

SOCIAL CHANGE

Social change forced progress following World War II. Europe changed from a 44-hour week to a 40-hour week, which helped usher in the golden age of rock climbing, particularly in Britain. The shorter working week gave men and women from the industrial cities more time in the outdoors. Advances in man-made materials, brought about before and during the war, had a direct impact on climbing. Light plimsolls or "vibrams" (rubber-soled boots) replaced nailed boots on the more difficult climbs and were a vast improvement. Nylon ropes, slings and karabiners made a big difference to safety. Greater availability meant greater protection and a rise in standards.

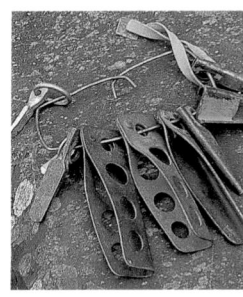

Commercialization

△ *Gravediggers,*
E8 (6c), North Wales
– a route which
symbolizes the
modern trend for
ascending hard,
traditionally
protected routes
using the type of
tactics that are
normally associated
with sport climbing.

While the spirit of fun and fair play that was generated by the early pioneers of rock climbing is still very much alive today, the rapid force of change is re-shaping the cutting edge of the sport. Gone is the light-hearted touch; the modern extreme climber is unashamedly competitive and dedicated. As standards rise and the level of commercialization in climbing increases, it is common practice for those at the top end to take their training and preparation as seriously as any Olympic athlete. The lure of lucrative sponsorship deals and competition prize money now make it possible for a few climbers to make a comfortable living from their sport. Far from being just a hobby, the addictiveness of climbing has a habit of turning into a full-blown obsession, even for those who operate at a more modest level. Heated debates rage over grades and ethical practices, often spilling over on to the pages of the climbing magazines.

SPECIALIZATION

Perhaps the most notable characteristic of modern climbing is the rate at which it has become increasingly specialized. It is now possible for two different people who would categorize themselves as rock climbers to be participating in very different sports. Just as the term "runner" says nothing about whether an individual is a sprinter or runs marathons, the term "rock climber" has become a generalization that is rendered almost obsolete. Whether it is sport climbing, big-wall aiding, free soloing, competitions or bold traditional climbing, the ethics are different, the climbing style is different and the attitudes towards training and preparation could not be more diverse.

WORLD GRADING SYSTEMS

There are now in excess of ten different grading systems used worldwide today to categorize the difficulty of different types of rock climbing. The most popular systems are:

● WORLD GRADING SYSTEM

Britain	USA	Australia	France	UIAA*
Difficult	5.3	11	2	II
Very Difficult	5.4	12	3	III
Severe (4a)**	5.5	12/13	4	IV/IV+
Hard Severe (4b)	5.6	13/14	5	V-
Very Severe (4c)	5.7	15	5/5+	V
Hard Very Severe (5a)	5.8/9	16/17	5+	VI-
E1*** (5b)	5.10a/b	18/19	6a/6a+	VI/VI+
E2 (5c)	5.10c/d	20/21	6b/6b+	VII-/VII
E3 (6a)	5.11a/b/c	22/23/24	6c/6c+/7a	VII+/VIII-

*   UIAA stands for Union Internationale des Associations d'Alpinistes.
**   The British technical grade is given in brackets. This shows how hard the hardest move on a climb will be.
***   E stands for Extreme!
The grades shown above are just a sample selection to illustrate equivalents. Grades in all countries are open-ended; they will continue to increase as long as people attempt harder climbs.

△ *Bouldering, while providing a great way to hone your skills for longer rock climbs, has now become a separate sport in its own right.*

△ *With the aid of bolt protection, sport routes provide the opportunity to focus on the physical and technical challenges of climbing.*

△ *Top roping on an indoor leading wall: a convenient way of staying in shape during the off-season or an independent sport if you are a competition climber.*

(for free climbing) French, British, German, USA, Australian, Norwegian; (for aid climbing) the "A" grades or USA big-wall grades; (for mountaineering-style rock routes) Alpine or UIAA; and (for bouldering) the "B" system, "V" system and Fontainebleau grades.

To the novice climber who is struggling to get to grips with grading in their own country, the thought of travelling abroad and having to tackle all these various systems can be daunting. Fortunately, most guidebooks offer user-friendly conversion tables to help you know what you are letting yourself in for.

As climbing becomes more advanced and specialized, grading systems have adapted and evolved to express the varying nature of the objective difficulties that may be encountered on a particular climb. For example, the early British system used a simple adjectival grade to make an overall assessment of the climb: Moderate (Mod), Difficult (Diff), Severe (S), Very Severe (VS), Extremely Severe (XS). When it was first developed, no climber could possibly have conceived the need for a grade any harder than XS, but it was soon realized that the Extremely Severe grades would need to be extended. They now range from E1 up to E10 at the time of writing. These British

descriptive grades would embrace all aspects of overall climbing difficulty, including strenuousness, seriousness, availability of protection, level of commitment required, presence of hazards such as loose rock, and so on. However, concurrent with the development of the "E" grades was the realization that this system was still incapable of differentiating between the overall difficulty of a climb and the technical difficulty of its hardest move.

◁ *Arriving at the crux of a climb – this is the hardest technical move or sequence on the pitch. Modern grading systems use a numerical grade to quantify the technical difficulty of the hardest move.*

Grade and ethical debates

By definition, grading is a subjective issue and differences between the heights, builds, climbing styles and opinions of individuals make it impossible to have an entirely standardized system. The main discrepancy that crops up time and again in grading debates is the breadth of each grade and the arbitrary points at which grades seem to overlap. For this reason, climbers are often reluctant to commit themselves and state a definitive grade for a particular route, preferring instead to take the safe option of saying, for example, "Maybe hard French 6c or easy 6c+". Grading first ascents can be especially difficult, as new routers must bear in mind that most routes clean up (by the removal of dirt, lichen and loose holds) after repeat traffic. In addition, the first ascentionist must cope with the increased psychological pressure from not knowing whether a climb is possible or how hard it will be. A combination of these factors may lead to some new routes being downgraded by as much as two or three grades after repeat ascents.

ETHICAL CONTROVERSIES

Inherently linked with the issue of grading is the complicated and highly contentious issue of the style in which an ascent is made. There is no disputing the fact that when rock climbing evolved as a break-off sport from mountaineering, the idea was to start at the bottom of a cliff and climb it to the top, placing all protection during the ascent and with no prior knowledge of the route. It seems clear and, indeed, if everyone adhered to this simple code there would be no need for ethical debate. The problem comes when individuals reach their own physical and mental limits in climbing using the traditional ethic, but still desire to push things further. At this point it always seems easier to bend the rules rather than spend years of training in an attempt to improve your skills further. Then, with the passage of time, as more and more climbers bend the rules in a similar manner, a new code of practice becomes accepted. It was an inevitable consequence that the use of pre-placed protection (including bolts), pre-inspection of climbs by abseil (rappel), and even top-rope rehearsal prior to the lead would become commonplace if harder routes were to be ascended. The open-minded will embrace both the old (on-sight) style and the new (pre-rehearsed) style.

▷ *Some climbers still bitterly dispute the arrival of so-called modern ethics, arguing that they merely serve to bring the climbs down to the level of the climber.*

▽ *An in situ hanger bolt – the answer to the safe future of climbing or the death of long-standing ethics and traditions?*

△ *Free soloing is arguably the purest form of climbing, though with the most serious consequences for failure.*

△ *A sea-cliff route that can only be reached by abseil (rappel) automatically carries with it a level of seriousness and commitment.*

△ *A traditional crag where the bolt-free ethic preserves the adventurous character of mountain rock climbing.*

● **CLIMBING TERMS**

Traditional climbing Climbing that puts emphasis on traditional values. This mainly centres on climbing a route using leader-placed protection, which is removed by the second climber, and on climbing without rehearsing or pre-inspecting the route.

Sport climbing A style of climbing that uses bolts as the main form of protection, allowing the climber to concentrate on technique and hard moves.

Big-wall climbing Climbing on big walls that usually take several days to complete. Special techniques, such as aid climbing, sack hauling, and sleeping on portaledges, have all been developed to support this style of climbing.

Aid climbing Climbing that is carried out using pegs (pitons), nuts and other equipment to directly help an ascent, as opposed to being used solely for protection. Equipment can be pulled on or stood in to assist ascent. Aid climbing is usually practised when time is short or where the route is too hard to be climbed in a purer style.

Free climbing Climbing that makes use of natural hand and foot holds only, using the rope and protection only as back-up. Contrast this with aid climbing, in which equipment is used to pull on or stand in to assist ascent.

Free soloing Climbing without ropes or any form of protection. A fall while soloing may be fatal.

Bouldering A form of soloing, but the climber reaches no greater height than they can reasonably safely fall from. It is most often carried out on boulders around 3m–5m (10ft–16ft) high.

Route preparation practices

△ Extreme, traditionally protected routes are still made by modern climbers today.

The question of which tactics are considered acceptable in the preparation of a new route by a first ascentionist is another highly contentious issue in climbing. If you take the standpoint that all routes should be attempted on-sight, then once again there is no need for discussion. Some incredible new lines have been climbed from the ground up, often with holds being brushed and loose rock being prized off while leading. However, the practicalities of new routing mean that most climbers will settle for a compromise and abseil (rappel) the line first to clean it and make an assessment of available protection. There are, of course, environmental implications to this procedure and excessive "gardening" may present a threat to rare flora or damage softer rocks if a hard brush is over-used. Worse still and now deemed as highly unacceptable is the use of a chisel or drill to improve or manufacture holds. Sadly, chipping has become a widespread practice in certain countries which have failed to appreciate their rock as a non-renewable resource. Climbing is still such a young sport and nobody is entitled to make the assumption that a piece of rock is unclimbable. Future generations of more talented climbers may succeed!

A SPORT WITHOUT RULES

The beauty of climbing has always been that it has no rules and yet it is this very fact that opens the floodgates to an endless list of ethical issues. Of course, it is up to the individual to take their own personal standpoint, provided it does not jeopardize the activities

◁ With a battery-powered cordless drill, expansion bolts can be placed in a matter of minutes on suitable rock.

of other climbers. While it is easy to be drawn into debates concerning those practices that are on the borderline of ethical acceptability, hopefully there is no further contention over the biggest ethical crimes.

A more complicated issue is whether glue or epoxy resins should be considered acceptable for the purpose of stabilizing loose rock. Some would argue that this is tolerable, provided that the hold is not improved and that the presence of the glue is highly discrete. Other nations have an almost free-for-all attitude to this type of issue and if a hold breaks off they simply bolt an artificial resin hold on in its place, perhaps smearing glue over it to make it less of an eyesore. If the distinction between indoor and outdoor climbing is to remain, these practices are to be condemned.

USING PEGS (PITONS) AND BOLTS

Another important issue faced by prospective new routers is whether to make use of various forms of fixed or in-situ protection, namely pegs (pitons) or bolts. The argument in favour of pegs is that their placement is still very much governed by the availability of natural cracks and that they cause less damage to the rock than bolts. However, any aid climber knows that the repeated placement and removal of pegs eventually causes hairline seams to be widened into finger cracks. The alternative is for them to be left in place, but here there is the risk that they will corrode away and become highly dangerous. For these reasons many modern free climbers will choose not to place pegs but climb without protection, creating a climb with a higher overall level of seriousness.

With regards to the placement of expansion bolts using either a battery-powered cordless

△ *An abseil (rappel) inspection of a climb will provide an abundance of information which may make a subsequent ascent less taxing.*

● STYLES OF ASCENT

On-sight The purest form of traditional ascent, where the climber starts from the bottom and climbs to the top in one push with no falls, placing all protection on the lead and with no prior knowledge of the intricacies of the climb.

Flash (beta flash) As with on-sight but using prior knowledge of moves, protection or both.

Ground-up (yo-yo) This is essentially a failed on-sight ascent where the climber falls, lowers to the ground and then either pulls the ropes through or, alternatively, top-ropes back up to their high point, either to complete the climb or repeat the same process until eventually the route succumbs.

Pre-inspection This ethic may be applied to traditional or sport climbs by making a prior abseil (rappel) inspection of a climb to clean or examine holds, or assess protection opportunities. If any moves are practised during the abseil then the ascent should be classified as a redpoint.

Redpoint A term developed for sport climbing to describe the process of repeatedly practising the moves of a climb (either by top-rope or repeated leader falls) before eventually completing it in one push, leading, clipping all protection and without falls.

Headpoint A term coined to describe the use of redpointing tactics to ascend bold, naturally protected climbs.

Day ascent The ethical ideal for multipitch free routes. It is common for those routes, which were first climbed with the use of fixed ropes over several days, to be attempted in a day by repeat ascentionists.

drill or a hand drill, this is perhaps the most over-scrutinized ethical issue in climbing. Countries such as France or Spain accept bolting universally, which means that the use of traditional forms of protection has all but died out, except in high mountainous regions. Countries such as Britain held out against the overwhelming pressure for bolting and then eventually succumbed to the use of bolts in certain designated areas. Other countries, such as the United States and Norway, have a policy of minimal bolting on certain crags, with cracklines tending to be climbed on natural protection and the blank faces between them often being equipped with bolts. Needless to say it is the type of rock that tends to have the greatest influence on the decision to use bolts. Smoother, less fractured rocks such as limestone offer far less in the way of natural protection and hence become obvious targets for bolting. Any climber who is uncertain of a national policy on fixed protection is advised to consult their governing associations (or relevant guidebooks) before they equip a new line.

◁ *Controversy over bolts: these old ring bolts have been chopped, being deemed out of place in an area that maintains a long tradition of adventure climbing.*

GETTING STARTED

There are many ways in which you can get started in the sport of rock climbing. Today, one of the most popular is to find an indoor climbing wall. Many towns and cities have climbing clubs, which will welcome new members. This is an ideal way to benefit from the experience of other members. Outdoor centres run courses on climbing and safe practice. Whichever route you choose, you will need to consider the equipment you buy and, once on the rock, your climbing technique. This chapter will help you in these first steps, pointing you in the direction of those all-important early experiences.

Opposite: *Rock climbing is an exciting and demanding sport. Developing good technique early on will stand anyone in good stead for future, harder climbs.*

Choosing clothing

Clothing should be chosen according to the environment in which you intend to climb. What you wear in winter on a heated indoor climbing wall might also be what you wear outside in summer on a hot day – shorts and a t-shirt. However, climbing outside carries an element of uncertainty not found indoors – that of the weather and its changeable nature. It is always wise to carry layers of clothing, providing warmth (fleece or wool), windproof protection and maybe even waterproof protection. Today there is an enormous choice of clothing, covering every conceivable situation and designed to fit all shapes and sizes. Most manufacturers offer key lines in both male and female designs. Consider carefully what you require your clothing for. That way, you will avoid wasting your money.

FABRICS

There are no rights and wrongs about what you should wear to climb in. Personal preference will influence you. However, some fabrics are better than others for different situations. For example, cotton is comfortable and absorbs sweat, but it is not hardwearing, does not dry quickly and does not keep you warm. You might choose it if you are climbing indoors. Man-made fabrics, such as polyester and

◁ It is important to dress for the occasion – and of course with some style! In hot climates, being cool and comfortable will enhance enjoyment.

▷ A breezy day by the sea or on a mountain crag may require full body cover, but be sure that what you wear is light and unrestrictive.

nylon, are hardwearing and dry quickly. Some wick sweat away from your skin. You might choose them when climbing outdoors. Fleece is a fine example of such a fabric and is available in many guises.

If you like tight-fitting clothes, make sure they stretch. Modern fabrics allow manufacturers to be inventive with design, style and variety. Lycra fabrics are perhaps the stretchiest of all; garments fit snugly around the body but do not restrict movement in any way. Lycra in itself is not hardwearing and is usually mixed with other fabrics to provide durability. Out on the crags, walls and boulders, clothing is subject to constant abrasion, which makes this an important consideration.

Close-fitting clothing, particularly fleece, can be quite clammy, especially on hot, sunny days or when you are working hard. It will feel uncomfortable and cause overheating, which saps valuable energy. A great many climbers prefer looser clothing.

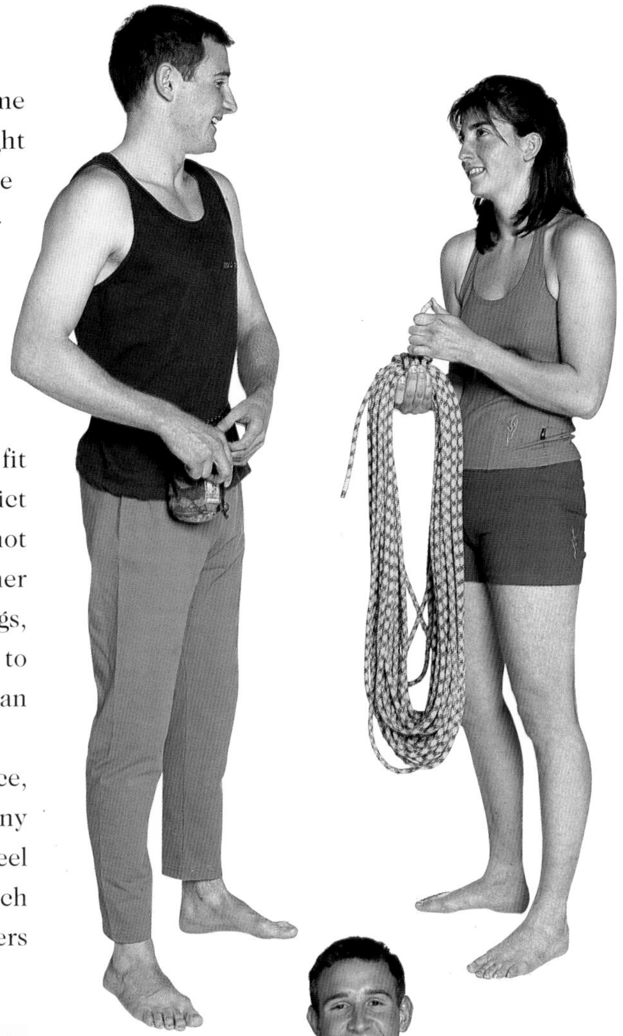

◁ *For indoor climbing or outside on warm sunny days, light clothing is perfectly adequate, though you'll certainly have to carry something warmer as well when outdoors.*

▽ *For warmer wear, if you choose the "baggy" look make sure that clothing doesn't obstruct gear handling. Stretch fleece wear is warm and snug-fitting for a more "sporty" look.*

● MOISTURE CONTROL

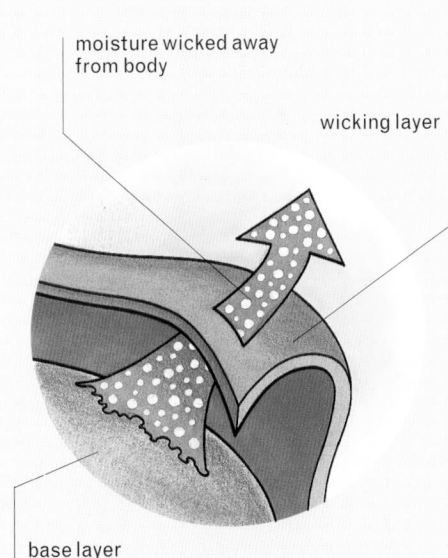

moisture wicked away from body

wicking layer

base layer

△ *During any exertion, the body gives off moisture in the form of sweat. It is important to get rid of this, to avoid your body over-cooling once you stop working. Man-made fibres do this by wicking moisture away from the skin.*

Choosing equipment

To begin climbing at its most basic level, that of bouldering (either indoors or out), you will need very few pieces of specialist equipment. To get the most out of the activity, you will need a pair of rock shoes and a chalk bag. You might also wish to wear a helmet when you start out on your climbing career. It is highly recommended that you do wear a helmet, but more experienced climbers will often choose not to. At the end of the day, it is a matter of personal preference, but there is no doubt that helmets have saved lives.

▷ *You can have plenty of fun with just a pair of rock shoes and a chalk bag. Equipment is expensive and to begin with you might seek to borrow from friends or to hire from professional outlets.*

ROCK SHOES

The choice of footwear depends entirely on your sphere of activity. If you choose to climb only on indoor walls and to boulder, a light and snug-fitting pair of slipper-style rock shoes is adequate. This type gives a high degree of sensitivity in feeling the holds on which you place your feet. This is advantageous to an experienced climber but the benefits may not be appreciated fully at a beginner level. Slipper-style shoes do not offer much in the way of support and protection for the feet, so if you intend to climb on more adventurous rock you will need to consider this factor and choose something more robust.

The sturdier and more supportive the shoe, the less sensitive it will be to standing on tiny edges or smearing holds. Fortunately, the greatest diversity of shoe design is found in the range of shoes intended for the widest application. As with clothing, not all styles or models will fit all shapes and sizes of feet. It is important to try on as many different shoes as you can. Even so, finding a shoe that is comfortable in the shop does not necessarily mean that it will be comfortable out on the crag. Climbing in hot conditions for hours at a time encourages

● LOOKING AFTER YOUR CLIMBING SHOES

Rock shoes are expensive. They will last longer and give better performance if you take a little time to look after them. Keep the soles clean by wiping them after use. This is especially important after using them outdoors, where grit, mud and sand can all stick to the rubber soles, detracting from their amazing friction properties. Always be sure to wipe them before setting off on a climb.

Rock shoes can be repaired by specialist companies once they start to wear out. This is done by replacing worn-out rands and toe caps, and also the sole, if necessary.

△ *A selection of footwear: two shoe styles, two boots and a slipper.*

feet to swell, and though shoes will stretch a little with use, they might become uncomfortably tight. Very painful feet are not usually conducive to pleasurable climbing experiences.

CHALK AND CHALK BAGS

The use of chalk to increase hand grip is widespread. Chalk absorbs moisture from the fingertips and allows the climber to hold on with greater confidence, which also means the climber endures that little bit longer. Chalk is available in block form and is broken into tiny pieces and carried on a waistband in a small pouch, called a chalk bag. This bag need only be big enough to get the fingers of one hand into at one time. Some indoor walls have banned the use of this type of chalk for reasons of health and cleanliness. Certainly if you fall upside down, a deluge of chalk dust is likely to fall on to your belayer and pollute the air. Chalk balls go some way to alleviating this problem. These are chalk-filled secure muslin (cheesecloth) bags that are simply kept in the chalk bag itself. When squeezed, chalk is released through small holes in the muslin. It is also possible to buy very large chalk bags intended for communal use.

CRASHMATS

If you get really serious about your bouldering you might want to consider acquiring a crashmat. There are a number of types available, some of which fold up into quite small packages and are easy to carry, yet still provide adequate cushioning.

▷ *All you need for sport climbing – shoes, harness, chalk bag, quickdraws and a rope.*

△ *A chalk bag and chalk ball.*

▷ *Bouldering is very much a social activity and though you may find that there will always be someone to "spot" you if you fall off, a crashmat is very reassuring if you are likely to land on your back.*

● HELMETS

There are many different types available commercially. Most are made from plastic or fibreglass, although some new designs have used the cycle helmet model and use very light polystyrene. Things to look out for are weight (most people prefer light helmets), durability (some designs will only take one knock and should then be retired), and fit. They are designed to take an impact from above (in the event of falling stones) and the sides. If a helmet does sustain a major impact, it should be replaced.

△ *A good all-purpose helmet.*

△ *An ill-fitting helmet.*

More equipment

△ *A simple and inexpensive adjustable harness is fine for starting out.*

△ *A well-padded harness for rock climbing. This will be comfortable and provide plenty of gear loops for equipment.*

△ *A fully adjustable harness is preferable for all-round climbing use, including winter and alpine mountaineering.*

Climbing beyond bouldering implies the use of more equipment. You will need a rope, harness, belay device, screwgate or locking karabiner, and some quickdraws. This equipment will enable you to start climbing at an indoor wall and on sport routes outside. However, many walls have quickdraws already in place in bolts on the routes for leading and ropes for bottom-roping. You may also be able to hire rock shoes, harnesses and anything else you require.

CHOOSING A HARNESS

More than any other item of gear, harnesses present the widest variety of design and style. This can make it difficult to decide on the most suitable type for your chosen style of climbing. If you climb only on indoor walls and outdoors on sport climbs that are protected by in situ bolts, you will have little need for anything more sophisticated than the simplest and lightest harness available. For comfort, it is better to opt for a harness with a fixed-size waist belt and padded leg loops. You will not need to carry heavy equipment on the harness, nor are you likely to require it to fit over bulky clothing. However, if you plan to climb on high mountain routes, you might like to consider a fully adjustable harness. This will enable you to fit it over whatever clothing you need to wear.

BELAY DEVICES

The belay device and karabiner that you choose are likely to be suitable for almost any climbing situation, either indoors or outdoors, so consider carefully what you buy and you will certainly save money at a later date. However, some climbing walls stipulate the type of device that should be used. In Britain

this is rarely the case, but there are many indoor venues in other countries that insist on a device that has a "fail-safe" mechanism such as the Petzl Gri-Gri. Proper training in the safe operation of whatever device you use is essential and it is quite possible that on a first visit to an indoor wall you will be asked to demonstrate your belaying skills prior to being permitted to climb.

KARABINERS

A belay device needs a screwgate or "locking" karabiner, usually a HMS (or pear-shaped) one. This allows the rope to run smoothly through a belay device and lessens the chance of a tangle occurring or the rope jamming. Snaplink karabiners are used in quickdraws for speedy clipping – the rope goes into the bent gate.

◁ *A belay device with screwgate or locking karabiner.*

◁ *The Gri-Gri is a belay device with a fail-safe mechanism.*

▽ *A few quickdraws will allow you to lead sport climbs.*

ROPES

Ropes come in two main strengths: full (or single) and half (or double). A full rope can be used on its own, whereas a half rope must be used in conjunction with another half rope. Full ropes have traditionally been 11 mm in thickness (although today this has been reduced to 9.8 mm), and half ropes 9 mm in thickness. In terms of length, you can buy standard 45 m (148 ft), 50 m (164 ft), 55 m (180 ft) and even 60 m (197 ft) ropes. Obviously, the thicker and longer a rope, the heavier it will be.

You can also buy ropes that have been treated to repel water. These are useful for climbing outdoors but not necessary if you only climb indoors. This treatment inevitably puts the price of the rope up.

It is important to read the accompanying manufacturer's safety notes when you buy your rope. They will give a recommended life-span (dependent on how often you use it), and how many heavy falls it could take (see The Fall Factor, page 135).

Ropes are expensive and you may not feel inclined to use your best climbing rope on a climbing wall. The chances are that you will spend a great deal of time at the wall attempting routes that are beyond your ability and consequently might take numerous, though short, falls on to the rope. The longevity of a rope reduces considerably the more frequently it is subjected to a fall. Even short falls will stretch a rope and eventually its ability to

absorb shock will diminish. The ends of the rope will also be subjected to considerably greater wear and tear than the middle part. If you visit climbing walls regularly, say three or four times a week, and you can afford to, it is a good idea to buy a rope that is designed to be used exclusively for this purpose. Manufacturers now produce short ropes specifically to meet this market demand. If you have an old rope that has been retired from more serious use, you could also consider cutting out the worn bits and using that. Be certain though that there is still sufficient life in the rope to justify its continued use.

△ *The accoutred climber. Buy what you need as you gain more experience. The rope is perhaps the single most expensive item of gear you will need but taking care of it will make it last for many years.*

● CROSS-SECTION OF ROPE

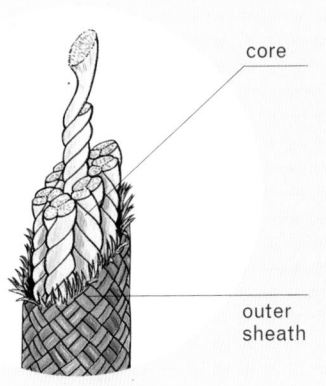

core

outer sheath

◁ *Modern ropes are dynamic – they stretch. This property absorbs the energy of a fall. The inner core provides the greatest contribution to strength and elasticity, with the sheath acting as a protective cover.*

△ *A rope bag is useful for keeping the rope clean and for ease of carrying.*

Why warm up?

THE MAIN MUSCLE GROUPS

FRONT VIEW OF MUSCLE GROUPS

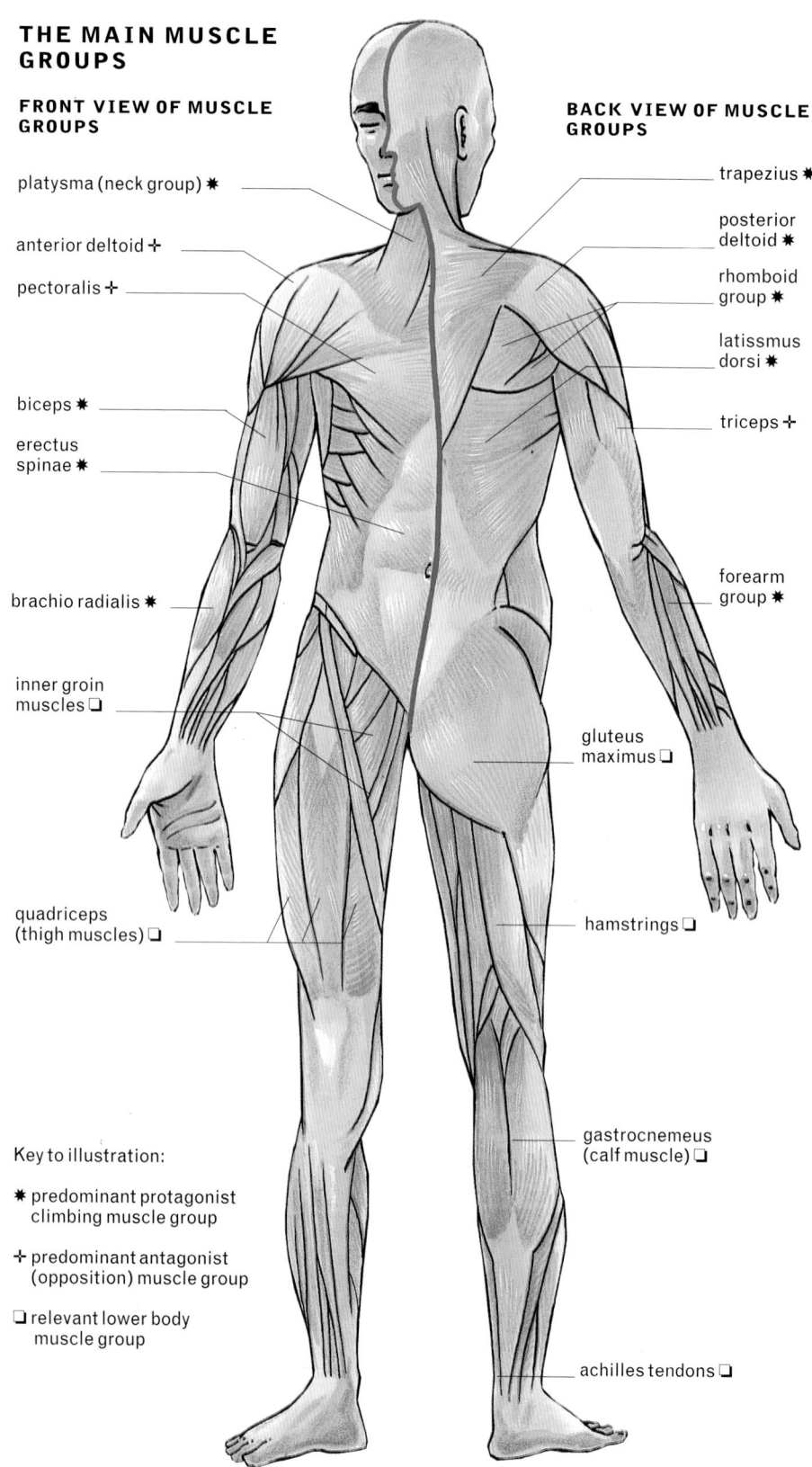

platysma (neck group) ✻

anterior deltoid ✛

pectoralis ✛

biceps ✻

erectus spinae ✻

brachio radialis ✻

inner groin muscles ❏

quadriceps (thigh muscles) ❏

BACK VIEW OF MUSCLE GROUPS

trapezius ✻

posterior deltoid ✻

rhomboid group ✻

latissmus dorsi ✻

triceps ✛

forearm group ✻

gluteus maximus ❏

hamstrings ❏

gastrocnemeus (calf muscle) ❏

achilles tendons ❏

Key to illustration:

✻ predominant protagonist climbing muscle group

✛ predominant antagonist (opposition) muscle group

❏ relevant lower body muscle group

Whether you are about to attempt your very first climb or compete in the final of a top international competition, the importance of warming up for climbing cannot be stressed enough. Most climbers are notoriously lazy when it comes to correct preparation practices; after all, if you don't take climbing that seriously, then why should you prepare for it as if it were an athletic sport? Climbing is one of the most punishing activities ever invented for joints and connective tissues, and yet many of its participants still seem to hold the belief that injury is something that only happens to other people. Equally surprising are the numbers who have suffered the odd tweaked tendon or muscle and yet completely fail to learn from their previous mistakes. Of course, there are other factors, aside from warming up, that will have some influence on your ability to avoid injury: the amount of rest you take between climbs or climbing days, your sleep patterns and your nutritional intake, to name but a few. But in the short term, the most important variable will be the effectiveness of your pre-climbing preparation routine.

IMPROVE YOUR CLIMBING

If the threat of injury is not a good enough incentive, then the other main reason to warm up is that it helps you to climb better. We all know how it feels to arrive at work having just fallen out of bed – mental and physical attunement take their time and you simply cannot expect your muscles to be able to pull their hardest or be smooth and co-ordinated if you

◁ *Climbing puts tremendous stress on muscles and joints. It is worth knowing a little about your anatomy to help avoid injury.*

△ Build up gradually before launching into steep, dynamic climbing.

△ Even on remote mountain crags, it pays to have a quick boulder around before commencing a longer, more committed climb.

◁ It may help your warm-up routine to have a few practice routes that you know well. Climbing them will indicate how in-tune and warmed-up you really are.

jump from a sedentary state straight into your hardest climb or boulder problem. A warm-up routine also gives you sufficient time to filter out the cluttered chaotic thoughts generated by your work or social schedule, and focus in on the task of climbing.

A SYSTEMATIC APPROACH

How many times at the crag or climbing wall have you seen people arrive looking as if they lack direction? Then while getting changed or chatting to a friend they will go through the motions of a warm-up by performing a few violent helicopter-style arm circles, yank their fingers backwards and forwards and then finish with a half-hearted bouncing touch of the toes? The irony is that some of the bizarre and extreme forms of so-called warm-up that you occasionally witness are potentially more damaging than climbing itself! It is very important to learn safe practices from the very start and to adopt a consistent approach to warming up every time you climb. After all, the warm-up is an ideal time to gauge how good you are feeling, and whether or not you have recovered from your previous climbing session. Climbers who are well in tune with their warm-up will use a series of benchmark exercises as a gauge for how hard they should push themselves throughout the remainder of the session proper. It is also worth taking the time to practise a few standard routine warm-up routes or problems at your regular climbing venues. These will also give clues as to how well you are performing on a particular day.

Progression

▽ Your warm-up will play a vital role in the outcome of a steep strenuous ascent such as this 8a sport climb.

The most important thing about a warm-up is that it must introduce increasing overload to the relevant climbing muscle groups in a gradual and controlled manner over a reasonable time period. To go "too hard too soon" is to ruin your warm-up. You will know when you have done this by the fact that you won't climb anything harder than your so-called warm-up route or boulder problem in the rest of the session. If you are at a crag that has no suitable easy routes and you are forced to warm up on something difficult, make yourself stop intermittently and take rests between individual moves (if a top rope or the protection permits) and treat the exercise as if you were warming up for bouldering. Although less desirable, this is far better than jumping straight on something hard and heading for the inevitable burn-out. If you are pushed for time, then you may be able to cut out certain less relevant parts of your warm-up routine. However, the progressive build-up of effort must always stay if you are to avoid injury, even if it means less climbing time as a result.

SPECIFICITY

Certain core elements of your warm-up must be consistent, while others should vary according to the specific type of climbing that you are about to do. It may sound obvious, but why perform lots of laborious leg stretches if you only plan to go on a steep bouldering wall or fingerboard board? However, if you are about to attempt a leg-contorting slab route you will need to put more time into calf, thigh and groin stretches. It is also vital to make your warm-up intensity-specific. Use easy boulder problems to warm up for bouldering or power-training sessions and use easy traverses, circuits or routes to prepare for longer endurance climbing.

THE FOUR-POINT WARM-UP GUIDE

This covers the core areas of a suggested warm-up routine for climbing. It is laid out in

△ *Jogging on the spot provides a good way of raising your pulse at the beginning of your warm-up session.*

▷ *Some light climbing, where careful attention is paid to form and control, should always precede more strenuous climbing.*

the order in which you should do them, to get the most out of your warm-up. The stages are:

① Pulse raiser
② General mobility
③ Specific stretching
④ Progressive climbing build-up

PULSE RAISER

If you are slogging up a steep hill to reach a distant mountain crag, then you can happily forget this first stage. But if you are stepping out of your car to the foot of a roadside sport climbing venue or a climbing wall, then you will need to do something to get your heart and lungs going before you attempt to do any stretching, let alone climbing. By raising your pulse for approximately 3–5 minutes, with a quick jog, skip or some on-the-spot style exercises, you will increase overall blood flow, warm the muscles and generally trigger your body into exercise mode. This vital part of the warm-up also serves to soften joint cartilage in preparation for the impacts of strenuous exercise.

GENERAL MOBILITY

Before you attempt to stretch, it pays to do some controlled circular movements. For example, both the shoulders and hips can be gently rotated to warm the joints up, and to get your muscles, tendons and joints used to working through a full range of motion. To save time, you can combine these with some finger clenches, either with or without the use of a wrist exerciser. Violent swinging movements are definitely out – especially when the spine is involved. Use a smooth "front-crawl"-style swimming action for your arms.

Upper body stretches

As an overall rule your core stretches, which should be common to every climbing session, are the fingers and forearms, elbow tendon insertions, shoulders and neck. For steep rock, pay particular attention to your back and sides, and for lower angled rock, make sure you go through your leg stretches.

FINGER STRETCHES

First perform some finger clenches, either with or without a grip exerciser. Then carefully work through each individual finger and thumb joint, stretching them both ways for approximately 6–8 seconds and up to three times each. Apply even, progressive pressure with no sharp tugging. You can maybe do this on the journey to the crag or wall to save time.

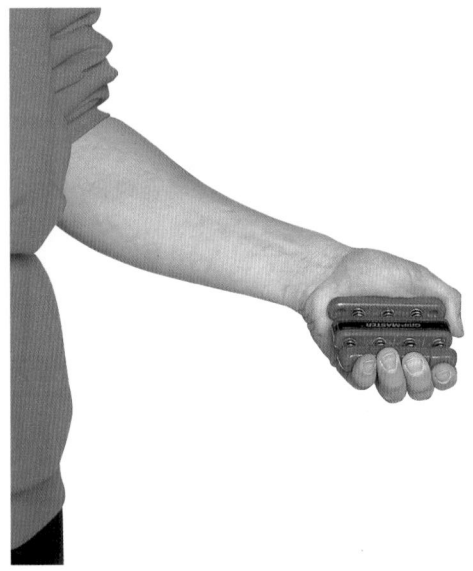

△ *Finger clenches with or without a grip exerciser will develop finger and overall hand strength.*

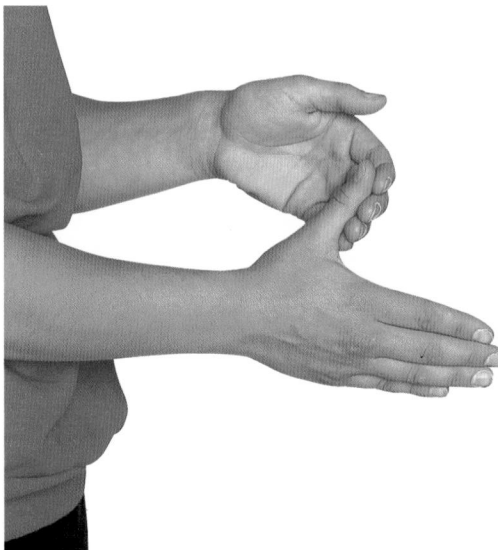

△ *The thumb stretch.*

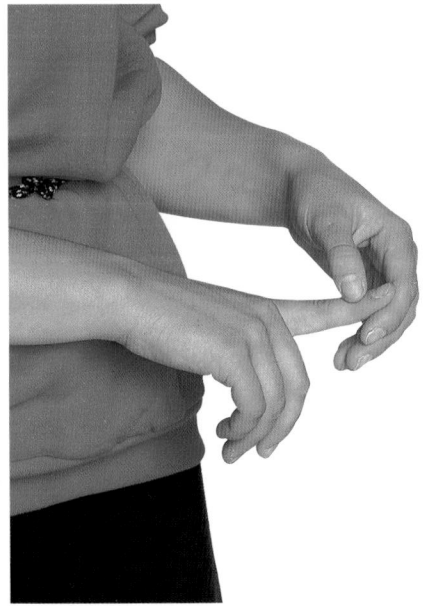

△ *First joint finger stretch.*

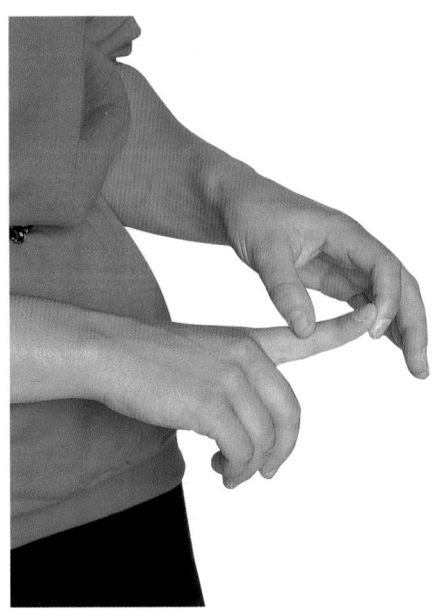

△ *Second joint finger stretch.*

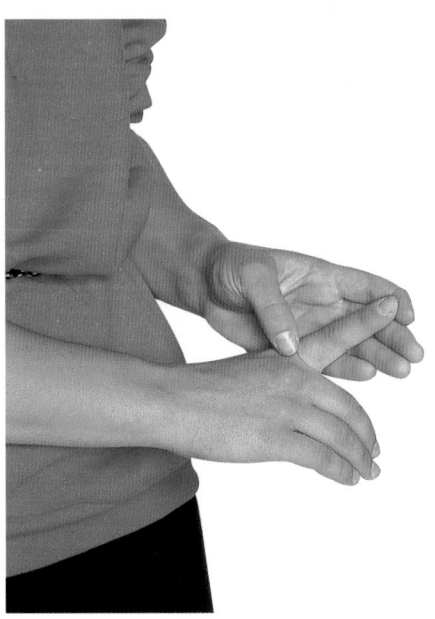

△ *Third joint finger stretch.*

ELBOW AND FOREARM STRETCH

Hold one arm out straight in front of you, clasp the fingers with your spare hand and bend your wrist and fingers back, so as to take up the tension on the flexor tendon insertion to the elbow. Hold for 8–12 seconds and repeat three times for each arm.

SHOULDER STRETCHES

Stand upright, grasp your elbow and bring your upper arm behind your head, applying gentle downward pressure to stretch the deltoid muscles. Then hold your arm out straight in front of you and pull it sideways across your body. Hold each stretch for 8–12 seconds and repeat three times.

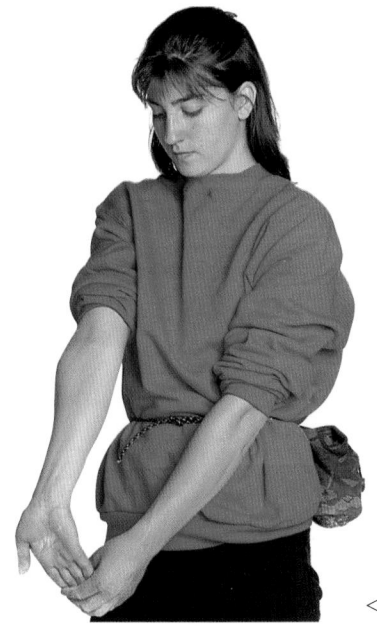

◁ Forearm stretch.

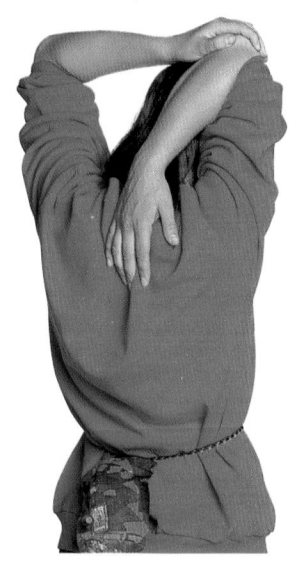

△ Shoulder stretch (1).

△ Shoulder stretch (2).

NECK STRETCH

Stand or sit upright, then gently bend your neck to one side, back to the centre and then to the other side, to the front and then to the back, always returning to the centre first each time. Do not rotate your neck.

BACK STRETCHES

For your lats (the large wing-like muscles down your sides), stand legs apart and slightly bent, then lean sideways stretching the leading arm over your head so as to feel the tension in your sides. Place the other hand on your hip or thigh for support. For your upper middle back muscles (rhomboid and teres groups) simply hold both arms out in front with hands clenched together, then curl your arms and shoulders forward.

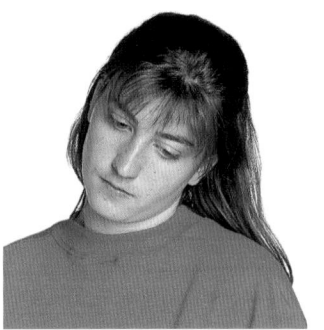

△ Side neck stretch.   △ Rear neck stretch.

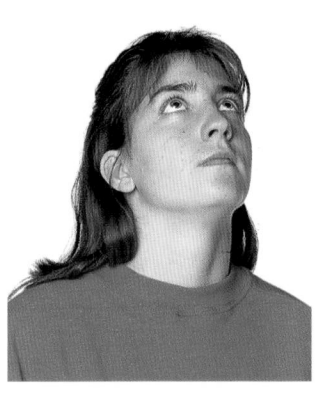

◁ Front neck stretch.

△ Upper back stretch.

△ Side stretch.

Lower body stretches

For warming-up purposes, lower body stretches can be kept to an absolute minimum. Choose one basic exercise for each muscle group, namely the groin, thighs, hamstrings and calves.

All these exercises can be performed on the rock or wall to help you combine your flexibility work with an element of climbing technique.

This provides a fun way of breaking up the monotony of an extensive pre-climbing stretching routine.

It is worth consulting an elementary yoga or flexibility training manual for more detailed information. However, it is worth prioritizing the following flexibility exercises, which are especially good for the inner thigh.

THIGH AND QUADRICEPS STRETCH

Stand straight, bending one leg up behind you. Hold your ankle to keep it in position. To increase the stretch, gently push hips forward.

CALF STRETCH

Place both hands against the wall and stretch one leg out straight behind you. Repeat with the other leg.

◁ *A good exercise to prepare you for rock-overs or high step-ups.*

▷ *This exercise stretches the relevant muscles for standing on small holds.*

HAMSTRING STRETCH

Sit on the ground, stretching one leg out in front of you, and fold the other leg in. Now gently stretch your upper body forwards.

◁ *You can also do this hamstring stretch by standing straight-legged and bending forward to touch the toes. Never bounce, but hold the stretch for 8–12 seconds.*

FRONT SPLITS

Although ideal for improving your ability for wide bridging moves, this commonly known exercise requires some care and preferably a few easier groin stretches first to help you work up to it. Simply face front with feet pointing forwards and slowly and carefully ease yourself into a bridge position.

▷ *The leg raise and groin stretch.*

▽ *Front splits and bridge stretch.*

FROG STRETCH

This simple exercise can be performed either standing or lying face down on the floor with your feet slightly wider than shoulder-width apart. Lower your hips towards your feet, turning your knees outwards in a ballet dancer's "plié" position. A great stretch for improving your ability to get your weight close in to the rock.

▷ *The inner thigh frog stretch.*

Progressive build-up

Now for the really important part. You are warm, mobile and fully stretched, so the final stage is to subject your muscles and tendons to gradually increasing overload (climbing or climbing-related movements of heightened intensity). As mentioned before, use longer sequences to prepare for endurance climbing and shorter programmes to build up for bouldering. Try, also, to make the moves in your warm-up sequences specific to the crag or wall you are about to use. For example, warm up on steep rock if that's what you are mainly going to be doing. Your first movements should be so easy that you barely notice them; use these to relax, stretch out and to tune in mentally to the sensation of climbing. Then, with the use of intermittent rest, build up until you are almost ready for maximum effort. Once you reach this stage, stop and rest for anything between 6–15 minutes

▽ *After you have warmed up and done some light climbing, it is worthwhile to do some more mobility exercises.*

△ *Even outside you can warm up by doing some easy bouldering, before launching yourself on a hard route.*

● THE WARM-UP SURVIVAL GUIDE

• Always ensure that all the main three finger grip angles are utilized during the warm-up: crimp, half crimp, and open hand. If necessary try to incorporate slopers, pinches or other more specific types of fingerhold if you know they will be required.

• Ensure that all main arm positions are worked through the full range of motion during the warm-up: pull-down, side-pull, reverse side-pull and undercut.

• Try to climb fluidly, smoothly and in control and only attempt faster dynamic moves to recruit your power and timing towards the end of the warm-up.

• For longer endurance climbing, you will always climb better after incorporating a primary pump into your warm-up to open the capillaries and to activate your body's lactic acid transfer systems.

• The different finger grip angles and arm positions are described on pages 54–59. There is in reality an infinite number, but they break down into specific types of holds.

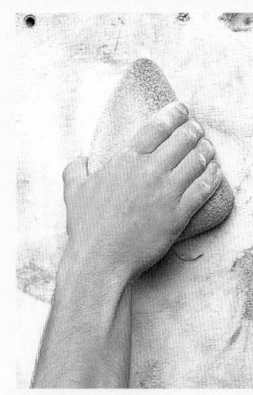
△ Pinching.

△ Using an undercut hold indoors.

▷ Using an undercut hold on a crag.

before you commence with the climbing session proper. It's worth taking a small amount of fluid and having a light secondary stretch during this period.

PUTTING IT ALL TOGETHER
While this chapter proposes an optimum warming-up model for climbing, it is not intended as a comprehensive guide and should be adapted to suit the requirements of individuals. Above all else, you should warm up in a way that suits your own mental and physical conditioning. Remember that it is always better to make the effort to do something, no matter how simple, for your warm-up and if you're going to set the time aside then you may as well do it properly. After all, the purpose here is to give yourself the best chance of climbing well in addition to avoiding a possible injury.

Training and technique

Regardless of your level of fitness or strength, technique is always the deciding factor in climbing. You can incorporate some aspects of technique into your training programme. They will help develop your flexibilty, as well as atune you to more difficult climbing moves. Establishing a repertoire of moves is an important aspect of mental training. These techniques will be looked at again later in the book.

▷ Frogging – a technique that demands flexibility.

FROGGING

This is a technique that can be used to help bring your centre of gravity in close on vertical or overhanging rock. It is especially relevant where you have either one central foothold or two very close footholds. The idea is to push your hips in as close to the rock as possible by turning your legs out in a sort of ballet dancer's "plié" movement. The more flexible your inner groin, the better you will be at this. Thus, frogging can provide that crucial means of resting when all else is letting you down.

▷ The Egyptian – a good technique for use on steep or overhanging rock.

THE EGYPTIAN

So named because of the extreme dropped knee posture that is adopted during these moves, the Egyptian is a useful and cunning method of keeping your centre of gravity as close to the rock as possible when climbing on steep ground. It applies to situations where you have two high footholds either side of you on rock which is usually in excess of 5 degrees overhanging. The idea is to "twist into" the next move by dropping the knee on the same side as the hand that you are about to reach with (the passive side) and turning your body to face the hold that you are currently holding on with (the active side). This brings your hips in close and perpendicular to the rock and creates torque between the footholds which, in turn, will reduce the loading on your arms. The secret is to co-ordinate your Egyptians fluidly between moves and, where the ground dictates, to switch continuously from one Egyptian to the other.

FLAGGING

This is a subtle conterbalancing technique which can be used as a quick and efficient substitute for swapping feet. It applies mainly to situations on steep rock where you only have one central foothold and thus require that fine degree of balance to make the next move. The idea is to pass your free leg either inside you or behind you and hang your body straight down, so as to form a stable "tripod" position with your three points of contact. Then, having completed the move, simply rectify yourself so you are set up to move on.

△ Inner flagging.

△ Outer flagging.

SIDE HEEL-HOOKING

The basic heel-hook is well known and is useful for turning the lips of roofs or for making traverses on very steep ground. However, the side heel-hook can be used far more frequently if the user is sufficiently creative and flexible. In situations where you have a large flat hold just to one side of your waist, simply lift your leg and rotate your foot outwards in such a manner that enables you to get the side of your heel on to the hold. Use it, and then when you're halfway through the move and have gained sufficient height, re-adjust to using your toe. Side heel-hooks can feel weird and insecure the first few times you try them, but like all techniques you will feel comfortable with them the more you practise.

◁ A heel-hook in action at an indoor climbing wall.

● TRAINING TERMS

Overload is the term used to describe the healthy, desirable stresses and strains that are placed on the connective tissues and joints during physical training. It does not necessarily imply the use of excessive or dangerous forces which may cause injury to the climber. See also Chapter 6, Advanced Training.

Intensity in climbing refers to the relationship between the length of climbing and the difficulty of the moves. For example a short boulder problem would be described as high intensity, whereas a long sea cliff climb would be regarded as low intensity. See also Chapter 6, Advanced Training.

Circuits are either random or pre-determined sequences of moves which usually work their way across, diagonally, up and down an indoor or outdoor bouldering wall. See also Chapter 6, Advanced Training.

Timing is the term used to describe the ability of a climber to use neuromuscular co-ordination to pull up and catch a handhold at high speed.

Primary pump is the act of climbing to deliberately induce a light burning cramp into your forearms to prime them for a more severe pump later on in the session.

First steps

Contrary to popular belief, you do not have to be super-muscular with the tenacity of a limpet to be a rock climber. Images in the climbing press do have a tendency to promote this point of view, but there are hundreds of thousands of climbs around the world that require little more than good balance and a head for heights. The first steps on rock can have such a profound influence over subsequent feelings towards this great sport that it is important to take them carefully. A course run by trained and qualified personnel is one of the better ways to be

introduced, but many people develop a deep affinity for the sport through friends who are themselves committed climbers. There need be no limitations of age, height or weight for those first steps – whether as a child or pensioner, when you put feet and hands to rock matters little, for there are levels to suit all.

FIRST STEPS

More and more people are introduced to rock climbing through the medium of climbing walls indoors. This is no bad thing, for it does at least allow the beginner to concentrate on

△ *Modern instructional techniques allow you to progress to leading easy climbs within a few days of taking your first steps on rock.*

◁ *An idyllic pose high above a valley. For many climbers, the thrill of an exposed situation spices up the whole experience.*

△ *Climbing walls are a good medium through which to learn the basics of movement, but try to avoid the steep and strenuous climbs when starting out.*

◁ *As the rock climb gets steeper you will definitely need muscles and tenacity – and a great deal of experience.*

▽ *An ideal angle on which to begin. Concentrate on precise footwork and learn to trust the friction properties of your footwear.*

movement in a friendly atmosphere that is always warm and dry. Not all climbing walls have suitable facilities for beginners. They are usually too steep and require strength combined with good technique, normally acquired over a period of time. The ideal beginner's venue is a low-angled slab where much of the body weight is taken over the feet rather than relying on arm strength to maintain contact with the rock.

An outdoor crag can be more suitable because of the infinite variety of low-angled rock that can be found. The major disadvantage is, of course, that you cannot guarantee finding warm and dry conditions! Wet rock tends to be very slippery and cold wet rock is

certain to put you off forever. Given that ideal conditions are available you should try to find a venue that has a profusion of easy-angled rock with little or nothing in the way of potential danger. Low boulders are ideal, even more so if they have lush grassy ground beneath them or soft sand. Make sure, too, that you are able to descend from the boulder with ease either off the back or by climbing down an easy way. Put on your shoes, and a helmet if there is a chance of loose rock or a fall, and you're away. It is always important to ensure that your feet are dry before you set foot on to the rock. This can be done by wiping the sole on the inside of a trouser leg, with your hand or with a rag specifically carried for this purpose.

Feet and friction

Good footwork is one of the main foundations for good climbing. The skill of precise foot placement enables better balance and movement. Your legs are much stronger than your arms, and the more you learn to use them, the farther and longer you will be able to climb. Most beginners concentrate on where to put their hands, ignoring their feet entirely. This approach should be resisted. You must learn to trust your feet, even on the smallest of holds. The use of rock shoes, with their excellent friction properties, makes this much easier to do.

EASY-ANGLED ROCK

Find a really low-angled piece of rock, say around 25 to 30 degrees, and simply walk around on it. At this angle you will find that it's easily possible to manage without using your hands. Take the opportunity to become acquainted with the superb friction properties of your rock shoes. Try standing on a small ledge of rock with the inside or outside edge of the shoe. Avoid high-stepping movements. Though there are times in rock climbing when you need to make a big step up, a good deal of energy can be saved by utilizing intermediate,

▽ Spend some time before a climb simply walking around on rock without the need for handholds.

△ Economy of effort is essential in rock climbing. Try to avoid high stepping movements when taking those first steps.

perhaps smaller, footholds to reach a more secure one. Keep looking down at your feet and slowly begin to develop precision about where you place them. Each time you put your foot on a hold, it should be placed deliberately and, hardest of all, with confidence that it will stick in place. Try to use only the friction between shoe sole and rock to create a foothold. This is known as "smearing".

USING FOOTHOLDS

Having gained some confidence in the stickiness of the shoes, it's time to move on to techniques of standing on specific and obvious holds or ledges. Find a piece of rock that is a little bit steeper and where hands placed against the surface can be used for balance. Balance only, remember! You don't need to use them to pull up on just yet. It was once thought that climbing is more efficient and safer if you maintain three points of contact with the rock at all times, and lean out and away from the rock so that you have a clear view of your feet and the rock in front of you. While this may be useful for easier climbs, in the grand scheme of things it may misdirect you and make later climbing experiences much less efficient.

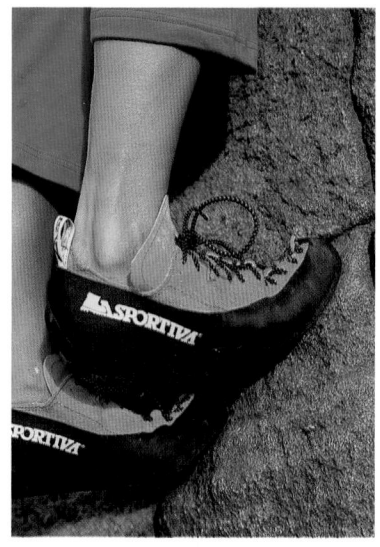

△ The technique of "smearing" the shoes over the rock surface is well illustrated here.

▷ The feet are smeared and the hands are used mainly for balance, though some support may be gained by curling the fingers over the smallest of edges.

● USING SMALL STEPS

It is a good idea to get into the habit of taking small steps up as you climb. This may mean using footholds that are not particularly good. However, it is better to use them and move up for better holds, rather than stretching too high to get to the better holds straight away. Over-reaching immediately puts you off balance and will also put a greater strain on your muscles.

Experiment at your local indoor wall or crag. Choose an easy route (either short, easy bouldering problems or a longer route – but use a rope and be belayed!). Try it first making big reaches with both hands and feet. Now do it again, but taking small steps and making smaller controlled moves. What did you notice?

△ Keep the hands low to avoid over-stretching.

△ Having made the step up, the next handhold is reached.

More footwork

As you gain confidence in your feet, you will come to trust the smaller footholds generally found on harder climbs. Be creative about your approach to footwork, and remember to experiment with your balance, finding out what works and what does not.

▷ When standing on well-defined ledges, however large or small, try to use the inside of the foot. This will allow you to get your weight closer in to the rock and directly over the foothold.

▷ A similar technique is used here, but the outside of one foot is also used to aid upward progress.

EDGING

Look down towards your feet and try to pick out small or large edges, protrusions and depressions in the rock surface. Each one you find could be a foothold and you should try to use them all, even if it means taking 20 steps to gain a few feet of height. You will quickly discover that by using these features each placement of the foot gains greater security than if it was just smeared on to the hold. If you find an edge that is difficult or uncomfortable to stand on with the front of the shoe, experiment by turning your foot sideways and putting either the inside or the outside edge of the shoe on the hold. This technique will be instantly more comfortable, for the simple reason that you are able to gain more support from the shoe across its width than its length because there is a good deal more rigidity and less leverage

△ *Using the inside and outside of the shoe means you can get more of your foot in contact with the rock, and will ultimately be more comfortable.*

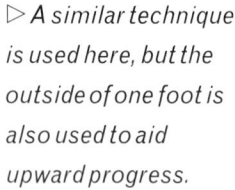

● CLIMBING BLINDFOLD

At this stage there are lots of little exercises you can do to make learning more fun. One suggestion is to try climbing with a blindfold on and ask a colleague to talk you through the moves. Not only will this help you to gain more awareness of body movement, but the person talking you through the sequence will have to visualize the most efficient sequence for you to follow. Concentrate on being very precise with each foot and handhold. Think about your balance. Being blindfold should help you with this. Be prepared to make lots of small adjustments to your position to find the most efficient body shape to adapt to in the circumstances.

◁ *Steeper rock and smaller footholds demand precise footwork and the confidence to stand around while fixing protection or working out the next move.*

across the sole. When you use the sides of the shoe in this way, it is called "edging". As you venture on to steeper rock, this technique becomes increasingly important.

CROSSING YOUR FEET

Like the often repeated adage regarding three points of contact at all times, ignore those that suggest you should never cross your feet one in front of the other. On a traverse it will be considerably easier if you are able to cross your feet, for it will put you in a good position to transfer body weight over to the next foothold. It is very important that you don't attempt too large a step. Normally your ability to stretch and flex your limbs will dictate the extent to which you can step, so be aware of what your body tells you. If you clearly cannot cope with the stretch, look for alternative and intermediate holds.

△ **1** *By crossing one leg inside the other, you are well placed to move comfortably towards the next suitable foothold.*

△ **2** *The move completed. You are now ready to repeat the sequence and move on to the next holds.*

Using handholds

Handholds are more easily seen, generally speaking, than footholds. They are at eye level, or thereabouts. However, they come in all shapes and sizes and at all angles. You will need to experiment to find the best use of them.

JUGS, FINGERHOLDS AND SIDE-PULLS

Having gained some confidence with your feet, it's time to move on to the hands. We have already experimented a little with the hands for balance. Having an edge to curl your fingers over increases the feeling of security, but we are not yet ready to use holds to pull our body weight up the rock – that has to wait for much steeper occasions. To begin, select a section of rock at a 45–50 degree angle and long enough so that you can make several consecutive

moves horizontally or at a slight rising diagonal across the surface. This sideways movement is called "traversing". The benefits of traversing are that you don't need to climb too high above the ground and that you will also get more continuous movement.

Now you need to look not only at your feet and decide where to put them, but also to consider using your hands to make life easier. You will need to use a variety of handholds. The simplest ones to use are those that you pull on from directly below. No doubt these will sometimes feel large and occasionally so small that they might appear inadequate. Large handholds that you can curl all of the fingers of one hand over are usually called "jugs". Climbers, in their early days on rock, also refer to them as "thank God" holds for

▷ *Holds over which you can comfortably curl your hand are sometimes called "thank God" holds. These are the most welcome holds to find on any climb.*

△ *More large handholds, this time inside and along the edges of a diagonal crack. Use your imagination when looking for holds to grip on to.*

It is always a good idea to remove your watch and any rings or other jewellery. Some types of handholds can be very taxing on your fingers and arms, and may cause damage to anything you happen to be wearing. Apart from scratches to your jewellery, you may also suffer damage to yourself if your jewellery becomes trapped. The forces involved could dent a ring into your finger, for example.

◁ *Small fingerholds are surprisingly secure, particularly if there is an incut lip to the edge of the hold.*

obvious reasons! Holds that you can only get half the length of your fingers on, or your fingertips only, are called "fingerholds".

With these two types of handhold you have enough to be able to climb most moderately graded rock. But other less obvious handholds exist, and to get the best out of them you will need to experiment. For example, a handhold found to lie vertically with the cliff face may at first seem useless. However, if it is pulled on from the side, with your feet positioned to keep you in balance, this type of hold will be found usable. They are called "side-pulls". Side-pulls are great holds to use when traversing, as they help you to pull your body across the rock and to transfer weight from foot to foot. You need to keep a keen eye out for the infinite variety of handholds available. A canny climber will look for, find and use even the most obscure hold to aid progress, so don't dismiss anything lightly.

◁ *Leaning sideways off a hold will allow you to let go with one hand to reach upward and diagonally. In this case, the climber will be able to let go with the right hand and reach up to better holds above.*

Planning your moves

The key to climbing efficiently is to be able to read the rock you are about to climb. This will require some imagination (what will it be like to be up there in that position?) and your past experience, and then planning ahead.

CLIMBING MOVES IN SEQUENCE

To climb a section of rock, whether it is a traverse or straight up, you should try to look upon it as a sequence of interlinked movements. To link the movements successfully, you'll need to look beyond the section of rock immediately in front of you and determine where your sequence will end before beginning the next. Sometimes this will be three or four moves and sometimes considerably more. For example, if you have a clear view of a place where you think you can comfortably stand that is about 3 m (10 ft) above, plan a sequence of moves to reach that point.

READING THE ROCK

To successfully plan a sequence of moves, you'll need to look very carefully at the availability of handholds and footholds over the

△ **1** *The objective is clear – first you need to stand up on the right foot and find suitable holds for the hands.*

△ **2** *Pull your weight over on to the right foot and stand up. Keeping as much weight on your right foot as possible ...*

△ **3** *... reach up with your right hand for the jug. Here, this sequence of three moves will gain you 1 m (3 ft) in height.*

△ **1** *In this sequence, notice how the feet change position but the left hand stays on the same hold.*

△ **2** *The left hand remains in place to aid balance while an intermediate hold is used by the right hand.*

△ **3** *The left hand changes from a pull hold to a push hold and the feet can be comfortably moved higher, now that there is a secure hold for the right hand.*

section of rock. You will need to think ahead in terms of how you might use the available holds and in what order. An interesting insight into this takes place at indoor climbing competitions. A climber taking part in an indoor climbing competition is allowed to see the route they have to climb a little before they actually have to do it. They will stand at the bottom of the route and scrutinize the holds, trying to visualize where they will be when they get to certain points, how their weight will be distributed, where their hands and feet will be and what technique they might use to move up. They will break the route down into manageable sections. To some extent, all climbers with experience will learn to do this to a certain level to help them cope with the climb they are about to do. Quite often there are many different ways to link holds and moves together in a sequence. These variations depend on what you see, what you think you might be able to use, how far you can

reach and your experience or ability to visualize the moves – often referred to as being able to "read the rock". The way one person climbs a sequence is not necessarily the way that another might link it together, though it is quite right to say that having seen someone climb a piece of rock the next climber to attempt it has a distinct advantage.

● **VERTICAL CHESS**

Some people find it helpful to consider the analogy between climbing and a game of chess. There are an infinite number of moves that you could make but only a few that will lead you into a winning position – and, of course, it is the winning moves that matter most! You might try a bouldering sequence several times, attempting the moves differently each time. Try to gauge which sequence was the most efficient and energy-saving. Try also to analyze what makes a sequence a success or a failure. Climbers often talk about their minds being in tune with what they are trying to do on one day, but out of tune on others. Getting it right is as much a mental achievement as a physical one.

Moving on – a real route

Having spent a few hours practising the basic skills of movement on rock, it is time to move on to something a little more adventurous. The most natural progression is to attempt a short climb on a bottom rope. For advice on how to set up the system, see Chapter 3.

USING A ROPE

When you first climb using a rope, you may feel differently about the whole experience of climbing. There is more to think about than simply making moves. The harness and rope may get in the way, but you will soon get used to them. At this stage try to find a climb that is not too steep, is well endowed with handholds and footholds, and offers a diversity of rock features – by doing so you are assured of success. An ideal height for the climb would be around 10 m (30 ft). Ideals, of course, are rarely

achievable! Before starting out on the climb, stand back and take a good look at the route you think you might take. Look for obvious ledges or breaks in the cliff face, places where you might be able to pause and rest to consider the remainder of the ascent. The knowledge that you gain from this perusal can be used to your advantage in breaking down the climb into short sections that are easier to cope with. You must of course keep the final goal in mind, but don't let it hinder your ability to think calmly.

Remembering the analogy with a game of chess, plan a sequence of moves and put them to the test. If it doesn't quite work out the way you had planned but you still succeed, it matters little. If you find that your calculated sequence doesn't quite work, take a moment to re-think. Do not just look at the rock immediately in front of your nose. Look to the sides of the line you are to take. Quite often there

◁ *A short climb, well endowed with holds of all kinds. Here the climber is safeguarded by using a bottom rope safety system.*

▷ *The same climb being safeguarded with a top rope method. There are advantages and disadvantages to both methods and much will depend on the situation you find yourself in.*

△ Grooves and corners should be straddled for comfort and energy-efficient climbing.

will be holds off to one side or the other that are not immediately obvious but that you can put a foot or hand on for maintaining balance or resting. They may not be quite the types of big holds you are looking for or expecting to find, but experimentation is quite likely to prove worthwhile.

Grooves and corners in the rock face are usually straddled with both feet and hands for comfort. This is called "bridging" and is a particularly restful and economic way to climb, because much of your body weight is supported by the feet and legs. Find places where you can experiment with taking one hand off, or even both, in order to gain a rest. Climbing on a top rope is totally safe, and though your weight might sag on to the rope, you'll not fall off in the truest sense – it'll only be a slump! Armed with this knowledge, you can forget those worries and concentrate on the task in hand.

Some people find it a useful exercise to climb the same route several times. Each ascent should become more efficient in terms of energy expended and you will learn a great deal about body movement and awareness.

However, rock in all its infinite variety offers so many different combinations of moves that it is as well not to ponder for too long on any particular climb. You need to extend your experience to include widely differing styles of climbing in order to make progress.

△ An easy-angled slab makes an ideal first climb. Slabs can be surprisingly tiring on the feet and legs, so try to vary the position of your feet frequently.

◁ The climbing wall is an ideal place to try things that might be a little too difficult. If you want to attempt something strenuous don't get too demoralized if you find your strength wanes quickly. Your stamina will improve with practice.

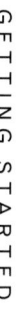

Longer climbs

The next stage is to move on to longer climbs, either single pitch or multi-pitch (see also Chapter 3). Exactly the same principles of movement apply, but bear in mind that you may have to keep energy levels running for longer. It is vitally important to conserve energy and you would do well to take moments out to deliberately rest during the climb. This means finding a position that is relatively comfortable (by bridging, for example) and allowing yourself time to re-evaluate the situation, to settle yourself into a good frame of mind and to grow accustomed to the situation you find yourself in.

It is in situations like this that your attitude to climbing is important. Your combination of mental and physical resilience will be re-evaluated. A confident approach, tempered with sound judgement and good technique, will stand you in good stead.

COPING WITH EXPOSURE

Many people find sufficient encouragement and motivation to continue from the early steps on low boulders or short single-pitch climbs to attempt longer climbs, but fail to take heed of the fact that longer climbs may have a frightening element that they hadn't bargained for – a big drop below! This is known as "exposure" and it comes in differing degrees and affects individuals in various ways. A small minority of people are so intimidated that they limit themselves ever after to short climbs; but for the majority of others, exposure adds that extra little bit of spice to the outing. Coping with exposure and maintaining concentration on the task of climbing do not always mix well together.

THE FEAR FACTOR

The fear factor has a considerable influence on your ability to climb and the feeling of an airy and forbidding space below your feet tends to

◁ *It is more difficult to find places to rest weary arms on harder climbs, but with imagination and control it is often possible to find something.*

△ *Longer, steeper climbs will inevitably require a certain amount of stamina in equal proportion to strength.*

▷ *The sound of the sea crashing on the rocks below will often add to a feeling of exposure and intimidation.*

preoccupy the mind with all kinds of negative thoughts. Mental preparation for this and taking the time to grow with your surroundings are as important as the actual skills of moving over the rock. Unfortunately it is not so easy to practise in a controlled environment, because the fear factor only kicks in when being scared becomes a reality. Everyone who climbs has their own way of overcoming this factor. There are those who seem oblivious to it but they are few in number. Taking time to mentally stand back and consider your position, and to concentrate on the moves that lie ahead, are important ways to overcome the fear factor.

The way forward

Be selective when you choose climbs to undertake. Pay close attention to the grade and the style of the climb. Those route descriptions found in guidebooks that mention things like "an awkward and strenuous chimney" or "make a bold move up the slightly impending arete" or "a thin and worrying sequence leads to a good jug" or "difficult for the short" or "an airy traverse" – are best avoided. They are coded descriptions for things that might be truly scary!

Enlist the company of a sympathetic friend with whom you can share your experiences. You may have encounters that turn out to be monumental and memorable adventures, which can be recounted years and hundreds of thousands of feet of rock later as happy, innocent moments through which a great deal of experience was gained.

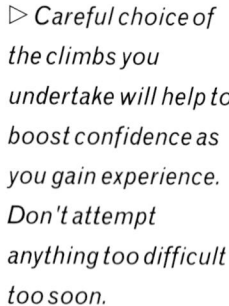

▷ *Careful choice of the climbs you undertake will help to boost confidence as you gain experience. Don't attempt anything too difficult too soon.*

△ *A guidebook will help you to find your way but don't expect it to give you a blow-by-blow account of how to climb.*

STARTING TO LEAD

Progress is not normally a hasty affair. However, quite soon after taking your first steps you may want to begin leading your own climbs. Being on the "sharp" end of the rope is a much riskier proposition, so the first climbs you undertake on the lead should be well within your ability. You will need to learn how to place all the protection equipment you carry, how to arrange your own anchor points and stances, and, above all, choose the way ahead based on what you see and the information given in guidebooks. If you begin climbing on a course staffed by qualified personnel, you are likely to be given the opportunity to lead a very short time after starting out. This is no bad thing, for you will quickly learn to appreciate the finer points of climbing and become more attuned to the rock.

Many people take their first leads alongside an instructor who is attached to a fixed rope by means of a mechanical ascending device. The instructor moves up alongside the student

△ Take a long look at the route before setting off and try to work out in advance where the line goes.

◁ Differing types of rock require particular techniques and are not always suited to all climbers.

▽ Leading with an instructor alongside provides a valuable learning experience.

and, because they don't need to hold on to the rock at all, is able to stop and talk the student through runner placements, selection of line to climb and even ways to make sequences of moves. It is an invaluable method of learning and one in which progress can be made relatively quickly and painlessly. Of course you may discover that leading is not for you. There are thousands of climbers who have absolutely no desire whatsoever to lead, but still get great rewards from rock climbing.

Though there are superstars who shine through within a few years of starting out, for many the road is slower. This has advantages in that by the time you are climbing difficult rock the experience amassed stands you in good stead where safety is concerned. However you begin and however long you

climb, savour those first innocent steps into the vertical world – they are but a tantalizing morsel of the riches beyond.

Defining your terms

Thumb sprags, slopers, crimps and smears are all climbing holds and key words of the rock climber's world. But to the uninitiated they are probably meaningless – this chapter should bring enlightenment! In previous pages we have already mentioned a few holds that are commonly used and simple techniques to employ them to best effect. As you gain more experience, you'll discover that a broader repertoire of holds is required. What follows is a brief look at these types of holds, and where and how they can be used most effectively.

JUG, BUCKET OR "THANK GOD" HOLD

These are huge holds that you can curl all your hand over, rather like holding on to the rungs of a ladder (see also page 44). Jugs instill great confidence for the simple reason that you can hang off them without strength draining away too quickly. Any jug that appears at the end of a particularly harrowing sequence of moves is always very welcome, hence its more descriptive term of "thank God" hold. Large holds are often a good place to linger, taking a well-earned rest (or semi-rest). You can also look ahead to see what's in store.

▷ *The ultimate "thank God" hold. The only worry is whether or not it will bear the full weight of the climber!*

FINGERHOLDS

These are small versions of jugs. The finest fingerhold to use is one that has a small lip to it or is incut at the back. Though you might only be able to curl the ends of your fingers over the edge, it is generally sufficient for a fairly strong pull. Fingerholds are sometimes flat and are fine to pull on from directly below but much harder to hang on to if they are at shoulder level. Normally you'd use a flat fingerhold with fingers bent 90 degrees at the main joint. If, however, you can only get the very tips of your fingers on the hold, you must arch the main joint above the hold and keep the fingers rigid. It helps to place your thumb over the first finger as well so that it can take some of the load. This is sometimes referred to as a "crimp". You might also find some relief from levering your thumb against a protrusion or edge if it's available. By levering inwards or pushing outwards, it makes the fingers feel more securely gripped to the rock.

▽ A tiny ledge can be crimped (as held by the lower hand) or held with the tips of the fingers.

△ A flat edge can be gripped with at least half the length of the fingers to provide a secure hold.

△ An incut fingerhold, though small, usually feels very positive.

Creative handholds

As we found out on pages 44–45, handholds are not always what they seem. Sometimes, to get the most out of them, you need to be a little creative in your use of them. Here are a few more tips on how to use marginal holds or to create a hold where there doesn't appear to be one!

SLOPER OR ROUNDED HOLD

These types of hold do not generally instill confidence and are particularly worrying the smaller they become. A sloper that you can get your whole hand over can be made to feel fairly secure provided that you can keep your whole arm and body weight directly below it. Basically, what you do is to try to smear the whole hand over the rock and rely on friction and pressure to hold the hand in place.

Sometimes you can slot fingers into tiny depressions in the rock to give valuable extra purchase. Slopers, though they are found on most types of rock, are more prevalent on sandstone and gritstone, and granite that has been worn by water. The classic, if not particularly encouraging, place to come across slopers is at the top of a gritstone crag. Often you can achieve extra pulling power and grip by smearing part of your arm over the rock as well.

PALMING

This is exactly what it says it is – pushing on the inside of the palm. It can be implemented in several ways, each of which is applicable to different types of move. One of the ways it is most usefully employed is where you have a good positive handhold for one hand and need

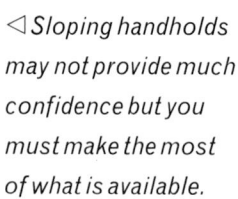
◁ Sloping handholds may not provide much confidence but you must make the most of what is available.

▷ Imaginative use of a "palming" technique allows the climber to make a high step.

to make a clean, big step up on to a good foothold. Pulling up on the jug with one hand and pushing down on the rock with the palm of the other lightens the weight on each arm, pushes you further away from the cliff face and allows you to make a high step up. Another application for palming is in climbing corners or grooves where there are few handholds. By pressurizing each palm on either side of the corner or groove, you can relieve enough weight from one foot at a time in order to move them higher. There are climbs where this technique, along with smearing for the feet, are the only techniques that will get you up the climb. Needless to say, climbing long sections of rock devoid of any other types of handholds and footholds can be a harrowing experience.

UNDERCLING

Undercling holds are used in many different ways and, when used imaginatively, prove to be one of the most versatile of all for resting between sequences of moves. The most frequently found use for the undercling is in situations where you are confronted with having to make a move over an overlap or

△ *An undercut hold is less tiring on the arms when resting.*

▷ *Undercut holds will also allow you to lean out and look up the rock to see where you are going.*

▽ *Relying wholly on friction for both feet and for both hands requires confidence in the friction properties between boot and rock, and skin and rock.*

overhang. These features on a rock face often have a crack running horizontally beneath which the hands can be slotted in, with the palms facing upwards. Pulling outwards on your arms allows you to arch your back out and pop your head over the obstacle to see what lies ahead. Once you have found suitable handholds over the lip, you can move one hand over while keeping the other firmly gripped in the undercling. Having taken a good grip of the hold over the lip, release the undercling and move the hand up to another hold and pull yourself around or over the overhang. You can use underclings in many other situations. Basically, any hold that you can get your fingers or your whole hand into from underneath is an undercling. Even if there isn't a hole or crack, a small edge might suffice. On steeper rock underclings are used to best advantage to help you rest and recover enough for the next sequence of moves.

More creative handholds

The weakest link in your body climbing machine is in the fingers. Once you have progressed on to steeper, harder climbs, this will become apparent. To use the types of holds described here, you will need to build up your finger strength.

PINCH-GRIP

Whenever you use a hold between fingers and thumb it's called a pinch-grip. They come in many shapes and sizes, from small and rounded to large and square, and can be used sideways, lengthways or on a diagonal. One of the typical features of limestone rock is the tufa, which is a calciferous flow that hardens over time and usually stands proud of the rock surface. Tufa is the ultimate pinch-grip hold as there are quite often little indents into which you can place your fingers for extra grip. You can also pinch sharp edges of rock in a fairly open-handed grip and gain some security for an upward, or sideways pull. Small knobbles

of rock that protrude from the surface are another type of pinch-grip. A good way to train for increasing the power of your pinch-grip is to lift concrete building blocks – it also toughens the ends of your fingers!

POCKETS

Pockets or holes in the rock are most commonly found on limestone crags, but they are by no means exclusive to limestone. They vary in size tremendously from holes that you can only insert one or two fingers into, to great big ones that you can get both hands in at the same time. They are frequently deep enough to get most of the length of the fingers into, and so even though they might be small they offer excellent grip if you have the finger strength to hang on and pull up. Pockets sometimes have a lip on the upper inside and, having used one to pull up on, you may then be able to turn it into an undercling hold when you move above it.

△ *An open-handed pinch-grip is useful for maintaining balance.*

△ *A finger pocket combined with a pinch-grip by the thumb.*

△ *A one-finger pocket requires strong fingers.*

△ *Here, the weight is taken mainly over the left foot with layaway handholds to maintain the climber's position.*

▷ *The left hand has an open-hand pinch-grip held in an undercut position, while the right hand holds an inverted side-pull or layaway.*

SIDE-PULLS OR LAYAWAYS

Side-pulls are commonly used to allow you to lean sideways to reach another hold that would otherwise be difficult to get to. They are also used to pull yourself sideways on to a foothold that is off to one side or the other. The sides of cracks, regardless of size, can be used to pull sideways on, or to layaway off, and so also can any edges that run vertically on the rock surface. They can also be used to gain a rest, provided the rest of the body is in balance. Simply lean away from the hold and try to keep your arm straight. An arm that is straight rests on the bones and joints, and saves the muscles from becoming more fatigued in the process.

Unusual positions

There are usually several ways in which to overcome an obstacle. However, some of these ways will be more efficient in terms of energy expended than others. This is where good technique comes in to play. Here are a few special techniques to try out, experiment with and then make part of your everyday climbing repertoire.

LAYBACKING

Laybacking is a technique that requires the hands and feet to work in unison. The handholds you use are layaways or side-pulls and feet are usually smeared or placed on any available edges. It is a powerful series of moves in which the hands pull in one direction and the feet push in another. Such is the force generated that in a full-on layback if your hands lose their grip you'll almost certainly catapult out and away from the rock! As a series of linked moves, laybacking is very strenuous indeed and it is sometimes very difficult to take one hand off to place or remove protection. When you do take one hand off, the balance of power between feet and hands is altered and there is a tendency to swing outwards towards the direction of your feet. This rather unnerving phenomenon is known by climbers as "barn-dooring". Layback techniques can also be used as an isolated move to gain holds higher up either on the side of a crack or on small edges in the rock surface.

△ **1** *The layback position uses opposing forces from feet and hands.*

△ **2** *As your feet get closer to your hands, the forces increase.*

△ **3** *Maintain pressure on the feet and one hand, and move the other hand up.*

△ **4** *Now move your feet up again towards your hands ...*

△ **5** *... and keep going for as long as you need to.*

MANTLESHELFING

This is a technique rather than a hold, as such. The simplest scenario is one in which you have a ledge to get on to but there are no holds above the ledge that you can reach or use. It requires considerable effort on steep ground, where you might find it difficult to use your feet to help you. You have to reach up to the edge of the ledge and take hold of it with both hands, about shoulder width apart. You then give an almighty heave to bring your shoulders level with the ledge. If you are able, you should try to run your feet up the rock using the smearing technique. Using the momentum you have initiated, keep going upwards until you can turn one hand around into a palming pressure hold on the ledge and lock the arm by bending it at the elbow and throwing your head and shoulders over the top of it. You need to hold that position momentarily while you get the other arm into a similar position, and from there you straighten your arms with another heave and at the same time bring one foot up on to the ledge just on the outside of one arm. Transfer your weight immediately on to this foot and push up on your leg with all your might. As the leg straightens you can bring the other foot up on to the ledge and, in one dynamic movement, stand up.

That is the theory; the practice is considerably different and in the majority of instances you'll end up throwing yourself on to the ledge with a belly roll and then, accompanied by a great deal of leg kicking, nudge the rest of your body on until you are lying sideways on the ledge. Not as graceful but almost as effective!

△ **1** *Get a good grip of the ledge and walk your feet up as high as possible.*

△ **2** *Change the hand grip to a push down and straighten the arms.*

△ **3** *Move one foot up on the ledge by the side of your hands.*

◁ **4** *It is important to keep the arms as straight as is feasibly possible.*

▷ **5** *Finally bring up the second foot and stand up. Mantleshelfing requires a good deal of flexibility in the legs and body.*

Chimneying

This is a technique that you will either love or hate! Chimneys are large fissures in a rock face that will accommodate an entire climber. They can be so tight that there is very little room to manoeuvre, just wide enough to have your back on one side and feet on the other, or so broad that you have to straddle across them with arms and legs spread wide. The techniques for differing widths vary slightly. The classic technique is called back-and-footing. The clearest way to interpret this technique is that you push your back against one wall of the chimney while your feet push against the other and you use these opposing forces to hold you in position.

You don't even need to have handholds and footholds; pressure is sufficient. Although it's easy to hold yourself in, moving up can feel insecure if you take the pressure off. The correct technique for upward progress is vital. Place the palms of both hands on either side of you and just above buttock level. Pressurize them, push your back slightly away from the wall and move up until your buttocks are just above your hands, then immediately lean on to your back. Keeping your palms against the rock, you can then move your feet up, one at a time, until they are on the same level as your bottom. Repeat this process until you reach the end of the chimney. It is helpful if your legs

△ *A classic back-and-foot position.*

△ *The technique of upward progress alternates between these two body positions (left and above).*

△ *In narrower chimneys it may be possible to utilize the knee for extra security.*

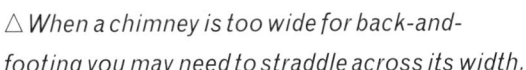

△ When a chimney is too wide for back-and-footing you may need to straddle across its width.

◁ A tight chimney will be awkward but will feel very secure. Note the pressure or palming handhold used to wedge the body more tightly and to help push upwards.

◁ By squirming with the body and pushing with all your might on feet and hands, it is possible to move upwards.

don't have to be stretched fully out; a little bend at the knees helps you to exert greater pressure. Make sure that you take only short movements each time in order to maintain the security of the wedge and, if you can, use footholds and handholds to advantage.

Tight chimneys that allow little room for movement are climbed using similar principles but upward progress is achieved more by a wriggling technique in combination with pressure on either side of the chimney. When a chimney is so wide that back-and-footing is impossible, you will need to straddle the gap. Handholds and footholds are more crucial to success, as it is often quite difficult to get a high degree of opposing pressure to keep you in place. By their very nature, chimneys are fairly dark and dingy places and it can be extremely difficult to actually see the rock features in order to find holds – allow your eyes time to accustom to the poor light.

Jamming

Jamming is a technique used in smooth-sided, virtually holdless cracks. If you are adept at using them and a suitable crack exists, you might also jam as an alternative to using normal handholds. The technique is exactly as the term "jamming" suggests;

what it doesn't tell you, though, is how painful it can be if executed incorrectly, damaging the hand in the process.

HAND JAMS

A crack that is suitable for a hand jam is called a "hand crack". Clearly, what might be a hand crack for a person with small hands is likely to be a tight hand crack for someone larger. Assuming that you can get your hand into the crack, place it open-handed. Find a spot where there is about 1–2 cm (½–¾ in) clearance either side of the hand then push the thumb

◁▽ *A nearly perfect hand crack will provide very secure jams. On first acquaintance jamming may seem painful, but as you gain more experience a good jam becomes something of a "thank God" type of hold.*

into the palm of the hand. As you do, arch your hand across the crack so that the fingers are pushing against one side and the back of your hand against the other. It is important to stretch the skin as tightly as you can across the back of the hand, as this will prevent the skin from getting too badly damaged. Once you feel the tightening action happen, continue to arch your hand as much as possible. This will tighten the jam and make it much more secure – though it will be difficult to believe it at first! Now you can put some weight on it and see if it works.

FIST JAMS

When a crack is too large for a hand jam, it may be possible to jam your fist into it. The basic theory is very similar in that you need to keep the skin taut across your hand, and you must keep the pressure on as long as you need the jam to grip. There are two ways to jam the fist. One is quite simply to make a fist and the other is with the thumb pressed inside curled fingers.

Fist jams can be used effectively in parallel-sided cracks or in tapered cracks. Normally you would use them with the back of the hand

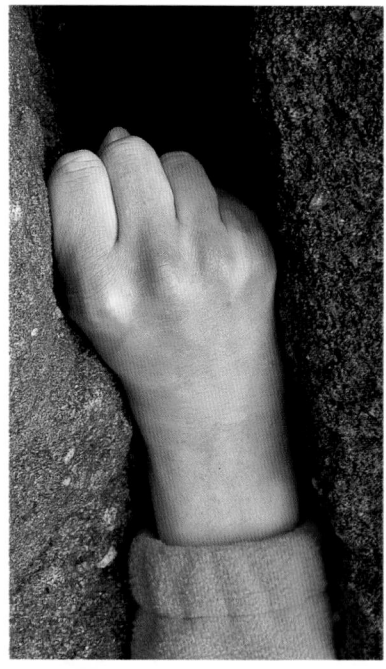

△ *A well-placed hand jam – push the thumb into the palm and arch your hand across the crack to create a sound hold.*

△ *When a crack is too wide for a hand jam, try wedging the fist into the crack. Make sure that the thumb is tucked inside the palm.*

facing out from the crack but in a great many situations you will find them more comfortable to use if the inside of the hand faces outwards. One hand each way is a useful technique to employ for repeated fist-jamming movements.

● FOOT JAMS

Any part of the body can be used to jam with. The toes, or better still, the whole foot, can be utilized in a suitable-sized crack. Toes can be jammed into narrow cracks, about the size you would use for your fingers or hands. The whole foot can be used, either straight in, or placed sideways if the crack is large enough. You must be careful, however, not to jam your foot too deeply into a crack. It is remarkably easy to get a foot well and truly wedged in. This will make moving up impossible! Try to achieve a jam that gives enough security to use successfully, but will not prove a hindrance when moving on.

▷ *This shows a foot jam wedged sideways across a wide crack.*

More jamming

Once you have worked on and perfected the more obvious jamming techniques, you can move on to the more esoteric. Once again, an immunity to pain will help!

FINGER JAMS OR LOCKS

If a crack is obviously too narrow for the whole of your hand, you might need to jam part of it. In an extreme case this might mean just the tips of your fingers, but hopefully the majority of the time it will be at least half the length of your fingers. If you can get your hand in up to the knuckles, the crack is called a tight hand crack. If you can get the fingers in up to the middle joint, it's called a finger crack.

The easiest and least painful way to jam the fingers is to find a constriction in the crack through which your fingers will not slip, regardless of how much pressure is put on them. It is possible to take your body weight

on one or two fingers alone, if they are well placed. If the crack is parallel-sided, you must twist the fingers into the crack to create a "camming" action. This is effected by placing the fingers in with the thumb pointing downwards and trying to bend your wrist through 90 degrees. If you are able to lever the thumb against one side of the crack, it helps. It is possible to make a finger jam with the thumb facing upwards, by applying similar principles. It tends to be much more painful though.

KNEE-BARS

The knee-bar is another type of jammed hold. It is particularly useful for gaining a rest or increasing security, and is essential for off-width crack climbing. In its simplest form, it requires a foothold and a constriction in the crack just above knee level against which the knee can be wedged. The other foot must either find a suitable foothold to the side or just

▽ Long sections of thin finger-crack climbing demand a few years' climbing experience.

△ A finger jam, where the finger is simply wedged into a constriction in the crack, is secure but sometimes a little painful.

△ With this style of finger jam or lock, two fingers are intertwined to form a wider profile for greater security.

△**1** *This is a strenuous and technical sequence on very steep rock.*

△**2** *A bold laybacking move gains a tiring position where strength may wane rapidly.*

△**3** *Judicious use of a knee-bar allows the climber to release both hands to rest!*

simply be held in place with pressure and friction. You must commit yourself fully to the locking position that can be achieved in order for the technique to be effective. Even on vertical rock faces, it is possible to let go with both hands and hang from a knee-bar.

OFF-WIDTH CRACKS

Quite possibly the most feared of all crack types, off-widths are cracks that are too wide to jam fists and feet into and too narrow to get your whole body into. There are some climbers who are attracted to off-widths, have honed the technique and make any ascent look childishly simple. They are a rare breed, specializing in esoteric arts. Most people avoid any climb with the mention of the word off-width associated with it.

Techniques to cope with an off-width crack are, in theory, straightforward. You basically have to wedge any part of your body into the crack, according to the width. Most of the time you should be able to get a shoulder, one arm and a half a leg in. The rest of your body hangs out of the crack groping around for any kind of

purchase possible. In order to wedge the bits of your body in the crack, you often have to get yourself into some incredibly contorted positions and might even use your head as a wedge! Upward progress is a harrowing experience and at best tenuous.

◁ *Off-width crack climbing is perhaps the most awkward of all styles of climbing. There are, however, a few who delight in the struggle.*

Gymnastic moves

You have already come across some of these techniques in the warm-up section of this chapter. It needs to be stressed that some are difficult, and should only be practised once you are fully warmed up. Needless to say, they may one day prove to be the only way of successfully completing a hard route or sequence of moves.

DYNO

A dyno is a movement rather than a hold. The term is an abridgement of "dynamic leap", and it requires a great deal in the way of confidence, agility, strength and technique. Normally you would only resort to a dyno if the rock between you and the next hold is obviously devoid of anything remotely usable, and the hold you are jumping for is a good one. It goes without saying that should you fail to reach your hold, or if the hold is not as good as you thought, then a fall is the inevitable consequence. You should be prepared for this, placing good runners to protect yourself, and ensuring that the person belaying you is aware of the move you are about to make and is ready for a possible fall. Of course, if you are bouldering, then there should be no problem – you simply fall to the ground if you fail.

THE FIGURE-OF-FOUR

This is a particularly difficult move, though it does enable you to reach holds that may otherwise be out of reach. To carry out a figure-of-four successfully you will need a few very good handholds. Take one leg over your arm, which remains in place on its hold. This leg can now be used by you to move up by pressing down on your arm. You should then be able to reach high with the free hand.

△**1** *The climber "psyches up" for a big dyno move – success requires total commitment and belief.*

△**2** *Having reached the hold solves only half the problem; there is still a very strenuous move to make.*

△ *The figure-of-four is surprisingly comfortable and effective for making long reaches on steep rock.*

HEEL-HOOK

A heel-hook is a particularly useful hold for climbing overhangs. A well- positioned heel can take considerable pressure off the arms and can also be used as a lever for pulling yourself over the lip of an overhang. It does require a considerable amount of flexibility and confidence.

△1 *Get a good grip of the handholds over the lip of the roof and hang straight off them. Throw one of your feet up to the hand level and hook the heel of the shoe on to a ledge or protrusion.*

△2 *Pull up on your arms at the same time as levering on your leg. When you get your shoulders to hand level, convert the grip into a downward pressure hold and push your shoulders up.*

△ 3 *Now for the really strenuous bit – lever up on the foot and reach for higher holds with the hands. For a firmer foothold, shift your body weight over the foot as soon as possible.*

ROCK-OVER

A rock-over is a very useful technique to get to grips with. It consists of shifting your balance and weight from a foot on a lower foothold to one on a higher foothold. As this sequence demonstrates, it is another gymnastic move, requiring strong leg muscles and a developed sense of balance.

△1 *Select the foothold to use – the higher the step, the more difficult the rock-over will be.*

△2 *Having placed your foot on the hold, pull your body weight over towards the foot.*

△3 *Transfer all your weight on to the foot and push up with your leg using all your strength.*

Strength and technique

The first few climbs of your newly discovered sport will undoubtedly be fairly low-angled and of an easy grade. As you gain experience and familiarity with movement on rock, your confidence will increase and you'll doubtless have higher aspirations. From here on in the climbs you embark on will become steeper and the holds smaller and fewer. Those less precise techniques that you might have been able to get away with on easier-angled rock will create undesirable difficulties on steeper ground and harder climbs. Shoddy footwork is not forgiven, bad planning may lead you into corners from which there is no escape, and tiring arms lead to waning strength and confidence.

△ *Low-angled climbs, where you can take most of the weight on your feet, are ideal for developing precise technique.*

BUILDING STRENGTH

There is an enormous amount you can do to improve your strength, which in the long term will help you to climb better. Building up arm and finger strength pays very quick dividends, for example. There are exercises that you can do to help, but at the end of the day climbing is by far the best way to train. This is where the climbing wall comes into its own. Within the confines of the indoor environment you are able to concentrate fully on a well thought-out training programme that will build both strength and ability on a gradual but effective platform. The belief you have in yourself to hang around on small holds for long periods of time contributes massively to success.

TECHNIQUE

Strength in itself is not the answer. Good technique is important – perhaps even more important. Developing good technique is only achieved through many hours on rock. Like many sports there are those who appear to be born rock climbers. To these people movement on rock seems to be second nature, but unfortunately we are not all equal in this respect. Talented climbers display a natural ability and body awareness that allows them to move fluently over the rock in total control of both body and mind. Such movement, like all things done competently, is a pleasure to witness. One of the great things about rock climbing is that this level of performance is within the grasp of almost anybody who perseveres. The lessons we learn on early climbs are the foundation stones for harder ones later on in our career. The basics of good footwork and the ability to work out sequences of moves apply equally, regardless of the grade of the climb.

173. HONDURAS: RELATIONS AMONG MAIN NATIONAL ACCOUNTS AGGREGATES, AT CURRENT PRICES

(Millions of lempiras)

1978	1979	1980	1981	1982	1983	
1 550	1 744	1 973	2 083	2 221	2 450	*Compensation of employees*
1 685	1 938	2 198	2 323	2 552	2 572	*Plus: Operating surplus*[1]
166	200	261	285	245	251	*Plus: Consumption of fixed capital*
3 401	3 882	4 432	4 691	5 018	5 273	1. *Equals:* **Gross domestic product at factor cost**
434	499	547	611	602	637	*Plus: Indirect taxes*
4	3	3	9	38	19	*Less: Subsidies*
3 814	4 378	4 976	5 293	5 582	5 891	2. *Equals:* **Gross domestic product at market prices**
150	210	275	269	385	268	*Less: Net factor income paid to the rest of the world*
3 664	4 168	4 701	5 024	5 197	5 623	3. *Equals:* **Gross national product at market prices**
166	200	261	285	245	251	*Less: Consumption of fixed capital*
3 498	3 968	4 440	4 739	4 952	5 372	4. *Equals:* **National income at market prices**
...	...	...	...	...	...	*Plus: Other net current transfers received from the rest of the world*
...	...	...	...	...	...	5. *Equals:* **National disposable income at market prices**
3 023	3 499	4 074	4 559	4 879	5 232	*Less: Total final consumption expenditure*
...	...	...	...	...	...	6. *Equals:* **National saving**
...	...	...	...	...	...	*Less: Surplus of the nation on current transactions*
821	893	1 042	840	582	679	7. *Equals:* **Net capital formation**
166	200	261	285	245	251	*Plus: Consumption of fixed capital*
987	1 093	1 303	1 125	827	930	8. *Equals:* **Gross capital formation**

[1] *Data not published by the original source. Obtained by difference.*

II. CUENTAS NACIONALES

174. HONDURAS: PRODUCTO INTERNO BRUTO POR CLASE DE ACTIVIDAD ECONOMICA, AL COSTO DE FACTORES

(Millones de lempiras)

Clase de actividad	1960	1965	1970	1975	1977
	A precios corrientes				
1. Agricultura, caza, silvicultura y pesca	212	352	424	597	964
2. Explotación de minas y canteras	10	17	28	52	56
3. Industrias manufactureras	76	115	181	316	436
4. Electricidad, gas y agua	4	9	18	36	45
5. Construcción	24	34	63	108	145
6. Comercio al por mayor y al por menor, restaurantes y hoteles [1]	81	117	158	239	371
7. Transportes, almacenamiento y comunicaciones	42	59	104	157	219
8. Establecimientos financieros, seguros, bienes inmuebles y servicios prestados a las empresas [2]	62	87	142	235	313
Viviendas	52	68	102	153	188
9. Servicios comunales, sociales y personales [3]	105	136	189	282	358
Servicios gubernamentales	24	28	44	66	101
Subtotal	616	926	1 307	2 022	2 907
Menos: Comisión imputada de los servicios bancarios	...	...	...	...	...
Total: Producto interno bruto	616	926	1 307	2 022	2 907
	A precios constantes de 1966				
1. Agricultura, caza, silvicultura y pesca	239	347	407	389	449
2. Explotación de minas y canteras	12	17	26	33	30
3. Industrias manufactureras	86	117	170	195	236
4. Electricidad, gas y agua	5	8	14	23	22
5. Construcción	31	36	42	54	64
6. Comercio al por mayor y al por menor, restaurantes y hoteles [1]	93	123	140	153	201
7. Transportes, almacenamiento y comunicaciones	56	64	81	97	107
8. Establecimientos financieros, seguros, bienes inmuebles y servicios prestados a las empresas [2]	68	86	119	161	186
Viviendas	53	66	88	111	123
9. Servicios comunales, sociales y personales [3]	128	147	173	208	239
Servicios gubernamentales	30	31	40	45	60
Subtotal	718	945	1 172	1 313	1 534
Menos: Comisión imputada de los servicios bancarios	...	...	...	...	...
Total: Producto interno bruto	718	945	1 172	1 313	1 534

[1] Restaurantes y hoteles se incluyen en Servicios comunales, sociales y personales.
[2] Servicios prestados a las empresas se incluyen en Servicios comunales, sociales y personales.
[3] Incluye Restaurantes y hoteles y Servicios prestados a las empresas.

174. HONDURAS: GROSS DOMESTIC PRODUCT BY KIND OF ECONOMIC ACTIVITY, AT FACTOR COST

(Millions of lempiras)

1978	1979	1980	1981	1982	1983	Kind of activity
			At current prices			
1 048	1 135	1 263	1 313	1 381	1 450	1. *Agriculture, hunting, forestry and fishing*
73	104	96	97	108	114	2. *Mining and quarrying*
517	602	681	716	754	785	3. *Manufacturing*
54	72	98	118	121	128	4. *Electricity, gas and water*
201	230	267	258	301	320	5. *Construction*
453	497	587	625	666	692	6. *Wholesale and retail trade, restaurants and hotels* [1]
257	299	332	364	389	403	7. *Transport, storage and communications*
365	434	515	556	585	629	8. *Finance, insurance, real estate and business services* [2]
215	256	297	322	349	377	*Dwellings*
433	509	593	644	713	752	9. *Community, social and personal services* [3]
122	161	197	223	255	276	*Government services*
3 401	3 882	4 432	4 691	5 018	5 273	*Subtotal*
...	...	...	...	...	...	*Less: Imputed bank service charges*
3 401	3 882	4 432	4 691	5 018	5 273	*Total: Gross domestic product*
			At constant 1966 prices			
485	518	539	548	552	567	1. *Agriculture, hunting, forestry and fishing*
37	43	38	36	39	39	2. *Mining and quarrying*
259	289	295	296	279	268	3. *Manufacturing*
26	31	34	37	36	36	4. *Electricity, gas and water*
67	72	74	71	74	75	5. *Construction*
221	222	230	232	228	220	6. *Wholesale and retail trade, restaurants and hotels* [1]
115	• 120	120	125	126	123	7. *Transport, storage and communications*
203	209	217	215	211	209	8. *Finance, insurance, real estate and business services* [2]
132	136	143	142	142	141	*Dwellings*
265	285	292	291	301	290	9. *Community, social and personal services* [3]
68	83	86	90	93	93	*Government services*
1 678	1 780	1 839	1 851	1 846	1 827	*Subtotal*
...	...	...	...	...	...	*Less: Imputed bank service charges*
1 678	1 780	1 839	1 851	1 846	1 827	*Total: Gross domestic product*

[1] *Restaurants and hotels are included in Community, social and personal services.*
[2] *Business services are included in Community, social and personal services.*
[3] *Including Restaurants and hotels and Business services.*

175. HONDURAS: INGRESOS Y GASTOS DE LOS HOGARES, INCLUIDAS LAS EMPRESAS NO FINANCIERAS NO CONSTITUIDAS EN SOCIEDAD [1]

(Millones de lempiras)

	1960	1965	1970	1975	1976	1977
1. Remuneración de los asalariados	286	394	582	1 021	1 140	1 341
2. Renta neta de la propiedad y de la empresa	282	413	567	813	920	1 162
3. Prestaciones de seguridad social	...	...	...	...	...	...
4. Donaciones de asistencia social	...	...	...	...	...	...
5. Transferencias corrientes n.e.p. de residentes	2	3	7	10	17	22
6. Transferencias corrientes n.e.p. del resto del mundo	1	3	11	17	15	16
Total: Ingresos corrientes	571	813	1 167	1 863	2 092	2 541
7. Gasto de consumo final	524	754	1 073	1 772	1 963	2 246
8. Impuestos directos	8	13	30	82	83	101
9. Contribuciones a la seguridad social	-	4	...	...	...	...
10. Transferencias corrientes n.e.p. a residentes	1	1	4	8	7	8
11. Transferencias corrientes n.e.p. al resto del mundo	2	2	5	7	8	7
12. Ahorro	36	39	55	-6	31	179
Total: Egresos corrientes	571	813	1 167	1 863	2 092	2 541

[1] Comprende Instituciones privadas sin fines de lucro que sirven a los hogares.
[2] Dato no publicado por la fuente original. Estimado por diferencia para igualar Ingresos y egresos totales.

176. HONDURAS: INGRESOS Y GASTOS DEL GOBIERNO GENERAL

(Millones de lempiras)

	1960	1965	1970	1975	1977	1978
1. Renta de la propiedad y de la empresa	2	4	7	42	28	30
2. Impuestos indirectos	61[1]	87[1]	124	185	364	397
3. Impuestos directos	11	18	44	86	107	141
4. Contribuciones a la seguridad social	-	4	6	19	27	32
5. Transferencias corrientes n.e.p. de residentes	1	1	4	8	8	6
6. Transferencias corrientes n.e.p. del resto del mundo	7	8	9	29	25	32
Total: Ingresos corrientes	82	122	194	369	559	638
7. Gasto de consumo final	74	102	166	278	417	463
8. Renta de la propiedad	2[4]	4[4]	8[4]	20[4]	32[4]	37[4]
9. Subsidios	-3[5]	-4[5]	-15	-36	-50	-33
10. Prestaciones de seguridad social	...	...	...	...	...	...
11. Transferencias corrientes n.e.p. a residentes	2	3	7	10	22	19
12. Transferencias corrientes n.e.p. al resto del mundo	-	1	2	5	6	8
13. Ahorro	7	16	26	92	132	144
Total: Egresos corrientes	82	122	194	369	559	638

[1] Incluye Utilidades de las empresas públicas.
[2] Incluye Contribuciones a la seguridad social.
[3] Se incluye en Impuestos directos.
[4] Se refiere a Intereses de la deuda pública.
[5] Incluye Pérdidas de las empresas públicas.

175. HONDURAS: INCOME AND OUTLAY OF HOUSEHOLDS, INCLUDING PRIVATE UNINCORPORATED NON-FINANCIAL ENTERPRISES [1]

(Millions of lempiras)

1978	1979	1980	1981	1982	
1 567	1 744	1 972	2 054	2 221	1. Compensation of employees
1 308	1 476	1 700	1 779	1 854	2. Net property and entrepreneurial income
...	...	...	...	...	3. Social security benefits
...	...	...	...	...	4. Social assistance grants
19	22	31	30	31	5. Current transfers n.e.c. from residents
19	29	30	35	33	6. Current transfers n.e.c. from the rest of the world
2 913	3 271	3 733	3 898	4 139	Total: Current receipts
2 560	2 955	3 386	3 756	3 959	7. Final consumption expenditure
128	146	212	165	171	8. Direct taxes
...	...	...	...	...	9. Social security contributions
6	13	14	15	17	10. Current transfers n.e.c. to residents
9	15	15	17	15	11. Current transfers n.e.c. to rest of the world
210	142	106	-55	-23[2]	12. Saving
2 913	3 271	3 733	3 898	4 139	Total: Current disbursements

[1] Includes Private non-profit institutions serving households.
[2] Data not published by original source. Estimated by difference between Total current receipts and disbursements.

176. HONDURAS: INCOME AND OUTLAY OF THE GENERAL GOVERNMENT

(Millions of lempiras)

1979	1980	1981	1982	1983	
76	77	89	96	107	1. Property and entrepreneurial income
453	496	538	542	544	2. Indirect taxes
171	255	203	235	272[2]	3. Direct taxes
36	45	48	42	[3]	4. Social security contributions
13	14	15	30	32	5. Current transfers n.e.c. from residents
42	44	50	47	75	6. Current transfers n.e.c. from the rest of the world
791	931	943	992	1 030	Total: Current receipts
544	682	766	805	889	7. Final consumption expenditure
48[4]	58[4]	57[4]	81[4]	119[4]	8. Property income
-43	-48	-64	-23	-73	9. Subsidies
...	...	...	...	...	10. Social security benefits
22	31	30	42	44	11. Current transfers n.e.c. to residents
15	16	13	5	5	12. Current transfers n.e.c. to rest of the world
205	192	141	82	46	13. Saving
791	931	943	992	1 030	Total: Current disbursements

[1] Including Profits from public enterprises.
[2] Includes Contribution to social security.
[3] Included in Direct taxes.
[4] Refers to public interest debt.
[5] Including Losses from public enterprises.

359

177. JAMAICA: PRODUCTO INTERNO BRUTO POR TIPO DE GASTO, A PRECIOS DE MERCADO

(Millones de dólares de Jamaica)

Tipo de gasto	1960	1965	1969		1970
			A precios corrientes		
1. Gasto de consumo final del gobierno general	43.4	69.8	117.4	102.6	137.3
2. Gasto privado de consumo final	338.5	468.7	634.2	607.7	713.1
3. Variación de existencias	4.6	4.8	7.0	33.7	2.5
4. Formación bruta de capital fijo	99.2	124.2	251.1	315.3	367.2
Construcción	50.6[1]	61.1[1]	126.1[1]	...	...
Maquinaria y equipo	48.6[2]	63.1[2]	126.0[2]	...	...
5. Exportaciones de bienes y servicios	169.9	235.8	365.0	364.9	389.0
6. Menos: Importaciones de bienes y servicios	181.6	248.8	417.9	431.4	438.0
Total: Producto interno bruto	471.2	656.0	957.8	992.7	1 171.1
Discrepancia estadística	-2.7[3]	1.5[3]	1.0[3]	-0.1[3]	-
			A precios constantes de:		
		1960		1974	
1. Gasto de consumo final del gobierno general	43.4	59.5	...	...	...
2. Gasto privado de consumo final	338.5	430.7	...	...	...
3. Variación de existencias	4.6	3.7	...	...	...
4. Formación bruta de capital fijo	99.2	108.9	...	...	...
Construcción	50.6[1]	...	...	...	...
Maquinaria y equipo	48.6[2]	...	...	...	...
5. Exportaciones de bienes y servicios	169.9	243.4	...	...	...
6. Menos: Importaciones de bienes y servicios	181.6	240.9	...	...	...
Total: Producto interno bruto	471.2	605.3[4]	...	1 770.2	1 982.2
Discrepancia estadística	-2.7[3]	-	...	...	...

[1] Incluye Inversión bruta fija en tierras.
[2] Incluye Inversión en exploraciones e investigaciones.
[3] Diferencia para obtener el total de Producto interno bruto a precios de mercado.
[4] Incluye Discrepancia estadística.

177. JAMAICA: GROSS DOMESTIC PRODUCT BY TYPE OF EXPENDITURE, AT MARKET PRICES

(Millions of Jamaica dollars)

1975	1978	1979	1980	1981	1982	Type of expenditure
			At current prices			
477.1	749.9	824.6	985.7	1 118.0	1 297.5	1. General government final consumption expenditure
1 716.0	2 362.5	2 701.4	3 114.7	3 551.5	3 908.6	2. Private final consumption expenditure
60.5	69.8	65.4	47.1	159.8	2.2	3. Increase in stocks
609.6	498.9	748.1	690.1	954.3	1 153.6	4. Gross fixed capital formation
300.8	301.8	393.7	361.5	457.1	574.7	Construction
308.8	197.0	354.5	328.6	497.2	578.9	Machinery and equipment
917.0	1 575.2	2 065.0	2 425.8	2 510.3	2 265.5	5. Exports of goods and services
1 186.1	1 525.2	2 133.1	2 525.2	3 057.6	2 955.1	6. Less: Imports of goods and services
2 594.1	3 731.1	4 271.4	4 738.2	5 236.3	5 672.3	**Total:** Gross domestic product
-	-	-	-	-	-	Statistical discrepancy
		At constant prices of:				
		1974				
...	...	...	...	...	...	1. General government final consumption expenditure
...	...	...	...	...	...	2. Private final consumption expenditure
...	...	...	...	...	...	3. Increase in stocks
...	...	...	...	...	...	4. Gross fixed capital formation
...	...	...	...	...	...	Construction
...	...	...	...	...	...	Machinery and equipment
...	...	...	...	...	...	5. Exports of goods and services
...	...	...	...	...	...	6. Less: Imports of goods and services
2 143.8	1 968.5	1 941.2	1 837.5	1 897.7	1 900.9	**Total:** Gross domestic product
...	...	...	...	...	...	Statistical discrepancy

[1] Including Gross fixed investment in land.
[2] Including Investigation and exploration investment.
[3] Difference in order to estimate the total value of the Gross domestic product at market prices.
[4] Including Statistical discrepancy.

II. CUENTAS NACIONALES

173. JAMAICA: RELACIONES ENTRE PRINCIPALES AGREGADOS DE CUENTAS NACIONALES, A PRECIOS CORRIENTES

(Millones de dólares de Jamaica)

	1960	1965	1969		1970
Remuneración de los asalariados	228.4	325.3	462.0	487.2	587.0
Más: Excedente de explotación	171.4	223.3	340.2	325.1	369.3
Más: Consumo de capital fijo	31.9	45.7	66.7	93.0	117.0
1. Igual: **Producto interno bruto al costo de factores**	431.7	594.3	868.9	905.3	1 073.3
Más: Impuestos indirectos	42.1	67.1	109.2	95.8	105.5
Menos: Subsidios	2.6	5.3	9.1	8.4	7.7
2. Igual: **Producto interno bruto a precios de mercado**	471.2	656.1	969.0	992.7	1 171.1
Menos: Remuneración neta de factores pagada al resto del mundo	16.7	18.7	52.9	51.2	50.9
3. Igual: **Producto nacional bruto a precios de mercado**	454.5	637.4	916.1	941.5	1 120.2
Menos: Consumo de capital fijo	31.9	45.7	66.7	93.0	117.0
4. Igual: **Ingreso nacional a precios de mercado**	422.6	591.7	849.4	848.5	1 003.1
Más: Otras transferencias corrientes netas procedentes del resto del mundo	11.9	9.8	14.1	14.8	22.3
5. Igual: **Ingreso nacional disponible a precios de mercado**	434.5	601.5	863.5	863.3	1 025.4
Menos: Gasto total de consumo final	381.9	538.5	761.1	710.3	850.4
6. Igual: **Ahorro nacional**	52.6	63.0	102.4	153.0	175.0
Menos: Excedente de la nación por transacciones corrientes	-16.5	-22.0	-91.7	-102.9	-77.7
7. Igual: **Formación neta de capital**	71.8	83.5	192.9	255.7	252.7
Más: Consumo de capital fijo	31.9	45.7	66.7	93.0	117.0
8. Igual: **Formación bruta de capital**	103.7	129.2	259.6	348.7	369.7
Discrepancia estadística	-2.6[1]	-1.5[1]	-1.2[1]	-0.2[1]	-

[1] Dato no publicado en la fuente original. Obtenido por diferencia entre Ahorro nacional y Formación neta de capital.

178. JAMAICA: RELATIONS AMONG MAIN NATIONAL ACCOUNTS AGGREGATES, AT CURRENT PRICES

(Millions of Jamaica dollars)

1975	1978	1979	1980	1981	1982	
1 448.6	1 942.4	2 180.1	2 433.4	2 777.3	3 261.1	Compensation of employees
676.2	1 174.1	1 339.4	1 466.7	1 468.2	1 257.8	Plus: Operating surplus
230.6	342.7	393.7	422.8	485.5	537.3	Plus: Consumption of fixed capital
2 355.4	3 459.2	3 913.2	4 322.9	4 731.0	5 056.2	1. Equals: **Gross domestic product at factor cost**
270.0	473.8	505.8	493.8	585.8	697.1	Plus: Indirect taxes
31.3	201.9	147.6	78.5	80.5	81.0	Less: Subsidies
2 594.1	3 731.1	4 271.4	4 738.2	5 236.3	5 672.3	2. Equals: **Gross domestic product at market prices**
-19.7	151.5	256.9	318.2	292.7	279.4	Less: Net factor income paid to the rest of the world
2 613.8	3 579.6	4 014.5	4 420.0	4 943.6	5 392.9	3. Equals: **Gross national product at market prices**
230.6	342.7	393.7	422.8	585.8	537.3	Less: Consumption of fixed capital
2 383.2	3 236.9	3 620.8	3 997.2	4 458.1	4 855.5	4. Equals: **National income at market prices**
19.1	23.2	123.7	145.7	219.6	222.7	Plus: Other net current transfers received from the rest of the world
2 402.3	3 260.1	3 744.5	4 142.9	4 677.7	5 078.2	5. Equals: **National disposable income at market prices**
2 193.1	3 112.4	3 526.0	4 100.4	4 669.5	5 206.1	Less: Total final consumption expenditure
209.2	147.7	218.5	42.5	8.2	-127.9	6. Equals: **National saving**
-230.3	-78.3	-201.3	-271.9	-620.3	-746.3	Less: Surplus of the nation on current transactions
439.5	226.0	419.9	314.4	628.6	618.5	7. Equals: **Net capital formation**
230.6	342.7	393.7	422.8	485.5	537.3	Plus: Consumption of fixed capital
670.1	568.7	813.6	737.2	1 114.1	1 155.8	8. Equals: **Gross capital formation**
-	-	-	-	-	-	Statistical discrepancy

[1] Data not published by the original source. Estimated by difference between National saving and Net capital formation.

179. JAMAICA: PRODUCTO INTERNO BRUTO POR CLASE DE ACTIVIDAD ECONOMICA, A PRECIOS DE MERCADO [1]

(Millones de dólares de Jamaica)

Clase de actividad	1960	1965	1969	1970
	A precios corrientes			
1. Agricultura, caza, silvicultura y pesca	51.9	69.1	74.4	76.7	78.4
2. Explotación de minas y canteras	41.6	57.7	124.7	123.2	147.8
3. Industrias manufactureras	58.7	89.3	120.5	160.0	183.8
4. Electricidad, gas y agua	4.5	8.0	11.1	10.6	11.8
5. Construcción	51.1	63.6	105.3	125.0	155.7
6. Comercio al por mayor y al por menor, restaurantes y hoteles [2]	88.0	99.7	108.8	197.9	222.5
7. Transportes, almacenamiento y comunicaciones	33.4	43.9	62.5	55.9	64.5
8. Establecimientos financieros, seguros, bienes inmuebles y servicios prestados a las empresas	29.7[3]	46.8[3]	69.5[3]	119.7[3]	154.6
Viviendas	13.5	20.5	24.8	40.2[4]	52.1[4]
9. Servicios comunales, sociales y personales	72.8[5]	116.2[5]	181.9[5]	143.3[6]	176.2[6]
Servicios gubernamentales	26.6	44.6	77.5	76.8	91.6
Subtotal	**431.7**	**594.3**	**858.7**	**1 012.3**	**1 195.3**
Menos: Comisión imputada de los servicios bancarios	...	...	...	19.6	24.2
Más: Derechos de importación	...	...	...	...	...
Total: Producto interno bruto	**431.7[1]**	**594.3[1]**	**858.8[1]**	**992.7**	**1 171.1**
	A precios constantes de:				
		1960		**1974**	
1. Agricultura, caza, silvicultura y pesca	51.9	58.5	56.6	141.4	149.8
2. Explotación de minas y canteras	41.6	54.6	70.0	108.2	139.7
3. Industrias manufactureras	58.7	83.0	97.5	328.0	348.1
4. Electricidad, gas y agua	4.5	8.1	62.9	15.2	16.4
5. Construcción	51.1	58.4	12.0	216.3	261.7
6. Comercio al por mayor y al por menor, restaurantes y hoteles [2]	77.8	94.0	81.4	400.7	423.2
7. Transportes, almacenamiento y comunicaciones	33.4	52.2	67.2	97.9	109.1
8. Establecimientos financieros, seguros, bienes inmuebles y servicios prestados a las empresas	29.7[3]	37.5[3]	42.7[3]	246.0	272.7US
Viviendas	13.5	15.2	16.1	172.1[4]	194.1[4]
9. Servicios comunales, sociales y personales	82.9[5]	97.6[5]	153.4[5]	266.8[6]	314.1[6]
Servicios gubernamentales	28.7	36.4	56.5	150.7	180.1
Subtotal	**431.6**	**543.9**	**643.7**	**1 820.5**	**2 034.8**
Menos: Comisión imputada de los servicios bancarios	...	...	...	50.3	52.6
Más: Derechos de importación	...	...	...	...	...
Total: Producto interno bruto	**431.6[1]**	**543.9**	**643.7[1]**	**1 770.2**	**1 982.2**
Discrepancia estadística	-	-	-	-	

[1] Entre los años 1960 y 1969 (de la serie antigua), las cifras están expresadas al costo de factores.
[2] Restaurantes y hoteles están incluidos en Servicios comunales, sociales y personales.
[3] Servicios prestados a las empresas están incluidos en Servicios comunales, sociales y personales.
[4] Incluye Servicios prestados a las empresas.
[5] Incluye Restaurantes y hoteles y Servicios prestados a las empresas.
[6] Incluye Restaurantes y hoteles.
[7] Obtenido por diferencia para obtener el total del Producto interno bruto.

179. JAMAICA: GROSS DOMESTIC PRODUCT BY KIND OF ECONOMIC ACTIVITY, AT MARKET PRICES [1]

(Millions of Jamaica dollars)

1975	1978	1979	1980	1981	1982	Kind of activity
		At current prices				
190.6	296.1	310.3	385.1	398.9	398.8	1. Agriculture, hunting, forestry and fishing
220.8	510.4	622.5	678.0	543.5	336.6	2. Mining and quarrying
444.1	636.7	691.8	762.2	811.9	925.9	3. Manufacturing
38.9	84.2	89.6	75.2	84.7	96.4	4. Electricity, gas and water
252.4	252.1	311.3	279.1	368.4	466.6	5. Construction
508.0	619.8	758.6	913.1	1 091.7	1 226.4	6. Wholesale and retail trade, restaurants and hotels [2]
156.9	227.8	250.9	243.9	267.8	325.0	7. Transport, storage and communications
361.4	465.5	533.8	616.6	777.7	892.6	8. Finance, insurance, real estate and business services
252.4[4]	319.8[4]	368.8[4]	407.6[4]	505.8[4]	586.0[4]	Dwellings
500.6[6]	742.4[6]	805.0[6]	927.3[6]	1 059.3[6]	1 211.0[6]	9. Community, social and personal services
327.8	509.2	566.0	679.4	770.7	890.3	Government services
2 673.4	3 835.0	4 373.9	4 880.5	5 403.9	5 879.3	*Subtotal*
79.6	104.0	102.5	142.3	167.6	207.0	Less: Imputed bank service charges
...	...	..	...	...	...	Plus: Import duties
2 594.1	3 731.0	4 271.4	4 738.2	5 236.3	5 672.3	**Total: Gross domestic product**
		At constant prices of: 1974				
156.0	178.0	160.6	150.6	156.4	145.9	1. Agriculture, hunting, forestry and fishing
157.2	150.4	148.0	162.7	164.8	117.0	2. Mining and quarrying
396.5	331.9	318.3	287.5	291.1	303.2	3. Manufacturing
23.1	23.7	23.3	23.6	23.9	23.9	4. Electricity, gas and water
210.8	138.5	137.4	98.3	99.9	112.7	5. Construction
413.0	306.3	293.7	273.1	287.8	304.4	6. Wholesale and retail trade, restaurants and hotels [2]
142.6	129.4	129.9	124.5	125.6	130.8	7. Transport, storage and communications
306.5	308.2	306.9	314.1	331.0	333.4	8. Finance, insurance, real estate and business services
211.9[4]	210.4[4]	216.0[4]	215.4[4]	222.6[4]	233.6[4]	Dwellings
407.0[6]	471.3[6]	478.1[6]	470.2[6]	482.9[6]	493.5[6]	9. Community, social and personal services
265.1	344.1	360.5	358.5	369.5	370.9	Government services
2 212.7	2 037.5	1 996.2	1 904.6	1 963.4	1 964.8	*Subtotal*
68.9	68.0	55.0	67.1	65.8	64.0	Less: Imputed bank service charges
...	...	...	...	...	...	Plus: Import duties
2 143.8	1 968.5	1 941.2	1 837.5	1 897.7	1 900.9	**Total: Gross domestic product**
-	1.0[7]	-	-	0.1[7]	0.1[7]	Statistical discrepancy

[1] From 1960 to 1969 (of the old series), the figures are expressed at factor cost.
[2] Restaurants and hotels are included in Community, social and personal services.
[3] Business services are included in Community, social and personal services.
[4] Including Business services.
[5] Including Restaurants and hotels and Business services.
[6] Including Restaurants and hotels.
[7] Obtained by difference in order to estimate the total value of the Gross domestic product.

II. CUENTAS NACIONALES

180. JAMAICA: INGRESOS Y GASTOS DEL GOBIERNO GENERAL

(Millones de dólares de Jamaica)

	1960	1965	1969		1970
1. Renta de la propiedad y de la empresa	0.7	1.3	1.6	20.3	24.6
2. Impuestos indirectos	42.1	67.1	109.2	95.8	105.5
3. Impuestos directos	[1]	[1]	79.2	62.9	79.9
4. Contribuciones a la seguridad social	23.0[2]	40.1[2]	8.9	8.9	9.2
5. Transferencias corrientes n.e.p. de residentes	0.5	1.0	1.7	3.1	3.2
6. Transferencias corrientes n.e.p. del resto del mundo	4.0	2.5	11.0	...	...
Total: Ingresos corrientes	**70.4**	**111.8**	**211.6**	**191.0**	**222.4**
7. Gasto de consumo final	43.4	69.8	121.8	102.5	137.3
8. Renta de la propiedad	...	...	...	12.4	15.8
9. Subsidios	2.6	5.3	9.1	8.4	7.7
10. Prestaciones de seguridad social	...	...	...	0.7	0.7
11. Transferencias corrientes n.e.p. a residentes	7.9	13.0	24.7	11.2	10.9
12. Transferencias corrientes n.e.p. al resto del mundo	4.3	7.0	11.6	...	...
13. Ahorro	12.1	16.6	44.2	55.8	50.0
Total: Egresos corrientes	**70.3**	**111.8**	**211.6**	**191.0**	**222.4**

[1] Se incluye en Contribuciones a la seguridad social.
[2] Incluye Impuestos indirectos.

180. JAMAICA: INCOME AND OUTLAY OF THE GENERAL GOVERNMENT

(Millions of Jamaica dollars)

1975	1978	1979	1980	1981	1982	
43.6	45.1	57.5	75.4	73.5	67.7	1. *Property and entrepreneurial income*
269.9	415.2	505.8	493.8	585.8	697.1	2. *Indirect taxes*
327.1	526.1	605.1	725.4	780.2	778.1	3. *Direct taxes*
19.5	36.1	38.7	48.0	53.1	73.1	4. *Social security contributions*
8.1	11.1	11.5	14.7	21.2	21.1	5. *Current transfers n.e.c. from residents*
...	...	...	...	...	...	6. *Current transfers n.e.c. from the rest of the world*
668.2	**1 033.6**	**1 218.6**	**1 357.3**	**1 513.8**	**1 637.1**	***Total: Current receipts***
477.1	749.9	824.6	985.7	1 118.1	1 297.6	7. *Final consumption expenditure*
58.1	187.3	249.7	349.2	430.8	601.5	8. *Property income*
31.3	201.9	147.6	78.5	80.5	81.0	9. *Subsidies*
6.4	11.8	12.7	18.7	21.7	35.0	10. *Social security benefits*
25.8	46.3	47.2	52.5	57.8	71.8	11. *Current transfers n.e.c. to residents*
...	...	...	...	...	...	12. *Current transfers n.e.c. to rest of the world*
69.5	-163.6	-63.2	-127.3	-195.1	-449.8	13. *Saving*
668.2	**1 033.6**	**1 218.6**	**1 357.3**	**1 513.8**	**1 637.1**	***Total: Current disbursements***

[1] *Included in Social security contributions.*
[2] *Including Indirect taxes.*

181. MEXICO: PRODUCTO INTERNO BRUTO POR TIPO DE GASTO, A PRECIOS DE MERCADO

(Millones de pesos)

Tipo de gasto	1960	1965	1970	1975	1978
			A precios corrientes		
1. Gasto de consumo final del gobierno general	9 497	17 667	32 575	32 243.2	113 493.1	255 197.1
2. Gasto privado de consumo final	114 725	182 042	300 775	319 521.8	755 923.5	1 543 833.2
3. Variación de existencias	4 157	10 513	11 447	12 295.4	25 008.1	59 235.1
4. Formación bruta de capital fijo	25 507	44 295	82 300	88 660.6	235 607.1	492 425.3
Construcción	14 043	23 042	44 643	50 755.4	135 522.1	288 605.2
Maquinaria y equipo	11 464	21 253	37 657	37 905.2	100 085.0	203 820.1
5. Exportaciones de bienes y servicios	15 566	23 424	34 312	34 430.5	75 839.0	244 706.6
6. Menos: Importaciones de bienes y servicios	18 941	25 913	42 709	42 880.1	105 821.0	257 999.4
Total: Producto interno bruto	150 511	252 028	418 700	444 271.4	1 100 049.8	2 337 397.9

			A precios constantes de:		
		1960		1970	
1. Gasto de consumo final del gobierno general	9 497	15 329	22 157	32 243.2	54 018.1	62 448.1
2. Gasto privado de consumo final	114 725	152 384	213 352	319 521.8	425 435.7	490 806.1
3. Variación de existencias	4 157	9 230	8 971	12 295.4	18 534.7	21 672.8
4. Formación bruta de capital fijo	25 507	39 054	61 605	88 660.6	132 316.1	142 799.3
Construcción	14 043	19 461	31 240	50 755.4	71 742.7	82 185.4
Maquinaria y equipo	11 464	19 593	30 365	37 905.2	60 573.4	60 613.9
5. Exportaciones de bienes y servicios	15 566	21 360	25 798	34 430.5	43 231.5	64 499.3
6. Menos: Importaciones de bienes y servicios	18 941	25 037	35 283	42 880.1	63 560.3	70 243.3
Total: Producto interno bruto	150 511	212 320	296 600	444 271.4	609 975.8	711 982.3

181. MEXICO: GROSS DOMESTIC PRODUCT BY TYPE OF EXPENDITURE, AT MARKET PRICES

(Millions of pesos)

1979	1980	1981	1982	1983	Type of expenditure
		At current prices			
334 315.9	462 838.2	684 537.4	1 057 557.1	1 590 312.6	1. General government final consumption expenditure
1 975 879.1	2 651 488.5	3 583 821.5	5 776 093.6	10 356 004.0	2. Private final consumption expenditure
77 588.4	169 841.1	193 246.1	- 98 040.7	499 923.6	3. Increase in stocks
718 454.8	1 032 920.2	1 509 365.7	2 098 829.6	2 972 280.4	4. Gross fixed capital formation
404 709.8	587 726.9	856 158.5	...	...	Construction
313 745.0	445 193.3	653 207.2	...	...	Machinery and equipment
343 283.5	537 241.4	701 552.9	1 636 502.7	3 340 558.9	5. Exports of goods and services
381 995.3	577 839.0	798 138.0	1 053 852.9	1 617 385.8	6. Less: Imports of goods and services
3 067 526.4	4 276 490.4	5 874 385.6	9 417 089.4	17 141 693.7	Total: Gross domestic product
		At constant prices of:			
		1970			
68 433.7	74 957.5	82 501.2	84 440.2	83 335.4	1. General government final consumption expenditure
534 218.5	574 502.6	616 706.5	623 356.2	576 610.9	2. Private final consumption expenditure
21 704.0	38 609.6	46 354.6	4 172.7	8 809.0	3. Increase in stocks
171 714.2	197 364.5	226 427.4	190 312.8	137 240.7	4. Gross fixed capital formation
92 923.3	104 562.7	116 410.8	110 498.5	...	Construction
78 790.9	92 801.8	110 016.6	79 814.3	...	Machinery and equipment
72 328.8	76 746.2	81 499.5	92 641.7	103 270.7	5. Exports of goods and services
91 236.6	120 325.9	144 724.4	91 085.0	53 093.1	6. Less: Imports of goods and services
777 162.6	841 854.5	908 764.8	903 838.6	856 173.6	Total: Gross domestic product

182. MEXICO: RELACIONES ENTRE PRINCIPALES AGREGADOS DE CUENTAS NACIONALES, A PRECIOS CORRIENTES

(Millones de pesos)

	1960	1965	1970		1975	1978
Remuneración de los asalariados	46 918	81 708	147 748	158 453.5	418 899.0	885 660.6
Más: Excedente de explotación	87 089	143 243	221 442	240 375.9	558 503.1	1 177 303.9
Más: Consumo de capital fijo	10 170	16 014	28 710	23 800.5	59 722.3	136 197.2
1. Igual: **Producto interno bruto al costo de factores**	144 177	240 965	397 900	422 629.9	1 037 124.4	2 199 161.7
Más: Impuestos indirectos	6 334[1]	11 063[1]	20 800[1]	24 761.3	79 149.3	175 254.5
Menos: Subsidios	[2]	[2]	[2]	3 119.8	16 223.9	37 018.3
2. Igual: **Producto interno bruto a precios de mercado**	150 511	252 028	418 700	444 271.4	1 100 049 8	2 337 397.9
Menos: Remuneración neta de factores pagada al resto del mundo	768	1 529	4 121	5 626.0	17 929.0	52 504.3
3. Igual: **Producto nacional bruto a precios de mercado**	149 743	250 499	414 579	438 645.4	1 082 120.8	2 284 893.6
Menos: Consumo de capital fijo	10 170	16 014	28 710	23 800.5	59 722.3	136 197.2
4. Igual: **Ingreso nacional a precios de mercado**	139 573	234 485	385 869	414 844.9	1 022 398.5	2 148 696.4
Más: Otras transferencias corrientes netas procedentes del resto del mundo	383	81	691	692.0	1 751.0	4 471.0
5. Igual: **Ingreso nacional disponible a precios de mercado**	139 956	234 566	386 560	415 536.9	1 024 149.5	2 153 167.4
Menos: Gasto total de consumo final	124 222	199 709	333 350	351 765.0	869 416.6	1 799 030.3
6. Igual: **Ahorro nacional**	15 734	34 857	53 210	63 771.9	154 732.9	354 137.1
Menos: Excedente de la nación por transacciones corrientes	-3 760	-3 937	-11 827	-13 383.6	-46 160.0	-61 326.1
7. Igual: **Formación neta de capital**	19 494	38 794	65 037	77 155.5	200 892.9	415 463.2
Más: Consumo de capital fijo	10 170	16 014	28 710	23 800.5	59 722.3	136 197.2
8. Igual: **Formación bruta de capital**	29 664	54 808	93 747	100 956.0	260 615.2	551 660.4

[1] Incluye Subsidios.
[2] Se incluye en Impuestos indirectos.

182. MEXICO: RELATIONS AMONG MAIN NATIONAL ACCOUNTS AGGREGATES, AT CURRENT PRICES

(Millions of pesos)

1979	1980	1981	1982	1983	
1 157 160.1	1 542 177.2	2 194 201.5	3 371 968.7	4 932 391.0	Compensation of employees
1 525 044.7	2 142 909.4	2 876 012.1	4 581 296.7	9 449 414.4	Plus: Operating surplus
178 389.9	236 591.6	327 828.6	528 075.4	992 850.0	Plus: Consumption of fixed capital
2 860 594.7	3 921 678.2	5 398 042.2	8 481 340.8	15 374 655.4	1. Equals: **Gross domestic product at factor cost**
260 314.1	434 393.7	598 565.4	1 181 153.1	2 305 453.0	Plus: Indirect taxes
53 382.4	79 581.5	122 222.0	245 404.5	538 414.7	Less: Subsidies
3 067 526.4	4 276 490.4	5 874 385.6	9 417 089.4	17 141 693.7	2. Equals: **Gross domestic product at market prices**
77 141.0	117 224.7	200 156.0	508 949.2	1 041 747.5	Less: Net factor income paid to the rest of the world
2 990 385.4	4 159 265.7	5 674 229.6	8 908 140.2	16 099 946.2	3. Equals: **Gross national product at market prices**
178 389.9	236 591.6	327 828.6	528 075.4	992 850.0	Less: Consumption of fixed capital
2 811 995.5	3 922 674.1	5 346 401.0	8 380 064.8	15 107 096.2	4. Equals: **National income at market prices**
5 105.6	6 158.5	7 498.2	16 854.2	53 506.8	Plus: Other net current transfers received from the rest of the world
2 817 101.1	3 928 832.6	5 353 899.2	8 396 919.0	15 160 603.0	5. Equals: **National disposable income at market prices**
2 310 195.0	3 114 326.7	4 268 358.9	6 833 650.7	11 946 316.6	Less: Total final consumption expenditure
506 906.1	814 505.9	1 085 540.3	1 563 268.3	3 214 286.4	6. Equals: **National saving**
-110 747.2	-151 663.8	-289 242.9	90 554.8	734 932.4	Less: Surplus of the nation on current transactions
617 653.3	966 169.7	1 374 783.2	1 472 713.5	2 479 354.0	7. Equals: **Net capital formation**
178 389.9	236 591.6	327 828.6	528 075.4	992 850.0	Plus: Consumption of fixed capital
796 043.2	1 202 761.3	1 702 611.8	2 000 788.9	3 472 204.0	8. Equals: **Gross capital formation**

[1] Including Subsidies.
[2] Included in Indirect taxes.

183. MEXICO: PRODUCTO INTERNO BRUTO POR CLASE DE ACTIVIDAD ECONOMICA, A PRECIOS DE MERCADO

(Millones de pesos)

Clase de actividad	1960	1965	1970	1970	1975	1978
			A precios corrientes			
1. Agricultura, caza, silvicultura y pesca	23 970	36 386	47 435	54 123.2	123 153.0	239 570.8
2. Explotación de minas y canteras	7 395	11 918	17 680	11 190.3	31 729.5	79 496.8
3. Industrias manufactureras	28 931	52 925	95 900	105 203.0	256 701.0	550 963.9
4. Electricidad, gas y agua	1 502	3 425	6 181	5 146.7	9 793.1	24 476.8
5. Construcción	6 105	10 131	21 401	23 530.2	65 810.6	139 415.1
6. Comercio al por mayor y al por menor, restaurantes y hoteles	46 880	76 334	124 125	115 162.9	277 033.1	560 355.9
7. Transportes, almacenamiento y comunicaciones	4 996	7 268	11 072	21 357.4	62 611.8	150 428.5
8. Establecimientos financieros, seguros, bienes inmuebles y servicios prestados a las empresas	13 888	23 068	38 831	50 209.7	104 285.9	208 729.6
Viviendas	11 051	18 249	30 115	41 808.4 [1]	83 410.7 [1]	164 708.2 [1]
9. Servicios comunales, sociales y personales	18 363	33 085	60 677	63 743.5	181 054.7	409 466.8
Servicios gubernamentales	7 399	13 740	25 971	12 542.3	40 432.3	81 105.6
Subtotal	152 030	254 540	423 302	449 666.9	1 112 172.7	2 362 904.2
Menos: Comisión imputada de los servicios bancarios	1 519	2 512	4 602	5 395.5	12 122.9	25 506.3
Más: Derechos de importación	...	...	...	...	...	...
Total: Producto interno bruto	150 511	252 028	418 700	444 271.4	1 100 049.8	2 337 397.9
		A precios constantes de:				
		1960			**1970**	
1. Agricultura, caza, silvicultura y pesca	23 970	30 222	34 535	54 123.2	62 725.6	72 199.7
2. Explotación de minas y canteras	7 395	9 954	14 154	11 190.3	14 972.3	19 524.8
3. Industrias manufactureras	28 931	45 251	69 060	105 203.0	148 057.7	176 816.5
4. Electricidad, gas y agua	1 502	2 769	5 357	5 146.7	8 235.1	10 723.7
5. Construcción	6 105	8 534	13 583	23 530.2	32 792.2	36 531.8
6. Comercio al por mayor y al por menor, restaurantes y hoteles	46 880	67 368	94 491	115 162.9	157 978.3	179 045.2
7. Transportes, almacenamiento y comunicaciones	4 996	6 443	9 395	21 357.4	37 904.0	47 780.2
8. Establecimientos financieros, seguros, bienes inmuebles y servicios prestados a las empresas	13 888	17 516	23 108	50 209.7	66 196.5	74 623.0
Viviendas	11 051	13 889	18 098	41 808.4 [1]	55 501.8 [1]	61 524.5 [1]
9. Servicios comunales, sociales y personales	18 363	26 547	36 484	63 743.5	88 209.2	103 256.9
Servicios gubernamentales	7 399	11 834	17 097	12 542.3	21 211.7	23 284.9
Subtotal	152 030	214 604	300 167	449 666.9	617 070.9	720 501.8
Menos: Comisión imputada de los servicios bancarios	1 519	2 284	3 567	5 395.5	7 095.1	8 519.5
Más: Derechos de importación	...	...	...	...	...	...
Total: Producto interno bruto	150 511	212 320	296 600	444 271.4	609 975.8	711 982.3

[1] Se refiere al alquiler de inmuebles.

183. MEXICO: GROSS DOMESTIC PRODUCT BY KIND OF ECONOMIC ACTIVITY, AT MARKET PRICES

(Millions of pesos)

1979	1980	1981	1982	1983	Kind of activity
		At current prices			
281 262.4	357 131.1	477 463.3	693 316.7	1 358 919.1	1. Agriculture, hunting, forestry and fishing
131 564.1	291 374.1	369 523.2	934 280.9	2 047 407.3	2. Mining and quarrying
714 612.9	985 013.1	1 311 492.7	2 000 785.5	3 870 597.1	3. Manufacturing
31 243.8	42 034.9	52 361.8	77 344.0	155 357.9	4. Electricity, gas and water
194 120.5	276 192.9	409 317.9	589 827.1	878 252.6	5. Construction
743 435.5	999 555.8	1 361 225.3	2 146 407.6	3 821 762.1	6. Wholesale and retail trade, restaurants and hotels
199 694.1	279 111.6	388 791.6	604 377.7	1 138 648.3	7. Transport, storage and communications
259 688.0	336 895.2	470 296.7	710 463.3	1 195 662.5	8. Finance, insurance, real estate and business services
196 510.6[1]	250 735.3[1]	340 923.9[1]	...	...	Dwellings
545 311.4	756 971.1	1 104 880.4	1 767 376.3	2 819 765.1	9. Community, social and personal services
102 887.2	141 046.1	205 882.8	...	...	Government services
3 100 932.7	4 324 279.8	5 945 352.9	9 309 999.7	17 286 372.0	*Subtotal*
33 406.3	47 789.4	70 967.3	107 089.7	144 678.2	Less: Imputed bank service charges
...	...	...	...	...	Plus: Import duties
3 067 526.4	4 276 490.4	5 874 385.6	9 417 089.4	17 141 693.8	**Total:** Gross domestic product
		At constant prices of: 1970			
70 692.0	75 703.8	80 299.4	79 821.5	82 131.1	1. Agriculture, hunting, forestry and fishing
22 397.4	27 390.7	31 593.1	34 497.5	33 557.8	2. Mining and quarrying
195 613.7	209 681.9	224 326.2	217 852.2	202 026.3	3. Manufacturing
11 829.5	12 593.9	13 646.7	14 554.1	14 655.0	4. Electricity, gas and water
41 296.9	46 379.1	51 851.8	49 259.2	40 392.5	5. Construction
200 006.1	216 174.0	234 490.9	230 032.3	207 034.4	6. Wholesale and retail trade, restaurants and hotels
55 199.4	62 970.1	69 710.4	67 086.2	63 859.6	7. Transport, storage and communications
78 569.7	82 168.4	86 113.2	88 624.8	90 481.2	8. Finance, insurance, real estate and business services
63 610.2[1]	65 842.4[1]	67 993.1[1]	69 990.6[1]	71 333.7[1]	Dwellings
111 372.3	119 777.7	128 948.5	134 643.8	135 095.1	9. Community, social and personal services
25 236.8	27 826.5	30 362.7	31 685.9	32 636.9	Government services
786 977.0	852 839.6	920 980.2	916 371.2	869 233.0	*Subtotal*
9 814.4	10 985.1	12 215.4	12 533.0	13 059.4	Less: Imputed bank service charges
...	...	...	...	...	Plus: Import duties
777 162.6	841 854.5	908 764.8	903 838.6	856 173.6	**Total:** Gross domestic product

[1] It refers to rental of real estate.

184. NICARAGUA: PRODUCTO INTERNO BRUTO POR TIPO DE GASTO,
A PRECIOS DE MERCADO

(Millones de córdobas)

Tipo de gasto	1960	1965	1970		1975
			A precios corrientes		
1. Gasto de consumo final del gobierno general	203.5	316.6	521.4	521.4	1 007.3
2. Gasto privado de consumo final	1 853.3	2 942.8	4 037.6	4 097.6	8 608.6
3. Variación de existencias	51.5	83.9	119.6	121.1	-181.7
4. Formación bruta de capital fijo	300.3	745.7	891.2	891.2	2 510.3
Construcción	110.0	266.5	354.6	354.6	1 137.2
Maquinaria y equipo	190.3	479.2	536.6	536.6	1 373.1
5. Exportaciones de bienes y servicios	528.5	1 162.0	1 453.2	1 453.2	3 122.0
6. Menos: Importaciones de bienes y servicios	588.7	1 285.2	1 586.9	1 586.9	4 112.5
Total: Producto interno bruto	2 348.4	3 965.8	5 436.1	5 497.6	10 954.0
			A precios constantes de:		
		1958		1980	
1. Gasto de consumo final del gobierno general	199.9	237.2	293.9	1 416.8	1 963.5
2. Gasto privado de consumo final	1 858.9	2 909.1	3 365.7	15 151.1	18 861.1
3. Variación de existencias	52.6	85.1	102.6	441.9	-426.5
4. Formación bruta de capital fijo	296.1	742.8	825.5	2 975.0	4 451.0
Construcción	105.8	253.8	320.7	1 459.2	2 608.3
Maquinaria y equipo	190.3	489.0	504.8	1 515.8	1 842.7
5. Exportaciones de bienes y servicios	573.8	1 205.4	1 403.2	4 584.2	6 728.4
6. Menos: Importaciones de bienes y servicios	588.7	1 311.4	1 326.6	4 482.8	5 841.6
Total: Producto interno bruto	2 392.6	3 868.2	4 664.3	20 086.2	25 735.9

184. NICARAGUA: GROSS DOMESTIC PRODUCT BY TYPE OF EXPENDITURE, AT MARKET PRICES

(Millions of córdobas)

1978	1979	1980	1981	1982	1983	Type of expenditure
		At current prices				
1 762.4	2 590.9	4 106.6	5 375.6	6 649.2	10 360.2	1. General government final consumption expenditure
10 132.0	10 739.1	18 380.9	19 534.3	21 203.6	22 091.4	2. Private final consumption expenditure
-281.6	-1 800.0	481.6	567.0	653.3	1 083.1	3. Increase in stocks
2 179.9	966.9	2 882.5	5 054.6	4 497:1	6 101.3	4. Gross fixed capital formation
853.3	341.8	1 268.6	1 711.3	1 781.8	1 930.3	Construction
1 326.6	625.1	1 613.9	3 343.3	2 715.3	4 171.0	Machinery and equipment
5 159.7	6 099.7	5 039.3	5 470.5	4 529.9	6 039.6	5. Exports of goods and services
4 685.8	4 083.3	8 999.3	10 229.2	7 836.5	10 061.4	6. Less: Imports of goods and services
14 266.6	14 513.3	21 891.6	25 772.8	29 696.6	35 614.2	*Total:* Gross domestic product
		At constant prices of:				
		1980				
2 842.6	3 044.5	4 106.6	4 658.2	5 445.7	7 464.1	1. General government final consumption expenditure
19 998.0	14 595.9	18 380.9	16 007.2	13 977.8	13 740.4	2. Private final consumption expenditure
-534.3	-2 469.1	481.6	507.2	501.2	709.3	3. Increase in stocks
3 431.4	1 202.2	2 882.5	4 693.7	3 800.7	3 966.4	4. Gross fixed capital formation
1 752.2	452.7	1 268.6	1 530.7	1 161.9	943.9	Construction
1 679.2	749.5	1 613.9	3 163.0	2 638.8	3 022.5	Machinery and equipment
7 413.4	8 483.6	5 039.3	5 788.9	5 323.0	5 416.7	5. Exports of goods and services
6 101.3	4 955.5	8 999.3	8 603.2	6 269.4	7 458.4	6. Less: Imports of goods and services
27 049.8	19 901.6	21 891.6	23 052.0	22 779.0	23 838.5	*Total:* Gross domestic product

II. CUENTAS NACIONALES

185. NICARAGUA: RELACIONES ENTRE PRINCIPALES AGREGADOS DE CUENTAS NACIONALES, A PRECIOS CORRIENTES

(Millones de córdobas)

	1960	1965	1970	1975
Remuneración de los asalariados	1 245.7	2 155.9	2 906.1	...	9 483.0 [1]
Más: Excedente de explotación	793.4	1 281.2	1 853.4	...	[2]
Más: Consumo de capital fijo	93.9	158.6	217.4	219.9	438.2
1. Igual: **Producto interno bruto al costo de factores**	2 133.0	3 595.7	4 976.9	5 038.4	9 921.2
Más: Impuestos indirectos	215.4 [3]	370.1 [3]	459.2 [3]	459.2 [3]	1 032.8 [3]
Menos: Subsidios	[4]	[4]	[4]	[4]	[4]
2. Igual: **Producto interno bruto a precios de mercado**	2 348.4	3 965.8	5 436.1	5 497.6	10 954.0
Menos: Remuneración neta de factores pagada al resto del mundo	12.6	77.0	176.4	176.4	406.9
3. Igual: **Producto nacional bruto a precios de mercado**	2 335.8	3 888.8	5 259.7	5 321.2	10 547.1
Menos: Consumo de capital fijo	93.9	158.6	217.4	219.9	438.2
4. Igual: **Ingreso nacional a precios de mercado**	2 241.9	3 730.2	5 042.3	5 101.3	10 108.9
Más: Otras transferencias corrientes netas procedentes del resto del mundo	21.0	45.5	43.7	...	117.0
5. Igual: **Ingreso nacional disponible a precios de mercado**	2 262.9	3 775.7	5 086.0	...	10 225.9
Menos: Gasto total de consumo final	2 056.8	3 259.4	4 559.0	4 619.0	9 615.9
6. Igual: **Ahorro nacional**	206.1	516.3	527.0	...	610.0
Menos: Excedente de la nación por transacciones corrientes	-51.8	-154.7	-266.4	...	-1 280.4
7. Igual: **Formación neta de capital**	257.9	671.0	793.4	792.4	1 890.4
Más: Consumo de capital fijo	93.9	158.6	217.4	219.9	438.2
8. Igual: **Formación bruta de capital**	351.8	829.6	1 010.8	1 012.3	2 328.6

[1] Incluye Excedente de explotación.
[2] Se incluye en Remuneración de los asalariados.
[3] Incluye Subsidios.
[4] Se incluye en Impuestos indirectos.

185. NICARAGUA: RELATIONS AMONG MAIN NATIONAL ACCOUNTS AGGREGATES, AT CURRENT PRICES

(Millions of córdobas)

1978	1979	1980	1981	1982	1983	
12 366.1 [1]	12 585.0 [1]	19 653.1 [1]	21 364.6 [1]	24 045.6 [1]	27 603.3 [1]	*Compensation of employees*
[2]	[2]	[2]	[2]	[2]	[2]	*Plus: Operating surplus*
570.7	580.5	875.7	1 030.9	1 187.9	1 424.6	*Plus: Consumption of fixed capital*
12 936.8	13 165.5	20 528.8	22 395.5	25 233.5	29 027.9	1. *Equals:* **Gross domestic product at factor cost**
1 329.8 [3]	1 347.8 [3]	1 362.8 [3]	3 377.3 [3]	4 463.1 [3]	6 586.3 [3]	*Plus: Indirect taxes*
[4]	[4]	[4]	[4]	[4]	[4]	*Less: Subsidies*
14 266.6	14 513.3	21 891.6	25 772.8	29 696.6	35 614.2	2. *Equals:* **Gross domestic product at market prices**
690.5	740.0	922.6	1 015.6	1 462.2	784.3	*Less: Net factor income paid to the rest of the world*
13 576.1	13 773.3	20 969.0	24 757.2	28 234.4	34 829.9	3. *Equals:* **Gross national product at market prices**
570.7	580.5	875.7	1 030.9	1 187.9	1 424.6	*Less: Consumption of fixed capital*
13 005.4	13 192.8	20 093.3	23 726.3	27 046.5	33 405.3	4. *Equals:* **National income at market prices**
68.1	845.2	800.1	697.0	497.8	...	*Plus: Other net current transfers received from the rest of the world*
13 073.5	14 038.0	20 893.4	24 423.3	27 544.3	...	5. *Equals:* **National disposable income at market prices**
11 894.4	13 330.0	22 487.5	24 910.0	27 852.8	32 451.6	*Less: Total final consumption expenditure*
1 179.1	708.0	-1 594.1	-486.7	-308.5	...	6. *Equals:* **National saving**
-148.5	2 121.6	-4 082.5	-5 077.3	-4 271.0	...	*Less: Surplus of the nation on current transactions*
1 327.6	-1 413.6	2 488.4	4 590.6	3 962.5	5 759.8	7. *Equals:* **Net capital formation**
570.7	580.5	875.7	1 030.9	1 187.9	1 424.6	*Plus: Consumption of fixed capital*
1 898.3	- 833.1	3 364.1	5 621.6	5 150.4	7 184.4	8. *Equals:* **Gross capital formation**

[1] *Including Operating surplus.*
[2] *Included in Compensation of employees.*
[3] *Including Subsidies.*
[4] *Included in Indirect taxes.*

186. NICARAGUA: PRODUCTO INTERNO BRUTO POR CLASE DE ACTIVIDAD ECONOMICA, A PRECIOS DE MERCADO

(Millones de córdobas)

Clase de actividad	1960	1965	1970	1975	1978
			A precios corrientes		
1. Agricultura, caza, silvicultura y pesca	557.1	996.8	1 353.2	1 392.4	2 462.6	3 708.5
2. Explotación de minas y canteras	29.9	49.2	33.5	33.5	39.1	98.5
3. Industrias manufactureras	376.5	700.0	1 110.8	1 110.8	2 459.9	3 341.6
4. Electricidad, gas y agua	30.9	61.8	84.1	84.1	174.8	287.0
5. Construcción	54.3	128.2	173.3	173.3	603.9	453.1
6. Comercio al por mayor y al por menor, restaurantes y hoteles	522.8 [1]	829.5 [1]	1 153.3 [1]	1 167.5 [1]	2 300.7	2 784.3
7. Transportes, almacenamiento y comunicaciones	132.9	210.8	293.1	296.7	585.7	670.8
8. Establecimientos financieros, seguros, bienes inmuebles y servicios prestados a las empresas	280.7 [2]	368.9 [2]	494.8 [2]	494.8 [2]	923.2 [2]	1 177.6 [2]
Viviendas	245.3	267.6	351.2	351.2	615.4	760.7
9. Servicios comunales, sociales y personales	363.3 [3]	620.6 [3]	740.0 [3]	744.5 [3]	1 404.1 [4]	1 750.2 [4]
Servicios gubernamentales	160.2	252.9	374.8	374.8	709.5	1 081.9
Subtotal	2 348.4	3 965.8	5 436.1	5 497.6	10 954.0	14 271.6
Menos: Comisión imputada de los servicios bancarios	...	...	...	...	...	...
Más: Derechos de importación	...	...	...	...	...	...
Total: Producto interno bruto	2 348.4	3 965.8	5 436.1	5 497.6	10 954.0	14 271.6
			A precios constantes de:		
		1958		1980		
1. Agricultura, caza, silvicultura y pesca	589.1	1 027.8	1 073.1	4 834.1	6 131.0	6 991.6
2. Explotación de minas y canteras	28.3	43.9	32.3	712.8	566.7	639.6
3. Industrias manufactureras	374.0	727.0	1 071.0	4 191.7	5 578.0	6 401.5
4. Electricidad, gas y agua	31.7	63.3	91.8	315.0	413.2	534.5
5. Construcción	52.2	122.1	158.3	722.1	1 385.1	930.4
6. Comercio al por mayor y al por menor, restaurantes y hoteles	536.2 [1]	849.9 [1]	1 008.1 [1]	4 292.1 [1]	5 517.2	5 375.1
7. Transportes, almacenamiento y comunicaciones	136.3	216.0	256.2	1 090.8	1 404.5	1 295.0
8. Establecimientos financieros, seguros, bienes inmuebles y servicios prestados a las empresas	287.9 [2]	378.0 [2]	443.0 [2]	1 549.9 [2]	1 691.4 [2]	1 846.9 [2]
Viviendas	251.6	274.2	317.5	1 018.0	949.7	1 042.1
9. Servicios comunales, sociales y personales	356.9 [3]	440.2 [3]	530.5 [3]	2 377.7 [3]	3 048.8 [4]	3 035.2 [4]
Servicios gubernamentales	157.4	189.4	211.3	1 018.5	1 383.0	1 745.0
Subtotal	2 392.6	3 868.2	4 664.3	20 086.2	25 735.9	27 049.8
Menos: Comisión imputada de los servicios bancarios	...	...	...	...	...	...
Más: Derechos de importación	...	...	...	...	...	...
Total: Producto interno bruto	2 392.6	3 868.2	4 664.3	20 086.2	25 735.9	27 049.8

[1] Restaurantes y hoteles se incluyen en Servicios comunales, sociales y personales.
[2] Servicios prestados a las empresas se incluyen en Servicios comunales, sociales y personales.
[3] Incluye Restaurantes y hoteles y Servicios prestados a las empresas.
[4] Incluye Servicios prestados a las empresas.

186. NICARAGUA: GROSS DOMESTIC PRODUCT BY KIND OF ECONOMIC ACTIVITY, AT MARKET PRICES

(Millions of córdobas)

1979	1980	1981	1982	1983	Kind of activity
		At current prices			
4 107.5	4 947.0	5 279.0	6 273.2	7 792.5	1. *Agriculture, hunting, forestry and fishing*
75.3	266.2	299.8	286.8	362.0	2. *Mining and quarrying*
3 571.4	5 492.0	6 709.5	7 511.5	9 105.8	3. *Manufacturing*
326.4	525.4	701.3	799.9	758.2	4. *Electricity, gas and water*
181.5	522.3	654.0	710.6	1 025.0	5. *Construction*
2 409.1	4 370.7	5 190.4	6 090.3	6 913.7	6. *Wholesale and retail trade, restaurants and hotels*
731.0	1 329.0	1 577.9	1 852.7	2 101.4	7. *Transport, storage and communications*
1 086.3 [2]	1 530.7 [2]	1 894.4	2 214.3	2 675.6	8. *Finance, insurance, real estate and business services*
580.0	764.6	913.7	1 277.3	1 591.6	*Dwellings*
2 024.8 [4]	2 908.3 [4]	3 466.5	3 957.3	4 880.0	9. *Community, social and personal services*
1 391.5	1 757.4	2 110.7	2 356.6	3 075.5	*Government services*
14 513.3	21 891.6	25 772.8	29 696.6	35 614.2	*Subtotal*
...	...	...	...	...	*Less: Imputed bank service charges*
...	...	...	...	...	*Plus: Import duties*
14 513.3	21 891.6	25 772.8	29 696.6	35 614.2	*Total: Gross domestic product*
		At constant prices of: 1980			
5 911.8	4 947.0	5 448.7	5 605.9	5 960.6	1. *Agriculture, hunting, forestry and fishing*
268.9	266.2	281.8	261.9	248.5	2. *Mining and quarrying*
4 650.3	5 492.0	5 647.7	5 551.7	5 807.1	3. *Manufacturing*
475.8	525.4	467.5	455.5	378.9	4. *Electricity, gas and water*
240.4	522.3	576.7	429.6	501.2	5. *Construction*
3 346.0	4 370.7	4 557.0	4 474.9	4 551.5	6. *Wholesale and retail trade, restaurants and hotels*
1 015.3	1 329.0	1 385.3	1 360.3	1 383.4	7. *Transport, storage and communications*
1 468.4 [2]	1 530.7 [2]	1 646.2	1 538.9	1 603.4	8. *Finance, insurance, real estate and business services*
765.2	764.6	800.8	838.1	854.8	*Dwellings*
2 514.7 [4]	2 908.3 [4]	3 041.1	3 100.3	3 403.9	9. *Community, social and personal services*
1 635.1	1 757.4	1 846.6	1 928.5	2 215.8	*Government services*
19 891.6	21 891.6	23 052.0	22 779.0	23 838.5	*Subtotal*
...	...	...	...	...	*Less: Imputed bank service charges*
...	...	...	...	...	*Plus: Import duties*
19 891.6	21 891.6	23 052.0	22 779.0	23 838.5	*Total: Gross domestic product*

[1] *Restaurants and hotels are included in Community, social and personal services.*
[2] *Business services are included in Community, social and personal services.*
[3] *Including Restaurants and hotels and Business services.*
[4] *Including Business services.*

II. CUENTAS NACIONALES

187. PANAMA: PRODUCTO INTERNO BRUTO POR TIPO DE GASTO, A PRECIOS DE MERCADO

(Millones de balboas)

Tipo de gasto	1960	1965	1970		1975
			A precios corrientes		
1. Gasto de consumo final del gobierno general	46.9	72.4	149.8	152.3	353.3
2. Gasto privado de consumo final	322.9	484.9	654.7	618.8	1 054.1
3. Variación de existencias	6.4	15.7	20.3	22.4	31.9
4. Formación bruta de capital fijo	61.4	100.1	255.6	261.9	535.5
Construcción	38.9	52.1	127.6	148.4	328.3
Maquinaria y equipo	22.5	48.0	128.0	113.5	207.2
5. Exportaciones de bienes y servicios	127.3[1]	240.2[1]	390.1[1]	388.2[1]	865.4[1]
6. Menos: Importaciones de bienes y servicios	149.1	253.4	424.7	422.4	999.4
Total: Producto interno bruto	**415.8**	**659.9**	**1 045.8**	**1 021.2**	**1 840.8**
			A precios constantes de:		
		1960		1970	
1. Gasto de consumo final del gobierno general	46.9	67.0	102.4	152.3	234.3
2. Gasto privado de consumo final	322.9	470.5	621.8	618.8	733.0
3. Variación de existencias	6.4	15.7	20.3	22.4	18.7
4. Formación bruta de capital fijo	61.4	97.1	221.9	261.9	361.0
Construcción	38.9	51.3	112.5	148.4	209.4
Maquinaria y equipo	22.5	45.8	109.4	113.5	151.6
5. Exportaciones de bienes y servicios	127.3[1]	223.4[1]	324.5[1]	388.2[1]	467.0[1]
6. Menos: Importaciones de bienes y servicios	149.1	256.4	396.4	422.4	528.3
Total: Producto interno bruto	**415.8**	**617.3**	**894.5**	**1 021.2**	**1 285.7**

[1] Incluye sueldos y salarios recibidos por los residentes de Panamá que trabajan en la Zona del Canal de Panamá.

187. PANAMA: GROSS DOMESTIC PRODUCT BY TYPE OF EXPENDITURE, AT MARKET PRICES

(Millions of balboas)

1978	1979	1980	1981	1982	1983	Type of expenditure
			At current prices			
482.9	567.2	680.5	812.9	962.6	1 067.8	1. General government final consumption expenditure
1 431.7	1 693.8	2 009.5	2 107.4	2 311.5	2 370.5	2. Private final consumption expenditure
45.4	124.5	120.5	87.6	-0.8	17.0	3. Increase in stocks
606.3	661.2	866.4	1 079.6	1 185.4	925.9	4. Gross fixed capital formation
377.5	419.6	564.4	682.2	851.3	622.1	Construction
228.8	241.6	302.0	397.4	334.1	303.8	Machinery and equipment
986.4[1]	1 124.8[1]	1 567.1	1 632.0	1 689.6	1 695.9	5. Exports of goods and services
1 100.2	1 371.3	1 685.2	1 841.5	1 869.4	1 697.7	6. Less: Imports of goods and services
2 452.5	2 800.2	3 558.8	3 878.0	4 278.9	4 379.4	**Total:** Gross domestic product
			At constant prices of:			
			1970			
261.5	269.1	284.8	334.9	365.5	380.4	1. General government final consumption expenditure
877.0	931.6	952.4	945.7	997.6	999.2	2. Private final consumption expenditure
23.4	52.2	46.3	37.3	0.5	12.7	3. Increase in stocks
303.2	299.9	365.3	426.1	430.1	333.1	4. Gross fixed capital formation
192.6	185.4	224.0	248.6	289.3	204.5	Construction
110.6	114.5	141.3	177.5	140.8	128.6	Machinery and equipment
538.8[1]	531.6[1]	764.5	740.7	800.1	806.4	5. Exports of goods and services
553.1	568.1	667.5	665.9	675.2	605.5	6. Less: Imports of goods and services
1 450.8	1 516.3	1 745.8	1 818.8	1 918.6	1 926.3	**Total:** Gross domestic product

[1]Including wages and salaries received by residents of Panama working in the Panama Canal Zone.

II. CUENTAS NACIONALES

188. PANAMA: RELACIONES ENTRE PRINCIPALES AGREGADOS DE CUENTAS NACIONALES, A PRECIOS CORRIENTES

(Millones de balboas)

	1960	1965	1970		1975
Remuneración de los asalariados	266.5	428.4	677.4	511.0	942.8
Más: Excedente de explotación	82.4	126.6	189.8	378.4	666.6
Más: Consumo de capital fijo	32.3	55.8	95.1	53.0	91.8
1. Igual: **Producto interno bruto al costo de factores**	381.2	610.8	962.3	942.4	1 701.2
Más: Impuestos indirectos	34.8	49.1	83.6	81.4	142.5
Menos: Subsidios	0.2	0.0	0.1	2.6	2.9
2. Igual: **Producto interno bruto a precios de mercado**	415.8	659.9	1 045.8	1 021.2	1 840.8
Menos: Remuneración neta de factores pagada al resto del mundo	12.4	15.8	26.4	26.5	19.5
3. Igual: **Producto nacional bruto a precios de mercado**	403.4	644.1	1 019.4	994.7	1 821.3
Menos: Consumo de capital fijo	32.3	55.8	95.1	53.0	91.8
4. Igual: **Ingreso nacional a precios de mercado**	371.1	588.3	924.3	941.7	1 729.5
Más: Otras transferencias corrientes netas procedentes del resto del mundo	-0.7	4.1	3.3	-1.8	-15.8
Menos: Gasto total de consumo final	369.8	557.3	804.5	771.1	1 407.4
6. Igual: **Ahorro nacional**	0.6	35.1	123.1	168.8	306.3
Menos: Excedente de la nación por transacciones corrientes	-34.9	-25.0	-57.7	-62.5	-169.3
7. Igual: **Formación neta de capital**	35.5	60.1	180.8	231.3	475.6
Más: Consumo de capital fijo	32.3	55.8	95.1	53.0	91.8
8. Igual: **Formación bruta de capital**	67.8	115.9	275.9	284.3	567.4

188. PANAMA: RELATIONS AMONG MAIN NATIONAL ACCOUNTS
AGGREGATES, AT CURRENT PRICES

(Millions of balboas)

1978	1979	1980	1981	1982	1983	
1 218.7	1 392.8	1 624.6	1 800.2	2 049.5	2 123.0	*Compensation of employees*
882.9	998.4	1 413.9	1 516.5	1 600.6	1 595.3	*Plus: Operating surplus*
134.9	157.3	252.1	279.7	320.9	331.2	*Plus: Consumption of fixed capital*
2 236.5	2 548.5	3 290.6	3 596.4	3 971.0	4 049.5	1. *Equals:* **Gross domestic product at factor cost**
221.7	255.1	269.7	285.4	313.7	337.6	*Plus: Indirect taxes*
5.7	3.4	1.5	3.8	5.8	7.7	*Less: Subsidies*
2 452.5	2 800.2	3 558.8	3 878.0	4 278.9	4 379.4	2. *Equals:* **Gross domestic product at market prices**
57.4	102.8	110.0	78.6	138.9	-1.7	*Less: Net factor income paid to the rest of the world*
2 395.1	2 697.4	3 448.8	3 799.4	4 140.0	4 381.1	3. *Equals:* **Gross national product at market prices**
134.9	157.3	252.1	279.7	320.9	331.2	*Less: Consumption of fixed capital*
2 260.2	2 540.1	3 196.7	3 519.7	3 819.1	4 049.9	4. *Equals:* **National income at market prices**
-18.3	-4.4	14.3	31.2	36.0	41.0	*Plus: Other net current transfers received from the rest of the world*
1 914.6	2 261.0	2 690.0	2 920.3	3 274.1	3 438.3	*Less: Total final consumption expenditure*
327.3	274.7	521.0	630.6	581.0	652.6	6. *Equals:* **National saving**
-189.5	-353.7	-213.8	-256.9	-282.7	40.9	*Less: Surplus of the nation on current transactions*
516.8	628.4	734.8	887.5	863.7	611.7	7. *Equals:* **Net capital formation**
134.9	157.3	252.1	279.7	320.9	331.2	*Plus: Consumption of fixed capital*
651.7	785.7	986.9	1 167.2	1 184.6	942.9	8. *Equals:* **Gross capital formation**

189. PANAMA: PRODUCTO INTERNO BRUTO POR CLASE DE ACTIVIDAD ECONOMICA, A PRECIOS DE MERCADO

(Millones de balboas)

Clase de actividad	1960	1965	1970	1975	1978
			A precios corrientes		
1. Agricultura, caza, silvicultura y pesca	95.7	157.7	200.4	149.1	205.6	288.5
2. Explotación de minas y canteras	1.1	1.9	2.5	1.9	3.2	4.1
3. Industrias manufactureras	54.5	101.3	166.4	127.3	236.0	252.6
4. Electricidad, gas y agua	8.4	11.9	19.0	21.8	41.4	82.5
5. Construcción	22.9	35.2	61.2	68.2	151.5	172.7
6. Comercio al por mayor y al por menor, restaurantes y hoteles	57.9[1]	89.8[1]	146.4[1]	161.0	318.4	422.7
7. Transportes, almacenamiento y comunicaciones	19.3	30.8	56.8	61.2	129.3	217.8
8. Establecimientos financieros, seguros, bienes inmuebles y servicios prestados a las empresas	44.8[2]	62.4[2]	105.8[2]	122.1	242.7	346.5
Viviendas	34.5	44.1	65.5	72.3	133.1	189.9
9. Servicios comunales, sociales y personales	111.2[3]	168.9[3]	287.3[3]	282.3[4]	510.9[4]	678.5[4]
Servicios gubernamentales	11.4	13.7	29.5	117.8[5]	241.8[5]	329.7[5]
Subtotal	415.8	659.9	1 045.8	994.9	1 839.0	2 465.9
Menos: Comisión imputada de los servicios bancarios	...	...	...	10.6	42.4	70.4
Más: Derechos de importación	...	...	...	36.9	44.2	57.0
Total: Producto interno bruto	415.8	659.9	1 045.8	1 021.2	1 840.8	2 452.5
			A precios constantes de:		
		1960			1970	
1. Agricultura, caza, silvicultura y pesca	95.7	132.2	161.1	149.1	158.6	189.1
2. Explotación de minas y canteras	1.1	1.7	2.3	1.9	2.5	2.2
3. Industrias manufactureras	54.5	98.1	153.6	127.3	147.0	154.9
4. Electricidad, gas y agua	8.4	14.5	26.0	21.8	38.3	46.7
5. Construcción	22.9	34.9	54.0	68.2	96.9	102.5
6. Comercio al por mayor y al por menor, restaurantes y hoteles	57.9[1]	85.8[1]	126.6[1]	161.0	191.0	219.6
7. Transportes, almacenamiento y comunicaciones	19.3	32.9	59.6	61.2	116.0	145.1
8. Establecimientos financieros, seguros, bienes inmuebles y servicios prestados a las empresas	44.8[2]	61.0[2]	94.9[2]	122.1	178.8	199.7
Viviendas	34.5	43.4	60.1	72.3	103.3	114.2
9. Servicios comunales, sociales y personales	111.2[3]	156.2[3]	216.4[3]	282.3[4]	365.8[4]	397.8[4]
Servicios gubernamentales	11.4	15.7	23.4	117.8[5]	169.9[5]	187.6[5]
Subtotal	415.8	617.3	894.5	994.9	1 294.9	1 457.6
Menos: Comisión imputada de los servicios bancarios	...	...	...	10.6	30.1	33.3
Más: Derechos de importación	...	...	...	36.9	20.9	26.5
Total: Producto interno bruto	415.8	617.3	894.5	1 021.2	1 285.7	1 450.8

[1] Restaurantes y hoteles se incluyen en Servicios comunales, sociales y personales.
[2] Servicios prestados a las empresas se incluyen en Servicios comunales, sociales y personales.
[3] Incluye Restaurantes y hoteles, Servicios prestados a las empresas y Servicios prestados a la Zona del Canal de Panamá.
[4] Para el período 1970-1979 incluye Servicios prestados a la Zona del Canal de Panamá. Desde 1980, las actividades que se desarrollaban en esta área se distribuyeron en las respectivas actividades e incluyen la Comisión del Canal de Panamá, que es una empresa residente que vende servicios relacionados con el transporte, a precios de mercado.
[5] Se refiere a los Productores de servicios gubernamentales.

189. PANAMA: GROSS DOMESTIC PRODUCT BY KIND OF ECONOMIC ACTIVITY, AT MARKET PRICES

(Millions of balboas)

1979	1980	1981	1982	1983	Kind of activity
		At current prices			
304.2	320.4	359.3	371.2	410.1	1. *Agriculture, hunting, forestry and fishing*
4.4	6.8	8.7	9.3	10.0	2. *Mining and quarrying*
293.3	356.0	375.6	394.0	391.1	3. *Manufacturing*
95.0	113.8	142.4	152.6	153.5	4. *Electricity, gas and water*
194.4	258.4	295.2	378.4	269.0	5. *Construction*
493.6	618.2	667.6	681.3	652.0	6. *Wholesale and retail trade, restaurants and hotels*
263.6	408.2	427.4	497.0	582.6	7. *Transport, storage and communications*
430.1	503.2	587.4	663.7	715.1	8. *Finance, insurance, real estate and business services*
215.6	247.9	278.4	319.1	...	*Dwellings*
795.1[4]	1 042.9[4]	1 114.5[4]	1 277.7[4]	1 331.3[4]	9. *Community, social and personal services*
399.4[5]	446.4[5]	468.5[5]	534.2[5]	602.6[5]	*Government services*
2 873.7	**3 627.9**	**3 978.1**	**4 425.2**	**4 514.7**	*Subtotal*
141.6	147.5	183.7	237.4	231.6	*Less: Imputed bank service charges*
68.1	78.4	83.6	91.1	96.3	*Plus: Import duties*
2 800.2	**3 558.8**	**3 878.0**	**4 278.9**	**4 379.4**	*Total: Gross domestic product*
		At constant prices of: 1970			
181.0	173.7	188.1	185.2	194.4	1. *Agriculture, hunting, forestry and fishing*
2.4	3.1	3.8	4.1	4.4	2. *Mining and quarrying*
172.0	182.1	176.1	179.9	176.1	3. *Manufacturing*
52.4	53.5	56.2	59.2	65.7	4. *Electricity, gas and water*
102.4	124.3	128.3	154.7	106.6	5. *Construction*
240.9	256.4	252.9	251.0	235.2	6. *Wholesale and retail trade, restaurants and hotels*
155.4	207.6	216.5	251.1	310.6	7. *Transport, storage and communications*
222.9	227.2	243.5	252.6	262.9	8. *Finance, insurance, real estate and business services*
118.2	121.9	125.2	129.2	133.0	*Dwellings*
417.0[4]	537.0[4]	579.9[4]	619.4[4]	607.6[4]	9. *Community, social and personal services*
196.5[5]	201.2[5]	222.9[5]	232.1[5]	242.3[5]	*Government services*
1 546.4	**1 764.9**	**1 845.3**	**1 957.2**	**1 958.5**	*Subtotal*
56.4	47.2	54.2	68.2	64.9	*Less: Imputed bank service charges*
26.3	28.1	27.7	29.6	32.7	*Plus: Import duties*
1 516.3	**1 745.8**	**1 818.8**	**1 918.6**	**1 926.3**	*Total: Gross domestic product*

[1] *Restaurants and hotels are included in Community, social and personal services.*
[2] *Business services are included in Community, social and personal services.*
[3] *Including Restaurants and hotels, Business services and Services to the Panama Canal Zone.*
[4] *For the period 1970-1979, includes Services to the Panama Canal Zone. Since 1980, activities in this area were distributed over the respective activities and include the Panama Canal Commission, a resident enterprise which sells transport-related services at market prices.*
[5] *Refers to Producers of government services.*

385

190. PANAMA: INGRESOS Y GASTOS DEL GOBIERNO GENERAL

(Millones de balboas)

	1960	1965	1970		1975	1978
1. Renta de la propiedad y de la empresa	10.0	17.0	25.0	26.5[1]	56.9[1]	59.6[1]
2. Impuestos indirectos	34.8	49.1	83.6	81.4	142.5	221.7
3. Impuestos directos	10.8	22.2	54.4	55.7	117.5	136.7
4. Contribuciones a la seguridad social	8.4	20.6	41.5	43.8	93.3	154.2
5. Transferencias corrientes n.e.p. de residentes	-0.7[2]	-2.6[2]	-4.3[2]	45.7	79.3	97.8
6. Transferencias corrientes n.e.p. del resto del mundo	5.0	10.5	8.8	9.4	8.6	15.6
Total: Ingresos corrientes	68.3	116.8	209.0	262.5	498.1	685.6
7. Gasto de consumo final	46.9	72.4	149.8	152.3	353.3	482.9
8. Renta de la propiedad	...	...	...	11.2	42.3	78.5
9. Subsidios	0.2	0.0	0.1	2.6	2.9	5.7
10. Prestaciones de seguridad social	5.4	10.6	23.6	18.2	45.9	74.8
11. Transferencias corrientes n.e.p. a residentes	1.6	2.9	14.3	19.5	35.5	40.4
12. Transferencias corrientes n.e.p. al resto del mundo	0.3	0.6	1.8	1.8	2.3	2.8
13. Ahorro	13.9	30.3	19.4	56.9	15.9	0.5
Total: Egresos corrientes	68.3	116.8	209.0	262.5	498.1	685.6

Nota: Las cifras del período 1950-1959 no son comparables con las del resto de la serie.
[1] Incluye Excedente de explotación y Retiros de la renta empresarial de las cuasisociedades públicas.
[2] Incluye Intereses de la deuda pública.

190. PANAMA: INCOME AND OUTLAY OF THE GENERAL GOVERNMENT

(Millions of balboas)

1979	1980	1981	1982	1983	
63.5 [1]	88.5 [1]	96.8 [1]	105.6 [1]	133.6 [1]	1. *Property and entrepreneurial income*
255.1	269.7	285.4	313.7	337.6	2. *Indirect taxes*
170.9	226.6	284.2	300.8	354.0	3. *Direct taxes*
191.0	227.7	272.3	327.9	349.2	4. *Social security contributions*
139.0	219.9	250.3	245.4	268.3	5. *Current transfers n.e.c. from residents*
16.5	26.3	32.4	40.2	45.7	6. *Current transfers n.e.c. from the rest of the world*
836.0	**1 058.7**	**1 221.4**	**1 333.6**	**1 488.4**	*Total:* Current receipts
567.2	680.5	812.9	962.6	1 067.8	7. *Final consumption expenditure*
129.1	187.4	230.3	316.5	292.5	8. *Property income*
3.4	1.5	3.8	5.8	7.7	9. *Subsidies*
87.2	99.1	121.7	134.6	149.6	10. *Social security benefits*
65.7	94.3	112.3	140.5	226.3	11. *Current transfers n.e.c. to residents*
3.0	4.4	5.9	6.3	8.4	12. *Current transfers n.e.c. to rest of the world*
-19.6	-8.5	-65.5	-232.7	-263.9	13. *Saving*
836.0	**1 058.7**	**1 221.4**	**1 333.6**	**1 488.4**	*Total:* Current disbursements

Note: The figures for the period 1950-1959 are not comparable with those of the rest of the series.
[1] *Including Operating surplus and Entrepreneurial income from public quasi-corporations.*
[2] *Including Interests on the public debt.*

191. PARAGUAY: PRODUCTO INTERNO BRUTO POR TIPO DE GASTO, A PRECIOS DE MERCADO

(Millones de guaraníes)

Tipo de gasto	1960	1962	1970	1975
		A precios corrientes		
1. Gasto de consumo final del gobierno general	2 611.0	3 204.0	6 748.1	11 971.8
2. Gasto privado de consumo final	29 919.0	37 476.9	58 041.5	141 077.7
3. Variación de existencias	118.7	460.5	150.8	6 350.0
4. Formación bruta de capital fijo	4 281.8	5 237.0	10 882.8	39 543.0
Construcción	...	2 669.2	5 462.5	18 850.0
Maquinaria y equipo	...	2 567.8	5 420.3	20 693.0
5. Exportaciones de bienes y servicios	5 236.3	5 739.8	11 176.0	29 331.0
6. Menos: Importaciones de bienes y servicios	6 586.1	6 670.5	12 078.0	37 835.0
Total: Producto interno bruto	35 580.7	45 447.7	74 921.2	190 438.5

Tipo de gasto	A precios constantes de:				
	1967		1982		
1. Gasto de consumo final del gobierno general	8 427.0	7 990.0	14 902	25 720.0	28 956
2. Gasto privado de consumo final	88 768.0	84 158.0	161 987	230 899.0	317 410
3. Variación de existencias	385.0	1 327.0	2 144	629.0	15 338
4. Formación bruta de capital fijo	9 096.0	9 503.0	15 180	35 917.0	63 472
Construcción	...	...	...	...	30 257
Maquinaria y equipo	...	...	...	...	33 215
5. Exportaciones de bienes y servicios	15 048.0	20 948.0	30 052	42 015.0	52 005
6. Menos: Importaciones de bienes y servicios	19 476.0	11 718.0	19 336	39 861.0	60 730
Total: Producto interno bruto	102 248.0	112 208.0	204 988	295 319.0	416 451
Discrepancia estadística	-	-	59[1]	-	-

[1]Cifra no publicada por la fuente original. Obtenida por diferencia.

II. NATIONAL ACCOUNTS

191. PARAGUAY: GROSS DOMESTIC PRODUCT BY TYPE OF EXPENDITURE, AT MARKET PRICES

(Millions of guaraníes)

1978	1979	1980	1981	1982	1983	Type of expenditure
		At current prices				
21 500.0	24 710.0	34 732.0	48 625.0	52 272.0	58 024.0	1. General government final consumption expenditure
225 241.0	306 501.0	399 296.0	504 074.0	552 019.0	642 198.0	2. Private final consumption expenditure
6 461.0	6 830.0	8 550.0	10 064.0	12 045.0	10 720.0	3. Increase in stocks
81 256.0	116 142.0	152 654.0	194 219.0	176 871.0	164 509.0	4. Gross fixed capital formation
40 710.0	61 066.0	90 308.0	123 000.0	115 632.0	128 351.0	Construction
40 546.0	55 076.0	62 346.0	71 219.0	61 239.0	36 158.0	Machinery and equipment
59 413.0	69 133.0	77 599.0	79 107.0	89 461.0	70 054.0	5. Exports of goods and services
71 329.0	92 802.0	112 372.0	127 400.0	145 628.0	127 391.0	6. Less: Imports of goods and services
322 542.0	430 514.0	560 459.0	708 689.0	737 040.0	818 114.0	Total: Gross domestic product
		At constant prices of:				
		1982				
40 245	37 494	42 803	51 126	52 272	53 919	1. General government final consumption expenditure
409 266	403 714	472 573	524 562	552 019	543 425	2. Private final consumption expenditure
12 354	10 179	10 776	10 741	12 045	9 404	3. Increase in stocks
126 174	150 834	183 699	216 762	176 871	145 183	4. Gross fixed capital formation
63 215	79 307	108 673	137 277	115 632	113 185	Construction
62 959	71 527	75 026	79 485	61 239	31 998	Machinery and equipment
74 452	132 693	110 070	83 358	89 461	75 734	5. Exports of goods and services
110 759	120 522	135 225	142 188	145 628	112 736	6. Less: Imports of goods and services
551 732	614 392	684 686.0	744 361	737 040	714 929	Total: Gross domestic product
-	-	-	-	-	-	Statistical discrepancy

[1] Figure not published by the original source. Obtained by difference.

192. PARAGUAY: RELACIONES ENTRE PRINCIPALES AGREGADOS DE CUENTAS NACIONALES, A PRECIOS CORRIENTES

(Millones de guaraníes)

	1960	1965	1970	1975	1977
Remuneración de los asalariados	31 162.7[1]	19 977.4	25 770.0	65 260.0	91 600.0
Más: Excedente de explotación	[2]	29 334.9	39 703.5	107 499.5	137 121.0
Más: Consumo de capital fijo	2 216.0	3 411.3	3 962.0	9 800.0	24 621.0
1. Igual: **Producto interno bruto al costo de factores**	33 378.7	52 723.6	69 435.5	182 559.5	253 342.0
Más: Impuestos indirectos	2 202.0[3]	3 172.5	5 507.1	7 940.2	10 342.0
Menos: Subsidios	[4]	4.2	21.4	61.2	72.0
2. Igual: **Producto interno bruto a precios de mercado**	35 580.7	55 891.9	74 921.2	190 438.5	263 612.0
Menos: Remuneración neta de factores pagada al resto del mundo	187.6	609.8	1 816.0	1 536.0	-359.0
3. Igual: **Producto nacional bruto a precios de mercado**	35 393.1	55 282.1	73 105.2	188 902.5	263 971.0
Menos: Consumo de capital fijo	2 216.0	3 411.3	3 962.0	9 800.0	24 621.0
4. Igual: **Ingreso nacional a precios de mercado**	33 177.1	51 870.8	69 143.2	179 102.5	239 359.0
Más: Otras transferencias corrientes netas procedentes del resto del mundo	[5]	[5]	[5]	[5]	[5]
5. Igual: **Ingreso nacional disponible a precios de mercado**	33 177.1	51 870.8	69 143.2	179 102.5	239 359.0
Menos: Gasto total de consumo final	32 530.0	47 906.0	64 789.6	153 049.5	206 415.0
6. Igual: **Ahorro nacional**[6]	647.1	3 964.8	4 353.6	26 053.0	32 935.0
Menos: Excedente de la nación por transacciones corrientes	-1 537.4	-1 054.0	-2 718.0	-10 040.0	-7 516.0
7. Igual: **Formación neta de capital**	2 184.5	5 018.8	7 071.6	36 093.0	40 451.0
Más: Consumo de capital fijo	2 216.0	3 411.3	3 962.0	9 800.0	24 621.0
8. Igual: **Formación bruta de capital**	4 400.5	8 430.1	11 033.6	45 893.0	65 072.0

[1] Incluye Excedente de explotación.
[2] Incluido en Remuneración de los asalariados.
[3] Incluye Subsidios.
[4] Incluido en Impuestos indirectos.
[5] Incluido en Excedente de la nación por transacciones corrientes.
[6] No incluye Otras transferencias corrientes netas procedentes del resto del mundo.

192. PARAGUAY: RELATIONS AMONG MAIN NATIONAL ACCOUNTS AGGREGATES, AT CURRENT PRICES

(Millions of guaraníes)

1978	1979	1980	1981	1982	1983	
106 100.0	150 900.0	195 300.0	242 850.0	245 900.0	258 243.0	*Compensation of employees*
167 977.0	202 859.0	271 993.0	346 257.0	368 645.0	442 567.0	*Plus: Operating surplus*
32 253.0	49 190.0	58 630.0	77 688.0	74 285.0	72 184.0	*Plus: Consumption of fixed capital*
306 330.0	402 949.0	525 923.0	666 795.0	688 830.0	772 994.0	1. *Equals:* **Gross domestic product** **at factor cost**
16 297.0	27 586.0	34 578.0	41 946.0	48 297.0	45 166.0	*Plus: Indirect taxes*
85.0	21.0	42.0	52.0	87.0	46.0	*Less: Subsidies*
322 542.0	430 514.0	560 459.0	708 689.0	737 040.0	818 114.0	2. *Equals:* **Gross domestic product** **at market prices**
-1 773.0	-1 294.0	-5 261.0	-8 759.0	-8 263.0	-4 990.0	*Less: Net factor income paid to the rest of the world*
324 315.0	431 808.0	565 720.0	717 448.0	745 303.0	823 104.0	3. *Equals:* **Gross national product** **at market prices**
32 253.0	49 190.0	58 630.0	77 688.0	74 285.0	72 184.0	*Less: Consumption of fixed capital*
292 062.0	382 618.0	507 090.0	639 760.0	671 018.0	750 920.0	4. *Equals:* **National income at market prices**
5	5	5	5	5	5	*Plus: Other net current transfers received from the rest of the world*
292 062.0	382 618.0	507 090.0	639 760.0	671 018.0	750 920.0	5. *Equals:* **National disposable income** **at market prices**
246 741.0	331 211.0	434 028.0	552 699.0	604 291.0	700 222.0	*Less: Total final consumption expenditure*
45 321.0	51 407.0	73 062.0	87 061.0	66 727.00	50 698.0	6. *Equals:* **National saving**[6]
-10 843.0	-22 375.0	-29 512.0	-39 534.0	-47 904.0	-52 347.0	*Less: Surplus of the nation on current transactions*
55 464.0	73 782.0	102 574.0	126 595.0	114 631.0	103 045.0	7. *Equals:* **Net capital formation**
32 253.0	49 190.0	58 630.0	77 688.0	74 285.0	72 184.0	*Plus: Consumption of fixed capital*
87 717.0	122 972.0	161 204.0	204 283.0	188 916.0	175 229.0	8. *Equals:* **Gross capital formation**

[1] *Including Operating surplus.*
[2] *Included in Compensation of employees.*
[3] *Including Subsidies.*
[4] *Included in Indirect taxes.*
[5] *Included in Surplus of the nation on current transactions.*
[6] *Does not include Other net current transfers from the rest of the world.*

II. CUENTAS NACIONALES

193. PARAGUAY: PRODUCTO INTERNO BRUTO POR CLASE DE ACTIVIDAD
ECONOMICA, A PRECIOS DE MERCADO

(Millones de guaraníes)

Clase de actividad	1960	1965	1970	1975	1977
	A precios corrientes				
1. Agricultura, caza, silvicultura y pesca	13 006.8	20 516.6	24 024.2	70 284.0	89 924.7
2. Explotación de minas y canteras	58.7	104.1	82.9	364.8	685.3
3. Industrias manufactureras	5 771.6	8 665.6	12 497.7	29 758.8	44 974.3
4. Electricidad, gas y agua [1]	243.1	367.5	839.7	2 739.0	4 607.2
5. Construcción	786.9	1 358.4	2 075.7	7 163.0	10 560.0
6. Comercio al por mayor y al por menor, restaurantes y hoteles [2][3]	8 098.6	12 743.7	18 290.9	43 593.8	66 026.4
7. Transportes, almacenamiento y comunicaciones	1 248.8	2 403.6	2 950.4	7 599.8	10 263.9
8. Establecimientos financieros, seguros, bienes inmuebles y servicios prestados a las empresas	[4][5]	[4][5]	[4][5]	[4][5]	[4][5]
Viviendas	1 368.5	1 878.0	2 281.0	5 017.6	6 076.6
9. Servicios comunales, sociales y personales [6]	4 997.7	7 854.4	11 878.7	23 917.7	30 493.9
Servicios gubernamentales	1 436.2	2 148.4	3 943.0	6 493.6	10 283.1
Subtotal	35 580.7	55 891.9	74 921.2	190 438.5	263 612.3
Menos: Comisión imputada de los servicios bancarios	...	...	...	...	...
Más: Derechos de importación	...	...	...	...	...
Total: Producto interno bruto	35 580.7	55 891.9	74 921.2	190 438.5	263 612.3
	A precios constantes de 1982				
1. Agricultura, caza, silvicultura y pesca	66 593.8	82 680.0	89 846	128 157	141 963
2. Explotación de minas y canteras	199.8	359.0	219	731	1 276
3. Industrias manufactureras	28 762.1	39 367.0	54 267	70 036	86 626
4. Electricidad, gas y agua [1]	1 093.0	1 343.0	2 794	6 135	8 470
5. Construcción	3 751.7	4 880.0	7 141	13 491	20 889
6. Comercio al por mayor y al por menor, restaurantes y hoteles [2][3]	48 920.1	59 743.0	78 258	105 602	130 219
7. Transportes, almacenamiento y comunicaciones	8 125.5	10 131.0	11 702	18 699	21 608
8. Establecimientos financieros, seguros, bienes inmuebles y servicios prestados a las empresas	[4][5]	[4][5]	[4][5]	[4][5]	[4][5]
Viviendas	9 154.8	9 185.0	10 699	13 661	15 993
9. Servicios comunales, sociales y personales [6]	19 029.1	27 567.0	40 393	59 939	68 449
Servicios gubernamentales	7 961.9	9 831.0	16 955	17 929	20 276
Subtotal	185 630.0	235 255.0	295 319	416 451	495 493
Menos: Comisión imputada de los servicios bancarios	...	...	...	...	...
Más: Derechos de importación	...	...	...	...	...
Total: Producto interno bruto	185 630.0	235 255.0	295 319	416 451	495 493

[1] Incluye servicios sanitarios.
[2] Incluye Establecimientos financieros, seguros y bienes inmuebles, con excepción de Viviendas.
[3] Restaurantes y hoteles se incluyen en Servicios comunales, sociales y personales.
[4] Establecimientos financieros, seguros y bienes inmuebles, con excepción de Viviendas, se incluyen en Comercio al por mayor, al por menor, restaurantes y hoteles.
[5] Servicios prestados a las empresas se incluyen en Servicios comunales, sociales y personales.
[6] Incluye Restaurantes y hoteles y Servicios prestados a las empresas.

193. PARAGUAY: GROSS DOMESTIC PRODUCT BY KIND OF ECONOMIC ACTIVITY, AT MARKET PRICES

(Millions of guaraníes)

1978	1979	1980	1981	1982	1983	Kind of activity
		At current prices				
103 430.9	135 162.4	165 136.4	196 784.2	190 644.8	211 615.4	1. *Agriculture, hunting, forestry and fishing*
794.4	1 446.3	2 284.7	2 932.6	3 141.5	3 487.0	2. *Mining and quarrying*
54 418.9	69 609.7	92 337.6	118 469.1	120 966.4	134 272.6	3. *Manufacturing*
5 981.8	7 889.7	12 923.2	15 271.8	18 120.2	20 638.2	4. *Electricity, gas and water* [1]
15 470.0	23 205.1	34 317.1	46 739.9	49 544.3	54 994.1	5. *Construction*
83 985.6	112 656.2	144 869.9	188 378.3	196 157.6	217 210.0	6. *Wholesale and retail trade, restaurants and hotels* [2][3]
12 994.1	17 358.7	23 783.5	29 058.8	31 106.9	34 528.6	7. *Transport, storage and communications*
[4][5]	[4][5]	[4][5]	[4][5]	[4][5]	[4][5]	8. *Finance, insurance, real estate and business services*
7 492.5	11 228.6	14 993.0	20 090.6	22 501.4	24 976.6	*Dwellings*
37 973.5	51 957.1	69 813.5	90 963.6	104 857.5	116 391.7	9. *Community, social and personal services* [6]
12 709.9	14 595.2	19 115.0	26 678.0	32 857.6	36 471.9	*Government services*
322 541.7	430 513.8	560 458.8	708 688.9	737 040.6	818 114.0	*Subtotal*
...	...	...	...	...	...	*Less: Imputed bank service charges*
...	...	...	...	...	...	*Plus: Import duties*
322 541.7	430 513.8	560 458.8	708 688.9	737 040.6	818 114.0	**Total:** *Gross domestic product*
		At constant 1982 prices				
149 112	159 001	172 524	189 877	190 645	185 991	1. *Agriculture, hunting, forestry and fishing*
1 487	2 118	2 669	3 070	3 142	2 912	2. *Mining and quarrying*
96 712	106 289	120 422	125 613	120 966	115 861	3. *Manufacturing*
9 922	11 797	14 024	14 746	18 120	17 779	4. *Electricity, gas and water* [1]
27 573	35 845	45 164	52 707	49 544	46 720	5. *Construction*
148 841	167 446	185 028	200 570	196 158	190 171	6. *Wholesale and retail trade, restaurants and hotels* [2][3]
23 985	26 743	29 551	30 497	31 107	30 742	7. *Transport, storage and communications*
[4][5]	[4][5]	[4][5]	[4][5]	[4][5]	[4][5]	8. *Finance, insurance, real estate and business services*
17 833	19 705	21 479	22 961	22 501	21 448	*Dwellings*
76 267	85 448	93 825	104 320	104 857	103 305	9. *Community, social and personal services* [6]
21 879	24 044	25 728	31 593	32 857	32 172	*Government services*
551 732	614 392	684 686	744 361	737 040	714 929	*Subtotal*
...	...	...	...	...	...	*Less: Imputed bank service charges*
...	...	...	...	...	...	*Plus: Import duties*
551 732	614 392	684 686	744 361	737 040	714 929	**Total:** *Gross domestic product*

[1] *Including Sanitary services.*
[2] *Including Finance, insurance and real estate, with the exception of Dwellings.*
[3] *Restaurants and hotels are included in Community, social and personal services.*
[4] *Finance, insurance and real estate, with the exception of Dwellings, are included in Wholesale and retail trade, restaurants and hotels.*
[5] *Business services are included in Community, social and personal services.*
[6] *Including Restaurants and hotels and Business services.*

II. CUENTAS NACIONALES

194. PARAGUAY: INGRESOS Y GASTOS DE LOS HOGARES, INCLUIDAS LAS EMPRESAS NO FINANCIERAS NO CONSTITUIDAS EN SOCIEDAD [1]

(Millones de guaraníes)

	1965	1970	1975	1976	1977	1978
1. Remuneración de los asalariados	19 977.4	25 770.0	65 260.0	76 670	91 600	106 100
2. Renta neta de la propiedad y de la empresa	27 768.9	35 981.7	100 479.4	106 979	128 117	154 727
3. Prestaciones de seguridad social	...	...	...	...	...	...
4. Donaciones de asistencia social	...	...	...	...	...	...
5. Transferencias corrientes n.e.p. de residentes	500.9	1 570.3	1 966.3	2 188	2 414	3 798
6. Transferencias corrientes n.e.p. del resto del mundo	...	...	...	...	...	...
Total: Ingresos corrientes	48 247.2	63 322.0	167 705.7	185 837	222 131	264 625
7. Gasto de consumo final	44 112.2	58 041.5	142 969.8	155 172	190 062	225 241
8. Impuestos directos	...	...	...	...	...	...
9. Contribuciones a la seguridad social	853.4	1 277.9	2 661.7	3 271	4 691	6 484
10. Transferencias corrientes n.e.p. a residentes	483.1	744.1	1 011.9	1 034	2 323	1 024
11. Transferencias corrientes n.e.p. al resto del mundo	...	...	...	...	...	...
12. Ahorro	2 798.5	3 258.5	21 062.3	26 360	25 055	31 876
Total: Egresos corrientes	48 247.2	63 322.0	167 705.7	185 837	222 131	264 625

[1] Comprende Instituciones privadas sin fines de lucro que sirven a los hogares.

194. PARAGUAY: INCOME AND OUTLAY OF HOUSEHOLDS, INCLUDING PRIVATE UNINCORPORATED NON-FINANCIAL ENTERPRISES [1]

(Millions of guaraníes)

1979	1980	1981	1982	1983	
150 900	195 300	242 850	245 900	258 243	1. *Compensation of employees*
179 825	251 674	323 321	347 430	414 301	2. *Net property and entrepreneurial income*
...	...	...	...	...	3. *Social security benefits*
...	...	...	...	...	4. *Social assistance grants*
5 043	7 047	9 955	18 923	17 593	5. *Current transfers n.e.c. from residents*
...	...	...	...	...	6. *Current transfers n.e.c. from the rest of the world*
335 768	454 021	576 126	612 253	690 137	**Total:** *Current receipts*
306 501	399 296	504 074	552 019	642 198	7. *Final consumption expenditure*
...	...	...	...	...	8. *Direct taxes*
8 268	9 840	13 430	14 982	17 593	9. *Social security contributions*
1 191	1 452	1 952	2 591	3 348	10. *Current transfers n.e.c. to residents*
...	...	...	...	...	11. *Current transfers n.e.c. to rest of the world*
19 808	43 433	56 670	42 661	26 998	12. *Saving*
335 768	454 021	576 126	612 253	690 137	**Total:** *Current disbursements*

[1] *Including Private non-profit institutions serving households.*

II. CUENTAS NACIONALES

195. PARAGUAY: INGRESOS Y GASTOS DEL GOBIERNO GENERAL

(Millones de guaraníes)

	1965	1970	1975	1976	1977	1978
1. Renta de la propiedad y de la empresa	502.7	955.9	1 428.5	1 809.0	2 946.0	4 909.0
2. Impuestos indirectos	3 172.5	5 507.1	7 940.2	8 940.0	10 342.0	16 297.0
3. Impuestos directos	483.3	800.8	1 471.0	1 876.0	2 441.0	4 937.0
4. Contribuciones a la seguridad social	853.4	1 277.9	2 661.7	3 271.0	4 691.0	6 484.0
5. Transferencias corrientes n.e.p. de residentes	483.1	744.1	1 011.9	1 034.0	2 323.0	1 024.0
6. Transferencias corrientes n.e.p. del resto del mundo	...	...	...	...	...	...
Total: Ingresos corrientes	5 495.0	9 285.8	14 513.3	16 930.0	22 743.0	33 651.0
7. Gasto de consumo final	3 793.8	6 748.1	11 971.8	13 413.0	16 353.0	21 500.0
8. Renta de la propiedad [1]	246.5	101.6	115.4	110.0	54.0	53.0
9. Subsidios	4.2	21.4	61.2	69.0	72.0	85.0
10. Prestaciones de seguridad social	...	...	...	...	...	...
11. Transferencias corrientes n.e.p. a residentes	500.9	1 570.3	1 966.3	2 188.0	2 414.0	3 798.0
12. Transferencias corrientes n.e.p. al resto del mundo	...	...	...	...	...	...
13. Ahorro	949.6	844.4	398.6	1 150.0	3 850.0	8 215.0
Total: Egresos corrientes	5 495.0	9 285.8	14 513.3	16 930.0	22 743.0	33 651.0

[1] Se refiere sólo a Intereses de la deuda pública.

195. PARAGUAY: INCOME AND OUTLAY OF THE GENERAL GOVERNMENT

(Millions of guaraníes)

1979	1980	1981	1982	1983	
10 530.0	7 609.0	8 315.0	6 561.0	7 412.0	1. *Property and entrepreneurial income*
27 586.0	34 578.0	41 946.0	48 297.0	45 166.0	2. *Indirect taxes*
6 493.0	8 837.0	11 187.0	11 104.0	12 542.0	3. *Direct taxes*
8 268.0	9 840.0	13 430.0	14 982.0	17 593.0	4. *Social security contributions*
1 191.0	1 452.0	1 952.0	2 591.0	3 348.0	5. *Current transfers n.e.c. from residents*
...	...	...	...	...	6. *Current transfers n.e.c. from the rest of the world*
54 068.0	**62 316.0**	**76 830.0**	**83 535.0**	**86 061.0**	**Total:** *Current receipts*
24 710.0	34 732.0	48 625.0	52 272.0	58 024.0	7. *Final consumption expenditure*
75.0	126.0	107.0	87.0	91.0	8. *Property income* [1]
21.0	42.0	52.0	87.0	46.0	9. *Subsidies*
...	...	...	...	...	10. *Social security benefits*
5 043.0	7 047.0	9 955.0	18 923.0	17 593.0	11. *Current transfers n.e.c. to residents*
...	...	...	...	...	12. *Current transfers n.e.c. to rest of the world*
24 219.0	20 369.0	18 091.0	12 166.0	10 307.0	13. *Saving*
54 068.0	**62 316.0**	**76 830.0**	**83 535.0**	**86 061.0**	**Total:** *Current disbursements*

[1] *Refers only to Interest on public debt.*

II. CUENTAS NACIONALES

196. PERU: PRODUCTO INTERNO BRUTO POR TIPO DE GASTO, A PRECIOS DE MERCADO

(Millones de soles)

Tipo de gasto	1960	1965	1970	1975	1977
	A precios corrientes				
1. Gasto de consumo final del gobierno general	5 939	15 591	30 372	81 752	173 495
2. Gasto privado de consumo final	41 987	90 258	191 716	476 752	846 660
3. Variación de existencias	5 246	3 718	-190	6 141	-9 282
4. Formación bruta de capital fijo	11 572	23 491	35 601	117 018	180 637
Construcción	5 556	11 689	17 362	51 362	92 516
Maquinaria y equipo	6 016	11 802	18 239	65 656	88 121
5. Exportaciones de bienes y servicios	13 356	20 427	47 138	67 980	178 476
6. Menos: Importaciones de bienes y servicios	11 969	22 065	37 516	122 251	226 854
Total: Producto interno bruto	66 131	131 420	267 121	627 392	1 143 132
	A precios constantes de 1973				
1. Gasto de consumo final del gobierno general	20 860	32 428	40 053	60 458	72 658
2. Gasto privado de consumo final	120 100	179 510	240 220	303 375	317 887
3. Variación de existencias	18 273	12 619	1 482	3 052	-3 321
4. Formación bruta de capital fijo	26 016	42 415	43 222	84 851	60 526
Construcción	13 991	20 518	20 603	39 106	32 308
Maquinaria y equipo	12 025	21 897	22 619	45 745	28 218
5. Exportaciones de bienes y servicios	52 111	67 350	76 152	55 494	61 971
6. Menos: Importaciones de bienes y servicios	21 597	40 778	48 533	66 157	59 983
Total: Producto interno bruto	215 763	293 544	352 596	441 073	449 738

196. PERU: GROSS DOMESTIC PRODUCT BY TYPE OF EXPENDITURE, AT MARKET PRICES

(Millions of soles)

1978	1979	1980	1981	1982	1983	Type of expenditure
At current prices						
225 070	335 846	709 385	1 297 666	2 292 017	4 184 654	1. General government final consumption expenditure
1 315 097	2 264 444	3 713 599	6 621 001	10 892 330	20 553 819	2. Private final consumption expenditure
-10 296	-32 463	-1 348	58 825	-534 459	-900 000	3. Increase in stocks
260 508	476 788	953 717	1 800 401	3 114 232	4 626 937	4. Gross fixed capital formation
127 901	241 474	460 329	892 905	1 737 106	2 735 979	Construction
132 607	235 314	493 388	907 496	1 377 126	1 890 958	Machinery and equipment
371 098	911 424	1 332 380	1 697 452	2 814 375	6 099 737	5. Exports of goods and services
319 266	557 763	1 109 126	1 979 790	3 260 714	5 847 072	6. Less: Imports of goods and services
1 842 211	3 398 276	5 598 607	9 495 555	15 317 781	28 718 075	**Total: Gross domestic product**
At constant 1973 prices						
64 966	61 065	67 452	69 538	74 569	68 081	1. General government final consumption expenditure
304 479	320 989	343 779	357 530	354 090	317 896	2. Private final consumption expenditure
-2 191	-3 833	2 435	3 955	-6 595	-5 559	3. Increase in stocks
51 321	53 860	67 491	77 843	76 053	55 417	4. Gross fixed capital formation
28 686	29 581	34 782	38 225	38 659	30 813	Construction
22 635	24 279	32 709	39 618	37 394	24 604	Machinery and equipment
70 749	79 448	67 690	63 080	71 337	62 563	5. Exports of goods and services
41 854	45 590	64 999	69 283	65 003	48 752	6. Less: Imports of goods and services
447 470	465 939	483 848	502 663	504 451	449 646	**Total: Gross domestic product**

197. PERU: RELACIONES ENTRE PRINCIPALES AGREGADOS DE CUENTAS NACIONALES, A PRECIOS CORRIENTES

(Millones de soles)

	1960	1965	1970	1975	1977	1978
Remuneración de los asalariados	...	...	93 014	230 061	419 899	577 505
Más: Excedente de explotación	...	...	136 932	316 095	591 027	965 386
Más: Consumo de capital fijo	...	...	15 120	36 722	83 464	131 119
1. Igual: **Producto interno bruto al costo de factores**	...	...	245 066	582 878	1 094 390	1 674 010
Más: Impuestos indirectos	...	...	23 122	57 169	113 524	223 517
Menos: Subsidios	...	...	1 067	12 655	64 782	55 316
2. Igual: **Producto interno bruto a precios de mercado**	66 131	131 420	267 121	627 392	1 143 132	1 842 211
Menos: Remuneración neta de factores pagada al resto del mundo	...	...	4 511	8 687	34 507	87 689
3. Igual: **Producto nacional bruto a precios de mercado**	...	...	262 610	618 705	1 108 625	1 754 522
Menos: Consumo de capital fijo	...	...	15 120	36 722	83 464	131 119
4. Igual: **Ingreso nacional a precios de mercado**	...	...	247 490	581 983	1 025 161	1 623 403
Más: Otras transferencias corrientes netas procedentes del resto del mundo	...	...	3 197	1 731	3 943	7 562
5. Igual: **Ingreso nacional disponible a precios de mercado**	...	...	250 687	583 714	1 029 104	1 630 965
Menos: Gasto total de consumo final	47 926	105 849	222 088	558 504	1 020 155	1 540 167
6. Igual: **Ahorro nacional**	...	...	28 599	25 210	8 949	90 798
Menos: Excedente de la nación por transacciones corrientes	...	...	8 308	-61 227	-78 942	-28 295
7. Igual: **Formación neta de capital**	...	...	20 291	86 437	87 891	119 093
Más: Consumo de capital fijo	...	...	15 120	36 722	83 464	131 119
8. Igual: **Formación bruta de capital**	16 818	27 209	35 411	123 159	171 355	250 212

197. PERU: RELATIONS AMONG MAIN NATIONAL ACCOUNTS AGGREGATES, AT CURRENT PRICES

(Millions of soles)

1979	1980	1981	1982	1983	
938 259	1 673 504	2 989 743	5 158 657	8 995 726	*Compensation of employees*
1 892 543	2 954 365	4 904 549	7 440 910	15 184 211	*Plus: Operating surplus*
241 631	395 295	649 993	1 073 388	2 065 000	*Plus: Consumption of fixed capital*
3 072 433	5 023 164	8 544 285	13 672 955	26 244 937	1. *Equals:* **Gross domestic product** *at factor cost*
408 849	722 093	1 123 639	1 904 907	2 835 554	*Plus: Indirect taxes*
83 006	146 650	172 369	260 081	362 416	*Less: Subsidies*
3 398 276	5 598 607	9 495 555	15 317 781	28 718 075	2. *Equals:* **Gross domestic product** *at market prices*
211 867	235 915	424 108	720 638	1 840 318	*Less: Net factor income paid to the rest of the world*
3 186 409	5 362 692	9 071 447	14 597 143	26 877 757	3. *Equals:* **Gross national product** *at market prices*
241 631	395 295	649 993	1 073 388	2 065 000	*Less: Consumption of fixed capital*
2 944 778	4 967 397	8 421 454	13 523 755	24 812 757	4. *Equals:* **National income at market prices**
23 816	33 668	59 393	107 065	299 662	*Plus: Other net current transfers received from the rest of the world*
2 968 594	5 001 065	8 480 847	13 630 820	25 112 419	5. *Equals:* **National disposable income** *at market prices*
2 600 290	4 422 984	7 918 667	13 184 347	24 738 473	*Less: Total final consumption expenditure*
368 304	578 081	562 180	446 473	373 946	6. *Equals:* **National saving**
165 610	21 007	-647 053	-1 059 912	-1 287 991	*Less: Surplus of the nation on current transactions*
202 694	557 074	1 209 233	1 506 385	1 661 937	7. *Equals:* **Net capital formation**
241 631	395 295	649 993	1 073 388	2 065 000	*Plus: Consumption of fixed capital*
444 325	952 369	1 859 226	2 579 773	3 726 937	8. *Equals:* **Gross capital formation**

401

198. PERU: PRODUCTO INTERNO BRUTO POR CLASE DE ACTIVIDAD ECONOMICA, A PRECIOS DE MERCADO

(Millones de soles)

Clase de actividad	1960	1965	1970	1975	1977	1978
			A precios corrientes			
1. Agricultura, caza, silvicultura y pesca	...	...	43 698	87 034	148 526	200 018
2. Explotación de minas y canteras	...	...	18 214	28 476	80 945	185 338
3. Industrias manufactureras	...	...	63 447	156 493	293 229	508 715
4. Electricidad, gas y agua	...	...	1 933	4 742	10 653	18 740
5. Construcción	...	...	7 990	23 401	40 919	53 308
6. Comercio al por mayor y al por menor, restaurantes y hoteles	...	...	34 233	107 113	183 522	299 510
7. Transportes, almacenamiento y comunicaciones	...	...	14 334	41 013	85 058	118 428
8. Establecimientos financieros, seguros, bienes inmuebles y servicios prestados a las empresas	...	...	30 466	63 437	103 420	159 722
Viviendas	...	...	17 595	30 240	37 809	48 500
9. Servicios comunales, sociales y personales	...	...	49 258	110 040	204 837	299 218
Servicios gubernamentales	...	...	25 401 [1]	59 683 [1]	106 055 [1]	142 344 [1]
Subtotal	...	...	263 573	621 749	1 151 109	1 842 997
Menos: Comisión imputada de los servicios bancarios	...	...	4 370	12 134	26 461	40 996
Más: Derechos de importación	...	...	7 918	17 777	18 484	40 210
Total: Producto interno bruto	66 131	131 420	267 121	627 392	1 143 132	1 842 211
			A precios constantes de 1973			
1. Agricultura, caza, silvicultura y pesca	39 473	47 233	59 374	56 750	57 580	57 619
2. Explotación de minas y canteras	16 848	19 861	24 930	25 243	32 909	36 033
3. Industrias manufactureras	49 523	69 602	87 238	114 959	114 469	110 026
4. Electricidad, gas y agua	1 015	1 616	2 234	3 541	4 537	4 728
5. Construcción	7 308	10 589	10 455	17 009	15 107	13 551
6. Comercio al por mayor y al por menor, restaurantes y hoteles	63 499 [2]	88 283 [2]	44 630	66 256	61 605	60 152
7. Transportes, almacenamiento y comunicaciones	[3]	[3]	17 635	26 453	28 347	28 773
8. Establecimientos financieros, seguros, bienes inmuebles y servicios prestados a las empresas	[3]	[3]	39 103	49 769	52 304	53 632
Viviendas	15 902	18 529	20 969	25 671	26 542	26 818
9. Servicios comunales, sociales y personales	[3]	[3]	63 645	80 681	88 036	87 601
Servicios gubernamentales	19 297	28 454	33 971 [1]	44 908 [1]	49 918 [1]	49 969 [1]
Subtotal	212 865	284 167	349 244	440 661	454 894	452 115
Menos: Comisión imputada de los servicios bancarios	[3]	[3]	6 931	8 964	9 963	9 866
Más: Derechos de importación	2 898	9 377	10 283	9 376	4 807	5 221
Total: Producto interno bruto	215 763	293 544	352 596	441 073	449 738	447 470

[1] Incluye actividades de los Productores de servicios gubernamentales generadas en distintas ramas de la CIIU.
[2] Incluye Transportes, almacenamiento y comunicaciones, Establecimientos financieros, seguros, bienes inmuebles y servicios prestados a las empresas, Servicios comunales, sociales y personales y la deducción de la Comisión imputada de los servicios bancarios.
[3] Se incluyen en Comercio al por mayor y al por menor, restaurantes y hoteles.

198. PERU: GROSS DOMESTIC PRODUCT BY KIND OF ECONOMIC ACTIVITY, AT MARKET PRICES

(Millions of soles)

1979	1980	1981	1982	1983	Kind of activity
		At current prices			
326 609	474 707	871 824	1 250 224	2 318 561	1. *Agriculture, hunting, forestry and fishing*
483 103	655 430	934 263	1 484 802	3 179 487	2. *Mining and quarrying*
951 547	1 567 315	2 339 371	3 703 607	7 323 863	3. *Manufacturing*
33 172	49 527	90 468	177 539	320 991	4. *Electricity, gas and water*
83 581	159 605	307 246	566 313	887 524	5. *Construction*
575 449	1 028 403	1 864 595	3 014 918	4 869 093	6. *Wholesale and retail trade, restaurants, and hotels*
205 312	330 400	619 789	1 024 402	2 066 561	7. *Transport, storage and communications*
252 469	388 493	736 504	1 147 563	2 117 254	8. *Finance, insurance, real estate and business services*
62 077	86 877	133 905	195 599	342 457	*Dwellings*
494 786	913 596	1 697 392	2 859 987	5 644 066	9. *Community, social and personal services*
227 218 [1]	475 483 [1]	916 797 [1]	1 547 422 [1]	3 086 005 [1]	*Government services*
3 406 028	5 567 476	9 461 452	15 229 355	28 727 400	**Subtotal**
76 231	123 657	276 820	372 383	711 860	*Less: Imputed bank service charges*
68 479	154 788	310 923	460 809	702 535	*Plus: Import duties*
3 398 276	5 598 607	9 495 555	15 317 781	28 718 075	**Total:** *Gross domestic product*
		At constant 1973 prices			
60 215	56 877	62 952	64 290	57 078	1. *Agriculture, hunting, forestry and fishing*
39 324	39 477	38 245	40 750	37 612	2. *Mining and quarrying*
114 697	121 275	121 031	118 010	99 128	3. *Manufacturing*
5 071	5 347	5 859	6 187	5 924	4. *Electricity, gas and water*
14 170	16 833	18 693	19 123	15 107	5. *Construction*
63 269	67 024	70 818	68 485	57 294	6. *Wholesale and retail trade, restaurants and hotels*
30 152	32 443	34 216	34 123	31 092	7. *Transport, storage and communications*
55 115	57 457	59 758	61 368	58 226	8. *Finance, insurance, real estate and business services*
27 178	27 537	27 931	28 250	28 590	*Dwellings*
88 626	91 722	94 687	96 279	93 499	9. *Community, social and personal services*
50 150 [1]	52 449 [1]	54 527 [1]	55 984 [1]	55 984 [1]	*Government services*
470 640	488 455	506 259	508 615	454 960	**Subtotal**
10 306	11 740	12 410	11 583	10 969	*Less: Imputed bank service charges*
5 606	7 133	8 814	7 419	5 655	*Plus: Import duties*
465 939	483 848	502 663	504 451	449 646	**Total:** *Gross domestic product*

[1] *Including activities of Producers of government services generated in various branches of the ISIC.*
[2] *Including Transport, storage and communications, Finance, insurance, real estate and business services, Community, social and personal services, and deduction of Imputed bank service charges.*
[3] *Included in Wholesale and retail trade, restaurants and hotels.*

II. CUENTAS NACIONALES

199. PERU: INGRESOS Y GASTOS DEL GOBIERNO GENERAL [1]

(Millones de soles)

	1960	1965	1970		1975	1978
1. Renta de la propiedad y de la empresa	181 [2]	575 [2]	2 263 [2]	1 384	2 256	12 263
2. Impuestos indirectos	4 952 [3]	13 312 [3]	25 269 [3]	23 122	57 169	223 517
3. Impuestos directos	2 866	4 492	13 967	11 674	25 994	50 454
4. Contribuciones a la seguridad social	550	2 304	4 774	4 888	17 427	28 651
5. Transferencias corrientes n.e.p. de residentes	164	370	1 442	3 765	8 805	30 636
6. Transferencias corrientes n.e.p. del resto del mundo	...	...	...	31	44	100
Total: Ingresos corrientes	8 351	19 903	43 189	44 864	111 695	345 621
7. Gasto de consumo final	4 776	12 542	24 426	30 372	81 752	225 070
8. Renta de la propiedad	[5]	[5]	[5]	2 658	9 269	72 234
9. Subsidios	882	2 493	3 184	1 067	12 655	55 316
10. Prestaciones de seguridad social	...	...	...	901	4 803	14 208
11. Transferencias corrientes n.e.p. a residentes	1 141	5 247	10 936	3 460	6 696	50 110
12. Transferencias corrientes n.e.p. al resto del mundo	41	29	85	87	154	425
13. Ahorro	1 511	-408	-4 558	6 319	-3 634	-71 742
Total: Egresos corrientes	8 351	19 903	43 189	44 864	111 695	345 621

[1] La información para el período 1960-1970 no es comparable con las series del Producto interno bruto por origen sectorial o por tipo de gasto.
[2] Incluye Intereses de la deuda pública y Renta de la propiedad.
[3] Incluye Ingresos no tributarios provenientes de las empresas.
[4] Presenta diferencia con respecto al mismo concepto del cuadro 197.
[5] Incluido en Renta de la propiedad y de la empresa.

199. PERU: INCOME AND OUTLAY OF THE GENERAL GOVERNMENT [1]

(Millions of soles)

1979	1980	1981	1982	1983	
29 931	62 798	85 152	172 180	253 028	1. *Property and entrepreneurial income*
408 849	722 093	1 123 639	1 904 907	3 006 938 [4]	2. *Indirect taxes*
131 152	478 279	396 701	524 992	675 544	3. *Direct taxes*
55 752	114 163	228 230	318 519	501 621	4. *Social security contributions*
41 849	66 427	142 319	216 552	622 299	5. *Current transfers n.e.c. from residents*
95	149	194	370	654	6. *Current transfers n.e.c. from the rest of the world*
667 627	1 443 909	1 976 235	3 137 520	5 060 084	**Total:** *Current receipts*
335 846	709 385	1 297 666	2 292 017	4 184 654	7. *Final consumption expenditure*
123 512	205 986	320 246	432 314	753 108	8. *Property income*
83 006	146 650	172 369	260 081	362 416	9. *Subsidies*
22 534	39 606	71 868	126 873	211 115	10. *Social security benefits*
137 823	97 037	132 479	229 055	607 572	11. *Current transfers n.e.c. to residents*
488	2 235	2 541	3 194	3 985	12. *Current transfers n.e.c. to rest of the world*
-35 582	243 010	-20 934	-206 014	-1 062 766	13. *Saving*
667 627	1 443 909	1 976 235	3 137 520	5 060 084	**Total:** *Current disbursements*

[1] *Data for the period 1960-1970 are not comparable with the series on Gross domestic product by kind of economic activity or by type of expenditure.*
[2] *Including Public debt interest and Property income.*
[3] *Including Non-tax income from enterprises.*
[4] *Shows a difference with respect to same concept in table 197.*
[5] *Included in Property and entrepreneurial income.*

200. REPUBLICA DOMINICANA: PRODUCTO INTERNO BRUTO POR TIPO DE GASTO, A PRECIOS DE MERCADO

(Millones de pesos)

Tipo de gasto	1960	1965	1970	1975	1977
			A precios corrientes		
1. Gasto de consumo final del gobierno general	92.2	172.8	172.0	222.1	189.3
2. Gasto privado de consumo final [1]	491.4	718.8	1 137.7	2 495.6	3 589.3
3. Variación de existencias [2]	9.1	- 2.4	38.4	79.4	60.3
4. Formación bruta de capital fijo	75.7	89.2	245.9	802.7	939.2
Construcción	44.0	65.3	147.0	502.7	619.1
Maquinaria y equipo	31.7	23.9	98.9	300.0	320.1
5. Exportaciones de bienes y servicios	172.1	144.8	255.9	1 009.1	917.9
6. Menos: Importaciones de bienes y servicios	116.9	166.4	364.5	1 009.8	1 108.9
Total: Producto interno bruto	723.6	956.8	1 485.5	3 599.1	4 587.1

Tipo de gasto	A precios constantes de:					
	1962			1970		
1. Gasto de consumo final del gobierno general	91.0	162.6	124.5	172.0	179.3	151.5
2. Gasto privado de consumo final [1]	529.6	650.7	1 008.6	1 137.7	1 699.5	1 896.4
3. Variación de existencias [2]	9.2	-2.5	20.8	38.4	40.4	41.0
4. Formación bruta de capital fijo	67.3	83.7	218.3	245.9	571.7	577.9
Construcción	43.3	59.1	130.0	147.0	308.8	341.4
Maquinaria y equipo	24.0	24.6	88.3	98.9	262.9	236.5
5. Exportaciones de bienes y servicios	188.7	143.9	211.8	255.9	430.3	550.0
6. Menos: Importaciones de bienes y servicios	110.2	155.5	311.5	364.5	632.3	652.3
Total: Producto interno bruto	775.6	882.9	1 272.5	1 485.5	2 288.9	2 564.5

[1] Incluye una parte de Variación de existencias.
[2] Comprende sólo la Variación de existencias de maní, tabaco en rama y frijoles, y de las actividades de Minería e Industrias manufactureras.

200. DOMINICAN REPUBLIC: GROSS DOMESTIC PRODUCT BY TYPE OF EXPENDITURE, AT MARKET PRICES

(Millions of pesos)

1978	1979	1980	1981	1982	Type of expenditure
		At current prices			
271.1	419.6	504.0	693.4	778.4	1. General government final consumption expenditure
3 659.1	4 034.4	5 125.4	5 121.1	5 886.4	2. Private final consumption expenditure [1]
98.3	59.5	81.8	61.2	104.6	3. Increase in stocks [2]
1 031.9	1 334.7	1 566.9	1 640.3	1 540.9	4. Gross fixed capital formation
706.1	847.5	970.1	1 086.8	1 127.2	Construction
325.8	487.2	596.8	553.5	413.7	Machinery and equipment
828.0	1 134.9	1 271.3	1 512.6	1 141.8	5. Exports of goods and services
1 154.0	1 484.3	1 918.7	1 818.4	1 534.6	6. Less: Imports of goods and services
4 734.4	**5 498.8**	**6 630.7**	**7 210.2**	**7 917.5**	**Total:** Gross domestic product
		At constant prices of:			
		1970			
175.2	212.9	262.5	329.4	348.9	1. General government final consumption expenditure
1 887.1	1 901.2	2 212.9	2 211.4	2 238.6	2. Private final consumption expenditure [1]
60.8	34.0	52.2	30.7	53.0	3. Increase in stocks [2]
574.8	653.5	682.9	624.4	554.4	4. Gross fixed capital formation
353.2	371.5	399.8	397.5	381.9	Construction
221.6	282.0	283.1	226.9	172.5	Machinery and equipment
542.7	672.4	560.0	598.3	518.9	5. Exports of goods and services
621.1	735.9	866.6	774.4	642.9	6. Less: Imports of goods and services
2 619.5	**2 738.1**	**2 903.9**	**3 019.8**	**3 070.9**	**Total:** Gross domestic product

[1] Includes a part of Increase in stocks.
[2] Only includes Increase in stocks in the case of peanuts, raw tobacco and beans and of Mining and Manufacturing activities.

407

201. REPUBLICA DOMINICANA: RELACIONES ENTRE PRINCIPALES AGREGADOS DE CUENTAS NACIONALES, A PRECIOS CORRIENTES

(Millones de pesos)

	1960	1965	1970	1975	1976
Remuneración de los asalariados [1]	584.2	814.9	1 236.2	2 951.1	3 327.7
Más: Excedente de explotación	[2]	[2]	[2]	[2]	[2]
Más: Consumo de capital fijo	43.4	57.4	89.1	216.0	237.1
1. Igual: **Producto interno bruto al costo de factores**	627.6	872.3	1 325.3	3 167.1	3 564.8
Más: Impuestos indirectos	96.0 [3]	84.5 [3]	160.2 [3]	432.1 [3]	386.7 [3]
Menos: Subsidios	[4]	[4]	[4]	[4]	[4]
2. Igual: **Producto interno bruto a precios de mercado**	723.6	956.8	1 485.5	3 599.2	3 951.5
Menos: Remuneración neta de factores pagada al resto del mundo	9.6	12.0	25.1	112.8	123.8
3. Igual: **Producto nacional bruto a precios de mercado**	714.0	944.8	1 460.4	3 486.4	3 827.7
Menos: Consumo de capital fijo	43.4	57.4	89.1	216.0	237.1
4. Igual: **Ingreso nacional a precios de mercado**	670.6	887.4	1 371.3	3 270.4	3 590.6
Más: Otras transferencias corrientes netas procedentes del resto del mundo	...	...	...	39.0	46.5
5. Igual: **Ingreso nacional disponible a precios de mercado**	...	...	...	3 309.4	3 637.1
Menos: Gasto total de consumo final	583.6	891.6	1 309.7	2 717.7 [5]	3 234.4 [5]
6. Igual: **Ahorro nacional**	87.0 [6]	-4.2 [6]	61.6 [6]	591.6	402.7
Menos: Excedente de la nación por transacciones corrientes	45.6 [6]	-33.6 [6]	-133.6 [6]	-74.5	-241.9
7. Igual: **Formación neta de capital**	41.4	29.4	195.2	666.1	644.6
Más: Consumo de capital fijo	43.4	57.4	89.1	216.0	237.1
8. Igual: **Formación bruta de capital**	84.8	86.8	284.3	882.1 [7]	881.7 [7]

[1] Incluye Excedente de explotación.
[2] Incluido en Remuneración de los asalariados.
[3] Incluye Subsidios.
[4] Incluido en Impuestos indirectos.
[5] Incluye una parte de Variación de existencias.
[6] No incluye Otras transferencias corrientes netas procedentes del resto del mundo.
[7] Comprende sólo la Variación de existencias de maní, tabaco en rama y frijoles, y de las actividades de Minería e Industrias manufactureras.

201. DOMINICAN REPUBLIC: RELATIONS AMONG MAIN NATIONAL ACCOUNTS AGGREGATES, AT CURRENT PRICES

(Millions of pesos)

1977	1978	1979	1980	1981	1982	
3 864.9	4 056.5	4 716.5	5 729.0	6 240.2	6 973.6	*Compensation of employees* [1]
[2]	[2]	[2]	[2]	[2]	[2]	*Plus: Operating surplus*
272.7	275.5	326.7	394.5	429.0	471.1	*Plus: Consumption of fixed capital*
4 137.6	4 332.0	5 043.2	6 123.5	6 669.2	7 444.7	1. *Equals:* **Gross domestic product at factor cost**
462.8	421.4	464.0	507.7	541.1	472.8 [3]	*Plus: Indirect taxes*
13.3	19.0	8.4	0.5	0.1	[4]	*Less: Subsidies*
4 587.1	4 734.4	5 498.8	6 630.7	7 210.2	7 917.5	2. *Equals:* **Gross domestic product at market prices**
123.4	135.7	187.7	210.2	293.1	254.1	*Less: Net factor income paid to the rest of the world*
4 463.7	4 598.7	5 311.1	6 420.5	6 917.1	7 663.4	3. *Equals:* **Gross national product at market prices**
272.7	275.5	326.7	394.5	429.0	471.1	*Less: Consumption of fixed capital*
4 191.0	4 323.2	4 984.4	6 026.0	6 488.1	7 192.3	4. *Equals:* **National income at market prices**
50.1	149.8	205.8	187.8	193.0	205.0	*Plus: Other net current transfers received from the rest of the world*
4 241.1	4 473.0	5 190.2	6 213.8	6 681.1	7 397.3	5. *Equals:* **National disposable income at market prices**
3 778.6 [5]	3 930.2 [5]	4 454.0 [5]	5 629.4 [5]	5 814.5 [5]	6 664.8 [5]	*Less: Total final consumption expenditure*
462.5	542.8	736.2	584.4	866.6	732.5	6. *Equals:* **National saving**
-264.3	-311.9	-331.3	-669.0	-405.9	-441.9	*Less: Surplus of the nation on current transactions*
726.8	854.7	1 067.5	1 254.2	1 272.5	1 174.4	7. *Equals:* **Net capital formation**
272.7	275.5	326.7	394.5	429.0	471.1	*Plus: Consumption of fixed capital*
999.5 [7]	1 130.2 [7]	1 394.2 [7]	1 648.7 [7]	1 701.5 [7]	1 645.5 [7]	8. *Equals:* **Gross capital formation**

[1] *Including Operating surplus.*
[2] *Included in Compensation of employees.*
[3] *Including Subsidies.*
[4] *Included in Indirect taxes.*
[5] *Includes part of Increase in stocks.*
[6] *Does not include Other net current transfers from the rest of the world.*
[7] *Only includes Increase in stocks in the case of peanuts, raw tobacco and beans and of Mining and Manufacturing activities.*

II. CUENTAS NACIONALES

202. REPUBLICA DOMINICANA: PRODUCTO INTERNO BRUTO POR CLASE DE ACTIVIDAD ECONOMICA, A PRECIOS DE MERCADO

(Millones de pesos)

Clase de actividad	1960	1965	1970	1975	1977
	\multicolumn{5}{c}{A precios corrientes}				
1. Agricultura, caza, silvicultura y pesca	193.1	252.9	345.1	772.8	920.5
2. Explotación de minas y canteras	13.5	13.0	22.7	107.8	144.0
3. Industrias manufactureras	125.0	138.1	275.4	752.1	870.6
4. Electricidad, gas y agua [1]	7.5	11.4	17.5	30.1	32.9
5. Construcción	21.7	32.2	72.7	248.5	305.9
6. Comercio al por mayor y al por menor, restaurantes y hoteles	135.4 [2]	152.4 [2]	237.6	586.0	787.1
7. Transportes, almacenamiento y comunicaciones	33.2	49.9	114.8	217.8	282.9
8. Establecimientos financieros, seguros, bienes inmuebles y servicios prestados a las empresas	62.5 [3]	85.7 [3]	127.2	308.9	506.2
Viviendas	52.2	74.2	100.2	228.7	368.2
9. Servicios comunales, sociales y personales	131.7 [4][5]	221.2 [4][5]	272.4 [5]	575.2 [5]	737.0
Servicios gubernamentales	71.6	144.6	152.1	228.6	273.5
Subtotal	**723.6**	**956.8**	**1 485.4**	**3 599.2**	**4 587.1**
Menos: Comisión imputada de los servicios bancarios	...	...		...	...
Más: Derechos de importación	...	...	...	...	...
Total: Producto interno bruto	**723.6**	**956.8**	**1 485.4**	**3 599.2**	**4 587.1**
	\multicolumn{5}{c}{A precios constantes de:}				
	\multicolumn{3}{c}{1962}			\multicolumn{2}{c}{1970}	
1. Agricultura, caza, silvicultura y pesca	254.5	236.8	313.8	345.2	399.9	436.8
2. Explotación de minas y canteras	12.1	12.1	18.1	22.7	121.7	143.0
3. Industrias manufactureras	115.3	112.2	215.5	275.4	428.5	483.2
4. Electricidad, gas y agua [1]	8.1	10.4	19.7	17.5	30.0	39.3
5. Construcción	21.4	29.3	64.2	72.7	152.6	168.7
6. Comercio al por mayor y al por menor, restaurantes y hoteles	131.7 [2]	135.6 [2]	224.6	237.6	385.9	429.8
7. Transportes, almacenamiento y comunicaciones	36.2	52.1	82.6	114.8	182.7	211.8
8. Establecimientos financieros, seguros, bienes inmuebles y servicios prestados a las empresas	66.3 [3]	86.4 [3]	118.9	127.2	197.7	233.3
Viviendas	53.3	70.9	97.7	100.2	149.0	169.8
9. Servicios comunales, sociales y personales	130.0 [4][5]	208.0 [4][5]	215.1 [5]	272.4 [5]	389.9 [5]	418.6
Servicios gubernamentales	70.7	136.0	106.6	152.1	183.1	191.2
Subtotal	**775.6**	**882.9**	**1 272.5**	**1 485.5**	**2 288.9**	**2 564.5**
Menos: Comisión imputada de los servicios bancarios	...	...	...	...		...
Más: Derechos de importación	...	...	...	...	...	
Total: Producto interno bruto	**775.6**	**882.9**	**1 272.5**	**1 485.5**	**2 288.9**	**2 564.5**

[1] Se refiere sólo a Electricidad.
[2] Restaurantes y hoteles se incluyen en Servicios comunales, sociales y personales.
[3] Servicios prestados a las empresas se incluyen en Servicios comunales, sociales y personales.
[4] Incluye Restaurantes y hoteles y Servicios prestados a las empresas.
[5] Incluye gas y agua.

202. DOMINICAN REPUBLIC: GROSS DOMESTIC PRODUCT BY KIND OF ECONOMIC ACTIVITY, AT MARKET PRICES

(Millions of pesos)

1978	1979	1980	1981	1982	Kind of activity
		At current prices			
886.3	1 026.8	1 336.3	1 349.5	1 414.9	1. *Agriculture, hunting, forestry and fishing*
117.9	221.0	351.7	255.9	190.0	2. *Mining and quarrying*
879.7	928.6	1 015.4	1 133.1	1 454.9	3. *Manufacturing*
42.6	31.3	30.0	66.8	82.4	4. *Electricity, gas and water* [1]
349.0	418.8	479.4	537.1	557.0	5. *Construction*
732.8	861.0	1 047.8	1 173.6	1 321.4	6. *Wholesale and retail trade, restaurants and hotels*
322.3	354.9	362.3	390.5	423.9	7. *Transport, storage and communications*
557.7	647.3	794.0	967.9	998.8	8. *Finance, insurance, real estate and business services*
402.8	456.3	556.2	681.2	693.5	*Dwellings*
846.1 [5]	1 009.1 [5]	1 213.8 [5]	1 335.8 [5]	1 474.2 [5]	9. *Community, social and personal services*
326.3	469.1	551.8	608.0	663.3	*Government services*
4 734.4	5 498.8	6 630.7	7 210.2	7 917.5	**Subtotal**
...	...	...	...	...	*Less: Imputed bank service charges*
...	...	...	...	...	*Plus: Import duties*
4 734.4	5 498.8	6 630.7	7 210.2	7 917.5	**Total:** *Gross domestic product*
		At constant prices of: 1970			
456.7	461.7	484.2	510.8	532.7	1. *Agriculture, hunting, forestry and fishing*
114.3	146.5	124.6	133.5	85.0	2. *Mining and quarrying*
482.6	504.8	530.2	544.5	572.6	3. *Manufacturing*
42.9	43.7	49.0	53.4	48.4	4. *Electricity, gas and water* [1]
174.5	183.6	197.5	196.5	188.7	5. *Construction*
438.8	451.5	473.6	494.9	520.2	6. *Wholesale and retail trade, restaurants and hotels*
218.9	224.3	230.5	242.6	257.0	7. *Transport, storage and communications*
243.6	253.9	268.6	272.1	273.5	8. *Finance, insurance, real estate and business services*
177.2	186.0	198.1	198.8	197.0	*Dwellings*
447.2 [5]	468.1 [5]	545.7 [5]	571.5 [5]	592.8 [5]	9. *Community, social and personal services*
200.4	233.6	280.3	300.1	311.9	*Government services*
2 619.5	2 738.1	2 903.9	3 019.8	3 070.9	**Subtotal**
...	...	...	...	...	*Less: Imputed bank service charges*
...	...	...	...	...	*Plus: Import duties*
2 619.5	2 738.1	2 903.9	3 019.8	3 070.9	**Total:** *Gross domestic product*

[1] *Refers only to Electricity.*
[2] *Restaurants and hotels are included in Community, social and personal services.*
[3] *Business services are included in Community, social and personal services.*
[4] *Including Restaurants and hotels and Business services.*
[5] *Including gas and water.*

203. SAN CRISTOBAL Y NIEVES: PRODUCTO INTERNO BRUTO POR CLASE
DE ACTIVIDAD ECONOMICA, AL COSTO DE FACTORES

(Miles de dólares del Caribe oriental)

Clase de actividad	1977	1978	1979
	A precios corrientes		
1. Agricultura, caza, silvicultura y pesca	15 650	15 760	17 030
2. Explotación de minas y canteras	200	160	240
3. Industrias manufactureras	12 540	13 240	12 790
4. Electricidad, gas y agua	610	710	810
5. Construcción	6 590	5 490	8 120
6. Comercio al por mayor y al por menor, restaurantes y hoteles	7 620	10 080	12 920
7. Transportes, almacenamiento y comunicaciones	5 860	7 320	7 840
8. Establecimientos financieros, seguros, bienes inmuebles y servicios prestados a las empresas	9 050	9 320	11 090
Viviendas	5 260	5 310	6 510
9. Servicios comunales, sociales y personales	15 300	19 270	21 890
Servicios gubernamentales	11 750	15 740	17 920
Subtotal	73 420	81 350	92 730
Menos: Comisión imputada de los servicios bancarios	2 480	2 930	3 480
Total: Producto interno bruto	70 940	78 420	89 250
	A precios constantes de 1977		
1. Agricultura, caza, silvicultura y pesca	15 650	16 330	17 320
2. Explotación de minas y canteras	200	150	180
3. Industrias manufactureras	12 540	13 150	13 310
4. Electricidad, gas y agua	610	710	740
5. Construcción	6 590	4 940	6 090
6. Comercio al por mayor y al por menor, restaurantes y hoteles	7 620	8 600	9 680
7. Transportes, almacenamiento y comunicaciones	5 860	6 180	6 290
8. Establecimientos financieros, seguros, bienes inmuebles y servicios prestados a las empresas	9 050	8 940	9 460
Viviendas	5 260	5 310	5 400
9. Servicios comunales, sociales y personales	15 300	16 150	18 060
Servicios gubernamentales	11 750	12 840	14 690
Subtotal	73 420	75 150	81 130
Menos: Comisión imputada de los servicios bancarios	2 480	2 640	3 100
Total: Producto interno bruto	70 940	72 510	78 030

203. ST. CHRISTOPHER AND NEVIS: GROSS DOMESTIC PRODUCT BY KIND OF ECONOMIC ACTIVITY, AT FACTOR COST

(Thousands of East Caribbean dollars)

1980	1981	1982	Kind of activity
	At current prices		
21 560	19 710	27 910	1. *Agriculture, hunting, forestry and fishing*
320	330	290	2. *Mining and quarrying*
15 740	17 880	18 660	3. *Manufacturing*
880	1 110	1 250	4. *Electricity, gas and water*
10 580	10 850	9 770	5. *Construction*
14 690	19 190	18 910	6. *Wholesale and retail trade, restaurants and hotels*
10 010	14 970	16 220	7. *Transport, storage and communications*
11 910	13 320	14 070	8. *Finance, insurance, real estate and business services*
6 660	7 480	7 820	*Dwellings*
24 040	32 760	35 360	9. *Community, social and personal services*
18 840	26 190	28 060	*Government services*
109 730	130 120	142 440	*Subtotal*
4 360	3 990	4 260	*Less: Imputed bank service charges*
105 370	126 130	138 180	*Total: Gross domestic product*
	At constant 1977 prices		
16 590	16 690	16 670	1. *Agriculture, hunting, forestry and fishing*
230	240	200	2. *Mining and quarrying*
13 530	12 150	13 170	3. *Manufacturing*
880	940	1 000	4. *Electricity, gas and water*
7 720	7 990	7 190	5. *Construction*
9 960	11 920	11 500	6. *Wholesale and retail trade, restaurants and hotels*
6 880	9 290	9 410	7. *Transport, storage and communications*
9 780	9 760	9 830	8. *Finance, insurance, real estate and business services*
5 500	5 570	5 620	*Dwellings*
19 200	20 590	21 960	9. *Community, social and personal services*
15 450	16 300	17 460	*Government services*
84 820	89 560	90 930	*Subtotal*
3 590	3 060	3 070	*Less: Imputed bank service charges*
81 180	86 510	87 860	*Total: Gross domestic product*

204. SAN VICENTE Y LAS GRANADINAS: PRODUCTO INTERNO BRUTO POR TIPO DE GASTO, A PRECIOS DE MERCADO

(Millones de dólares del Caribe oriental, a precios corrientes)

Tipo de gasto	1975	1976
1. Gasto de consumo final del gobierno general	18.2	19.1
2. Gasto privado de consumo final	71.7	66.1
3. Variación de existencias	0.3	0.7
4. Formación bruta de capital fijo	18.4	17.1
Construcción	14.4	13.2[1]
Maquinaria y equipo	3.9	4.0
5. Exportaciones de bienes y servicios	16.5	24.7
6. Menos: Importaciones de bienes y servicios	53.9	44.4
Total: Producto interno bruto	71.1	83.2

[1] Incluye Discrepancia estadística.

205. SAN VICENTE Y LAS GRANADINAS: RELACIONES ENTRE PRINCIPALES AGREGADOS DE CUENTAS NACIONALES, A PRECIOS CORRIENTES

(Millones de dólares del Caribe oriental)

	1975	1976
Remuneración de los asalariados	37.8	40.9
Más: Excedente de explotación	17.8	24.5
Más: Consumo de capital fijo	5.0	5.6
1. Igual: **Producto interno bruto al costo de factores**	60.6	71.0
Más: Impuestos indirectos	10.7	12.4
Menos: Subsidios	0.1	0.1
2. Igual: **Producto interno bruto a precios de mercado** [1]	71.1	83.2
Menos: Remuneración neta de factores pagada al resto del mundo	...	...
3. Igual: **Producto nacional bruto a precios de mercado**	...	...
Menos: Consumo de capital fijo	5.0	5.6
4. Igual: **Ingreso nacional a precios de mercado**	...	...
Más: Otras transferencias corrientes netas procedentes del resto del mundo	...	...
5. Igual: **Ingreso nacional disponible a precios de mercado**	...	...
Menos: Gasto total de consumo final	89.9	85.2
6. Igual: **Ahorro nacional**	...	...
Menos: Excedente de la nación por transacciones corrientes	...	...
7. Igual: **Formación neta de capital**	13.6	12.2
Más: Consumo de capital fijo	5.0	5.6
8. Igual: **Formación bruta de capital**	18.6	17.8

[1] No coincide con la suma de los sumandos, por haberse redondeado las cifras.

204. SAINT VINCENT AND THE GRENADINES: GROSS DOMESTIC PRODUCT BY TYPE OF EXPENDITURE, AT MARKET PRICES

(Millions of East Caribbean dollars, at current prices)

1977	1978	1979	Type of expenditure
20.5	27.2	30.8	1. General government final consumption expenditure
101.1	121.7	154.6	2. Private final consumption expenditure
2.6	1.9	2.6	3. Increase in stocks
26.5	27.8	34.1	4. Gross fixed capital formation
17.7[1]	...	...	Construction
8.8	...	...	Machinery and equipment
26.8	44.0	39.8	5. Exports of goods and services
81.9	97.7	125.2	6. Less: Imports of goods and services
95.5	125.0	136.7	**Total:** Gross domestic product

[1] *Includes Statistical discrepancy.*

205. SAINT VINCENT AND THE GRENADINES: RELATIONS AMONG MAIN NATIONAL ACCOUNTS AGGREGATES, AT CURRENT PRICES

(Millions of East Caribbean dollars)

1977	1978	1979	
47.0	59.1	67.0	Compensation of employees
26.9	38.1	35.9	Plus: Operating surplus
6.3	9.1	10.7	Plus: Consumption of fixed capital
80.2	106.3	113.6	1. Equals: **Gross domestic product at factor cost**
15.4	18.8	23.3	Plus: Indirect taxes
0.1	0.1	0.1	Less: Subsidies
95.5	125.0	136.7	2. Equals: **Gross domestic product at market prices** [1]
...	...	...	Less: Net factor income paid to the rest of the world
...	...	...	3. Equals: **Gross national product at market prices**
6.3	9.1	10.7	Less: Consumption of fixed capital
...	...	...	4. Equals: **National income at market prices**
...	...	...	Plus: Other net current transfers received from the rest of the world
...	...	...	5. Equals: **National disposable income at market prices**
121.6	148.9	185.4	Less: Total final consumption expenditure
...	...	...	6. Equals: **National saving**
...	...	...	Less: Surplus of the nation on current transactions
22.8	20.6	26.0	7. Equals: **Net capital formation**
6.3	9.1	10.7	Plus: Consumption of fixed capital
29.1	29.7	36.7	8. Equals: **Gross capital formation**

[1] *As the figures have been rounded off, this total does not agree with the sum of the individual figures.*

206. SAN VICENTE Y LAS GRANADINAS: PRODUCTO INTERNO BRUTO POR CLASE DE ACTIVIDAD ECONOMICA, AL COSTO DE FACTORES

(Millones de dólares del Caribe oriental)

Clase de actividad	1960	1965	1970	1974	1975
		A precios corrientes			
1. Agricultura, caza, silvicultura y pesca	...	8.4	9.3	...	9.0
2. Explotación de minas y canteras	...	1.1 [1]	1.4 [1]	...	0.2
3. Industrias manufactureras	...	[2]	[2]	...	4.0
4. Electricidad, gas y agua	...	-	0.9	...	1.7
5. Construcción	...	1.6	3.8	...	8.7
6. Comercio al por mayor y al por menor, restaurantes y hoteles	...	4.5	7.2	...	8.6
7. Transportes, almacenamiento y comunicaciones	...	0.8	1.2	...	7.9
8. Establecimientos financieros, seguros, bienes inmuebles y servicios prestados a las empresas	...	3.9	5.1	...	8.4
Viviendas	...	2.8	...	...	...
9. Servicios comunales, sociales y personales	...	6.3	8.1	...	15.0
Servicios gubernamentales	...	5.0	6.5	...	13.0
Subtotal	....	26.6	37.0	...	63.6
Menos: Comisión imputada de los servicios bancarios	...	...	...	...	3.0
Total: Producto interno bruto	...	26.6	37.0	...	60.6
Discrepancia estadística	-	-	-	...	-
		A precios constantes de 1976			
1. Agricultura, caza, silvicultura y pesca	...	...	...	...	11.0
2. Explotación de minas y canteras	...	...	...	...	0.2
3. Industrias manufactureras	...	...	...	...	4.4
4. Electricidad, gas y agua	...	...	...	...	2.0
5. Construcción	...	...	...	...	9.7
6. Comercio al por mayor y al por menor, restaurantes y hoteles	...	...	...	...	9.6
7. Transportes, almacenamiento y comunicaciones	...	...	...	...	8.6
8. Establecimientos financieros, seguros, bienes inmuebles y servicios prestados a las empresas	...	...	...	...	9.3
Viviendas	...	...	...	...	...
9. Servicios comunales, sociales y personales	...	...	...	...	15.3
Servicios gubernamentales	...	...	...	...	...
Subtotal	...	...	...	...	70.1
Menos: Comisión imputada de los servicios bancarios	...	...	...	...	3.4
Total: Producto interno bruto	...	...	...	...	66.7

[1] Incluye Industrias manufactureras.
[2] Se incluye en Minas y canteras.
[3] Diferencia para obtener el total del Producto interno bruto.

206. SAINT VINCENT AND THE GRENADINES: GROSS DOMESTIC PRODUCT BY KIND OF ECONOMIC ACTIVITY, AT FACTOR COST

(Millions of East Caribbean dollars)

1976	1977	1978	1979	Kind of activity
	At current prices			
14.0	14.8	20.2	17.0	1. Agriculture, hunting, forestry and fishing
0.2	0.3	0.3	0.3	2. Mining and quarrying
4.4	5.9	10.3	13.1	3. Manufacturing
2.1	2.4	2.4	2.7	4. Electricity, gas and water
7.7	10.0	11.5	14.6	5. Construction
10.8	11.8	13.4	13.5	6. Wholesale and retail trade, restaurants and hotels
9.8	11.4	16.5	17.4	7. Transport, storage and communications
9.7	10.7	13.9	17.0	8. Finance, insurance, real estate and business services
...	...	...	...	Dwellings
17.4	20.9	23.3	24.8	9. Community, social and personal services
15.1	17.7	19.8	21.1	Government services
76.0	87.6	11.87	120.6	Subtotal
3.7	4.5	5.6	7.1	Less: Imputed bank service charges
71.0	80.2	106.1	113.5	Total: Gross domestic product
-1.4³	-2.8³	-	-	Statistical discrepancy
	At constant 1976 prices			
14.0	11.5	13.6	10.2	1. Agriculture, hunting, forestry and fishing
0.2	0.2	0.3	0.2	2. Mining and quarrying
4.4	5.3	8.6	9.7	3. Manufacturing
2.1	2.5	2.5	3.1	4. Electricity, gas and water
7.7	9.1	9.0	9.8	5. Construction
10.8	11.1	11.1	11.3	6. Wholesale and retail trade, restaurants and hotels
9.8	10.9	13.9	13.0	7. Transport, storage and communications
9.7	9.9	12.0	12.6	8. Finance, insurance, real estate and business services
...	...	...	...	Dwellings
16.0	17.2	18.0	19.0	9. Community, social and personal services
15.1	17.7	...	...	Government services
74.7	77.6	89.0	88.9	Subtotal
3.7	4.1	4.6	5.1	Less: Imputed bank service charges
71.0	73.5	84.3	83.8	Total: Gross domestic product

¹ Including Manufacturing.
² Included in Mining and quarrying.
³ Difference to give total Gross domestic product.

417

207. SANTA LUCIA: PRODUCTO INTERNO BRUTO POR CLASE DE ACTIVIDAD ECONOMICA, AL COSTO DE FACTORES

(Millones de dólares del Caribe oriental)

Clase de actividad	1965	1970	1974	1975
	A precios corrientes			
1. Agricultura, caza, silvicultura y pesca	12.7	13.8	...	16.1
2. Explotación de minas y canteras	1.7[1]	2.3[1]	...	1.5
3. Industrias manufactureras	[2]	[2]	...	7.4
4. Electricidad, gas y agua	0.6	1.4	...	2.8
5. Construcción	3.1	12.1	...	11.2
6. Comercio al por mayor y al por menor, restaurantes y hoteles	7.0	12.4	...	18.3
7. Transportes, almacenamiento y comunicaciones	1.0	2.0	...	8.5
8. Establecimientos financieros, seguros, bienes inmuebles y servicios prestados a las empresas	2.2[3]	5.2[3]	...	16.3[3]
Viviendas	...	3.0	...	...
9. Servicios comunales, sociales y personales	7.1[4]	13.6[4]	...	26.0[4]
Servicios gubernamentales	5.3	11.2	...	7.0
Subtotal	35.4	62.8	...	108.1
Menos: Comisión imputada de los servicios bancarios	...	...	...	...
Total: Producto interno bruto	34.9	62.9	...	108.1
Discrepancia estadística	-0.6[5]	0.1[5]	...	-
	A precios constantes de 1977			
1. Agricultura, caza, silvicultura y pesca	...	...	...	...
2. Explotación de minas y canteras	...	...	...	...
3. Industrias manufactureras	...	...	...	...
4. Electricidad, gas y agua	...	...	...	...
5. Construcción	...	...	...	...
6. Comercio al por mayor y al por menor, restaurantes y hoteles	...	...	...	...
7. Transportes, almacenamiento y comunicaciones	...	...	...	...
8. Establecimientos financieros, seguros, bienes inmuebles y servicios prestados a las empresas	...	...	...	...
Viviendas	...	...	...	...
9. Servicios comunales, sociales y personales	...	...	...	...
Servicios gubernamentales	...	...	...	...
Subtotal	...	...	...	...
Menos: Comisión imputada de los servicios bancarios	...	...	...	...
Total: Producto interno bruto	...	...	...	...

[1] Incluye Industrias manufactureras.
[2] Se incluye en Minas y canteras.
[3] Servicios prestados a las empresas se incluyen en Servicios comunales, sociales y personales.
[4] Incluye Servicios prestados a las empresas.
[5] Diferencia con el total del Producto interno bruto.

207. *SAINT LUCIA: GROSS DOMESTIC PRODUCT BY KIND OF ECONOMIC ACTIVITY, AT FACTOR COST*

(Millions of East Caribbean dollars)

1977	1979	1980	1981	1982	Kind of activity
		At current prices			
21.1	22.7	37.6	35.7	40.0	44.1	1. *Agriculture, hunting, forestry and fishing*
1.9	1.2	3.5	4.2	4.5	4.1	2. *Mining and quarrying*
12.6	13.8	24.2	27.1	27.5	29.9	3. *Manufacturing*
4.0	4.5	5.1	5.5	8.0	9.0	4. *Electricity, gas and water*
17.1	10.8	32.3	34.8	38.1	32.9	5. *Construction*
·31.7	35.6	56.1	57.8	58.0	58.0	6. *Wholesale and retail trade, restaurants and hotels*
12.2	19.1	24.8	28.7	30.7	33.0	7. *Transport, storage and communications*
22.1³	18.5	26.0	30.0	38.7	42.0	8. *Finance, insurance, real estate and business services*
...	9.0	11.1	14.1	16.8	18.1	*Dwellings*
34.3⁴	33.4	42.5	48.3	61.5	79.0	9. *Community, social and personal services*
8.1	27.3	34.2	37.7	49.5	66.4	*Government services*
157.0	159.6	252.1	272.1	307.0	332.0	*Subtotal*
...	7.2	10.8	12.0	17.8	19.6	*Less: Imputed bank service charges*
157.0	152.4	241.3	260.1	289.2	312.4	*Total: Gross domestic product*
-	-	-	-	-	-	*Statistical discrepancy*
		At constant 1977 prices			
...	22.7	26.9	21.2	22.4	25.2	1. *Agriculture, hunting, forestry and fishing*
...	1.2	3.0	3.5	3.1	2.4	2. *Mining and quarrying*
...	13.8	13.8	16.2	16.1	18.2	3. *Manufacturing*
...	4.5	5.9	5.7	5.8	6.1	4. *Electricity, gas and water*
...	10.8	23.8	23.2	23.5	20.3	5. *Construction*
...	35.6	41.2	41.8	41.4	39.1	6. *Wholesale and retail trade, restaurants and hotels*
...	19.1	21.0	20.2	19.5	19.7	7. *Transport, storage and communications*
...	18.5	20.9	21.1	22.6	23.5	8. *Finance, insurance, real estate and business services*
...	9.0	9.4	9.7	10.0	10.4	*Dwellings*
...	33.4	37.3	38.5	42.9	46.4	9. *Community, social and personal services*
...	27.3	30.4	31.1	35.6	39.1	*Government services*
...	159.6	193.8	191.4	197.3	200.9	*Subtotal*
...	-7.2	-9.3	-9.3	-10.4	-11.0	*Less: Imputed bank service charges*
...	152.4	184.5	182.1	186.9	189.9	*Total: Gross domestic product*

¹ *Including Manufacturing.*
² *Included in Mining and quarrying.*
³ *Business services are included in Community, social and personal services.*
⁴ *Including Business services.*
⁵ *Difference with total Gross domestic product.*

208. SURINAME: PRODUCTO INTERNO BRUTO POR TIPO DE GASTO, A PRECIOS DE MERCADO

(Millones de florines, a precios corrientes)

Tipo de gasto	1973	1974	1975	1976
1. Gasto de consumo final del gobierno general	116	133	137	123
2. Gasto privado de consumo final	387	403	493	586
3. Variación de existencias	1	1	1	1
4. Formación bruta de capital fijo[2]	156	245	353	304
Construcción	...	...	...	...
Maquinaria y equipo	...	...	...	...
5. Exportaciones de bienes y servicios	369	543	578	618
6. Menos: Importaciones de bienes y servicios	349	536	634	620
Total: Producto interno bruto[3]	680	789	926	1 012

[1] Se incluye en Formación bruta de capital fijo.
[2] Incluye Variación de existencias. Estas cifras no coinciden con las contenidas en el cuadro de Relaciones entre principales agregados de cuentas nacionales.
[3] Debido al redondeo estos totales no coinciden exactamente con la suma de sus parciales ni con las cifras contenidas en el cuadro de Relaciones entre principales agregados de cuentas nacionales.

209. SURINAME: RELACIONES ENTRE PRINCIPALES AGREGADOS DE CUENTAS NACIONALES, A PRECIOS CORRIENTES

(Millones de florines)

	1973	1974	1975	1976	1977
Remuneración de los asalariados	307	341	409	483	621
Más: Excedente de explotación	231	257	207	269	388
Más: Consumo de capital fijo	79	100	114	101	130
1. Igual: Producto interno bruto al costo de factores	617	694	730	853	1 139
Más: Impuestos indirectos	80	113	224	193	217
Menos: Subsidios	17	23	28	34	36
2. Igual: Producto interno bruto a precios de mercado	680	789	926	1 012	1 320
Menos: Remuneración neta de factores pagada al resto del mundo	70	46	26	67	61 ‹
3. Igual: Producto nacional bruto a precios de mercado	610	742	900	945	1 259
Menos: Consumo de capital fijo	79	100	114	101	130
4. Igual: Ingreso nacional a precios de mercado	531	642	786	844	1 129
Más: Otras transferencias corrientes netas procedentes del resto del mundo	-4	-6	-5	42	2
5. Igual: Ingreso nacional disponible a precios de mercado	527	636	781	886	1 131
Menos: Gasto total de consumo final	503	537	630	711	988
6. Igual: Ahorro nacional	24	99	151	175	143
Menos: Excèdente de la nación por transacciones corrientes	-53	-45	-87	-27	-147
7. Igual: Formación neta de capital	77	144	238	202	290
Más: Consumo de capital fijo	79	100	114	101	130
8. Igual: Formación bruta de capital	156	245[3]	353[3]	304[3]	419[3]
Discrepancia estadística	-	-4[4]	-	-	-
Discrepancia estadística	-	5[5]	-	-	-

[1] Incluye Subsidios.
[2] Incluido en Impuestos indirectos.
[3] Estas cifras difieren de las contenidas en el cuadro sobre Producto interno bruto por tipo de gasto.
[4] Cifras no publicadas por la fuente original. Obtenidas por diferencia entre el Producto interno bruto al costo de factores y sus respectivos sumandos.
[5] Cifras no publicadas por la fuente original. Obtenidas por diferencia entre el Producto interno bruto a precios de mercado y el Producto interno bruto al costo de factores.

420

208. SURINAME: GROSS DOMESTIC PRODUCT BY TYPE OF EXPENDITURE, AT MARKET PRICES

(Millions of guilders, at current prices)

1977	1978	1979	Type of expenditure
191	284	240	1. *General government final consumption expenditure*
797	952	1 051	2. *Private final consumption expenditure*
1	1	1	3. *Increase in stocks*
419	355	377	4. *Gross fixed capital formation*[2]
...	...	...	*Construction*
...	...	...	*Machinery and equipment*
707	814	917	5. *Exports of goods and services*
795	848	922	6. *Less: Imports of goods and services*
1 320	1 557	1 663	*Total: Gross domestic product*[3]

[1] *Included in Gross fixed capital formation.*
[2] *Including Increase in stocks. These figures do not coincide with those contained in the table on Relations among main national accounts aggregates.*
[3] *Because of rounding, these totals do not coincide exactly with the sum of the figures contained in the table on Relations among main national accounts aggregates.*

209. SURINAME: RELATIONS AMONG MAIN NATIONAL ACCOUNTS AGGREGATES, AT CURRENT PRICES

(Millions of guilders)

1978	1979	1980	1981	1982	1983	
732	...	...	...	...	...	*Compensation of employees*
437	...	...	...	...	...	*Plus: Operating surplus*
154	...	...	...	...	...	*Plus: Consumption of fixed capital*
1 323	1 425	1 524	1 785	1 975	2 079	1. *Equals:* **Gross domestic product at factor cost**
265	226[1]	238[1]	261[1]	230[1]	214[1]	*Plus: Indirect taxes*
30	[2]	[2]	[2]	[2]	[2]	*Less: Subsidies*
1 558[3]	1 651[3]	1 762	2 046	2 205	2 293	2. *Equals:* **Gross domestic product at market prices**
57	77	34	-20	-10	...	*Less: Net factor income paid to the rest of the world*
1 501	1 574	1 728	2 066	2 215	2 270	3. *Equals:* **Gross national product at market prices**
154	...	...	...	...	...	*Less: Consumption of fixed capital*
1 347	...	...	...	...	...	4. *Equals:* **National income at market prices**
-2	...	...	...	...	...	*Plus: Other net current transfers received from the rest of the world*
1 345	...	...	...	...	...	5. *Equals:* **National disposable income at market prices**
1 236	...	...	...	...	...	*Less: Total final consumption expenditure*
109	...	...	...	...	...	6. *Equals:* **National saving**
-93	...	...	...	...	...	*Less: Surplus of the nation on current transactions*
202	...	...	...	...	...	7. *Equals:* **Net capital formation**
154	...	...	...	...	...	*Plus: Consumption of fixed capital*
355[3]	...	...	...	...	...	8. *Equals:* **Gross capital formation**
-	-	-	-	-	-	*Statistical discrepancy*
-	-	-	-	-	-	*Statistical discrepancy*

[1] *Including Subsidies.*
[2] *Included in Indirect taxes.*
[3] *These figures differ from those contained in the table on Gross domestic product by type of expenditure.*
[4] *Figures not published by the original source. Estimated by difference between Gross domestic product at factor cost and the sums of the respective individual items.*
[5] *Figures not published by the original source. Estimated by difference between Gross domestic product at market prices and Gross domestic product at factor cost.*

210. SURINAME: PRODUCTO INTERNO BRUTO POR CLASE DE ACTIVIDAD ECONOMICA, AL COSTO DE FACTORES

(Millones de florines)

Clase de actividad	1960	1965	1970	1975	1978	1979
			A precios corrientes			
1. Agricultura, caza, silvicultura y pesca	23	35	...	84	138	146
2. Explotación de minas y canteras	58	72	...	179	264	275
3. Industrias manufactureras	[1]	[2]	...	45	101	113
4. Electricidad, gas y agua	[1]	36[3]	...	18	29	33
5. Construcción	[1]	[2]	...	15	69	66
6. Comercio al por mayor y al por menor, restaurantes y hoteles	[1]	...	...	124	215	236
7. Transportes, almacenamiento y comunicaciones	93[4]	11	...	32	55	60
8. Establecimientos financieros, seguros, bienes inmuebles y servicios prestados a las empresas	[1]	50	...	60	144	170
Viviendas	[1]	11	...	30	55	65
9. Servicios comunales, sociales y personales	[1]	67	...	173	315	339
Servicios gubernamentales	27	47	...	155	291	313
Subtotal	174	270	...	730	1 323	1 437
Menos: Comisión imputada de los servicios bancarios	...	...	...	...	...	...
Total: Producto interno bruto	174	270	...	730	1 323	1 437
Discrepancia estadística	...	-1[5]	...	-	-7[5]	-1[5]
			A precios constantes de 1973			
1. Agricultura, caza, silvicultura y pesca	...	...	...	...	...	...
2. Explotación de minas y canteras	...	...	...	...	...	...
3. Industrias manufactureras	...	...	...	...	...	...
4. Electricidad, gas y agua	...	...	...	...	...	...
5. Construcción	...	...	...	...	...	...
6. Comercio al por mayor y al por menor, restaurantes y hoteles	...	...	...	...	...	...
7. Transportes, almacenamiento y comunicaciones	...	...	...	...	...	...
8. Establecimientos financieros, seguros, bienes inmuebles y servicios prestados a las empresas	...	...	...	...	...	...
Viviendas	...	...	...	...	...	...
9. Servicios comunales, sociales y personales	...	...	...	...	...	...
Servicios gubernamentales	...	...	...	...	...	...
Subtotal	...	...	...	...	...	...
Menos: Comisión imputada de los servicios bancarios	...	...	...	...	...	...
Total: Producto interno bruto	...	...	...	...	...	...

[1] Se incluye en Transporte, almacenamiento y comunicaciones.
[2] Se incluye en Electricidad, gas y agua.
[3] Incluye Industrias manufactureras y Construcción.
[4] Incluye las actividades Industrias manufactureras, Electricidad, gas y agua, Construcción, Comercio al por mayor y al por menor, restaurantes y hoteles. Establecimientos financieros, seguros, bienes inmuebles y servicios prestados a las empresas, y Servicios comunales, sociales y personales.
[5] Cifras no publicadas por la fuente original. Estimadas por diferencia.

210. SURINAME: GROSS DOMESTIC PRODUCT BY KIND OF ECONOMIC ACTIVITY, AT FACTOR COST

(Millions of guilders)

1979	1980	1981	1982	1983	Kind of activity
		At current prices			
147	163	198	201	195	1. *Agriculture, hunting, forestry and fishing*
261	273	282	261	244	2. *Mining and quarrying*
113	131	181	198	209	3. *Manufacturing*
33	37	36	39	39	4. *Electricity, gas and water*
66	52	60	63	63	5. *Construction*
236	244	246	268	274	6. *Wholesale and retail trade, restaurants and hotels*
60	65	101	113	131	7. *Transport, storage and communications*
170	211	266	320	362	8. *Finance, insurance, real estate and business services*
65	72	78	87	93	*Dwellings*
339	348	415	512	562	9. *Community, social and personal services*
313	318	379	474	519	*Government services*
1 425	1 524	1 785	1 975	2 079	*Subtotal*
...	...	...	...	...	*Less: Imputed bank service charges*
1 425	1 524	1 785	1 975	2 079	*Total: Gross domestic product*
-	-	-	-	-	*Statistical discrepancy*
		At constant 1973 prices			
81	86	98	95	92	1. *Agriculture, hunting, forestry and fishing*
119	104	92	78	77	2. *Mining and quarrying*
66	71	94	103	109	3. *Manufacturing*
19	20	19	20	20	4. *Electricity, gas and water*
29	24	26	26	26	5. *Construction*
123	112	104	105	103	6. *Wholesale and retail trade, restaurants and hotels*
33	30	45	46	48	7. *Transport, storage and communications*
87	95	108	114	121	8. *Finance, insurance, real estate and business services*
34	33	33	34	35	*Dwellings*
240	229	228	243	251	9. *Community, social and personal services*
226	215	213	228	235	*Government services*
797	771	814	830	847	*Subtotal*
...	...	...	...	...	*Less: Imputed bank service charges*
797	771	814	830	847	*Total: Gross domestic product*

[1] *Included in Transport, storage and communications.*
[2] *Included in Electricity, gas and water.*
[3] *Including Manufacturing and Construction.*
[4] *Including Manufacturing, Electricity, gas and water, Construction, Wholesale and retail trade, restaurants and hotels, Finance, insurance, real estate and business services, and Community, social and personal services.*
[5] *Figures not published by the original source. Estimated residually.*

II. CUENTAS NACIONALES

211. SURINAME: INGRESOS Y GASTOS DE LOS HOGARES, INCLUIDAS LAS EMPRESAS NO FINANCIERAS NO CONSTITUIDAS EN SOCIEDAD [1]

(Millones de florines)

	1973	1974	1975	1976
1. Remuneración de los asalariados	307	341	409	483
2. Renta neta de la propiedad y de la empresa	95	159	138	137
3. Prestaciones de seguridad social	...	...	...	...
4. Donaciones de asistencia social [2]	7	9	20	8
5. Transferencias corrientes n.e.p. de residentes	[3]	[3]	[3]	[3]
6. Transferencias corrientes n.e.p. del resto del mundo	7	6	12	55
Total: Ingresos corrientes	416	515	579	683
7. Gasto de consumo final	387	403	493	586
8. Impuestos directos	13	14	20	24
9. Contribuciones a la seguridad social [4]	2	3	2	3
10. Transferencias corrientes n.e.p. a residentes	[5]	[5]	[5]	[5]
11. Transferencias corrientes n.e.p. al resto del mundo	10	12	16	13
12. Ahorro	4	82	45	57
Total: Egresos corrientes	416	515	579	683
Discrepancia estadística	-	1 [6]	3 [6]	-

[1] Comprende Instituciones privadas sin fines de lucro que sirven a los hogares.
[2] Incluye Transferencias corrientes n.e.p. de residentes.
[3] Se incluye en Donaciones de asistencia social.
[4] Incluye Transferencias corrientes n.e.p. a los residentes.
[5] Se incluye en Contribuciones a la seguridad social.
[6] Cifras no publicadas por la fuente original. Obtenidas por diferencia para igualar Egresos con Ingresos totales.

211. SURINAME: INCOME AND OUTLAY OF HOUSEHOLDS, INCLUDING PRIVATE UNINCORPORATED NON-FINANCIAL ENTERPRISES [1]

(Millions of guilders)

1977	1978	1979	
621	732	757	1. *Compensation of employees*
259	297	349	2. *Net property and entrepreneurial income*
...	...	...	3. *Social security benefits*
24	31	8	4. *Social assistance grants* [2]
[3]	[3]	[3]	5. *Current transfers n.e.c. from residents*
19	23	28	6. *Current transfers n.e.c. from the rest of the world*
923	1 083	1 142	*Total: Current receipts*
797	952	1 051	7. *Final consumption expenditure*
28	43	53	8. *Direct taxes*
2	2	3	9. *Social security contributions* [4]
[5]	[5]	[5]	10. *Current transfers n.e.c. to residents*
17	16	16	11. *Current transfers n.e.c. to rest of the world*
76	64	13	12. *Saving*
923	1 083	1 142	*Total: Current disbursements*
3 [6]	6 [6]	6 [6]	*Statistical discrepancy*

[1] *Includes Private non-profit institutions serving households.*
[2] *Including Current transfers n.e.c. from residents.*
[3] *Included in Social assistance grants.*
[4] *Including Current transfers n.e.c. to residents.*
[5] *Included in Social security contributions.*
[6] *Figures not published by the original source. Estimated by difference between Current receipts and Disbursements.*

II. CUENTAS NACIONALES

212. SURINAME: INGRESOS Y GASTOS DEL GOBIERNO GENERAL

(Millones de florines)

	1973	1974	1975	1976
1. Renta de la propiedad y de la empresa	24	13	19	25
2. Impuestos indirectos	80	113	224	193
3. Impuestos directos	56	56	48	68
4. Contribuciones a la seguridad social [1]	2	3	2	3
5. Transferencias corrientes n.e.p. de residentes	[2]	[2]	[2]	[2]
6. Transferencias corrientes n.e.p. del resto del mundo	...	...	...	...
Total: Ingresos corrientes	**162**	**185**	**293**	**289**
7. Gasto de consumo final	116	133	137	123
8. Renta de la propiedad	1	2	1	2
9. Subsidios	17	23	28	34 [3]
10. Prestaciones de seguridad social	7 [4]	9 [4]	20 [4]	[5]
11. Transferencias corrientes n.e.p. a residentes	[6]	[6]	[6]	8
12. Transferencias corrientes n.e.p. al resto del mundo	-	1	1	2
13. Ahorro	21	23	106	119
Total: Egresos corrientes	**162**	**185**	**293**	**289**
Discrepancia estadística	-	-6 [7]	-	1 [7]

[1] Incluye Transferencias corrientes n.e.p. de residentes.
[2] Se incluye en Contribuciones a la seguridad social.
[3] Incluye Prestaciones de seguridad social.
[4] Incluye Transferencias corrientes n.e.p. a residentes.
[5] Se incluye en Subsidios.
[6] Se incluye en Prestaciones de seguridad social.
[7] Cifras no publicadas por la fuente original. Obtenidas por diferencia para igualar Egresos con Ingresos totales.

212. SURINAME: INCOME AND OUTLAY OF THE GENERAL GOVERNMENT

(Millions of guilders)

1977	1978	1979	
15	18	23	1. *Property and entrepreneurial income*
217	265	251	2. *Indirect taxes*
87	117	123	3. *Direct taxes*
2	2	3	4. *Social security contributions* [1]
2	2	2	5. *Current transfers n.e.c. from residents*
...	...	...	6. *Current transfers n.e.c. from the rest of the world*
321	402	400	**Total:** *Current receipts*
191	284	240	7. *Final consumption expenditure*
1	3	5	8. *Property income*
36 [3]	30 [3]	25 [3]	9. *Subsidies*
5	5	5	10. *Social security benefits*
24	51	8	11. *Current transfers n.e.c. to residents*
2	9	1	12. *Current transfers n.e.c. to rest of the world*
67	45	121	13. *Saving*
321	402	400	**Total:** *Current disbursements*
-	-20 [7]	-	*Statistical discrepancy*

[1] *Including Current transfers n.e.c. from residents.*
[2] *Included in Social security contributions.*
[3] *Including Social security benefits.*
[4] *Including Current transfers n.e.c. to residents.*
[5] *Included in Subsidies.*
[6] *Included in Social security benefits.*
[7] *Figures not published by original source. Obtained by difference between Total current receipts and Disbursements.*

213. TRINIDAD Y TABAGO: PRODUCTO INTERNO BRUTO POR TIPO DE GASTO, A PRECIOS DE MERCADO [1]

(Millones de dólares de Trinidad y Tabago, a precios corrientes)

Tipo de gasto	1960		1966	1970	1975
1. Gasto de consumo final del gobierno general	87.8	173	176	241	708
2. Gasto privado de consumo final	555.1	848	863	1 098	2 516
3. Variación de existencias	17.6	1	[2]	[2]	[2]
4. Formación bruta de capital fijo	268.3	293	279 [3]	421 [3]	1 151 [3]
Construcción	148.7	...	...	...	...
Maquinaria y equipo	119.6	...	...	...	...
5. Exportaciones de bienes y servicios	551.7	881	483	659	2 876
6. Menos: Importaciones de bienes y servicios	562.2	846	467	685	1 866
Total: Producto interno bruto	918.3	1 350	1 334	1 734	5 385

[1] La información para el período 1966-1981 no es comparable con la serie del Producto interno bruto por origen sectorial.
[2] Se incluye en la Formación bruta de capital fijo.
[3] Incluye Variación de existencias.

213. TRINIDAD AND TOBAGO: GROSS DOMESTIC PRODUCT BY TYPE OF EXPENDITURE, AT MARKET PRICES[1]

(Millions of Trinidad and Tobago dollars, at current prices)

1976	1977	1978	1979	1980	1981	Type of expenditure
801	1 030	1 244	1 681	2 036	2 782	1. *General government final consumption expenditure*
2 802	3 554	4 035	5 093	6 025	7 141	2. *Private final consumption expenditure*
2	2	2	2	2	2	3. *Increase in stocks*
1 614[3]	2 220[3]	2 713[3]	3 457[3]	5 492[3]	5 216[3]	4. *Gross fixed capital formation*
...	...	...	...	...	...	*Construction*
...	...	...	...	...	...	*Machinery and equipment*
3 435	3 742	3 776	4 995	7 536	7 271	5. *Exports of goods and services*
2 445	2 779	3 390	4 345	5 684	5 961	6. *Less: Imports of goods and services*
6 207	4 767	8 378	10 881	15 402	16 449	**Total:** *Gross domestic product*

[1] *The data for the period 1966-1981 are not comparable with the series on Gross domestic product by kind of economic activity.*
[2] *Included in Gross fixed capital formation.*
[3] *Including Increase in stocks.*

214. TRINIDAD Y TABAGO: RELACIONES ENTRE PRINCIPALES AGREGADOS DE CUENTAS NACIONALES, A PRECIOS CORRIENTES

(Millones de dólares de Trinidad y Tabago)

	1960	1966	1970	1975
Remuneración de los asalariados	773 [1]	1 167 [1]	...	...	...
Más: Excedente de explotación	[2]	[2]	...	...	...
Más: Consumo de capital fijo	93	118	...	...	...
1. Igual: **Producto interno bruto al costo de factores**	866	1 285	1 265	1 631	5 246
Más: Impuestos indirectos	59	90	69 [3]	104 [3]	...
Menos: Subsidios	7	25	[4]	[4]	...
2. Igual: **Producto interno bruto a precios de mercado**	918	1 350	1 334	1 734	5 385
Menos: Remuneración neta de factores pagada al resto del mundo	89	100	...	...	...
3. Igual: **Producto nacional bruto a precios de mercado**	829	1 250	...	...	...
Menos: Consumo de capital fijo	93	118	...	...	...
4. Igual: **Ingreso nacional a precios de mercado**	736	1 132	...	...	...
Más: Otras transferencias corrientes netas procedentes del resto del mundo	-2	...	...	...	...
5. Igual: **Ingreso nacional disponible a precios de mercado**	734	...	...	...	...
Menos: Gasto total de consumo final	643	1 021	1 039	1 339	3 244
6. Igual: **Ahorro nacional**	91	106	...	...	...
Menos: Excedente de la nación por transacciones corrientes	-102	-70	...	...	...
7. Igual: **Formación neta de capital**	193	176	...	...	...
Más: Consumo de capital fijo	93	118	...	...	...
8. Igual: **Formación bruta de capital**	286	294	279	421	1 151

[1] Incluye Excedente de explotación.
[2] Se incluye en Remuneración de los asalariados.
[3] Incluye Subsidios.
[4] Se incluye en Impuestos indirectos.

214. TRINIDAD AND TOBAGO: RELATIONS AMONG MAIN NATIONAL ACCOUNTS AGGREGATES, AT CURRENT PRICES

(Millions of Trinidad and Tobago dollars)

1978	1979	1980	1981	1982	1983	
...	...	...	...	...	...	*Compensation of employees*
...	...	...	...	...	...	*Plus: Operating surplus*
...	...	...	...	...	...	*Plus: Consumption of fixed capital*
8 180	11 521	15 727	17 763	19 276	19 282	1. *Equals:* **Gross domestic product at factor cost**
...	...	...	...	...	...	*Plus: Indirect taxes*
...	...	...	...	...	...	*Less: Subsidies*
8 378	...	...	...	...	...	2. *Equals:* **Gross domestic product at market prices**
						Less: Net factor income paid to the
...	...	...	...	...	...	*rest of the world*
...	...	...	...	...	...	3. *Equals:* **Gross national product at market prices**
						Less: Consumption of fixed capital
...	...	...	...	...	...	4. *Equals:* **National income at market prices**
						Plus: Other net current transfers received
...	...	...	...	...	...	*from the rest of the world*
						5. *Equals:* **National disposable income**
...	...	...	...	...	...	**at market prices**
5 279	...	...	...	...	...	*Less: Total final consumption expenditure*
...	...	...	...	...	...	6. *Equals:* **National saving**
						Less: Surplus of the nation on current
...	...	...	...	...	...	*transactions*
...	...	...	...	...	...	7. *Equals:* **Net capital formation**
...	...	...	...	...	...	*Plus: Consumption of fixed capital*
2 713	...	...	...	...	...	8. *Equals:* **Gross capital formation**

[1] *Including Operating surplus.*
[2] *Included in Compensation of employees.*
[3] *Including Subsidies.*
[4] *Included in Indirect taxes.*

II. CUENTAS NACIONALES

215. TRINIDAD Y TABAGO: PRODUCTO INTERNO BRUTO POR CLASE DE ACTIVIDAD ECONOMICA, AL COSTO DE FACTORES

(Millones de dólares de Trinidad y Tabago)

Clase de actividad	1960	1966		1970		1975
		A precios corrientes				
1. Agricultura, caza, silvicultura y pesca	103.0	107.3	61	80	80	173
2. Explotación de minas y canteras	269.0	313.6	154	131	133	1 821
3. Industrias manufactureras	108.0	198.4	234	366	368	739
4. Electricidad, gas y agua	28.0	73.0	26	32	32	67
5. Construcción	41.0	56.2	68	95	111	387
6. Comercio al por mayor y al por menor, restaurantes y hoteles	117.0	[1]	230	283	283	615
7. Transportes, almacenamiento y comunicaciones	32.0	235.2[2]	190	240	240	419
8. Establecimientos financieros, seguros, bienes inmuebles y servicios prestados a las empresas	37.0	96.1	100	139	139	319
Viviendas	17.0	49.9	53	...	58	108
9. Servicios comunales, sociales y personales	131.0	205.1	202	265	245	706
Servicios gubernamentales	83.0	132.4	106	137	185	453
Subtotal	866.0	1 284.9	1 265	1 631	1 631	5 246
Menos: Comisión imputada de los servicios bancarios	...	...	...	...	...	...
Total: Producto interno bruto	866.0	1 284.9	1 265	1 631	1 631	5 246
		A precios constantes de 1970				
1. Agricultura, caza, silvicultura y pesca	...	70		80		80
2. Explotación de minas y canteras	...	143		133		202
3. Industrias manufactureras	...	273		368		311
4. Electricidad, gas y agua	...	26		32		44
5. Construcción	...	90		111		175
6. Comercio al por mayor y al por menor, restaurantes y hoteles	...	260		283		330
7. Transportes, almacenamiento y comunicaciones	...	229		240		283
8. Establecimientos financieros, seguros, bienes inmuebles y servicios prestados a las empresas	...	116		139		172
Viviendas	...	...		...		...
9. Servicios comunales, sociales y personales	...	202		245		295
Servicios gubernamentales	...	141		185		163
Subtotal	...	1 409		1 631		1 892
Menos: Comisión imputada de los servicios bancarios	...	...		...		...
Total: Producto interno bruto	...	1 409		1 631		1 892

[1] Se incluye en Transportes, almacenamiento y comunicaciones.
[2] Incluye Comercio al por mayor y al por menor, restaurantes y hoteles.

215. TRINIDAD AND TOBAGO: GROSS DOMESTIC PRODUCT BY KIND OF ECONOMIC ACTIVITY, AT FACTOR COST

(Millions of Trinidad and Tobago dollars)

1979	1980	1981	1982	1983	Kind of activity
At current prices					
328.6	322.9	372.9	428.7	469.2	1. *Agriculture, hunting, forestry and fishing*
3 380.8	5 917.8	5 792.9	4 751.0	3 821.8	2. *Mining and quarrying*
1 216.5	1 430.5	1 298.7	1 479.2	1 770.0	3. *Manufacturing*
159.1	157.7	131.8	208.8	217.8	4. *Electricity, gas and water*
1 562.0	1 947.8	2 541.6	3 117.2	2 898.2	5. *Construction*
1 224.7	1 571.2	1 779.9	2 179.0	2 070.3	6. *Wholesale and retail trade, restaurants and hotels*
1 255.7	1 564.7	1 752.3	2 224.7	2 376.5	7. *Transport, storage and communications*
801.6	977.9	1 140.5	1 536.2	1 796.8	8. *Finance, insurance, real estate and business services*
...	...	...	...	...	*Dwellings*
1 591.9	1 836.6	2 952.7	3 351.6	3 861.9	9. *Community, social and personal services*
1 063.6	1 172.4	2 030.3	2 269.7	2 603.8	*Government services*
11 520.	15 727.1	17 763.3	19 276.4	19 282.5	*Subtotal*
...	...	...	...	...	*Less: Imputed bank service charges*
11 520.	15 727.1	17 763.3	19 276.4	19 282.5	*Total: Gross domestic product*
At constant 1970 prices					
72.3	66.7	65.8	67.9	65.6	1. *Agriculture, hunting, forestry and fishing*
206.6	206.8	185.0	174.4	158.5	2. *Mining and quarrying*
382.1	429.9	398.9	410.1	402.1	3. *Manufacturing*
62.1	69.5	71.1	83.8	90.0	4. *Electricity, gas and water*
395.0	413.1	447.2	465.8	404.1	5. *Construction*
426.3	439.1	468.3	492.0	435.6	6. *Wholesale and retail trade, restaurants and hotels*
443.0	416.9	449.3	527.3	485.6	7. *Transport, storage and communications*
281.4	292.8	297.8	365.8	371.9	8. *Finance, insurance, real estate and business services*
...	...	...	...	...	*Dwellings*
365.6	375.9	411.6	394.4	389.0	9. *Community, social and personal services*
213.6	219.1	244.1	234.4	233.0	*Government services*
2 634.4	2 710.7	2 795.0	2 981.5	2 802.4	*Subtotal*
...	...	...	...	...	*Less: Imputed bank service charges*
2 634.4	2 710.7	2 795.0	2 981.5	2 802.4	*Total: Gross domestic product*

[1] Included in Transport, storage and communications.
[2] Including Wholesale and retail trade, restaurants and hotels.

216. URUGUAY: PRODUCTO INTERNO BRUTO POR TIPO DE GASTO, A PRECIOS DE MERCADO

(Pesos nuevos)

Tipo de gasto	1960	1965	1970	1975
	A precios corrientes			
	(miles / *thousands*)		(millones)	
1. Gasto de consumo final del gobierno general	1 228	7 653	92	1 116
2. Gasto privado de consumo final	10 727	35 596	448	6 244
3. Variación de existencias	347	-13	-	12
4. Formación bruta de capital fijo	2 045	5 653	69	1 090
Construcción [1]	1 371	3 916	40	770
Maquinaria y equipo	674	1 737	28	320
5. Exportaciones de bienes y servicios	1 952	9 963	73	1 317
6. Menos: Importaciones de bienes y servicios	2 716	6 342	81	1 613
Total: Producto interno bruto	**13 583**	**52 510**	**601**	**8 166**

	A precios constantes de:				
	1961			1978	
	(miles / *thousands*)			(millones)	
1. Gasto de consumo final del gobierno general	1 794	2 113	2 783	3 047	3 334
2. Gasto privado de consumo final	12 934	12 383	14 454	21 972	22 758
3. Variación de existencias	336	41	-12	-111	-84
4. Formación bruta de capital fijo	2 488	1 951	2 745	2 851	3 141
Construcción [1]	1 779	1 250	1 554	1 683	2 105
Maquinaria y equipo	709	701	1 191	1 168	1 036
5. Exportaciones de bienes y servicios	2 008	2 939	2 928	3 053	4 086
6. Menos: Importaciones de bienes y servicios	2 758	1 906	3 304	4 955	5 305
Total: Producto interno bruto	**16 802**	**17 521**	**19 594**	**25 857**	**27 930**

[1] Incluye plantaciones y cultivos permanentes.

216. URUGUAY: GROSS DOMESTIC PRODUCT BY TYPE OF EXPENDITURE, AT MARKET PRICES

(New pesos)

1978	1979	1980	1981	1982	1983	Type of expenditure
		At current prices				
		(millions)				
3 821	6 789	11 482	17 336	20 261	23 672	1. General government final consumption expenditure
22 919	43 441	69 890	91 147	95 655	138 735	2. Private final consumption expenditure
8	663	572	- 403	- 834	- 1 763	3. Increase in stocks
4 943	9 312	15 422	19 205	17 795	21 411	4. Gross fixed capital formation
3 215	6 143	10 551	14 037	13 552	14 856	Construction [1]
1 728	3 169	4 871	5 168	4 243	6 555	Machinery and equipment
5 530	9 400	13 861	17 987	18 072	44 308	5. Exports of goods and services
6 291	11 980	19 023	22 819	22 412	40 074	6. Less: Imports of goods and services
30 930	**57 625**	**92 204**	**122 453**	**128 537**	**186 289**	***Total: Gross domestic product***
		At constant prices of:				
		1978				
		(millions)				
3 821	4 302	4 244	4 562	4 486	4 253	1. General government final consumption expenditure
22 919	24 163	26 232	26 854	24 489	21 959	2. Private final consumption expenditure
8	250	206	- 179	- 350	- 355	3. Increase in stocks
4 943	5 882	6 255	6 067	4 878	3 551	4. Gross fixed capital formation
3 215	3 659	3 848	3 894	3 316	2 479	Construction [1]
1 728	2 223	2 407	2 173	1 562	1 072	Machinery and equipment
5 530	5 893	6 106	6 483	5 801	6 519	5. Exports of goods and services
6 291	7 652	8 235	8 318	7 276	5 395	6. Less: Imports of goods and services
30 930	**32 838**	**34 808**	**35 469**	**32 028**	**30 532**	***Total: Gross domestic product***

[1] Including plantations and permanent crops.

435

II. CUENTAS NACIONALES

217. URUGUAY: RELACIONES ENTRE PRINCIPALES AGREGADOS DE CUENTAS NACIONALES, A PRECIOS CORRIENTES

(Pesos nuevos)

	1960	1965	1970		1975
	(miles / *thousands*)			(millones)	
Remuneración de los asalariados	5 370	24 639	268 635	269	3 299
Más: Excedente de explotación	6 683	22 526	230 227	229	3 466
Más: Consumo de capital fijo	515	1 581	21 587	22	343
1. Igual: **Producto interno bruto al costo de factores**	12 568	48 746	520 449	520	7 108
Más: Impuestos indirectos	1 640	6 276	91 570	92	1 224
Menos: Subsidios	626	2 512	11 046	11	166
2. Igual: **Producto interno bruto a precios de mercado**	13 583	52 510	600 973	601	8 166
Menos: Remuneración neta de factores pagada al resto del mundo	74	580	6 202	6	168
3. Igual: **Producto nacional bruto a precios de mercado**	13 509	51 930	594 771	595	7 998
Menos: Consumo de capital fijo	515	1 581	21 587	22	343
4. Igual: **Ingreso nacional a precios de mercado**	12 994	50 349	573 184	573	7 655
Más: Otras transferencias corrientes netas procedentes del resto del mundo	-5	-60	2 775	3	35
5. Igual: **Ingreso nacional disponible a precios de mercado**	12 989	50 289	575 959	576	7 690
Menos: Gasto total de consumo final	11 955	43 249	540 454	540	7 360
6. Igual: **Ahorro nacional**	1 034	7 040	35 505	36	330
Menos: Excedente de la nación por transacciones corrientes	-843	2 981	-11 774	-11	-429
7. Igual: **Formación neta de capital**	1 877	4 059	47 279	47	759
Más: Consumo de capital fijo	515	1 581	21 587	22	343
8. Igual: **Formación bruta de capital**	2 392	5 640	68 866	69	1 102

[1] Incluye Excedente de explotación. Dato no publicado por la fuente original; obtenido por diferencia.
[2] Se incluye en Remuneración de los asalariados.

217. URUGUAY: RELATIONS AMONG MAIN NATIONAL ACCOUNTS AGGREGATES, AT CURRENT PRICES

(New pesos)

1978	1979	1980	1981	1982	1983	
			(millions)			
11 917	20 451	34 361	47 384	107 577 [1]	157 482 [1]	*Compensation of employees*
12 818	26 374	40 320	52 469	[2]	[2]	*Plus: Operating surplus*
1 557	2 933	4 858	6 050	5 605	6 744	*Plus: Consumption of fixed capital*
26 292	49 758	79 539	105 903	113 182	164 226	1. *Equals:* **Gross domestic product at factor cost**
5 357	8 864	14 552	19 239	19 057	26 753	*Plus: Indirect taxes*
719	997	1 887	2 689	3 702	4 690	*Less: Subsidies*
30 930	57 625	92 204	122 453	128 537	186 289	2. *Equals:* **Gross domestic product at market prices**
465	454	912	797	2 729	10 926	*Less: Net factor income paid to the rest of the world*
30 465	57 171	91 292	121 656	125 808	175 363	3. *Equals:* **Gross national product at market prices**
1 557	2 933	4 858	6 050	5 605	6 744	*Less: Consumption of fixed capital*
28 908	54 238	86 434	115 606	120 203	168 611	4. *Equals:* **National income at market prices**
44	56	79	105	145	380	*Plus: Other net current transfers received from the rest of the world*
28 952	54 294	86 513	115 711	120 348	168 999	5. *Equals:* **National disposable income at market prices**
26 740	50 230	81 372	108 483	115 916	162 407	*Less: Total final consumption expenditure*
2 212	4 064	5 141	7 228	4 432	6 592	6. *Equals:* **National saving**
-1 182	-2 978	-5 995	-5 524	-6 924	-6 312	*Less: Surplus of the nation on current transactions*
3 394	7 042	11 136	12 752	11 356	12 904	7. *Equals:* **Net capital formation**
1 557	2 933	4 858	6 050	5 605	6 744	*Plus: Consumption of fixed capital*
4 951	9 975	15 994	18 802	16 961	19 648	8. *Equals:* **Gross capital formation**

[1] *Includes Operating surplus. Data not published by the original source; obtained by difference.*
[2] *Included in Compensation of employees.*

218. URUGUAY: PRODUCTO INTERNO BRUTO POR CLASE DE ACTIVIDAD ECONOMICA, AL COSTO DE FACTORES

(Pesos nuevos)

Clase de actividad	1960	1965	1970	1975
	A precios corrientes			
	(miles / *thousands*)		(millones)	
1. Agricultura, caza, silvicultura y pesca	2 430	7 231	67	851
2. Explotación de minas y canteras	111	195	6	43
3. Industrias manufactureras	2 553	12 980	114	1 756
4. Electricidad, gas y agua	186	818	8	145
5. Construcción	649	1 812	20	336
6. Comercio al por mayor y al por menor, restaurantes y hoteles [1]	2 157	6 403	68	1 098
7. Transportes, almacenamiento y comunicaciones	943	3 746	45	542
8. Establecimientos financieros, seguros, bienes inmuebles y servicios prestados a las empresas [2]	1 310	4 097	49	648
Viviendas	771	1 749	28	320
9. Servicios comunales, sociales y personales [3]	2 229	11 464	143	1 689
Servicios gubernamentales	1 027	6 170	77	881
Subtotal	12 568	48 746	520	7 108
Menos: Comisión imputada de los servicios bancarios	...	...	...	...
Total: Producto interno bruto	12 568	48 746	520	7 108

Clase de actividad	A precios constantes de:				
	1961			1978	
	(miles / *thousands*)			(millones)	
1. Agricultura, caza, silvicultura y pesca	2 142	2 501	2 872	3 197	3 001
2. Explotación de minas y canteras	143	67	121	151	207
3. Industrias manufactureras	3 321	3 510	3 909	5 058	5 565
4. Electricidad, gas y agua	248	309	394	281	314
5. Construcción	920	613	755	686	876
6. Comercio al por mayor y al por menor, restaurantes y hoteles [1]	2 278	2 298	2 593	3 461	3 644
7. Transportes, almacenamiento y comunicaciones	1 331	1 378	1 385	1 485	1 563
8. Establecimientos financieros, seguros, bienes inmuebles y servicios prestados a las empresas	6	6	6	6	6
Viviendas	847	920	1 009	1 742	1 746
9. Servicios comunales, sociales y personales [7]	3 775	4 048	4 460	5 907	6 830
Servicios gubernamentales	1 543	1 682	2 079	2 333	2 524
Subtotal	15 005	15 644	17 498	21 968	23 746
Menos: Comisión imputada de los servicios bancarios	...	...	...	...	...
Total: Producto interno bruto	15 005	15 644	17 498	21 968	23 746

[1] Restaurantes y hoteles se incluyen en Servicios comunales, sociales y personales
[2] Servicios prestados a las empresas se incluyen en Servicios comunales, sociales y personales.
[3] Incluye Restaurantes y hoteles y Servicios prestados a las empresas.
[4] Se incluye en Industrias manufactureras.
[5] Incluye Explotación de minas y canteras.
[6] Con excepción de Viviendas, esta actividad se incluye en Servicios comunales, sociales y personales.
[7] Incluye Restaurantes y hoteles y Establecimientos financieros, seguros, bienes inmuebles y servicios prestados a las empresas, con excepción de Viviendas.

218. URUGUAY: GROSS DOMESTIC PRODUCT BY KIND OF ECONOMIC ACTIVITY, AT FACTOR COST

(New pesos)

1978	1979	1980	1981	1982	1983	Kind of activity
		At current prices (millions)				
2 946	6 020	8 860	9 987	9 841	19 051	1. *Agriculture, hunting, forestry and fishing*
255	565	1 191	1 613	1 413	2 080	2. *Mining and quarrying*
6 364	13 603	20 603	24 152	22 845	35 837	3. *Manufacturing*
366	562	1 185	1 774	2 170	3 780	4. *Electricity, gas and water*
1 326	2 544	4 182	5 965	5 815	6 278	5. *Construction*
4 359	8 503	12 273	15 436	13 860	21 944	6. *Wholesale and retail trade, restaurants and hotels* [1]
1 709	2 993	5 083	4 982	7 556	11 158	7. *Transport, storage and communications*
3 152	5 304	9 381	15 045	20 546	28 237	8. *Finance, insurance, real estate and business services* [2]
1 789	2 833	5 360	9 456	13 350	16 576	*Dwellings*
5 815	9 764	16 781	24 949	29 136	35 861	9. *Community, social and personal services* [3]
2 914	4 856	8 490	12 958	15 599	18 235	*Government services*
26 292	49 758	79 539	105 903	113 182	164 226	*Subtotal*
...	...	...	...	...	...	*Less: Imputed bank service charges*
26 292	49 758	79 539	105 903	113 182	164 226	*Total: Gross domestic product*
		At constant prices of: 1978 (millions)				
2 946	2 933	3 408	3 596	3 185	3 269	1. *Agriculture, hunting, forestry and fishing*
4	4	4	4	4	4	2. *Mining and quarrying*
6 363 [5]	6 815 [5]	6 980 [5]	6 662 [5]	5 536 [5]	5 148 [5]	3. *Manufacturing*
366	379	408	430	435	446	4. *Electricity, gas and water*
1 326	1 490	1 546	1 593	1 377	1 012	5. *Construction*
4 359	4 677	5 183	5 327	4 182	3 689	6. *Wholesale and retail trade, restaurants and hotels* [1]
1 709	1 885	2 041	2 025	1 811	1 724	7. *Transport, storage and communications*
6	6	6	6	6	6	8. *Finance, insurance, real estate and business services*
1 789	1798	1 830	1 848	1 861	1 874	*Dwellings*
7 434	7 937	8 204	8 692	8 838	8 792	9. *Community, social and personal services* [7]
2 914	3 143	3 147	...	...	...	*Government services*
26 292	27 914	29 600	30 173	27 225	25 954	*Subtotal*
...	...	...	...	...	...	*Less: Imputed bank service charges*
26 292	27 914	29 600	30 173	27 225	25 954	*Total: Gross domestic product*

[1] *Restaurants and hotels are included in Community, social and personal services.*
[2] *Business services are includes in Community, social and personal services.*
[3] *Including Restaurants and hotels and Business services.*
[4] *Included in Manufacturing.*
[5] *Including Mining and quarrying.*
[6] *With the exception of Dwellings, this item is included in Community, social and personal services.*
[7] *Including Restaurants and hotels and Finance, insurance, real estate and business services, with the exception of Dwellings.*

219. URUGUAY: INGRESOS Y GASTOS DE LOS HOGARES, INCLUIDAS LAS EMPRESAS NO FINANCIERAS NO CONSTITUIDAS EN SOCIEDAD [1]

(Pesos nuevos)

	1960	1965	1970	1975
	(miles / *thousands*)		(millones)	
1. Remuneración de los asalariados	5 370	24 639	268 635	487 [2]	6 568 [2]
2. Renta neta de la propiedad y de la empresa	6 306	21 709	219 109	[3]	[3]
3. Prestaciones de seguridad social	...	...	...	...	...
4. Donaciones de asistencia social	...	...	...	...	...
5. Transferencias corrientes n.e.p. de residentes	1 179	4 924	59 566	60	692
6. Transferencias corrientes n.e.p. del resto del mundo	...	...	...	...	13
Total: Ingresos corrientes	12 855	51 272	547 310	547	7 273
7. Gasto de consumo final	10 727	35 596	448 337	448	6 244
8. Impuestos directos	342	685	10 755	11	169
9. Contribuciones a la seguridad social	1 186	5 921	59 631	59	618
10. Transferencias corrientes n.e.p. a residentes	...	...	...	...	...
11. Transferencias corrientes n.e.p. al resto del mundo	...	...	-225	...	...
12. Ahorro	600	9 070	28 812	29	242
Total: Egresos corrientes	12 855	51 272	547 310	547	7 273

[1] Comprende las Instituciones privadas sin fines de lucro que sirven a los hogares.
[2] Incluye Renta neta de la propiedad y la empresa.
[3] Se incluye en Remuneración de los asalariados.

220. URUGUAY: INGRESOS Y GASTOS DEL GOBIERNO GENERAL

(Pesos nuevos)

	1960	1965	1970	1975
	(miles / *thousands*)		(millones)	
1. Renta de la propiedad y de la empresa	15	95	1 808	2	5
2. Impuestos indirectos	1 640	6 276	91 570	92	1 224
3. Impuestos directos	446	1 013	16 071	16	221
4. Contribuciones a la seguridad social	1 186	5 921	59 631	59	618
5. Transferencias corrientes n.e.p. de residentes	...	...	...	...	...
6. Transferencias corrientes n.e.p. del resto del mundo	...	...	2 550	3	22
Total: Ingresos corrientes	3 287	13 305	171 630	172	2 090
7. Gasto de consumo final	1 228	7 653	92 117	92	1 116
8. Renta de la propiedad	68	186	2 208	2	28
9. Subsidios	626	2 512	11 046	11	166
10. Prestaciones de seguridad social	...	...	...	...	...
11. Transferencias corrientes n.e.p. a residentes	1 179	4 924	59 566	60	692
12. Transferencias corrientes n.e.p. al resto del mundo	5	60	...	...	...
13. Ahorro	181	-2 030	6 693	7	88
Total: Egresos corrientes	3 287	13 305	171 630	172	2 090

219. URUGUAY: INCOME AND OUTLAY OF HOUSEHOLDS, INCLUDING PRIVATE UNINCORPORATED NON-FINANCIAL ENTERPRISES [1]

(New pesos)

1977	1978	1979	1980	1981	1982	
(millions)						
15 559[2]	23 766[2]	45 278[2]	71 727	96 738	103 723[2]	1. *Compensation of employees*
[3]	[3]	[3]	[3]	[3]	[3]	2. *Net property and entrepreneurial income*
...	...	...	...	...	...	3. *Social security benefits*
...	...	...	...	...	...	4. *Social assistance grants*
1 550	2 482	3 834	6 783	12 501	15 776	5. *Current transfers n.e.c. from residents*
9	9	12	18	23	31	6. *Current transfers n.e.c. from the rest of the world*
17 118	26 257	49 124	78 528	109 262	119 530	**Total:** *Current receipts*
15 018	22 919	43 441	69 890	91 147	95 655	7. *Final consumption expenditure*
413	420	542	1 533	1 324	1 568	8. *Direct taxes*
1 461	2 465	3 988	5 887	7 439	8 889	9. *Social security contributions*
...	...	...	...	...	...	10. *Current transfers n.e.c. to residents*
...	...	...	...	...	...	11. *Current transfers n.e.c. to rest of the world*
226	453	1 153	1 218	9 352	13 418	12. *Saving*
17 118	26 257	49 124	78 528	109 262	119 530	**Total:** *Current disbursements*

[1] *Including Private non-profit institutions serving households.*
[2] *Including Net property and entrepreneurial income.*
[3] *Included in Compensation of employees.*

220. URUGUAY: INCOME AND OUTLAY OF THE GENERAL GOVERNMENT

(New pesos)

1976	1977	1978	1979	1980	1981	
(millions)						
6	17	54	203	185	239	1. *Property and entrepreneurial income*
2 113	3 258	5 357	8 864	14 552	20 848	2. *Indirect taxes*
453	739	956	1 528	3 680	4 946	3. *Direct taxes*
973	1 461	2 465	3 988	5 887	6 384	4. *Social security contributions*
...	...	...	...	...	...	5. *Current transfers n.e.c. from residents*
32	22	35	44	61	82	6. *Current transfers n.e.c. from the rest of the world*
3 577	5 497	8 867	14 627	24 365	32 499	**Total:** *Current receipts*
1 755	2 451	3 821	6 789	11 482	16 809	7. *Final consumption expenditure*
75	28	86	97	290	440	8. *Property income*
349	488	719	996	1 887	763	9. *Subsidies*
...	...	...	...	...	...	10. *Social security benefits*
1 012	1 550	2 482	3 834	6 783	10 854	11. *Current transfers n.e.c. to residents*
...	...	...	...	...	...	12. *Current transfers n.e.c. to rest of the world*
386	980	1 759	2 911	3 923	3 633	13. *Saving*
3 577	5 497	8 867	14 627	24 365	32 499	**Total:** *Current disbursements*

221. VENEZUELA: PRODUCTO INTERNO BRUTO POR TIPO DE GASTO, A PRECIOS DE MERCADO

(Millones de bolívares)

Tipo de gasto	1960	1965	1968	1968	1970
			A precios corrientes		
1. Gasto de consumo final del gobierno general	3 684	4 682	5 926	5 557	6 635
2. Gasto privado de consumo final	14 352	21 689	25 795	22 893	27 267
3. Variación de existencias	-287 [1]	928 [1]	1 232 [1]	3 719	4 206
4. Formación bruta de capital fijo	4 797	6 974	9 382	10 355	11 537
Construcción	...	...	...	6 293	6 678
Maquinaria y equipo	...	...	...	4 062 [2]	4 859 [2]
5. Exportaciones de bienes y servicios	8 265	11 648	12 134	11 559	12 226
6. Menos: Importaciones de bienes y servicios	5 140	7 996	9 621	8 928	9 846
Total: Producto interno bruto	25 671	37 925	44 848	45 155	52 025
			A precios constantes de:		
		1957		1968	
1. Gasto de consumo final del gobierno general	3 095	3 846	4 737	...	...
2. Gasto privado de consumo final	13 904	17 657	20 112	...	...
3. Variación de existencias	-273 [1]	746 [1]	951 [1]	...	...
4. Formación bruta de capital fijo	4 725	5 558	6 707	10 355	10 949
Construcción	3 067	3 616	4 644	6 293	6 476
Maquinaria y equipo	1 658	1 942	2 063	4 062 [2]	4 473 [2]
5. Exportaciones de bienes y servicios	9 945	15 828	16 808	...	...
6. Menos: Importaciones de bienes y servicios	4 280	5 030	6 047	...	...
Total: Producto interno bruto	27 116	38 605	43 268	45 155	50 634

[1] Variación de existencias del ganado está incluida en Formación bruta de capital fijo.
[2] Incluye importación no controlada de equipo de transporte y ganadería.

221. VENEZUELA: GROSS DOMESTIC PRODUCT BY TYPE OF EXPENDITURE, AT MARKET PRICES

(Millions of bolívares)

1975	1979	1980	1981	1982	1983	Type of expenditure
			At current prices			
15 943	27 758	35 123	42 643	42 594	41 221	1. General government final consumption expenditure
56 286	110 329	135 375	160 533	182 239	188 562	2. Private final consumption expenditure
5 846	98	-1 354	-4 374	5 167	-10 770	3. Increase in stocks
30 598	65 553	64 145	69 783	70 163	53 735	4. Gross fixed capital formation
16 590	39 401	38 227	40 431	40 514	36 640	Construction
14 008 [2]	26 152 [2]	25 918 [2]	29 352 [2]	29 649 [2]	17 095	Machinery and equipment
39 278	64 024	85 463	89 614	75 197	74 517	5. Exports of goods and services
29 853	60 025	64 551	72 991	84 092	62 002	6. Less: Imports of goods and services
118 098	**207 737**	**254 201**	**285 208**	**291 268**	**285 263**	**Total:** Gross domestic product
		At constant prices of:				
		1968				
...	...	...	...	...	...	1. General government final consumption expenditure
...	...	...	...	...	...	2. Private final consumption expenditure
...	...	...	...	...	...	3. Increase in stocks
18 929	26 074	22 290	22 959	22 102	...	4. Gross fixed capital formation
9 778	14 696	12 129	11 688	10 716	...	Construction
9 151 [2]	11 378 [2]	10 161 [2]	11 271 [2]	11 386 [2]	...	Machinery and equipment
...	...	...	...	...	...	5. Exports of goods and services
...	...	...	...	...	...	6. Less: Imports of goods and services
64 417	**77 396**	**75 857**	**75 628**	**76 144**	**72 494**	**Total:** Gross domestic product

[1] *Increase in stocks of livestock is included in Gross fixed capital formation.*
[2] *Including non-registered imports, of transport equipment and cattle.*

II. CUENTAS NACIONALES

222. VENEZUELA: RELACIONES ENTRE PRINCIPALES AGREGADOS DE CUENTAS NACIONALES, A PRECIOS CORRIENTES

(Millones de bolívares)

	1960	1965	1968		1970	1975
Remuneración de los asalariados	11 645	16 284	20 099	17 712	21 098	45 807
Más: Excedente de explotación	9 824	16 675	18 386	20 962	23 267	60 196
Más: Consumo de capital fijo	2 422	3 211	4 229	4 075	4 824	7 523
1. Igual: **Producto interno bruto al costo de factores**	23 891	36 170	42 714	42 749	49 189	113 526
Más: Impuestos indirectos	1 831	1 915	2 237	2 522	2 947	5 599
Menos: Subsidios	51	160	103	116	111	1 027
2. Igual: **Producto interno bruto a precios de mercado**	25 671	37 925	44 848	45 155	52 025	118 098
Menos: Remuneración neta de factores pagada al resto del mundo	2 097	3 492	3 532	3 226	2 530	-344
3. Igual: **Producto nacional bruto a precios de mercado**	23 574	34 433	41 316	41 929	49 495	118 442
Menos: Consumo de capital fijo	2 422	3 211	4 229	4 075	4 824	7 523
4. Igual: **Ingreso nacional a precios de mercado**	...	...	...	37 854	44 671	110 919
Más: Otras transferencias corrientes netas procedentes del resto del mundo	...	...	...	-256	-308	-651
5. Igual: **Ingreso nacional disponible a precios de mercado**	21 152	31 222	37 087	37 598	44 363	110 268
Menos: Gasto total de consumo final	18 036	26 371	31 721	28 450	33 902	72 229
6. Igual: **Ahorro nacional**	3 116[1]	4 851[1]	5 366[1]	9 148	10 461	38 039
Menos: Excedente de la nación por transacciones corrientes	1 028[1]	160[1]	-1 019[1]	-851	-458	9 118
7. Igual: **Formación neta de capital**	2 088	4 691	6 385	9 999	10 919	28 921
Más: Consumo de capital fijo	2 422	3 211	4 229	4 075	4 824	7 523
8. Igual: **Formación bruta de capital**	4 510	7 902	10 614	14 074	15 743	36 444

[1] No incluye Otras transferencias corrientes netas procedentes del resto del mundo.

222. VENEZUELA: RELATIONS AMONG MAIN NATIONAL ACCOUNTS AGGREGATES, AT CURRENT PRICES

(Millions of bolívares)

1979	1980	1981	1982	1983	
86 602	105 143	119 642	124 529	124 785	*Compensation of employees*
99 574	123 958	137 281	135 297	117 091	*Plus: Operating surplus*
14 912	17 104	19 869	21 666	23 855	*Plus: Consumption of fixed capital*
201 088	246 205	276 792	281 492	265 731	1. *Equals:* **Gross domestic product** *at factor cost*
8 997	11 378	12 013	12 910	21 839	*Plus: Indirect taxes*
2 348	3 382	3 597	3 134	2 307	*Less: Subsidies*
207 737	254 201	285 208	291 268	285 263	2. *Equals:* **Gross domestic product** *at market prices*
759	-1 203	-2 247	6 553	9 736	*Less: Net factor income paid to the rest of the world*
206 978	255 404	287 455	284 715	275 527	3. *Equals:* **Gross national product** *at market prices*
14 912	17 104	19 869	21 666	23 855	*Less: Consumption of fixed capital*
192 066	238 300	267 586	263 049	251 672	4. *Equals:* **National income at market prices**
-1 742	-1 879	-1 750	-2 738	-1 752	*Plus: Other net current transfers received from the rest of the world*
190 324	236 421	265 836	260 311	249 920	5. *Equals:* **National disposable income** *at market prices*
138 087	170 498	203 176	224 833	229 783	*Less: Total final consumption expenditure*
52 237	65 923	62 660	35 478	20 137	6. *Equals:* **National saving**
1 498	20 236	17 120	-18 186	1 027	*Less: Surplus of the nation on current transactions*
50 739	45 687	45 540	53 664	19 110	7. *Equals:* **Net capital formation**
14 912	17 104	19 869	21 666	23 855	*Plus: Consumption of fixed capital*
65 651	62 791	65 409	75 330	42 965	8. *Equals:* **Gross capital formation**

[1] *Does not include Other net current transfers from the rest of the world.*

223. VENEZUELA: PRODUCTO INTERNO BRUTO POR CLASE DE ACTIVIDAD ECONOMICA, A PRECIOS DE MERCADO

(Millones de bolívares)

Clase de actividad	1960	1965	1968	1970	1975
			A precios corrientes		
1. Agricultura, caza, silvicultura y pesca	1 650	2 648	3 311	3 127	3 714	6 974
2. Explotación de minas y canteras	6 955	10 392	10 640	9 333	9 293	30 486
3. Industrias manufactureras	4 202[1]	24 885[2]	9 320[1]	7 330	8 319	18 851
4. Electricidad, gas y agua	[3]	[3]	[3]	693	845	1 407
5. Construcción	[3]	[3]	[3]	1 822	2 084	6 201
6. Comercio al por mayor y al por menor, restaurantes y hoteles	12 864[4]	[3]	21 577[4]	4 782	5 625	11 205
7. Transportes, almacenamiento y comunicaciones	[5]	[3]	[5]	4 215	5 458	11 063
8. Establecimientos financieros, seguros, bienes inmuebles y servicios prestados a las empresas	[5]	[3]	[5]	6 226	7 536	15 014
Viviendas	...	...	...	5 294[6]	6 415[6]	9 132[6]
9. Servicios comunales, sociales y personales	[5]	[3]	[5]	7 200	8 625	18 933
Servicios gubernamentales	...	...	...	4 817	5 771	12 914
Subtotal	25 671	37 925	44 848	44 728	51 499	120 134
Menos: Comisión imputada de los servicios bancarios	...	...	...	866	1 065	5 098
Más: Derechos de importación	...	...	...	1 293	1 591	3 062
Total: Producto interno bruto	25 671	37 925	44 848	45 155	52 025	118 098
			A precios constantes de:		
		1957			1968	
1. Agricultura, caza, silvicultura y pesca	1 987	2 546	2 938	3 127	3 544	4 236
2. Explotación de minas y canteras	8 205	9 874	10 205	9 333	9 780	6 594
3. Industrias manufactureras	2 930	4 515	5 121	7 330	8 264	10 634
4. Electricidad, gas y agua	371	738	1 041	693	859	1 483
5. Construcción	1 647	1 545	2 040	1 822	2 015	3 661
6. Comercio al por mayor y al por menor, restaurantes y hoteles	3 976[7]	5 455[7]	6 344[7]	4 782	5 416	7 364
7. Transportes, almacenamiento y comunicaciones	1 011	1 267	1 460	4 215	5 223	7 664
8. Establecimientos financieros, seguros, bienes inmuebles y servicios prestados a las empresas	[8]	[8]	[8]	6 226	7 226	11 739
Viviendas	1 851	2 383	2 833	5 294[6]	6 127[6]	7 849[6]
9. Servicios comunales, sociales y personales	5 138[9]	10 282[9]	11 286[9]	7 200	7 835	12 428
Servicios gubernamentales	1 256	1 406	1 692	4 817	5 082	7 850
Subtotal	27 116	38 605	43 268	44 728	50 162	65 803
Menos: Comisión imputada de los servicios bancarios	...	...	...	866	1 040	3 287
Más: Derechos de importación	...	...	...	1 293	1 512	1 901
Total: Producto interno bruto	27 116	38 605	43 268	45 155	50 634	64 417

[1] Incluye Electricidad, gas y agua y Construcción.
[2] Incluye Electricidad, gas y agua, Construcción, Comercio al por mayor, al por menor, restaurantes y hoteles, Transporte, almacenamiento y comunicaciones, Establecimientos financieros, seguros, bienes inmuebles y servicios prestados a las empresas, y Servicios comunales, sociales y personales.
[3] Se incluye en Industrias manufactureras.
[4] Incluye Transportes, almacenamiento y comunicaciones, Establecimientos financieros, seguros, bienes inmuebles y servicios prestados a las empresas, y Servicios comunales, sociales y personales.
[5] Se incluye en Comercio al por mayor y al por menor, restaurantes y hoteles.
[6] Se refiere a Bienes inmuebles y Servicios prestados a las empresas.
[7] Comprende Establecimientos financieros, seguros, bienes inmuebles y servicios prestados a las empresas, con excepción de Viviendas. No incluye Restaurantes y hoteles, que se incluyen en Servicios comunales, sociales y personales.
[8] Con excepción de Viviendas, Establecimientos financieros, seguros, bienes inmuebles y servicios prestados a las empresas se incluyen en Comercio al por mayor y al por menor, restaurantes y hoteles.
[9] Incluye Restaurantes y hoteles.

223. VENEZUELA: GROSS DOMESTIC PRODUCT BY KIND OF ECONOMIC ACTIVITY, AT MARKET PRICES

(Millions of bolívares)

1979	1980	1981	1982	1983	Kind of activity
		At current prices			
11 940	14 436	16 413	17 676	19 536	1. *Agriculture, hunting, forestry and fishing*
45 507	62 188	66 944	54 389	46 586	2. *Mining and quarrying*
34 743	41 197	43 089	46 784	49 261	3. *Manufacturing*
2 499	2 579	3 977	4 900	5 575	4. *Electricity, gas and water*
14 753	14 479	15 683	15 657	14 269	5. *Construction*
19 192	20 834	23 245	25 704	27 100	6. *Wholesale and retail trade, restaurants and hotels*
23 452	25 184	30 769	35 631	31 954	7. *Transport, storage and communications*
27 386	37 883	46 277	49 953	53 850	8. *Finance, insurance, real estate and business services*
16 132[6]	23 757[6]	28 903[6]	33 079[6]	34 560[6]	*Dwellings*
33 889	42 156	48 850	49 575	49 819	9. *Community, social and personal services*
23 621	30 078	34 903	35 222	34 508	*Government services*
213 361	260 936	295 247	300 269	297 950	*Subtotal*
10 693	13 104	16 378	15 879	16 664	*Less: Imputed bank service charges*
5 069	6 369	6 339	6 878	3 977	*Plus: Import duties*
207 737	254 201	285 208	291 268	285 263	*Total: Gross domestic product*
		At constant prices of: 1968			
4 677	4 765	4 676	4 843	4 863	1. *Agriculture, hunting, forestry and fishing*
6 526	6 103	5 948	5 340	4 923	2. *Mining and quarrying*
13 324	13 660	13 322	13 863	13 731	3. *Manufacturing*
1 933	1 950	2 256	2 533	2 730	4. *Electricity, gas and water*
5 519	4 609	4 511	4 131	3 572	5. *Construction*
8 211	6 907	6 724	6 897	6 830	6. *Wholesale and retail trade, restaurants and hotels*
9 851	9 805	10 155	10 508	8 848	7. *Transport, storage and communications*
14 504	14 023	15 133	14 645	14 975	8. *Finance, insurance, real estate and business services*
8 957[6]	8 721[6]	8 981[6]	9 312[6]	9 525[6]	*Dwellings*
15 656	16 205	16 281	15 948	15 522	9. *Community, social and personal services*
10 073	10 498	10 586	10 593	10 400	*Government services*
80 201	78 027	79 006	78 708	75 994	*Subtotal*
5 203	4 777	5 697	4 910	4 779	*Less: Imputed bank service charges*
2 398	2 607	2 319	2 346	1 279	*Plus: Import duties*
77 396	75 857	75 628	76 144	72 494	*Total: Gross domestic product*

[1] *Including Electricity, gas and water and Construction.*

[2] *Including Electricity, gas and water, Construction, Wholesale and retail trade, restaurants and hotels, Transport, storage and communications, Finance, insurance, real estate and business services and Community, social and personal services.*

[3] *Included in Manufacturing.*

[4] *Including Transport, storage and communications, Finance, insurance, real estate and business services, and Community, social and personal services.*

[5] *Included in Wholesale and retail trade, restaurants and hotels.*

[6] *Refers to Real estate and Business services.*

[7] *Including Finance, insurance, real estate and business services, with the exception of Dwellings. Does not include Restaurants and hotels, which are included in Community, social and personal services.*

[8] *Finance, insurance, real estate and business services with the exception of Dwellings, are included in Wholesale and retail trade, restaurants and hotels.*

[9] *Including Restaurants and hotels.*

II. CUENTAS NACIONALES

224. VENEZUELA: INGRESOS Y GASTOS DEL GOBIERNO GENERAL

(Millones de bolívares)

	1960	1965	1968	1969	1970
1. Renta de la propiedad y de la empresa	1 350	2 209	2 683	2 538	...
2. Impuestos indirectos	1 831	1 915	2 237	2 353	...
3. Impuestos directos	2 077	3 870	4 601	4 951	...
4. Contribuciones a la seguridad social	...	...	...	...	...
5. Transferencias corrientes n.e.p. de residentes	...	...	...	...	...
6. Transferencias corrientes n.e.p. del resto del mundo	...	...	...	...	...
Total: Ingresos corrientes	5 258	7 994	9 521	9 842	...
7. Gasto de consumo final	3 684	4 682	5 926	6 274	...
8. Renta de la propiedad	...	...	...	...	...
9. Subsidios	51	160	103	127	...
10. Prestaciones de seguridad social	...	...	...	...	...
11. Transferencias corrientes n.e.p. a residentes	381	445	620	696	...
12. Transferencias corrientes n.e.p. al resto del mundo	...	...	...	...	...
13. Ahorro	1 142	2 707	2 872	2 745	...
Total: Egresos corrientes	5 258	7 994	9 521	9 842	...

Nota: La cuenta ingresos y gastos del gobierno general se interrumpió a partir del año 1970 por insuficiencia de información, lo que pudo resolverse a partir del año 1978.

224. VENEZUELA: INCOME AND OUTLAY OF THE GENERAL GOVERNMENT

(Millions of bolívares)

1975	1978	1979	1980	1981	1982	
...	12 428	12 035	14 430	18 381	21 588	1. *Property and entrepreneurial income*
...	6 648	8 997	11 378	12 013	12 910	2. *Indirect taxes*
...	23 440	37 378	54 910	61 996	48 491	3. *Direct taxes*
...	2 718	3 062	4 258	5 397	4 734	4. *Social security contributions*
...	12 546	15 722	15 508	19 791	19 937	5. *Current transfers n.e.c. from residents*
...	-	-	-	-	-	6. *Current transfers n.e.c. from the rest of the world*
...	57 780	77 194	100 484	116 578	107 660	*Total: Current receipts*
...	24 056	27 758	35 123	42 643	42 594	7. *Final consumption expenditure*
...	2 515	2 915	5 585	5 992	6 399	8. *Property income*
...	2 104	2 348	3 382	3 597	3 134	9. *Subsidies*
...	780	905	1 298	1 584	1 783	10. *Social security benefits*
...	11 131	13 002	15 613	18 969	21 839	11. *Current transfers n.e.c. to residents*
...	108	92	135	167	138	12. *Current transfers n.e.c. to rest of the world*
...	17 086	30 174	39 348	43 626	31 773	13. *Saving*
...	57 780	77 194	100 484	116 578	107 660	*Total: Current disbursements*

Note: The General government income and expenditure account had not been calculated since 1970 because of lack of information; its calculation was resumed in 1978.

III. PRECIOS INTERNOS

225. INDICES ANUALES DE PRECIOS IMPLICITOS EN EL PRODUCTO INTERNO BRUTO

(Año base 1970 = 100)

País	Año base [1] *Base year* [1]	1960	1965	1975	1977	1978
Argentina	1970	16.7	49.0	1 412.9	19 521.5	50 521.7
Bolivia	1970	54.0	81.0	299.7	359.3	407.6
Brasil	1970	3.1	32.7	314.9	668.5	963.5
Colombia	1975	34.1	61.6	231.6	375.3	439.4
Costa Rica	1966	78.9	84.4	192.1	262.0	282.7
Chile	1977	6.6	23.5	40 299.5	287 687.0	450 301.0
Ecuador	1975	61.3	73.5	179.7	238.4	257.2
El Salvador	1962	95.6	96.4	133.5	193.8	195.4
Guatemala	1958	93.7	92.5	146.0	189.4	199.8
Guyana	1970	...	...	183.1	...	...
Haití	1976	72.02	90.2	170.7	226.0	222.7
Honduras	1966	77.9	89.4	138.2	170.0	181.8
Jamaica	1974	...	...	204.5	254.2	320.5
México	1970	70.8	84.7	180.4	281.2	328.3
Nicaragua	1980	85.1	88.8	155.9	184.0	193.2
Panamá	1970	85.5	91.4	143.2	156.6	169.0
Paraguay	1982	75.6	93.6	180.2	209.7	230.4
Perú	1973	40.5	59.1	187.7	335.3	543.1
República Dominicana	1970	79.7	92.8	157.2	178.9	180.7
Santa Lucía	1977	...	...	...	100.0	108.8
San Vicente y las Granadinas	1976	...	...	90.9	109.1	126.1
Suriname	1973	...	...	...	...	...
Trinidad y Tabago	1970	61.5	80.3	277.3	339.8	349.9
Uruguay	1978	2.8	10.3	1 260.3	2 921.1	4 310.3
Venezuela	1968	87.5	90.8	177.8	202.0	214.7

[1] Corresponde al año base más reciente del cálculo a precios constantes de las cuentas nacionales. Para Santa Lucía, San Vicente y las Granadinas y Suriname se incluyen los índices en la base original que se indica.

450

225. IMPLICIT ANNUAL PRICE INDEX OF GROSS DOMESTIC PRODUCT

(Base year 1970 = 100)

1979	1980	1981	1982	1983	Country
128 927.4	254 315.5	525 265.4	1 478 726.8	...	Argentina
481.8	669.5	855.5	2 294.2	9 494.7	Bolivia
1 518.7	2 954.7	5 844.2	11 479.5	28 240.6	Brazil
545.1	695.4	853.7	1 063.8	1 283.1	Colombia
308.5	366.6	517.4	952.8	1 206.3	Costa Rica
658 715.8	851 014.3	954 798.6	1 081 681.3	1 369 504.5	Chile
298.7	357.0	408.2	479.7	673.5	Ecuador
222.5	252.4	266.8	293.1	316.7	El Salvador
217.0	238.8	259.1	272.1	289.7	Guatemala
...	...	...	...	...	Guyana
229.1	278.8	296.0	305.7	330.5	Haiti
195.4	216.2	227.4	244.1	258.9	Honduras
372.4	437.4	474.6	519.2	593.8	Jamaica
394.7	508.0	646.4	1 041.9	2 002.1	Mexico
267.1	366.3	409.5	477.5	547.3	Nicaragua
184.7	203.8	213.2	223.0	227.3	Panama
275.2	322.7	375.3	394.2	451.1	Paraguay
962.2	1 526.5	2 492.2	4 006.0	8 426.1	Peru
200.8	228.3	238.8	257.8	...	Dominican Republic
130.8	142.8	154.7	164.5	...	Saint Lucia
135.6	...	...	...	...	Saint Vincent and the Grenadines
178.8	197.7	219.3	238.0	245.5	Suriname
437.3	580.3	635.5	646.5	688.1	Trinidad and Tobago
7 563.8	11 417.3	14 880.9	17 298.4	26 298.9	Uruguay
260.4	325.1	365.8	371.0	381.7	Venezuela

[1] Most recent base year used for national accounts calculations at constant prices. For St. Lucia, St. Vincent and the Grenadines and Suriname indexes using the original base year indicated are given.

III. PRECIOS INTERNOS

226. INDICES ANUALES DEL NIVEL GENERAL DE PRECIOS MAYORISTAS

(Año base 1970 = 100)

País	1960	1965	1975	1977	1978
Argentina	17.6	50.0	1 300.7	19.436.0	47 810.1
Brasil	3.0	44.1	273.8	559.0	769.1
Colombia	37.1	65.4	287.8	559.0	527.1
Costa Rica	78.3	82.7	221.7	260.5	280.7
Chile	9.0	28.1	80 546.8	481 241.4	687 931.9
El Salvador	89.3	92.1	154.6	306.6	245.7
Guatemala [1]	89.6	90.8	159.7	199.4	206.6
México [2]	79.0	86.7	166.7	289.0	333.3
Panamá	...	...	187.8	217.0	228.7
Perú	...	...	144.7	293.6	516.6
República Dominicana	82.8	99.7	176.0	187.3	185.2
Uruguay [3]	3.4	10.9	1 513.6	3 426.5	5 090.9
Venezuela	78.2	92.8	151.6	179.3	192.5

[1] Se refiere a la ciudad de Guatemala.
[2] Se refiere a la ciudad de México.
[3] Se refiere a Montevideo.

226. GENERAL ANNUAL WHOLESALE PRICE INDEXES

(Base year 1970 = 100)

1979	1980	1981	1982	1983	Country
119 189.1	209 090.3	438 217.6	1 561 073.1	7 195 435.4	Argentina
1 199.0	2 476.2	5 153.7	9 897.7	26 550.6	Brazil
673.9	836.8	1 038.2	1 304.8	1 588.3	Colombia
329.7	408.4	673.9	1 405.7	1 773.9	Costa Rica
1 027 839.4	1 434 395.1	1 564 767.6	1 677 253.0	2 440 699.9	Chile
278.5	285.9	302.5	326.6	348.2	El Salvador
227.9	264.3	295.3	278.2	281.5	Guatemala [1]
394.3	490.7	611.0	953.7	1 977.3	Mexico [2]
260.7	300.7	330.9	358.2	366.7	Panama
880.3	1 347.6	2 265.4	3 541.0	7 546.6	Peru
211.3	240.4	243.3	259.8	270.7	Dominican Republic
9 184.7	13 020.2	16 071.5	18 145.9	31 479.6	Uruguay [3]
210.3	258.5	287.4	310.5	331.8	Venezuela

[1] Index for Guatemala City.
[2] Index for México City.
[3] Index for Montevideo.

227. INDICES ANUALES DE PRECIOS AL CONSUMIDOR

a) Nivel General
(Año base 1970 = 100)

País	Cobertura geográfica	1960	1965	1975	1977	1978
Argentina	Capital Federal	14.5	41.3	1 187.7	17 286.0	47 641.7
Barbados	...	75.1	81.9	234.7	266.9	292.3
Bolivia	La Paz	58.6	75.1	255.3	288.4	318.3
Brasil	São Paulo	2.6	28.9	268.5	511.0	706.7
Colombia	Bogotá, D.E.	34.6	61.9	239.2	365.1	428.5
Costa Rica	San José	78.7	88.2	189.7	204.4	216.8
Chile	Gran Santiago	9.5	31.4	27 751.6	166 163.1	232 773.2
Ecuador	Quito	67.9	79.4	188.0	235.2	262.6
El Salvador	San Salvador / Mejicanos / Villa Delgado	93.7	95.0	151.1	180.8	204.8
Guatemala	Guatemala	92.2	92.8	100.0[2]	124.6	134.6
Guyana	Zona urbana	79.6	88.2	144.6	170.5	196.5
Haití	Puerto Príncipe	76.5	92.1	188.3	213.9	208.3
Honduras	Tegucigalpa	77.9	89.1	135.4	153.9	162.7
Jamaica	...	64.9	77.1	195.1	238.9	322.5
México	México, D.F.	76.7	84.2	176.7	259.1	303.0
Nicaragua	Area Metropolitana de Managua[3]	95.0	103.0	107.5	123.2	128.8
Panamá	Panamá	88.8	92.2	141.4	153.7	160.3
Paraguay	Asunción	71.7	93.9	172.8	197.4	218.4
Perú	Lima / Callao	40.2	62.8	181.4	334.5	527.4
República Dominicana	Santo Domingo, D.F.	90.3	94.8	165.5	201.3	208.5
Trinidad y Tabago	...	74.6	82.7	185.5	228.8	252.2
Uruguay	Montevideo	2.6	9.6	1 383.2	3 296.4	4 764.7
Venezuela	Area Metropolitana de Caracas	92.1	92.4	131.9	153.0	164.0

[1] Desde 1980 corresponde al índice nacional de los niveles de ingresos medios y bajos, en su conjunto, con base diciembre de 1979 = 100.
[2] Nueva serie. Año base 1975 = 100.
[3] Los datos de 1960 y 1965, tienen como base 1958 = 100 y a partir de 1975 el año base es 1974 = 100.

227. ANNUAL CONSUMER PRICE INDEXES

a) General Level
(Base year 1970 = 100)

1979	1980	1981	1982	1983	Geografical coverage	Country
123 635.3	248 216.6	507 543.8	1 343 857.4	5 964 160.4	Federal Capital	Argentina
330.8	377.9	433.0	477.6	502.8	...	Barbados
381.0	561.0	741.3	1 657.0	6 223.6	La Paz	Bolivia
1 061.3	1 889.6	3 697.0	7 008.7	16 508.9	São Paulo	Brazil
532.4	147.3 [1]	187.8 [1]	234.0 [1]	280.1 [1]	Bogotá	Colombia
236.7	279.5	383.1	728.4	966.1	San José City	Costa Rica
310 498.7	419 601.2	502 215.3	552 122.0	702 622.6	Greater Santiago	Chile
289.6	327.3	380.9	442.4	642.2	Quito	Ecuador
237.3	278.6	319.7	357.0	404.3	San Salvador / Mejicanos / Villa Delgado	El Salvador
150.0	166.1	185.1	185.4	...	Guatemala City	Guatemala
231.4	264.0	322.7	390.2	...	Urban Area	Guyana
235.4	277.3	296.3	320.0	...	Port-au-Prince	Haiti
182.4	215.4	235.6	257.7	280.6	Tegucigalpa	Honduras
415.4	527.6	596.2	636.2	...	...	Jamaica
357.0	451.5	579.1	920.0	1 857.3	México City	Mexico
190.8	258.2	319.7	399.0	...	Managua Metropolitan Area [3]	Nicaragua
173.0	196.9	211.2	220.2	224.9	Panamá City	Panama
279.9	342.7	390.4	416.8	472.9	Asunción	Paraguay
885.0	1 408.8	2 470.8	4 063.7	8 580.5	Lima / Callao	Peru
227.6	265.8	285.7	306.6	...	Santo Domingo	Dominican Republic
289.3	339.9	388.5	432.9	505.3	...	Trinidad and Tobago
7 949.9	12 996.1	17 420.6	20 729.3	30 927.4	Montevideo	Uruguay
184.2	226.8	260.0	285.9	303.0	Caracas Metropolitan Area	Venezuela

[1] *Since 1980 it refers to the national index for middle and low-income strata together, base December 1979 = 100.*
[2] *New series. Base year 1975 = 100.*
[3] *For 1960 and 1965, base year is 1958 = 100; from 1975 onwards, base year is 1974 = 100.*

III. PRECIOS INTERNOS

227. INDICES ANUALES DE PRECIOS AL CONSUMIDOR (conclusión)

b) Alimentos
(Año base 1970 = 100)

País	Cobertura geográfica	1960	1965	1975	1977	1978
Argentina	Capital Federal	15.3	43.4	1 134.7	18 621.1	49 009.5
Barbados	...	77.8	83.5	262.5	297.0	326.9
Bolivia	La Paz	61.9	68.8	285.7	316.4	348.2
Brasil	São Paulo	3.0	30.9	294.7	550.7	774.2
Colombia	Bogotá, D.E.	34.3	64.2	281.3	448.0	508.0
Costa Rica	San José	74.7	83.1	192.1	201.2	221.9
Chile	Gran Santiago	8.6	32.1	35 820.2	208 667.2	280 917.0
Ecuador	Quito	58.5	74.2	223.4	283.0	312.1
El Salvador	San Salvador / Mejicanos / Villa Delgado	93.7	89.6	154.3	178.9	198.1
Guatemala	Guatemala	91.4	91.8	100.0[2]	121.7	127.3
Guyana	Zona urbana	77.7	87.1	169.6	208.7	244.7
Haití	Puerto Príncipe	74.5	90.1	200.5	229.7	213.7
Honduras	Tegucigalpa	79.3	92.9	145.3	168.5	178.9
Jamaica	...	67.0	75.2	211.7	252.3	345.1
México	México, D.F.	79.2	85.6	185.9	262.4	305.8
Nicaragua	Area Metropolitana de Managua[3]	91.0	104.0	107.7	125.1	129.6
Panamá	Panamá	86.0	91.2	154.3	161.1	171.1
Paraguay	Asunción	70.1	99.0	191.6	222.2	251.0
Perú	Lima / Callao	42.2	64.9	200.0	370.1	591.8
República Dominicana	Santo Domingo, D.F.	92.3	99.7	182.7	194.2	188.3
Trinidad y Tabago	...	75.0	83.5	211.1	241.9	263.9
Uruguay	Montevideo	3.0	10.8	1 293.5	3 132.2	4 527.1
Venezuela	Area Metropolitana de Caracas	90.1	95.6	151.0	184.7	201.8

[1] Desde 1980 corresponde al índice nacional de los niveles de ingresos medios y bajos, en su conjunto, con base diciembre de 1979 = 100.
[2] Nueva serie. Año base 1975 = 100.
[3] Los datos de los años 1960 y 1965 tienen como base 1958 = 100; a partir de 1975 el año base es 1974 = 100.

227. ANNUAL CONSUMER PRICE INDEXES (concluded)

b) Food
(Base year 1970 = 100)

1979	1980	1981	1982	1983	Geografical coverage	Country
131 671.5	256 872.3	511 571.1	1 424 129.8	6 252 513.7	Federal Capital	Argentina
363.1	406.8	467.6	501.7	515.0	...	Barbados
413.1	609.7	824.6	1 846.4	7 454.2	La Paz	Bolivia
1 215.9	2 229.1	4 302.9	7 913.5	21 278.0	São Paulo	Brazil
627.6	152.3[1]	195.8	245.6	296.2	Bogotá	Colombia
250.0	304.3	416.0	834.4	1 174.6	San José City	Costa Rica
368 157.7	500 933.0	572 266.5	592 941.6	745 654.6	Greater Santiago	Chile
343.4	380.9	434.9	520.8	901.7	Quito	Ecuador
227.3	272.0	320.0	354.2	401.9	San Salvador / Mejicanos / Villa Delgado	El Salvador
140.4	156.1	173.6	168.8	...	Guatemala City	Guatemala
291.0	326.2	416.3	358.4	650.8	Urban Area	Guyana
247.1	312.8	337.2	354.8	...	Port-au-Prince	Haiti
199.2	233.2	250.2	267.0	281.2	Tegucigalpa	Honduras
460.5	614.3	677.7	719.1	...	...	Jamaica
364.8	459.3	581.0	876.8	1 675.5	México City	Mexico
211.7	315.6	...	825.7	...	Managua Metropolitan Area[3]	Nicaragua
188.6	212.3	231.8	245.5	259.7	Panamá City	Panama
324.9	386.1	426.3	441.3	517.0	Asunción	Paraguay
1 030.9	1 637.1	2 887.6	4 415.5	9 963.9	Lima / Callao	Peru
208.9	240.9	242.0	261.1	...	Santo Domingo	Dominican Republic
300.4	358.3	417.5	474.5	584.1	...	Trinidad and Tobago
7 738.6	12 221.7	15 352.9	17 150.0	26 430.6	Montevideo	Uruguay
235.4	313.3	371.2	407.3	439.1	Caracas Metropolitan Area	Venezuela

[1] Since 1980 it refers to the national index for middle and low-income strata together, base December 1979 = 100.
[2] New series. Base year 1975 = 100.
[3] For 1960 and 1965, base year is 1958 = 100; from 1975 onwards, base year is 1974 = 100.

IV. BALANCE DE PAGOS

228. AMERICA LATINA: [1] BALANCE DE PAGOS

(Millones de dólares)

	1960	1965	1970	1975	1977
Exportaciones de bienes y servicios	10 058.8	13 113.1	18 200.4	44 331.5	59 276.4
Bienes fob	8 415.5	11 079.7	14 484.2	36 109.5	49 267.8
Servicios [2]	1 643.4	2 033.4	3 716.2	8 226.2	10 007.4
Transporte y seguros	338.8	402.7	870.1	2 151.3	2 844.1
Viajes	819.0	1 150.5	1 881.2	3 765.1	4 061.2
Importaciones de bienes y servicios	10 043.0	11 921.5	18 802.0	52 803.4	62 986.5
Bienes fob	7 567.2	9 011.7	13 830.5	41 613.1	49 273.5
Servicios [2]	2 475.8	2 909.8	4 971.5	11 190.1	13 709.0
Transporte y seguros	1 063.0	1 184.2	2 033.2	5 554.7	6 471.3
Viajes	684.0	863.3	1 656.4	3 186.0	3 848.9
Balance de bienes	**848.3**	**2 068.0**	**653.7**	**-5 503.4**	**-6.2**
Balance comercial	**15.8**	**1 191.6**	**-601.6**	**-8 472.1**	**-3 710.0**
Servicios de factores	-1 184.9	-1 794.0	-2 887.0	-5 820.9	-8 556.8
Utilidades	-1 028.7	-1 432.6	-2 021.8	-2 540.8	-3 232.0
Intereses recibidos	22.1	59.7	315.1	1 902.4	2 262.4
Intereses pagados	-296.0	-556.1	-1 263.4	-5 120.9	-7 563.0
Otros	117.7	135.0	83.0	-59.7	-21.7
Transferencias unilaterales privadas	-82.1	37.8	99.1	213.9	386.5
Balance en cuenta corriente	**-1 251.1**	**-564.6**	**-3 389.5**	**-14 075.9**	**-11 880.3**
Transferencias unilaterales oficiales	127.5	202.3	186.6	331.7	259.5
Capital a largo plazo	1 075.7	691.3	3 257.6	13 641.6	16 994.6
Inversión directa	499.4	598.5	1 072.3	3 159.1	2 971.7
Inversión de cartera	-71.1	40.7	27.2	130.7	1 388.0
Otro capital a largo plazo	647.4	52.1	2 158.1	10 352.2	12 634.6
Sector oficial [3]	230.0	175.8	736.9	3 478.3	6 726.1
Préstamos recibidos	628.7	862.0	1 422.7	5 671.3	10 514.1
Amortizaciones	-337.3	-528.8	-840.0	-2 125.6	-3 542.7
Bancos comerciales [3]	1.5	1.6	582.0	2 250.1	1 472.8
Préstamos recibidos	1.5	6.7	966.2	3 097.7	3 708.7
Amortizaciones	0.0	-9.6	-385.3	-891.9	-2 648.7
Otros sectores [3]	415.9	-125.3	839.2	4 623.7	4 436.0
Préstamos recibidos	986.0	892.6	1 815.1	8 008.2	9 899.6
Amortizaciones	-597.7	-915.9	-973.7	-2 927.0	-4 863.2
Balance básico	**-47.9**	**329.0**	**54.7**	**-102.7**	**5 373.5**
Capital a corto plazo	379.5	-332.0	693.9	2 586.3	-1 380.0
Sector oficial	128.4	-355.0	-32.1	219.8	-813.5
Bancos comerciales	148.6	70.5	-20.4	582.1	327.1
Otros sectores	102.5	-47.5	746.4	1 784.4	-893.3
Errores y omisiones netos	-356.8	396.6	212.8	-1 851.2	1 698.7
Balance en cuenta de capital	**1 225.9**	**958.2**	**4 349.8**	**14 705.3**	**17 570.0**
Balance global [4]	**-25.2**	**393.6**	**960.3**	**629.5**	**5 689.5**
Variación total de las reservas (signo - indica aumento)	15.8	-409.8	-1 194.4	-425.9	-5 747.2
Oro monetario	225.8	54.5	10.0	-24.7	-47.2
Derechos especiales de giro	0.0	0.0	-272.2	141.6	-141.2
Posición de reserva en el FMI	-52.3	-4.8	-175.8	-447.0	5.0
Activos en divisas	-208.5	-453.5	-613.0	-150.7	-4 426.5
Otros activos	-1.8	27.3	10.7	-417.5	-1 071.3
Uso de crédito del FMI	52.6	-33.3	-154.1	473.3	-65.4

[1] Argentina, Barbados, Bolivia, Brasil, Colombia, Costa Rica, Chile, Ecuador, El Salvador, Guatemala, Guyana, Haití, Honduras, Jamaica, México, Nicaragua, Panamá, Paraguay, Perú, República Dominicana, Suriname, Trinidad y Tabago, Uruguay y Venezuela.
[2] Incluye Otros servicios no factoriales.
[3] Incluye Préstamos netos concedidos y Otros activos y pasivos.
[4] Es igual a Variación total de las reservas (con signo contrario) más Asientos de contrapartida.

458

(Millions of dollars)

1978	1979	1980	1981	1982	
65 145.2	86 497.7	111 885.0	119 991.9	107 342.6	*Exports of goods and services*
53 039.2	70 825.2	91 962.8	98 267.1	90 243.4	*Goods FOB*
12 109.8	15 675.3	19 922.1	21 725.4	17 097.6	*Services* [2]
3 059.7	3 924.2	5 241.4	5 667.8	5 297.5	*Transport and insurance*
5 553.3	7 009.8	8 676.5	9 926.8	7 082.9	*Travel*
73 403.9	92 603.1	121 444.7	132 735.9	111 042.5	*Imports of goods and services*
56 068.9	70 384.2	92 984.2	100 280.9	81 620.8	*Goods FOB*
17 333.1	22 215.8	28 464.9	32 457.2	29 417.8	*Services* [2]
7 405.3	9 099.2	12 010.2	12 903.4	10 761.9	*Transport and insurance*
5 963.0	7 839.1	10 248.2	12 355.8	9 641.0	*Travel*
-3 030.0	441.1	-1 021.2	-2 014.3	8 622.5	**Trade balance (goods)**
-8 258.4	-6 105.2	-9 559.8	-12 744.0	-3 700.1	**Trade balance (goods and services)**
-10 484.5	-14 209.5	-19 015.7	-28 967.0	-38 794.5	*Factor services*
-3 748.9	-4 445.8	-4 571.2	-5 378.7	-5 212.3	*Profits*
3 737.2	6 291.1	9 488.3	12 160.0	10 365.4	*Interest received*
-10 483.8	-15 942.9	-23 494.7	-34 886.4	-43 210.5	*Interest paid*
10.5	-113.0	-432.3	-863.6	-737.0	*Others*
329.2	425.3	521.5	660.3	174.9	*Private unrequited transfers*
-18 412.7	-19 886.0	-28 056.3	-41 051.6	-42 317.7	**Balance on current account**
389.4	631.1	730.2	771.9	838.6	*Official unrequited transfers*
25 731.4	22 850.8	29 244.6	46 028.7	35 338.5	*Long-term capital*
3 920.6	4 979.4	5 795.5	7 472.0	6 040.4	*Direct investment*
1 157.6	623.9	1 878.3	2 227.6	4 377.4	*Portfolio investment*
20 652.8	17 247.6	21 571.4	36 328.9	24 920.6	*Other long-term capital*
7 377.0	6 961.2	4 096.6	4 746.7	9 490.3	*Official sector* [3]
14 368.4	14 051.4	10 507.9	12 309.0	16 366.3	*Loans received*
-6 426.1	-6 961.0	-5 594.8	-6 925.9	-6 526.2	*Amortizations*
3 952.2	2 022.0	4 887.4	10 674.1	4 694.6	*Commercial banks* [3]
6 757.1	6 539.8	8 416.3	14 559.2	9 211.2	*Loans received*
-3 482.6	-3 841.9	-3 715.7	-4 446.8	-4 439.6	*Amortizations*
9 323.2	8 264.0	12 587.2	20 908.3	10 735.8	*Other sectors* [3]
18 394.2	19 807.2	21 851.3	33 303.4	23 033.0	*Loans received*
-8 277.3	-11 086.5	-9 652.6	-10 722.9	-11 990.4	*Amortizations*
7 708.0	3 595.5	1 918.2	5 748.7	-6 141.0	**Basic balance**
-1 451.8	3 916.9	5 953.6	2 452.1	-4 897.4	*Short-term capital*
928.8	430.5	1 189.4	950.8	7 440.4	*Official sector*
-240.2	1 226.4	3 124.4	7 930.8	629.7	*Commercial banks*
-2 140.2	2 260.3	1 639.8	-6 429.9	-12 967.9	*Other sectors*
1 825.6	1 963.7	-5 552.0	-10 590.1	-10 622.4	*Errors and omissions (net)*
26 493.2	29 360.2	30 384.9	38 668.3	20 655.4	**Capital account balance**
8 080.7	9 473.8	2 328.5	-2 383.4	-21 662.8	**Global balance** [4]
-8 087.0	-9 935.1	-2 985.7	...	...	*Total variation in reserves (minus sign indicates an increase)*
-59.2	-227.1	-730.4	-521.4	754.1	*Monetary gold*
-201.4	-746.8	225.5	...	...	*Special Drawing Rights*
-37.7	124.1	-587.2	...	...	*Reserve position in IMF*
-6 729.3	-6 352.2	2 905.6	...	...	*Foreign exchange assets*
-528.9	-2 889.2	-4 551.8	528.4	6 139.5	*Other assets*
-530.5	156.0	-248.0	...	...	*Use of IMF credit*

[1] *Argentina, Barbados, Bolivia, Brazil, Colombia, Costa Rica, Chile, Ecuador, El Salvador, Guatemala, Guyana, Haiti, Honduras, Jamaica, Mexico, Nicaragua, Panama, Paraguay, Perú, Dominican Republic, Suriname, Trinidad and Tobago, Uruguay and Venezuela.*
[2] *Non factorial services also included.*
[3] *Net loans received and Other assets and liabilities included.*
[4] *Equals to Total variation in reserves (with opposite sign) plus Counterpart items.*

459

229. AMERICA LATINA, PAISES NO EXPORTADORES DE PETROLEO:[1] BALANCE DE PAGOS

(Millones de dólares)

	1960	1965	1970	1975	1977
Exportaciones de bienes y servicios	5 298.8	6 991.4	10 644.8	24 338.5	35 352.9
Bienes fob	4 447.2	6 057.5	8 849.6	20 513.7	30 172.0
Servicios [2]	851.6	933.9	1 795.2	3 829.3	5 178.5
Transporte y seguros	272.8	295.7	597.7	1 365.1	1 862.0
Viajes	263.0	308.0	573.3	1 199.8	1 487.3
Importaciones de bienes y servicios	6 174.1	6 338.6	11 252.8	31 425.8	35 797.6
Bienes fob	4 652.4	4 793.5	8 521.5	25 355.0	28 491.9
Servicios [2]	1 521.7	1 545.1	2 731.3	6 069.3	7 302.8
Transporte y seguros	715.7	681.8	1 334.4	3 517.2	3 856.3
Viajes	311.6	297.0	662.2	1 236.1	1 397.0
Balance de bienes	-205.2	1 264.0	328.1	-4 841.4	1 679.7
Balance comercial	-875.3	652.8	-608.0	-7 087.3	-444.6
Servicios de factores	-407.9	-660.4	-1 629.1	-3 734.1	-5 617.5
Utilidades	-248.4	-348.0	-926.2	-956.5	-2 113.8
Intereses recibidos	18.4	37.6	171.3	945.4	1 192.5
Intereses pagados	-218.1	-394.7	-839.6	-3 633.7	-4 646.9
Otros	40.2	44.7	-34.7	-87.1	-46.8
Transferencias unilaterales privadas	7.2	103.2	99.3	220.1	473.1
Balance en cuenta corriente	-1 276.0	95.6	-2 137.8	-10 598.1	-5 588.9
Transferencias unilaterales oficiales	105.2	158.2	122.3	284.6	209.9
Capital a largo plazo	898.0	271.8	2 330.7	6 883.7	8 171.4
Inversión directa	576.4	276.0	746.4	1 575.0	2 247.1
Inversión de cartera	-5.8	11.8	64.0	45.1	32.7
Otro capital a largo plazo	327.4	-16.0	1 520.3	5 263.9	5 891.4
Sector oficial [3]	74.4	109.1	424.5	2 532.2	2 764.0
Préstamos recibidos	397.6	687.1	1 071.3	4 130.8	5 502.4
Amortizaciones	-285.0	-442.1	-671.7	-1 550.9	-2 599.9
Bancos comerciales [3]	1.5	1.6	522.0	470.1	164.9
Préstamos recibidos	1.5	6.7	617.2	1 008.7	1 436.0
Amortizaciones	0.0	-9.6	-96.3	-533.1	-1 269.4
Otros sectores [3]	251.5	-126.7	573.8	2 261.5	2 962.7
Préstamos recibidos	575.7	468.6	1 179.9	4 617.8	6 548.2
Amortizaciones	-355.2	-535.3	-612.6	-2 158.9	-3 342.8
Balance básico	-272.8	525.6	315.2	-3 429.8	2 792.2
Capital a corto plazo	431.9	-400.3	372.9	2 122.5	1 404.5
Sector oficial	266.4	-461.2	-23.9	143.4	-605.6
Bancos comerciales	75.2	127.1	-195.6	118.4	736.2
Otros sectores	90.3	-66.2	592.4	1 860.9	1 274.0
Errores y omisiones netos	-68.5	310.5	-34.3	-808.5	-374.2
Balance en cuenta de capital	1 366.6	340.2	2 790.5	8 478.0	9 411.1
Balance global [4]	90.6	435.8	652.7	-2 120.1	3 822.0
Variación total de las reservas (signo - indica aumento)	-105.7	-459.8	-836.2	2 184.9	-4 050.8
Oro monetario	-20.2	70.4	11.9	-22.8	-33.0
Derechos especiales de giro	0.0	0.0	-158.9	84.2	-58.8
Posición de reserva en el FMI	-17.3	3.3	-121.0	17.6	-56.2
Activos en divisas	-116.8	-492.5	-432.0	1 716.3	-3 634.4
Otros activos	-5.4	-1.7	-0.6	-84.5	-43.6
Uso de crédito del FMI	54.0	-39.3	-135.6	474.5	-224.3

[1] Argentina, Barbados, Brasil, Colombia, Costa Rica, Chile, El Salvador, Guatemala, Guyana, Haití, Honduras, Jamaica, Nicaragua, Panamá, Paraguay, República Dominicana, Suriname y Uruguay.
[2] Incluye Otros servicios no factoriales.
[3] Incluye Préstamos netos concedidos y Otros activos y pasivos.
[4] Es igual a Variación total de las reservas (con signo contrario) más Asientos de contrapartida.

229. LATIN AMERICA, NON-OIL EXPORTING COUNTRIES: [1] BALANCE OF PAYMENTS

(Millions of dollars)

1978	1979	1980	1981	1982	
38 226.6	46 975.6	56 716.7	59 162.2	52 477.5	*Exports of goods and services*
32 389.2	39 285.4	46 875.2	49 131.4	43 155.0	*Goods FOB*
5 838.6	7 693.0	9 842.6	10 029.9	9 319.9	*Services* [2]
2 037.2	2 540.9	3 553.3	3 887.7	3 534.7	*Transport and insurance*
1 787.2	2 233.4	2 574.5	2 807.9	2 679.9	*Travel*
40 306.1	53 603.5	70 369.0	70 504.2	58 196.3	*Imports of goods and services*
31 770.9	42 066.6	55 477.3	55 527.9	44 830.4	*Goods FOB*
8 535.0	11 535.3	14 893.4	14 978.6	13 363.2	*Services* [2]
4 187.3	5 479.7	7 348.3	7 469.3	6 236.0	*Transport and insurance*
1 925.9	2 822.7	3 548.0	3 185.7	2 791.1	*Travel*
618.2	**-2 781.2**	**-8 602.1**	**-6 397.0**	**-1 675.6**	**Trade balance (goods)**
-2 079.3	**-6 627.8**	**-13 652.3**	**-11 342.1**	**-5 718.9**	**Trade balance (goods and services)**
-6 703.0	-8 370.5	-11 200.0	-17 721.5	-23 253.9	*Factor services*
-2 380.2	-2 323.6	-1 962.7	-2 328.1	-2 918.7	*Profits*
2 104.6	3 963.7	5 646.4	6 543.0	5 959.7	*Interest received*
-6 394.3	-10 058.1	-14 829.1	-21 728.2	-25 907.1	*Interest paid*
-33.3	47.4	-51.4	-211.5	-386.6	*Others*
595.4	697.7	843.3	983.2	762.6	*Private unrequited transfers*
-8 187.0	**-14 297.1**	**-24 008.8**	**-28 080.9**	**-28 210.6**	**Balance on current account**
250.5	382.7	416.5	428.5	533.1	*Official unrequited transfers*
15 283.8	14 128.7	17 784.9	29 868.4	19 121.9	*Long-term capital*
2 814.1	3 314.0	3 233.0	4 248.3	3 922.4	*Direct investment*
197.1	1 094.6	664.5	1 156.9	2 140.7	*Portfolio investment*
12 272.5	9 720.2	13 888.0	24 463.2	13 058.8	*Other long-term capital*
4 467.0	4 965.4	2 602.3	3 107.5	4 492.9	*Official sector* [3]
9 140.7	7 597.9	5 629.6	6 466.8	7 960.6	*Loans received*
-4 305.9	-2 581.7	-2 459.1	-2 960.8	-3 016.5	*Amortizations*
2 195.9	1 329.2	3 553.0	7 117.5	2 536.7	*Commercial banks* [3]
3 355.4	2 996.7	5 836.7	9 806.5	5 992.8	*Loans received*
-1 150.5	-1 648.1	-2 268.3	-2 676.2	-3 385.7	*Amortizations*
5 609.2	3 425.3	7 732.5	14 238.4	6 029.2	*Other sectors* [3]
11 548.5	10 667.4	13 558.8	22 851.8	13 416.3	*Loans received*
-5 371.7	-6 673.1	-6 383.8	-7 432.5	-6 540.8	*Amortizations*
7 347.0	**214.0**	**-5 807.6**	**2 215.8**	**-8 555.8**	**Basic balance**
665.9	2 473.9	2 081.3	-4 826.6	1 113.1	*Short-term capital*
1 039.1	543.3	1 006.2	779.3	7 194.3	*Official sector*
800.0	315.2	826.4	1 676.3	52.6	*Commercial banks*
-1 173.2	1 615.8	248.8	-7 282.5	-6 133.9	*Other sectors*
415.7	924.1	-148.5	-63.0	-1 403.5	*Errors and omissions (net)*
16 615.2	**17 907.9**	**20 139.4**	**25 408.4**	**19 363.1**	**Capital account balance**
8 428.5	**3 610.4**	**-3 869.5**	**-2 672.7**	**-8 847.7**	**Global balance** [4]
-8 703.0	-3 948.4	3 539.9	...	...	*Total variation in reserves (minus sign indicates an increase)*
-50.1	-158.3	-551.0	-393.0	748.6	*Monetary gold*
-124.8	-354.7	70.3	...	...	*Special Drawing Rights*
-265.1	-103.4	-326.2	...	...	*Reserve position in IMF*
-7 759.8	-3 481.9	4 202.7	...	...	*Foreign exchange assets*
-35.6	-10.5	299.8	84.5	86.6	*Other assets*
-467.6	160.7	-156.0	...	...	*Use of IMF credit*

[1] *Argentina, Barbados, Brazil, Colombia, Costa Rica, Chile, El Salvador, Guatemala, Guyana, Haiti, Honduras, Jamaica, Nicaragua, Panama, Paraguay, Dominican Republic, Suriname and Uruguay.*
[2] *Non factorial services also included.*
[3] *Net loans received and Other assets and liabilities included.*
[4] *Equals to Total variation in reserves (with opposite sign) plus Counterpart items.*

461

230. AMERICA LATINA, PAISES EXPORTADORES DE PETROLEO: [1] BALANCE DE PAGOS

(Millones de dólares)

	1960	1965	1970	1975	1977	1978
Exportaciones de bienes y servicios	4 760.0	6 121.7	7 555.6	19 993.0	23 923.5	26 918.6
Bienes fob	3 968.3	5 022.2	5 634.6	15 595.8	19 095.8	20 650.0
Servicios [2]	791.8	1 099.5	1 921.0	4 396.9	4 828.9	6 271.2
Transporte y seguros	66.0	107.0	272.4	786.2	982.1	1 022.5
Viajes	556.0	842.5	1 307.9	2 565.3	2 573.9	3 766.1
Importaciones de bienes y servicios	3 868.9	5 582.9	7 549.2	21 377.6	27 188.9	33 097.8
Bienes fob	2 914.8	4 218.2	5 309.0	16 258.1	20 781.6	24 298.0
Servicios [2]	954.1	1 364.7	2 240.2	5 120.8	6 406.2	8 798.1
Transporte y seguros	347.3	502.4	698.8	2 037.5	2 615.0	3 218.0
Viajes	372.4	566.3	994.2	1 949.9	2 451.9	4 037.1
Balance de bienes	1 053.5	804.0	325.6	-662.0	-1 685.9	-3 648.2
Balance comercial	891.1	538.8	6.4	-1 384.8	-3 265.4	-6 179.1
Servicios de factores	-777.0	-1 133.6	-1 257.9	-2 086.8	-2 939.3	-3 781.5
Utilidades	-780.3	-1 084.6	-1 095.6	-1 584.3	-1 118.2	-1 368.7
Intereses recibidos	3.7	22.1	143.8	957.0	1 069.9	1 632.6
Intereses pagados	-77.9	-161.4	-423.8	-1 487.2	-2 916.1	-4 089.5
Otros	77.5	90.3	117.7	27.4	25.1	43.8
Transferencias unilaterales privadas	-89.3	-65.4	-0.2	-6.2	-86.6	-266.2
Balance en cuenta corriente	24.9	-660.2	-1 251.7	-3 477.8	-6 291.4	-10 225.7
Transferencias unilaterales oficiales	22.3	44.1	64.3	47.1	49.6	138.9
Capital a largo plazo	177.7	419.5	926.9	6 757.9	8 823.2	10 447.6
Inversión directa	-77.0	322.5	325.9	1 584.1	724.6	1 106.5
Inversión de cartera	-65.3	28.9	-36.8	85.6	1 355.3	960.5
Otro capital a largo plazo	320.0	68.1	637.8	5 088.3	6 743.2	8 380.3
Sector oficial [3]	155.6	66.7	312.4	946.1	3 962.1	2 910.0
Préstamos recibidos	231.1	174.9	351.4	1 540.5	5 011.7	5 227.7
Amortizaciones	-52.3	-86.7	-168.3	-574.7	-942.8	-2 120.2
Bancos comerciales [3]	0.0	0.0	60.0	1 780.0	1 307.9	1 756.3
Préstamos recibidos	0.0	0.0	349.0	2 089.0	2 272.7	3 401.7
Amortizaciones	0.0	0.0	-289.0	-358.8	-1 379.3	-2 332.1
Otros sectores [3]	164.4	1.4	265.4	2 362.2	1 473.3	3 714.0
Préstamos recibidos	410.3	424.0	635.2	3 390.4	3 351.4	6 845.7
Amortizaciones	-242.5	-380.6	-361.1	-768.1	-1 520.4	-2 905.6
Balance básico	224.9	-196.6	-260.5	3 327.1	2 581.3	361.0
Capital a corto plazo	-52.4	68.3	321.0	463.8	-2 784.5	-2 117.7
Sector oficial	-138.0	106.2	-8.2	76.4	-207.9	-110.3
Bancos comerciales	73.4	-56.6	175.2	463.7	-409.1	-1 040.2
Otros sectores	12.2	18.7	154.0	-76.5	-2 167.3	-967.0
Errores y omisiones netos	-288.3	86.1	247.1	-1 042.7	2 072.9	1 409.9
Balance en cuenta de capital	**-140.7**	**618.0**	**1 559.3**	**6 227.3**	**8 158.9**	**9 878.0**
Balance global [4]	**-115.8**	**-42.2**	**307.6**	**2 749.6**	**1 867.5**	**-347.8**
Variación total de las reservas (signo - indica aumento)	121.5	50.0	-358.2	-2 610.8	-1 696.4	616.0
Oro monetario	246.0	-15.9	-1.9	-1.9	-14.2	-9.1
Derechos especiales de giro	0.0	0.0	-113.3	57.4	-82.4	-76.6
Posición de reserva en el FMI	-35.0	-8.1	-54.8	-464.6	61.2	227.4
Activos en divisas	-91.7	39.0	-181.0	-1 867.0	-792.1	1 030.5
Otros activos	3.6	29.0	11.3	-333.0	-1 027.7	-493.3
Uso de crédito del FMI	-1.4	6.0	-18.5	-1.2	158.9	-62.9

[1] Bolivia, Ecuador, México, Perú, Trinidad y Tabago y Venezuela.
[2] Incluye Otros servicios no factoriales.
[3] Incluye Préstamos netos concedidos y Otros activos y pasivos.
[4] Es igual a Variación total de las reservas (con signo contrario) más Asientos de contrapartida.

230. LATIN AMERICA, OIL-EXPORTING COUNTRIES: [1] BALANCE OF PAYMENTS

(Millions of dollars)

1979	1980	1981	1982	1983	
39 522.1	55 168.3	60 829.7	54 865.1	...	Exports of goods and services
31 539.8	45 087.6	49 135.7	47 088.4	45 306.8	Goods FOB
7 982.3	10 079.5	11 695.5	7 777.7	...	Services [2]
1 383.3	1 688.1	1 780.1	1 762.8	1 886.0	Transport and insurance
4 776.4	6 102.0	7 118.9	4 403.0	3 904.7	Travel
38 999.6	51 075.7	62 231.7	52 846.2	...	Imports of goods and services
28 317.6	37 506.9	44 753.0	36 790.4	21 432.1	Goods FOB
10 680.5	13 571.5	17 478.6	16 054.6	...	Services [2]
3 619.5	4 661.9	5 434.1	4 525.9	3 391.2	Transport and insurance
5 016.4	6 700.2	9 170.1	6 849.9	3 602.9	Travel
3 222.3	**7 580.9**	**4 382.7**	**10 298.1**	**23 874.7**	**Trade balance (goods)**
522.6	**4 092.5**	**-1 401.9**	**2 018.8**	**...**	**Trade balance (goods and services)**
-5 839.0	-7 815.7	-11 245.5	-15 540.6	...	Factor services
-2 122.2	-2 608.5	-3 050.6	-2 293.6	...	Profits
2 327.4	3 841.9	5 617.0	4 405.7	2 898.8	Interest received
-5 884.8	-8 665.6	-13 158.2	-17 303.4	...	Interest paid
-160.4	-380.9	-652.1	-350.4	...	Others
-272.4	-321.8	-322.9	-587.7	...	Private unrequited transfers
-5 588.9	**-4 047.5**	**-12 970.7**	**-14 107.1**	**...**	**Balance on current account**
248.4	313.7	343.4	305.5	...	Official unrequited transfers
8 722.1	11 459.7	16 160.3	16 216.6	...	Long-term capital
1 665.4	2 562.5	3 223.7	2 118.0	...	Direct investment
-470.7	1 213.8	1 070.7	2 236.7	...	Portfolio investment
7 527.4	7 683.4	11 865.7	11 861.8	...	Other long-term capital
1 995.8	1 494.3	1 639.2	4 997.4	...	Official sector [3]
6 453.5	4 878.3	5 842.2	8 405.7	...	Loans received
-4 379.3	-3 135.7	-3 965.1	-3 509.7	...	Amortizations
692.8	1 334.4	3 556.6	2 157.9	...	Commercial banks [3]
3 543.1	2 579.6	4 752.7	3 218.4	...	Loans received
-2 193.8	-1 447.4	-1 770.6	-1 053.9	...	Amortizations
4 838.7	4 854.7	6 669.9	4 706.6	...	Other sectors [3]
9 139.8	8 292.5	10 451.6	9 616.7	...	Loans received
-4 413.4	-3 268.8	-3 290.4	-5 449.6	...	Amortizations
3 381.5	**7 725.8**	**3 532.9**	**2 414.8**	**...**	**Basic balance**
1 443.0	3 872.3	7 278.7	-6 010.5	...	Short-term capital
-112.8	183.2	171.5	246.1	...	Official sector
911.2	2 298.0	6 254.5	577.1	...	Commercial banks
644.5	1 391.0	852.6	-6 834.0	...	Other sectors
1 039.6	-5 403.5	-10 527.1	-9 218.9	...	Errors and omissions (net)
11 452.3	**10 245.5**	**13 259.9**	**1 292.3**	**...**	**Capital account balance**
5 863.4	**6 198.0**	**289.3**	**-12 815.1**	**1 401.4**	**Global balance** [4]
-5 986.7	-6 525.6	-1 504.3	...	...	Total variation in reserves *(minus sign indicates an increase)*
-68.8	-179.4	-128.4	5.5	-10.6	Monetary gold
-392.1	155.2	-156.7	...	...	Special Drawing Rights
227.5	-261.0	-85.4	...	...	Reserve position in IMF
-2 870.3	-1 297.1	-1 481.3	...	...	Foreign exchange assets
-2 878.7	-4 851.6	443.9	6 052.9	933.3	Other assets
-4.7	-92.0	-96.2	...	...	Use of IMF credit

[1] *Bolivia, Ecuador, Mexico, Peru, Trinidad and Tobago and Venezuela.*
[2] *Non factorial services also included.*
[3] *Net loans received and Other assets and liabilities included.*
[4] *Equals to Total variation in reserves (with opposite sign) plus Counterpart items.*

231. ARGENTINA: BALANCE DE PAGOS

(Millones de dólares)

	1960	1965	1970	1975	1977	1978
Exportaciones de bienes y servicios	1 270.9	1 603.0	2 104.0	3 498.0	6 587.7	7 482.6
Bienes fob	1 079.2	1 493.0	1 773.0	2 961.3	5 650.2	6 401.2
Servicios [1]	191.7	110.0	331.0	536.7	935.2	1 082.7
Transporte y seguros	116.7	53.0	140.0	199.1	439.0	474.7
Viajes	36.2	0.0	74.0	154.2	212.3	278.0
Importaciones de bienes y servicios	1 436.0	1 326.0	1 986.0	4 323.6	4 710.9	4 962.4
Bienes fob	1 106.0	1 062.0	1 499.0	3 510.1	3 799.2	3 488.4
Servicios [1]	330.0	264.0	487.0	813.5	911.7	1 474.0
Transporte y seguros	219.0	117.0	252.0	534.2	459.0	509.7
Viajes	75.1	49.0	130.0	93.5	187.6	588.2
Balance de bienes	**-26.8**	**431.0**	**274.0**	**-548.8**	**1 850.9**	**2 912.8**
Balance comercial	**-165.1**	**277.0**	**118.0**	**-825.6**	**1 876.8**	**2 520.2**
Servicios de factores	-57.0	-53.0	-278.0	-466.2	-781.5	-733.6
Utilidades	-31.6	-8.0	-70.0	-15.8	-368.0	-274.4
Intereses recibidos	0.0	5.0	26.0	54.6	127.6	315.2
Intereses pagados	-25.4	-50.0	-179.0	-467.4	-498.9	-720.1
Otros	0.0	0.0	-55.0	-37.6	-41.0	-54.4
Transferencias unilaterales privadas	-7.0	-4.0	0.0	6.1	32.7	47.7
Balance en cuenta corriente	**-229.1**	**220.0**	**-160.0**	**-1 285.8**	**1 126.8**	**1 835.5**
Transferencias unilaterales oficiales	1.0	2.0	-3.0	-1.2	-1.2	20.9
Capital a largo plazo	606.1	-248.0	120.0	-170.0	475.6	1 519.6
Inversión directa	332.0	43.0	11.0	0.0	143.8	273.4
Inversión de cartera	0.0	5.0	84.0	-55.9	-0.4	101.7
Otro capital a largo plazo	274.1	-296.0	25.0	-114.1	332.1	1 144.5
Sector oficial [2]	82.7	-134.0	-108.0	-72.8	-202.6	-953.9
Préstamos recibidos	154.2	119.0	46.0	227.0	99.0	47.2
Amortizaciones	-49.9	-231.0	-127.0	-275.6	-210.3	-913.9
Bancos comerciales [2]	0.0	-9.0	0.0	0.0	62.8	101.4
Préstamos recibidos	0.0	0.0	0.0	0.0	66.3	124.3
Amortizaciones	0.0	-9.0	0.0	0.0	-3.5	-21.7
Otros sectores [2]	191.4	-153.0	133.0	-41.3	472.0	1 997.0
Préstamos recibidos	231.7	121.0	315.0	359.4	1 047.3	3 745.3
Amortizaciones	-40.3	-274.0	-182.0	-400.7	-575.4	-1 588.3
Balance básico	**378.0**	**-26.0**	**-43.0**	**-1 457.0**	**1 601.2**	**3 376.0**
Capital a corto plazo	-24.0	59.0	131.0	372.7	109.2	-1 246.2
Sector oficial	-49.0	32.0	-33.0	35.2	-399.2	334.9
Bancos comerciales	25.0	58.0	-21.0	178.5	20.1	-27.1
Otros sectores	0.0	-31.0	185.0	159.1	488.3	-1 554.0
Errores y omisiones netos	-152.6	94.0	-12.0	3.6	134.5	9.3
Balance en cuenta de capital	**430.5**	**-93.0**	**236.0**	**205.2**	**719.3**	**302.4**
Balance global [3]	**201.4**	**127.0**	**76.0**	**-1 080.6**	**1 846.0**	**2 137.9**
Variación total de las reservas (signo - indica aumento)	-201.4	-127.0	-134.0	1 071.1	-1 827.0	-2 235.8
Oro monetario	-47.4	5.0	-5.0	0.0	-7.0	-3.9
Derechos especiales de giro	0.0	0.0	-59.0	61.9	0.7	-121.2
Posición de reserva en el FMI	0.0	0.0	-12.0	13.5	0.0	-169.4
Activos en divisas	-202.0	-88.0	-58.0	781.4	-1 710.0	-1 522.3
Otros activos	0.0	0.0	0.0	0.0	0.0	0.0
Uso de crédito del FMI	48.0	-44.0	0.0	214.3	-110.7	-419.1

[1] Incluye Otros servicios no factoriales.
[2] Incluye Préstamos netos concedidos y Otros activos y pasivos.
[3] Es igual a Variación total de las reservas (con signo contrario), más Asientos de contrapartida.

231. ARGENTINA: BALANCE OF PAYMENTS

(Millions of dollars)

1979	1980	1981	1982	1983	
9 176.6	9 890.9	10 853.8	9 182.8	9 290.6	Exports of goods and services
7 810.3	8 021.8	9 142.3	7 621.7	7 838.0	Goods FOB
1 366.4	1 870.5	1 710.3	1 560.0	1 453.6	Services [1]
604.8	809.7	887.3	713.1	754.7	Transport and insurance
266.3	345.1	412.5	609.8	453.0	Travel
8 773.5	13 081.5	11 610.3	6 515.9	5 821.8	Imports of goods and services
6 027.4	9 394.5	8 432.0	4 859.4	4 120.5	Goods FOB
2 744.8	3 688.3	3 179.5	1 655.4	1 700.2	Services [1]
905.5	1 271.2	1 163.7	732.8	736.6	Transport and insurance
1 265.8	1 791.5	1 472.1	566.1	507.4	Travel
1 782.8	-1 372.7	710.3	2 762.3	3 717.5	**Trade balance (goods)**
403.1	-3 190.6	-756.5	2 666.9	3 468.8	**Trade balance (goods and services)**
-972.9	-1 607.1	-3 931.8	-5 054.1	-5 922.4	Factor services
-428.4	-584.8	-737.6	-316.5	-424.5	Profits
680.7	1 229.2	887.1	526.4	440.1	Interest received
-1 174.8	-2 175.3	-3 850.9	-4 925.6	-5 425.5	Interest paid
-51.6	-76.2	-232.6	-338.5	-513.5	Others
34.9	23.4	-21.5	34.2	16.0	Private unrequited transfers
-534.9	-4 774.2	-4 712.2	-2 354.1	-2 436.4	**Balance on current account**
22.1	0.0	0.0	0.0	0.0	Official unrequited transfers
3 155.9	4 491.6	9 965.2	3 843.6	1 715.4	Long-term capital
265.2	787.9	943.3	257.3	183.2	Direct investment
223.4	153.2	1 123.0	1 888.0	1 139.6	Portfolio investment
2 667.4	3 550.5	7 898.8	1 698.3	392.7	Other long-term capital
-0.5	477.8	961.7	-44.0	376.3	Official sector [2]
50.0	510.0	1 034.5	229.6	2 496.7	Loans received
-42.6	-36.2	-47.9	-225.5	-2 109.8	Amortizations
198.1	-65.1	362.9	267.2	38.3	Commercial banks [2]
235.6	89.4	399.0	737.4	264.4	Loans received
-37.4	-154.5	-37.2	-469.0	-227.2	Amortizations
2 469.7	3 137.7	6 574.2	1 475.1	-21.9	Other sectors [2]
3 157.1	4 230.9	8 795.1	2 602.5	2 447.0	Loans received
-857.4	-1 228.6	-1 695.6	-650.3	-2 295.2	Amortizations
2 643.2	-282.6	5 253.0	1 489.5	-721.0	**Basic balance** [3]
1 341.3	-2 010.8	-8 244.0	-1 758.4	-1 288.6	Short-term capital
180.4	312.6	299.1	2 681.6	-90.9	Official sector
-285.6	-365.0	24.2	351.3	310.9	Commercial banks
1 446.6	-1 958.3	-8 567.3	-4 791.3	-1 508.6	Other sectors
243.3	-307.4	-205.4	-401.5	-440.0	Errors and omissions (net)
4 760.2	2 176.0	1 519.5	1 686.0	-13.1	**Capital account balance**
4 225.2	-2 598.2	-3 192.7	-668.2	-2 449.5	**Global balance** [3]
-4 423.7	2 665.9	3 452.1	761.8	2 507.5	Total variation in reserves *(minus sign indicates an increase)*
-2.6	-1.3	0.0	0.0	0.0	Monetary gold
-115.6	-1.1	-76.2	404.0	0.0	Special Drawing Rights
-33.5	-132.6	57.4	177.7	100.4	Reserve position in IMF
-4 271.9	2 800.8	3 471.0	180.1	1 233.9	Foreign exchange assets
0.0	0.0	0.0	0.0	0.0	Other assets
0.0	0.0	0.0	0.0	1 173.2	Use of IMF credit

[1] Non factorial services also included.
[2] Net-loans received and Other assets and liabilities included.
[3] Equals to Total variation in reserves (with opposite sign) plus Counterpart items.

232. BAHAMAS: BALANCE DE PAGOS

(Millones de dólares)

	1960	1965	1970	1975	1977	1978
Exportaciones de bienes y servicios	...	...	...	588.0	705.7	829.3
Bienes fob	...	...	...	117.3	135.9	146.4
Servicios [1]	...	...	...	470.8	569.8	683.0
Transporte y seguros	...	...	...	91.6	81.3	99.8
Viajes	...	...	...	313.5	412.4	494.7
Importaciones de bienes y servicios	...	...	...	470.6	541.3	643.0
Bienes fob	...	...	...	340.6	387.5	468.0
Servicios [1]	...	...	...	130.0	153.9	175.3
Transporte y seguros	...	...	...	40.1	46.0	58.8
Viajes	...	...	...	45.6	54.3	60.7
Balance de bienes	...	...	...	-223.4	-251.6	-321.7
Balance comercial	...	...	...	117.4	164.4	186.3
Servicios de factores	...	...	...	-64.0	-84.8	-130.1
Utilidades	...	...	...	0.0	0.0	0.0
Intereses recibidos	...	...	...	124.8	4.0	7.0
Intereses pagados	...	...	...	-182.9	-78.1	-119.1
Otros	...	...	...	-5.9	-10.7	-18.0
Transferencias unilaterales privadas	...	...	...	-14.9	-18.6	-22.2
Balance en cuenta corriente	...	...	...	38.5	61.1	34.0
Transferencias unilaterales oficiales	...	...	...	4.7	5.4	7.4
Capital a largo plazo	...	...	...	37.7	39.4	-25.1
Inversión directa	...	...	...	48.8	31.1	-1.2
Inversión de cartera	...	...	0.0	0.0	6.9	-2.3
Otro capital a largo plazo	...	...	...	-11.1	1.4	-21.6
Sector oficial [2]	...	...	...	-5.6	1.5	-3.2
Préstamos recibidos	...	...	...	0.0	6.4	1.3
Amortizaciones	...	...	...	-5.6	-4.9	-4.5
Bancos comerciales [2]	...	...	...	0.0	0.0	0.0
Préstamos recibidos	...	0.0	...	0.0	0.0	0.0
Amortizaciones	...	0.0	...	0.0	0.0	0.0
Otros sectores [2]	...	...	...	-5.5	-0.1	-18.4
Préstamos recibidos	...	...	...	11.7	21.4	10.6
Amortizaciones	...	...	...	-17.1	-21.5	-29.1
Balance básico	...	...	...	80.9	105.8	16.4
Capital a corto plazo	...	...	...	-23.6	10.5	0.3
Sector oficial	...	...	...	0.0	0.0	0.0
Bancos comerciales	...	...	...	-23.6	10.5	0.3
Otros sectores	...	...	...	0.0	0.0	0.0
Errores y omisiones netos	...	...	...	-53.6	-96.4	-26.0
Balance en cuenta de capital	...	...	...	-34.7	-41.5	-43.0
Balance global [3]	...	...	...	3.7	19.6	-9.0
Variación total de las reservas (signo - indica aumento)	...	...	...	-3.4	-19.6	8.8
Oro monetario	...	...	...	0.0	0.0	-0.1
Derechos especiales de giro	0.0	0.0	0.0	0.0	0.0	0.0
Posición de reserva en el FMI	0.0	0.0	0.0	0.3	-0.3	-0.2
Activos en divisas	...	...	4.4	-3.7	-19.4	9.1
Otros activos	...	...	...	0.0	0.0	0.0
Uso de crédito del FMI	0.0	0.0	0.0	0.0	0.0	0.0

[1] Incluye Otros servicios no factoriales.
[2] Incluye Préstamos netos concedidos y Otros activos y pasivos.
[3] Es igual a Variación total de las reservas (con signo contrario), más Asientos de contrapartida.

232. BAHAMAS: BALANCE OF PAYMENTS

(Millions of dollars)

1979	1980	1981	1982	1983	
941.6	1 147.1	1 143.6	1 148.9	1 208.6	Exports of goods and services
170.5	200.5	176.2	221.5	244.8	Goods FOB
770.9	946.6	967.3	927.5	963.7	Services [1]
113.2	207.7	186.5	131.9	139.9	Transport and insurance
561.7	595.5	639.2	655.7	703.7	Travel
785.8	1 022.8	1 053.5	1 051.8	1 125.5	Imports of goods and services
597.6	801.0	787.5	740.2	801.8	Goods FOB
188.2	221.9	266.1	311.5	323.8	Services [1]
74.0	76.2	82.9	88.4	90.1	Transport and insurance
53.6	70.6	91.1	104.2	95.6	Travel
-427.1	-600.5	-611.2	-518.8	-557.0	**Trade balance (goods)**
155.9	124.4	90.0	97.1	83.0	**Trade balance (goods and services)**
-136.1	-137.6	-161.6	-134.5	-141.8	Factor services
0.0	0.0	0.0	0.0	0.0	Profits
11.1	13.0	17.0	23.7	15.4	Interest received
-134.3	-126.7	-155.9	-138.7	-138.5	Interest paid
-12.9	-24.0	-22.7	-19.6	-18.7	Others
-15.8	-19.8	-13.9	-17.8	-10.5	Private unrequited transfers
3.9	-33.1	-85.4	-55.3	-69.3	**Balance on current account**
11.9	17.8	11.1	21.5	17.4	Official unrequited transfers
4.1	10.1	141.4	69.3	15.1	Long-term capital
9.6	4.0	34.4	2.8	-5.9	Direct investment
-3.2	-3.0	-3.1	-3.2	0.0	Portfolio investment
-2.3	9.1	110.1	69.7	21.0	Other long-term capital
-4.7	-4.7	34.3	46.4	18.4	Official sector [2]
0.5	0.0	38.2	51.8	20.1	Loans received
-5.2	-4.7	-3.8	-5.2	-1.6	Amortizations
0.0	0.0	0.0	0.0	0.0	Commercial banks [2]
0.0	0.0	0.0	0.0	0.0	Loans received
0.0	0.0	0.0	0.0	0.0	Amortizations
2.4	13.7	75.8	23.3	2.6	Other sectors [2]
23.7	51.8	99.9	43.6	27.2	Loans received
-21.3	-38.0	-24.2	-20.3	-24.6	Amortizations
19.9	-5.2	67.1	35.5	-36.8	**Basic balance** [3]
-19.4	-5.0	17.6	-1.0	-15.0	Short-term capital
0.0	0.0	0.0	0.0	0.0	Official sector
-19.4	-5.0	17.6	-1.0	-15.0	Commercial banks
0.0	0.0	0.0	0.0	0.0	Other sectors
14.3	20.7	-79.1	-23.7	61.4	Errors and omissions (net)
11.0	43.7	91.1	66.1	79.0	**Capital account balance**
14.9	10.7	5.7	10.9	9.6	**Global balance** [3]
-19.4	-14.5	-8.3	-13.4	...	Total variation in reserves (minus sign indicates an increase)
0.0	0.0	0.0	0.0	0.0	Monetary gold
-4.5	1.0	-3.7	0.7	...	Special Drawing Rights
0.1	-5.0	3.5	0.3	...	Reserve position in IMF
-14.9	-10.5	-8.1	-14.4	...	Foreign exchange assets
0.0	0.0	0.0	0.0	0.0	Other assets
0.0	0.0	0.0	0.0	...	Use of IMF credit

[1] Non factorial services also included.
[2] Net-loans received and Other assets and liabilities included.
[3] Equals to Total variation in reserves (with opposite sign) plus Counterpart items.

233. BARBADOS: BALANCE DE PAGOS

(Millones de dólares)

	1960	1965	1970	1975	1977	1978
Exportaciones de bienes y servicios	36.4	59.7	94.9	208.5	252.1	317.8
Bienes fob	20.4	32.0	35.8	94.5	85.3	110.9
Servicios [1]	16.0	27.7	59.1	114.0	166.7	206.8
Transporte y seguros	3.5	7.6	7.5	22.7	27.0	33.1
Viajes	8.9	15.2	40.4	77.2	111.1	137.7
Importaciones de bienes y servicios	51.9	80.3	141.6	253.2	315.1	364.0
Bienes fob	40.6	60.8	106.9	197.1	250.2	288.1
Servicios [1]	11.3	19.5	34.7	56.1	64.9	75.9
Transporte y seguros	4.8	9.1	16.5	31.7	32.6	41.3
Viajes	0.9	1.4	3.5	6.9	9.2	9.9
Balance de bienes	**-20.2**	**-28.8**	**-71.1**	**-102.6**	**-164.9**	**-177.2**
Balance comercial	**-15.5**	**-20.6**	**-46.7**	**-44.7**	**-63.0**	**-46.2**
Servicios de factores	2.7	3.3	-0.3	-4.0	-4.3	-1.8
Utilidades	-0.4	-0.7	-4.2	-8.0	-4.6	-5.1
Intereses recibidos	1.3	2.3	3.6	4.4	2.5	5.5
Intereses pagados	-1.0	-1.9	-2.6	-6.6	-6.5	-5.9
Otros	2.8	3.6	2.8	6.2	4.3	3.8
Transferencias unilaterales privadas	1.3	2.6	3.9	6.8	12.7	14.5
Balance en cuenta corriente	**-11.5**	**-14.7**	**-43.1**	**-41.9**	**-54.5**	**-33.4**
Transferencias unilaterales oficiales	0.7	0.7	1.3	0.5	3.2	2.1
Capital a largo plazo	5.2	6.7	12.3	22.8	35.5	24.2
Inversión directa	3.0	1.7	8.5	22.1	4.7	9.3
Inversión de cartera	1.0	4.4	-0.6	0.1	0.6	2.0
Otro capital a largo plazo	1.2	0.6	4.4	0.6	30.2	12.9
Sector oficial [2]	1.2	0.6	0.9	-0.5	14.6	12.5
Préstamos recibidos	0.0	0.0	1.1	0.8	18.1	13.5
Amortizaciones	0.0	0.0	0.0	-0.8	-2.8	-0.5
Bancos comerciales [2]	0.0	0.0	0.0	-2.2	6.3	4.8
Préstamos recibidos	0.0	0.0	0.0	0.0	6.2	2.4
Amortizaciones	0.0	0.0	0.0	-0.7	0.0	0.0
Otros sectores [2]	0.0	0.0	3.5	3.3	9.3	-4.4
Préstamos recibidos	0.0	0.0	0.0	0.0	6.2	0.0
Amortizaciones	0.0	0.0	0.0	0.0	0.0	-5.0
Balance básico	**-5.6**	**-7.3**	**-29.5**	**-18.6**	**-15.9**	**-7.1**
Capital a corto plazo	1.2	1.7	0.2	-1.6	-2.2	-0.5
Sector oficial	-0.5	0.0	-0.1	-0.1	-0.7	-0.6
Bancos comerciales	0.0	1.4	-0.9	-4.9	-7.4	-15.8
Otros sectores	1.7	0.3	1.2	3.4	5.8	15.9
Errores y omisiones netos	4.4	11.2	23.6	28.7	19.7	28.8
Balance en cuenta de capital	**11.5**	**20.3**	**37.3**	**50.6**	**56.2**	**54.5**
Balance global [3]	**0.0**	**5.6**	**-5.8**	**8.7**	**1.6**	**21.0**
Variación total de las reservas (signo - indica aumento)	0.0	-5.6	4.6	-0.3	1.1	-22.6
Oro monetario	0.0	0.0	0.0	0.0	0.0	-0.1
Derechos especiales de giro	0.0	0.0	0.0	0.2	-0.0	0.0
Posición de reserva en el FMI	0.0	0.0	-2.0	-1.4	-0.2	0.1
Activos en divisas	0.0	-5.6	-2.1	0.8	-8.8	-23.0
Otros activos	0.0	0.0	8.7	0.2	2.2	-0.1
Uso de crédito del FMI	0.0	0.0	0.0	0.0	7.9	0.6

[1] Incluye Otros servicios no factoriales.
[2] Incluye Préstamos netos concedidos y Otros activos y pasivos.
[3] Es igual a Variación total de las reservas (con signo contrario), más Asientos de contrapartida.

233. BARBADOS: BALANCE OF PAYMENTS

(Millions of dollars)

1979	1980	1981	1982	1983	
425.8	552.0	532.9	604.3	677.5	Exports of goods and services
131.5	180.8	162.7	208.2	272.3	Goods FOB
294.3	371.2	370.1	396.1	405.2	Services [1]
41.1	67.7	48.5	71.0	68.0	Transport and insurance
206.7	252.4	262.7	253.4	253.7	Travel
474.8	597.9	661.0	652.1	720.9	Imports of goods and services
378.4	479.0	521.4	501.1	565.0	Goods FOB
96.4	118.8	139.5	151.0	155.9	Services [1]
51.4	64.9	73.0	74.0	74.5	Transport and insurance
12.9	19.0	22.1	26.1	21.5	Travel
-246.9	-298.2	-358.7	-292.9	-292.7	**Trade balance (goods)**
-49.0	-45.9	-128.2	-47.8	-43.4	**Trade balance (goods and services)**
-7.2	-1.2	-8.5	-11.0	-19.2	Factor services
-5.6	-5.3	-8.3	-6.3	-4.3	Profits
8.0	9.9	9.2	10.7	9.9	Interest received
-14.0	-13.0	-18.0	-23.1	-29.6	Interest paid
4.3	7.2	8.7	7.4	4.7	Others
16.9	21.5	24.1	17.1	16.7	Private unrequited transfers
-39.3	-25.6	-112.5	-41.7	-46.0	**Balance on current account**
4.9	0.0	-6.1	6.1	4.0	Official unrequited transfers
-16.9	15.4	77.7	12.6	47.5	Long-term capital
5.0	0.9	7.1	4.4	16.3	Direct investment
-2.6	21.0	1.7	-0.8	-1.3	Portfolio investment
-19.4	-6.5	69.0	8.9	32.5	Other long-term capital
2.1	3.8	48.0	11.7	28.8	Official sector [2]
8.4	7.5	49.2	16.6	29.9	Loans received
-5.7	-3.3	-0.5	-2.0	0.0	Amortizations
-6.8	-3.8	0.8	3.4	12.3	Commercial banks [2]
0.0	0.0	1.7	3.2	12.6	Loans received
-6.5	-3.6	0.0	0.0	0.0	Amortizations
-14.6	-6.5	20.2	-6.2	-8.6	Other sectors [2]
0.0	8.1	42.2	15.6	11.9	Loans received
-0.8	0.0	0.0	0.0	0.0	Amortizations
-51.3	-10.3	-40.9	-23.1	5.5	**Basic balance** [3]
22.1	33.8	67.9	4.0	6.5	Short-term capital
0.8	0.3	47.0	-7.3	-1.0	Official sector
1.2	7.9	18.0	-5.2	3.5	Commercial banks
20.2	25.6	2.8	16.4	4.0	Other sectors
33.9	-6.6	-33.6	18.3	-4.5	Errors and omissions (net)
44.1	42.6	106.0	40.8	53.6	**Capital account balance**
4.8	16.9	-6.5	-0.9	7.6	**Global balance** [3]
-6.0	-20.5	-24.7	...	...	Total variation in reserves (minus sign indicates an increase)
-0.1	-1.4	-1.5	0.0	0.0	Monetary gold
-1.9	3.1	0.4	...	...	Special Drawing Rights
0.1	-2.6	0.6	...	...	Reserve position in IMF
-4.4	-13.4	-22.5	...	...	Foreign exchange assets
0.3	-0.7	0.5	0.3	0.1	Other assets
0.1	-5.6	-2.1	...	...	Use of IMF credit

[1] Non factorial services also included.
[2] Net-loans received and Other assets and liabilities included.
[3] Equals to Total variation in reserves (with opposite sign) plus Counterpart items.

234. BOLIVIA: BALANCE DE PAGOS

(Millones de dólares)

	1960	1965	1970	1975	1977	1978
Exportaciones de bienes y servicios	57.3	124.5	204.6	485.7	695.0	703.4
Bienes fob	54.2	115.1	190.4	444.7	634.3	627.3
Servicios [1]	3.2	9.4	14.2	40.9	60.7	76.1
Transporte y seguros	0.0	1.0	1.7	6.9	11.9	15.0
Viajes	0.5	1.8	2.5	18.9	29.0	35.0
Importaciones de bienes y servicios	87.5	160.9	178.9	617.6	758.9	945.8
Bienes fob	68.2	126.6	135.2	469.9	579.0	723.9
Servicios [1]	19.3	34.3	43.7	147.8	180.0	221.7
Transporte y seguros	11.3	22.1	28.6	99.0	103.1	139.9
Viajes	1.2	3.5	3.9	25.5	38.0	41.0
Balance de bienes	**-14.0**	**-11.5**	**55.2**	**-25.1**	**55.3**	**-96.7**
Balance comercial	**-30.2**	**-36.4**	**25.7**	**-132.0**	**-64.0**	**-242.4**
Servicios de factores	-0.8	-3.5	-25.4	-11.3	-68.9	-116.1
Utilidades	3.5	0.8	-17.0	14.8	-1.4	-17.8
Intereses recibidos	0.1	0.8	2.1	6.7	3.9	0.6
Intereses pagados	-2.4	-5.2	-10.1	-30.5	-69.2	-96.4
Otros	-2.0	0.1	-0.4	-2.3	-2.1	-2.6
Transferencias unilaterales privadas	0.2	1.1	1.5	3.4	2.4	5.4
Balance en cuenta corriente	**-30.7**	**-38.8**	**1.8**	**-139.9**	**-130.6**	**-353.0**
Transferencias unilaterales oficiales	12.8	14.9	2.4	9.7	12.6	21.5
Capital a largo plazo	15.8	24.2	33.2	158.9	325.3	292.6
Inversión directa	16.5	12.5	-75.9	53.4	-1.1	11.5
Inversión de cartera	0.0	0.0	0.0	0.0	0.0	0.0
Otro capital a largo plazo	-0.7	11.7	109.1	105.5	326.3	281.1
Sector oficial [2]	-2.7	8.3	93.6	50.3	168.9	114.3
Préstamos recibidos	2.4	11.2	21.6	69.2	220.7	326.5
Amortizaciones	-3.9	-1.1	-5.1	-18.6	-41.9	-203.0
Bancos comerciales [2]	0.0	0.0	0.0	0.0	0.0	0.0
Préstamos recibidos	0.0	0.0	0.0	0.0	0.0	0.0
Amortizaciones	0.0	0.0	0.0	0.0	0.0	0.0
Otros sectores [2]	2.0	3.4	15.5	55.2	157.5	166.8
Préstamos recibidos	10.4	11.8	31.0	117.9	238.2	275.0
Amortizaciones	-8.2	-8.4	-15.5	-62.7	-80.9	-108.1
Balance básico	**-2.1**	**0.3**	**37.4**	**28.8**	**207.3**	**-38.9**
Capital a corto plazo	1.1	12.0	2.0	-17.0	-61.0	39.9
Sector oficial	0.9	12.3	2.9	4.2	42.2	-53.0
Bancos comerciales	-0.1	-0.3	-1.9	-1.3	37.9	50.6
Otros sectores	0.3	0.0	1.0	-19.9	-141.0	42.3
Errores y omisiones netos	-3.1	1.3	-39.7	-47.1	-79.0	-84.9
Balance en cuenta de capital	**26.6**	**52.4**	**-2.1**	**104.5**	**197.9**	**269.5**
Balance global [3]	**-4.1**	**13.6**	**-0.3**	**-35.3**	**67.3**	**-83.6**
Variación total de las reservas (signo - indica aumento)	3.9	-14.1	-5.5	33.5	-44.0	55.3
Oro monetario	0.0	-2.0	-1.0	-1.9	-7.8	-1.8
Derechos especiales de giro	0.0	0.0	-2.7	-5.0	1.1	-11.4
Posición de reserva en el FMI	0.0	-1.1	0.0	0.0	-1.6	-2.7
Activos en divisas	0.3	-11.0	0.2	41.7	-59.6	55.5
Otros activos	5.0	0.0	0.0	0.0	23.9	-3.8
Uso de crédito del FMI	-1.4	0.0	-2.0	-1.2	0.0	19.5

[1] Incluye Otros servicios no factoriales.
[2] Incluye Préstamos netos concedidos y Otros activos y pasivos.
[3] Es igual a Variación total de las reservas (con signo contrario), más Asientos de contrapartida.

234. BOLIVIA: BALANCE OF PAYMENTS

(Millions of dollars)

1979	1980	1981	1982	1983	
854.6	1 043.2	1 011.7	912.5	853.6	Exports of goods and services
761.8	941.9	909.3	827.7	757.1	Goods FOB
92.8	101.3	102.7	84.8	96.5	Services [1]
28.8	32.4	34.0	26.5	36.0	Transport and insurance
36.9	40.0	36.1	30.0	40.0	Travel
1 081.0	953.5	994.5	632.9	719.2	Imports of goods and services
814.9	680.2	680.0	428.7	482.0	Goods FOB
266.0	273.4	314.4	204.2	237.2	Services [1]
177.0	168.0	196.1	100.8	130.3	Transport and insurance
45.0	52.0	49.9	40.0	20.0	Travel
-53.0	261.7	229.3	399.0	275.2	**Trade balance (goods)**
-226.4	89.7	17.3	279.5	134.4	**Trade balance (goods and services)**
-183.4	-263.8	-342.8	-417.5	-423.9	Factor services
-27.5	-19.0	-29.4	-24.0	-2.5	Profits
2.0	14.1	15.0	6.7	21.8	Interest received
-155.0	-255.9	-325.4	-397.4	-443.3	Interest paid
-2.8	-3.0	-2.8	-2.8	0.0	Others
11.4	8.1	13.3	16.7	18.1	Private unrequited transfers
-398.5	-166.2	-312.4	-121.3	-271.4	**Balance on current account**
40.7	47.9	26.3	28.8	88.5	Official unrequited transfers
257.5	252.1	473.0	181.8	436.2	Long-term capital
18.0	41.5	60.0	36.9	42.9	Direct investment
0.0	-2.6	0.0	0.0	0.0	Portfolio investment
239.5	213.2	413.0	145.0	393.3	Other long-term capital
88.8	263.8	310.2	123.4	416.7	Official sector [2]
148.6	333.9	328.1	138.3	74.0	Loans received
-56.7	-56.0	-52.8	-66.4	-65.8	Amortizations
77.1	-24.1	25.9	-11.7	-1.7	Commercial banks [2]
87.2	12.8	9.6	6.8	4.2	Loans received
-10.1	-21.2	-6.1	-18.7	-4.7	Amortizations
73.6	-26.5	76.9	33.2	-21.7	Other sectors [2]
151.1	94.1	95.9	65.8	20.9	Loans received
-77.5	-89.7	-55.0	-37.1	-33.6	Amortizations
-100.3	133.9	186.9	89.3	253.3	**Basic balance[3]**
147.4	-20.4	148.2	-6.6	-331.5	Short-term capital
191.8	-29.2	200.1	118.3	-242.9	Official sector
-10.5	-19.4	6.0	20.2	-16.3	Commercial banks
-34.0	28.2	-57.9	-145.2	-72.4	Other sectors
-27.9	-260.5	-329.2	-51.2	59.0	Errors and omissions (net)
417.5	19.1	318.5	152.9	252.3	**Capital account balance**
18.9	-147.1	6.2	31.6	-19.1	**Global balance[3]**
-24.3	136.5	-22.9	-38.0	13.8	Total variation in reserves (minus sign indicates an increase)
-1.7	-2.5	-2.9	-1.9	-0.9	Monetary gold
18.4	0.0	-0.1	0.1	-0.1	Special Drawing Rights
11.7	0.0	0.0	0.0	0.0	Reserve position in IMF
-38.7	72.1	6.5	-56.2	19.5	Foreign exchange assets
-14.3	6.2	-17.2	5.1	-7.8	Other assets
0.2	60.6	-9.1	14.9	3.0	Use of IMF credit

[1] Non factorial services also included.
[2] Net-loans received and Other assets and liabilities included.
[3] Equals to Total variation in reserves (with opposite sign) plus Counterpart items.

IV. BALANCE DE PAGOS

235. BRASIL: BALANCE DE PAGOS

(Millones de dólares)

	1960	1965	1970	1975	1977	1978
Exportaciones de bienes y servicios	1 459.0	1 747.0	3 059.0	9 416.8	13 003.9	13 665.6
Bienes fob	1 270.0	1 596.0	2 739.0	8 493.0	11 921.6	12 473.0
Servicios [1]	189.0	151.0	320.0	927.4	1 082.3	1 191.3
Transporte y seguros	48.0	58.0	167.0	483.0	546.3	569.6
Viajes	24.0	30.0	30.0	71.8	54.9	68.9
Importaciones de bienes y servicios	1 786.0	1 280.0	3 295.0	14 323.0	14 645.2	16 495.3
Bienes fob	1 293.0	941.0	2 507.0	12 042.0	12 021.9	13 631.7
Servicios [1]	493.0	339.0	788.0	2 279.9	2 620.9	2 863.5
Transporte y seguros	131.0	88.0	349.0	1 434.5	1 522.4	1 580.0
Viajes	72.0	31.0	160.0	420.7	228.9	254.2
Balance de bienes	**-23.0**	**655.0**	**232.0**	**-3 548.9**	**-100.4**	**-1 158.6**
Balance comercial	**-327.0**	**467.0**	**-236.0**	**-4 906.3**	**-1 641.3**	**-2 829.7**
Servicios de factores	-194.0	-258.0	-622.0	-2 105.5	-3 471.8	-4 278.1
Utilidades	-60.0	-102.0	-387.0	-531.6	-1 332.4	-1 535.0
Intereses recibidos	3.0	10.0	49.0	366.3	360.6	644.2
Intereses pagados	-137.0	-166.0	-291.0	-1 862.1	-2 463.7	-3 343.3
Otros	0.0	0.0	7.0	-75.7	-36.3	-45.2
Transferencias unilaterales privadas	-13.0	39.0	-3.0	12.5	-4.7	69.8
Balance en cuenta corriente	**-534.0**	**248.0**	**-861.0**	**-6 996.9**	**-5 115.5**	**-7 039.2**
Transferencias unilaterales oficiales	17.0	36.0	24.0	-9.8	3.6	2.6
Capital a largo plazo	149.0	132.0	1 217.0	4 936.2	6 041.2	10 087.9
Inversión directa	141.0	154.0	407.0	1 190.3	1 687.6	1 882.5
Inversión de cartera	0.0	0.0	0.0	0.0	0.0	0.0
Otro capital a largo plazo	8.0	-22.0	810.0	3 745.9	4 353.6	8 205.4
Sector oficial [2]	14.0	58.0	130.0	1 653.3	2 406.3	3 965.2
Préstamos recibidos	151.0	250.0	469.0	2 329.7	4 097.6	6 239.9
Amortizaciones	-137.0	-82.0	-330.0	-667.3	-1 690.6	-2 062.0
Bancos comerciales [2]	0.0	0.0	479.0	424.4	450.5	1 853.5
Préstamos recibidos	0.0	0.0	571.0	935.6	1 270.5	2 897.8
Amortizaciones	0.0	0.0	-92.0	-510.1	-818.9	-1 043.0
Otros sectores [2]	-6.0	-80.0	201.0	1 668.2	1 496.8	2 386.7
Préstamos recibidos	265.0	113.0	430.0	2 870.4	3 394.8	4 978.5
Amortizaciones	-270.0	-132.0	-228.0	-1 007.7	-1 622.9	-2 169.3
Balance básico	**-368.0**	**416.0**	**380.0**	**-2 070.5**	**929.3**	**3 051.3**
Capital a corto plazo	322.0	-419.0	75.0	1 446.6	220.1	1 272.8
Sector oficial	241.0	-439.0	-14.0	-6.3	-317.7	499.0
Bancos comerciales	16.0	20.0	-247.0	-94.8	237.3	896.7
Otros sectores	65.0	0.0	336.0	1 547.7	300.5	-122.9
Errores y omisiones netos	10.0	212.0	39.0	-438.2	-628.4	299.9
Balance en cuenta de capital	**498.0**	**-39.0**	**1 354.0**	**5 931.1**	**5 636.4**	**11 665.8**
Balance global [3]	**-36.0**	**209.0**	**493.0**	**-1 065.8**	**520.9**	**4 626.6**
Variación total de las reservas (signo - indica aumento)	36.0	-219.0	-530.0	1 236.7	-710.5	-4 639.5
Oro monetario	40.0	28.0	0.0	0.0	-7.0	-3.9
Derechos especiales de giro	0.0	0.0	-62.0	8.8	-11.5	-29.6
Posición de reserva en el FMI	0.0	0.0	-105.0	6.2	-6.1	13.3
Activos en divisas	-18.0	-267.0	-363.0	1 221.7	-685.8	-4 619.3
Otros activos	-1.0	0.0	0.0	0.0	0.0	0.0
Uso de crédito del FMI	15.0	20.0	0.0	0.0	0.0	0.0

[1] Incluye Otros servicios no factoriales.
[2] Incluye Préstamos netos concedidos y Otros activos y pasivos.
[3] Es igual a Variación total de las reservas (con signo contrario), más Asientos de contrapartida.

235. BRAZIL: BALANCE OF PAYMENTS

(Millions of dollars)

1979	1980	1981	1982	1983	
16 706.6	21 857.5	25 523.4	21 966.7	23 618.9	*Exports of goods and services*
15 244.4	20 131.5	23 275.5	20 172.3	21 905.7	*Goods FOB*
1 464.8	1 726.0	2 247.8	1 791.0	1 712.1	*Services* [1]
704.6	843.5	1 101.5	1 013.4	1 118.8	*Transport and insurance*
73.6	124.9	242.4	66.5	39.6	*Travel*
21 725.3	27 792.5	27 200.2	24 761.9	19 539.9	*Imports of goods and services*
17 961.3	22 954.7	22 091.4	19 395.4	15 434.3	*Goods FOB*
3 763.9	4 837.8	5 108.8	5 365.4	4 105.7	*Services* [1]
2 104.2	2 758.3	2 786.2	2 460.4	2 025.2	*Transport and insurance*
310.0	367.3	406.6	912.9	430.7	*Travel*
-2 716.9	-2 823.1	1 184.0	777.0	6 471.5	**Trade balance (goods)**
-5 018.7	-5 935.0	-1 676.9	-2 795.2	4 079.0	**Trade balance (goods and services)**
-5 478.0	-7 040.7	-10 274.0	-13 509.2	-11 025.3	*Factor services*
-1 356.2	-719.7	-1 112.0	-2 141.4	-1 452.8	*Profits*
1 157.1	1 146.5	1 143.6	1 197.7	707.5	*Interest received*
-5 260.7	-7 455.7	-10 305.8	-12 550.3	-10 267.0	*Interest paid*
-16.8	-9.2	-1.1	-14.1	-12.9	*Others*
11.7	127.8	188.6	-10.7	106.1	*Private unrequited transfers*
-10 482.4	-12 847.9	-11 760.0	-16 314.1	-6 842.3	**Balance on current account**
5.2	42.1	9.6	2.4	2.2	*Official unrequited transfers*
6 466.2	7 104.1	11 659.4	8 010.8	1 851.5	*Long-term capital*
2 222.7	1 544.1	2 312.9	2 533.8	1 372.0	*Direct investment*
659.1	354.0	-1.6	-0.9	-285.9	*Portfolio investment*
3 584.4	5 206.0	9 348.1	5 478.0	765.4	*Other long-term capital*
3 370.2	-14.3	60.1	1 744.2	3 132.3	*Official sector* [2]
4 664.6	1 841.3	1 649.6	3 367.8	4 679.4	*Loans received*
-1 277.7	-1 366.0	-1 319.5	-1 286.4	-1 649.9	*Amortizations*
486.4	2 104.9	4 053.9	1 680.8	-1 520.0	*Commercial banks* [2]
1 980.5	4 004.7	6 408.7	4 239.5	1 136.0	*Loans received*
-1 494.1	-1 916.8	-2 360.6	-2 558.6	-2 656.1	*Amortizations*
-272.3	3 115.4	5 234.1	2 053.0	-846.9	*Other sectors* [2]
4 248.5	6 084.6	9 632.7	6 674.7	2 527.0	*Loans received*
-3 781.2	-3 394.0	-3 760.8	-4 264.3	-3 358.4	*Amortizations*
-4 011.0	-5 701.7	-91.1	-8 300.8	-4 988.6	**Basic balance** [3]
-122.2	2 572.4	1 132.3	3 476.0	3 681.9	*Short-term capital*
274.2	-31.0	-6.3	3 878.9	4 756.4	*Official sector*
-422.4	607.7	1 039.4	-135.7	-710.3	*Commercial banks*
26.0	1 995.7	99.2	-267.2	-364.2	*Other sectors*
1 233.3	-342.5	-418.1	-368.7	-588.2	*Errors and omissions (net)*
7 582.5	9 378.7	12 380.9	11 119.5	4 946.3	**Capital account balance**
-2 899.9	-3 469.3	620.9	-5 194.6	-1 896.0	**Global balance** [3]
2 859.7	3 321.8	-746.9	4 157.3	1 213.8	*Total variation in reserves (minus sign indicates an increase)*
0.0	-103.2	-129.7	824.1	-155.9	*Monetary gold*
-143.6	-0.6	-68.1	452.0	0.0	*Special Drawing Rights*
-60.0	-103.3	80.4	-23.0	287.0	*Reserve position in IMF*
3 063.3	3 301.0	-844.3	2 245.0	-714.0	*Foreign exchange assets*
0.0	227.9	214.8	108.7	-297.4	*Other assets*
0.0	0.0	0.0	550.5	2 094.1	*Use of IMF credit*

[1] *Non factorial services also included.*
[2] *Net-loans received and Other assets and liabilities included.*
[3] *Equals to Total variation in reserves (with opposite sign) plus Counterpart items.*

IV. BALANCE DE PAGOS

236. COLOMBIA: BALANCE DE PAGOS

(Millones de dólares)

	1960	1965	1970	1975	1977	1978
Exportaciones de bienes y servicios	574.0	694.0	977.0	2 134.5	3 403.3	3 958.8
Bienes fob	480.2	581.0	788.0	1 716.8	2 713.3	3 206.4
Servicios [1]	93.8	113.0	189.0	417.7	690.0	752.5
Transporte y seguros	39.1	62.0	95.0	174.8	290.7	305.5
Viajes	22.7	28.0	54.0	163.9	245.2	283.0
Importaciones de bienes y servicios	634.4	636.0	1 126.0	2 026.4	2 760.0	3 426.7
Bienes fob	496.4	430.0	802.0	1 424.2	1 978.9	2 564.1
Servicios [1]	138.0	206.0	324.0	602.2	781.1	862.6
Transporte y seguros	69.7	89.0	163.0	276.8	382.9	420.7
Viajes	28.3	50.0	66.0	154.2	199.6	229.1
Balance de bienes	**-16.2**	**151.0**	**-14.0**	**292.6**	**734.4**	**642.3**
Balance comercial	**-60.4**	**58.0**	**-149.0**	**108.1**	**643.3**	**532.1**
Servicios de factores	-39.6	-91.0	-180.0	-261.0	-261.5	-283.0
Utilidades	-27.1	-25.0	-91.0	-68.0	-86.4	-121.4
Intereses recibidos	2.4	0.0	16.0	55.9	65.4	123.9
Intereses pagados	-14.9	-54.0	-105.0	-250.1	-252.2	-304.2
Otros	0.0	-12.0	0.0	1.2	11.7	18.8
Transferencias unilaterales privadas	0.4	4.0	-4.0	26.7	53.7	45.1
Balance en cuenta corriente	**-99.6**	**-29.0**	**-333.0**	**-126.3**	**435.5**	**294.2**
Transferencias unilaterales oficiales	5.3	8.0	40.0	17.0	4.7	27.5
Capital a largo plazo	-9.4	43.0	227.0	295.0	230.0	95.2
Inversión directa	2.5	10.0	39.0	35.2	43.2	67.6
Inversión de cartera	-3.5	-4.0	-2.0	-1.2	-2.3	-2.5
Otro capital a largo plazo	-8.4	37.0	190.0	261.0	189.1	30.0
Sector oficial [2]	-54.7	-7.0	127.0	172.4	11.7	30.0
Préstamos recibidos	10.6	54.0	173.0	231.9	87.6	155.2
Amortizaciones	-58.8	-58.0	-46.0	-53.4	-74.7	-102.7
Bancos comerciales [2]	0.0	0.0	0.0	0.0	0.0	0.0
Préstamos recibidos	0.0	0.0	0.0	0.0	0.0	0.0
Amortizaciones	0.0	0.0	0.0	0.0	0.0	0.0
Otros sectores [2]	46.3	44.0	63.0	88.6	177.5	0.0
Préstamos recibidos	24.3	62.0	148.0	259.8	332.7	207.8
Amortizaciones	-7.9	-17.0	-85.0	-171.2	-155.3	-207.8
Balance básico	**-103.7**	**22.0**	**-66.0**	**185.8**	**670.2**	**416.9**
Capital a corto plazo	2.1	-83.0	102.0	-116.6	-256.9	13.8
Sector oficial	2.4	-2.0	-13.0	-21.9	-3.5	15.0
Bancos comerciales	11.4	15.0	57.0	1.2	-203.1	13.8
Otros sectores	-11.7	-96.0	58.0	-95.9	-50.2	-15.0
Errores y omisiones netos	43.8	67.0	-18.0	9.7	158.8	18.8
Balance en cuenta de capital	**41.8**	**35.0**	**351.0**	**204.0**	**136.6**	**154.0**
Balance global [3]	**-57.8**	**6.0**	**18.0**	**77.7**	**572.1**	**448.2**
Variación total de las reservas (signo - indica aumento)	42.7	-16.0	-36.0	-72.3	-660.6	-675.5
Oro monetario	-7.2	23.0	9.0	-29.1	-12.8	-56.3
Derechos especiales de giro	0.0	0.0	0.0	7.2	-3.7	-17.9
Posición de reserva en el FMI	-21.0	0.0	0.0	2.1	-41.3	2.3
Activos en divisas	74.0	-15.0	6.0	-52.4	-602.8	-603.6
Otros activos	-3.1	0.0	0.0	0.0	0.0	0.0
Uso de crédito del FMI	0.0	-24.0	-51.0	0.0	0.0	0.0

[1] Incluye Otros servicios no factoriales.
[2] Incluye Préstamos netos concedidos y Otros activos y pasivos.
[3] Es igual a Variación total de las reservas (con signo contrario), más Asientos de contrapartida.

474

236. COLOMBIA: BALANCE OF PAYMENTS

(Millions of dollars)

1979	1980	1981	1982	1983	
4 525.9	5 315.4	4 292.1	4 435.9	4 032.6	Exports of goods and services
3 506.5	4 062.1	3 219.1	3 214.9	3 002.8	Goods FOB
1 019.4	1 253.4	1 073.0	1 221.0	1 029.8	Services [1]
334.6	433.4	479.9	437.2	397.8	Transport and insurance
357.9	402.2	376.2	382.0	402.1	Travel
3 919.9	5 456.0	6 025.5	6 703.5	6 086.9	Imports of goods and services
2 996.1	4 300.3	4 762.6	5 404.1	4 758.7	Goods FOB
923.8	1 155.8	1 262.9	1 299.4	1 328.2	Services [1]
431.5	648.2	727.5	793.8	781.7	Transport and insurance
236.4	223.9	253.5	213.1	284.5	Travel
510.3	-238.2	-1 543.5	-2 189.3	-1 755.9	**Trade balance (goods)**
605.9	-140.6	-1 733.4	-2 267.6	-2 054.3	**Trade balance (goods and services)**
-215.8	-183.5	-404.5	-796.0	-857.6	Factor services
-49.1	-41.6	-121.5	-139.1	-73.8	Profits
249.4	471.2	632.0	497.9	185.0	Interest received
-456.1	-627.3	-936.3	-1 146.0	-950.7	Interest paid
40.1	14.3	21.2	-8.8	-18.2	Others
99.5	165.3	242.9	166.7	173.2	Private unrequited transfers
489.7	-158.8	-1 894.9	-2 896.9	-2 738.7	**Balance on current account**
1.3	0.0	0.0	2.2	0.0	Official unrequited transfers
724.8	797.8	1 622.5	1 609.6	1 331.4	Long-term capital
104.7	48.2	212.2	337.8	285.5	Direct investment
-11.6	-2.6	-1.2	-6.6	0.0	Portfolio investment
631.8	752.3	1 411.5	1 278.4	1 045.9	Other long-term capital
396.6	505.0	772.3	323.5	131.5	Official sector [2]
600.8	679.4	1 007.0	505.6	330.4	Loans received
-188.6	-127.5	-185.1	-177.7	-198.9	Amortizations
0.0	0.0	0.0	0.0	0.0	Commercial banks [2]
0.0	0.0	0.0	0.0	0.0	Loans received
0.0	0.0	0.0	0.0	0.0	Amortizations
235.1	247.3	639.1	955.0	914.3	Other sectors [2]
511.6	437.3	990.5	1 207.8	1 359.2	Loans received
-276.5	-190.0	-351.4	-252.8	-444.9	Amortizations
1 215.8	639.1	-272.4	-1 285.1	-1 407.3	**Basic balance**[3]
175.7	40.3	389.1	346.7	-237.4	Short-term capital
-22.0	-56.0	35.4	37.5	92.0	Official sector
376.0	171.8	188.7	131.4	-4.3	Commercial banks
-178.3	-75.5	165.1	177.7	-325.1	Other sectors
68.5	374.8	316.0	64.0	-265.2	Errors and omissions (net)
969.0	1 213.0	2 327.7	2 021.4	828.8	**Capital account balance**
1 458.7	1 054.2	432.8	-875.5	-1 909.9	**Global balance**[3]
-1 551.7	-1 311.4	-198.8	711.3	1 782.4	Total variation in reserves (minus sign indicates an increase)
-74.9	-324.1	-288.9	-168.9	-177.5	Monetary gold
-45.3	-13.6	-30.6	-39.7	-19.3	Special Drawing Rights
-6.3	-49.2	-30.4	-16.0	-81.0	Reserve position in IMF
-1 425.2	-924.5	151.1	936.0	2 060.1	Foreign exchange assets
0.0	0.0	0.0	0.0	0.0	Other assets
0.0	0.0	0.0	0.0	0.0	Use of IMF credit

[1] Non factorial services also included.
[2] Net-loans received and Other assets and liabilities included.
[3] Equals to Total variation in reserves (with opposite sign) plus Counterpart items.

237. COSTA RICA: BALANCE DE PAGOS

(Millones de dólares)

	1960	1965	1970	1975	1977	1978
Exportaciones de bienes y servicios	104.5	135.8	276.9	596.3	958.7	1 007.7
Bienes fob	87.0	111.7	231.0	493.1	827.8	863.9
Servicios [1]	17.5	24.1	45.9	103.2	130.8	143.9
Transporte y seguros	2.9	6.5	13.3	28.5	35.1	28.2
Viajes	6.9	10.5	22.1	51.7	62.3	72.4
Importaciones de bienes y servicios	120.9	197.9	341.1	757.6	1 120.4	1 274.2
Bienes fob	98.9	160.9	286.8	627.2	925.1	1 049.4
Servicios [1]	22.0	37.0	54.3	130.4	195.2	224.9
Transporte y seguros	13.1	21.4	34.7	81.6	114.8	129.5
Viajes	5.2	10.1	12.7	35.0	51.4	61.6
Balance de bienes	**-11.9**	**-49.2**	**-55.8**	**-134.2**	**-97.4**	**-185.5**
Balance comercial	**-16.4**	**-62.1**	**-64.2**	**-161.4**	**-161.7**	**-266.4**
Servicios de factores	-3.7	-14.1	-15.8	-65.9	-79.6	-113.3
Utilidades	-2.6	-8.4	-3.8	-24.2	-18.4	-26.9
Intereses recibidos	0.3	0.5	1.0	4.2	9.5	16.3
Intereses pagados	-1.4	-5.5	-10.8	-41.0	-67.9	-99.8
Otros	0.0	-0.7	-2.2	-5.0	-2.7	-2.9
Transferencias unilaterales privadas	0.8	4.9	3.4	9.5	15.4	15.9
Balance en cuenta corriente	**-19.3**	**-71.3**	**-76.6**	**-217.8**	**-226.0**	**-364.0**
Transferencias unilaterales oficiales	3.3	3.5	2.5	0.1	0.4	0.8
Capital a largo plazo	14.0	33.0	43.8	238.0	299.6	352.7
Inversión directa	1.6	0.1	26.4	69.0	62.5	47.0
Inversión de cartera	-0.4	2.8	-0.4	0.0	3.5	20.9
Otro capital a largo plazo	12.8	30.1	17.8	169.0	233.6	284.8
Sector oficial [2]	11.7	2.4	0.3	59.5	81.1	114.3
Préstamos recibidos	14.9	33.3	11.0	82.0	99.5	241.3
Amortizaciones	-2.6	-28.8	-9.2	-22.0	-17.7	-120.1
Bancos comerciales [2]	1.5	5.9	0.3	18.2	37.2	-11.5
Préstamos recibidos	1.5	6.4	3.9	24.3	50.7	11.6
Amortizaciones	0.0	-0.5	-3.5	-6.1	-13.5	-23.2
Otros sectores [2]	-0.4	21.8	17.2	91.3	115.2	182.0
Préstamos recibidos	0.7	34.1	27.3	164.0	235.8	332.8
Amortizaciones	-1.1	-12.3	-10.1	-72.7	-120.6	-150.7
Balance básico	**-2.0**	**-34.8**	**-30.3**	**20.3**	**73.9**	**-10.5**
Capital a corto plazo	1.9	14.9	25.4	-67.1	64.2	88.3
Sector oficial	0.2	-1.3	2.4	-21.6	4.0	57.3
Bancos comerciales	-1.8	5.7	0.3	-0.4	5.3	2.3
Otros sectores	3.5	10.5	22.7	-45.2	55.0	28.7
Errores y omisiones netos	-1.1	15.5	-10.5	32.4	-27.4	-50.7
Balance en cuenta de capital	**18.1**	**66.9**	**61.2**	**203.4**	**336.8**	**391.3**
Balance global [3]	**-1.2**	**-4.4**	**-15.4**	**-14.4**	**110.8**	**27.3**
Variación total de las reservas (signo - indica aumento)	1.2	4.4	11.6	16.7	-108.2	-18.3
Oro monetario	0.0	0.0	0.0	0.0	-0.5	-0.3
Derechos especiales de giro	0.0	0.0	-0.2	-2.0	-5.3	2.8
Posición de reserva en el FMI	-0.1	0.0	-4.0	0.0	0.0	-10.2
Activos en divisas	1.2	-1.2	17.1	-4.7	-89.8	4.0
Otros activos	0.1	-1.5	-1.3	11.3	-10.7	-10.8
Uso de crédito del FMI	0.0	7.1	0.0	12.1	-1.9	-3.9

[1] Incluye Otros servicios no factoriales.
[2] Incluye Préstamos netos concedidos y Otros activos y pasivos.
[3] Es igual a Variación total de las reservas (con signo contrario), más Asientos de contrapartida.

237. COSTA RICA: BALANCE OF PAYMENTS

(Millions of dollars)

1979	1980	1981	1982	1983	
1 097.4	1 198.3	1 175.3	1 115.6	1 133.6	Exports of goods and services
942.0	1 000.8	1 002.5	869.0	870.7	Goods FOB
156.1	196.9	172.9	247.6	262.1	Services [1]
32.8	48.3	33.3	56.9	60.0	Transport and insurance
73.8	84.9	95.6	132.9	132.9	Travel
1 518.7	1 657.5	1 302.4	1 042.8	1 147.6	Imports of goods and services
1 257.2	1 375.2	1 090.5	804.9	892.8	Goods FOB
261.8	282.6	213.3	237.6	253.8	Services [1]
155.2	176.6	128.4	129.9	134.2	Transport and insurance
63.4	60.4	48.5	43.9	52.3	Travel
-315.2	-374.3	-88.1	64.1	-22.0	**Trade balance (goods)**
-421.3	-459.2	-127.1	72.8	-13.9	**Trade balance (goods and services)**
-149.6	-218.4	-307.8	-407.2	-367.7	Factor services
-16.7	-16.0	5.0	5.0	-2.6	Profits
10.9	15.6	20.3	24.2	38.9	Interest received
-140.3	-215.8	-329.2	-433.1	-401.1	Interest paid
-3.6	-2.2	-3.8	-3.2	-2.9	Others
16.5	19.8	27.2	29.6	23.1	Private unrequited transfers
-554.4	-657.8	-407.6	-304.8	-358.5	**Balance on current account**
-4.3	-5.3	-0.1	6.3	41.8	Official unrequited transfers
352.9	402.2	215.4	-90.0	1 401.4	Long-term capital
42.4	48.2	66.2	26.5	49.7	Direct investment
0.0	124.1	0.4	0.4	0.0	Portfolio investment
310.5	229.9	148.9	-116.9	1 351.7	Other long-term capital
220.7	81.0	113.7	-148.7	1 368.1	Official sector [2]
304.3	111.5	169.1	125.6	1 404.9	Loans received
-79.2	-25.2	-48.3	-261.8	-52.8	Amortizations
34.9	9.4	-17.8	-20.2	-6.7	Commercial banks [2]
62.9	32.2	11.4	6.1	1.1	Loans received
-27.8	-22.6	-29.2	-26.5	-7.7	Amortizations
54.9	139.5	53.1	52.0	-9.6	Other sectors [2]
357.5	266.9	186.4	167.9	69.4	Loans received
-302.5	-127.4	-133.4	-115.8	-79.0	Amortizations
-205.8	-261.0	-192.3	-388.5	1 084.8	**Basic balance**[3]
6.1	422.5	42.4	351.0	-1 164.2	Short-term capital
2.1	286.9	45.5	426.7	-870.9	Official sector
5.8	32.0	5.1	41.5	-77.7	Commercial banks
-1.7	103.6	-8.3	-117.2	-215.6	Other sectors
80.4	-71.2	100.0	164.2	132.5	Errors and omissions (net)
435.6	749.4	357.8	430.5	412.2	**Capital account balance**
-118.8	91.6	-49.9	125.7	53.8	**Global balance**[3]
112.6	-33.4	64.7	-124.8	27.7	Total variation in reserves (minus sign indicates an increase)
-0.3	0.0	27.6	-6.5	-0.5	Monetary gold
-2.0	5.9	0.0	-0.1	-2.9	Special Drawing Rights
0.3	9.9	0.0	0.0	0.0	Reserve position in IMF
77.0	-42.9	14.2	-94.6	-82.3	Foreign exchange assets
11.6	-5.5	-23.0	-13.8	14.4	Other assets
26.0	-0.8	45.8	-9.8	99.0	Use of IMF credit

[1] Non factorial services also included.
[2] Net-loans received and Other assets and liabilities included.
[3] Equals to Total variation in reserves (with opposite sign) plus Counterpart items.

IV. BALANCE DE PAGOS

238. CHILE: BALANCE DE PAGOS

(Millones de dólares)

	1960	1965	1970	1975	1977	1978
Exportaciones de bienes y servicios	550.5	792.0	1 247.0	1 838.2	2 603.6	2 940.9
Bienes fob	480.0	692.0	1 113.0	1 590.5	2 185.6	2 460.2
Servicios [1]	70.5	100.0	134.0	248.9	418.0	482.0
Transporte y seguros	18.2	38.0	61.0	104.4	149.4	232.9
Viajes	33.9	45.0	50.0	82.6	81.7	108.9
Importaciones de bienes y servicios	663.2	716.0	1 148.0	2 049.5	2 870.9	3 620.8
Bienes fob	472.3	530.0	867.0	1 520.1	2 150.6	2 885.9
Servicios [1]	190.9	186.0	281.0	529.4	720.4	734.9
Transporte y seguros	98.4	125.0	138.0	289.0	342.1	420.7
Viajes	67.4	30.0	87.0	112.9	205.5	130.2
Balance de bienes	7.7	162.0	246.0	70.4	35.0	-425.7
Balance comercial	-112.7	76.0	99.0	-211.3	-267.4	-679.8
Servicios de factores	-64.6	-128.0	-196.0	-291.4	-379.4	-505.8
Utilidades	-46.1	-62.0	-104.0	-8.5	-23.4	-32.6
Intereses recibidos	0.0	0.0	27.0	3.6	17.5	41.3
Intereses pagados	-18.5	-66.0	-119.0	-280.5	-358.4	-497.0
Otros	0.0	0.0	0.0	-6.1	-14.0	-16.3
Transferencias unilaterales privadas	12.7	10.0	2.0	3.6	80.6	75.1
Balance en cuenta corriente	-164.6	-42.0	-95.0	-497.8	-567.4	-1 110.5
Transferencias unilaterales oficiales	34.4	-1.0	4.0	8.5	16.3	22.5
Capital a largo plazo	46.7	115.0	140.0	172.4	50.2	1 509.9
Inversión directa	29.0	-38.0	-79.0	49.8	16.3	176.5
Inversión de cartera	-8.6	-4.0	-10.0	-6.1	-7.0	0.0
Otro capital a largo plazo	26.3	157.0	229.0	128.7	40.9	1 333.4
Sector oficial [2]	11.7	148.0	150.0	204.0	-157.6	166.5
Préstamos recibidos	27.3	154.0	154.0	388.5	218.3	587.2
Amortizaciones	-6.8	-18.0	-76.0	-184.6	-357.3	-420.7
Bancos comerciales [2]	0.0	0.0	0.0	13.4	7.0	290.5
Préstamos recibidos	0.0	0.0	0.0	14.6	17.5	295.5
Amortizaciones	0.0	0.0	0.0	-1.2	-10.5	-3.8
Otros sectores [2]	14.6	9.0	79.0	-88.6	191.5	876.4
Préstamos recibidos	41.4	77.0	145.0	230.7	667.8	1 438.5
Amortizaciones	-26.8	-68.0	-66.0	-320.5	-477.5	-562.1
Balance básico	-83.5	72.0	49.0	-316.9	-500.9	421.9
Capital a corto plazo	33.7	-30.0	-27.0	140.8	556.9	449.5
Sector oficial	24.7	8.0	5.0	65.6	43.2	13.8
Bancos comerciales	-0.7	-16.0	-6.0	-59.5	127.3	57.6
Otros sectores	9.7	-22.0	-26.0	134.8	386.4	378.1
Errores y omisiones netos	52.2	8.0	57.0	-109.3	115.6	-127.7
Balance en cuenta de capital	167.0	92.0	174.0	212.5	737.9	1 854.2
Balance global [3]	2.4	50.0	79.0	-285.3	170.5	743.7
Variación total de las reservas (signo - indica aumento)	-2.4	-50.0	-100.0	184.3	-124.6	-683.1
Oro monetario	-3.5	-1.0	2.0	6.1	-1.2	-1.3
Derechos especiales de giro	0.0	0.0	-22.0	-7.4	-11.0	39.5
Posición de reserva en el FMI	0.0	0.0	0.0	0.0	0.0	-49.5
Activos en divisas	20.0	-48.0	-24.0	-6.0	-11.0	-654.0
Otros activos	0.1	0.0	0.0	0.0	0.0	0.0
Uso de crédito del FMI	-19.0	-1.0	-56.0	191.6	-101.4	-17.8

[1] Incluye Otros servicios no factoriales.
[2] Incluye Préstamos netos concedidos y Otros activos y pasivos.
[3] Es igual a Variación total de las reservas (con signo contrario), más Asientos de contrapartida.

238. CHILE: BALANCE OF PAYMENTS

(Millions of dollars)

1979	1980	1981	1982	1983	
4 618.9	5 967.5	5 007.9	4 641.3	4 626.1	Exports of goods and services
3 834.7	4 705.0	3 835.8	3 706.2	3 851.9	Goods FOB
784.2	1 262.5	1 172.1	936.2	774.2	Services [1]
347.5	433.4	372.6	318.0	269.5	Transport and insurance
149.9	174.4	200.5	124.8	95.2	Travel
5 217.1	7 023.1	8 252.9	5 019.9	3 986.6	Imports of goods and services
4 190.0	5 469.0	6 512.5	3 643.2	2 838.1	Goods FOB
1 027.1	1 554.0	1 740.4	1 376.7	1 148.5	Services [1]
584.0	872.0	941.0	623.8	511.2	Transport and insurance
165.4	200.4	220.5	195.4	213.9	Travel
-355.3	-764.0	-2 676.7	62.9	1 013.8	**Trade balance (goods)**
-598.2	-1 055.5	-3 245.0	-378.7	639.5	**Trade balance (goods and services)**
-696.4	-1 028.2	-1 595.4	-2 034.7	-1 800.8	Factor services
-41.3	-82.0	-121.5	-128.1	-77.0	Profits
126.6	304.6	601.4	505.6	187.1	Interest received
-761.0	-1 151.9	-1 943.3	-2 298.5	-1 813.7	Interest paid
-20.7	-98.9	-132.1	-113.7	-97.3	Others
87.9	63.8	36.6	40.8	49.2	Private unrequited transfers
-1 205.4	-2 020.0	-4 805.1	-2 372.5	-1 111.1	**Balance on current account**
16.8	49.5	71.9	68.4	42.8	Official unrequited transfers
1 785.5	2 242.5	3 578.8	1 680.3	1 214.8	Long-term capital
232.6	170.5	362.0	384.2	151.9	Direct investment
50.4	0.0	0.0	0.0	0.0	Portfolio investment
1 502.6	2 072.0	3 216.7	1 296.1	1 063.0	Other long-term capital
95.6	-192.6	-496.4	133.6	1 149.6	Official sector [2]
581.4	279.8	154.5	295.9	1 300.4	Loans received
-484.5	-472.5	-641.5	-162.3	-150.8	Amortizations
524.6	1 438.2	2 496.3	326.8	-8.6	Commercial banks [2]
593.0	1 616.5	2 729.8	701.0	134.7	Loans received
-50.4	-147.1	-215.8	-309.1	-161.5	Amortizations
882.4	826.5	1 216.9	835.7	-78.1	Other sectors [2]
1 692.5	1 645.1	2 205.0	1 613.0	511.2	Loans received
-810.1	-818.7	-961.0	-788.3	-589.2	Amortizations
596.9	272.0	-1 154.4	-623.8	146.5	**Basic balance** [3]
470.3	999.6	1 189.8	-646.9	-694.0	Short-term capital
3.9	100.2	126.2	15.5	112.3	Official sector
38.8	468.6	252.3	68.4	-410.6	Commercial banks
427.7	430.8	811.3	-730.9	-395.7	Other sectors
-12.9	50.8	100.2	-69.6	29.9	Errors and omissions (net)
2 261.0	3 341.0	4 940.7	1 032.2	594.6	**Capital account balance**
1 055.6	1 321.1	135.6	-1 340.3	-516.5	**Global balance** [3]
-1 061.3	-1 330.9	-163.7	1 111.8	424.3	Total variation in reserves (minus sign indicates an increase)
-43.9	-89.8	0.0	-2.2	46.0	Monetary gold
-1.6	25.2	-15.3	-0.8	14.1	Special Drawing Rights
0.8	-32.9	6.8	-3.5	77.8	Reserve position in IMF
-847.8	-1 176.6	-81.4	1 160.3	-313.2	Foreign exchange assets
0.0	0.0	0.0	0.0	0.0	Other assets
-168.7	-56.7	-73.8	-42.0	599.6	Use of IMF credit

[1] Non factorial services also included.
[2] Net-loans received and Other assets and liabilities included.
[3] Equals to Total variation in reserves (with opposite sign) plus Counterpart items.

239. ECUADOR: BALANCE DE PAGOS

(Millones de dólares)

	1960	1965	1970	1975	1977	1978
Exportaciones de bienes y servicios	154.9	198.4	258.6	1 109.7	1 592.5	1 703.5
Bienes fob	146.3	181.0	234.9	1 012.8	1 400.8	1 529.2
Servicios [1]	8.6	17.4	23.7	96.9	191.7	174.3
Transporte y seguros	0.0	0.0	1.1	40.6	92.9	49.5
Viajes	3.8	7.4	8.5	28.8	48.5	64.9
Importaciones de bienes y servicios	152.3	201.6	359.3	1 294.9	1 774.0	2 166.7
Bienes fob	109.8	151.8	249.6	1 006.3	1 360.5	1 704.0
Servicios [1]	42.5	49.8	109.7	288.6	413.5	462.7
Transporte y seguros	17.6	27.3	45.2	160.5	256.5	283.0
Viajes	4.3	7.6	9.4	35.5	81.6	96.7
Balance de bienes	**36.5**	**29.2**	**-14.7**	**6.6**	**40.3**	**-174.8**
Balance comercial	**2.6**	**-3.2**	**-100.7**	**-185.2**	**-181.5**	**-463.2**
Servicios de factores	-22.8	-25.0	-29.2	-67.1	-196.1	-278.9
Utilidades	-20.5	-20.2	-19.2	-57.6	-118.6	-115.8
Intereses recibidos	0.0	0.0	0.3	17.0	25.5	36.9
Intereses pagados	-2.3	-4.8	-10.3	-26.6	-76.4	-176.4
Otros	0.0	0.0	0.0	0.0	-26.6	-23.7
Transferencias unilaterales privadas	1.4	2.2	7.7	13.5	0.4	12.0
Balance en cuenta corriente	**-18.8**	**-26.0**	**-122.2**	**-238.8**	**-377.2**	**-730.2**
Transferencias unilaterales oficiales	5.8	7.1	9.2	18.8	35.8	28.9
Capital a largo plazo	22.4	20.0	110.4	199.7	590.9	782.0
Inversión directa	8.0	7.4	88.6	95.3	34.4	48.6
Inversión de cartera	0.0	0.0	-0.3	0.0	52.0	0.0
Otro capital a largo plazo	14.4	12.6	22.1	104.4	504.5	733.4
Sector oficial [2]	11.1	3.6	28.5	62.9	440.2	351.6
Préstamos recibidos	15.9	9.7	47.5	90.0	487.4	497.5
Amortizaciones	-3.1	-5.5	-19.0	-26.3	-41.8	-138.7
Bancos comerciales [2]	0.0	0.0	0.0	0.0	0.0	62.7
Préstamos recibidos	0.0	0.0	0.0	0.0	0.0	64.1
Amortizaciones	0.0	0.0	0.0	0.0	0.0	-0.8
Otros sectores [2]	3.3	9.0	-6.4	41.5	64.3	319.1
Préstamos recibidos	8.7	13.2	1.7	59.1	122.7	469.1
Amortizaciones	-5.4	-4.2	-8.1	-17.6	-58.4	-88.0
Balance básico	**9.4**	**1.1**	**-2.6**	**-20.3**	**249.5**	**80.8**
Capital a corto plazo	-9.9	2.2	16.6	2.7	-87.6	-119.6
Sector oficial	-0.2	0.9	10.4	47.6	-100.9	3.4
Bancos comerciales	-2.0	-1.4	6.2	-7.4	-25.7	2.8
Otros sectores	-7.7	2.7	0.0	-37.5	39.0	-125.7
Errores y omisiones netos	-2.3	-15.0	-2.1	-47.5	-49.9	44.2
Balance en cuenta de capital	**16.0**	**14.3**	**134.1**	**173.7**	**489.3**	**735.6**
Balance global [3]	**-2.8**	**-11.7**	**11.9**	**-65.1**	**112.1**	**5.4**
Variación total de las reservas (signo - indica aumento)	2.8	11.7	-7.7	65.2	-146.2	-13.0
Oro monetario	0.4	0.1	3.1	0.0	-0.6	-0.3
Derechos especiales de giro	0.0	0.0	-0.1	0.6	-2.6	-3.8
Posición de reserva en el FMI	0.0	3.0	0.0	-4.2	0.0	-10.4
Activos en divisas	2.5	2.6	-12.2	68.9	-143.0	1.5
Otros activos	-0.1	0.0	0.0	0.0	0.0	0.0
Uso de crédito del FMI	0.0	6.0	1.5	0.0	0.0	0.0

[1] Incluye Otros servicios no factoriales.
[2] Incluye Préstamos netos concedidos y Otros activos y pasivos.
[3] Es igual a Variación total de las reservas (con signo contrario), más Asientos de contrapartida.

239. ECUADOR: BALANCE OF PAYMENTS

(Millions of dollars)

1979	1980	1981	1982	1983	
2 410.7	2 866.5	2 913.5	2 689.9	2 623.0	*Exports of goods and services*
2 150.5	2 544.2	2 544.2	2 343.0	2 365.0	*Goods FOB*
260.2	322.4	369.3	347.0	258.0	*Services* [1]
109.0	112.6	151.4	139.0	140.0	*Transport and insurance*
79.7	130.8	131.0	131.0	97.0	*Travel*
2 709.6	3 013.7	3 217.7	3 058.0	2 033.0	*Imports of goods and services*
2 096.8	2 241.8	2 361.5	2 181.0	1 408.0	*Goods FOB*
612.8	771.8	856.2	876.9	625.0	*Services* [1]
295.1	327.6	368.4	163.9	105.0	*Transport and insurance*
155.8	228.2	250.0	249.9	178.0	*Travel*
53.7	302.5	182.7	162.1	957.0	**Trade balance (goods)**
-298.8	-147.2	-304.2	-368.1	590.0	**Trade balance (goods and services)**
-355.7	-524.8	-722.4	-847.0	-718.0	*Factor services*
-94.4	-110.6	-100.0	-80.0	-100.0	*Profits*
67.7	109.1	86.9	44.0	65.0	*Interest received*
-328.9	-523.2	-709.1	-811.0	-683.0	*Interest paid*
0.0	0.0	0.0	0.0	0.0	*Others*
0.4	0.0	0.0	0.0	0.0	*Private unrequited transfers*
-654.1	-671.8	-1 026.6	-1 215.0	-128.0	**Balance on current account**
29.5	30.2	25.0	20.0	24.0	*Official unrequited transfers*
689.7	763.1	1 076.8	162.0	...	*Long-term capital*
63.4	70.0	60.0	40.0	50.0	*Direct investment*
0.0	0.0	0.0	0.0	...	*Portfolio investment*
626.2	693.1	1 016.8	122.0	...	*Other long-term capital*
344.4	609.2	897.7	-261.0	...	*Official sector* [2]
951.7	795.4	1 283.4	192.0	...	*Loans received*
-601.0	-175.8	-377.9	-437.0	...	*Amortizations*
1.2	4.8	1.8	0.0	...	*Commercial banks* [2]
2.2	7.9	7.2	7.9	...	*Loans received*
-0.8	-1.0	-0.9	-1.0	...	*Amortizations*
280.6	79.0	117.3	383.0	...	*Other sectors* [2]
593.3	496.1	462.5	1 112.0	...	*Loans received*
-374.2	-416.4	-344.6	-728.0	...	*Amortizations*
65.0	121.4	75.2	-1 033.0	...	**Basic balance** [3]
-23.5	217.2	-360.0	921.1	...	*Short-term capital*
8.7	-30.1	0.9	585.0	...	*Official sector*
-9.8	-17.1	-5.4	50.0	...	*Commercial banks*
-22.4	264.3	-355.5	286.0	...	*Other sectors*
3.0	-68.3	-85.7	-228.2	...	*Errors and omissions (net)*
698.3	941.9	656.1	874.7	273.9	**Capital account balance**
44.2	270.1	-370.5	-340.3	145.9	**Global balance** [3]
-86.5	-291.0	380.7	328.1	-145.9	*Total variation in reserves (minus sign indicates an increase)*
-0.3	0.0	0.0	0.0	0.0	*Monetary gold*
-11.5	1.1	-9.4	33.6	-0.1	*Special Drawing Rights*
-2.0	-15.4	-0.9	28.7	-12.0	*Reserve position in IMF*
-72.8	-276.7	391.0	265.8	-328.2	*Foreign exchange assets*
0.0	0.0	0.0	0.0	0.0	*Other assets*
0.0	0.0	0.0	0.0	194.4	*Use of IMF credit*

[1] *Non factorial services also included.*
[2] *Net-loans received and Other assets and liabilities included.*
[3] *Equals to Total variation in reserves (with opposite sign) plus Counterpart items.*

IV. BALANCE DE PAGOS

240. EL SALVADOR: BALANCE DE PAGOS

(Millones de dólares)

	1960	1965	1970	1975	1977	1978
Exportaciones de bienes y servicios	116.9	212.2	255.9	593.4	1 088.6	923.1
Bienes fob	102.6	190.0	236.1	533.0	973.5	801.7
Servicios [1]	14.3	22.2	19.8	60.3	115.0	121.4
Transporte y seguros	1.4	2.2	1.5	13.1	19.3	23.0
Viajes	6.4	6.1	8.5	18.5	31.8	36.7
Importaciones de bienes y servicios	141.6	230.5	251.9	673.4	1 069.6	1 208.1
Bienes fob	111.5	185.7	194.7	550.7	861.0	951.0
Servicios [1]	30.1	44.8	57.2	122.6	208.6	256.9
Transporte y seguros	13.1	20.3	26.3	61.1	87.7	98.0
Viajes	10.4	14.3	20.4	33.9	57.9	103.3
Balance de bienes	**-8.9**	**4.3**	**41.4**	**-17.7**	**112.4**	**-149.4**
Balance comercial	**-24.7**	**-18.3**	**4.0**	**-80.0**	**19.0**	**-285.0**
Servicios de factores	-3.9	-7.6	-9.6	-40.3	-27.7	-52.2
Utilidades	-3.0	-5.2	-7.4	-23.2	-25.7	-26.0
Intereses recibidos	0.3	1.6	3.5	5.3	19.6	14.5
Intereses pagados	-1.2	-4.2	-5.6	-22.9	-31.5	-49.0
Otros	0.0	0.2	-0.1	0.5	9.9	8.3
Transferencias unilaterales privadas	0.2	9.7	12.4	25.1	30.4	44.8
Balance en cuenta corriente	**-28.4**	**-16.2**	**6.8**	**-95.2**	**21.6**	**-292.3**
Transferencias unilaterales oficiales	0.8	3.6	1.9	2.3	9.2	6.5
Capital a largo plazo	7.4	22.1	-1.4	94.7	38.3	175.8
Inversión directa	4.5	7.2	3.7	13.1	18.7	23.4
Inversión de cartera	0.0	-0.2	0.0	0.0	0.7	4.0
Otro capital a largo plazo	2.9	15.1	-5.1	81.6	18.9	148.4
Sector oficial [2]	1.8	7.9	-3.5	23.6	24.5	115.4
Préstamos recibidos	3.7	9.9	5.4	70.4	42.3	126.8
Amortizaciones	-1.2	-2.4	-7.6	-45.4	-15.8	-9.9
Bancos comerciales [2]	0.0	0.0	0.0	0.0	0.0	0.0
Préstamos recibidos	0.0	0.0	0.0	0.0	0.0	0.0
Amortizaciones	0.0	0.0	0.0	0.0	0.0	0.0
Otros sectores [2]	1.1	7.2	-1.6	58.0	-5.6	32.9
Préstamos recibidos	1.6	8.7	4.4	89.1	47.9	54.5
Amortizaciones	-0.5	-1.0	-5.2	-29.6	-71.3	-31.4
Balance básico	**-20.2**	**9.5**	**7.3**	**1.8**	**69.1**	**-110.1**
Capital a corto plazo	12.3	-3.6	7.9	18.2	5.7	194.7
Sector oficial	0.1	1.4	-3.1	-4.5	-0.9	23.7
Bancos comerciales	8.4	-7.8	2.4	-15.8	20.4	3.9
Otros sectores	3.8	2.8	8.6	38.5	-13.8	167.1
Errores y omisiones netos	-2.5	-3.1	-13.0	9.7	-33.9	-29.0
Balance en cuenta de capital	**18.0**	**19.0**	**-4.6**	**124.8**	**19.4**	**347.8**
Balance global [3]	**-10.4**	**2.8**	**2.2**	**29.6**	**41.0**	**55.5**
Variación total de las reservas (signo - indica aumento)	10.4	-5.2	-6.4	-30.3	-41.0	-56.9
Oro monetario	0.4	-1.4	0.0	0.0	-0.2	0.0
Derechos especiales de giro	0.0	0.0	0.0	-0.2	-4.8	-0.4
Posición de reserva en el FMI	0.0	0.0	0.0	0.0	-6.2	-5.3
Activos en divisas	4.2	-2.8	1.1	-29.2	-14.9	-51.2
Otros activos	0.1	-1.0	0.0	0.0	0.0	0.0
Uso de crédito del FMI	5.7	0.0	-7.5	-1.0	-14.9	0.0

[1] Incluye Otros servicios no factoriales.
[2] Incluye Préstamos netos concedidos y Otros activos y pasivos.
[3] Es igual a Variación total de las reservas (con signo contrario), más Asientos de contrapartida.

240. EL SALVADOR: BALANCE OF PAYMENTS

(Millions of dollars)

1979	1980	1981	1982	1983	
1 265.8	1 215.4	924.3	822.5	921.0	*Exports of goods and services*
1 132.3	1 075.3	798.1	704.1	732.0	*Goods FOB*
133.5	140.0	126.3	118.3	189.0	*Services* [1]
24.4	25.4	20.3	22.5	46.0	*Transport and insurance*
24.9	13.4	14.1	20.0	22.0	*Travel*
1 255.3	1 170.3	1 160.9	1 040.5	1 072.0	*Imports of goods and services*
954.7	897.0	898.4	825.9	803.0	*Goods FOB*
300.6	273.5	262.6	214.6	269.0	*Services* [1]
106.8	83.9	112.6	72.2	117.0	*Transport and insurance*
117.1	106.1	69.2	59.9	64.0	*Travel*
177.7	178.3	-100.3	-121.8	-71.0	**Trade balance (goods)**
10.5	45.0	-236.5	-218.0	-151.0	**Trade balance (goods and services)**
-40.4	-63.3	-74.2	-105.1	-148.0	*Factor services*
-44.8	-41.1	-40.3	-45.5	-80.0	*Profits*
39.5	18.5	12.9	14.4	15.0	*Interest received*
-72.2	-71.7	-72.5	-98.1	-131.0	*Interest paid*
37.1	31.1	25.8	24.1	48.0	*Others*
45.0	17.3	39.1	51.7	60.0	*Private unrequited transfers*
14.9	-0.9	-271.6	-271.4	-239.0	**Balance on current account**
6.5	31.5	21.1	119.0	148.0	*Official unrequited transfers*
78.3	174.3	125.7	255.0	...	*Long-term capital*
-9.9	5.9	-5.8	-1.0	...	*Direct investment*
-5.7	-1.0	0.0	-1.0	...	*Portfolio investment*
93.9	169.5	131.5	257.0	270.0	*Other long-term capital*
82.9	167.4	131.4	251.1	146.0	*Official sector* [2]
100.3	200.7	205.2	358.5	173.0	*Loans received*
-16.3	-29.2	-69.1	-87.1	-27.0	*Amortizations*
0.0	3.3	-0.2	-0.1	128.0	*Commercial banks* [2]
0.0	4.3	0.0	0.7	268.0	*Loans received*
0.0	-0.9	-0.2	-0.9	-140.0	*Amortizations*
11.0	-1.2	0.4	6.1	-4.0	*Other sectors* [2]
21.6	35.9	28.4	36.4	...	*Loans received*
-10.6	-37.1	-28.1	-30.4	...	*Amortizations*
99.6	204.9	-124.8	102.7	...	**Basic balance** [3]
-127.4	37.6	75.6	-36.3	...	*Short-term capital*
-14.7	194.3	96.3	-65.2	...	*Official sector*
-2.2	-67.3	-11.0	28.9	...	*Commercial banks*
-110.5	-89.4	-9.8	0.0	...	*Other sectors*
-106.2	-317.3	0.2	-95.5	...	*Errors and omissions (net)*
-148.6	-73.8	222.6	242.0	418.0	**Capital account balance**
-133.7	-74.7	-48.9	-29.4	179.0	**Global balance** [3]
127.7	69.1	42.6	27.1	...	*Total variation in reserves (minus sign indicates an increase)*
-0.3	-0.3	0.0	0.0	...	*Monetary gold*
-7.5	17.4	-0.1	-1.7	...	*Special Drawing Rights*
0.3	11.2	0.0	0.0	...	*Reserve position in IMF*
135.2	33.9	5.9	-34.9	...	*Foreign exchange assets*
0.0	0.0	0.0	0.0	...	*Other assets*
0.0	6.9	36.9	63.7	...	*Use of IMF credit*

[1] *Non factorial services also included.*
[2] *Net-loans received and Other assets and liabilities included.*
[3] *Equals to Total variation in reserves (with opposite sign) plus Counterpart items.*

IV. BALANCE DE PAGOS

241. GUATEMALA: BALANCE DE PAGOS

(Millones de dólares)

	1960	1965	1970	1975	1977	1978
Exportaciones de bienes y servicios	131.5	226.1	349.5	782.9	1 335.2	1 297.5
Bienes fob	115.9	192.1	297.1	640.9	1 160.2	1 092.4
Servicios [1]	15.6	34.0	52.4	141.9	175.0	205.1
Transporte y seguros	2.9	7.7	10.9	22.3	28.4	33.4
Viajes	5.8	5.9	12.1	78.1	66.1	67.4
Importaciones de bienes y servicios	152.1	256.7	336.7	860.3	1 433.4	1 651.4
Bienes fob	124.8	206.1	266.6	672.4	1 086.9	1 283.7
Servicios [1]	27.3	50.6	70.1	188.0	346.4	367.8
Transporte y seguros	17.1	24.2	35.4	85.5	171.5	141.6
Viajes	3.5	16.5	14.5	54.8	99.7	107.7
Balance de bienes	**-8.9**	**-14.0**	**30.5**	**-31.4**	**73.3**	**-191.3**
Balance comercial	**-20.6**	**-30.6**	**12.8**	**-77.5**	**-98.2**	**-353.9**
Servicios de factores	-5.0	-11.5	-38.2	-66.0	-32.9	-32.2
Utilidades	-4.3	-11.7	-29.9	-50.5	-32.8	-34.9
Intereses recibidos	0.9	2.7	4.2	14.2	33.0	49.9
Intereses pagados	-1.6	-2.5	-12.5	-29.7	-32.2	-47.1
Otros	0.0	0.0	0.0	0.0	-0.6	-0.1
Transferencias unilaterales privadas	0.1	3.5	17.4	78.3	94.0	115.0
Balance en cuenta corriente	**-25.5**	**-38.6**	**-8.0**	**-65.2**	**-37.1**	**-271.2**
Transferencias unilaterales oficiales	14.5	4.0	0.1	-0.5	1.9	0.8
Capital a largo plazo	21.5	39.4	55.0	168.6	199.2	267.8
Inversión directa	16.8	14.1	29.4	80.0	97.4	127.2
Inversión de cartera	1.6	5.2	1.5	-2.4	5.4	11.6
Otro capital a largo plazo	3.1	20.1	24.1	91.1	96.4	129.0
Sector oficial [2]	4.7	8.2	11.1	52.3	68.0	102.2
Préstamos recibidos	7.3	18.1	20.5	63.0	82.2	116.9
Amortizaciones	-1.8	-7.0	-8.9	-9.1	-14.2	-14.7
Bancos comerciales [2]	0.0	0.0	-0.4	-0.1	0.0	0.0
Préstamos recibidos	0.0	0.0	0.0	0.0	0.0	0.0
Amortizaciones	0.0	0.0	0.0	0.0	0.0	0.0
Otros sectores [2]	-1.6	11.9	13.4	38.9	28.4	26.8
Préstamos recibidos	1.5	13.2	17.8	48.9	43.4	58.0
Amortizaciones	-3.1	-2.0	-4.7	-21.2	-24.0	-41.4
Balance básico	**10.5**	**4.8**	**47.1**	**103.0**	**164.0**	**-2.6**
Capital a corto plazo	5.7	24.9	-27.9	11.9	44.3	129.5
Sector oficial	-1.2	0.5	-0.5	0.0	0.2	7.6
Bancos comerciales	1.8	8.5	-6.5	2.9	3.3	1.2
Otros sectores	5.1	15.9	-20.9	9.0	40.8	120.7
Errores y omisiones netos	-6.2	-20.9	-3.8	-10.7	-26.5	-58.5
Balance en cuenta de capital	**35.5**	**47.4**	**23.4**	**169.3**	**218.7**	**339.4**
Balance global [3]	**10.0**	**8.8**	**15.4**	**104.1**	**181.6**	**68.3**
Variación total de las reservas (signo - indica aumento)	-10.0	-8.8	-14.6	-102.6	-182.0	-68.2
Oro monetario	0.0	1.2	2.5	0.0	-0.7	-0.3
Derechos especiales de giro	0.0	0.0	-2.1	0.6	-0.7	-1.1
Posición de reserva en el FMI	0.0	3.8	0.0	0.5	-1.1	-1.7
Activos en divisas	-10.0	-13.3	-4.6	-103.5	-176.1	-69.7
Otros activos	0.0	-0.5	0.7	-0.1	-3.3	4.7
Uso de crédito del FMI	0.0	0.0	-11.1	0.0	0.0	0.0

[1] Incluye Otros servicios no factoriales.
[2] Incluye Préstamos netos concedidos y Otros activos y pasivos.
[3] Es igual a Variación total de las reservas (con signo contrario), más Asientos de contrapartida.

241. GUATEMALA: BALANCE OF PAYMENTS

(Millions of dollars)

1979	1980	1981	1982	1983	
1 472.6	1 730.5	1 453.6	1 307.0	1 172.3	*Exports of goods and services*
1 221.4	1 519.9	1 299.0	1 199.6	1 092.1	*Goods FOB*
251.2	210.6	154.7	107.5	80.1	*Services* [1]
40.3	43.3	32.9	26.5	17.5	*Transport and insurance*
81.7	61.6	30.5	12.0	6.8	*Travel*
1 792.3	1 958.5	2 023.8	1 630.2	1 314.1	*Imports of goods and services*
1 401.6	1 472.6	1 540.0	1 284.3	1 056.3	*Goods FOB*
390.5	485.9	483.8	346.1	257.5	*Services* [1]
160.8	187.0	187.9	140.5	98.9	*Transport and insurance*
120.1	164.0	133.1	100.3	89.5	*Travel*
-180.2	47.3	-241.1	-84.7	35.8	**Trade balance (goods)**
-319.7	-228.0	-570.2	-323.1	-141.8	**Trade balance (goods and services)**
-12.7	-45.1	-85.8	-114.8	-113.2	*Factor services*
-44.7	-41.8	-48.8	-40.8	-38.5	*Profits*
78.1	75.1	55.0	20.0	26.9	*Interest received*
-46.0	-92.0	-109.3	-101.3	-102.0	*Interest paid*
0.0	13.9	17.2	7.2	0.5	*Others*
123.3	108.6	89.3	62.0	29.8	*Private unrequited transfers*
-208.9	-164.6	-566.5	-376.1	-225.0	**Balance on current account**
3.2	1.2	1.4	0.9	0.8	*Official unrequited transfers*
257.7	246.5	415.6	341.0	240.0	*Long-term capital*
117.0	110.6	127.1	77.2	44.9	*Direct investment*
5.4	3.9	0.2	0.4	0.1	*Portfolio investment*
135.4	132.1	288.3	263.4	195.1	*Other long-term capital*
112.3	106.3	219.0	142.2	200.7	*Official sector* [2]
130.0	120.9	246.2	196.7	343.6	*Loans received*
-18.0	-17.7	-27.3	-54.6	-143.0	*Amortizations*
0.0	0.0	0.0	0.0	0.0	*Commercial banks* [2]
0.0	0.0	0.0	0.0	0.0	*Loans received*
0.0	0.0	0.0	0.0	0.0	*Amortizations*
23.1	25.8	69.3	121.2	-5.7	*Other sectors* [2]
59.8	24.7	99.6	121.3	10.8	*Loans received*
-47.3	-10.1	-42.3	-14.9	-17.9	*Amortizations*
52.0	83.1	-149.5	-34.2	15.8	**Basic balance** [3]
-33.3	-323.1	-140.3	28.6	112.7	*Short-term capital*
1.8	59.0	44.3	15.5	-24.6	*Official sector*
24.0	2.2	-6.8	13.7	71.1	*Commercial banks*
-59.1	-384.3	-177.8	-0.6	66.1	*Other sectors*
-44.4	-18.0	-11.3	-32.5	-77.9	*Errors and omissions (net)*
183.3	-93.2	265.3	337.6	276.0	**Capital account balance**
-25.7	-257.7	-301.2	-38.5	51.0	**Global balance** [3]
18.9	250.6	304.6	16.2	-63.5	*Total variation in reserves (minus sign indicates an increase)*
-0.4	0.0	0.0	0.0	0.0	*Monetary gold*
-9.1	1.7	20.0	2.6	-0.6	*Special Drawing Rights*
-1.8	-9.1	18.0	9.7	-8.2	*Reserve position in IMF*
56.1	259.2	257.0	25.2	-89.0	*Foreign exchange assets*
-25.9	-1.2	-101.6	-15.4	-0.5	*Other assets*
0.0	0.0	111.3	-5.8	34.7	*Use of IMF credit*

[1] Non factorial services also included.
[2] Net-loans received and Other assets and liabilities included.
[3] Equals to Total variation in reserves (with opposite sign) plus Counterpart items.

242. GRANADA: BALANCE DE PAGOS

(Millones de dólares)

	1960	1965	1970	1975	1977
Exportaciones de bienes y servicios	...	...	...	...	28.9
Bienes fob	...	...	6.0	12.3	14.3
Servicios [1]	...	...	...	...	14.6
Transporte y seguros	...	...	...	0.0	0.0
Viajes	...	...	...	8.9	11.6
Importaciones de bienes y servicios	...	...	...	...	32.9
Bienes fob	...	...	20.1	21.9	28.5
Servicios [1]	...	...	...	...	4.4
Transporte y seguros	...	...	...	2.3	2.8
Viajes	...	...	...	1.0	1.2
Balance de bienes	...	...	-14.1	-9.6	-14.3
Balance comercial	...	...	...	...	-4.0
Servicios de factores	...	...	...	...	0.1
Utilidades	...	...	...	...	0.0
Intereses recibidos	...	...	...	0.0	0.3
Intereses pagados	...	...	...	...	-0.2
Otros	...	...	...	...	0.0
Transferencias unilaterales privadas	...	...	...	3.0	4.5
Balance en cuenta corriente	...	...	...	-0.3	0.6
Transferencias unilaterales oficiales	...	...	...	0.0	0.7
Capital a largo plazo	...	...	...	...	1.7
Inversión directa	...	...	...	...	-0.1
Inversión de cartera	...	...	...	...	0.0
Otro capital a largo plazo	...	...	...	...	1.8
Sector oficial [2]	...	...	...	0.0	1.7
Préstamos recibidos	...	...	...	0.0	1.9
Amortizaciones	...	...	...	...	-0.2
Bancos comerciales [2]	...	...	...	...	0.0
Préstamos recibidos	...	...	...	...	0.0
Amortizaciones	...	...	...	...	0.0
Otros sectores [2]	...	...	...	...	0.1
Préstamos recibidos	...	...	...	...	0.1
Amortizaciones	...	...	...	...	0.0
Balance básico	...	...	...	...	3.0
Capital a corto plazo	...	...	...	...	0.9
Sector oficial	...	...	...	...	0.0
Bancos comerciales	...	...	...	...	0.9
Otros sectores	...	...	...	...	0.0
Errores y omisiones netos	...	...	...	-0.2	-4.0
Balance en cuenta de capital	...	...	...	-0.2	-0.7
Balance global [3]	...	...	...	-0.5	-0.1
Variación total de las reservas (signo - indica aumento)	...	...	...	0.6	-2.1
Oro monetario	...	...	...	0.0	0.0
Derechos especiales de giro	0.0	0.0	0.0	-0.1	0.1
Posición de reserva en el FMI	0.0	0.0	0.0	0.0	0.0
Activos en divisas	...	...	...	-0.3	-1.9
Otros activos	...	...	...	0.0	-0.3
Uso de crédito del FMI	0.0	0.0	0.0	0.9	0.1

[1] Incluye Otros servicios no factoriales.
[2] Incluye Préstamos netos concedidos y Otros activos y pasivos.
[3] Es igual a Variación total de las reservas (con signo contrario) más Asientos de contrapartida.

242. GRENADA: BALANCE OF PAYMENTS

(Millions of dollars)

1978	1979	1980	1981	1982	
33.3	39.3	33.9	32.9	32.9	Exports of goods and services
16.9	21.4	17.4	19.0	18.6	Goods FOB
16.4	17.9	16.5	13.9	14.3	Services [1]
0.0	0.0	0.0	0.0	0.1	Transport and insurance
14.4	15.3	16.5	13.9	13.0	Travel
40.7	52.6	60.9	70.8	83.3	Imports of goods and services
33.4	44.8	52.3	57.4	64.8	Goods FOB
7.3	7.8	8.6	13.4	18.4	Services [1]
3.3	4.5	5.2	5.7	9.0	Transport and insurance
4.0	3.3	3.2	3.9	3.3	Travel
-16.5	-23.4	-34.9	-38.4	-46.2	**Trade balance (goods)**
-7.4	-13.3	-27.0	-37.9	-50.3	**Trade balance (goods and services)**
-0.1	0.1	0.3	0.1	-0.0	Factor services
0.0	0.0	0.0	0.0	-0.1	Profits
0.3	0.5	0.7	0.8	1.1	Interest received
-0.4	-0.4	-0.4	-0.7	-1.1	Interest paid
0.0	0.0	0.0	0.0	0.0	Others
7.0	8.0	13.4	14.6	18.1	Private unrequited transfers
-0.5	-5.2	-13.3	-23.2	-32.2	**Balance on current account**
0.8	6.9	12.7	12.9	15.5	Official unrequited transfers
2.5	3.0	2.0	7.4	8.9	Long-term capital
1.4	0.0	0.0	0.0	1.9	Direct investment
-0.5	0.0	0.1	-0.3	0.0	Portfolio investment
1.6	3.0	1.9	7.7	7.0	Other long-term capital
1.6	2.7	2.0	7.6	7.0	Official sector [2]
1.8	2.9	2.2	7.9	7.5	Loans received
-0.2	-0.2	-0.2	-0.3	-0.5	Amortizations
0.0	0.0	0.0	0.0	0.0	Commercial banks [2]
0.0	0.0	0.0	0.0	0.0	Loans received
0.0	0.0	0.0	0.0	0.0	Amortizations
0.0	0.3	-0.1	0.1	0.0	Other sectors [2]
0.0	0.3	0.2	0.2	0.2	Loans received
0.0	-0.0	-0.2	-0.0	-0.2	Amortizations
2.8	4.7	1.4	-2.9	-7.8	**Basic balance**
-0.6	-0.4	0.7	0.6	7.2	Short-term capital
0.2	0.4	0.3	0.8	0.8	Official sector
-0.8	-0.8	0.4	-0.2	6.4	Commercial banks
0.0	0.0	0.0	0.0	0.0	Other sectors
-0.4	-1.8	-0.5	-1.4	-5.3	Errors and omissions (net)
2.3	7.7	14.9	19.4	26.3	**Capital account balance**
1.8	2.5	1.6	-3.8	-6.0	**Global balance** [3]
0.8	-5.8	...	...	...	Total variation in reserves (minus sign indicates an increase)
-0.0	0.0	0.0	0.0	0.0	Monetary gold
0.0	-0.0	0.0	...	...	Special Drawing Rights
0.0	0.0	0.0	...	...	Reserve position in IMF
0.4	-5.4	...	...	...	Foreign exchange assets
0.3	-0.1	-0.4	0.8	0.0	Other assets
0.1	-0.3	-0.9	...	...	Use of IMF credit

[1] Non factorial services also included.
[2] Net loans received and Other assets and liabilities included.
[2] Equals to Total variation in reserves (with opposite sign) plus Counterpart items.

IV. BALANCE DE PAGOS

243. GUYANA: BALANCE DE PAGOS

(Millones de dólares)

	1960	1965	1970	1975	1977	1978
Exportaciones de bienes y servicios	81.4	114.6	145.6	370.3	275.5	313.8
Bienes fob	74.8	103.3	129.0	351.4	259.3	295.6
Servicios [1]	6.6	11.3	16.6	18.9	16.1	18.2
Transporte y seguros	2.3	1.9	3.1	3.3	4.0	5.0
Viajes	0.6	1.1	3.4	2.5	3.4	3.4
Importaciones de bienes y servicios	90.0	120.7	151.0	370.0	347.5	313.6
Bienes fob	77.5	95.2	119.9	305.8	286.7	253.5
Servicios [1]	12.5	25.5	31.1	64.1	60.8	60.1
Transporte y seguros	8.6	12.7	17.1	36.8	37.5	34.8
Viajes	0.9	3.4	3.0	5.2	3.4	5.1
Balance de bienes	**-2.7**	**8.1**	**9.1**	**45.5**	**-27.4**	**42.1**
Balance comercial	**-8.6**	**-6.1**	**-5.4**	**0.4**	**-71.9**	**0.1**
Servicios de factores	-9.1	-14.4	-15.9	-18.9	-21.6	-23.3
Utilidades	-9.3	-13.9	-14.2	-7.6	-2.7	-0.6
Intereses recibidos	1.3	2.7	1.0	1.5	0.0	0.0
Intereses pagados	-1.1	-3.2	-2.7	-12.7	-19.0	-22.7
Otros	0.0	0.0	0.0	0.0	0.0	0.0
Transferencias unilaterales privadas	-0.1	-1.3	-0.5	-4.4	-3.5	0.3
Balance en cuenta corriente	**-17.8**	**-21.8**	**-21.8**	**-22.9**	**-97.1**	**-22.9**
Transferencias unilaterales oficiales	2.7	6.3	0.0	-1.7	-0.4	-6.8
Capital a largo plazo	6.7	9.2	17.1	97.4	41.3	32.8
Inversión directa	3.0	9.4	9.0	0.8	-1.8	0.0
Inversión de cartera	-0.5	-0.3	-0.2	3.8	-1.1	-1.5
Otro capital a largo plazo	4.2	0.1	8.3	92.8	44.1	34.3
Sector oficial [2]	4.2	0.9	8.3	65.0	23.6	22.9
Préstamos recibidos	5.1	2.3	9.7	51.4	35.4	41.9
Amortizaciones	-0.9	-1.2	-1.2	-4.5	-6.3	-12.6
Bancos comerciales [2]	0.0	0.0	0.0	0.0	0.0	0.0
Préstamos recibidos	0.0	0.0	0.0	0.0	0.0	0.0
Amortizaciones	0.0	0.0	0.0	0.0	0.0	0.0
Otros sectores [2]	0.0	-0.8	0.0	27.8	20.5	11.4
Préstamos recibidos	0.0	0.0	0.0	27.8	36.9	56.8
Amortizaciones	-0.5	-0.8	0.0	0.0	-10.7	-37.8
Balance básico	**-8.4**	**-6.3**	**-4.7**	**72.7**	**-56.2**	**3.1**
Capital a corto plazo	4.3	10.7	-0.2	-3.9	35.3	-8.1
Sector oficial	0.0	-0.6	0.7	0.0	-1.5	-1.8
Bancos comerciales	4.3	10.3	0.9	-3.4	4.2	4.0
Otros sectores	0.0	1.0	-1.8	-0.5	32.6	-10.4
Errores y omisiones netos	4.9	-3.8	2.7	-19.1	9.6	21.4
Balance en cuenta de capital	**18.6**	**22.4**	**19.5**	**72.7**	**85.7**	**39.6**
Balance global [3]	**0.8**	**0.6**	**-2.3**	**49.8**	**-11.4**	**16.7**
Variación total de las reservas (signo - indica aumento)	-0.8	-3.6	0.1	-45.7	12.0	-14.8
Oro monetario	0.0	0.0	0.0	0.0	-0.4	-0.3
Derechos especiales de giro	0.0	0.0	-0.1	0.3	0.8	-0.4
Posición de reserva en el FMI	0.0	0.0	-0.6	-3.6	0.0	0.0
Activos en divisas	-0.8	-3.6	0.8	-34.7	3.4	-35.0
Otros activos	0.0	0.0	0.0	-1.6	7.2	2.4
Uso de crédito del FMI	0.0	0.0	0.0	-6.1	0.9	18.5

[1] Incluye Otros servicios no factoriales.
[2] Incluye Préstamos netos concedidos y Otros activos y pasivos.
[3] Es igual a Variación total de las reservas (con signo contrario), más Asientos de contrapartida.

243. GUYANA: BALANCE OF PAYMENTS

(Millions of dollars)

1979	1980	1981	1982	1983	
311.2	408.7	369.4	264.1	225.0	*Exports of goods and services*
292.8	388.9	346.4	241.4	193.5	*Goods FOB*
18.5	19.8	23.0	22.6	31.5	*Services* [1]
5.6	5.9	9.3	8.4	11.7	*Transport and insurance*
3.2	3.9	3.7	2.6	4.2	*Travel*
360.1	493.7	498.5	348.6	324.0	*Imports of goods and services*
288.8	386.4	399.6	254.1	225.9	*Goods FOB*
71.3	107.2	98.9	94.5	98.2	*Services* [1]
40.1	52.6	51.1	42.6	44.3	*Transport and insurance*
6.3	8.5	10.7	12.0	14.0	*Travel*
4.0	2.5	-53.2	-12.7	-32.4	**Trade balance (goods)**
-48.8	-85.0	-129.1	-84.6	-99.0	**Trade balance (goods and services)**
-34.4	-42.7	-54.5	-48.9	-57.5	*Factor services*
0.0	0.0	-0.5	-4.4	-4.7	*Profits*
3.7	1.8	3.1	0.3	0.3	*Interest received*
-38.1	-44.5	-57.2	-44.8	-53.1	*Interest paid*
0.0	0.0	0.0	0.0	0.0	*Others*
0.3	1.0	4.2	-5.9	-4.3	*Private unrequited transfers*
-83.1	-126.8	-179.5	-139.4	-160.8	**Balance on current account**
0.3	-1.8	-4.1	-1.9	3.3	*Official unrequited transfers*
28.2	79.9	128.9	10.2	-22.2	*Long-term capital*
0.6	0.7	-1.8	4.4	4.7	*Direct investment*
3.5	2.6	0.0	0.0	0.0	*Portfolio investment*
24.0	76.7	130.7	5.7	-26.9	*Other long-term capital*
19.9	86.3	126.3	9.6	-8.0	*Official sector* [2]
50.8	125.7	155.2	88.2	65.6	*Loans received*
-24.4	-32.7	-17.1	-70.2	-73.6	*Amortizations*
0.0	0.0	0.0	0.0	0.0	*Commercial banks* [2]
0.0	0.0	0.0	0.0	0.0	*Loans received*
0.0	0.0	0.0	0.0	0.0	*Amortizations*
4.1	-9.6	4.4	-3.9	-18.9	*Other sectors* [2]
80.5	52.2	15.1	10.5	0.0	*Loans received*
-79.7	-61.8	-10.6	-13.0	-18.9	*Amortizations*
-54.7	-48.7	-54.7	-131.2	-179.8	**Basic balance** [3]
5.7	5.3	47.8	87.4	118.8	*Short-term capital*
0.6	6.9	17.8	22.9	65.8	*Official sector*
0.3	-2.2	7.1	4.9	-2.2	*Commercial banks*
4.8	0.7	22.9	59.7	55.3	*Other sectors*
-8.1	0.3	-11.4	43.3	61.3	*Errors and omissions (net)*
26.0	83.6	161.2	139.0	161.3	**Capital account balance**
-57.1	-43.2	-18.3	-0.4	0.4	**Global balance** [3]
54.5	37.4	10.3	...	...	*Total variation in reserves (minus sign indicates an increase)*
-0.3	0.0	0.0	0.0	0.0	*Monetary gold*
-0.0	3.7	-1.0	...	...	*Special Drawing Rights*
0.0	0.0	0.0	...	...	*Reserve position in IMF*
40.9	1.1	7.9	...	...	*Foreign exchange assets*
0.0	0.0	3.2	0.0	0.0	*Other assets*
13.9	32.6	0.2	...	...	*Use of IMF credit*

[1] *Non factorial services also included.*
[2] *Net-loans received and Other assets and liabilities included.*
[3] *Equals to Total variation in reserves (with opposite sign) plus Counterpart items.*

IV. BALANCE DE PAGOS

244. HAITI: BALANCE DE PAGOS

(Millones de dólares)

	1960	1965	1970	1975	1977	1978
Exportaciones de bienes y servicios	54.4	44.9	52.9	106.0	174.1	211.2
Bienes fob	38.1	37.8	39.1	71.2	137.7	150.0
Servicios [1]	16.3	7.1	13.8	34.7	36.5	61.2
Transporte y seguros	2.6	0.9	0.9	0.5	1.5	2.2
Viajes	8.1	1.4	6.6	22.0	29.8	53.0
Importaciones de bienes y servicios	58.1	62.2	69.6	159.8	263.1	309.0
Bienes fob	43.4	42.6	47.8	122.1	199.9	207.5
Servicios [1]	14.7	19.6	21.8	37.6	63.1	101.6
Transporte y seguros	5.2	6.7	9.8	24.7	40.0	49.1
Viajes	3.8	5.6	4.3	4.2	6.0	28.2
Balance de bienes	-5.3	-4.8	-8.7	-50.9	-62.2	-57.5
Balance comercial	-3.7	-17.3	-16.7	-53.8	-89.0	-97.8
Servicios de factores	-4.1	-5.2	-3.5	-8.5	-12.1	-14.7
Utilidades	-3.5	-3.0	-3.2	-7.7	-7.8	-9.1
Intereses recibidos	0.0	0.0	0.0	0.0	0.0	0.4
Intereses pagados	-0.6	-2.2	-0.4	-0.9	-4.4	-6.0
Otros	0.0	0.0	0.1	0.0	0.0	0.0
Transferencias unilaterales privadas	2.6	4.7	14.8	22.0	31.0	28.8
Balance en cuenta corriente	-5.2	-17.8	-5.4	-40.4	-70.1	-83.9
Transferencias unilaterales oficiales	6.6	4.1	7.1	13.4	32.6	39.2
Capital a largo plazo	0.7	2.0	2.8	22.3	70.4	41.5
Inversión directa	0.1	1.0	2.8	2.7	8.0	10.0
Inversión de cartera	0.0	0.0	0.0	0.0	0.0	0.0
Otro capital a largo plazo	0.6	1.0	0.0	19.7	62.4	31.5
Sector oficial [2]	0.6	1.0	-0.3	13.8	42.6	20.8
Préstamos recibidos	1.5	1.7	0.9	16.6	44.9	34.2
Amortizaciones	-0.3	-0.8	-1.3	-2.8	-2.3	-2.8
Bancos comerciales [2]	0.0	0.0	0.0	0.0	0.0	0.0
Préstamos recibidos	0.0	0.0	0.0	0.0	0.0	0.0
Amortizaciones	0.0	0.0	0.0	0.0	0.0	0.0
Otros sectores [2]	0.0	0.0	0.3	5.9	19.8	10.7
Préstamos recibidos	0.0	0.0	0.3	9.3	25.9	17.0
Amortizaciones	0.0	0.0	0.0	-3.4	-6.1	-6.4
Balance básico	2.1	-11.7	4.5	-4.6	32.9	-3.2
Capital a corto plazo	1.3	5.6	-2.3	11.5	-0.7	-3.8
Sector oficial	-0.4	1.0	0.5	0.4	0.1	0.2
Bancos comerciales	0.3	0.8	0.0	11.1	-0.8	-4.0
Otros sectores	1.4	3.8	-2.8	0.0	0.0	0.0
Errores y omisiones netos	-1.2	5.2	-1.0	-20.0	-19.8	20.9
Balance en cuenta de capital	7.4	16.9	6.6	27.2	82.4	97.9
Balance global [3]	2.2	-0.9	1.2	-13.2	12.3	14.1
Variación total de las reservas (signo - indica aumento)	-2.2	0.9	-3.7	12.4	-13.0	-5.6
Oro monetario	0.0	0.0	0.0	0.0	-0.1	-0.2
Derechos especiales de giro	0.0	0.0	-0.1	0.3	-0.2	-3.0
Posición de reserva en el FMI	0.0	0.0	0.0	0.0	0.0	-3.1
Activos en divisas	-0.9	0.9	-1.1	2.8	-8.0	0.4
Otros activos	0.0	0.0	0.2	0.0	0.0	0.0
Uso de crédito del FMI	-1.3	0.0	-2.7	9.4	-4.6	0.4

[1] Incluye Otros servicios no factoriales.
[2] Incluye Préstamos netos concedidos y Otros activos y pasivos.
[3] Es igual a Variación total de las reservas (con signo contrario), más Asientos de contrapartida.

490

244. HAITI: BALANCE OF PAYMENTS

(Millions of dollars)

1979	1980	1981	1982	1983	
212.9	305.6	240.4	269.7	267.7	*Exports of goods and services*
138.0	215.8	150.4	173.8	178.5	*Goods FOB*
75.0	89.8	90.0	95.9	89.2	*Services* [1]
3.4	5.6	6.7	6.7	8.7	*Transport and insurance*
64.7	76.5	74.6	79.6	69.9	*Travel*
330.2	483.8	563.5	519.1	524.4	*Imports of goods and services*
220.0	319.0	398.2	336.4	351.9	*Goods FOB*
110.1	164.9	165.2	182.7	172.6	*Services* [1]
48.0	82.8	95.2	91.4	102.6	*Transport and insurance*
32.5	40.6	31.0	41.0	24.2	*Travel*
-82.0	-103.3	-247.8	-162.6	-173.5	***Trade balance (goods)***
-117.2	-178.2	-323.1	-249.4	-256.8	***Trade balance (goods and services)***
-13.4	-14.2	-13.0	-13.8	-12.0	*Factor services*
-7.1	-8.4	-7.2	-7.9	-4.5	*Profits*
0.4	0.5	0.6	0.6	1.1	*Interest received*
-6.8	-6.4	-6.4	-6.4	-8.7	*Interest paid*
0.0	0.0	0.0	0.0	0.0	*Others*
34.1	52.1	64.5	81.0	60.8	*Private unrequited transfers*
-96.6	-140.3	-271.6	-182.2	-208.0	***Balance on current account***
41.7	36.7	65.3	49.2	63.6	*Official unrequited transfers*
63.7	64.6	92.8	44.3	46.5	*Long-term capital*
12.0	13.1	8.3	7.0	8.7	*Direct investment*
0.0	0.0	0.0	0.0	0.0	*Portfolio investment*
51.6	51.6	84.5	37.3	37.9	*Other long-term capital*
44.0	49.0	27.7	33.6	32.0	*Official sector* [2]
41.2	51.6	32.2	38.5	34.8	*Loans received*
-3.1	-2.5	-4.5	-3.8	-2.6	*Amortizations*
0.0	0.0	0.0	0.0	0.0	*Commercial banks* [2]
0.0	0.0	0.0	0.0	0.0	*Loans received*
0.0	0.0	0.0	0.0	0.0	*Amortizations*
7.6	2.6	56.8	3.8	5.9	*Other sectors* [2]
11.5	9.9	60.6	8.4	12.4	*Loans received*
-3.9	-7.4	-3.9	-4.6	-6.5	*Amortizations*
8.8	-39.0	-113.5	-88.7	-97.8	***Basic balance*** [3]
-0.8	-1.0	-5.9	-11.8	-2.1	*Short-term capital*
1.4	1.6	-0.4	0.0	0.0	*Official sector*
-2.2	-2.6	-5.5	-11.8	-2.1	*Commercial banks*
0.0	0.0	0.0	0.0	0.0	*Other sectors*
0.1	11.0	62.1	55.1	67.2	*Errors and omissions (net)*
104.7	111.2	214.2	136.8	175.2	***Capital account balance***
8.1	-29.1	-57.5	-45.4	-32.8	***Global balance*** [3]
-24.1	26.1	50.3	3.3	23.6	*Total variation in reserves (minus sign indicates an increase)*
-5.3	-3.7	2.2	0.9	0.0	*Monetary gold*
-2.4	4.5	2.9	-0.2	-0.0	*Special Drawing Rights*
-3.0	6.1	0.0	-0.1	0.0	*Reserve position in IMF*
-11.5	22.2	15.2	-15.7	-4.8	*Foreign exchange assets*
0.0	0.0	0.0	0.0	0.0	*Other assets*
-1.9	-3.1	30.1	18.4	28.3	*Use of IMF credit*

[1] *Non factorial services also included.*
[2] *Net-loans received and Other assets and liabilities included.*
[3] *Equals to Total variation in reserves (with opposite sign) plus Counterpart items.*

491

245. HONDURAS: BALANCE DE PAGOS

(Millones de dólares)

	1960	1965	1970	1975	1977	1978
Exportaciones de bienes y servicios	70.6	138.7	196.5	344.5	580.6	687.3
Bienes fob	63.1	128.2	178.2	309.6	529.8	626.1
Servicios [1]	7.5	10.5	18.3	34.7	50.8	61.2
Transporte y seguros	1.5	2.0	5.1	10.2	19.3	22.4
Viajes	1.2	2.9	4.1	10.7	13.8	16.8
Importaciones de bienes y servicios	76.6	136.4	244.3	445.5	654.9	776.6
Bienes fob	64.1	113.2	203.4	372.4	550.1	654.5
Servicios [1]	12.5	23.2	40.9	73.1	104.7	122.1
Transporte y seguros	8.0	11.7	20.5	34.0	54.4	63.6
Viajes	1.7	5.6	11.9	15.3	21.5	23.2
Balance de bienes	-1.0	15.0	-25.2	-62.8	-20.3	-28.4
Balance comercial	-6.0	2.3	-47.8	-101.0	-74.3	-89.3
Servicios de factores	9.1	-13.0	-22.6	-28.8	-68.7	-85.3
Utilidades	8.9	-11.8	-20.0	-10.7	-39.0	-47.2
Intereses recibidos	0.7	1.4	2.3	5.7	12.1	17.9
Intereses pagados	-0.5	-2.6	-4.9	-23.9	-42.1	-56.2
Otros	0.0	0.0	0.0	0.1	0.4	0.3
Transferencias unilaterales privadas	-0.5	0.4	2.9	4.9	3.9	4.5
Balance en cuenta corriente	2.6	-10.3	-67.5	-124.9	-138.9	-170.0
Transferencias unilaterales oficiales	3.2	3.3	3.7	12.7	10.3	12.9
Capital a largo plazo	-4.9	10.8	40.1	131.5	148.7	175.7
Inversión directa	-7.6	6.3	8.4	7.0	8.9	13.1
Inversión de cartera	-0.3	-0.5	0.0	0.0	0.0	-0.5
Otro capital a largo plazo	3.0	5.0	31.7	124.5	139.9	163.0
Sector oficial [2]	2.3	2.8	19.4	89.4	33.6	50.1
Préstamos recibidos	4.3	5.6	23.3	96.8	57.3	73.4
Amortizaciones	-1.4	-2.3	-3.4	-5.9	-16.5	-19.7
Bancos comerciales [2]	0.0	0.0	-0.2	1.7	12.7	0.6
Préstamos recibidos	0.0	0.0	0.3	5.7	18.8	17.2
Amortizaciones	0.0	0.0	-0.5	-4.0	-6.1	-16.5
Otros sectores [2]	0.7	2.2	12.5	33.4	93.5	112.3
Préstamos recibidos	0.9	2.9	15.1	52.9	134.4	159.9
Amortizaciones	-0.2	-0.7	-2.6	-19.5	-40.9	-42.7
Balance básico	0.9	3.8	-23.7	19.3	20.1	18.5
Capital a corto plazo	0.2	6.3	10.0	34.2	52.9	-21.4
Sector oficial	0.2	1.2	-0.2	34.2	10.6	-6.3
Bancos comerciales	0.7	2.1	5.3	0.8	9.9	-16.7
Otros sectores	-0.7	3.0	4.9	-0.8	32.3	1.5
Errores y omisiones netos	-0.7	-3.9	0.9	-0.4	-6.5	12.5
Balance en cuenta de capital	-2.2	16.5	54.6	178.4	205.3	179.5
Balance global [3]	0.4	6.2	-12.9	53.4	66.3	9.5
Variación total de las reservas (signo - indica aumento)	-0.4	-6.1	9.8	-54.0	-66.2	-9.8
Oro monetario	0.0	0.0	0.0	0.0	-0.5	0.0
Derechos especiales de giro	0.0	0.0	-0.2	1.8	-1.2	0.6
Posición de reserva en el FMI	0.0	0.0	4.8	0.0	0.0	-8.2
Activos en divisas	-0.9	-3.7	6.2	-54.4	-47.7	3.0
Otros activos	0.0	0.0	-1.0	-0.5	-2.5	0.0
Uso de crédito del FMI	0.5	-2.4	0.0	-0.9	-14.3	-5.2

[1] Incluye Otros servicios no factoriales.
[2] Incluye Préstamos netos concedidos y Otros activos y pasivos.
[3] Es igual a Variación total de las reservas (con signo contrario), más Asientos de contrapartida.

245. HONDURAS: BALANCE OF PAYMENTS

(Millions of dollars)

1979	1980	1981	1982	1983	
838.4	941.7	883.5	767.0	796.8	Exports of goods and services
756.6	850.3	783.8	676.5	694.5	Goods FOB
81.4	91.4	99.8	90.4	102.3	Services [1]
30.2	40.0	38.8	36.9	44.4	Transport and insurance
20.9	24.5	30.5	25.0	22.5	Travel
930.4	1 126.5	1 060.7	822.9	917.2	Imports of goods and services
783.4	954.0	898.6	680.7	761.0	Goods FOB
147.0	172.5	162.0	142.2	156.2	Services [1]
78.8	98.1	89.7	69.3	78.1	Transport and insurance
28.7	31.0	26.8	22.9	20.5	Travel
-26.8	-103.7	-114.9	-4.2	-66.5	**Trade balance (goods)**
-92.0	-184.8	-177.1	-56.0	-120.4	**Trade balance (goods and services)**
-119.9	-153.5	-153.1	-202.3	-149.3	Factor services
-68.1	-77.7	-43.6	-45.0	-30.0	Profits
19.6	24.2	17.9	15.0	12.2	Interest received
-72.0	-100.1	-127.5	-171.8	-131.0	Interest paid
0.4	0.1	0.1	-0.4	-0.4	Others
6.8	7.5	8.8	9.1	9.7	Private unrequited transfers
-204.9	-330.8	-321.3	-249.3	-260.1	**Balance on current account**
13.6	14.1	18.6	21.0	34.9	Official unrequited transfers
180.0	266.2	209.3	168.3	180.4	Long-term capital
28.2	5.9	-3.7	13.8	21.0	Direct investment
-0.1	0.0	-0.2	-0.2	0.1	Portfolio investment
151.9	260.3	213.2	154.7	159.3	Other long-term capital
56.1	53.5	22.5	76.9	52.5	Official sector [2]
78.6	94.4	77.1	125.0	104.4	Loans received
-19.4	-30.5	-40.6	-38.1	-43.1	Amortizations
-14.6	1.6	4.7	-2.0	-2.5	Commercial banks [2]
8.8	12.1	18.3	3.2	2.1	Loans received
-23.4	-10.5	-13.6	-5.2	-4.6	Amortizations
110.5	205.3	186.0	79.7	109.3	Other sectors [2]
205.3	277.6	244.7	142.1	173.6	Loans received
-94.8	-72.4	-78.3	-62.4	-64.3	Amortizations
-11.4	-50.6	-93.4	-60.1	-44.8	**Basic balance**[3]
50.6	12.0	28.2	19.3	-24.9	Short-term capital
-1.4	-8.9	49.3	39.1	-38.0	Official sector
42.5	-8.2	-34.8	17.7	7.7	Commercial banks
9.6	29.0	13.7	-37.4	5.3	Other sectors
-19.5	-38.8	-6.7	-5.2	22.4	Errors and omissions (net)
225.1	253.3	249.4	203.5	212.8	**Capital account balance**
20.1	-77.6	-71.9	-45.8	-47.3	**Global balance**[3]
-25.0	72.9	68.9	52.8	39.3	Total variation in reserves (minus sign indicates an increase)
-0.3	-0.3	0.0	0.0	0.0	Monetary gold
-6.4	10.1	-1.6	-0.2	-0.4	Special Drawing Rights
0.2	8.0	0.0	0.0	-4.4	Reserve position in IMF
-18.5	41.2	50.5	-11.0	3.4	Foreign exchange assets
0.0	-1.2	-2.6	-2.1	-2.0	Other assets
0.0	15.0	22.7	66.1	42.8	Use of IMF credit

[1] Non factorial services also included.
[2] Net-loans received and Other assets and liabilities included.
[3] Equals to Total variation in reserves (with opposite sign) plus Counterpart items.

IV. BALANCE DE PAGOS

246. JAMAICA: BALANCE DE PAGOS

(Millones de dólares)

	1960	1965	1970	1975	1977
Exportaciones de bienes y servicios	233.0	331.9	499.3	1 050.7	949.5
Bienes fob	164.6	216.7	341.4	808.6	737.8
Servicios [1]	68.4	115.2	157.9	242.1	211.8
Transporte y seguros	12.9	20.2	27.6	74.4	74.4
Viajes	40.3	64.7	95.5	128.5	105.5
Importaciones de bienes y servicios	260.5	350.9	590.0	1 284.9	891.1
Bienes fob	187.6	254.8	449.0	969.6	666.7
Servicios [1]	72.9	96.1	141.0	315.3	224.3
Transporte y seguros	41.7	43.7	87.8	193.4	147.5
Viajes	6.7	11.8	15.5	52.2	11.9
Balance de bienes	**-23.0**	**-38.1**	**-107.6**	**-161.0**	**71.1**
Balance comercial	**-27.5**	**-19.0**	**-90.7**	**-234.2**	**58.5**
Servicios de factores	-15.9	-28.6	-84.7	-76.2	-120.7
Utilidades	-30.9	-44.8	-103.9	-59.1	-29.0
Intereses recibidos	4.2	6.9	15.2	21.6	9.7
Intereses pagados	-3.8	-4.9	-9.5	-65.2	-109.4
Otros	14.6	14.2	13.5	26.5	7.9
Transferencias unilaterales privadas	17.1	19.9	26.9	22.7	15.1
Balance en cuenta corriente	**-26.3**	**-27.7**	**-148.5**	**-287.8**	**-47.1**
Transferencias unilaterales oficiales	-0.3	-2.8	-4.4	5.0	5.0
Capital a largo plazo	19.6	22.7	160.7	227.9	51.6
Inversión directa	13.2	14.3	161.4	-1.8	-9.7
Inversión de cartera	8.6	6.4	-6.4	-4.1	0.0
Otro capital a largo plazo	-2.2	2.0	5.7	233.8	61.3
Sector oficial [2]	-0.3	2.0	2.0	153.7	56.0
Préstamos recibidos	0.0	2.0	9.4	159.4	108.0
Amortizaciones	-0.3	0.0	-3.1	-4.0	-50.9
Bancos comerciales [2]	0.0	0.0	0.0	0.0	0.0
Préstamos recibidos	0.0	0.0	0.0	0.0	0.0
Amortizaciones	0.0	0.0	0.0	0.0	0.0
Otros sectores [2]	-1.9	0.0	3.7	80.1	5.3
Préstamos recibidos	0.0	0.0	0.0	115.1	35.6
Amortizaciones	0.0	0.0	0.0	-20.9	-39.9
Balance básico	**-7.0**	**-7.8**	**7.8**	**-54.9**	**9.6**
Capital a corto plazo	8.7	11.6	-0.4	94.8	-22.4
Sector oficial	-2.0	0.0	2.4	25.6	47.1
Bancos comerciales	8.7	11.6	0.0	2.3	-0.1
Otros sectores	2.0	0.0	-2.8	66.9	-69.4
Errores y omisiones netos	-2.5	-4.1	7.3	-83.0	-1.3
Balance en cuenta de capital	**25.5**	**27.4**	**163.3**	**244.5**	**32.8**
Balance global [3]	**-0.8**	**-0.3**	**14.8**	**-43.2**	**-14.2**
Variación total de las reservas (signo - indica aumento)	0.8	1.6	-24.9	39.0	14.6
Oro monetario	0.0	0.0	0.0	0.0	0.0
Derechos especiales de giro	0.0	0.0	-6.4	1.2	-16.4
Posición de reserva en el FMI	0.0	0.0	-0.2	0.0	0.0
Activos en divisas	2.2	1.1	-14.6	63.6	1.1
Otros activos	-1.4	0.5	-3.7	-25.0	2.9
Uso de crédito del FMI	0.0	0.0	0.0	-0.7	27.0

[1] Incluye Otros servicios no factoriales.
[2] Incluye Préstamos netos concedidos y Otros activos y pasivos.
[3] Es igual a Variación total de las reservas (con signo contrario) más Asientos de contrapartida.

246. JAMAICA: BALANCE OF PAYMENTS

(Millions of dollars)

1978	1979	1980	1981	1982	
1 113.0	1 165.1	1 358.9	1 400.3	1 244.7	*Exports of goods and services*
831.1	818.2	962.7	974.0	767.4	Goods FOB
282.0	346.9	396.2	426.3	477.3	Services [1]
100.2	114.1	113.8	97.6	97.9	Transport and insurance
146.9	195.4	240.7	284.4	336.2	Travel
1 032.3	1 197.6	1 386.0	1 682.0	1 603.2	*Imports of goods and services*
750.1	882.4	1 038.2	1 296.7	1 208.9	Goods FOB
282.2	315.0	347.8	385.2	394.4	Services [1]
182.2	202.8	216.7	246.4	243.7	Transport and insurance
10.4	10.9	11.7	13.8	30.1	Travel
81.0	**-64.2**	**-75.5**	**-322.7**	**-441.5**	**Trade balance (goods)**
80.8	**-32.4**	**-27.1**	**-281.7**	**-358.6**	**Trade balance (goods and services)**
-156.6	-186.6	-229.6	-179.5	-195.2	*Factor services*
-92.1	-81.7	-111.9	-2.9	28.6	Profits
8.9	7.9	11.5	14.7	13.2	Interest received
-95.7	-129.1	-151.1	-213.3	-248.3	Interest paid
22.3	16.3	22.0	22.1	11.4	Others
15.1	70.0	81.7	123.3	134.5	*Private unrequited transfers*
-60.6	**-149.0**	**-175.1**	**-337.8**	**-419.2**	**Balance on current account**
10.6	10.1	9.0	0.9	15.9	*Official unrequited transfers*
-95.4	-25.2	231.3	127.7	355.7	*Long-term capital*
-26.5	-26.4	27.7	-11.6	-15.8	Direct investment
0.0	0.0	0.0	0.0	0.0	Portfolio investment
-68.9	1.2	203.6	139.3	371.5	Other long-term capital
108.3	55.0	278.5	150.0	383.9	Official sector [2]
278.1	178.7	395.4	403.9	641.7	Loans received
-167.5	-121.1	-115.1	-253.9	-257.8	Amortizations
0.0	0.0	0.0	0.0	0.0	Commercial banks [2]
0.0	0.0	0.0	0.0	0.0	Loans received
0.0	0.0	0.0	0.0	0.0	Amortizations
-177.2	-53.9	-75.0	-10.7	-12.4	Other sectors [2]
0.0	0.0	46.9	38.4	37.3	Loans received
-177.2	-53.9	-121.8	-49.1	-49.7	Amortizations
-145.4	**-164.1**	**65.2**	**-209.2**	**-47.6**	**Basic balance**
56.1	3.1	38.1	11.7	-64.9	*Short-term capital*
66.4	-6.5	71.3	4.2	-112.7	Official sector
4.8	2.7	-11.5	18.5	-12.0	Commercial banks
-15.0	6.8	-21.7	-11.1	59.8	Other sectors
36.1	-4.1	-30.2	-17.3	-5.4	*Errors and omissions (net)*
7.4	-16.4	248.2	123.2	301.2	**Capital account balance**
-53.2	-165.4	73.1	-214.6	-118.0	**Global balance** [3]
62.4	165.9	-82.9	170.2	...	*Total variation in reserves (minus sign indicates an increase)*
0.0	0.0	0.0	0.0	0.0	Monetary gold
11.5	5.3	0.5	-1.3	...	Special Drawing Rights
0.0	0.0	0.0	-2.8	...	Reserve position in IMF
-22.7	-10.3	-41.6	23.8	...	Foreign exchange assets
0.0	0.0	0.4	-9.9	9.5	Other assets
73.6	170.9	-42.2	160.4	...	Use of IMF credit

[1] Non factorial services also included.
[2] Net loans received and Other assets and liabilities included.
[3] Equals to Total variation in reserves (with opposite sign) plus Counterpart items.

247. MEXICO: BALANCE DE PAGOS

(Millones de dólares)

	1960	1965	1970	1975	1977	1978
Exportaciones de bienes y servicios	1 319.5	1 953.0	2 745.0	6 066.2	7 792.2	10 743.2
Bienes fob	779.5	1 146.0	1 348.0	3 006.8	4 603.6	6 246.3
Servicios [1]	540.0	807.0	1 397.0	3 059.3	3 188.6	4 496.9
Transporte y seguros	0.2	0.0	47.0	180.8	199.7	250.3
Viajes	521.3	775.0	1 171.0	2 168.5	2 122.2	3 208.3
Importaciones de bienes y servicios	1 521.2	2 091.0	3 417.0	8 466.0	7 665.0	11 336.1
Bienes fob	1 131.0	1 492.0	2 236.0	6 278.4	5 624.5	7 991.6
Servicios [1]	390.2	599.0	1 181.0	2 187.6	2 040.5	3 344.5
Transporte y seguros	64.8	85.0	179.0	525.5	487.2	778.6
Viajes	261.6	414.0	755.0	1 355.2	1 183.1	2 151.7
Balance de bienes	**-351.5**	**-346.0**	**-888.0**	**-3 271.5**	**-1 020.9**	**-1 745.3**
Balance comercial	**-201.7**	**-138.0**	**-672.0**	**-2 399.9**	**127.2**	**-592.8**
Servicios de factores	-111.5	-249.0	-451.0	-1 783.1	-2 150.6	-2 770.6
Utilidades	-141.6	-236.0	-359.0	-840.5	-400.6	-675.9
Intereses recibidos	0.0	0.0	67.0	116.7	168.3	404.5
Intereses pagados	-48.9	-103.0	-282.0	-1 094.0	-1 979.0	-2 575.7
Otros	79.0	90.0	123.0	34.7	60.6	76.5
Transferencias unilaterales privadas	-6.9	-5.0	48.0	114.1	153.0	104.0
Balance en cuenta corriente	**-320.1**	**-392.0**	**-1 075.0**	**-4 068.9**	**-1 870.4**	**-3 259.4**
Transferencias unilaterales oficiales	2.0	0.0	7.0	26.5	16.5	88.1
Capital a largo plazo	90.2	169.0	626.0	4 667.2	4 611.1	5 120.6
Inversión directa	-38.1	214.0	323.0	609.0	556.3	823.8
Inversión de cartera	-60.8	37.0	-19.0	155.9	1 345.3	737.1
Otro capital a largo plazo	189.1	-82.0	322.0	3 902.3	2 709.5	3 559.6
Sector oficial [2]	-10.0	-8.0	9.0	366.0	1 076.7	361.5
Préstamos recibidos	0.0	36.0	22.0	376.9	1 143.5	856.6
Amortizaciones	0.0	-37.0	-13.0	-10.9	-66.8	-495.1
Bancos comerciales [2]	0.0	0.0	60.0	1 730.2	893.4	1 006.3
Préstamos recibidos	0.0	0.0	349.0	2 089.0	2 272.7	3 337.6
Amortizaciones	0.0	0.0	-289.0	-358.8	-1 379.3	-2 331.3
Otros sectores [2]	199.1	-74.0	253.0	1 806.2	739.5	2 191.8
Préstamos recibidos	363.2	308.0	522.0	2 263.9	1 787.4	4 245.8
Amortizaciones	-164.1	-328.0	-257.0	-463.2	-982.2	-2 036.7
Balance básico	**-227.9**	**-223.0**	**-442.0**	**624.7**	**2 757.1**	**1 949.3**
Capital a corto plazo	99.8	-62.0	219.0	774.2	-2 430.7	-1 420.7
Sector oficial	-4.1	-12.0	-12.0	-7.3	-292.4	-0.6
Bancos comerciales	62.9	-40.0	151.0	482.4	-468.9	-836.8
Otros sectores	41.0	-10.0	80.0	299.1	-1 669.4	-583.3
Errores y omisiones netos	118.0	218.0	244.0	-1 229.2	49.3	-98.2
Balance en cuenta de capital	**310.0**	**325.0**	**1 096.0**	**4 238.6**	**2 247.3**	**3 692.3**
Balance global [3]	**-10.1**	**-67.0**	**21.0**	**169.8**	**376.9**	**432.9**
Variación total de las reservas (signo - indica aumento)	16.0	78.0	-82.0	-143.3	-332.1	-411.0
Oro monetario	6.0	11.0	-8.0	0.0	-5.8	-6.3
Derechos especiales de giro	0.0	0.0	-48.0	57.3	-55.9	1.1
Posición de reserva en el FMI	0.0	-10.0	-23.0	5.3	0.0	0.0
Activos en divisas	10.0	48.0	-4.0	-208.4	-405.1	-193.6
Otros activos	0.0	29.0	1.0	2.6	-3.5	-1.5
Uso de crédito del FMI	0.0	0.0	0.0	0.0	138.3	-210.5

[1] Incluye Otros servicios no factoriales.
[2] Incluye Préstamos netos concedidos y Otros activos y pasivos.
[3] Es igual a Variación total de las reservas (con signo contrario), más Asientos de contrapartida.

247. MEXICO: BALANCE OF PAYMENTS

(Millions of dollars)

1979	1980	1981	1982	1983	
15 129.2	23 458.0	28 884.4	26 895.0	26 431.7	Exports of goods and services
9 300.3	16 066.7	19 938.1	22 081.4	22 235.4	Goods FOB
5 828.9	7 390.0	8 947.4	4 814.7	4 194.1	Services [1]
320.6	446.2	476.3	425.3	477.9	Transport and insurance
4 184.7	5 243.2	6 346.5	3 500.4	3 040.5	Travel
16 704.3	25 683.4	33 542.3	21 310.9	12 479.9	Imports of goods and services
12 129.7	18 896.8	24 037.6	14 434.2	7 723.0	Goods FOB
4 573.3	6 789.2	9 504.6	6 876.7	4 755.8	Services [1]
1 121.5	1 934.0	2 389.0	1 730.4	1 224.1	Transport and insurance
2 931.0	4 174.4	6 155.1	3 205.2	1 900.2	Travel
-2 829.4	-2 830.1	-4 099.5	7 647.1	14 512.4	**Trade balance (goods)**
-1 575.1	-2 225.4	-4 657.9	5 584.1	13 951.8	**Trade balance (goods and services)**
-4 108.3	-6 209.0	-9 530.7	-11 598.5	-9 095.2	Factor services
-945.2	-1 386.7	-1 898.0	-1 331.9	-307.9	Profits
695.7	1 021.6	1 385.8	1 324.4	1 066.3	Interest received
-3 708.8	-5 476.2	-8 383.5	-11 264.3	-9 866.5	Interest paid
-150.0	-367.7	-635.0	-327.9	12.8	Others
130.5	131.5	114.2	91.8	112.0	Private unrequited transfers
-5 552.9	-8 305.5	-14 074.5	-5 921.5	4 967.5	**Balance on current account**
94.5	144.4	175.3	168.6	243.0	Official unrequited transfers
5 199.8	7 775.7	13 044.3	11 056.4	4 310.7	Long-term capital
1 332.2	2 184.9	2 536.5	1 398.9	496.6	Direct investment
-393.2	-75.1	986.9	654.4	-544.2	Portfolio investment
4 260.8	5 665.9	9 520.8	9 003.1	4 358.3	Other long-term capital
-180.4	655.3	618.4	2 774.7	4 250.6	Official sector [2]
1 751.7	1 148.9	1 803.1	3 157.8	5 194.7	Loans received
-1 933.3	-493.6	-1 184.6	-384.3	-943.1	Amortizations
1 269.5	1 133.7	2 973.5	2 169.6	-39.4	Commercial banks [2]
3 453.7	2 558.9	4 735.9	3 203.7	963.8	Loans received
-2 182.9	-1 425.2	-1 763.6	-1 034.2	-1 001.0	Amortizations
3 171.7	3 876.9	5 928.9	4 058.8	147.1	Other sectors [2]
6 124.0	5 491.2	7 912.2	6 774.6	2 154.4	Loans received
-2 967.8	-1 627.3	-1 623.8	-3 386.5	-2 173.0	Amortizations
-258.6	**-385.4**	**-854.9**	5 303.4	9 521.3	**Basic balance** [3]
-58.1	5 180.2	10 147.4	-1 931.9	-5 045.5	Short-term capital
0.0	67.3	-15.9	-136.7	0.0	Official sector
1 077.0	2 317.1	6 127.3	-439.8	796.1	Commercial banks
-1 135.1	2 795.8	4 036.0	-1 355.4	-5 841.6	Other sectors
597.7	-3 770.0	-8 594.5	-7 482.5	-2 455.0	Errors and omissions (net)
5 835.2	9 330.2	14 774.9	1 811.6	-2 945.6	**Capital account balance**
282.3	1 024.7	700.5	-4 110.0	2 021.9	**Global balance** [3]
-355.7	-938.4	-762.4	...	...	Total variation in reserves (minus sign indicates an increase)
-2.6	-3.9	-7.1	7.4	-9.7	Monetary gold
-144.2	56.1	-33.8	...	...	Special Drawing Rights
0.0	-127.5	-59.5	...	...	Reserve position in IMF
-46.3	-727.3	-661.9	...	...	Foreign exchange assets
0.0	0.0	0.0	0.0	0.0	Other assets
-162.7	-135.7	0.0	...	...	Use of IMF credit

[1] Non factorial services also included.
[2] Net-loans received and Other assets and liabilities included.
[3] Equals to Total variation in reserves (with opposite sign) plus Counterpart items.

IV. BALANCE DE PAGOS

248. NICARAGUA: BALANCE DE PAGOS

(Millones de dólares)

	1960	1965	1970	1975	1977	1978
Exportaciones de bienes y servicios	79.1	171.8	213.1	446.7	719.3	720.2
Bienes fob	63.8	149.2	178.6	374.9	636.2	646.0
Servicios [1]	15.3	22.6	34.5	71.8	83.1	74.1
Transporte y seguros	5.7	8.1	9.7	24.5	29.0	28.2
Viajes	2.0	4.8	13.2	26.3	33.9	25.3
Importaciones de bienes y servicios	87.7	188.7	228.5	588.5	841.3	657.7
Bienes fob	56.4	133.9	178.6	482.1	704.2	553.3
Servicios [1]	31.3	54.8	49.9	106.4	137.2	104.3
Transporte y seguros	15.7	30.4	24.2	55.7	68.2	55.7
Viajes	5.3	13.4	15.1	32.3	46.2	59.8
Balance de bienes	7.4	15.3	0.0	-107.2	-68.1	92.8
Balance comercial	-8.6	-16.9	-15.4	-141.8	-122.0	62.5
Servicios de factores	-2.8	-12.8	-30.2	-59.9	-71.1	-96.9
Utilidades	-2.1	-12.2	-22.9	-23.8	-28.3	-34.6
Intereses recibidos	0.2	2.3	3.7	8.4	9.7	7.6
Intereses pagados	-0.9	-2.9	-10.1	-38.7	-49.9	-66.9
Otros	0.0	0.0	-0.9	-5.7	-2.8	-3.3
Transferencias unilaterales privadas	0.2	2.5	2.5	4.1	0.7	0.1
Balance en cuenta corriente	-11.2	-27.2	-43.1	-197.5	-192.4	-34.3
Transferencias unilaterales oficiales	2.7	4.0	3.6	12.5	10.5	9.4
Capital a largo plazo	5.0	16.5	45.9	178.2	211.1	135.0
Inversión directa	1.7	8.2	15.0	10.9	10.0	7.0
Inversión de cartera	0.0	0.0	0.0	0.0	0.0	0.0
Otro capital a largo plazo	3.3	8.3	30.9	167.3	201.0	128.0
Sector oficial [2]	3.1	-0.4	11.8	106.1	139.9	122.6
Préstamos recibidos	0.4	2.9	15.1	113.3	171.6	152.5
Amortizaciones	-1.3	-2.3	-2.9	-6.3	-27.3	-24.2
Bancos comerciales [2]	0.0	4.5	1.6	-2.8	-0.5	-6.9
Préstamos recibidos	0.0	0.0	0.0	0.0	0.0	0.0
Amortizaciones	0.0	0.0	0.0	0.0	0.0	0.0
Otros sectores [2]	0.2	4.2	17.5	64.0	61.6	12.3
Préstamos recibidos	1.6	6.9	24.7	80.9	96.8	58.1
Amortizaciones	-1.4	-2.7	-7.2	-16.9	-35.1	-45.8
Balance básico	-3.5	-6.7	6.4	-6.8	29.2	110.1
Capital a corto plazo	3.2	31.8	2.5	48.9	-16.3	-184.0
Sector oficial	0.0	0.5	0.2	-3.5	8.2	-12.8
Bancos comerciales	-0.3	17.2	-2.1	22.6	55.1	55.5
Otros sectores	3.5	14.1	4.4	29.9	-79.6	-226.7
Errores y omisiones netos	0.2	-6.9	-0.7	-1.5	-3.6	-9.6
Balance en cuenta de capital	11.1	45.4	51.3	238.2	201.5	-49.2
Balance global [3]	-0.1	18.2	8.2	40.7	9.1	-83.5
Variación total de las reservas (signo - indica aumento)	0.1	-18.2	-11.4	-41.3	-9.4	83.0
Oro monetario	-0.1	0.0	0.0	0.0	-0.4	-0.1
Derechos especiales de giro	0.0	0.0	-1.0	1.7	-0.5	-1.0
Posición de reserva en el FMI	0.0	0.0	0.0	0.0	0.0	0.0
Activos en divisas	0.2	-18.3	-3.9	-18.8	-1.8	98.7
Otros activos	0.0	0.1	-1.2	-30.0	1.1	-14.8
Uso de crédito del FMI	0.0	0.0	-5.3	5.8	-7.7	0.2

[1] Incluye Otros servicios no factoriales.
[2] Incluye Préstamos netos concedidos y Otros activos y pasivos.
[3] Es igual a Variación total de las reservas (con signo contrario), más Asientos de contrapartida.

248. NICARAGUA: BALANCE OF PAYMENTS

(Millions of dollars)

1979	1980	1981	1982	1983	
672.2	494.7	553.3	446.8	463.1	*Exports of goods and services*
615.9	450.5	508.2	406.1	428.5	Goods FOB
56.3	44.4	45.0	40.7	34.5	Services [1]
22.0	13.1	14.7	11.8	10.5	Transport and insurance
18.3	21.6	22.5	20.0	4.9	Travel
510.7	908.6	1 036.8	829.0	925.3	*Imports of goods and services*
388.9	802.9	922.5	723.5	778.4	Goods FOB
121.8	105.7	114.4	105.5	146.9	Services [1]
30.9	51.4	57.8	49.3	50.5	Transport and insurance
47.5	31.0	15.0	20.0	7.4	Travel
227.0	-352.5	-414.2	-317.4	-349.9	**Trade balance (goods)**
161.5	-413.9	-483.6	-382.2	-462.2	**Trade balance (goods and services)**
-72.9	-89.2	-92.7	-140.0	-60.5	*Factor services*
-12.7	-20.6	0.0	-5.2	-1.4	Profits
6.5	19.3	28.3	8.7	6.5	Interest received
-65.4	-87.9	-121.0	-143.5	-65.7	Interest paid
-1.3	0.0	0.0	0.0	0.0	Others
1.4	12.4	13.2	7.9	3.6	*Private unrequited transfers*
90.1	-490.5	-563.0	-514.2	-519.1	**Balance on current account**
90.2	111.5	57.1	43.5	75.7	*Official unrequited transfers*
125.3	343.3	596.3	441.6	557.0	*Long-term capital*
2.8	0.0	0.0	0.0	7.7	Direct investment
0.0	0.0	0.0	0.0	0.0	Portfolio investment
122.5	343.3	596.3	441.6	549.3	Other long-term capital
68.9	326.2	514.3	435.3	555.4	Official sector [2]
85.4	343.9	580.7	486.0	594.0	Loans received
-16.5	-17.7	-66.3	-50.7	-38.6	Amortizations
56.1	17.4	82.0	20.4	33.5	Commercial banks [2]
56.1	21.7	86.4	28.7	37.6	Loans received
0.0	-4.3	-4.4	-8.3	-4.1	Amortizations
-2.5	-0.3	0.0	-14.1	-39.6	Other sectors [2]
14.6	0.0	0.0	0.0	0.0	Loans received
-17.1	-0.3	0.0	-14.1	-39.6	Amortizations
305.6	-35.7	90.3	-29.1	113.7	**Basic balance** [3]
-266.9	-137.3	-37.3	-49.0	-20.0	*Short-term capital*
0.0	0.0	0.0	0.0	0.0	Official sector
0.0	0.0	0.0	0.0	0.0	Commercial banks
-266.9	-137.3	-37.3	-49.0	-20.0	Other sectors
-43.9	-20.7	-0.4	143.7	-24.5	*Errors and omissions (net)*
-95.3	296.9	615.8	579.8	588.2	**Capital account balance**
-5.3	-193.7	52.7	65.6	69.1	**Global balance** [3]
-8.6	225.4	...	...	...	*Total variation in reserves (minus sign indicates an increase)*
-0.5	0.0	0.0	0.0	0.0	Monetary gold
5.6	0.0	...	...	...	Special Drawing Rights
0.0	0.0	...	...	...	Reserve position in IMF
-74.9	120.0	...	...	...	Foreign exchange assets
6.6	113.4	10.0	-11.5	0.0	Other assets
54.7	-7.9	...	...	...	Use of IMF credit

[1] Non factorial services also included.
[2] Net-loans received and Other assets and liabilities included.
[3] Equals to Total variation in reserves (with opposite sign) plus Counterpart items.

IV. BALANCE DE PAGOS

249. PANAMA: BALANCE DE PAGOS

(Millones de dólares)

	1960	1965	1970	1975	1977	1978
Exportaciones de bienes y servicios	97.0	185.3	380.6	843.2	898.6	938.1
Bienes fob	39.0	92.5	130.3	330.9	288.5	301.9
Servicios [1]	58.0	92.8	250.3	512.4	610.1	636.3
Transporte y seguros	6.4	14.7	31.4	151.6	133.0	105.2
Viajes	25.1	41.0	82.8	137.0	176.6	200.9
Importaciones de bienes y servicios	142.9	240.5	419.9	987.5	991.3	1 094.1
Bienes fob	108.7	192.4	331.0	823.1	790.4	862.1
Servicios [1]	34.2	48.1	88.9	164.4	200.9	232.0
Transporte y seguros	17.1	26.9	45.8	100.0	111.7	127.5
Viajes	7.1	10.0	22.7	32.2	34.8	37.2
Balance de bienes	**-69.7**	**-99.9**	**-200.7**	**-492.2**	**-501.9**	**-560.3**
Balance comercial	**-45.9**	**-55.2**	**-39.3**	**-144.2**	**-92.7**	**-156.0**
Servicios de factores	13.5	21.5	-28.9	-19.5	-60.4	-50.8
Utilidades	-11.5	-15.1	-19.4	2.7	-20.8	-16.2
Intereses recibidos	2.2	0.0	12.6	374.3	482.2	794.6
Intereses pagados	-1.1	-5.3	-22.1	-400.2	-524.9	-832.2
Otros	23.9	41.9	0.0	3.6	3.2	2.9
Transferencias unilaterales privadas	-5.3	-5.8	-10.9	-25.6	-29.9	-33.6
Balance en cuenta corriente	**-37.7**	**-39.5**	**-79.1**	**-189.4**	**-183.0**	**-240.3**
Transferencias unilaterales oficiales	6.1	9.7	14.9	20.8	27.6	31.4
Capital a largo plazo	21.9	22.6	119.8	185.4	-113.1	452.8
Inversión directa	17.3	15.2	33.4	7.6	10.9	-0.8
Inversión de cartera	-0.4	-0.1	-1.1	1.1	12.6	70.1
Otro capital a largo plazo	5.0	7.5	87.5	176.7	-136.6	383.5
Sector oficial [2]	6.8	2.8	37.8	66.4	89.9	341.3
Préstamos recibidos	7.8	6.5	61.6	89.1	122.8	684.8
Amortizaciones	-0.4	-1.9	-22.9	-22.5	-31.5	-343.5
Bancos comerciales [2]	0.0	0.2	41.7	15.3	-410.9	-33.4
Préstamos recibidos	0.0	0.3	42.0	15.4	1.1	0.0
Amortizaciones	0.0	-0.1	-0.3	-0.1	-411.8	-33.4
Otros sectores [2]	-1.8	4.5	8.0	94.9	184.4	75.6
Préstamos recibidos	0.0	5.2	9.6	119.4	245.9	212.7
Amortizaciones	-0.2	-0.4	-1.8	-21.5	-58.8	-143.9
Balance básico	**-9.7**	**-7.2**	**55.6**	**16.8**	**-268.5**	**244.0**
Capital a corto plazo	10.8	3.9	15.4	77.8	331.1	-155.9
Sector oficial	1.9	1.4	0.1	-1.8	3.4	5.1
Bancos comerciales	9.9	5.8	19.5	93.2	377.3	-162.0
Otros sectores	-1.0	-3.3	-4.2	-13.6	-49.6	1.0
Errores y omisiones netos	2.3	3.9	-71.7	-117.4	-70.1	-1.8
Balance en cuenta de capital	**41.1**	**40.1**	**78.5**	**166.6**	**175.7**	**326.6**
Balance global [3]	**3.4**	**0.6**	**-0.6**	**-22.8**	**-7.2**	**86.4**
Variación total de las reservas (signo - indica aumento)	-3.4	-0.6	-4.0	16.2	9.8	-78.4
Oro monetario	0.0	0.0	0.0	0.0	0.0	0.0
Derechos especiales de giro	0.0	0.0	-3.2	-4.7	0.6	0.3
Posición de reserva en el FMI	0.0	0.0	-1.0	0.0	0.0	-4.8
Activos en divisas	-3.4	-0.6	2.6	9.4	7.5	-75.1
Otros activos	0.0	0.0	0.3	0.0	0.0	0.0
Uso de crédito del FMI	0.0	0.0	-2.7	11.4	1.8	1.2

[1] Incluye Otros servicios no factoriales.
[2] Incluye Préstamos netos concedidos y Otros activos y pasivos.
[3] Es igual a Variación total de las reservas (con signo contrario), más Asientos de contrapartida.

249. PANAMA: BALANCE OF PAYMENTS

(Millions of dollars)

1979	1980	1981	1982	1983	
1 129.6	1 503.5	1 606.5	1 603.2	1 577.0	*Exports of goods and services*
355.6	374.6	343.4	344.9	317.0	*Goods FOB*
774.0	1 128.9	1 263.1	1 258.4	1 260.0	*Services* [1]
128.4	506.9	578.8	574.4	608.0	*Transport and insurance*
213.6	168.4	170.7	172.0	170.0	*Travel*
1 366.0	1 670.9	1 831.1	1 856.4	1 626.0	*Imports of goods and services*
1 085.7	1 317.1	1 440.9	1 441.3	1 246.0	*Goods FOB*
280.2	353.6	390.2	415.1	380.0	*Services* [1]
159.6	218.0	238.5	243.4	210.0	*Transport and insurance*
48.5	56.0	65.1	78.5	72.0	*Travel*
-730.1	-942.6	-1 097.6	-1 096.4	-929.0	***Trade balance (goods)***
-236.4	-167.4	-224.6	-253.1	-49.0	***Trade balance (goods and services)***
-87.0	-142.5	-222.7	-230.5	-300.0	*Factor services*
-38.0	-52.5	-31.4	-34.8	-40.0	*Profits*
1 435.0	2 107.3	2 821.8	2 815.9	2 200.0	*Interest received*
-1 495.4	-2 199.5	-3 018.8	-3 017.3	-2 466.0	*Interest paid*
11.4	2.1	5.7	5.7	6.0	*Others*
-39.3	-53.6	-49.1	-54.8	-60.0	*Private unrequited transfers*
-362.7	-363.4	-496.3	-538.4	-409.0	***Balance on current account***
51.6	41.3	77.9	84.7	100.0	*Official unrequited transfers*
314.0	295.2	275.0	1 385.1	...	*Long-term capital*
49.7	45.2	37.1	277.4	...	*Direct investment*
203.9	16.1	25.4	261.5	...	*Portfolio investment*
60.3	233.9	212.5	846.1	...	*Other long-term capital*
114.3	215.0	84.3	368.1	...	*Official sector* [2]
225.3	284.1	217.3	553.1	...	*Loans received*
-111.0	-65.9	-131.4	-183.4	...	*Amortizations*
42.9	41.5	134.4	256.0	...	*Commercial banks* [2]
43.0	41.6	134.5	256.1	...	*Loans received*
-0.1	-0.1	-0.1	-0.1	...	*Amortizations*
-96.9	-22.6	-6.2	222.0	...	*Other sectors* [2]
98.6	113.4	139.8	334.1	...	*Loans received*
-196.0	-136.4	-146.5	-113.1	...	*Amortizations*
2.8	-26.9	-143.4	931.3	...	***Basic balance*** [3]
391.3	-429.1	-151.3	-1 308.9	...	*Short-term capital*
-3.2	1.7	2.4	4.7	...	*Official sector*
432.9	-385.1	-85.3	-629.6	...	*Commercial banks*
-38.4	-45.7	-68.4	-684.0	...	*Other sectors*
-421.5	467.2	221.1	363.6	...	*Errors and omissions (net)*
335.4	374.7	422.6	524.4	440.0	***Capital account balance***
-27.3	11.3	-73.7	-14.0	31.0	***Global balance*** [3]
20.8	-17.2	66.4	9.2	...	*Total variation in reserves (minus sign indicates an increase)*
0.0	0.0	-1.7	0.0	...	*Monetary gold*
0.1	3.7	-1.9	-0.9	3.8	*Special Drawing Rights*
1.5	-7.0	10.3	0.0	-9.1	*Reserve position in IMF*
30.2	4.5	-11.0	19.9	-100.3	*Foreign exchange assets*
0.0	0.0	0.0	0.0	...	*Other assets*
-11.0	-18.4	70.6	-9.8	108.8	*Use of IMF credit*

[1] *Non factorial services also included.*
[2] *Net-loans received and Other assets and liabilities included.*
[3] *Equals to Total variation in reserves (with opposite sign) plus Counterpart items.*

250. PARAGUAY: BALANCE DE PAGOS

(Millones de dólares)

	1960	1965	1970	1975	1977	1978
Exportaciones de bienes y servicios	43.6	66.4	89.3	222.2	390.1	434.4
Bienes fob	37.3	60.8	65.3	188.0	327.1	356.1
Servicios [1]	6.3	5.6	24.0	34.1	62.9	78.3
Transporte y seguros	1.3	1.4	2.5	2.3	2.5	2.4
Viajes	0.9	0.6	14.2	10.3	35.4	40.4
Importaciones de bienes y servicios	55.3	76.9	98.4	282.4	432.2	527.7
Bienes fob	44.7	56.7	76.6	227.3	360.1	431.9
Servicios [1]	10.6	20.2	21.8	55.0	72.2	95.7
Transporte y seguros	5.9	9.1	9.0	31.9	43.9	64.5
Viajes	1.7	3.0	5.1	11.8	16.5	19.7
Balance de bienes	**-7.4**	**4.1**	**-11.3**	**-39.3**	**-32.9**	**-75.9**
Balance comercial	**-11.7**	**-10.5**	**-9.1**	**-60.2**	**-42.1**	**-93.3**
Servicios de factores	-1.5	-3.0	-12.5	-26.0	-17.7	-25.4
Utilidades	-0.4	-1.2	-5.2	-19.4	-20.1	-42.3
Intereses recibidos	0.0	0.1	0.4	6.3	12.5	17.7
Intereses pagados	-1.1	-1.9	-7.7	-18.2	-26.4	-36.6
Otros	0.0	0.0	0.0	5.3	16.2	35.8
Transferencias unilaterales privadas	0.8	1.1	2.3	1.0	0.7	0.6
Balance en cuenta corriente	**-12.4**	**-12.4**	**-19.3**	**-85.2**	**-59.2**	**-118.1**
Transferencias unilaterales oficiales	2.7	3.1	2.9	13.0	0.5	·5.3
Capital a largo plazo	5.7	9.9	18.8	86.0	85.2	166.5
Inversión directa	2.8	3.1	3.8	24.4	21.7	19.7
Inversión de cartera	0.0	0.0	0.0	0.0	0.0	0.0
Otro capital a largo plazo	2.9	6.8	15.0	61.6	63.5	146.9
Sector oficial [2]	0.1	1.5	7.1	19.5	30.7	56.1
Préstamos recibidos	1.6	3.3	9.5	23.1	38.3	64.9
Amortizaciones	-0.9	-0.8	-2.4	-3.6	-7.6	-8.6
Bancos comerciales [2]	0.0	0.0	0.0	6.9	0.1	0.1
Préstamos recibidos	0.0	0.0	0.0	13.1	4.4	6.3
Amortizaciones	0.0	0.0	0.0	-6.2	-4.3	-6.3
Otros sectores [2]	2.8	5.3	7.9	35.1	32.7	90.6
Préstamos recibidos	2.7	6.0	11.6	49.5	54.5	118.1
Amortizaciones	-0.8	-2.1	-4.1	-14.4	-21.8	-27.5
Balance básico	**-4.0**	**0.6**	**2.4**	**13.7**	**26.5**	**53.7**
Capital a corto plazo	1.5	-0.9	8.0	11.0	105.7	107.8
Sector oficial	0.4	-0.2	-1.0	-2.9	3.3	7.3
Bancos comerciales	-0.2	2.6	2.7	-2.8	3.7	8.6
Otros sectores	1.3	-3.3	6.3	16.8	98.7	91.9
Errores y omisiones netos	-0.2	5.8	-5.0	3.9	-20.3	17.2
Balance en cuenta de capital	**9.7**	**17.9**	**24.7**	**113.9**	**170.9**	**296.5**
Balance global [3]	**-2.7**	**5.5**	**5.4**	**28.7**	**111.7**	**178.4**
Variación total de las reservas (signo - indica aumento)	2.7	-5.5	-7.2	-27.8	-112.3	-179.5
Oro monetario	0.0	-0.9	0.0	0.0	-0.2	-0.3
Derechos especiales de giro	0.0	0.0	-2.5	0.4	-0.3	-0.6
Posición de reserva en el FMI	0.0	-0.5	-1.0	0.3	-1.3	-0.5
Activos en divisas	2.9	-4.3	-3.7	-28.4	-108.6	-179.8
Otros activos	0.0	0.2	0.0	0.0	-1.9	1.6
Uso de crédito del FMI	-0.2	0.0	0.0	0.0	0.0	0.0

[1] Incluye Otros servicios no factoriales.
[2] Incluye Préstamos netos concedidos y Otros activos y pasivos.
[3] Es igual a Variación total de las reservas (con signo contrario), más Asientos de contrapartida.

250. PARAGUAY: BALANCE OF PAYMENTS

(Millions of dollars)

1979	1980	1981	1982	1983	
513.6	565.8	566.5	617.3	475.9	Exports of goods and services
384.5	400.4	398.6	396.2	326.2	Goods FOB
129.1	165.6	167.9	221.0	149.7	Services [1]
3.1	4.0	4.6	2.1	1.7	Transport and insurance
69.4	90.7	80.2	59.0	48.9	Travel
731.3	841.8	978.0	1 063.1	709.0	Imports of goods and services
577.1	675.4	772.3	711.3	551.6	Goods FOB
154.1	166.6	205.5	351.7	157.4	Services [1]
93.3	104.4	118.4	105.7	75.2	Transport and insurance
31.4	34.6	38.0	42.3	44.2	Travel
-192.6	-275.0	-373.8	-315.1	-225.4	**Trade balance (goods)**
-217.7	-276.1	-411.5	-445.8	-233.1	**Trade balance (goods and services)**
4.4	-10.5	31.4	53.1	-20.5	Factor services
-18.5	-54.3	-38.0	-12.6	-38.6	Profits
45.1	76.7	102.4	122.1	63.0	Interest received
-55.0	-81.0	-92.9	-95.5	-77.5	Interest paid
32.8	48.2	59.9	39.1	32.6	Others
3.1	3.1	2.5	1.5	1.4	Private unrequited transfers
-210.2	-283.5	-377.7	-391.2	-252.3	**Balance on current account**
4.3	1.6	3.3	3.5	4.8	Official unrequited transfers
135.7	192.2	168.4	265.5	289.3	Long-term capital
50.3	31.8	32.0	36.7	4.9	Direct investment
0.0	0.0	7.1	7.9	3.3	Portfolio investment
85.4	160.5	129.4	220.9	281.0	Other long-term capital
9.9	85.3	39.3	60.5	138.7	Official sector [2]
21.1	97.7	59.5	82.6	162.1	Loans received
-11.2	-12.5	-20.3	-22.1	-23.4	Amortizations
3.1	0.8	10.7	10.7	7.2	Commercial banks [2]
8.9	7.2	16.7	16.3	10.3	Loans received
-5.8	-6.2	-6.1	-5.6	-3.1	Amortizations
72.4	74.4	79.4	149.7	135.2	Other sectors [2]
113.1	134.8	141.5	217.0	168.5	Loans received
-40.8	-60.4	-60.8	-52.0	-33.4	Amortizations
-70.3	-89.7	-206.0	-122.1	41.8	**Basic balance**[3]
223.3	260.7	262.6	73.5	-43.2	Short-term capital
14.9	3.3	11.8	10.5	22.1	Official sector
-9.3	-14.1	-13.4	0.6	7.4	Commercial banks
217.7	271.5	264.2	62.5	-72.7	Other sectors
8.9	-20.0	-13.1	-13.8	5.9	Errors and omissions (net)
372.0	434.3	421.2	328.6	256.8	**Capital account balance**
161.8	150.8	43.5	-62.6	4.5	**Global balance**[3]
-165.1	-152.8	-43.2	121.3	47.6	Total variation in reserves (minus sign indicates an increase)
-3.9	-0.3	0.4	0.2	0.2	Monetary gold
-3.8	-1.8	-3.4	-8.5	-5.7	Special Drawing Rights
-2.3	-8.2	-10.3	-1.1	-3.3	Reserve position in IMF
-154.3	-142.8	-30.1	132.8	60.4	Foreign exchange assets
-0.8	0.3	0.4	-2.0	-4.0	Other assets
0.0	0.0	0.0	0.0	0.0	Use of IMF credit

[1] Non factorial services also included.
[2] Net-loans received and Other assets and liabilities included.
[3] Equals to Total variation in reserves (with opposite sign) plus Counterpart items.

251. PERU: BALANCE DE PAGOS

(Millones de dólares)

	1960	1965	1970	1975	1977	1978
Exportaciones de bienes y servicios	494.1	772.0	1 224.0	1 688.9	2 131.0	2 400.6
Bienes fob	444.4	685.0	1 034.0	1 290.6	1 725.7	1 940.7
Servicios [1]	49.7	87.0	190.0	398.2	406.5	461.2
Transporte y seguros	14.2	35.0	69.0	153.0	175.1	179.3
Viajes	17.8	25.0	52.0	91.1	112.1	141.5
Importaciones de bienes y servicios	426.4	845.0	971.0	3 037.8	2 688.4	2 070.6
Bienes fob	326.6	653.0	699.0	2 389.4	2 164.0	1 599.9
Servicios [1]	99.8	192.0	272.0	648.4	524.4	469.4
Transporte y seguros	58.3	116.0	131.0	350.9	324.6	262.7
Viajes	19.5	39.0	60.0	83.8	36.2	32.6
Balance de bienes	**117.8**	**32.0**	**335.0**	**-1 098.8**	**-438.3**	**340.8**
Balance comercial	**67.7**	**-73.0**	**253.0**	**-1 348.9**	**-557.4**	**330.0**
Servicios de factores	-66.0	-91.0	-133.0	-241.6	-422.1	-578.8
Utilidades	-58.7	-62.0	-73.0	-14.6	-53.7	-84.1
Intereses recibidos	0.1	4.0	15.0	34.0	12.9	14.0
Intereses pagados	-7.4	-33.0	-75.0	-261.0	-381.3	-508.8
Otros	0.0	0.0	0.0	0.0	0.0	0.0
Transferencias unilaterales privadas	2.5	5.0	26.0	17.0	4.7	3.8
Balance en cuenta corriente	**4.2**	**-159.0**	**146.0**	**-1 573.5**	**-976.0**	**-243.8**
Transferencias unilaterales oficiales	3.7	11.0	56.0	32.8	52.5	53.9
Capital a largo plazo	-2.0	124.0	-17.0	1 293.1	955.4	264.6
Inversión directa	18.2	38.0	-70.0	315.7	54.9	26.2
Inversión de cartera	0.0	-3.0	-7.0	0.0	0.0	0.0
Otro capital a largo plazo	-20.2	89.0	60.0	977.4	900.5	238.4
Sector oficial [2]	-29.1	35.0	57.0	630.1	882.8	224.8
Préstamos recibidos	12.8	43.0	99.0	811.1	1 285.1	1 102.3
Amortizaciones	-39.9	-8.0	-95.0	-208.8	-395.2	-867.6
Bancos comerciales [2]	0.0	0.0	0.0	0.0	0.0	0.0
Préstamos recibidos	0.0	0.0	0.0	0.0	0.0	0.0
Amortizaciones	0.0	0.0	0.0	0.0	0.0	0.0
Otros sectores [2]	8.9	54.0	3.0	347.2	17.7	13.6
Préstamos recibidos	10.4	78.0	74.0	571.9	117.9	96.2
Amortizaciones	-2.3	-36.0	-71.0	-224.6	-100.3	-82.6
Balance básico	**5.9**	**-24.0**	**185.0**	**-247.7**	**31.9**	**74.7**
Capital a corto plazo	9.2	77.0	98.0	-57.1	149.5	-100.8
Sector oficial	4.3	56.0	-11.0	36.4	108.6	-37.2
Bancos comerciales	4.0	-6.0	23.0	57.1	38.6	-65.8
Otros sectores	0.9	27.0	86.0	-150.6	2.3	2.2
Errores y omisiones netos	2.5	-38.0	-35.0	-190.6	-112.7	52.9
Balance en cuenta de capital	**13.4**	**174.0**	**102.0**	**1 078.2**	**1 042.4**	**268.1**
Balance global [3]	**17.6**	**15.0**	**248.0**	**-495.4**	**66.4**	**24.3**
Variación total de las reservas (signo - indica aumento)	-17.6	-15.0	-187.0	498.3	-60.4	-5.6
Oro monetario	-14.4	0.0	-15.0	0.0	0.0	-0.1
Derechos especiales de giro	0.0	0.0	-14.0	2.0	-0.2	-2.9
Posición de reserva en el FMI	-1.0	0.0	0.0	1.7	0.0	0.0
Activos en divisas	-2.0	-15.0	-140.0	495.8	-67.7	-29.5
Otros activos	-0.2	0.0	0.0	-1.2	-13.1	-101.3
Uso de crédito del FMI	0.0	0.0	-18.0	0.0	20.6	128.2

[1] Incluye Otros servicios no factoriales.
[2] Incluye Préstamos netos concedidos y Otros activos y pasivos.
[3] Es igual a Variación total de las reservas (con signo contrario), más Asientos de contrapartida.

(Millions of dollars)

1979	1980	1981	1982	1983	
4 101.1	4 649.7	4 019.3	4 075.6	3 728.0	Exports of goods and services
3 519.3	3 898.8	3 249.7	3 293.5	3 016.5	Goods FOB
581.8	750.9	769.6	782.0	711.5	Services [1]
254.7	283.7	286.2	293.4	261.8	Transport and insurance
174.6	291.5	262.5	251.8	209.2	Travel
2 502.2	3 887.0	4 888.8	4 819.6	3 688.7	Imports of goods and services
1 955.3	3 062.3	3 802.9	3 721.3	2 722.8	Goods FOB
546.9	824.7	1 087.2	1 097.2	965.9	Services [1]
319.4	433.1	559.4	525.3	446.6	Transport and insurance
45.3	106.7	175.3	205.3	191.2	Travel
1 564.0	836.6	-553.1	-427.7	293.7	**Trade balance (goods)**
1 598.9	762.7	-869.5	-744.0	39.4	**Trade balance (goods and services)**
-936.4	-835.0	-1 019.8	-1 034.1	-1 132.8	Factor services
-392.5	-291.7	-251.9	-118.0	-137.4	Profits
55.9	201.4	203.5	109.0	114.0	Interest received
-601.0	-743.4	-970.2	-1 025.0	-1 110.4	Interest paid
0.0	0.0	0.0	0.0	0.0	Others
0.0	0.0	0.0	0.0	0.0	Private unrequited transfers
662.5	-72.3	-1 889.4	-1 777.0	-1 092.4	**Balance on current account**
121.7	134.0	166.2	170.9	222.8	Official unrequited transfers
697.9	272.6	429.0	1 142.8	1 237.0	Long-term capital
70.1	26.8	125.2	47.9	37.6	Direct investment
0.0	0.0	0.0	0.0	0.0	Portfolio investment
627.8	245.7	303.8	1 094.8	1 199.4	Other long-term capital
660.1	181.8	169.7	937.3	1 284.0	Official sector [2]
1 684.4	1 580.9	1 612.6	2 043.2	2 577.0	Loans received
-1 007.5	-1 391.3	-1 439.4	-1 105.9	-1 292.0	Amortizations
0.0	0.0	0.0	0.0	0.0	Commercial banks [2]
0.0	0.0	0.0	0.0	0.0	Loans received
0.0	0.0	0.0	0.0	0.0	Amortizations
-32.3	63.9	134.1	157.6	-84.6	Other sectors [2]
89.1	181.0	294.4	377.5	131.4	Loans received
-118.8	-117.1	-160.4	-221.1	-217.0	Amortizations
1 482.1	334.2	-1 294.2	-463.3	367.4	**Basic balance** [3]
-370.0	500.8	59.0	-112.8	-6.3	Short-term capital
-299.6	90.0	-17.1	-263.1	61.4	Official sector
-52.5	13.3	77.9	27.4	-2.1	Commercial banks
-17.9	397.5	-1.8	122.9	-65.6	Other sectors
-36.0	-185.7	509.5	438.3	-426.8	Errors and omissions (net)
413.6	725.5	1 165.9	1 638.0	1 026.7	**Capital account balance**
1 076.1	653.2	-723.5	-139.0	-65.7	**Global balance** [3]
-1 065.8	-606.6	565.2	121.9	...	Total variation in reserves (minus sign indicates an increase)
-63.6	-173.0	-118.4	0.0	0.0	Monetary gold
-100.2	93.9	1.3	-21.7	32.5	Special Drawing Rights
0.0	0.0	0.0	0.0	...	Reserve position in IMF
-1 030.5	-553.2	769.4	-118.8	...	Foreign exchange assets
-29.4	42.5	0.0	0.0	0.0	Other assets
157.8	-16.9	-87.1	262.4	...	Use of IMF credit

[1] Non factorial services also included.
[2] Net-loans received and Other assets and liabilities included.
[3] Equals to Total variation in reserves (with opposite sign) plus Counterpart items.

252. REPUBLICA DOMINICANA: BALANCE DE PAGOS

(Millones de dólares)

	1960	1965	1970	1975	1977	1978
Exportaciones de bienes y servicios	172.1	144.7	257.0	1 009.9	927.2	828.1
Bienes fob	157.4	125.5	214.0	893.9	780.5	675.5
Servicios [1]	4.7	19.2	43.0	116.2	146.8	152.5
Transporte y seguros	3.5	4.3	9.3	16.1	19.0	19.7
Viajes	3.0	3.3	16.4	58.8	92.4	92.3
Importaciones de bienes y servicios	116.9	166.4	364.2	1 009.0	1 097.0	1 154.0
Bienes fob	90.3	120.7	278.0	772.7	849.3	862.4
Servicios [1]	26.6	45.7	86.2	236.3	247.7	291.6
Transporte y seguros	11.3	16.6	40.7	124.2	103.4	110.9
Viajes	5.1	19.9	37.0	75.2	102.2	126.3
Balance de bienes	**67.1**	**4.8**	**-64.0**	**121.2**	**-68.8**	**-186.9**
Balance comercial	**55.2**	**-21.7**	**-107.2**	**1.0**	**-169.8**	**-325.9**
Servicios de factores	-9.6	-12.0	-25.9	-112.8	-98.4	-135.7
Utilidades	-8.6	-7.5	0.0	-77.9	-28.8	-40.7
Intereses recibidos	1.3	1.0	1.5	5.2	12.3	20.8
Intereses pagados	-2.3	-5.5	-27.4	-40.1	-81.8	-115.8
Otros	0.0	0.0	0.0	0.0	0.0	0.0
Transferencias unilaterales privadas	-3.0	12.4	30.4	34.2	136.1	146.4
Balance en cuenta corriente	**42.6**	**-21.3**	**-102.7**	**-77.6**	**-132.0**	**-315.4**
Transferencias unilaterales oficiales	-0.1	65.2	0.8	4.9	3.5	3.5
Capital a largo plazo	-20.8	7.7	109.5	159.2	218.8	174.7
Inversión directa	1.0	-8.1	71.6	63.9	71.5	63.6
Inversión de cartera	-0.8	0.0	0.0	0.0	0.0	0.0
Otro capital a largo plazo	-21.0	15.8	37.9	95.3	147.3	111.1
Sector oficial [2]	-20.5	7.5	30.6	54.6	102.5	133.1
Préstamos recibidos	0.0	8.8	40.8	92.3	127.8	157.8
Amortizaciones	-20.5	-0.7	-10.2	-37.8	-24.1	-24.9
Bancos comerciales [2]	0.0	0.0	0.0	0.0	-0.8	-0.8
Préstamos recibidos	0.0	0.0	0.0	0.0	0.0	0.0
Amortizaciones	0.0	0.0	0.0	0.0	-0.8	-0.8
Otros sectores [2]	-0.5	8.3	7.3	40.7	45.7	-21.3
Préstamos recibidos	0.0	10.4	12.5	72.0	105.2	56.1
Amortizaciones	-0.5	-2.1	-5.2	-31.3	-59.5	-77.4
Balance básico	**21.7**	**51.6**	**7.6**	**86.4**	**90.2**	**-137.2**
Capital a corto plazo	-14.7	-57.5	4.2	10.0	-24.1	29.0
Sector oficial	-0.2	-14.9	4.6	24.0	-17.2	39.6
Bancos comerciales	-9.9	-16.9	-7.9	-39.8	9.5	19.4
Otros sectores	-4.6	-25.7	7.5	25.7	-16.3	-29.9
Errores y omisiones netos	-28.1	10.3	-16.8	-69.0	-16.9	69.2
Balance en cuenta de capital	**-63.7**	**25.7**	**97.7**	**105.0**	**181.4**	**276.4**
Balance global [3]	**-21.1**	**4.4**	**-5.0**	**27.4**	**49.4**	**-38.9**
Variación total de las reservas (signo - indica aumento)	21.1	-4.4	-0.4	-25.2	-50.2	41.4
Oro monetario	0.1	0.0	0.0	0.2	-0.8	0.0
Derechos especiales de giro	0.0	0.0	0.0	1.2	0.7	0.2
Posición de reserva en el FMI	3.8	0.0	0.0	0.0	0.0	0.0
Activos en divisas	11.9	-9.4	7.7	-26.6	-57.3	26.0
Otros activos	0.0	0.0	0.0	0.0	-12.1	12.0
Uso de crédito del FMI	5.3	5.0	-8.1	0.0	19.4	3.2

[1] Incluye Otros servicios no factoriales.
[2] Incluye Préstamos netos concedidos y Otros activos y pasivos.
[3] Es igual a Variación total de las reservas (con signo contrario), más Asientos de contrapartida.

252. DOMINICAN REPUBLIC: BALANCE OF PAYMENTS

(Millions of dollars)

1979	1980	1981	1982	1983	
1 134.9	1 271.3	1 512.6	1 141.8	1 222.0	*Exports of goods and services*
868.6	962.0	1 188.0	767.7	783.0	*Goods FOB*
266.3	309.4	324.6	374.0	439.0	*Services* [1]
22.2	25.6	31.4	21.2	27.0	*Transport and insurance*
123.9	172.6	206.4	266.1	326.0	*Travel*
1 484.2	1 918.7	1 818.4	1 534.7	1 572.0	*Imports of goods and services*
1 137.5	1 519.7	1 451.7	1 257.2	1 297.0	*Goods FOB*
346.8	399.0	366.7	277.3	275.0	*Services* [1]
131.5	174.5	154.1	137.6	141.0	*Transport and insurance*
158.1	165.8	127.8	87.0	77.0	*Travel*
-268.9	-557.7	-263.7	-489.5	-514.0	**Trade balance (goods)**
-349.4	-647.4	-305.8	-392.9	-350.0	**Trade balance (goods and services)**
-187.7	-210.2	-293.1	-254.0	-299.0	*Factor services*
-57.1	-65.5	0.0	0.0	0.0	*Profits*
31.9	41.8	11.8	4.4	5.0	*Interest received*
-162.5	-186.5	-304.9	-258.4	-304.0	*Interest paid*
0.0	0.0	0.0	0.0	0.0	*Others*
177.0	183.1	182.9	190.0	195.0	*Private unrequited transfers*
-360.1	-674.5	-416.0	-456.9	-454.0	**Balance on current account**
28.8	4.7	10.1	15.0	20.0	*Official unrequited transfers*
160.3	423.1	230.8	262.4	505.0	*Long-term capital*
17.1	92.7	79.7	-1.4	35.0	*Direct investment*
0.0	0.0	0.0	0.0	0.0	*Portfolio investment*
143.3	330.5	151.1	263.9	470.0	*Other long-term capital*
165.1	268.1	225.9	290.1	562.0	*Official sector* [2]
314.1	305.2	285.6	392.9	723.0	*Loans received*
-142.2	-37.1	-59.7	-102.8	-161.0	*Amortizations*
7.1	0.0	-7.3	-0.9	0.0	*Commercial banks* [2]
7.9	0.0	0.0	0.0	1.0	*Loans received*
-0.8	0.0	-7.3	-0.9	-1.0	*Amortizations*
-28.9	62.3	-67.6	-25.4	-92.0	*Other sectors* [2]
53.4	163.2	29.2	25.9	15.0	*Loans received*
-82.3	-100.9	-96.9	-51.3	-107.0	*Amortizations*
-170.9	-246.6	-175.1	-179.5	71.0	**Basic balance** [3]
241.3	250.3	198.3	34.3	-255.0	*Short-term capital*
101.0	87.7	9.2	162.3	-97.0	*Official sector*
-15.9	91.9	192.9	-45.4	-271.0	*Commercial banks*
156.2	70.7	-3.8	-82.6	113.0	*Other sectors*
-72.7	29.9	15.3	-0.7	6.0	*Errors and omissions (net)*
357.6	708.0	454.4	311.0	276.0	**Capital account balance**
-2.5	33.6	38.4	-146.0	-178.0	**Global balance** [3]
-7.8	-44.3	-53.9	160.4	146.2	*Total variation in reserves (minus sign indicates an increase)*
0.0	-4.9	-5.1	16.4	12.0	*Monetary gold*
-3.4	9.5	-1.9	1.3	0.4	*Special Drawing Rights*
0.0	0.0	0.0	0.0	-7.7	*Reserve position in IMF*
-81.2	27.3	-21.5	94.8	-34.0	*Foreign exchange assets*
0.1	-0.4	-0.1	0.1	0.0	*Other assets*
76.7	-75.8	-25.4	47.7	175.5	*Use of IMF credit*

[1] *Non factorial services also included.*
[2] *Net-loans received and Other assets and liabilities included.*
[3] *Equals to Total variation in reserves (with opposite sign) plus Counterpart items.*

253. SURINAME: BALANCE DE PAGOS

(Millones de dólares)

	1960	1965	1970	1975	1977	1978
Exportaciones de bienes y servicios	52.7	70.8	156.3	325.4	396.4	473.7
Bienes fob	44.4	59.4	136.6	277.2	346.1	411.1
Servicios [1]	8.3	11.4	19.7	48.2	50.4	62.4
Transporte y seguros	2.3	2.6	3.9	7.3	8.0	7.3
Viajes	1.5	2.5	3.4	7.6	13.6	18.0
Importaciones de bienes y servicios	60.2	104.2	141.0	355.0	439.4	467.9
Bienes fob	48.3	84.4	104.1	242.1	324.0	343.5
Servicios [1]	11.9	19.8	36.9	112.9	115.2	124.5
Transporte y seguros	7.0	11.4	14.4	40.6	56.8	62.6
Viajes	1.5	3.0	8.5	34.2	19.0	23.1
Balance de bienes	**-3.9**	**-25.0**	**32.5**	**35.1**	**22.1**	**67.6**
Balance comercial	**-7.5**	**-33.4**	**15.3**	**-29.6**	**-43.0**	**5.8**
Servicios de factores	-15.8	-17.6	-40.2	-12.1	-40.2	-37.6
Utilidades	-14.9	-15.5	-38.4	-19.4	-43.1	-41.1
Intereses recibidos	0.3	0.8	2.8	10.1	6.7	7.5
Intereses pagados	-0.1	-0.4	-4.7	-2.4	-0.6	-0.6
Otros	-1.1	-2.5	0.1	-0.4	-3.0	-3.3
Transferencias unilaterales privadas	0.2	0.2	-0.3	-5.9	2.1	3.9
Balance en cuenta corriente	**-23.1**	**-50.8**	**-25.2**	**-47.7**	**-80.9**	**-27.9**
Transferencias unilaterales oficiales	3.5	4.7	12.7	178.8	77.6	55.5
Capital a largo plazo	13.0	43.4	6.7	-97.0	-13.1	14.7
Inversión directa	8.7	34.5	-5.0	0.0	-12.6	-7.7
Inversión de cartera	0.0	0.0	0.0	0.0	-0.1	-0.1
Otro capital a largo plazo	4.3	8.9	11.7	-97.0	-0.4	22.5
Sector oficial [2]	3.6	7.9	11.5	-136.2	-1.2	21.2
Préstamos recibidos	3.8	11.7	12.1	14.0	0.0	22.2
Amortizaciones	0.0	-3.8	-0.6	-150.2	-1.2	-0.9
Bancos comerciales [2]	0.0	0.0	0.0	0.0	0.0	0.0
Préstamos recibidos	0.0	0.0	0.0	0.0	0.0	0.0
Amortizaciones	0.0	0.0	0.0	0.0	0.0	0.0
Otros sectores [2]	0.7	1.0	0.2	39.2	0.8	1.3
Préstamos recibidos	0.0	0.5	0.0	39.2	0.8	1.3
Amortizaciones	0.0	-0.2	0.0	0.0	0.0	0.0
Balance básico	**-6.6**	**-2.7**	**-5.8**	**34.1**	**-16.3**	**42.2**
Capital a corto plazo	3.5	6.7	2.2	2.7	-1.6	-0.6
Sector oficial	0.2	-0.2	1.3	1.6	-1.3	-0.5
Bancos comerciales	-0.1	1.6	0.9	1.1	-0.1	-2.4
Otros sectores	3.4	5.3	0.0	0.0	-0.2	2.3
Errores y omisiones netos	1.0	0.7	11.3	10.1	0.2	0.3
Balance en cuenta de capital	**21.0**	**55.5**	**32.9**	**94.6**	**63.1**	**69.6**
Balance global [3]	**-2.1**	**4.7**	**7.7**	**46.9**	**-17.8**	**41.7**
Variación total de las reservas (signo - indica aumento)	2.1	-4.7	-7.3	-35.9	17.7	-27.9
Oro monetario	-2.5	0.0	0.0	0.0	0.0	17.7
Derechos especiales de giro	0.0	0.0	0.0	0.0	0.0	0.0
Posición de reserva en el FMI	0.0	0.0	0.0	0.0	0.0	-6.3
Activos en divisas	4.6	-4.7	-4.0	-23.8	16.2	-32.2
Otros activos	0.0	0.0	-3.3	-12.0	1.5	-7.1
Uso de crédito del FMI	0.0	0.0	0.0	0.0	0.0	0.0

[1] Incluye Otros servicios no factoriales.
[2] Incluye Préstamos netos concedidos y Otros activos y pasivos.
[3] Es igual a Variación total de las reservas (con signo contrario), más Asientos de contrapartida.

253 SURINAME: BALANCE OF PAYMENTS

(Millions of dollars)

1979	1980	1981	1982	1983	
513.9	613.0	565.7	509.5	434.5	*Exports of goods and services*
444.0	514.3	473.9	428.6	366.9	*Goods FOB*
69.5	98.5	91.9	80.9	67.5	*Services* [1]
9.7	45.1	37.8	35.4	26.4	*Transport and insurance*
21.0	18.6	17.4	12.0	4.3	*Travel*
512.6	657.9	700.1	667.0	578.7	*Imports of goods and services*
369.9	454.1	506.5	460.3	401.8	*Goods FOB*
142.8	203.8	193.7	206.6	176.8	*Services* [1]
71.7	126.3	123.6	110.0	91.7	*Transport and insurance*
32.0	33.6	28.8	35.6	34.5	*Travel*
74.1	60.2	-32.6	-31.7	-34.9	**Trade balance (goods)**
1.3	-44.9	-134.4	-157.5	-144.2	**Trade balance (goods and services)**
-45.2	-20.0	11.5	6.6	-11.2	*Factor services*
-53.6	-39.5	-19.5	-24.7	-24.7	*Profits*
13.3	25.0	35.2	35.4	15.8	*Interest received*
-0.9	-1.6	-1.3	-1.1	-1.5	*Interest paid*
-4.0	-3.8	-2.6	-2.8	-0.9	*Others*
7.0	6.5	3.7	-2.5	-7.9	*Private unrequited transfers*
-37.2	-58.3	-119.1	-153.6	-163.5	**Balance on current account**
80.8	73.8	94.8	96.9	2.5	*Official unrequited transfers*
-16.5	10.3	33.4	10.9	50.4	*Long-term capital*
-15.5	10.1	34.7	-6.2	45.7	*Direct investment*
0.0	0.0	-1.0	-1.2	0.0	*Portfolio investment*
-1.0	0.1	-0.4	18.3	4.7	*Other long-term capital*
-1.7	-1.6	-2.3	-1.3	-1.6	*Official sector* [2]
0.0	0.0	0.0	0.0	0.0	*Loans received*
-1.7	-1.6	-1.3	-0.7	-1.2	*Amortizations*
0.0	0.0	0.0	0.0	0.0	*Commercial banks* [2]
0.0	0.0	0.0	0.0	0.0	*Loans received*
0.0	0.0	0.0	0.0	0.0	*Amortizations*
0.6	1.7	1.9	19.6	6.3	*Other sectors* [2]
0.6	1.7	1.7	19.6	6.3	*Loans received*
0.0	0.0	0.0	0.0	0.0	*Amortizations*
27.1	25.7	9.1	-45.9	-110.6	**Basic balance** [3]
-0.5	-0.7	3.7	1.6	-0.6	*Short-term capital*
1.3	-0.8	2.6	1.4	0.8	*Official sector*
1.0	-7.0	0.0	-6.3	14.5	*Commercial banks*
-2.8	7.1	1.1	6.4	-15.9	*Other sectors*
-0.1	0.7	0.8	1.2	1.3	*Errors and omissions (net)*
64.0	84.3	132.1	110.9	53.7	**Capital account balance**
26.8	26.0	13.0	-42.7	-109.8	**Global balance** [3]
-31.0	-23.7	-16.4	41.2	...	*Total variation in reserves (minus sign indicates an increase)*
0.0	0.0	0.0	0.0	0.0	*Monetary gold*
-3.4	0.7	-3.6	-3.1	...	*Special Drawing Rights*
-0.1	-3.8	0.9	0.5	...	*Reserve position in IMF*
-33.6	-16.7	-15.1	33.8	...	*Foreign exchange assets*
6.1	-4.0	1.4	10.0	-5.0	*Other assets*
0.0	0.0	0.0	0.0	...	*Use of IMF credit*

[1] *Non factorial services also included.*
[2] *Net-loans received and Other assets and liabilities included.*
[3] *Equals to Total variation in reserves (with opposite sign) plus Counterpart items.*

IV. BALANCE DE PAGOS

254. TRINIDAD Y TABAGO: BALANCE DE PAGOS

(Millones de dólares)

	1960	1965	1970	1975	1977	1978
Exportaciones de bienes y servicios	225.0	486.8	344.4	1 289.9	1 548.4	1 564.7
Bienes fob	160.0	413.1	225.3	987.3	1 175.2	1 222.0
Servicios [1]	65.0	73.7	119.1	302.6	373.1	342.8
Transporte y seguros	31.0	46.0	56.6	143.9	187.3	144.0
Viajes	8.9	12.3	23.9	78.3	94.0	111.1
Importaciones de bienes y servicios	176.5	507.4	385.0	853.7	1 152.8	1 409.4
Bienes fob	133.8	440.8	276.2	651.6	860.0	1 044.4
Servicios [1]	42.7	66.6	108.8	202.0	292.8	364.8
Transporte y seguros	21.6	45.0	77.0	125.8	169.8	198.8
Viajes	9.9	12.2	22.9	33.4	51.7	66.2
Balance de bienes	**26.2**	**-27.7**	**-50.9**	**335.7**	**315.2**	**177.5**
Balance comercial	**48.5**	**-20.6**	**-40.6**	**436.2**	**395.6**	**155.4**
Servicios de factores	-53.9	-60.1	-66.3	-83.3	-190.3	-74.7
Utilidades	-56.6	-63.2	-59.4	-102.4	-252.0	-170.9
Intereses recibidos	3.4	6.3	5.4	43.2	77.1	124.9
Intereses pagados	-1.2	-3.4	-7.4	-19.2	-8.6	-22.3
Otros	0.5	0.2	-4.9	-5.0	-6.8	-6.4
Transferencias unilaterales privadas	1.1	0.3	2.6	-10.9	-15.9	-20.8
Balance en cuenta corriente	**-4.3**	**-80.4**	**-104.3**	**342.0**	**189.4**	**59.8**
Transferencias unilaterales oficiales	-2.0	12.1	-4.3	-10.3	-15.3	-17.2
Capital a largo plazo	40.7	63.3	83.3	43.2	230.8	270.6
Inversión directa	44.4	62.6	83.2	93.0	83.6	128.8
Inversión de cartera	0.3	-3.1	1.5	-1.1	-1.1	99.5
Otro capital a largo plazo	-4.0	3.8	-1.4	-48.7	148.3	42.2
Sector oficial [2]	0.0	3.8	-3.7	-34.5	143.1	3.6
Préstamos recibidos	0.0	7.0	4.3	5.1	156.4	3.4
Amortizaciones	0.0	-3.1	-7.2	-12.6	-3.6	-3.9
Bancos comerciales [2]	0.0	0.0	0.0	0.0	0.0	0.0
Préstamos recibidos	0.0	0.0	0.0	0.0	0.0	0.0
Amortizaciones	0.0	0.0	0.0	0.0	0.0	0.0
Otros sectores [2]	-4.0	0.0	2.3	-14.2	5.1	38.6
Préstamos recibidos	0.0	0.0	0.5	0.0	7.6	8.1
Amortizaciones	0.0	0.0	-1.5	0.0	-4.4	-20.5
Balance básico	**34.4**	**-5.0**	**-25.3**	**374.9**	**404.9**	**313.3**
Capital a corto plazo	13.6	-0.9	-4.6	-5.9	51.6	16.9
Sector oficial	3.7	0.0	-0.5	-13.0	-9.8	-15.4
Bancos comerciales	9.9	-0.9	-4.1	7.0	6.7	19.3
Otros sectores	0.0	0.0	0.0	0.0	54.8	13.0
Errores y omisiones netos	-49.4	2.8	10.9	89.2	-12.6	7.3
Balance en cuenta de capital	**2.9**	**77.3**	**85.3**	**116.3**	**254.5**	**277.6**
Balance global [3]	**-1.4**	**-3.1**	**-19.0**	**458.3**	**443.9**	**337.4**
Variación total de las reservas (signo - indica aumento)	1.4	1.4	12.0	-364.9	-461.7	-333.6
Oro monetario	0.0	0.0	0.0	0.0	0.0	-0.6
Derechos especiales de giro	0.0	0.0	-0.5	0.7	-6.0	-7.2
Posición de reserva en el FMI	0.0	0.0	-3.8	-16.0	-1.2	-5.3
Activos en divisas	2.5	1.4	6.0	-345.3	-460.9	-310.7
Otros activos	-1.1	0.0	10.3	-4.2	6.4	-9.8
Uso de crédito del FMI	0.0	0.0	0.0	0.0	0.0	0.0

[1] Incluye Otros servicios no factoriales.
[2] Incluye Préstamos netos concedidos y Otros activos y pasivos.
[3] Es igual a Variación total de las reservas (con signo contrario), más Asientos de contrapartida.

254. TRINIDAD AND TOBAGO: BALANCE OF PAYMENTS

(Millions of dollars)

1979	1980	1981	1982	1983	
2 067.7	3 182.8	3 062.5	2 735.0	...	*Exports of goods and services*
1 648.9	2 585.5	2 531.2	2 211.2	2 273.7	*Goods FOB*
418.9	597.3	531.3	523.7	...	*Services* [1]
197.3	300.4	236.7	215.1	223.9	*Transport and insurance*
122.2	153.1	155.3	180.7	205.7	*Travel*
1 803.4	2 409.1	2 484.7	3 391.1	...	*Imports of goods and services*
1 316.9	1 748.9	1 748.1	2 441.5	2 315.4	*Goods FOB*
486.4	660.3	736.6	949.6	...	*Services* [1]
253.0	350.6	354.1	482.0	440.4	*Transport and insurance*
101.6	139.7	167.3	225.0	262.3	*Travel*
331.9	836.6	783.1	-230.3	-41.7	**Trade balance (goods)**
264.3	773.6	577.8	-656.1	...	**Trade balance (goods and services)**
-252.6	-311.1	-204.1	-113.3	...	*Factor services*
-349.9	-479.0	-421.1	-338.9	...	*Profits*
159.8	232.3	344.7	357.0	230.8	*Interest received*
-54.9	-54.3	-113.4	-111.7	...	*Interest paid*
-7.6	-10.2	-14.3	-19.7	...	*Others*
-27.1	-43.6	-67.2	-81.3	...	*Private unrequited transfers*
-15.4	**419.0**	**306.5**	**-850.6**	...	**Balance on current account**
-18.6	-22.0	-23.5	-58.5	...	*Official unrequited transfers*
434.0	335.9	327.1	518.3	...	*Long-term capital*
93.8	184.6	258.1	341.5	...	*Direct investment*
-3.9	-19.1	1.3	0.3	...	*Portfolio investment*
344.1	170.5	67.7	176.5	...	*Other long-term capital*
57.1	74.4	-95.0	105.9	...	*Official sector* [2]
60.5	231.8	34.4	133.1	207.2	*Loans received*
-4.3	-163.9	-19.0	-24.6	-122.6	*Amortizations*
0.0	0.0	0.0	0.0	0.0	*Commercial banks* [2]
0.0	0.0	0.0	0.0	0.0	*Loans received*
0.0	0.0	0.0	0.0	0.0	*Amortizations*
287.0	96.1	162.7	70.7	...	*Other sectors* [2]
116.4	88.2	71.2	2.8	...	*Loans received*
-14.6	-10.9	-17.1	-9.3	...	*Amortizations*
400.0	**732.9**	**610.1**	**-390.8**	...	**Basic balance** [3]
-61.6	-109.2	-23.9	33.6	...	*Short-term capital*
-11.1	-17.6	-29.5	0.0	...	*Official sector*
-28.4	31.4	13.3	3.0	35.6	*Commercial banks*
-22.1	-123.0	-7.8	30.6	...	*Other sectors*
5.4	9.4	111.8	265.2	...	*Errors and omissions (net)*
359.0	**214.1**	**391.4**	**758.6**	...	**Capital account balance**
343.7	**633.1**	**697.8**	**-92.1**	**-836.7**	**Global balance** [3]
-333.9	-642.2	-565.1	...	...	*Total variation in reserves (minus sign indicates an increase)*
-0.6	0.0	0.0	0.0	0.0	*Monetary gold*
-19.1	-4.6	-14.1	...	...	*Special Drawing Rights*
-10.8	-30.6	-10.9	...	...	*Reserve position in IMF*
-303.0	-607.1	-540.1	...	...	*Foreign exchange assets*
-0.4	0.0	0.0	0.0	0.0	*Other assets*
0.0	0.0	0.0	...	...	*Use of IMF credit*

[1] *Non factorial services also included.*
[2] *Net-loans received and Other assets and liabilities included.*
[3] *Equals to Total variation in reserves (with opposite sign) plus Counterpart items.*

255. URUGUAY: BALANCE DE PAGOS

(Millones de dólares)

	1960	1965	1970	1975	1977	1978
Exportaciones de bienes y servicios	171.2	252.5	290.0	551.0	808.5	912.8
Bienes fob	129.4	196.3	224.1	384.9	611.5	686.1
Servicios [1]	41.8	56.2	65.9	166.1	197.0	226.7
Transporte y seguros	1.6	4.6	8.0	27.0	36.1	44.2
Viajes	35.5	45.0	42.6	98.1	117.5	137.2
Importaciones de bienes y servicios	239.8	168.3	319.6	676.2	914.3	970.3
Bienes fob	187.9	123.1	203.1	494.0	686.7	709.8
Servicios [1]	51.9	45.2	116.5	182.1	227.5	260.4
Transporte y seguros	29.0	18.6	50.2	81.5	79.9	94.9
Viajes	15.0	19.0	45.0	61.6	95.7	108.7
Balance de bienes	**-58.5**	**73.2**	**21.0**	**-109.2**	**-75.2**	**-23.7**
Balance comercial	**-68.6**	**84.2**	**-29.6**	**-125.2**	**-105.8**	**-57.5**
Servicios de factores	-6.6	-15.4	-24.8	-71.1	-67.9	-76.7
Utilidades	-1.0	0.0	-1.7	-3.8	-2.5	0.0
Intereses recibidos	0.0	0.3	1.5	3.8	11.6	18.4
Intereses pagados	-5.6	-15.7	-24.6	-71.1	-77.1	-95.2
Otros	0.0	0.0	0.0	0.0	0.0	0.0
Transferencias unilaterales privadas	-0.3	-0.6	-0.9	-1.5	2.1	1.4
Balance en cuenta corriente	**-75.5**	**68.2**	**-55.3**	**-197.8**	**-171.6**	**-132.7**
Transferencias unilaterales oficiales	1.1	3.8	10.2	8.3	4.6	5.8
Capital a largo plazo	10.6	-16.2	-4.4	135.1	100.9	152.4
Inversión directa	5.8	0.0	0.0	0.0	66.0	128.8
Inversión de cartera	-2.5	-2.9	-0.8	109.8	20.8	-8.6
Otro capital a largo plazo	7.3	-13.3	-3.6	25.4	14.1	32.2
Sector oficial [2]	1.4	-1.0	-11.5	8.1	0.4	38.4
Préstamos recibidos	4.1	4.0	8.9	81.5	51.7	102.9
Amortizaciones	-0.9	-1.1	-19.0	-55.1	-48.8	-56.7
Bancos comerciales [2]	0.0	0.0	0.0	-4.7	0.5	-2.4
Préstamos recibidos	0.0	0.0	0.0	0.0	0.5	0.3
Amortizaciones	0.0	0.0	0.0	-4.7	0.0	-1.8
Otros sectores [2]	5.9	-12.3	7.9	22.0	13.3	-3.9
Préstamos recibidos	4.3	7.7	18.6	29.4	36.3	53.1
Amortizaciones	-1.9	-20.0	-10.7	-7.4	-23.0	-57.0
Balance básico	**-63.8**	**55.8**	**-49.5**	**-54.4**	**-66.2**	**25.4**
Capital a corto plazo	58.2	16.6	46.9	30.6	203.3	-55.1
Sector oficial	48.6	-49.0	23.8	19.4	16.3	-8.8
Bancos comerciales	1.7	7.2	6.8	26.1	74.3	-39.8
Otros sectores	7.9	58.4	16.3	-14.9	112.7	-6.5
Errores y omisiones netos	7.8	-80.4	-23.6	-38.0	42.1	158.6
Balance en cuenta de capital	**77.7**	**-76.2**	**29.1**	**136.0**	**351.0**	**261.5**
Balance global [3]	**2.2**	**-8.0**	**-26.2**	**-61.8**	**179.3**	**128.8**
Variación total de las reservas (signo - indica aumento)	-2.2	8.0	17.6	43.9	-201.0	-173.9
Oro monetario	0.0	16.5	3.4	0.0	-1.2	-0.8
Derechos especiales de giro	0.0	0.0	-0.1	12.9	-6.0	-4.5
Posición de reserva en el FMI	0.0	0.0	0.0	0.0	0.0	-21.8
Activos en divisas	-2.0	-9.0	5.5	19.1	-140.0	-4.0
Otros activos	-0.2	0.5	0.0	-26.8	-28.0	-23.5
Uso de crédito del FMI	0.0	0.0	8.8	38.6	-25.8	-119.3

[1] Incluye Otros servicios no factoriales.
[2] Incluye Préstamos netos concedidos y Otros activos y pasivos.
[3] Es igual a Variación total de las reservas (con signo contrario), más Asientos de contrapartida.

255. URUGUAY: BALANCE OF PAYMENTS

(Millions of dollars)

1979	1980	1981	1982	1983	
1 194.2	1 526.0	1 700.7	1 537.3	1 411.9	Exports of goods and services
788.1	1 058.5	1 229.7	1 256.4	1 156.9	Goods FOB
406.1	467.5	471.1	281.0	255.0	Services [1]
72.1	88.6	91.7	81.3	71.3	Transport and insurance
268.2	298.1	283.0	106.0	89.7	Travel
1 503.5	2 143.8	2 098.1	1 585.5	1 194.8	Imports of goods and services
1 166.2	1 668.2	1 592.1	1 038.4	740.0	Goods FOB
337.3	475.6	506.0	547.0	454.8	Services [1]
123.6	161.4	174.2	115.6	84.6	Transport and insurance
135.7	202.6	203.1	304.0	259.2	Travel
-378.0	-609.6	-362.4	217.9	416.8	Trade balance (goods)
-309.3	-617.7	-397.4	-48.1	217.1	Trade balance (goods and services)
-54.8	-100.1	-73.8	-196.8	-287.9	Factor services
0.0	0.0	0.0	0.0	0.0	Profits
50.0	67.7	145.7	147.2	62.6	Interest received
-107.8	-167.8	-219.6	-344.0	-350.4	Interest paid
3.0	0.0	0.0	0.0	0.0	Others
1.6	2.0	2.9	10.4	11.0	Private unrequited transfers
-362.7	-715.8	-468.2	-234.6	-59.8	Balance on current account
5.6	6.6	6.8	0.0	0.0	Official unrequited transfers
358.8	404.4	345.5	515.0	643.6	Long-term capital
215.5	289.5	48.6	-13.7	5.6	Direct investment
-31.1	-6.8	3.1	-6.8	-15.6	Portfolio investment
174.4	121.7	293.8	535.6	653.6	Other long-term capital
154.0	107.6	109.7	422.6	329.4	Official sector [2]
162.9	180.5	140.0	456.3	531.2	Loans received
-18.5	-65.9	-26.5	-29.5	-197.7	Amortizations
-2.6	4.8	-2.9	-5.4	36.8	Commercial banks [2]
0.0	7.0	0.0	0.6	42.8	Loans received
-1.8	-1.7	-1.7	-1.5	-9.0	Amortizations
23.0	9.2	187.1	118.3	287.4	Other sectors [2]
41.2	25.6	200.9	182.2	345.6	Loans received
-18.2	-16.5	-13.8	-63.8	-58.1	Amortizations
1.7	-304.8	-115.9	280.4	583.8	Basic balance [3]
94.2	310.7	302.8	566.9	-359.0	Short-term capital
8.7	-22.9	-5.1	82.9	40.9	Official sector
127.6	307.3	86.9	240.2	-66.6	Commercial banks
-42.1	26.3	221.0	243.8	-333.2	Other sectors
-10.9	89.5	-161.4	-1 264.0	-295.3	Errors and omissions (net)
447.7	811.2	493.8	-182.1	-10.6	Capital account balance
85.0	95.4	25.6	-416.7	-70.4	Global balance [3]
-4.2	-112.2	-50.7	497.3	71.2	Total variation in reserves
-25.5	-21.7	3.7	84.6	52.0	Monetary gold
-19.7	1.4	-9.8	41.0	-2.0	Special Drawing Rights
0.4	-12.7	1.0	33.1	-10.0	Reserve position in IMF
49.0	-50.0	-37.0	240.0	-122.0	Foreign exchange assets
-8.5	-29.2	-8.6	2.8	11.5	Other assets
0.0	0.0	0.0	96.0	141.7	Use of IMF credit

[1] Non factorial services also included.
[2] Net-loans received and Other assets and liabilities included.
[3] Equals to Total variation in reserves (with opposite sign) plus Counterpart items.

IV. BALANCE DE PAGOS

256. VENEZUELA: BALANCE DE PAGOS

(Millones de dólares)

	1960	1965	1970	1975	1977	1978
Exportaciones de bienes y servicios	2 509.2	2 587.0	2 779.0	9 352.6	10 164.4	9 803.2
Bienes fob	2 383.9	2 482.0	2 602.0	8 853.6	9 556.2	9 084.5
Servicios [1]	125.3	105.0	177.0	499.0	608.3	719.9
Transporte y seguros	20.6	25.0	97.0	261.0	315.2	384.4
Viajes	3.7	21.0	50.0	179.7	168.1	205.3
Importaciones de bienes y servicios	1 505.0	1 777.0	2 238.0	7 107.6	13 149.8	15 169.2
Bienes fob	1 145.4	1 354.0	1 713.0	5 462.5	10 193.6	11 234.2
Servicios [1]	359.6	423.0	525.0	1 646.4	2 955.0	3 935.0
Transporte y seguros	173.7	207.0	238.0	775.8	1 273.8	1 555.0
Viajes	75.9	90.0	143.0	416.5	1 061.3	1 648.9
Balance de bienes	**1 238.5**	**1 128.0**	**889.0**	**3 391.1**	**-637.5**	**-2 149.7**
Balance comercial	**1 004.2**	**810.0**	**541.0**	**2 245.0**	**-2 985.3**	**-5 366.1**
Servicios de factores	-522.0	-705.0	-553.0	99.6	88.7	37.6
Utilidades	-506.4	-704.0	-568.0	-584.0	-291.9	-304.2
Intereses recibidos	0.1	11.0	54.0	739.4	782.2	1 051.7
Intereses pagados	-15.7	-12.0	-39.0	-55.9	-401.6	-709.9
Otros	0.0	0.0	0.0	0.0	0.0	0.0
Transferencias unilaterales privadas	-87.6	-69.0	-86.0	-143.3	-231.2	-370.6
Balance en cuenta corriente	**394.6**	**36.0**	**-98.0**	**2 201.3**	**-3 126.6**	**-5 699.1**
Transferencias unilaterales oficiales	0.0	-1.0	-6.0	-30.4	-52.5	-36.3
Capital a largo plazo	10.6	19.0	91.0	395.8	2 109.7	3 717.2
Inversión directa	-126.0	-12.0	-23.0	417.7	-3.5	67.6
Inversión de cartera	-4.8	-2.0	-12.0	-69.2	-40.9	123.9
Otro capital a largo plazo	141.4	33.0	126.0	47.4	2 154.1	3 525.6
Sector oficial [2]	186.3	24.0	128.0	-128.7	1 250.4	1 854.2
Préstamos recibidos	200.0	68.0	157.0	188.2	1 718.6	2 441.4
Amortizaciones	-5.4	-32.0	-29.0	-297.5	-393.5	-411.9
Bancos comerciales [2]	0.0	0.0	0.0	49.8	414.5	687.3
Préstamos recibidos	0.0	0.0	0.0	0.0	0.0	0.0
Amortizaciones	0.0	0.0	0.0	0.0	0.0	0.0
Otros sectores [2]	-44.9	9.0	-2.0	126.3	489.2	984.1
Préstamos recibidos	17.6	13.0	6.0	377.6	1 077.6	1 751.5
Amortizaciones	-62.5	-4.0	-8.0	0.0	-294.2	-569.7
Balance básico	**405.2**	**54.0**	**-13.0**	**2 566.7**	**-1 069.4**	**-2 018.2**
Capital a corto plazo	-166.2	40.0	-10.0	-233.1	-406.3	-533.4
Sector oficial	-142.6	49.0	2.0	8.5	44.4	-7.5
Bancos comerciales	-1.3	-8.0	1.0	-74.1	2.3	-210.3
Otros sectores	-22.3	-1.0	-13.0	-167.6	-453.0	-315.5
Errores y omisiones netos	-354.0	-83.0	69.0	382.5	2 277.8	1 488.6
Balance en cuenta de capital	**-509.6**	**-25.0**	**144.0**	**516.0**	**3 927.5**	**4 634.9**
Balance global [3]	**-115.0**	**11.0**	**46.0**	**2 717.3**	**800.9**	**-1 064.2**
Variación total de las reservas (signo - indica aumento)	115.0	-12.0	-88.0	-2 699.6	-652.0	1 323.9
Oro monetario	254.0	-25.0	19.0	0.0	0.0	0.0
Derechos especiales de giro	0.0	0.0	-48.0	1.8	-18.8	-52.4
Posición de reserva en el FMI	-34.0	0.0	-28.0	-451.4	64.0	245.8
Activos en divisas	-105.0	13.0	-31.0	-1 919.7	344.2	1 507.3
Otros activos	0.0	0.0	0.0	-330.2	-1 041.4	-376.9
Uso de crédito del FMI	0.0	0.0	0.0	0.0	0.0	0.0

[1] Incluye Otros servicios no factoriales.
[2] Incluye Préstamos netos concedidos y Otros activos y pasivos.
[3] Es igual a Variación total de las reservas (con signo contrario), más Asientos de contrapartida.

514

256. VENEZUELA: BALANCE OF PAYMENTS

(Millions of dollars)

1979	1980	1981	1982	1983	
14 958.8	19 968.1	20 938.3	17 557.1	15 949.8	*Exports of goods and services*
14 159.0	19 050.5	19 963.2	16 331.6	14 659.1	*Goods FOB*
799.7	917.6	975.2	1 225.5	1 289.7	*Services* [1]
472.9	512.8	595.5	663.5	746.4	*Transport and insurance*
178.3	243.4	187.5	309.1	312.3	*Travel*
14 199.1	15 129.0	17 103.7	19 633.7	9 820.1	*Imports of goods and services*
10 004.0	10 876.9	12 122.9	13 583.7	6 780.9	*,Goods FOB*
4 195.1	4 252.1	4 979.6	6 050.0	3 040.2	*Services* [1]
1 453.5	1 448.6	1 567.1	1 523.5	1 044.8	*Transport and insurance*
1 737.7	1 999.2	2 372.5	2 924.5	1 051.2	*Travel*
4 155.1	8 173.6	7 840.2	2 747.9	7 878.1	**Trade balance (goods)**
759.7	4 839.1	3 834.6	-2 076.6	6 129.7	**Trade balance (goods and services)**
-2.6	328.0	574.3	-1 530.2	-2 226.4	*Factor services*
-312.7	-321.5	-350.2	-400.8	-202.1	*Profits*
1 346.3	2 263.4	3 581.1	2 564.6	1 400.9	*Interest received*
-1 036.2	-1 612.6	-2 656.6	-3 694.0	-3 425.2	*Interest paid*
0.0	0.0	0.0	0.0	0.0	*Others*
-387.6	-417.8	-383.2	-614.9	-193.6	*Private unrequited transfers*
369.5	**4 749.3**	**4 025.7**	**-4 221.7**	**3 708.6**	**Balance on current account**
-19.4	-20.8	-25.9	-24.3	0.0	*Official unrequited transfers*
1 443.2	2 060.3	810.1	3 155.3	264.1	*Long-term capital*
87.9	54.7	183.9	252.8	-62.0	*Direct investment*
-73.6	1 310.6	82.5	1 582.0	531.5	*Portfolio investment*
1 429.0	695.0	543.6	1 320.4	-205.3	*Other long-term capital*
1 025.8	-290.2	-261.8	1 317.1	81.3	*Official sector* [2]
1 856.6	787.4	780.6	2 741.3	973.1	*Loans received*
-776.5	-855.1	-891.4	-1 491.5	-840.5	*Amortizations*
-655.0	220.0	555.4	0.0	0.0	*Commercial banks* [2]
0.0	0.0	0.0	0.0	0.0	*Loans received*
0.0	0.0	0.0	0.0	0.0	*Amortizations*
1 058.1	765.3	250.0	3.3	-286.6	*Other sectors* [2]
2 065.9	1 941.9	1 615.4	1 284.0	504.7	*Loans received*
-860.5	-1 007.4	-1 089.5	-1 067.6	-702.6	*Amortizations*
1 793.3	**6 788.8**	**4 809.8**	**-1 090.8**	**3 972.7**	**Basic balance** [3]
1 808.8	-1 896.3	-2 692.0	-4 913.9	-879.0	*Short-term capital*
-2.6	102.8	33.0	-57.4	-17.1	*Official sector*
-64.6	-27.3	35.4	916.3	-565.7	*Commercial banks*
1 876.0	-1 971.8	-2 760.4	-5 772.9	-296.2	*Other sectors*
497.4	-1 128.4	-2 139.0	-2 160.5	-2 937.6	*Errors and omissions (net)*
3 728.7	**-985.3**	**-4 046.9**	**-3 943.5**	**-3 553.5**	**Capital account balance**
4 098.2	**3 764.0**	**-21.2**	**-8 165.3**	**155.1**	**Global balance** [3]
-4 120.5	-4 183.9	-1 099.8	7 634.7	-97.9	*Total variation in reserves (minus sign indicates an increase)*
0.0	0.0	0.0	0.0	0.0	*Monetary gold*
-135.5	8.7	-100.6	5.0	87.0	*Special Drawing Rights*
228.6	-87.5	-14.1	-113.0	-166.0	*Reserve position in IMF*
-1 379.0	795.1	-1 446.2	1 694.9	-960.0	*Foreign exchange assets*
-2 834.6	-4 900.3	461.1	6 047.8	941.1	*Other assets*
0.0	0.0	0.0	0.0	0.0	*Use of IMF credit*

[1] Non factorial services also included.
[2] Net-loans received and Other assets and liabilities included.
[3] Equals to Total variation in reserves (with opposite sign) plus Counterpart items.

257. DEUDA EXTERNA TOTAL DESEMBOLSADA

(Saldo a fines del año en millones de dólares)

País	1978	1979	1980
Argentina	12 496	19 034	27 162
Bolivia [2]	1 762	1 941	2 220
Brasil [3]	52 285	58 907	68 354
Colombia	4 247	5 117	6 277
Costa Rica	1 870	2 333	3 183
Chile [4]	6 664	8 484	11 084
Ecuador	2 975	3 554	4 652
El Salvador	986	939	1 176
Guatemala	821	934	1 053
Haití [2]	210	248	290
Honduras	971	1 280	1 510
México	33 946	39 685	49 349
Nicaragua [2]	961	1 131	1 579
Panamá [2]	1 774	2 009	2 211
Paraguay	669	733	861
Perú	9 324	9 334	9 594
República Dominicana	1 309	1 565	1 839
Uruguay	1 240	1 679	2 156
Venezuela [7]	16 383	23 071	26 509
Total	150 893	181 978	221 059
Países exportadores de petróleo	64 390	77 585	92 324
Países no exportadores de petróleo	86 503	104 393	128 735

[1] Cifras preliminares.
[2] Corresponde a la deuda pública.
[3] Incluye la deuda total de mediano y largo plazo más la deuda de corto plazo con las instituciones financieras que proporcionan información al Banco de Pagos Internacionales.
[4] Deuda de corto, mediano y largo plazo; excluye la deuda con el FMI y los créditos de corto plazo para operaciones de comercio exterior.
[5] Cifras no comparables con la de los años anteriores a 1982, debido a la inclusión de la deuda de los bancos comerciales de México.
[6] Incluye la deuda de Bancos comerciales. Estimaciones sobre la base de información proporcionada por la Secretaría de Hacienda y Crédito Público.
[7] Incluye la deuda pública más la deuda no garantizada de largo y corto plazo con instituciones financieras que proporcionan información al Banco de Pagos Internacionales.

(Balance at end of year in millions of dollars)

1981	1982	1983[1]	Country
35 671	43 634	45 500	*Argentina*
2 450	2 373	3 065	*Bolivia*[2]
78 580	87 580	96 500	*Brazil*[3]
7 930	9 421	10 405	*Colombia*
3 360	3 497	3 848	*Costa Rica*
15 542	17 153	17 431	*Chile*[4]
5 868	6 187	6 689	*Ecuador*
1 471	1 683	2 000	*El Salvador*
1 409	1 504	1 766	*Guatemala*
372	410	446	*Haiti*[2]
1 708	1 800	2 079	*Honduras*
72 007	85 000[5][6]	90 000[5][6]	*Mexico*
2 163	2 797	3 385	*Nicaragua*[2]
2 338	2 820	3 275	*Panama*[2]
949	1 204	1 469	*Paraguay*
9 683	11 097	12 418	*Peru*
1 837	1 921	2 572	*Dominican Republic*
3 129	4 255	4 589	*Uruguay*
29 000	31 000	33 500	*Venezuela*[7]
275 422	315 336[5]	340 937[5]	*Total*
118 963	135 657[5]	145 672[5]	*Oil exporting countries*
156 459	179 679	195 265	*Non-oil exporting countries*

[1] *Preliminary figures.*
[2] *Corresponds to public debt.*
[3] *Includes total medium and long-term debt plus short-term debt with financial institutions reporting to the Bank for International Settlements.*
[4] *Short, medium and long-term debt, excluding indebtedness with IMF and short-term credit for external trade transactions.*
[5] *Figures not comparable with those for years before 1982, because of inclusion of debt of Mexican commercial banks.*
[6] *Includes commercial bank debt. Estimates based on data provided by the Ministry of Finance and Public Credit.*
[7] *Includes public debt and long and short-term non-guaranteed debt with financial institutions reporting to the Bank for International Settlements.*

258. INDICES DE QUANTUM DE LAS EXPORTACIONES DE BIENES [1]

(Año base 1970 = 100)

País	1960	1965	1970	1975	1977
Argentina	66.2	89.4	100.0	77.8	156.3
Barbados	55.6	87.4	100.0	89.1	116.8
Bolivia	56.9	65.4	100.0	119.4	136.5
Brasil	51.4	64.0	100.0	157.9	172.1
Colombia	69.3	81.9	100.0	152.0	93.4
Costa Rica	40.1	48.7	100.0	137.4	141.9
Chile	77.0	98.5	100.0	126.2	159.1
Ecuador	63.6	90.6	100.0	176.4	178.0
El Salvador	46.1	85.9	100.0	138.2	116.3
Guatemala	42.5	69.5	100.0	143.2	162.0
Guyana	71.9	94.3	100.0	92.6	74.7
Haití	116.1	107.9	100.0	106.4	132.7
Honduras	45.3	73.7	100.0	103.3	118.0
Jamaica	64.9	85.3	100.0	94.3	84.0
México	76.1	99.9	100.0	119.9	147.5
Nicaragua	40.8	89.6	100.0	141.8	154.5
Panamá	36.4	70.8	100.0	106.1	112.0
Paraguay	67.1	93.1	100.0	130.8	169.4
Perú	73.5	92.9	100.0	71.5	86.8
República Dominicana	109.8	74.3	100.0	149.9	196.3
Suriname	40.7	52.5	100.0	114.9	111.3
Trinidad y Tabago	63.3	164.6	100.0	77.1	83.5
Uruguay	61.7	91.9	100.0	109.8	157.8
Venezuela	77.0	94.4	100.0	63.9	58.3
Total	66.0	85.9	100.0	111.2	127.7
Países exportadores de petróleo [2]	74.3	97.1	100.0	85.8	93.5
Países no exportadores de petróleo	60.6	78.7	100.0	127.4	149.4

[1] Según valores del Balance de pagos.
[2] Se refiere a Bolivia, Ecuador, México, Perú, Trinidad y Tabago y Venezuela.

258. INDEXES OF VOLUME OF EXPORTS OF GOODS [1]

(Base year 1970 = 100)

1978	1979	1980	1981	1982	1983	Country
171.1	169.0	147.8	172.6	163.5	181.6	Argentina
134.6	159.5	182.1	159.8	240.2	...	Barbados
121.3	124.0	115.0	114.8	108.2	96.1	Bolivia
193.5	216.7	265.1	331.3	309.4	357.0	Brazil
130.7	155.3	153.8	148.0	135.7	132.0	Colombia
151.9	157.4	148.2	164.9	151.3	155.1	Costa Rica
170.7	203.3	221.9	213.5	249.2	260.4	Chile
210.0	208.1	195.9	204.0	203.6	222.9	Ecuador
117.7	158.8	150.0	121.4	102.2	112.4	El Salvador
150.6	169.2	183.4	163.2	163.3	170.5	Guatemala
88.0	80.6	79.1	65.4	48.5	...	Guyana
147.3	141.4	191.6	142.5	163.2	174.9	Haiti
133.4	165.2	154.3	154.5	139.0	145.6	Honduras
95.2	93.2	83.3	84.1	...	...	Jamaica
192.0	225.7	278.9	331.3	421.8	474.3	Mexico
165.4	163.7	103.8	127.3	108.2	126.3	Nicaragua
120.8	117.7	101.5	90.6	107.1	97.9	Panama
202.3	204.6	205.1	189.3	215.5	195.7	Paraguay
99.8	120.5	106.8	100.3	113.4	100.3	Peru
164.6	189.3	145.4	167.1	154.3	147.2	Dominican Republic
119.2	121.1	117.1	97.8	...	...	Suriname
85.4	80.3	80.6	69.4	62.5	...	Trinidad and Tobago
165.1	145.7	172.2	204.3	223.2	221.8	Uruguay
57.6	64.4	59.0	55.8	48.8	45.2	Venezuela
142.4	**157.7**	**166.9**	**185.1**	...	...	**Total**
107.1	121.9	128.9	138.6	158.9	...	Oil exporting countries [2]
164.9	180.4	191.1	214.8	...	...	Non-oil exporting countries

[1] *According to Balance of payments values.*
[2] *Refers to Bolivia, Ecuador, Mexico, Peru, Trinidad and Tobago and Venezuela.*

259. INDICES DEL VALOR UNITARIO DE LAS EXPORTACIONES DE BIENES FOB [1]

(Año base 1970 = 100)

País	1960	1965	1970	1975	1977
Argentina	91.9	94.2	100.0	214.8	203.9
Barbados	102.5	102.2	100.0	296.2	204.1
Bolivia	50.0	92.4	100.0	195.6	244.1
Brasil	90.2	91.1	100.0	196.4	252.9
Colombia	88.0	90.0	100.0	143.3	368.7
Costa Rica	94.0	99.3	100.0	155.4	252.5
Chile	56.0	63.1	100.0	113.2	123.4
Ecuador	98.0	85.0	100.0	244.5	335.0
El Salvador	94.3	93.7	100.0	163.4	354.5
Guatemala	91.8	93.0	100.0	150.7	241.1
Guyana	80.6	84.9	100.0	294.3	269.0
Haití	83.9	89.6	100.0	171.2	265.3
Honduras	78.2	97.6	100.0	168.3	252.0
Jamaica	74.3	74.4	100.0	251.2	257.3
México	76.0	85.1	100.0	186.0	231.6
Nicaragua	87.6	93.2	100.0	148.1	230.6
Panamá	82.3	100.3	100.0	239.3	197.6
Paraguay	85.2	100.0	100.0	220.1	295.8
Perú	58.5	71.3	100.0	174.5	192.3
República Dominicana	67.0	79.0	100.0	278.6	185.8
Suriname	79.9	82.8	100.0	176.6	227.5
Trinidad y Tabago	112.1	111.4	100.0	568.4	624.8
Uruguay	93.6	95.3	100.0	156.4	172.9
Venezuela	119.0	101.0	100.0	532.4	629.9
Total	**88.1**	**89.1**	**100.0**	**224.2**	**266.5**
Países exportadores de petróleo [2]	94.7	91.8	100.0	322.6	362.5
Países no exportadores de petróleo	82.9	86.9	100.0	181.9	228.2

[1] Según valores del Balance de pagos.
[2] Se refiere a Bolivia, Ecuador, México, Perú, Trinidad y Tabago y Venezuela.

259. INDEXES OF UNIT VALUE OF EXPORTS OF GOODS, FOB [1]

(Base year 1970 = 100)

1978	1979	1980	1981	1982	1983	Country
211.0	260.7	306.2	298.7	262.9	243.4	*Argentina*
230.1	230.3	277.3	284.4	242.1	...	*Barbados*
271.6	322.7	430.3	416.2	401.6	413.9	*Bolivia*
235.3	256.8	277.3	256.5	238.0	224.0	*Brazil*
311.2	286.6	335.2	276.0	300.6	288.6	*Colombia*
246.1	259.0	292.3	263.1	248.6	243.1	*Costa Rica*
129.5	169.5	190.5	161.4	133.6	132.9	*Chile*
309.9	439.9	553.0	530.9	490.0	451.8	*Ecuador*
288.6	302.0	303.7	278.5	291.8	275.8	*El Salvador*
244.1	242.9	279.0	267.8	247.2	215.6	*Guatemala*
260.4	281.5	381.3	410.4	385.6	...	*Guyana*
260.4	249.5	288.1	270.0	272.4	261.0	*Haiti*
263.4	257.0	309.3	284.6	273.1	267.6	*Honduras*
255.7	257.2	338.4	339.1	...	...	*Jamaica*
241.3	305.7	427.3	446.5	388.4	347.8	*Mexico*
218.7	210.6	243.0	223.6	210.2	190.0	*Nicaragua*
191.8	232.0	283.1	290.8	247.1	248.4	*Panama*
269.6	287.8	299.0	322.5	281.6	255.2	*Paraguay*
188.1	282.4	353.0	313.5	280.8	290.9	*Peru*
191.7	214.4	309.2	332.1	232.5	248.6	*Dominican Republic*
252.5	268.4	321.4	354.7	...	...	*Suriname*
635.1	911.5	1 423.7	1 619.4	1 570.5	...	*Trinidad and Tobago*
185.4	241.4	274.4	268.6	251.1	232.7	*Uruguay*
605.8	844.8	1241.0	1 375.2	1 287.5	1 247.3	*Venezuela*
257.1	**310.2**	**380.4**	**366.4**	...	...	*Total*
342.1	459.1	621.0	629.3	526.0	...	*Oil exporting countries* [2]
222.0	246.1	277.2	258.5	...	...	*Non-oil exporting countries*

[1] *According to Balance of payments values.*
[2] *Refers to Bolivia, Ecuador, Mexico, Peru, Trinidad and Tobago and Venezuela.*

260. INDICES DE LA RELACION DE PRECIOS DEL INTERCAMBIO DE BIENES FOB/CIF [1]

(Año base 1970 = 100)

País	1960	1965	1970	1975	1977
Argentina	104.9	109.2	100.0	100.7	86.3
Barbados	123.4	111.3	100.0	165.2	103.4
Bolivia	59.2	99.8	100.0	111.0	119.8
Brasil	104.4	93.9	100.0	85.4	100.8
Colombia	97.7	96.3	100.0	81.5	189.8
Costa Rica	101.1	107.6	100.0	77.9	121.7
Chile	63.9	68.4	100.0	53.2	51.3
Ecuador	99.1	83.7	100.0	159.0	194.8
El Salvador	116.1	107.0	100.0	87.4	179.9
Guatemala	124.6	110.8	100.0	70.2	120.4
Guyana	96.0	90.3	100.0	140.1	118.4
Haití	93.2	94.2	100.0	92.8	124.8
Honduras	106.8	125.3	100.0	91.4	114.2
Jamaica	89.5	80.9	100.0	111.6	98.1
México	100.5	89.7	100.0	105.7	122.9
Nicaragua	110.2	112.3	100.0	79.4	112.5
Panamá	87.7	105.8	100.0	110.7	82.1
Paraguay	101.4	112.4	100.0	106.1	139.8
Perú	70.9	72.9	100.0	104.0	101.6
República Dominicana	73.6	82.3	100.0	149.4	89.5
Suriname	95.1	89.7	100.0	95.5	110.4
Trinidad y Tabago	135.1	121.1	100.0	322.8	317.9
Uruguay	114.6	100.3	100.0	75.4	80.8
Venezuela	164.4	111.0	100.0	335.3	344.6
Total	**107.3**	**96.5**	**100.0**	**116.3**	**127.6**
Países exportadores de petróleo [2]	124.3	97.7	100.0	193.2	195.7
Países no exportadores de petróleo	96.1	95.7	100.0	84.9	98.8

[1] Según valores del Balance de pagos.
[2] Se refiere a Bolivia, Ecuador, México, Perú, Trinidad y Tabago y Venezuela.

260. INDEXES OF MERCHANDISE TERMS OF TRADE FOB/CIF [1]

(Base year 1970 = 100)

1978	1979	1980	1981	1982	1983	Country
79.9	81.1	94.2	89.1	82.2	79.5	Argentina
110.1	95.7	101.1	97.0	85.8	...	Barbados
121.2	120.6	143.6	134.8	132.1	140.4	Bolivia
87.6	79.9	67.4	56.1	54.0	53.9	Brazil
150.1	129.6	126.3	97.7	110.9	113.3	Colombia
100.2	98.6	95.8	81.6	73.4	70.1	Costa Rica
49.8	53.4	49.0	38.6	34.4	36.7	Chile
171.7	211.7	237.6	213.2	196.9	183.4	Ecuador
132.8	121.9	103.9	90.7	90.0	83.8	El Salvador
114.3	96.4	93.8	85.7	74.6	63.2	Guatemala
109.2	106.3	114.3	118.3	115.9	...	Guyana
114.4	98.2	100.7	90.4	85.9	80.9	Haiti
113.8	103.4	106.4	92.2	87.5	86.6	Honduras
90.7	82.1	85.7	81.8	...	...	Jamaica
118.6	132.5	164.3	162.4	133.4	128.5	Mexico
97.0	81.5	78.7	69.5	62.3	54.4	Nicaragua
75.2	75.3	76.2	75.2	61.1	60.8	Panama
123.8	111.3	98.7	102.3	86.2	81.0	Paraguay
86.8	117.2	131.1	107.8	94.7	95.3	Peru
85.5	86.6	103.2	106.0	72.7	78.9	Dominican Republic
106.5	93.8	93.7	99.5	...	...	Suriname
293.7	391.0	545.2	596.5	601.9	...	Trinidad and Tobago
84.7	90.1	81.4	72.0	71.6	72.1	Uruguay
309.6	401.1	509.9	505.6	499.0	508.9	Venezuela
114.4	**119.2**	**124.9**	**113.6**	...	...	**Total**
171.2	206.0	244.0	229.5	192.2	...	Oil exporting countries [2]
89.0	83.6	78.7	68.6	...	...	Non-oil exporting countries

[1] *According to Balance of payments values.*
[2] *Refers to Bolivia, Ecuador, Mexico, Peru, Trinidad and Tobago and Venezuela.*

261. INDICES DE QUANTUM DE LAS IMPORTACIONES DE BIENES FOB [1]

(Año base 1970 = 100)

País	1960	1965	1970	1975	1977
Argentina	82.4	82.1	100.0	108.4	106.4
Barbados	45.3	61.5	100.0	103.0	118.8
Bolivia	58.6	100.1	100.0	197.6	209.9
Brasil	58.9	38.3	100.0	206.5	189.5
Colombia	68.1	57.1	100.0	101.1	127.2
Costa Rica	36.2	60.4	100.0	108.4	155.1
Chile	60.2	65.5	100.0	81.2	101.8
Ecuador	42.5	58.5	100.0	266.9	323.9
El Salvador	70.0	108.8	100.0	150.7	224.7
Guatemala	63.6	92.4	100.0	115.2	203.8
Guyana	76.0	83.7	100.0	119.2	103.9
Haití	99.0	92.7	100.0	138.1	194.6
Honduras	43.2	72.2	100.0	99.2	121.5
Jamaica	49.5	61.2	100.0	92.2	54.3
México	66.9	70.0	100.0	159.8	134.0
Nicaragua	39.4	90.9	100.0	144.3	192.1
Panamá	33.9	60.8	100.0	112.8	97.1
Paraguay	68.4	82.9	100.0	140.3	221.0
Perú	55.8	93.9	100.0	204.6	164.2
República Dominicana	35.0	44.8	100.0	148.1	146.7
Suriname	54.5	87.2	100.0	125.4	150.6
Trinidad y Tabago	57.8	172.7	100.0	134.3	158.9
Uruguay	111.8	63.0	100.0	115.3	157.2
Venezuela	92.8	86.4	100.0	203.7	328.5
Total	66.0	70.2	100.0	155.3	170.1
Países exportadores de petróleo [2]	71.9	84.0	100.0	184.5	212.9
Países no exportadores de petróleo	62.2	61.6	100.0	137.0	143.5

[1] Según valores del Balance de pagos.
[2] Se refiere a Bolivia, Ecuador, México, Perú, Trinidad y Tabago y Venezuela.

261. INDEXES OF VOLUME OF IMPORTS OF GOODS, FOB [1]

(Base year 1970 = 100)

1978	1979	1980	1981	1982	1983	Country
87.2	122.9	189.8	166.3	100.8	89.4	*Argentina*
129.0	146.8	162.0	165.3	166.2	...	*Barbados*
236.8	220.3	162.4	159.4	103.1	119.9	*Bolivia*
200.7	220.5	218.8	189.8	172.9	146.5	*Brazil*
154.4	169.3	201.3	210.0	249.2	234.0	*Colombia*
146.6	164.9	153.7	116.1	81.1	87.5	*Costa Rica*
126.4	149.4	156.4	173.4	105.1	88.6	*Chile*
385.2	408.0	388.4	383.4	354.2	231.0	*Ecuador*
224.2	196.9	155.7	148.7	129.4	123.6	*El Salvador*
225.3	207.4	182.7	182.7	143.2	114.1	*Guatemala*
87.5	89.8	93.4	93.1	62.5	...	*Guyana*
188.1	178.9	227.6	275.3	216.7	221.1	*Haiti*
137.9	154.1	159.0	141.6	106.2	119.9	*Honduras*
56.4	60.0	54.6	64.7	...	...	*Jamaica*
176.0	235.3	324.4	391.0	221.4	127.8	*Mexico*
136.8	83.9	143.7	159.1	118.5	122.8	*Nicaragua*
99.7	102.7	100.6	107.0	102.1	86.8	*Panama*
258.0	286.9	283.3	314.0	278.7	225.6	*Paraguay*
105.4	115.9	161.9	186.5	178.9	126.6	*Peru*
137.4	164.1	178.5	164.5	139.4	146.2	*Dominican Republic*
137.4	121.1	121.9	130.5	...	...	*Suriname*
174.2	204.7	241.1	233.6	342.1	...	*Trinidad and Tobago*
159.2	212.3	238.6	205.4	144.2	112.2	*Uruguay*
337.9	280.4	261.5	260.5	309.4	163.4	*Venezuela*
179.6	**194.1**	**217.8**	**222.4**	...	...	**Total**
230.3	240.3	277.2	307.5	253.7	...	*Oil exporting countries* [2]
148.1	165.3	180.8	169.4	...	...	*Non-oil exporting countries*

[1] *According to Balance of payments values.*
[2] *Refers to Bolivia, Ecuador, Mexico, Peru, Trinidad and Tobago and Venezuela.*

262. INDICES DE VALOR UNITARIO DE LAS IMPORTACIONES DE BIENES FOB [1]

(Año base 1970 = 100)

País	1960	1965	1970	1975	1977
Argentina	89.5	86.2	100.0	216.1	238.2
Barbados	83.9	92.5	100.0	179.0	197.0
Bolivia	86.1	93.5	100.0	175.9	204.0
Brasil	87.5	98.0	100.0	232.6	253.1
Colombia	90.9	94.0	100.0	175.6	194.0
Costa Rica	95.4	92.8	100.0	201.8	208.0
Chile	90.5	93.3	100.0	216.0	243.7
Ecuador	103.6	104.0	100.0	151.0	168.3
El Salvador	81.9	87.6	100.0	187.6	196.8
Guatemala	73.6	83.6	100.0	219.0	200.1
Guyana	85.1	94.8	100.0	214.0	230.1
Haití	91.8	96.2	100.0	185.0	214.9
Honduras	73.0	77.1	100.0	184.5	222.6
Jamaica	84.4	92.7	100.0	234.3	273.3
México	75.6	95.3	100.0	175.7	187.8
Nicaragua	80.1	82.5	100.0	187.1	205.2
Panamá	96.8	95.7	100.0	220.4	245.8
Paraguay	85.3	89.3	100.0	211.4	212.7
Perú	83.7	99.5	100.0	167.1	188.6
República Dominicana	92.7	96.9	100.0	187.7	208.3
Suriname	85.2	93.0	100.0	185.5	206.6
Trinidad y Tabago	83.8	92.4	100.0	175.7	195.9
Uruguay	82.7	96.2	100.0	210.9	215.1
Venezuela	72.1	91.5	100.0	156.6	181.1
Total	83.0	92.8	100.0	193.8	209.4
Países exportadores de petróleo [2]	76.3	94.6	100.0	166.0	183.9
Países no exportadores de petróleo	87.7	91.3	100.0	217.1	233.0

[1] Según valores del Balance de pagos.
[2] Se refiere a Bolivia, Ecuador, México, Perú, Trinidad y Tabago y Venezuela.

262. INDEXES OF UNIT VALUE OF IMPORTS OF GOODS, FOB[1]

(Base year 1970 = 100)

1978	1979	1980	1981	1982	1983	Country
266.8	327.3	330.2	338.2	321.6	307.5	Argentina
208.9	241.2	276.6	295.1	282.0	...	Barbados
226.1	273.5	309.7	315.5	307.5	297.3	Bolivia
270.9	324.9	418.4	464.2	447.5	420.2	Brazil
207.1	220.7	266.3	282.8	270.4	253.5	Colombia
249.6	265.9	311.9	327.5	345.9	355.8	Costa Rica
263.4	323.6	403.3	433.2	399.8	369.6	Chile
177.2	205.9	231.3	246.8	246.7	244.2	Ecuador
217.8	249.0	295.9	310.3	327.9	333.6	El Salvador
213.7	253.5	302.3	316.2	336.3	347.1	Guatemala
241.7	268.2	345.0	358.1	339.3	...	Guyana
230.8	257.3	293.2	302.6	324.7	332.9	Haiti
233.4	249.9	295.0	311.9	315.1	312.1	Honduras
296.1	327.3	423.4	446.1	...	...	Jamaica
203.0	230.5	260.5	275.0	291.6	270.3	Mexico
226.4	259.4	312.9	324.6	341.9	354.8	Nicaragua
261.3	319.5	395.4	406.7	426.7	433.5	Panama
218.6	262.6	311.2	321.1	333.2	319.2	Paraguay
217.1	241.4	270.6	291.8	297.7	307.6	Peru
225.8	249.3	306.3	317.4	324.4	319.1	Dominican Republic
240.2	293.3	357.8	372.7	...	...	Suriname
217.0	233.0	262.6	270.9	258.4	...	Trinidad and Tobago
219.5	270.5	344.3	381.7	354.6	324.7	Uruguay
194.1	208.2	242.8	271.7	256.3	242.2	Venezuela
225.7	**262.2**	**308.6**	**326.0**	...	...	**Total**
198.8	222.0	254.8	274.1	273.1	...	Oil exporting countries [2]
251.8	298.6	360.0	384.6	...	...	Non-oil exporting countries

[1] *According to Balance of payments values.*
[2] *Refers to Bolivia, Ecuador, Mexico, Peru, Trinidad and Tobago and Venezuela.*

263. INDICES DEL PODER DE COMPRA DE LAS EXPORTACIONES DE BIENES [1]

(Año base 1970 = 100)

País	1960	1965	1970	1975	1977
Argentina	69.5	97.6	100.0	78.3	134.9
Barbados	68.7	97.2	100.0	147.4	120.8
Bolivia	33.7	65.3	100.0	132.5	163.6
Brasil	53.7	60.1	100.0	134.8	173.4
Colombia	67.6	78.9	100.0	123.9	177.2
Costa Rica	40.5	52.4	100.0	107.0	172.8
Chile	49.2	67.4	100.0	67.2	81.6
Ecuador	63.0	75.9	100.0	280.4	346.7
El Salvador	53.5	91.9	100.0	120.8	209.2
Guatemala	52.9	77.1	100.0	100.5	195.1
Guyana	69.0	85.2	100.0	129.7	88.5
Haití	108.3	101.8	100.0	98.8	165.5
Honduras	48.4	92.4	100.0	94.4	134.7
Jamaica	58.1	69.0	100.0	105.3	82.4
México	76.5	89.6	100.0	126.8	181.3
Nicaragua	44.9	100.6	100.0	112.5	173.8
Panamá	31.9	74.9	100.0	117.6	92.0
Paraguay	68.0	104.6	100.0	138.8	236.8
Perú	52.1	67.7	100.0	74.4	88.2
República Dominicana	80.8	61.1	100.0	224.0	175.8
Suriname	38.7	47.1	100.0	109.7	123.0
Trinidad y Tabago	85.6	199.3	100.0	248.9	265.5
Uruguay	70.7	92.2	100.0	82.8	127.5
Venezuela	126.5	104.8	100.0	214.3	200.9
Total	71.9	83.1	100.0	132.6	161.4
Países exportadores de petróleo [2]	93.5	95.6	100.0	169.1	182.9
Países no exportadores de petróleo	58.2	75.1	100.0	109.4	147.8

[1] Según valores del Balance de pagos.
[2] Se refiere a Bolivia, Ecuador, México, Perú, Trinidad y Tabago y Venezuela.

263. INDEXES OF PURCHASING POWER OF EXPORTS OF GOODS[1]

(Base year 1970 = 100)

1978	1979	1980	1981	1982	1983	Country
136.8	137.1	139.1	153.8	134.3	144.4	*Argentina*
148.2	152.7	184.1	154.9	206.2	...	*Barbados*
147.0	149.5	165.1	154.7	143.0	134.8	*Bolivia*
169.5	173.2	178.7	185.9	167.0	192.5	*Brazil*
196.3	201.2	194.2	144.7	150.5	149.6	*Colombia*
152.3	155.3	142.1	134.6	111.0	108.7	*Costa Rica*
85.0	108.6	108.7	82.5	85.7	95.6	*Chile*
360.7	440.6	465.5	435.0	400.9	408.8	*Ecuador*
156.3	193.6	155.8	110.1	91.9	94.2	*El Salvador*
172.2	163.1	172.0	139.9	121.8	107.8	*Guatemala*
96.1	85.7	90.4	77.4	56.2	...	*Guyana*
168.4	138.9	192.9	128.8	140.1	141.5	*Haiti*
151.8	170.9	164.1	142.4	121.6	126.1	*Honduras*
86.3	76.5	71.4	68.9	...	...	*Jamaica*
227.8	299.1	458.4	537.9	562.7	609.4	*Mexico*
160.4	133.5	81.7	88.5	67.4	68.7	*Nicaragua*
90.8	88.6	77.3	68.1	65.5	59.5	*Panama*
250.5	227.6	202.5	193.5	185.7	158.5	*Paraguay*
86.6	141.3	140.1	108.1	107.4	95.5	*Peru*
140.8	163.9	150.0	177.2	112.1	116.2	*Dominican Republic*
127.0	113.6	109.8	97.3	...	...	*Suriname*
250.7	314.0	439.5	413.8	376.0	...	*Trinidad and Tobago*
139.9	131.2	140.2	147.1	159.9	160.0	*Uruguay*
178.4	258.4	300.8	282.1	243.3	229.9	*Venezuela*
160.6	**190.5**	**214.8**	**212.2**	...	...	**Total**
182.8	252.8	316.8	318.7	303.3	...	*Oil exporting countries* [2]
146.4	150.9	149.9	144.3	...	...	*Non-oil exporting countries*

[1] *According to Balance of payments values.*
[2] *Refers to Bolivia, Ecuador, Mexico, Peru, Trinidad and Tobago and Venezuela.*

VI. COMERCIO EXTERIOR

264. **VALOR DE LAS EXPORTACIONES DE BIENES** [1]

a) **A precios corrientes**
(Millones de dólares fob)

País	1960	1965	1970	1975	1977
Argentina	1 079.2	1 493.0	1 773.0	2 961.3	5 650.2
Barbados	20.4	32.0	35.8	94.5	85.3
Bolivia	54.2	115.1	190.4	444.7	634.3
Brasil	1 270.0	1 596.0	2 739.0	8 493.0	11 921.6
Colombia	480.2	581.0	788.0	1 716.8	2 713.3
Costa Rica	87.0	111.7	231.0	493.1	827.8
Chile	480.0	692.0	1 113.0	1 590.5	2 185.6
Ecuador	146.3	181.0	234.9	1 012.8	1 400.8
El Salvador	102.6	190.0	236.1	533.0	973.5
Guatemala	115.9	192.1	297.1	640.9	1 160.2
Guyana	74.8	103.3	129.0	351.4	259.3
Haití	38.1	37.8	39.1	71.2	137.7
Honduras	63.1	128.2	178.2	309.6	529.8
Jamaica	164.6	216.7	341.4	808.6	737.8
México	779.5	1 146.0	1 348.0	3 006.8	4 603.6
Nicaragua	63.8	149.2	178.6	374.9	636.2
Panamá	39.0	92.5	130.3	330.9	288.5
Paraguay	37.3	60.8	65.3	188.0	327.1
Perú	444.4	685.0	1 034.0	1 290.6	1 725.7
República Dominicana	157.4	125.5	214.0	893.9	780.5
Suriname	44.4	59.4	136.6	277.2	346.1
Trinidad y Tabago	160.0	413.1	225.3	987.3	1 175.2
Uruguay	129.4	196.3	224.1	384.9	611.5
Venezuela	2 383.9	2 482.0	2 602.0	8 853.6	9 556.2
Total	8 415.5	11 079.7	14 484.2	36 109.5	49 267.8
Países exportadores de petróleo [2]	3 968.3	5 022.2	5 634.6	15 595.8	19 095.8
Países no exportadores de petróleo	4 447.2	6 057.5	8 849.6	20 513.7	30 172.0

[1] Según valores del Balance de pagos.
[2] Se refiere a Bolivia, Ecuador, México, Perú, Trinidad y Tabago y Venezuela.

264. VALUE OF EXPORTS OF GOODS [1]

a) *At current prices*
(Millions of dollars, FOB)

1978	1979	1980	1981	1982	1983	Country
6 401.2	7 810.3	8 021.8	9 142.3	7 621.7	7 838.0	Argentina
110.9	131.5	180.8	162.7	208.2	272.3	Barbados
627.3	761.8	941.9	909.3	827.7	757.1	Bolivia
12 473.0	15 244.4	20 131.5	23 275.5	20 172.3	21 905.7	Brazil
3 206.4	3 506.5	4 062.1	3 219.1	3 214.9	3 002.8	Colombia
863.9	942.0	1 000.8	1 002.5	869.0	870.7	Costa Rica
2 460.2	3 834.7	4 705.0	3 835.8	3 706.2	3 851.9	Chile
1 529.2	2 150.5	2 544.2	2 544.2	2 343.0	2 365.0	Ecuador
801.7	1 132.3	1 075.3	798.1	704.1	732.0	El Salvador
1 092.4	1 221.4	1 519.9	1 299.0	1 199.6	1 092.1	Guatemala
295.6	292.8	388.9	346.4	241.4	193.5	Guyana
150.0	138.0	215.8	150.4	173.8	178.5	Haiti
626.1	756.6	850.3	783.8	676.5	694.5	Honduras
831.1	818.2	962.7	974.0	767.4	...	Jamaica
6 246.3	9 300.3	16 066.7	19 938.1	22 081.4	22 235.4	Mexico
646.0	615.9	450.5	508.2	406.1	428.5	Nicaragua
301.9	355.6	374.6	343.4	344.9	317.0	Panama
356.1	384.5	400.4	398.6	396.2	326.2	Paraguay
1 940.7	3 519.3	3 898.8	3 249.7	3 293.5	3 016.5	Peru
675.5	868.6	962.0	1 188.0	767.7	783.0	Dominican Republic
411.1	444.0	514.3	473.9	428.6	366.9	Suriname
1 222.0	1 648.9	2 585.5	2 531.2	2 211.2	2 273.7	Trinidad and Tobago
686.1	788.1	1 058.5	1 229.7	1 256.4	1 156.9	Uruguay
9 084.5	14 159.0	19 050.5	19 963.2	16 331.6	14 659.1	Venezuela
53 039.2	70 825.2	91 962.8	98 267.1	90 243.4	...	**Total**
20 650.0	31 539.8	45 087.6	49 135.7	47 088.4	45 306.8	Oil exporting countries [2]
32 389.2	39 285.4	46 875.2	49 131.4	43 155.0	...	Non-oil exporting countries

[1] *According to Balance of payments values.*
[2] *Refers to Bolivia, Ecuador, Mexico, Peru, Trinidad and Tobago and Venezuela.*

264. VALOR DE LAS EXPORTACIONES DE BIENES [1] (conclusión)

b) A precios constantes de 1970
(Millones de dólares fob)

País	1960	1965	1970	1975	1977
Argentina	1 174.3	1 584.9	1 773.0	1 378.6	2 771.0
Barbados	19.9	31.3	35.8	31.9	41.8
Bolivia	108.4	124.6	190.4	227.3	259.9
Brasil	1 408.0	1 751.9	2 739.0	4 324.4	4 713.9
Colombia	545.7	645.6	788.0	1 198.1	735.9
Costa Rica	92.6	112.5	231.0	317.3	327.8
Chile	857.1	1 096.7	1 113.0	1 405.1	1 771.2
Ecuador	149.3	212.9	234.9	414.3	418.1
El Salvador	108.8	202.8	236.1	326.2	274.6
Guatemala	126.3	206.6	297.1	425.3	481.2
Guyana	92.8	121.7	129.0	119.4	96.4
Haití	45.4	42.2	39.1	41.6	51.9
Honduras	80.7	131.4	178.2	184.0	210.2
Jamaica	221.5	291.3	341.4	321.9	286.8
México	1 025.7	1 346.7	1 348.0	1 616.6	1 987.8
Nicaragua	72.8	160.1	178.6	253.2	275.9
Panamá	47.4	92.2	130.3	138.3	146.0
Paraguay	43.8	60.8	65.3	85.4	110.6
Perú	759.7	960.7	1 034.0	739.6	897.4
República Dominicana	234.9	158.9	214.0	320.8	420.1
Suriname	55.6	71.7	136.6	157.0	152.1
Trinidad y Tabago	142.7	370.8	225.3	173.7	188.1
Uruguay	138.2	206.0	224.1	246.1	353.7
Venezuela	2 003.3	2 457.4	2 602.0	1 663.0	1 517.1
Total	9 554.9	12 441.7	14 484.2	16 109.1	18 489.5
Países exportadores de petróleo [2]	4 189.1	5 473.1	5 634.6	4 834.5	5 268.4
Países no exportadores de petróleo	5 365.8	6 968.6	8 849.6	11 274.6	13 221.1

[1] Según valores del Balance de pagos.
[2] Se refiere a Bolivia, Ecuador, México, Perú, Trinidad y Tabago y Venezuela.

264. VALUE OF EXPORTS OF GOODS[1] (concluded)

b) At constant 1970 prices
(Millions of dollars, FOB)

1978	1979	1980	1981	1982	1983	Country
3 033.7	2 995.9	2 619.8	3 060.7	2 899.1	3 220.2	Argentina
48.2	57.1	65.2	57.2	86.0	...	Barbados
231.0	236.1	218.9	218.5	206.1	182.9	Bolivia
5 300.9	5 936.3	7 259.8	9 074.3	8 475.8	9 779.4	Brazil
1 030.3	1 223.5	1 211.8	1 166.3	1 069.5	1 040.5	Colombia
351.0	363.7	342.4	381.0	349.6	358.2	Costa Rica
1 899.7	2 262.3	2 469.8	2 376.6	2 774.1	2 898.3	Chile
493.4	488.9	460.1	479.2	478.2	523.5	Ecuador
277.8	374.9	354.1	286.6	241.3	265.4	El Salvador
447.5	502.8	544.8	485.0	485.3	506.6	Guatemala
113.5	104.0	102.0	84.4	62.6	...	Guyana
57.6	55.3	74.9	55.7	63.8	68.4	Haiti
237.7	294.4	274.9	275.4	247.7	259.5	Honduras
325.0	318.1	284.5	287.2	...	...	Jamaica
2 588.6	3 042.3	3 760.0	4 465.4	5 685.2	6 393.2	Mexico
295.4	292.4	185.4	227.3	193.2	225.5	Nicaragua
157.4	153.3	132.3	118.1	139.6	127.6	Panama
132.1	133.6	133.9	123.6	140.7	127.8	Paraguay
1 031.7	1 246.2	1 104.5	1 036.6	1 172.9	1 037.0	Peru
352.3	405.1	311.1	357.7	330.2	315.0	Dominican Republic
162.8	165.4	160.0	133.6	...	...	Suriname
192.4	180.9	181.6	156.3	140.8	...	Trinidad and Tobago
370.1	326.5	385.8	457.8	500.3	497.1	Uruguay
1 499.6	1 676.0	1 535.1	1 451.7	1 268.5	1 175.3	Venezuela
20 629.7	22 835.0	24 172.7	26 816.2	...	...	Total
6 036.7	6 870.4	7 260.2	7 807.7	8 951.7	...	Oil exporting countries [2]
14 593.0	15 964.6	16 912.5	19 008.5	...	...	Non-oil exporting countries

[1] According to Balance of payments values.
[2] Refers to Bolivia, Ecuador, Mexico, Peru, Trinidad and Tobago and Venezuela.

265. EXPORTACIONES TOTALES POR GRUPOS DE PRODUCTOS

a) Productos primarios / *Primary products*
(Millones de dólares fob / *Millons of dollars, FOB*)

País / Country	1960	1965	1970	1975	1980	1981
Argentina	1 034.9	1 409.2	1 527.2	2 243.4	6 164.9	...
Barbados	23.2	36.4	27.2	77.4	...	...
Bolivia	67.7	111.4	218.5	511.5	1 013.6	...
Brasil /*Brazil*	1 240.4	1 470.0	2 318.4	6 541.9	12 640.2	14 183.5
Colombia	457.6	505.3	653.1	1 156.6	3 169.8	2 149.2
Costa Rica	88.0	95.4	188.5	364.0	739.3	...
Chile	464.8	665.1	1 183.0	1 526.5	3 758.9	...
Ecuador	145.2	175.3	186.3	872.1	2 429.0	...
El Salvador	110.2	156.5	162.7	391.3	465.3	...
Guatemala	109.3	161.2	209.0	459.0	1 126.8	...
Guyana	71.2	91.5	126.1	315.0	357.6	...
Honduras	61.0	120.5	156.1	261.2	711.7	...
Jamaica	146.6	179.8	173.9	350.0	889.1	...
México / *Mexico*	640.9	852.1	814.1	2 063.7	13 574.9	...
Nicaragua	59.4	140.8	150.8	319.2	356.8	...
Panamá / *Panama*	25.9	77.4	105.0	273.3	319.0	...
Paraguay	23.0	52.5	58.9	155.9	296.6	276.3
Perú / *Peru*	443.0	658.5	1 033.0	1 264.6	2 756.2	...
República Dominicana / *Dominican Republic*	175.9	122.7	207.7	708.4	537.8	...
Trinidad y Tabago / *Trinidad and Tobago*	158.4	154.7	188.5	940.9	3 910.9	3 474.2
Uruguay	121.1	180.7	196.8	266.8	657.2	855.5
Venezuela	2 380.8	2 465.5	2 616.0	8 897.8	18 963.2	...
Total	8 048.5	9 882.5	12 500.8	29 960.5	74 838.8	...

b) Productos manufacturados / *Manufactured products*
(Millones de dólares fob / *Millions of dollars, FOB*)

País / *Country*	1960	1965	1970	1975	1980	1981
Argentina	44.3	84.2	245.9	717.9	1 856.5	...
Barbados	0.7	1.1	11.8	29.8	...	...
Bolivia	0.1	0.8	6.9	18.6	19.4	...
Brasil /*Brazil*	28.4	123.5	420.5	2 128.0	7 491.9	9 108.9
Colombia	6.9	33.8	78.5	308.3	775.3	806.3
Costa Rica	1.0	16.4	42.7	130.1	292.2	...
Chile	25.2	22.8	50.6	134.8	1 059.2	...
Ecuador	2.4	2.9	3.3	25.0	77.2	...
El Salvador	6.5	32.2	65.6	121.2	254.7	...
Guatemala	3.4	25.7	81.2	164.5	359.4	...
Guyana	2.8	4.5	4.1	37.8	25.4	...
Honduras	1.4	6.1	13.7	32.1	101.7	...
Jamaica	9.5	30.0	161.0	419.3	53.4	...
México / *Mexico*	122.3	268.3	391.3	929.4	1 732.6	...
Nicaragua	3.5	7.3	27.8	56.0	57.1	...
Panamá / *Panama*	0.1	0.6	1.2	13.1	31.6	...
Paraguay	4.0	4.8	5.2	18.2	13.6	19.2
Perú / *Peru*	3.6	5.3	14.8	50.0	552.8	...
República Dominicana / *Dominican Republic*	4.5	2.8	5.9	185.4	166.1	...
Trinidad y Tabago / *Trinidad and Tobago*	16.1	31.0	55.2	76.0	166.2	286.6
Uruguay	8.3	10.5	35.9	114.4	401.8	361.2
Venezuela	3.1	16.5	31.0	111.8	329.6	...
Total	298.1	737.5	1 754.1	5 821.7	15 817.7	...

266. VALOR DE LAS IMPORTACIONES DE BIENES [1]

a) A precios corrientes
(Millones de dólares fob)

País	1960	1965	1970	1975	1977
Argentina	1 106.0	1 062.0	1 499.0	3 510.1	3 799.2
Barbados	40.6	60.8	106.9	197.1	250.2
Bolivia	68.2	126.6	135.2	469.9	579.0
Brasil	1 293.0	941.0	2 507.0	12 042.0	12 021.9
Colombia	496.4	430.0	802.0	1 424.2	1 978.9
Costa Rica	98.9	160.9	286.8	627.2	925.1
Chile	472.3	530.0	867.0	1 520.1	2 150.6
Ecuador	109.8	151.8	249.6	1 006.3	1 360.5
El Salvador	111.5	185.7	194.7	550.7	861.0
Guatemala	124.8	206.1	266.6	672.4	1 086.9
Guyana	77.5	95.2	119.9	305.8	286.7
Haití	43.4	42.6	47.8	122.1	199.9
Honduras	64.1	113.2	203.4	372.4	550.1
Jamaica	187.6	254.8	449.0	969.6	666.7
México	1 131.0	1 492.0	2 236.0	6 278.4	5 624.5
Nicaragua	56.4	133.9	178.6	482.1	704.2
Panamá	108.7	192.4	331.0	823.1	790.4
Paraguay	44.7	56.7	76.6	227.3	360.1
Perú	326.6	653.0	699.0	2 389.4	2 164.0
República Dominicana	90.3	120.7	278.0	772.7	849.3
Suriname	48.3	84.4	104.1	242.1	324.0
Trinidad y Tabago	133.8	440.8	276.2	651.6	860.0
Uruguay	187.9	123.1	203.1	494.0	686.7
Venezuela	1 145.4	1 354.0	1 713.0	5 462.5	10 193.6
Total	7 567.2	9 011.7	13 830.5	41 613.1	49 273.5
Países exportadores de petróleo [2]	2 914.8	4 218.2	5 309.0	16 258.1	20 781.6
Países no exportadores de petróleo	4 652.4	4 793.5	8 521.5	25 355.0	28 491.9

[1] Según valores del Balance de pagos.
[2] Se refiere a Bolivia, Ecuador, México, Perú, Trinidad y Tabago y Venezuela.

266. VALUE OF IMPORTS OF GOODS [1]

a) At current prices
(Millions of dollars, FOB)

1978	1979	1980	1981	1982	1983	Country
3 488.4	6 027.4	9 394.5	8 432.0	4 859.4	4 120.5	*Argentina*
288.1	378.4	479.0	521.4	501.1	565.0	*Barbados*
723.9	814.9	680.2	680.0	428.7	482.0	*Bolivia*
13 631.7	17 961.3	22 954.7	22 091.4	19 395.4	15 434.3	*Brazil*
2 564.1	2 996.1	4 300.3	4 762.6	5 404.1	4 758.7	*Colombia*
1 049.4	1 257.2	1 375.2	1 090.5	804.9	892.8	*Costa Rica*
2 885.9	4 190.0	5 469.0	6 512.5	3 643.2	2 838.1	*Chile*
1 704.0	2 096.8	2 241.8	2 361.5	2 181.0	1 408.0	*Ecuador*
951.0	954.7	897.0	898.4	825.9	803.0	*El Salvador*
1 283.7	1 401.6	1 472.6	1 540.0	1 284.3	1 056.3	*Guatemala*
253.5	288.8	386.4	399.6	254.1	225.9	*Guyana*
207.5	220.0	319.0	398.2	336.4	351.9	*Haiti*
654.5	783.4	954.0	898.6	680.7	761.0	*Honduras*
750.1	882.4	1 038.2	1 296.7	1 208.9	...	*Jamaica*
7 991.6	12 129.7	18 896.8	24 037.6	14 434.2	7 723.0	*Mexico*
553.3	388.9	802.9	922.5	723.5	778.4	*Nicaragua*
862.1	1 085.7	1 317.1	1 440.9	1 441.3	1 246.0	*Panama*
431.9	577.1	675.4	772.3	711.3	551.6	*Paraguay*
1 599.9	1 955.3	3 062.3	3 802.9	3 721.3	2 722.8	*Peru*
862.4	1 137.5	1 519.7	1 451.7	1 257.2	1 297.0	*Dominican Republic*
343.5	369.9	454.1	506.5	460.3	401.8	*Suriname*
1 044.4	1 316.9	1 748.9	1 748.1	2 441.5	2 315.4	*Trinidad and Tobago*
709.8	1 166.2	1 668.2	1 592.1	1 038.4	740.0	*Uruguay*
11 234.2	10 004.0	10 876.9	12 122.9	13 583.7	6 780.9	*Venezuela*
56 068.9	**70 384.2**	**92 984.2**	**100 280.9**	**81 620.8**	...	**Total**
24 298.0	28 317.6	37 506.9	44 753.0	36 790.4	21 432.1	*Oil exporting countries* [2]
31 770.9	42 066.6	55 477.3	55 527.9	44 830.4	...	*Non-oil exporting countries*

[1] *According to Balance of payments values.*
[2] *Refers to Bolivia, Ecuador, Mexico, Peru, Trinidad and Tobago and Venezuela.*

266. VALOR DE LAS IMPORTACIONES DE BIENES [1]

b) A precios constantes de 1970
(Millones de dólares fob)

País	1960	1965	1970	1975	1977
Argentina	1 235.1	1 231.4	1 499.0	1 624.3	1 595.0
Barbados	48.4	65.7	106.9	110.1	127.0
Bolivia	79.2	135.4	135.2	267.1	283.8
Brasil	1 477.2	960.4	2 507.0	5 178.1	4 750.0
Colombia	546.3	457.6	802.0	810.9	1 020.1
Costa Rica	103.7	173.3	286.8	310.8	444.7
Chile	521.6	567.8	867.0	703.6	882.5
Ecuador	106.0	146.0	249.6	666.3	808.5
El Salvador	136.2	211.9	194.7	293.5	437.5
Guatemala	169.6	246.4	266.6	307.1	543.2
Guyana	91.1	100.4	119.9	142.9	124.6
Haití	47.3	44.3	47.8	66.0	93.0
Honduras	87.8	146.8	203.4	201.8	247.1
Jamaica	222.4	274.9	449.0	413.9	243.9
México	1 495.4	1 565.0	2 236.0	3 572.5	2 995.3
Nicaragua	70.4	162.3	178.6	257.7	343.1
Panamá	112.3	201.1	331.0	373.5	321.5
Paraguay	52.4	63.5	76.6	107.5	169.3
Perú	390.0	656.1	699.0	1 430.3	1 147.5
República Dominicana	97.4	124.5	278.0	411.7	407.8
Suriname	56.7	90.8	104.1	130.5	156.8
Trinidad y Tabago	159.7	476.9	276.2	370.8	438.9
Uruguay	227.1	128.0	203.1	234.2	319.2
Venezuela	1 589.2	1 479.4	1 713.0	3 489.2	5 627.3
Total	9 122.5	9 709.9	13 830.5	21 474.3	23 527.6
Países exportadores de petróleo [2]	3 819.5	4 458.8	5 309.0	9 796.2	11 301.3
Países no exportadores de petróleo	5 303.0	5 251.1	8 521.5	11 678.1	12 226.3

[1] Según valores del Balance de pagos.
[2] Se refiere a Bolivia, Ecuador, México, Perú, Trinidad y Tabago y Venezuela.

b) At constant 1970 prices
(Millions of dollars, FOB)

1978	1979	1980	1981	1982	1983	Country
1 307.6	1 841.7	2 845.4	2 492.9	1 510.8	1 339.8	Argentina
137.9	156.9	173.2	176.7	177.7	...	Barbados
320.1	297.9	219.6	215.5	139.4	162.1	Bolivia
5 032.3	5 528.2	5 486.3	4 759.5	4 334.3	3 672.8	Brazil
1 237.9	1 357.6	1 614.6	1 684.1	1 998.3	1 877.0	Colombia
420.4	472.8	440.9	333.0	232.7	250.9	Costa Rica
1 095.5	1 294.9	1 356.1	1 503.3	911.2	767.9	Chile
961.5	1 018.4	969.4	957.0	884.1	576.5	Ecuador
436.6	383.4	303.1	289.5	251.9	240.7	El Salvador
600.7	552.9	487.1	487.0	381.9	304.3	Guatemala
104.9	107.7	112.0	111.6	74.9	...	Guyana
89.9	85.5	108.8	131.6	103.6	105.7	Haiti
280.4	313.5	323.4	288.1	216.0	243.8	Honduras
253.3	269.6	245.2	290.7	...	...	Jamaica
3 936.4	5 261.5	7 253.3	8 742.4	4 950.8	2 857.0	Mexico
244.4	149.9	256.6	284.2	211.6	219.4	Nicaragua
329.9	339.8	333.1	354.3	337.8	287.4	Panama
197.6	219.8	217.0	240.5	213.5	172.8	Paraguay
736.9	810.0	1 131.5	1 303.3	1 250.2	885.2	Peru
382.0	456.3	496.2	457.4	387.5	406.4	Dominican Republic
143.0	126.1	126.9	135.9	...	...	Suriname
481.2	565.3	665.9	645.2	944.9	...	Trinidad and Tobago
323.4	431.1	484.5	417.1	292.8	227.9	Uruguay
5 788.1	4 804.0	4 479.4	4 462.3	5 300.5	2 799.3	Venezuela
24 841.9	26 844.8	30 129.5	30 763.1	...	...	Total
12 224.2	12 757.1	14 719.1	16 325.7	13 469.9	...	Oil exporting countries [2]
12 617.7	14 087.7	15 410.4	14 437.4	...	...	Non-oil exporting countries

[1] According to Balance of payments values.
[2] Refers to Bolivia, Ecuador, Mexico, Peru, Trinidad and Tobago and Venezuela.

539

267. IMPORTACIONES DE BIENES SEGUN GRUPOS DE LA CUODE [1]

a) Bienes de consumo no duraderos
(Millones de dólares)

País	1960	1965	1970	1975
Argentina	40.3	52.8	84.5	137.9
Bolivia	14.8	20.3	22.5	67.5
Brasil	60.2	70.4	178.8	429.3
Colombia	34.7	9.1	47.3	90.0
Costa Rica	18.5	26.7	58.6	97.6
Chile	58.1	54.1	80.0	85.2
Ecuador	16.3	20.0	26.0	67.6
El Salvador	25.6	40.9	45.2	101.6
Guatemala	22.1	34.0	48.5	111.1
Haití	10.0	15.5	20.2	50.6
Honduras	13.7	23.2	44.3	65.5
México	74.3	89.7	186.6	381.1
Nicaragua	12.8	26.9	39.6	77.9
Panamá	36.8	41.8	68.7	94.2
Paraguay	3.4	4.4	13.3	29.3
Perú	42.1	84.2	71.9	162.6
República Dominicana	15.3	18.6	54.6	140.6
Uruguay	20.8	7.3	12.5	23.8
Venezuela	291.5	155.0	184.2	443.3
Total	811.3	794.9	1 287.3	2 656.7

[1] Se está revisando la información presentada de acuerdo con un nuevo método computarizado que permite clasificar en forma más directa las partidas nacionales por grupos de la Clasificación del Comercio Exterior según Uso o Destino Económico (CUODE).

a) Non-durable consumer goods
(Millions of dollars)

1977	1978	1979	1980	1981	Country
135.8	190.9	591.7	979.0	859.6	Argentina
74.3	101.8	103.0	83.0	82.9	Bolivia
535.5	647.9	1 017.8	815.9	609.0	Brazil
162.2	316.1	254.2	307.4	331.4	Colombia
141.0	162.0	195.0	174.0	111.0	Costa Rica
181.1	288.2	367.0	651.2	...	Chile
85.2	85.8	87.0	123.4	104.3	Ecuador
157.8	204.0	215.0	273.0	267.0	El Salvador
174.9	211.4	225.5	218.1	224.6	Guatemala
77.2	75.0	79.6	110.5	...	Haiti
86.6	102.7	120.8	154.9	160.0	Honduras
235.8	347.5	608.0	1 263.0	...	Mexico
110.6	98.1	77.7	215.0	182.0	Nicaragua
102.5	133.5	165.9	201.2	...	Panama
37.3	54.7	74.6	79.7	...	Paraguay
86.3	78.4	88.2	193.7	...	Peru
121.0	115.1	132.6	165.7	...	Dominican Republic
38.7	38.3	65.1	102.9	...	Uruguay
817.9	1 168.6	1 119.4	1 244.2	...	Venezuela
3 361.7	4 420.0	5 588.1	7 355.8	...	Total

[1] This information is being revised under a new computerized system which makes it possible to classify national items more directly by groups of the Foreign Trade Classification by Economic Use or Destination (CUODE).

267. IMPORTACIONES DE BIENES SEGUN GRUPOS DE LA CUODE[1] (continuación 1)

b) Bienes de consumo duraderos
(Millones de dólares)

País	1960	1965	1970	1975
Argentina	38.6	17.1	32.9	66.0
Bolivia	8.1	12.8	9.8	60.3
Brasil	21.7	9.4	45.6	184.7
Colombia	23.9	8.2	43.1	78.4
Costa Rica	12.2	19.7	30.5	46.4
Chile	20.2	25.0	45.4	52.4
Ecuador	9.4	10.4	16.7	48.2
El Salvador	15.8	20.0	23.5	34.4
Guatemala	14.2	26.1	31.5	53.8
Haití	13.8	9.5	13.2	30.1
Honduras	8.1	12.9	23.1	29.3
México	83.5	100.7	157.6	320.0
Nicaragua	8.2	17.7	19.2	44.0
Panamá	20.7	27.0	46.5	49.8
Paraguay	1.7	2.8	5.0	15.5
Perú	30.5	64.4	16.4	85.2
República Dominicana	9.4	9.4	37.6	61.3
Uruguay	8.0	2.2	3.8	21.1
Venezuela	188.2	173.1	224.9	386.3
Total	536.2	568.4	826.3	1 667.2

[1] Se está revisando la información presentada de acuerdo con un nuevo método computarizado que permite clasificar en forma más directa las partidas nacionales por grupos de la Clasificación del Comercio Exterior según Uso o Destino Económico (CUODE).

b) **Durable consumer goods**
(Millions of dollars)

1977	1978	1979	1980	1981	Country
69.3	112.6	390.3	1 227.5	1 056.2	Argentina
55.7	65.4	87.6	76.5	77.1	Bolivia
173.5	214.9	218.8	199.4	159.2	Brazil
125.7	187.4	196.8	312.2	336.2	Colombia
104.0	117.0	138.0	215.0	129.0	Costa Rica
205.2	252.2	362.7	797.6	...	Chile
82.6	92.7	93.5	126.7	98.4	Ecuador
57.7	62.0	53.0	34.0	17.0	El Salvador
110.6	123.7	132.9	122.8	116.6	Guatemala
45.5	44.1	51.1	63.6	...	Haiti
52.6	62.9	74.0	82.8	77.0	Honduras
112.4	151.1	250.4	310.9	...	Mexico
70.8	49.8	19.5	43.0	47.0	Nicaragua
65.1	78.0	84.2	102.8	...	Panama
23.6	29.9	40.9	48.9	...	Paraguay
94.0	82.3	97.0	242.2	...	Peru
52.6	48.9	48.7	103.3	...	Dominican Republic
38.7	38.0	85.9	170.0	...	Uruguay
1 149.2	1 218.0	1 230.0	1 650.7	...	Venezuela
2 688.8	3 030.9	3 655.3	5 929.9	...	Total

[1] This information is being revised under a new computerized system which makes it possible to classify national items more directly by groups of the Foreign Trade Classification by Economic Use or Destination (CUODE).

267. IMPORTACIONES DE BIENES SEGUN GRUPOS DE LA CUODE [1] (continuación 2)

c) Combustibles
(Millones de dólares)

País	1960	1965	1970	1975
Argentina	167.8	115.2	79.6	513.9
Bolivia	2.4	1.2	1.1	7.2
Brasil	262.7	222.9	377.4	3 526.8
Colombia	9.8	3.2	3.4	14.5
Costa Rica	5.8	8.1	11.3	73.8
Chile	52.6	31.7	56.0	301.2
Ecuador	4.3	14.9	16.4	18.1
El Salvador	7.1	9.9	5.2	51.2
Guatemala	10.0	14.5	14.9	103.3
Haití	1.9	1.6	3.6	12.5
Honduras	6.0	6.6	13.9	68.5
México	46.6	35.6	73.2	330.7
Nicaragua	6.5	7.3	11.4	72.9
Panamá	12.6	44.2	65.9	355.4
Paraguay	3.4	5.8	7.4	35.9
Perú	17.2	20.9	12.2	314.8
República Dominicana	10.1	9.7	18.6	144.2
Uruguay	31.4	25.3	33.8	164.5
Venezuela	12.5	8.9	23.6	31.7
Total	670.7	587.5	828.9	6 141.1

[1] Se está revisando la información presentada de acuerdo con un nuevo método computarizado que permite clasificar en forma más directa las partidas nacionales por grupos de la Clasificación del Comercio Exterior según Uso o Destino Económico (CUODE).

267. IMPORTS OF GOODS BY CUODE GROUPS[1] *(continued 2)*

c) Fuels
(Millions of dollars)

1977	1978	1979	1980	1981	Country
673.5	472.7	1 086.4	1 062.1	998.2	Argentina
7.4	6.5	13.5	12.2	13.1	Bolivia
4 482.2	4 877.9	7 279.5	10 715.8	12 130.4	Brazil
186.8	204.5	322.2	562.8	724.1	Colombia
92.0	118.0	183.8	104.0	73.0	Costa Rica
449.1	480.4	888.7	959.6	...	Chile
9.4	11.1	13.5	23.3	25.8	Ecuador
92.8	83.0	122.1	151.0	170.0	El Salvador
144.1	167.7	242.0	338.7	369.1	Guatemala
25.4	26.9	34.5	35.8	...	Haiti
71.0	76.4	113.0	171.2	159.0	Honduras
126.3	156.2	202.7	272.0	...	Mexico
97.3	89.0	75.7	174.0	202.0	Nicaragua
282.1	229.0	337.8	423.0	...	Panama
62.0	84.2	125.3	169.3	...	Paraguay
377.8	78.4	11.0	31.1	...	Peru
201.4	224.0	314.7	355.5	...	Dominican Republic
186.0	228.7	264.7	467.6	...	Uruguay
31.1	58.5	65.5	184.8	....	Venezuela
7 599.7	7 673.1	11 696.1	16 213.8	...	*Total*

[1] *This information is being revised under a new computerized system which makes it possible to classify national items more directly by groups of the Foreign Trade Classification by Economic Use or Destination (CUODE).*

267. IMPORTACIONES DE BIENES SEGUN GRUPOS DE LA CUODE[1] (continuación 3)

d) Materias primas y productos intermedios para la agricultura y la industria
(Millones de dólares)

País	1960	1965	1970	1975
Argentina	448.1	620.9	908.7	2 360.6
Bolivia	19.0	44.9	58.8	192.0
Brasil	518.2	523.8	1 172.3	4 877.8
Colombia	210.7	195.9	355.0	766.3
Costa Rica	41.0	69.0	121.3	275.7
Chile	163.3	269.3	352.4	586.5
Ecuador	34.6	60.2	103.2	300.9
El Salvador	41.4	69.8	92.4	237.4
Guatemala	51.3	85.8	132.0	253.4
Haití	0.7	1.0	1.2	6.7
Honduras	25.5	46.0	72.5	124.7
México	474.6	680.9	1 022.1	2 693.0
Nicaragua	25.2	57.8	66.7	174.7
Panamá	32.9	55.5	82.7	206.2
Paraguay	9.1	16.8	17.5	43.8
Perú	147.1	266.9	297.2	1 058.1
República Dominicana	33.4	36.9	96.4	297.3
Uruguay	92.8	71.3	108.9	232.1
Venezuela	287.1	547.4	728.8	2 545.7
Total	2 656.0	3 720.1	5 790.1	17 232.9

[1] Se está revisando la información presentada de acuerdo con un nuevo método computarizado que permite clasificar en forma más directa las partidas nacionales por grupos de la Clasificación del Comercio Exterior según Uso o Destino Económico (CUODE).

267. IMPORTS OF GOODS BY CUODE GROUPS[1] *(continued 3)*

d) Raw materials and intermediate products for agriculture and industry
(Millions of dollars)

1977	1978	1979	1980	1981	Country
1 816.8	1 539.6	2 475.4	3 442.5	2 959.4	Argentina
189.4	203.5	251.3	203.4	196.1	Bolivia
4 772.3	5 522.1	7 292.7	8 661.3	6 862.3	Brazil
849.7	1 230.3	1 383.1	1 896.0	1 977.0	Colombia
394.0	401.0	455.0	660.0	615.0	Costa Rica
808.8	1 089.7	1 342.6	1 684.4	...	Chile
510.4	520.3	748.6	823.1	832.9	Ecuador
339.2	334.0	352.0	336.0	317.0	El Salvador
396.6	428.3	458.2	523.7	542.0	Guatemala
9.0	9.9	16.0	29.1	...	Haiti
186.5	221.2	266.8	297.7	302.0	Honduras
2 831.6	3 105.3	4 709.2	7 655.8	...	Mexico
257.5	217.8	126.1	309.0	309.0	Nicaragua
224.4	272.7	320.0	379.4	...	Panama
58.0	69.4	109.3	120.4	...	Paraguay
728.8	983.9	1 069.4	1 494.6	...	Peru
355.1	386.0	449.7	706.8	...	Dominican Republic
270.9	257.8	493.6	461.8	...	Uruguay
3 530.4	3 737.9	3 765.4	4 225.2	...	Venezuela
18 529.4	20 530.7	26 084.4	33 910.2	...	Total

[1] *This information is being revised under a new computerized system which makes it possible to classify national items more directly by groups of the Foreign Trade Classification by Economic Use or Destination (CUODE).*

267. IMPORTACIONES DE BIENES SEGUN GRUPOS DE LA CUODE [1] (continuación 4)

e) Materiales de construcción
(Millones de dólares)

País	1960	1965	1970	1975
Argentina	68.2	53.6	101.9	140.4
Bolivia	2.0	2.1	8.8	24.6
Brasil	34.9	7.4	47.0	340.2
Colombia	24.4	3.6	21.5	35.4
Costa Rica	9.1	12.8	19.8	34.7
Chile	19.1	18.8	26.1	34.6
Ecuador	8.7	8.1	19.7	68.3
El Salvador	8.8	14.4	10.4	29.7
Guatemala	9.1	12.7	17.0	37.5
Haití	2.1	1.5	2.1	10.9
Honduras	3.4	5.8	11.4	15.9
México	21.7	27.6	37.5	118.3
Nicaragua	3.6	8.9	13.7	27.7
Panamá	5.6	7.4	15.3	15.5
Paraguay	1.5	1.9	2.6	5.6
Perú	11.0	25.2	13.0	126.5
República Dominicana	5.2	3.2	14.1	46.9
Uruguay	6.3	1.9	2.1	8.1
Venezuela	76.5	69.4	59.3	310.3
Total	321.2	286.3	443.3	1 431.1

[1] Se está revisando la información presentada de acuerdo con un nuevo método computarizado que permite clasificar en forma más directa las partidas nacionales por grupos de la Clasificación del Comercio Exterior según Uso o Destino Económico (CUODE).

267. IMPORTS OF GOODS BY CUODE GROUPS[1] (continued 4)

e) Construction materials
(Millions of dollars)

1977	1978	1979	1980	1981	Country
106.0	132.4	227.9	348.0	...	Argentina
44.6	42.0	68.3	57.0	56.6	Bolivia
192.2	183.0	193.0	274.1	472.5	Brazil
28.4	44.7	63.1	98.3	159.6	Colombia
42.3	87.0	79.0	94.0	64.0	Costa Rica
31.4	45.0	50.6	85.1	...	Chile
92.3	89.4	82.8	119.9	89.8	Ecuador
50.5	77.0	72.0	57.0	57.0	El Salvador
80.0	86.2	100.6	92.6	99.9	Guatemala
14.6	14.6	16.5	20.4	...	Haiti
28.5	31.9	41.4	49.4	42.0	Honduras
125.0	166.2	509.0	621.8	...	Mexico
32.0	25.6	14.7	36.0	41.0	Nicaragua
24.7	29.2	32.0	40.6	...	Panama
11.8	12.8	12.9	19.0	...	Paraguay
53.7	56.8	61.7	69.2	...	Peru
39.7	27.5	42.6	42.5	...	Dominican Republic
12.4	9.2	23.2	31.1	...	Uruguay
445.2	464.5	604.4	554.4	...	Venezuela
1 455.3	1 625.0	2 295.7	2 710.4	...	*Total*

[1] This information is being revised under a new computerized system which makes it possible to classify national items more directly by groups of the Foreign Trade Classification by Economic Use or Destination (CUODE).

267. IMPORTACIONES DE BIENES SEGUN GRUPOS DE LA CUODE [1] (continuación 5)

f) Bienes de capital para la agricultura
(Millones de dólares)

País	1960	1965	1970	1975
Argentina	49.9	12.0	12.5	20.1
Bolivia	0.8	0.9	3.2	7.2
Brasil	73.3	14.7	26.0	266.7
Colombia	28.8	13.2	13.0	29.0
Costa Rica	4.4	4.3	6.4	20.1
Chile	11.8	12.3	17.0	20.4
Ecuador	4.9	4.3	7.5	48.9
El Salvador	2.1	4.0	2.8	11.6
Guatemala	4.2	9.6	6.5	19.4
Haití	-	0.2	0.1	0.6
Honduras	2.5	4.5	8.4	14.2
México	26.3	51.2	46.9	124.8
Nicaragua	2.4	9.8	3.5	12.4
Panamá	2.0	3.2	8.4	17.2
Paraguay	0.4	1.2	1.8	5.5
Perú	6.6	14.2	8.3	25.8
República Dominicana	1.3	3.0	10.1	32.4
Uruguay	2.5	5.7	11.4	14.1
Venezuela	25.9	46.8	40.7	183.6
Total	250.1	215.1	234.5	874.0

[1] Se está revisando la información presentada de acuerdo con un nuevo método computarizado que permite clasificar en forma más directa las partidas nacionales por grupos de la Clasificación del Comercio Exterior según Uso o Destino Económico (CUODE).

267. IMPORTS OF GOODS BY CUODE GROUPS[1] (continued 5)

f) Capital goods for agriculture
(Millions of dollars)

1977	1978	1979	1980	1981	Country
44.0	41.0	71.5	115.4	63.6	Argentina
16.7	16.2	21.2	18.7	18.9	Bolivia
71.3	48.9	39.1	43.4	29.4	Brazil
44.6	54.3	39.3	63.1	66.1	Colombia
28.4	37.0	37.0	29.0	19.0	Costa Rica
16.9	30.0	38.0	38.8	...	Chile
28.0	26.4	31.3	38.2	44.1	Ecuador
17.0	18.5	12.3	7.8	5.5	El Salvador
33.5	35.2	23.3	18.6	16.3	Guatemala
0.7	0.9	1.3	2.3	...	Haiti
19.2	21.3	29.6	22.3	19.0	Honduras
77.9	113.4	238.4	427.5	...	Mexico
22.9	11.9	4.3	24.0	30.0	Nicaragua
16.4	20.7	24.9	31.9	...	Panama
20.6	20.4	24.6	21.2	...	Paraguay
11.5	25.5	41.9	69.2	...	Peru
9.9	13.2	9.7	21.2	...	Dominican Republic
14.6	10.6	38.4	41.6	...	Uruguay
227.8	152.6	107.7	123.2	...	Venezuela
721.9	**698.0**	**833.8**	**1 157.4**	...	**Total**

[1] This information is being revised under a new computerized system which makes it possible to classify national items more directly by groups of the Foreign Trade Classification by Economic Use or Destination (CUODE).

267. IMPORTACIONES DE BIENES SEGUN GRUPOS DE LA CUODE[1] (continuación 6)

g) Bienes de capital para la industria
(Millones de dólares)

País	1960	1965	1970	1975
Argentina	261.4	230.1	374.2	540.1
Bolivia	18.2	33.0	26.4	92.6
Brasil	250.8	155.7	662.6	3 170.6
Colombia	128.6	164.2	218.7	269.1
Costa Rica	13.5	30.0	50.6	106.8
Chile	106.4	132.0	210.1	274.0
Ecuador	16.2	28.9	47.3	230.1
El Salvador	13.8	32.0	26.1	109.7
Guatemala	17.7	32.9	43.1	99.8
Haití	2.0	1.6	3.3	10.1
Honduras	8.9	14.4	31.6	61.6
México	343.9	488.7	762.4	1 838.9
Nicaragua	8.4	21.6	33.8	85.3
Panamá	13.4	23.4	50.7	81.9
Paraguay	6.5	12.5	12.3	38.3
Perú	67.0	161.9	136.1	609.1
República Dominicana	19.1	14.6	57.3	118.0
Uruguay	35.2	20.0	33.1	44.9
Venezuela	205.2	317.9	460.2	1 526.1
Total	1 536.2	1 915.4	3 239.9	9 307.0

[1] Se está revisando la información presentada de acuerdo con un nuevo método computarizado que permite clasificar en forma más directa las partidas nacionales por grupos de la Clasificación del Comercio Exterior según Uso o Destino Económico (CUODE).

267. IMPORTS OF GOODS BY CUODE GROUPS[1] *(continued 6)*

g) **Capital goods for industry**
(Millions of dollars)

1977	1978	1979	1980	1981	Country
845.3	988.9	1 189.7	2 378.6	2 378.4	*Argentina*
154.7	228.6	254.2	225.4	238.8	*Bolivia*
2 292.2	2 632.0	3 025.9	3 112.8	2 926.3	*Brazil*
409.7	517.0	603.1	955.1	1 113.2	*Colombia*
144.0	166.0	232.0	197.0	160.0	*Costa Rica*
499.8	510.3	759.2	988.1	...	*Chile*
400.5	491.9	567.2	570.2	547.2	*Ecuador*
156.2	177.7	146.0	83.6	66.2	*El Salvador*
176.6	226.5	226.4	193.2	221.3	*Guatemala*
15.5	15.4	19.7	26.8	...	*Haiti*
89.3	126.4	133.8	178.8	157.0	*Honduras*
1 441.3	2 306.5	3 639.9	5 732.1	...	*Mexico*
117.3	73.9	31.4	61.0	119.0	*Nicaragua*
95.4	112.9	144.6	175.2	...	*Panama*
54.6	52.2	77.1	77.4	...	*Paraguay*
422.0	470.4	606.4	986.0	...	*Peru*
136.9	130.4	136.2	183.9	...	*Dominican Republic*
129.2	103.4	144.8	297.1	...	*Uruguay*
2 940.3	3 589.5	2 944.4	3 079.6	...	*Venezuela*
10 520.8	12 919.9	14 882.0	19 501.9	...	*Total*

[1] *This information is being revised under a new computerized system which makes it possible to classify national items more directly by groups of the Foreign Trade Classification by Economic Use or Destination (CUODE).*

267. IMPORTACIONES DE BIENES SEGUN GRUPOS DE LA CUODE [1] (conclusión)

h) Bienes de capital para el transporte
(Millones de dólares)

País	1960	1965	1970	1975
Argentina	165.3	94.7	97.5	166.5
Bolivia	5.7	17.6	27.8	99.3
Brasil	236.8	89.1	268.3	767.7
Colombia	51.6	55.3	138.4	205.8
Costa Rica	5.7	7.3	17.8	38.3
Chile	65.9	59.6	143.2	172.6
Ecuador	20.0	17.4	36.2	156.4
El Salvador	7.5	8.8	7.3	24.9
Guatemala	9.2	12.2	12.1	52.5
Haití	1.7	2.9	3.3	10.6
Honduras	3.5	7.9	14.8	19.1
México	107.5	81.3	170.8	762.2
Nicaragua	2.4	8.6	9.7	21.2
Panamá	3.2	5.6	18.2	48.8
Paraguay	6.3	6.0	8.6	19.6
Perú	50.0	78.4	66.9	196.1
República Dominicana	6.1	4.6	17.2	58.6
Uruguay	16.8	15.2	26.2	30.8
Venezuela	93.9	122.2	170.3	892.9
Total	859.1	694.7	1 254.6	3 743.9

[1] Se está revisando la información presentada de acuerdo con un nuevo método computarizado que permite clasificar en forma más directa las partidas nacionales por grupos de la Clasificación del Comercio Exterior según Uso o Destino Económico (CUODE).

267. IMPORTS OF GOODS BY CUODE GROUPS[1] (concluded)

b) Capital goods for transport
(Millions of dollars)

1977	1978	1979	1980	1981	Country
469.7	354.5	665.7	910.0	792.3	Argentina
74.3	120.4	147.3	122.9	122.3	Bolivia
735.7	888.3	737.4	1 137.9	889.8	Brazil
212.9	252.1	371.2	467.8	491.6	Colombia
64.4	78.0	78.0	56.0	40.0	Costa Rica
217.3	300.2	400.7	607.6	...	Chile
295.9	308.7	356.8	408.2	494.3	Ecuador
58.1	71.8	49.0	29.2	20.2	El Salvador
89.8	101.3	88.5	74.0	62.8	Guatemala
15.8	15.7	19.2	24.1	...	Haiti
47.0	50.0	51.2	61.0	41.0	Honduras
930.9	1 208.8	1 728.7	2 934.1	...	Mexico
53.3	29.9	10.5	25.0	60.0	Nicaragua
47.4	59.3	71.1	88.3	...	Panama
39.3	59.2	56.2	63.6	...	Paraguay
143.9	174.4	227.1	363.3	...	Peru
74.4	72.3	81.5	70.9	...	Dominican Republic
35.0	29.7	90.4	108.0	...	Uruguay
1 190.6	1 284.7	1 201.9	1 244.2	...	Venezuela
4 795.7	5 489.3	6 432.4	8 796.1	...	Total

[1] This information is being revised under a new computerized system which makes it possible to classify national items more directly by groups of the Foreign Trade Classification by Economic Use or Destination (CUODE).

268. COMERCIO INTRARREGIONAL DE BIENES TOTALES, 1960

(Sobre la base de las exportaciones fob en millones de dólares)

Procedencia \ Destino	Argentina	Bolivia	Brasil Brazil	Colombia	Chile	Ecuador	México Mexico	Paraguay
Argentina	-	2.3	82.8	0.3	41.7	0.1	0.8	8.5
Bolivia	3.9	-	4.0	...	0.3	...	...	...
Brasil	56.5	0.5	-	0.2	11.6	...	0.1	1.1
Colombia	0.1	...	...	-	1.0	0.4	0.1	...
Chile	17.9	1.8	5.8	1.0	-	0.7	0.4	...
Ecuador	...	...	...	2.7	2.4	-	...	...
México	0.6	...	1.2	1.2	1.4	...	-	...
Paraguay	7.7	...	...	...	...	...	...	-
Perú	9.4	2.9	2.1	0.8	16.5	3.1	0.8	...
Uruguay	2.4	...	0.3	0.1	0.3	...	...	0.1
Venezuela	68.3	...	84.8	1.6	9.4	3.0	0.1	3.5
Total ALALC	**166.8**	**7.5**	**181.0**	**7.9**	**84.6**	**7.3**	**2.3**	**13.2**
Costa Rica	...	...	...	0.5	...	...	...	...
El Salvador	...	...	...	...	...	...	0.1	...
Guatemala	...	...	...	...	...	...	0.2	...
Honduras	...	...	...	...	...	...	...	...
Nicaragua	...	...	...	...	...	...	...	...
Total MCCA	**...**	**...**	**...**	**0.5**	**...**	**...**	**0.3**	**...**
Barbados	...	...	...	...	...	...	...	...
Guyana	...	...	...	...	...	...	...	...
Jamaica	...	...	...	...	...	...	...	...
Trinidad y Tabago	...	...	8.9	0.1	...	...	...	...
Bahamas	...	...	...	...	...	...	0.1	...
Haití	...	...	...	...	...	...	...	...
Panamá	...	...	...	...	...	...	...	...
República Dominicana	...	...	...	...	...	...	...	...
Suriname	...	...	...	...	...	...	...	...
Total Región	**166.8**	**7.5**	**189.9**	**8.5**	**84.6**	**7.3**	**2.7**	**13.2**
Mundo	**1 230.9**	**60.0**	**1 382.8**	**455.0**	**494.6**	**117.0**	**1 174.8**	**45.7**

268. INTRAREGIONAL TRADE IN TOTAL GOODS, 1960

(Based on exports FOB in millions of dollars)

Perú *Peru*	Uruguay	Venezuela	Total ALALC LAFTA	Costa Rica	El Salvador	Guatemala	Destination / Origin
15.5	12.9	5.4	170.3	...	...	...	*Argentina*
0.1	...	...	8.3	...	...	...	*Bolivia*
0.4	16.7	1.4	88.5	...	...	...	*Brazil*
3.2	...	1.4	6.2	1.3	...	...	*Colombia*
3.4	1.1	0.9	33.0	...	...	...	*Chile*
0.1	...	2.9	8.1	...	...	...	*Ecuador*
0.7	0.1	2.9	8.1	1.1	1.9	2.7	*Mexico*
...	1.2	...	8.9	...	...	...	*Paraguay*
-	0.7	0.5	36.8	0.2	...	...	*Peru*
0.1	-	...	3.3	...	...	...	*Uruguay*
1.8	23.2	-	195.7	1.1	1.4	1.2	*Venezuela*
25.3	55.9	15.4	567.2	3.7	3.3	3.9	*Total LAFTA*
0.4	...	0.2	1.1	-	0.6	0.8	*Costa Rica*
...	...	...	0.1	0.8	-	6.1	*El Salvador*
...	...	0.7	0.9	0.1	4.4	-	*Guatemala*
...	...	1.7	1.7	0.1	6.5	2.0	*Honduras*
...	...	0.2	0.2	1.2	1.3	...	*Nicaragua*
0.4	...	2.8	4.0	2.2	12.8	8.9	*Total CACM*
...	...	...	...	...	...	...	*Barbados*
...	...	...	...	...	...	...	*Guyana*
...	...	0.2	0.2	...	...	...	*Jamaica*
...	...	1.0	10.0	...	...	...	*Trinidad and Tobago*
...	...	...	0.1	...	...	...	*Bahamas*
...	...	...	...	...	...	...	*Haiti*
...	...	0.1	0.1	...	...	...	*Panama*
...	...	...	...	...	...	...	*Dominican Republic*
...	...	0.6	0.6	...	...	...	*Suriname*
25.7	55.9	20.1	582.2	5.9	16.1	12.8	*Total Region*
324.0	208.1	1 037.3	6 530.2	93.3	106.5	124.3	*World*

557

268. COMERCIO INTRARREGIONAL DE BIENES TOTALES, 1960 (conclusión)

(Sobre la base de las exportaciones fob en millones de dólares)

Procedencia \ Destino	Honduras	Nicaragua	Total MCCA CACM	Barbados	Guyana	Jamaica	Trinidad y Tabago Trinidad and Tobago
Argentina	...	...	...	...	...	...	...
Bolivia	...	...	...	...	...	...	...
Brasil	...	...	...	...	...	...	1.1
Colombia	...	...	1.3	...	...	...	6.5
Chile	...	...	...	...	...	...	0.1
Ecuador	...	...	...	...	...	...	...
México	0.6	0.8	7.1	...	...	...	...
Paraguay	...	...	...	...	...	...	...
Perú	...	0.3	0.5	...	...	...	...
Uruguay	...	...	...	...	...	...	...
Venezuela	0.2	1.4	5.3	0.7	...	1.0	72.0
Total ALALC	0.8	2.5	14.2	0.7	...	1.0	79.7
Costa Rica	...	1.0	2.4	...	...	...	...
El Salvador	4.0	1.4	12.3	...	...	...	...
Guatemala	0.4	0.1	5.0	...	...	...	...
Honduras	-	0.1	8.7	...	...	1.2	...
Nicaragua	...	-	2.5	...	...	...	...
Total MCCA	4.4	2.6	30.9	...	...	1.2	...
Barbados	...	...	...	-	0.4	...	0.9
Guyana	...	...	...	1.6	-	3.3	5.6
Jamaica	...	...	...	...	1.4	-	1.2
Trinidad y Tabago	...	...	...	...	6.9	...	-
Bahamas	...	...	...	...	...	0.1	...
Haití	...	...	...	...	...	...	...
Panamá	...	...	...	...	...	...	...
República Dominicana	...	...	...	...	...	...	...
Suriname	...	...	...	...	...	...	0.1
Total Región	5.2	5.1	45.1	2.3	8.7	5.6	87.5
Mundo	58.9	56.4	439.4	34.3	69.5	173.8	269.4

268. INTRAREGIONAL TRADE IN TOTAL GOODS, 1960 (concluded)

(Based on exports FOB in millions of dollars)

Bahamas	Haití *Haiti*	Panamá *Panama*	República Dominicana *Dominican Republic*	Suriname	Total región *region*	Mundo *World*	Destination / Origin
...	...	0.2	...	...	170.5	1 079.6	*Argentina*
...	...	...	...	...	8.3	67.9	*Bolivia*
...	...	...	...	...	89.6	1 270.9	*Brazil*
...	...	1.0	...	...	15.0	465.1	*Colombia*
...	...	4.4	...	...	37.5	489.7	*Chile*
...	...	0.1	...	...	8.2	104.6	*Ecuador*
...	...	6.6	...	...	21.8	764.4	*Mexico*
...	...	...	...	...	8.9	27.0	*Paraguay*
...	...	5.1	...	...	42.4	431.5	*Peru*
...	...	...	...	...	3.3	129.5	*Uruguay*
3.8	...	3.0	...	...	281.5	2 517.7	*Venezuela*
3.8	**...**	**20.4**	**...**	**...**	**687.0**	**7 347.9**	**Total LAFTA**
...	...	1.1	...	...	4.6	87.7	*Costa Rica*
...	...	0.2	...	...	12.6	116.7	*El Salvador*
...	...	...	...	...	5.9	112.8	*Guatemala*
...	...	...	...	...	11.6	64.3	*Honduras*
...	...	0.1	...	...	2.8	62.7	*Nicaragua*
...	**...**	**1.4**	**...**	**...**	**37.5**	**444.2**	**Total CACM**
...	...	...	...	...	1.3	23.9	*Barbados*
...	...	...	...	...	10.5	74.3	*Guyana*
0.3	...	...	...	...	3.1	158.4	*Jamaica*
...	...	...	...	...	16.9	287.1	*Trinidad and Tobago*
-	...	...	...	...	0.2	10.9	*Bahamas*
...	-	...	...	...	...	38.0	*Haiti*
...	...	-	...	...	0.1	19.4	*Panama*
...	...	...	-	0.3	0.3	180.4	*Dominican Republic*
...	...	...	...	-	0.7	44.1	*Suriname*
4.1	**...**	**21.8**	**...**	**0.3**	**757.6**	**8 628.6**	**Total Region**
75.7	42.1	267.7	76.1	43.9	8 022.1	...	*World*

269. COMERCIO INTRARREGIONAL DE BIENES TOTALES, 1965

(Sobre la base de las exportaciones fob en millones de dólares)

Procedencia \ Destino	Argentina	Bolivia	Brasil *Brazil*	Colombia	Chile	Ecuador	México *Mexico*	Paraguay
Argentina	-	7.6	107.1	7.1	53.4	0.6	6.7	10.6
Bolivia	0.9	-	1.3	...	0.7	...	...	...
Brasil	141.0	1.2	-	2.9	19.0	...	8.9	2.3
Colombia	5.5	...	0.4	-	0.8	3.9	0.5	...
Chile	26.5	0.8	14.1	1.9	-	1.4	2.8	0.1
Ecuador	2.7	0.1	...	6.3	1.7	-	0.2	...
México	7.4	0.2	5.4	5.5	12.3	1.3	-	...
Paraguay	14.7	...	...	...	...	...	...	-
Perú	19.7	1.2	5.3	4.3	17.4	1.4	4.3	...
Uruguay	3.1	...	5.4	4.6	0.9	...	0.3	0.2
Venezuela	26.1	...	79.9	1.2	16.8	7.8	0.1	...
Total ALALC	**247.6**	**11.1**	**218.9**	**33.8**	**123.0**	**16.4**	**23.8**	**13.2**
Costa Rica	...	...	...	0.3	...	...	...	...
El Salvador	...	...	...	...	...	...	...	...
Guatemala	...	...	...	...	...	...	...	...
Honduras	...	...	...	...	...	...	...	...
Nicaragua	...	...	...	0.2	...	...	...	...
Total MCCA	**...**	**...**	**...**	**0.5**	**...**	**...**	**...**	**...**
Barbados	...	...	...	...	...	...	...	...
Guyana	...	...	...	...	...	...	...	...
Jamaica	...	...	...	...	...	...	...	...
Trinidad y Tabago	0.7	...	2.2	0.1	...	...	...	...
Bahamas	...	...	...	...	...	...	...	...
Haití	...	...	...	...	...	...	...	...
Panamá	...	...	...	0.1	...	...	...	...
República Dominicana	...	...	...	...	...	...	...	...
Suriname	...	...	...	...	...	...	...	...
Total Región	**248.3**	**11.1**	**221.1**	**34.5**	**123.0**	**16.4**	**23.8**	**13.2**
Mundo	**1 114.6**	**101.3**	**939.4**	**414.3**	**581.7**	**156.4**	**1 640.5**	**58.3**

269. INTRAREGIONAL TRADE IN TOTAL GOODS, 1965

(Based on exports FOB in millions of dollars)

Perú Peru	Uruguay	Venezuela	Total ALALC LAFTA	Costa Rica	El Salvador	Guatemala	Destination / Origin
37.6	8.0	7.9	246.6	...	...	...	Argentina
0.6	...	...	3.5	...	...	...	Bolivia
12.0	11.2	3.2	201.7	...	...	...	Brazil
5.2	0.3	2.8	19.4	2.6	...	1.1	Colombia
4.6	1.9	2.3	56.4	...	...	...	Chile
1.9	0.3	0.1	13.3	0.1	0.1	0.1	Ecuador
3.5	0.8	7.4	43.8	2.5	4.4	5.0	Mexico
...	2.2	...	16.9	...	...	...	Paraguay
-	1.7	7.0	62.3	...	...	...	Peru
1.0	-	0.1	15.6	...	...	...	Uruguay
7.2	15.5	-	154.6	2.1	8.0	9.8	Venezuela
73.6	**41.9**	**30.8**	**834.1**	**7.3**	**12.5**	**16.0**	*Total LAFTA*
1.7	...	...	2.0	-	4.7	4.3	Costa Rica
...	...	...	...	4.7	-	20.3	El Salvador
...	...	0.1	0.1	4.3	19.6	-	Guatemala
...	...	...	...	1.5	13.2	5.2	Honduras
...	...	...	0.2	4.2	3.9	1.7	Nicaragua
1.7	**...**	**0.1**	**2.3**	**14.7**	**41.4**	**31.5**	*Total CACM*
...	...	...	...	...	...	...	Barbados
...	...	...	...	...	...	...	Guyana
...	...	0.1	0.1	...	...	...	Jamaica
...	...	0.8	3.8	...	...	...	Trinidad and Tobago
...	...	...	...	...	...	...	Bahamas
...	...	...	...	...	...	...	Haiti
...	...	0.2	0.3	0.5	...	...	Panama
...	...	0.9	0.9	...	...	...	Dominican Republic
...	...	...	...	...	...	...	Suriname
75.3	**41.9**	**32.9**	**841.5**	**22.5**	**53.9**	**47.5**	*Total Region*
684.0	**125.9**	**1 192.0**	**7 008.4**	**151.3**	**186.6**	**211.0**	*World*

VI. COMERCIO EXTERIOR

269. COMERCIO INTRARREGIONAL DE BIENES TOTALES, 1965 (conclusión)

(Sobre la base de las exportaciones fob en millones de dólares)

Procedencia \ Destino	Honduras	Nicaragua	Total MCCA CACM	Barbados	Guyana	Jamaica	Trinidad y Tabago *Trinidad and Tobago*
Argentina	...	...	...	1.0	...	...	0.4
Bolivia	...	...	...	...	...	...	...
Brasil	...	...	...	...	...	...	0.1
Colombia	...	1.2	4.9	...	...	...	28.2
Chile	...	...	...	...	...	...	...
Ecuador	...	0.1	0.4	...	...	...	...
México	0.9	2.4	15.2	...	...	...	...
Paraguay	...	...	...	...	...	...	...
Perú	...	...	...	...	...	...	...
Uruguay	...	...	...	...	...	...	...
Venezuela	...	4.3	24.2	5.7	...	18.9	98.8
Total ALALC	**0.9**	**8.0**	**44.7**	**6.7**	**...**	**18.9**	**127.5**
Costa Rica	3.0	6.3	18.3	...	...	...	...
El Salvador	14.1	6.2	45.3	...	...	...	...
Guatemala	6.6	5.2	35.7	...	0.8	....	...
Honduras	-	1.2	21.1	...	...	1.8	...
Nicaragua	2.6	-	12.4	...	...	...	...
Total MCCA	**26.3**	**18.9**	**132.8**	**...**	**0.8**	**1.8**	**...**
Barbados	...	...	...	-	0.4	0.1	1.0
Guyana	...	...	...	1.5	-	2.1	8.8
Jamaica	1.1	...	1.1	0.4	0.6	-	1.1
Trinidad y Tabago	...	...	...	...	9.5	2.1	-
Bahamas	...	...	...	...	...	0.1	...
Haití	...	...	...	...	...	...	...
Panamá	...	...	0.5	...	...	...	...
República Dominicana	...	...	...	...	...	...	...
Suriname	...	...	...	...	...	...	0.2
Total Región	**28.3**	**26.9**	**179.1**	**8.6**	**11.3**	**25.1**	**138.6**
Mundo	**108.1**	**139.6**	**796.6**	**43.2**	**84.6**	**256.6**	**418.3**

269. INTRAREGIONAL TRADE IN TOTAL GOODS, 1965 (concluded)

(Based on exports FOB in millions of dollars)

Bahamas	Haití *Haiti*	Panamá *Panama*	República Dominicana *Dominican Republic*	Suriname	Total región *region*	Mundo *World*	Destination / Origin
...	...	0.5	2.2	...	250.7	1 492.5	*Argentina*
...	...	...	...	...	3.5	131.9	*Bolivia*
0.2	...	0.2	...	...	202.2	1 595.7	*Brazil*
...	...	4.3	...	...	56.8	538.9	*Colombia*
...	...	0.4	...	...	56.8	687.8	*Chile*
...	...	0.1	...	... -	13.8	227.4	*Ecuador*
13.5	...	8.9	...	...	81.4	1 142.0	*Mexico*
...	...	...	...	...	16.9	57.3	*Paraguay*
...	...	...	...	...	62.3	667.6	*Peru*
...	...	...	...	...	15.6	191.3	*Uruguay*
10.4	...	35.7	1.5	...	349.8	2 784.2	*Venezuela*
24.1	...	**50.1**	**3.7**	...	**1 109.8**	**9 516.6**	***Total LAFTA***
...	...	1.9	...	...	22.2	111.9	*Costa Rica*
...	...	0.3	...	...	45.6	188.4	*El Salvador*
...	...	...	...	...	36.6	185.9	*Guatemala*
...	...	...	...	..	22.9	127.3	*Honduras*
...	...	0.3	...	...	12.9	149.0	*Nicaragua*
...	...	2.5	...	...	140.2	762.5	***Total CACM***
...	...	...	...	...	1.5	37.5	*Barbados*
...	...	...	...	...	12.4	97.3	*Guyana*
3.2	...	...	...	...	6.5	213.6	*Jamaica*
...	...	...	...	...	15.4	401.8	*Trinidad and Tobago*
-	...	...	...	...	0.1	18.5	*Bahamas*
...	-	...	...	...	...	45.0	*Haiti*
...	...	-	...	...	0.8	69.2	*Panama*
...	...	...	-	...	0.9	123.2	*Dominican Republic*
...	...	...	...	-	0.2	57.3	*Suriname*
27.3	...	52.6	3.7	...	1 287.8	11 342.5	***Total Region***
163.7	35.9	385.5	125.1	69.3	9 387.2	...	*World*

270. COMERCIO INTRARREGIONAL DE BIENES TOTALES, 1970

(Sobre la base de las exportaciones fob en millones de dólares)

Procedencia \ Destino	Argentina	Bolivia	Brasil *Brazil*	Colombia	Chile	Ecuador	México *Mexico*	Paraguay
Argentina	-	15.8	138.6	13.9	91.5	2.4	16.0	15.1
Bolivia	10.8	-	1.0	...	2.4	...	...	...
Brasil	186.0	8.0	-	7.0	24.0	1.0	20.0	11.0
Colombia	11.5	...	1.4	-	5.2	7.9	1.6	...
Chile	78.5	1.1	24.4	6.1	-	2.6	10.5	0.2
Ecuador	3.6	0.1	1.3	5.0	5.6	-	0.5	0.1
México	14.1	0.3	14.7	13.0	15.7	1.8	-	0.2
Paraguay	17.6	...	1.1	0.2	1.5	0.6	0.7	-
Perú	13.9	2.0	8.3	9.5	6.74	2.9	13.6	0.1
Uruguay	6.4	0.2	12.4	3.1	2.0	0.1	1.0	1.6
Venezuela	29.5	...	59.4	10.6	11.6	8.5	7.1	...
Total ALALC	**371.9**	**27.5**	**262.6**	**68.4**	**166.2**	**27.8**	**71.0**	**28.3**
Costa Rica	...	...	...	0.2	...	0.1	0.3	...
El Salvador	...	...	...	...	...	0.3	...	...
Guatemala	...	0.2	...	...	...	0.1	0.7	...
Honduras	...	...	...	0.2	...	...	...	...
Nicaragua	...	...	...	0.1	...	...	0.9	...
Total MCCA	**...**	**0.2**	**...**	**0.5**	**...**	**0.5**	**1.9**	**...**
Barbados	...	...	...	...	...	...	...	...
Guyana	0.7	...	0.1	0.2	0.1	...	0.6	...
Jamaica	...	...	...	...	...	...	...	...
Trinidad y Tabago	0.4	...	14.1	0.7	...	...	0.4	...
Bahamas	0.1	...	0.1	0.2	...	...	0.2	...
Haití	...	...	...	...	...	...	...	...
Panamá	...	...	...	0.1	...	...	1.0	...
República Dominicana	...	...	...	0.3	...	...	...	...
Suriname	0.3	...	0.1	...	...	...	...	...
Total Región	**373.4**	**27.7**	**277.0**	**70.4**	**166.3**	**28.3**	**75.1**	**28.3**
Mundo	**1 773.0**	**136.0**	**2 566.0**	**818.0**	**856.0**	**289.0**	**671.0**	**75.0**

270. INTRAREGIONAL TRADE IN TOTAL GOODS, 1970

(Based on exports FOB in millions of dollars)

Perú *Peru*	Uruguay	Venezuela	Total ALALC *LAFTA*	Costa Rica	El Salvador	Guatemala	Destination Origin
31.7	28.2	12.6	365.8	0.5	0.2	0.7	Argentina
6.1	...	...	20.3	...	...	...	Bolivia
8.00	31.0	8.0	304.0	...	...	...	Brazil
21.7	0.1	5.1	54.5	2.1	0.5	1.6	Colombia
9.0	16.3	3.3	152.0	...	...	...	Chile
3.9	...	0.1	20.2	0.1	0.1	0.1	Ecuador
8.1	2.9	21.9	92.7	5.0	3.2	8.8	Mexico
0.2	2.6	...	24.5	...	...	...	Paraguay
-	1.2	5.4	63.6	0.1	0.3	0.1	Peru
2.1	-	0.3	29.2	...	...	0.1	Uruguay
8.0	2.6	-	137.3	8.7	5.1	17.2	Venezuela
98.8	**84.9**	**56.7**	**1 264.1**	**16.5**	**9.4**	**28.6**	**Total LAFTA**
...	...	0.1	0.7	-	10.5	11.1	Costa Rica
...	...	0.1	0.4	19.5	-	39.7	El Salvador
0.1	...	0.1	1.2	20.1	38.8	-	Guatemala
...	...	...	0.2	7.2	...	7.5	Honduras
...	...	0.1	1.1	18.4	7.8	7.2	Nicaragua
0.1	**...**	**0.4**	**3.6**	**65.2**	**57.1**	**65.5**	**Total CACM**
...	...	...	...	...	...	...	Barbados
...	...	0.2	1.9	...	...	...	Guyana
...	...	0.6	0.6	...	...	0.7	Jamaica
...	...	1.2	16.8	...	...	...	Trinidad and Tobago
...	...	0.1	0.7	...	...	...	Bahamas
...	...	...	...	...	...	...	Haiti
...	...	...	1.1	2.3	0.1	0.2	Panama
...	...	1.1	1.4	...	...	...	Dominican Republic
...	...	...	0.4	...	...	...	Suriname
98.9	**84.9**	**60.3**	**1 290.6**	**84.0**	**66.6**	**95.0**	**Total Region**
660.0	**241.0**	**1 610.0**	**11 695.0**	**275.0**	**208.0**	**287.0**	**World**

270. COMERCIO INTRARREGIONAL DE BIENES TOTALES, 1970 (conclusión)

(Sobre la base de las exportaciones fob en millones de dólares)

Destino / Procedencia	Honduras	Nicaragua	Total MCCA CACM	Barbados	Guyana	Jamaica	Trinidad y Tabago Trinidad and Tobago
Argentina	0.1	0.3	1.8	1.0	...	0.9	0.5
Bolivia	...	...	...	...	...	...	...
Brasil	...	1.0	1.0	...	...	1.0	3.0
Colombia	1.0	1.4	6.6	0.2	...	0.4	3.2
Chile	...	...	...	...	...	...	...
Ecuador	...	0.1	0.4	...	...	...	...
México	1.7	2.4	21.1	...	0.2	0.6	0.3
Paraguay	...	...	...	...	...	...	...
Perú	...	0.2	0.7	...	...	0.1	2.3
Uruguay	...	...	0.1	...	...	...	0.1
Venezuela	9.6	9.2	49.8	3.4	0.1	30.9	106.9
Total ALALC	**12.4**	**14.6**	**81.5**	**4.6**	**0.3**	**33.9**	**116.3**
Costa Rica	11.6	12.9	46.1	...	...	0.1	...
El Salvador	...	14.4	73.6	...	...	...	...
Guatemala	28.9	14.5	102.3	...	...	0.3	...
Honduras	-	4.2	18.9	0.4	...	2.2	0.6
Nicaragua	12.6	-	46.0	...	...	1.1	...
Total MCCA	**53.1**	**46.0**	**286.9**	**0.4**	**...**	**3.7**	**0.6**
Barbados	...	...	...	-	0.6	0.4	1.8
Guyana	...	...	...	...	-	...	...
Jamaica	0.2	0.2	1.1	2.0	1.9	-	4.8
Trinidad y Tabago	0.2	0.2	0.4	8.6	16.3	5.8	-
Bahamas	...	0.2	0.2	0.1	...	0.6	0.1
Haití	...	...	...	...	...	0.1	...
Panamá	0.1	0.4	3.1	...	...	...	...
República Dominicana	...	...	...	...	...	0.1	...
Suriname	...	...	...	...	0.3	...	0.1
Total Región	**66.0**	**61.6**	**373.2**	**15.7**	**19.4**	**44.6**	**123.7**
Mundo	**204.0**	**187.0**	**1 161.0**	**87.0**	**114.0**	**480.0**	**430.0**

270. INTRAREGIONAL TRADE IN TOTAL GOODS, 1970 (concluded)

(Based on exports FOB in millions of dollars)

Bahamas	Haití Haiti	Panamá Panama	República Dominicana Dominican Republic	Suriname	Total región region	Mundo World	Destination / Origin
0.2	0.1	1.1	0.2	...	371.6	1 773.1	Argentina
...	...	...	...	...	20.3	228.3	Bolivia
2.0	...	4.0	1.0	1.0	317.0	2 739.0	Brazil
...	...	4.0	1.1	...	70.0	728.6	Colombia
...	...	0.5	...	...	152.5	1 245.9	Chile
...	...	0.5	...	...	21.1	210.3	Ecuador
2.1	0.5	6.5	1.2	0.1	125.3	1 312.8	Mexico
...	...	...	...	...	24.5	74.1	Paraguay
0.1	...	0.9	...	...	67.7	1 047.9	Peru
...	...	...	...	...	29.4	232.7	Uruguay
11.1	0.1	55.1	4.6	0.9	400.2	3 203.7	Venezuela
15.5	**0.7**	**72.6**	**8.1**	**2.0**	**1 599.6**	**12 786.4**	**Total LAFTA**
...	...	6.8	0.3	...	54.0	227.0	Costa Rica
...	...	0.7	0.2	...	74.9	236.2	El Salvador
...	0.1	1.7	0.8	...	106.4	290.2	Guatemala
...	0.2	1.9	4.9	..	29.3	172.0	Honduras
...	0.3	0.9	...	..	49.4	180.1	Nicaragua
...	**0.6**	**12.0**	**6.2**	**...**	**314.0**	**1 105.5**	**Total CACM**
0.1	...	...	...	0.1	3.0	45.5	Barbados
...	...	...	...	0.4	2.3	133.4	Guyana
3.6	...	...	...	...	14.0	339.7	Jamaica
...	...	...	...	...	47.9	481.5	Trinidad and Tobago
-	0.1	1.4	0.1	0.1	3.4	86.7	Bahamas
0.2	-	...	0.3	...	0.6	40.5	Haiti
...	...	-	0.2	0.1	4.5	106.5	Panama
...	0.2	0.2	-	...	1.9	213.5	Dominican Republic
0.1	...	...	0.1	-	1.0	133.9	Suriname
19.5	**1.6**	**86.2**	**15.0**	**2.7**	**1 981.8**	**15 473.1**	**Total Region**
290.0	67.0	655.0	278.0	88.0	15 345.0	...	**World**

271. COMERCIO INTRARREGIONAL DE BIENES TOTALES, 1975

(Sobre la base de las exportaciones fob en millones de dólares)

Procedencia \ Destino	Argentina	Bolivia	Brasil *Brazil*	Colombia	Chile	Ecuador	México *Mexico*	Paraguay
Argentina	-	63.8	213.5	16.3	130.6	11.4	178.6	37.3
Bolivia	135.0	-	18.5	1.4	5.8	13.3	0.9	0.5
Brasil	381.0	122.0	-	29.0	100.0	27.0	128.0	118.0
Colombia	27.8	6.5	8.6	-	23.9	36.1	5.8	0.3
Chile	166.4	13.4	98.0	25.0	-	19.1	10.0	1.4
Ecuador	9.3	0.3	5.8	26.3	78.0	-	602	0.1
México	36.0	1.0	92.0	24.0	15.0	10.0	-	1.0
Paraguay	49.7	...	6.2	0.2	1.0	0.1	2.2	-
Perú	34.9	5.5	35.6	15.9	82.8	10.1	9.9	...
Uruguay	29.6	2.8	65.5	3.0	2.2	0.4	2.3	3.7
Venezuela	48.0	...	95.0	22.0	30.0	8.0	65.0	...
Total ALALC	917.7	215.3	638.7	163.1	469.3	135.5	408.9	162.3
Costa Rica	...	0.1	0.2	0.5	0.2	6.3	9.5	...
El Salvador	...	0.1	0.2	...	...	0.1	6.1	...
Guatemala	...	0.2	0.4	0.1	...	0.3	3.6	...
Honduras	1.4	...	0.5	1.0	...	1.3	0.8	...
Nicaragua	0.2	...	0.2	...	...	...	0.4	...
Total MCCA	1.6	0.4	1.5	1.6	0.2	8.0	20.4	...
Barbados	...	...	0.1	0.1	...	...	...	...
Guyana	1.5	...	0.8	0.3	...	...	3.2	...
Jamaica	...	...	1.6	0.1	...	...	...	...
Trinidad y Tabago	...	...	3.3	0.2	...	...	1.7	...
Bahamas	8.5	...	1.4	0.1	...	10.8	8.6	...
Haití	...	...	...	...	...	...	...	...
Panamá	...	...	...	0.9	...	0.5	...	...
República Dominicana	...	...	1.9	0.2	...	0.2	...	...
Suriname	...	...	...	...	...	...	...	...
Total Región	929.3	215.7	649.3	166.6	469.5	155.0	442.8	162.3
Mundo	3 603.0	597.0	11 529.0	1 509.0	1 603.0	1 119.0	7 858.0	266.0

271. INTRAREGIONAL TRADE IN TOTAL GOODS, 1975

(Based on exports FOB in millions of dollars)

Perú *Peru*	Uruguay	Venezuela	Total ALALC *LAFTA*	Costa Rica	El Salvador	Guatemala	Destination / Origin
29.6	40.8	33.7	755.6	1.7	0.6	1.3	*Argentina*
7.4	4.1	0.2	187.1	...	...	...	*Bolivia*
93.0	88.0	107.0	1 193.0	3.0	3.0	4.0	*Brazil*
33.7	0.6	89.6	232.9	5.6	3.8	10.7	*Colombia*
25.0	7.3	23.9	389.5	0.7	1.6	0.2	*Chile*
103.3	0.1	1.4	230.8	1.0	0.2	0.1	*Ecuador*
29.0	5.0	57.0	270.0	27.0	14.0	25.0	*Mexico*
0.4	2.3	0.8	62.9	...	...	...	*Paraguay*
-	1.4	9.1	205.2	0.7	1.2	0.3	*Peru*
2.2	-	0.5	112.2	...	...	...	*Uruguay*
87.0	16.0	-	371.0	49.0	63.0	53.0	*Venezuela*
410.6	165.6	323.2	4 010.2	88.7	87.4	94.6	*Total LAFTA*
0.1	...	1.4	18.3	-	27.9	31.2	*Costa Rica*
0.1	...	0.1	6.7	32.9	-	79.5	*El Salvador*
...	...	0.4	5.0	37.5	74.9	-	*Guatemala*
...	0.1	2.0	7.1	6.2	...	12.2	*Honduras*
0.2	...	0.7	1.7	37.3	21.3	21.5	*Nicaragua*
0.4	0.1	4.6	38.8	113.9	124.1	144.4	*Total CACM*
...	...	0.2	0.4	...	...	...	*Barbados*
0.2	...	0.7	6.7	...	...	...	*Guyana*
...	0.4	3.0	5.1	0.1	0.5	1.4	*Jamaica*
1.0	0.6	1.8	8.6	1.9	0.9	13.4	*Trinidad and Tobago*
12.9	...	5.1	47.4	0.1	...	2.4	*Bahamas*
...	...	...	...	...	...	...	*Haiti*
...	...	1.0	2.4	4.8	1.7	3.0	*Panama*
...	...	2.9	5.2	...	...	...	*Dominican Republic*
...	...	...	...	...	...	...	*Suriname*
425.1	166.7	342.5	4 124.8	209.5	214.6	259.2	*Total Region*
2 551.0	462.0	4 946.0	36 043.0	596.0	573.0	741.0	*World*

271. **COMERCIO INTRARREGIONAL DE BIENES TOTALES, 1975 (conclusión)**

(Sobre la base de las exportaciones fob en millones de dólares)

Procedencia \ Destino	Honduras	Nicaragua	Total MCCA CACM	Barbados	Guyana	Jamaica	Trinidad y Tabago Trinidad and Tobago
Argentina	0.5	0.6	4.7	0.8	...	1.6	0.4
Bolivia	...	...	...	...	...	...	...
Brasil	7.0	1.0	18.0	1.0	4.0	6.0	6.0
Colombia	1.1	2.3	23.5	1.0	0.1	0.9	1.5
Chile	...	0.5	3.0	0.1	...	...	0.1
Ecuador	...	...	0.4	...	...	0.1	...
México	8.0	8.0	82.0	...	...	2.0	1.0
Paraguay	...	...	...	...	...	...	...
Perú	...	0.1	2.3	...	...	0.3	0.5
Uruguay	...	...	...	...	...	...	...
Venezuela	56.0	53.0	274.0	18.0	...	141.0	15.0
Total ALALC	**72.6**	**65.5**	**407.9**	**20.9**	**4.1**	**151.9**	**24.5**
Costa Rica	12.8	35.3	107.2	...	...	0.4	0.1
El Salvador	...	29.3	141.7	...	...	...	...
Guatemala	22.7	33.9	169.0	...	...	4.0	0.2
Honduras	-	12.4	30.8	1.5	0.1	5.3	1.6
Nicaragua	12.5	-	92.6	...	...	0.6	0.1
Total MCCA	**48.0**	**110.9**	**541.3**	**1.5**	**0.1**	**10.3**	**2.0**
Barbados	...	...	...	-	1.7	4.3	6.1
Guyana	...	...	...	4.6	-	21.8	19.6
Jamaica	0.6	0.8	3.4	5.5	7.7	-	15.3
Trinidad y Tabago	0.4	0.4	17.0	21.1	54.5	54.6	-
Bahamas	...	0.1	2.6	...	...	2.2	...
Haití	...	...	...	...	...	0.1	0.2
Panamá	0.3	2.9	12.7	1.3	0.4	0.4	...
República Dominicana	0.1	...	0.1	...	...	0.7	0.1
Suriname	...	...	...	...	...	...	...
Total Región	**122.0**	**180.6**	**985.0**	**54.9**	**68.5**	**246.3**	**67.8**
Mundo	**353.0**	**443.0**	**2 706.0**	**173.0**	**296.0**	**982.0**	**1 983.0**

271. INTRAREGIONAL TRADE IN TOTAL GOODS, 1975 (concluded)

(Based on exports FOB in millions of dollars)

Bahamas	Haití Haiti	Panamá Panama	República Dominicana Dominican Republic	Suriname	Total región region	Mundo World	Destination / Origin
0.1	...	2.4	0.5	...	766.1	2 961.0	Argentina
...	...	...	...	...	187.1	521.5	Bolivia
77.0	2.0	30.0	7.0	3.0	1 347.0	8 668.0	Brazil
...	1.3	21.4	20.9	0.3	303.8	1 470.2	Colombia
...	...	1.0	...	...	393.7	1 660.8	Chile
...	...	83.3	...	...	314.6	935.9	Ecuador
3.0	1.0	14.0	7.0	...	380.0	2 916.0	Mexico
...	...	...	...	...	62.9	176.7	Paraguay
...	...	2.0	0.2	...	210.5	1 247.0	Peru
...	0.1	0.1	...	...	112.4	383.9	Uruguay
42.0	...	112.0	109.0	...	1 082.0	8 800.0	Venezuela
122.1	**4.4**	**266.2**	**144.6**	**3.3**	**5 160.1**	**29 741.0**	**Total LAFTA**
...	...	16.4	0.5	0.1	143.0	493.3	Costa Rica
...	...	5.6	0.4	...	154.4	514.2	El Salvador
...	0.4	5.1	2.6	...	186.3	623.5	Guatemala
...	...	4.9	15.3	...	66.6	303.2	Honduras
...	0.2	1.0	0.1	...	96.3	375.2	Nicaragua
...	0.6	33.0	18.9	0.1	646.6	2 309.4	**Total CACM**
0.2	0.2	...	...	0.4	13.3	106.5	Barbados
...	...	...	0.2	2.5	55.4	362.9	Guyana
1.0	1.4	2.0	1.2	1.0	43.6	783.9	Jamaica
3.5	0.2	0.4	0.5	36.5	196.9	1 775.2	Trinidad and Tobago
-	0.1	45.4	0.2	3.7	101.6	2 508.3	Bahamas
0.2	-	...	0.5	...	1.0	81.2	Haiti
...	0.1	-	0.1	0.9	18.3	277.8	Panama
...	1.6	0.5	-	0.3	8.5	893.8	Dominican Republic
...	...	...	...	-	...	255.4	Suriname
127.0	**8.6**	**347.5**	**166.2**	**48.7**	**6 245.3**	**39 095.4**	**Total Region**
1 759.0	**226.0**	**2 575.0**	**886.0**	**280.0**	**47 909.0**	...	**World**

272. COMERCIO INTRARREGIONAL DE BIENES TOTALES, 1977

(Sobre la base de las exportaciones fob en millones de dólares)

Procedencia \ Destino	Argentina	Bolivia	Brasil *Brazil*	Colombia	Chile	Ecuador	México *Mexico*	Paraguay
Argentina	-	112.9	464.8	64.8	274.9	21.1	74.3	84.7
Bolivia	141.8	-	20.5	4.0	8.8	...	2.5	0.1
Brasil	374.0	144.0	-	62.0	130.0	22.0	107.0	185.0
Colombia	40.9	2.9	4.0	-	12.0	48.0	8.9	0.4
Chile	143.9	20.5	283.1	34.5	-	24.9	6.4	3.3
Ecuador	13.8	0.3	5.0	46.1	87.9	-	5.5	0.4
México	32.0	2.0	150.0	32.0	27.0	26.0	-	2.0
Paraguay	35.8	...	16.3	0.2	8.7	...	0.7	-
Perú	21.2	12.1	63.4	18.6	37.3	21.7	34.0	0.1
Uruguay	36.4	0.8	96.4	4.8	3.0	0.5	2.0	9.4
Venezuela	52.0	...	139.0	129.0	114.0	8.0	10.0	...
Total ALALC	**891.8**	**295.5**	**1 242.5**	**396.0**	**703.6**	**172.2**	**251.3**	**285.4**
Costa Rica	0.2	0.1	0.1	0.6	0.1	1.2	3.7	...
El Salvador	...	...	...	...	...	0.1	2.2	0.1
Guatemala	...	0.4	0.1	0.1	0.7	0.8	5.9	...
Honduras	...	...	0.1	0.8	...	...	0.1	...
Nicaragua	...	0.1	...	0.1	...	...	7.5	...
Total MCCA	**0.2**	**0.6**	**0.3**	**1.6**	**0.8**	**2.1**	**19.4**	**0.1**
Barbados	...	...	...	0.1	...	...	...	...
Guyana	2.0	...	1.3	0.8	...	...	3.9	...
Jamaica	...	...	...	...	...	0.1	0.1	0.7
Trinidad y Tabago	...	...	0.1	1.3	...	...	5.8	0.1
Bahamas	17.2	...	0.6	0.1	...	...	0.2	...
Haití	...	...	...	...	...	0.3	...	...
Panamá	...	...	...	4.6	0.1	0.2	...	...
República Dominicana	...	...	...	0.1	0.1	...	...	...
Suriname	...	...	0.6	1.3	...	...	...	...
Total Región	**911.2**	**296.1**	**1 245.4**	**405.9**	**704.6**	**174.9**	**280.7**	**286.3**
Mundo	**4 107.0**	**776.0**	**11 999.0**	**2 247.0**	**2 379.0**	**1 670.0**	**7 223.0**	**467.0**

272. INTRAREGIONAL TRADE IN TOTAL GOODS, 1977

(Based on exports FOB in millions of dollars)

Perú Peru	Uruguay	Venezuela	Total ALALC LAFTA	Costa Rica	El Salvador	Guatemala	Destination / Origin
46.5	96.9	130.8	1 371.7	11.2	1.4	4.4	Argentina
5.6	5.2	0.5	189.0	...	...	...	Bolivia
56.0	205.0	199.0	1 484.0	7.0	5.0	8.0	Brazil
28.5	0.4	219.2	365.2	5.6	3.1	4.5	Colombia
12.3	11.5	51.4	591.8	...	...	...	Chile
115.3	0.2	8.3	282.8	0.1	0.5	0.1	Ecuador
12.0	3.0	89.0	375.0	25.0	16.0	43.0	Mexico
0.1	12.9	0.3	75.0	...	...	...	Paraguay
-	1.6	20.0	230.0	1.8	2.0	0.2	Peru
2.8	-	1.1	157.2	...	...	0.1	Uruguay
154.0	21.0	-	627.0	31.0	71.0	68.0	Venezuela
433.1	357.7	719.6	5 748.7	81.7	99.0	128.3	Total LAFTA
...	...	20.1	26.1	-	47.7	53.4	Costa Rica
...	...	0.3	2.7	50.6	-	125.7	El Salvador
0.8	...	0.5	9.3	46.9	105.9	-	Guatemala
...	...	5.8	6.8	8.0	...	21.6	Honduras
...	...	8.8	16.5	48.3	33.7	34.7	Nicaragua
0.8	...	35.5	61.4	153.8	187.3	235.4	Total CACM
...	...	0.3	0.4	...	...	...	Barbados
0.2	...	4.5	12.7	...	...	...	Guyana
0.1	0.7	14.3	16.0	0.6	0.8	1.7	Jamaica
...	0.9	2.2	10.4	2.0	0.8	10.2	Trinidad and Tobago
2.8	...	0.3	21.2	...	...	13.1	Bahamas
...	...	0.4	0.7	...	0.1	0.1	Haiti
...	...	2.7	7.6	9.1	3.0	3.3	Panama
...	...	13.1	13.3	...	...	...	Dominican Republic
...	...	7.5	9.4	...	...	...	Suriname
437.0	359.3	800.4	5 901.8	247.2	291.0	392.1	Total Region
1 664.0	759.0	8 688.0	41 979.0	923.0	893.0	1 167.0	World

272. COMERCIO INTRARREGIONAL DE BIENES TOTALES, 1977 (conclusión)

(Sobre la base de las exportaciones fob en millones de dólares)

Procedencia \ Destino	Honduras	Nicaragua	Total MCCA CACM	Barbados	Guyana	Jamaica	Trinidad y Tabago Trinidad and Tobago
Argentina	3.5	0.9	21.4	1.9	0.3	1.4	1.6
Bolivia	...	...	...	...	...	...	...
Brasil	8.0	5.0	33.0	3.0	3.0	9.0	6.0
Colombia	3.2	2.3	18.7	0.4	...	0.4	3.5
Chile	...	...	...	...	...	...	...
Ecuador	...	...	0.7	...	...	...	...
México	14.0	14.0	112.0	...	...	2.0	2.0
Paraguay	...	...	...	...	...	...	...
Perú	0.5	0.5	5.0	...	...	0.3	0.5
Uruguay	...	...	0.1	0.5	...	0.4	0.4
Venezuela	30.0	79.0	279.0	16.0	...	111.0	18.0
Total ALALC	**59.2**	**101.7**	**469.9**	**21.8**	**3.3**	**124.5**	**32.0**
Costa Rica	17.1	55.6	173.8	...	...	0.1	...
El Salvador	...	39.2	215.5	...	...	0.1	0.5
Guatemala	29.1	40.5	222.4	...	...	0.3	...
Honduras	-	13.9	43.5	...	...	...	5.7
Nicaragua	17.3	-	134.0	0.1	...	...	0.7
Total MCCA	**63.5**	**149.2**	**789.2**	**0.1**	**...**	**0.5**	**6.9**
Barbados	...	...	...	-	1.7	2.3	10.5
Guyana	...	...	...	5.3	-	14.4	16.7
Jamaica	0.8	1.1	5.0	9.0	10.2	-	28.2
Trinidad y Tabago	23.1	0.8	36.9	26.5	62.3	25.0	-
Bahamas	0.1	...	13.2	...	...	0.1	...
Haití	2.0	...	2.2	0.4	0.1	0.1	...
Panamá	2.4	6.5	24.3	...	...	0.6	1.2
República Dominicana	0.2	...	0.2	0.5	...	0.5	0.3
Suriname	...	...	...	0.2	0.5	...	0.3
Total Región	**151.3**	**259.3**	**1 340.9**	**63.8**	**78.1**	**168.0**	**96.1**
Mundo	**542.0**	**730.0**	**4 255.0**	**219.0**	**261.0**	**729.0**	**2 327.0**

272. INTRAREGIONAL TRADE IN TOTAL GOODS, 1977 (concluded)

(Based on exports FOB in millions of dollars)

Bahamas	Haití *Haiti*	Panamá *Panama*	República Dominicana *Dominican Republic*	Suriname	Total región *region*	Mundo *World*	Destination / Origin
0.2	0.1	22.8	17.7	0.7	1 439.8	5 651.5	*Argentina*
...	...	...	...	...	189.0	718.4	*Bolivia*
1.0	6.0	14.0	23.0	7.0	1 589.0	12 152.0	*Brazil*
10.7	1.2	20.2	4.8	1.5	426.6	2 432.7	*Colombia*
...	...	...	...	...	591.8	2 189.2	*Chile*
...	...	122.5	...	...	406.0	1 200.4	*Ecuador*
9.0	...	14.0	9.0	...	523.0	4 171.0	*Mexico*
...	...	...	...	...	75.0	278.9	*Paraguay*
...	...	6.5	0.2	...	242.5	1 676.4	*Peru*
0.2	...	1.5	...	...	160.3	607.5	*Uruguay*
52.0	...	93.0	130.0	...	1 326.0	9 548.0	*Venezuela*
73.1	**7.3**	**294.5**	**184.7**	**9.2**	**6 969.0**	**40 626.0**	***Total ALALC***
...	1.3	22.5	4.0	0.5	228.3	797.5	*Costa Rica*
...	0.1	4.4	0.3	0.3	223.9	974.4	*El Salvador*
...	2.4	8.9	3.1	0.2	246.6	1 187.3	*Guatemala*
...	...	...	...	...	56.0	503.5	*Honduras*
...	0.4	2.2	0.1	...	154.0	636.8	*Nicaragua*
...	**4.2**	**38.0**	**7.5**	**1.0**	**908.8**	**4 099.5**	***Total CACM***
0.1	0.1	...	...	0.6	15.7	95.4	*Barbados*
...	...	...	...	0.3	49.4	252.4	*Guyana*
1.6	2.1	2.0	1.4	1.8	77.3	745.8	*Jamaica*
0.8	0.5	4.1	4.3	60.2	231.0	2 175.8	*Trinidad and Tobago*
-	0.1	13.8	0.2	...	48.6	3 260.6	*Bahamas*
0.1	-	...	0.7	0.1	4.4	143.3	*Haiti*
...	0.1	-	7.6	0.5	41.9	243.0	*Panama*
...	5.4	0.1	-	0.4	20.7	782.9	*Dominican Republic*
...	0.2	...	0.3	-	10.9	309.7	*Suriname*
75.7	**20.0**	**352.5**	**206.7**	**74.1**	**8 377.7**	**52 734.0**	***Total Region***
2 702.0	**342.0**	**2 954.0**	**947.0**	**360.0**	**57 075.0**	**...**	***World***

273. COMERCIO INTRARREGIONAL DE BIENES TOTALES, 1978

(Sobre la base de las exportaciones fob en millones de dólares)

Procedencia \ Destino	Argentina	Bolivia	Brasil Brazil	Colombia	Chile	Ecuador	México Mexico	Paraguay
Argentina	-	125.8	577.0	38.9	202.5	20.0	108.6	127.5
Bolivia	120.1	-	28.5	5.8	19.1	1.0	3.4	...
Brasil	348.0	134.0	-	113.0	192.0	44.0	178.0	224.0
Colombia	25.0	2.3	3.4	-	12.4	40.6	5.2	0.2
Chile	165.7	18.7	253.4	41.6	-	20.4	15.3	4.0
Ecuador	13.9	0.7	15.9	81.6	76.6	-	19.3	0.2
México	26.0	2.0	113.0	39.0	29.0	28.0	-	1.0
Paraguay	24.1	0.1	20.4	0.2	13.5	...	1.2	-
Perú	13.5	24.1	51.0	34.6	30.5	38.1	6.5	0.2
Uruguay	38.2	1.0	127.0	3.3	6.8	0.4	1.5	9.6
Venezuela	44.0	0.2	127.0	99.4	135.0	4.2	24.0	...
Total ALALC	**818.5**	**308.9**	**1 316.6**	**457.4**	**717.4**	**196.7**	**363.0**	**366.7**
Costa Rica	0.2	0.1	0.1	2.6	0.1	0.9	0.6	...
El Salvador	...	...	...	0.4	0.1	...	...	...
Guatemala	0.2	0.4	0.1	0.1	0.1	0.9	5.3	...
Honduras	0.3	...	...	2.5	...	...	2.0	...
Nicaragua	...	...	...	0.1	...	...	0.4	...
Total MCCA	**0.7**	**0.5**	**0.2**	**5.7**	**0.3**	**1.8**	**6.5**	**...**
Barbados	...	...	...	...	...	...	...	...
Guyana	1.6	...	1.2	0.6	0.2	...	4.8	...
Jamaica	...	...	...	0.1	..	...	0.1	1.2
Trinidad y Tabago	...	...	0.1	2.2	...	0.1	...	0.1
Bahamas	3.6	...	23.2	0.1	...	...	1.5	...
Haití	...	...	...	0.2	...	1.1	...	...
Panamá	...	...	0.1	3.5	0.2	0.2	0.1	...
República Dominicana	0.1	...	...	0.2	...	...	...	...
Suriname	...	...	6.1	2.5	...	...	...	...
Total Región	**824.5**	**309.4**	**1 347.5**	**472.5**	**718.1**	**199.9**	**376.0**	**368.0**
Mundo	**4 389.0**	**886.0**	**13 741.0**	**2 932.0**	**2 899.0**	**1 734.0**	**10 191.0**	**656.0**

273. INTRAREGIONAL TRADE IN TOTAL GOODS, 1978

(Based on exports FOB in millions of dollars)

Perú Peru	Uruguay	Venezuela	Total ALALC LAFTA	Costa Rica	El Salvador	Guatemala	Destination / Origin
45.9	121.5	147.2	1 514.9	3.3	2.8	3.9	*Argentina*
7.0	0.2	2.1	187.2	...	...	...	*Bolivia*
34.0	133.0	217.0	1 617.0	27.0	7.0	11.0	*Brazil*
12.1	0.3	197.8	299.3	4.1	2.2	4.7	*Colombia*
9.5	13.5	63.5	605.6	...	...	...	*Chile*
2.9	0.1	15.5	226.7	0.5	0.2	0.2	*Ecuador*
13.0	4.0	128.0	383.0	34.0	25.0	53.0	*Mexico*
0.1	7.0	0.2	66.8	...	...	...	*Paraguay*
-	2.5	33.9	234.9	...	...	...	*Peru*
0.9	-	2.8	191.5	...	...	...	*Uruguay*
17.3	5.0	-	456.1	10.0	71.0	86.0	*Venezuela*
142.7	**287.1**	**808.0**	**5 783.0**	**78.9**	**108.2**	**158.8**	**Total LAFTA**
2.4	...	1.2	8.2	-	49.5	61.6	*Costa Rica*
...	...	0.2	0.7	60.3	-	144.5	*El Salvador*
0.2	...	1.5	8.8	60.3	120.6	-	*Guatemala*
...	...	7.2	10.2	11.5	...	27.3	*Honduras*
0.3	...	2.1	2.9	55.1	37.0	34.2	*Nicaragua*
2.9	...	**12.2**	**30.8**	**187.2**	**207.1**	**267.6**	**Total CACM**
...	...	0.3	0.3	0.1	...	...	*Barbados*
0.5	...	2.1	11.0	...	...	...	*Guyana*
...	1.1	18.0	20.5	0.1	0.7	1.0	*Jamaica*
...	1.2	2.7	6.4	1.0	1.0	9.2	*Trinidad and Tobago*
5.6	...	0.2	34.2	0.1	...	5.7	*Bahamas*
...	...	0.5	1.8	...	0.2	0.1	*Haiti*
...	..	3.1	7.2	11.8	4.1	2.4	*Panama*
...	...	54.5	54.8	...	...	0.2	*Dominican Republic*
...	...	15.0	23.6	...	...	...	*Suriname*
151.7	**289.4**	**916.6**	**5 973.6**	**279.2**	**321.3**	**445.0**	**Total Region**
1 542.0	777.0	9 546.0	49 203.0	1 093.0	1 011.0	1 302.0	*World*

273. COMERCIO INTRARREGIONAL DE BIENES TOTALES, 1978 (conclusión)

(Sobre la base de las exportaciones fob en millones de dólares)

Procedencia \ Destino	Honduras	Nicaragua	Total MCCA CACM	Barbados	Guyana	Jamaica	Trinidad y Tabago Trinidad and Tobago
Argentina	4.3	1.6	15.9	3.0	...	4.0	2.8
Bolivia	...	...	...	...	...	...	...
Brasil	16.0	4.0	65.0	3.0	1.0	3.0	7.0
Colombia	3.2	2.4	16.6	0.3	0.1	0.7	3.4
Chile	...	...	...	...	...	...	...
Ecuador	...	0.1	1.0	...	...	...	...
México	16.0	10.0	138.0	...	1.0	4.0	...
Paraguay	...	...	...	...	...	0.3	...
Perú	...	...	...	...	...	...	...
Uruguay	...	...	...	0.3	...	2.1	0.1
Venezuela	19.0	62.0	248.0	10.0	1.0	130.0	19.0
Total ALALC	**58.5**	**80.1**	**484.5**	**16.6**	**3.1**	**144.1**	**32.3**
Costa Rica	21.7	45.8	178.6	0.1	0.1	0.1	1.0
El Salvador	...	29.0	233.8	...	...	...	0.4
Guatemala	36.5	37.6	255.0	...	...	0.9	...
Honduras	-	11.9	50.7	1.0	...	3.6	5.2
Nicaragua	19.9	-	146.2	...	...	0.1	0.3
Total MCCA	**78.1**	**124.3**	**864.3**	**1.1**	**0.1**	**4.7**	**6.9**
Barbados	...	...	0.1	-	1.5	3.7	15.6
Guyana	...	...	...	2.0	-	15.3	22.0
Jamaica	1.0	1.2	4.0	8.1	3.0	-	27.0
Trinidad y Tabago	22.9	...	34.1	25.6	54.9	27.0	-
Bahamas	0.1	0.1	6.0	...	0.6	...	...
Haití	...	...	0.3	...	0.3	0.5	0.1
Panamá	0.7	7.6	26.6	...	0.5	...	0.1
República Dominicana	0.4	0.1	0.7	...	...	1.5	...
Suriname	...	...	...	0.1	0.1	0.3	0.7
Total Región	**161.7**	**213.4**	**1 420.6**	**53.5**	**64.1**	**197.1**	**104.7**
Mundo	**625.0**	**560.0**	**4 521.0**	**252.0**	**233.0**	**803.0**	**1 755.0**

273. INTRAREGIONAL TRADE IN TOTAL GOODS, 1978 (concluded)

(Based on exports FOB in millions of dollars)

Bahamas	Haití Haiti	Panamá Panama	República Dominicana Dominican Republic	Suriname	Total región region	Mundo World	Destination / Origin
0.6	1.0	11.4	5.3	0.1	1 559.0	6 401.6	Argentina
..	...	...	...	...	187.2	723.6	Bolivia
1.0	2.0	51.0	13.0	8.0	1 771.0	12 650.0	Brazil
0.3	1.2	19.8	4.1	0.9	346.7	2 857.5	Colombia
...	...	17.1	5.6	...	628.3	2 383.1	Chile
...	...	189.1	...	...	416.8	1 493.5	Ecuador
3.0	1.0	22.0	13.0	...	565.0	5 954.0	Mexico
...	...	0.1	...	...	67.2	257.0	Paraguay
...	...	...	...	...	234.9	1 932.3	Peru
...	...	0.1	...	...	194.1	682.0	Uruguay
38.0	...	53.0	132.0	...	1 087.1	8 672.1	Venezuela
42.9	5.2	363.6	173.0	9.0	7 057.3	44 006.7	Total LAFTA
...	0.5	27.3	6.1	0.3	222.3	814.4	Costa Rica
...	...	6.8	0.4	0.1	242.2	848.4	El Salvador
...	0.1	11.5	3.4	...	279.7	1 089.5	Guatemala
...	...	0.1	4.8	...	75.6	591.2	Honduras
...	...	3.0	0.2	...	152.7	646.0	Nicaragua
...	0.6	48.7	14.9	0.4	972.5	3 989.5	Total CACM
0.5	0.1	...	...	0.8	22.6	129.8	Barbados
...	...	...	...	0.1	50.4	291.1	Guyana
2.2	3.5	4.6	2.6	1.4	76.9	764.5	Jamaica
2.7	0.2	1.7	8.0	58.7	219.3	2 018.1	Trinidad and Tobago
-	0.1	...	...	...	41.1	1 418.5	Bahamas
0.4	-	...	0.8	...	4.2	159.0	Haiti
0.1	1.0	-	7.4	0.2	43.1	244.7	Panama
...	3.3	0.2	-	0.3	60.8	673.3	Dominican Republic
...	0.1	...	0.1	-	25.0	442.2	Suriname
48.8	14.1	418.8	207.0	70.9	8 573.2	54 137.5	Total Region
2 437.0	357.0	3 501.0	984.0	371.0	64 417.0	...	World

274. COMERCIO INTRARREGIONAL DE BIENES TOTALES, 1979

(Sobre la base de las exportaciones fob en millones de dólares)

Procedencia \ Destino	Argentina	Bolivia	Brasil Brazil	Colombia	Chile	Ecuador	México Mexico	Paraguay
Argentina	-	120.0	886.0	52.0	160.0	16.0	122.0	184.0
Bolivia	114.5	-	38.8	6.5	28.2	0.6	1.5	...
Brasil	718.0	127.0	-	165.0	363.0	35.0	292.0	324.0
Colombia	46.5	2.3	6.1	-	29.3	53.8	10.9	0.3
Chile	275.6	19.8	383.7	61.9	-	28.8	44.1	5.1
Ecuador	30.3	0.6	6.1	64.6	151.2	-	21.6	0.4
México	38.0	2.0	150.0	45.0	38.0	24.0	-	1.0
Paraguay	51.0	0.1	29.1	0.4	7.2	...	2.5	-
Perú [1]	51.7	36.2	97.4	73.1	47.8	54.5	20.8	0.1
Uruguay	97.1	1.8	182.4	2.9	12.7	1.0	2.2	12.0
Venezuela	73.0	...	229.0	147.0	126.0	9.0	35.0	...
Total ALALC	1 495.7	309.8	2 008.6	618.4	963.4	222.7	552.6	526.9
Costa Rica	0.8	0.7	4.5	2.2	0.1	2.6	0.4	...
El Salvador	...	...	...	...	0.4	4.8	0.1	...
Guatemala	0.1	0.3	0.2	0.1	0.1	0.5	11.7	0.2
Honduras	...	...	0.5	1.4	...	...	...	...
Nicaragua	0.2	...	0.9	0.3	...	...	0.5	...
Total MCCA	1.1	1.0	6.1	4.0	0.6	7.9	12.7	0.2
Barbados	...	...	0.3	...	...	...	...	...
Guyana	1.5	...	2.3	0.7	...	...	6.7	...
Jamaica	0.4	...	...	...	...	0.1	0.1	0.8
Trinidad y Tabago	0.3	...	...	0.7	...	0.2	14.4	0.2
Bahamas [1]	44.0	...	24.1	0.2	...	...	1.0	...
Haití [1]	...	...	...	...	...	...	...	...
Panamá	...	0.1	0.1	3.9	0.3	0.4	3.4	...
República Dominicana	...	...	...	0.4	0.1	...	...	...
Suriname [1]	...	...	27.0	...	...	...	...	...
Total Región	1 543.0	310.9	2 068.5	628.3	964.4	231.3	590.9	528.1
Mundo	8 155.0	802.0	18 016.0	3 672.0	3 746.0	2 002.0	14 594.0	940.0

[1] Estimaciones.

274. INTRAREGIONAL TRADE IN TOTAL GOODS, 1979

(Based on exports FOB in millions of dollars)

Perú Peru	Uruguay	Venezuela	Total ALALC LAFTA	Costa Rica	El Salvador	Guatemala	Destination / Origin
73.0	239.0	161.0	2 013.0	6.0	2.0	3.0	Argentina
10.5	0.4	3.1	204.1	...	...	...	Bolivia
44.0	208.0	198.0	2 474.0	16.0	7.0	14.0	Brazil
13.7	0.6	347.9	511.4	5.6	3.3	10.8	Colombia
19.8	17.2	71.2	927.2	...	...	...	Chile
9.2	2.2	33.9	320.1	1.5	0.2	0.2	Ecuador
12.0	10.0	95.0	415.0	36.0	25.0	53.0	Mexico
...	13.6	0.1	104.0	...	...	...	Paraguay
-	6.2	61.7	449.5	4.8	5.9	0.9	Peru [1]
0.7	-	2.6	315.4	0.1	...	0.1	Uruguay
15.0	52.0	-	686.0	37.0	98.0	91.0	Venezuela
197.9	549.2	974.5	8 419.7	107.0	141.4	173.0	Total LAFTA
2.4	...	1.3	15.0	-	48.1	61.8	Costa Rica
0.4	...	0.1	5.8	66.8	-	176.4	El Salvador
...	...	0.5	13.7	71.3	153.3	-	Guatemala
...	...	4.8	6.7	14.1	...	31.7	Honduras
0.2	...	1.3	3.4	37.4	17.9	21.5	Nicaragua
3.0	...	8.0	44.6	189.6	219.3	291.4	Total CACM
...	...	5.7	6.0	...	...	...	Barbados
0.3	...	13.7	25.2	...	...	...	Guyana
0.1	0.8	20.1	22.4	0.1	0.3	0.6	Jamaica
...	2.3	2.4	20.5	1.4	...	35.7	Trinidad and Tobago
7.9	0.1	0.2	77.5	...	...	...	Bahamas [1]
...	...	0.2	0.2	0.1	...	0.1	Haiti [1]
0.2	...	3.7	12.1	16.7	4.2	1.9	Panama
...	0.1	49.1	49.7	0.2	...	0.1	Dominican Republic
...	...	11.2	38.2	...	...	...	Suriname [1]
209.4	552.5	1 088.8	8 716.1	315.1	365.2	502.8	Total Region
2 085.0	1 243.0	9 469.0	64 724.0	1 246.0	985.0	1 419.0	World

[1] Estimated.

274. COMERCIO INTRARREGIONAL DE BIENES TOTALES, 1979 (conclusión)

(Sobre la base de las exportaciones fob en millones de dólares)

Procedencia / Destino	Honduras	Nicaragua	Total MCCA CACM	Barbados	Guyana	Jamaica	Trinidad y Tabago Trinidad and Tobago
Argentina	3.0	0.0	16.0	2.0	...	1.0	...
Bolivia	...	...	...	...	...	...	...
Brasil	18.0	1.0	56.0	4.0	2.0	1.0	11.0
Colombia	4.0	0.7	24.4	0.3	...	4.3	6.5
Chile	...	...	...	...	...	...	...
Ecuador	0.2		2.1	...	...	...	...
México	19.0	4.0	137.0	...	...	3.0	1.0
Paraguay	...	...	...	...	...	...	...
Perú [1]	...	...	11.6	0.1	...	...	3.0
Uruguay	0.1	...	0.3	0.1	...	0.1	...
Venezuela	51.0	74.0	351.0	20.0	...	141.0	23.0
Total ALALC	**95.3**	**81.7**	**598.4**	**26.5**	**2.0**	**150.4**	**44.5**
Costa Rica	26.1	39.5	175.5	0.3	0.1	3.8	0.7
El Salvador	...	23.5	266.7	...	...	0.2	0.5
Guatemala	50.3	31.6	306.5	...	...	0.5	0.1
Honduras	-	14.2	60.0	1.8	...	3.3	4.5
Nicaragua	13.3	-	90.1	...	...	...	0.2
Total MCCA	**89.7**	**108.8**	**898.8**	**2.1**	**0.1**	**7.8**	**6.0**
Barbados	...	...	...	-	1.5	2.6	18.4
Guyana	...	...	...	4.2	-	17.6	20.3
Jamaica	0.4	0.1	1.5	11.3	6.3	-	35.1
Trinidad y Tabago	26.7	...	63.8	44.3	72.4	31.0	-
Bahamas [1]	0.1	...	0.1	...	0.9	...	...
Haití [1]	...	...	0.2	0.4	0.5	0.2	...
Panamá	1.6	5.1	29.5	...	...	0.1	0.1
República Dominicana	0.3	...	0.6	0.7	0.6	0.3	0.1
Suriname [1]	...	...	...	0.2	...	0.4	1.1
Total Región	**214.1**	**195.7**	**1 592.9**	**89.7**	**84.3**	**210.5**	**125.6**
Mundo	**736.0**	**349.0**	**4 735.0**	**369.0**	**285.0**	**931.0**	**1 721.0**

[1] Estimaciones.

274. INTRAREGIONAL TRADE IN TOTAL GOODS, 1979 (concluded)

(Based on exports FOB in millions of dollars)

Bahamas	Haití Haiti	Panamá Panama	República Dominicana Dominican Republic	Suriname	Total región region	Mundo World	Destination Origin
1.0	2.0	12.0	1.0	...	2 048.0	7 810.0	Argentina
...	...	...	...	...	204.1	761.8	Bolivia
2.0	4.0	35.0	10.0	8.0	2 607.0	15 250.0	Brazil
...	1.0	35.4	4.9	0.8	589.0	3 300.4	Colombia
...	...	10.1	11.0	...	948.3	3 764.3	Chile
...	...	190.2	...	...	512.4	2 070.6	Ecuador
1.0	1.0	20.0	13.0	...	591.0	8 983.0	Mexico
...	...	...	...	...	104.0	305.2	Paraguay
...	...	2.0	4.4	...	470.7	3 239.0	Peru[1]
...	...	0.4		...	316.3	788.9	Uruguay
66.0	...	170.0	165.0	...	1 622.0	14 317.0	Venezuela
70.0	8.0	475.1	209.3	8.8	10 012.8	60 590.2	Total LAFTA
0.3	0.6	35.5	5.3	0.5	237.6	934.0	Costa Rica
...	...	6.4	0.4		280.0	1 052.8	El Salvador
...	0.4	14.1	4.5	...	339.8	1 243.4	Guatemala
...	...	2.7	4.0	...	83.0	721.1	Honduras
...	0.2	1.0	0.4	...	95.3	560.8	Nicaragua
0.3	1.2	59.7	14.6	0.5	1 035.7	4 512.1	Total CACM
0.5	0.2	0.3	...	1.1	30.6	150.8	Barbados
...	...	...	...	0.2	67.5	289.9	Guyana
6.5	1.2	4.0	1.8	4.0	94.1	819.5	Jamaica
11.2	0.4	11.1	13.8	89.9	358.4	2 064.9	Trinidad and Tobago
-	0.2	...	...	...	78.7	2 267.5	Bahamas[1]
0.4	-	0.2	1.1	...	3.2	284.9	Haiti[1]
0.1	0.3	-	3.6	0.3	46.1	291.2	Panama
...	4.4	0.3	-	0.5	57.2	874.8	Dominican Republic
...	...	...	0.2	-	40.1	469.8	Suriname[1]
89.0	15.9	550.7	244.4	105.3	11 824.4	72 615.6	Total Region
2 310.0	400.0	3 313.0	1 251.0	360.0	79 399.0	...	World

[1] Estimated.

275. COMERCIO INTRARREGIONAL DE BIENES TOTALES, 1980

(Sobre la base de las exportaciones fob en millones de dólares)

Procedencia \ Destino	Argentina	Bolivia	Brasil *Brazil*	Colombia	Chile	Ecuador	México *Mexico*	Paraguay
Argentina	-	133.4	765.1	39.0	217.6	17.5	121.3	189.4
Bolivia	245.2	-	36.3	9.8	46.9	1.6	2.9	...
Brasil	1 092.0	180.0	-	136.0	451.0	50.0	470.0	409.0
Colombia	68.7	2.2	9.0	-	64.3	77.3	19.9	0.6
Chile	289.1	26.4	448.3	76.9	-	21.7	67.8	7.7
Ecuador	48.0	0.6	34.4	68.6	214.8	-	13.1	0.3
México	44.0	3.0	349.0	48.0	27.0	41.0	-	-
Paraguay	74.2	0.6	40.2	0.1	11.3	-	4.0	-
Perú	59.4	69.2	124.2	55.9	45.0	83.8	90.7	0.5
Uruguay	142.3	1.7	191.0	3.6	23.3	0.8	5.1	14.6
Venezuela	56.0	...	678.0	273.0	242.0	17.0	24.0	...
Total ALALC	**2 118.9**	**417.1**	**2 675.5**	**710.9**	**1 343.2**	**310.7**	**818.8**	**622.1**
Costa Rica	2.2	1.7	2.9	3.6	1.7	1.4	1.1	...
El Salvador	0.1	...	...	0.1	0.2	0.4	0.5	...
Guatemala	0.4	0.6	2.1	1.2	0.3	1.2	23.3	...
Honduras	0.3	...	0.9	1.1	...	...	0.6	...
Nicaragua [1]	0.1	0.1	...	0.5	...	0.1	0.2	...
Total MCCA	**3.1**	**2.4**	**5.9**	**6.5**	**2.2**	**3.1**	**25.7**	**...**
Barbados	...	...	...	...	...	...	...	...
Guyana [1]	1.5	...	2.8	´0.4	...	...	5.4	...
Jamaica	0.2	...	...	0.1	...	...	0.2	0.6
Trinidad y Tabago	8.2	...	15.9	1.6	...	2.9	...	0.1
Bahamas [1]	1.1	...	30.5	...	...	...	3.8	...
Haití [1]	...	...	...	0.4	...	...	...	...
Panamá	3.2	0.7	0.1	3.7	0.6	1.8	0.2	0.1
República Dominicana	...	...	...	0.9	0.7	...	...	...
Suriname [1]	...	...	13.5	0.1	...	...	...	...
Total Región	**2 136.2**	**420.2**	**2 744.2**	**724.6**	**1 346.7**	**318.5**	**854.1**	**622.9**
Mundo	**11 050.0**	**836.0**	**23 711.0**	**4 605.0**	**5 001.0**	**2 221.0**	**22 232.0**	**1 044.0**

[1] Estimaciones.

275. INTRAREGIONAL TRADE IN TOTAL GOODS, 1980

(Based on exports FOB in millions of dollars)

Perú Peru	Uruguay	Venezuela	Total ALALC LAFTA	Costa Rica	El Salvador	Guatemala	Destination / Origin
116.8	185.3	65.1	1 850.5	5.5	1.9	3.2	Argentina
32.3	0.6	4.8	380.4	...	...	...	Bolivia
130.0	311.0	230.0	3 459.0	20.0	3.0	12.0	Brazil
29.2	0.9	279.2	551.3	5.5	1.2	5.9	Colombia
70.7	29.6	78.8	1 117.0	...	...	...	Chile
12.7	5.1	42.1	439.7	1.9	0.2	0.5	Ecuador
26.0	8.0	62.0	608.0	96.0	12.0	59.0	Mexico
...	10.2	...	140.6	...	...	...	Paraguay
-	10.2	52.0	590.9	5.1	2.8	0.3	Peru
8.0	-	3.0	393.4	...	...	0.1	Uruguay
26.0	80.0	-	1 396.0	82.0	106.0	132.0	Venezuela
451.7	**640.9**	**817.0**	**10 926.8**	**216.0**	**127.1**	**213.0**	**Total LAFTA**
0.9	0.3	2.4	18.2	-	52.5	65.5	Costa Rica
...	...	0.4	1.7	67.5	-	173.6	El Salvador
0.2	...	1.3	30.6	89.8	194.0	-	Guatemala
...	...	2.2	5.1	17.6	...	41.2	Honduras
...	...	...	1.0	29.8	...	14.9	Nicaragua [1]
1.1	**0.3**	**6.3**	**56.6**	**204.7**	**246.5**	**295.2**	**Total CACM**
...	...	0.4	0.4	...	...	0.1	Barbados
0.9	...	...	11.0	...	...	...	Guyana [1]
...	0.8	13.3	15.2	0.1	...	0.1	Jamaica
2.1	3.5	2.2	36.5	1.9	...	47.6	Trinidad and Tobago
10.1	0.1	...	45.6	...	...	...	Bahamas [1]
...	...	...	0.4	...	0.4	0.2	Haiti [1]
0.2	0.5	5.1	16.2	22.6	4.6	7.0	Panama
...	0.2	84.3	86.1	0.9	...	0.1	Dominican Republic
...	...	...	13.6	...	...	...	Suriname [1]
466.1	**646.3**	**928.6**	**11 208.4**	**446.2**	**378.6**	**563.3**	**Total Region**
3 071.0	**1 717.0**	**10 261.0**	**85 749.0**	**1 348.0**	**834.0**	**1 622.0**	**World**

[1] Estimated.

585

275. COMERCIO INTRARREGIONAL DE BIENES TOTALES, 1980 (conclusión)

(Sobre la base de las exportaciones fob en millones de dólares)

Procedencia \ Destino	Honduras	Nicaragua	Total MCCA CACM	Barbados	Guyana	Jamaica	Trinidad y Tabago Trinidad and Tobago
Argentina	4.2	4.5	19.3	2.0	0.4	1.8	2.0
Bolivia	...	...	...	...	...	...	...
Brasil	16.0	18.0	69.0	7.0	7.0	2.0	24.0
Colombia	5.8	3.8	22.2	0.6	0.2	1.3	10.1
Chile	...	...	...	...	...	...	...
Ecuador	-	...	2.6	...	...	...	...
México	19.0	43.0	229.0			4.0	1.0
Paraguay	...	...	...			...	...
Perú	0.1	0.5	8.8	...	...	0.1	0.4
Uruguay	0.7	...	0.8	0.3		...	...
Venezuela	86.0	85.0	491.0	...	...	...	...
Total ALALC	**131.8**	**154.8**	**842.7**	**9.9**	**7.6**	**9.2**	**37.5**
Costa Rica	28.3	124.1	270.4	0.2	0.1	0.4	1.5
El Salvador	...	54.7	295.8	...	...	...	...
Guatemala	60.6	96.4	440.8	...	...	0.9	0.2
Honduras	-	32.6	91.4	0.3	...	0.2	5.8
Nicaragua [1]	6.8	-	51.5	...	...	...	...
Total MCCA	**95.7**	**307.8**	**1 149.9**	**0.5**	**0.1**	**1.5**	**7.5**
Barbados	...	...	0.1	-	1.1	6.8	26.1
Guyana [1]	...	...	...	4.0	-	22.2	21.7
Jamaica	0.1	...	0.3	9.8	3.6	-	34.7
Trinidad y Tabago	36.3	...	85.8	68.8	90.7	63.0	-
Bahamas [1]	0.1	...	0.1	...	1.1	...	1.6
Haití [1]	...	...	0.6	0.1	0.6	0.2	0.1
Panamá	1.5	10.7	46.4	...	0.5	1.5	0.1
República Dominicana	0.3	...	1.3	0.4	0.3	0.7	0.2
Suriname [1]	0.1	...	0.1	0.2	...	0.1	1.1
Total Región	**265.9**	**473.3**	**2 127.3**	**93.7**	**105.6**	**105.2**	**130.6**
Mundo	**903.0**	**839.0**	**5 546.0**	**444.0**	**335.0**	**1 016.0**	**2 384.0**

[1] Estimaciones.

275. INTRAREGIONAL TRADE IN TOTAL GOODS, 1980 *(concluded)*

(Based on exports FOB in millions of dollars)

Bahamas	Haití *Haiti*	Panamá *Panama*	República Dominicana *Dominican Republic*	Suriname	Total región *region*	Mundo *World*	Destination / Origin
1.1	0.3	14.0	1.4	0.1	1 892.9	8 024.8	*Argentina*
...	...	0.1	...	...	380.4	1 036.2	*Bolivia*
7.0	7.0	26.0	17.0	12.0	3 637.0	20 132.0	*Brazil*
0.4	1.4	59.2	6.0	1.6	654.3	3 945.0	*Colombia*
...	...	10.8	12.8	...	1 140.6	4 846.2	*Chile*
...	...	59.6	-	...	501.9	2 479.9	*Ecuador*
16.0	1.0	22.0	10.0	...	891.0	15 340.0	*Mexico*
...	...	...	...	...	140.6	310.2	*Paraguay*
126.6	...	102.3	0.1	...	829.2	3 914.7	*Peru*
0.2	...	0.3	...	...	395.0	1 058.0	*Uruguay*
...	...	...	...	...	1 887.0	19 226.0	*Venezuela*
151.3	**9.7**	**294.2**	**47.3**	**13.7**	**12 349.9**	**80 313.0**	***Total LAFTA***
...	0.7	41.8	3.1	0.3	336.7	980.9	*Costa Rica*
...	0.1	7.3	0.5	...	305.3	1 070.3	*El Salvador*
...	0.4	15.9	6.0	...	494.8	1 517.5	*Guatemala*
...	0.1	5.7	2.1	1.1	111.8	829.4	*Honduras*
...	0.4	3.3	...	...	56.2	547.8	*Nicaragua* [1]
...	**1.6**	**74.0**	**11.7**	**1.4**	**1 304.8**	**4 945.9**	***Total CACM***
0.5	0.4	0.1	0.1	1.5	37.1	214.7	*Barbados*
...	...	...	...	...	58.9	416.4	*Guyana* [1]
1.5	0.9	3.0	2.5	1.7	73.2	964.6	*Jamaica*
34.5	19.7	17.3	29.8	140.6	586.7	3 902.7	*Trinidad and Tobago*
-	0.2	...	...	...	48.6	2 459.9	*Bahamas* [1]
0.5	-	0.4	3.3	...	6.2	345.8	*Haiti* [1]
0.5	0.4	-	1.4	0.3	67.3	350.2	*Panama*
...	9.7	0.7	-	1.2	100.6	965.5	*Dominican Republic*
...	...	...	0.1	-	15.2	523.2	*Suriname* [1]
188.8	**42.6**	**389.7**	**96.2**	**160.4**	**14 648.5**	**95 401.9**	***Total Region***
3 856.0	**502.0**	**4 780.0**	**1 596.0**	**443.0**	**106 651.0**	**...**	***World***

[1] *Estimated.*

276. COMERCIO INTRARREGIONAL DE BIENES TOTALES, 1981

(Sobre la base de las exportaciones fob en millones de dólares)

Procedencia \ Destino	Argentina	Bolivia	Brasil Brazil	Colombia	Chile	Ecuador	México Mexico	Paraguay
Argentina	-	125.9	595.1	51.2	189.0	16.9	275.3	169.3
Bolivia	359.7	-	12.7	5.9	8.5	0.8	0.9	...
Brasil	880.0	255.0	-	204.0	641.0	69.0	643.0	450.0
Colombia	51.4	3.8	4.5	-	28.3	66.3	21.0	0.7
Chile	191.3	23.8	288.2	70.9	-	14.2	86.8	7.2
Ecuador	31.8	0.7	65.5	82.7	73.7	-	16.3	0.3
México	35.0	3.0	748.0	48.0	40.0	77.0	-	2.0
Paraguay	68.6	1.2	54.3	0.1	11.1	...	2.5	-
Perú	19.7	24.5	47.9	91.9	58.9	11.5	43.0	0.4
Uruguay	101.8	2.0	152.7	2.9	24.8	0.7	6.2	12.9
Venezuela	37.0	...	933.0	330.0	336.0	20.0	26.0	...
Total ALADI	**1 776.3**	**439.9**	**2 901.9**	**887.6**	**1 411.3**	**276.4**	**1 121.0**	**642.8**
Costa Rica	1.2	0.5	0.1	4.7	3.4	12.1	18.1	...
El Salvador	0.1	...	...	...	0.1	0.1	1.1	...
Guatemala	0.2	0.5	0.2	0.8	0.5	1.6	65.1	...
Honduras	...	...	0.7	1.1	...	...	0.9	...
Nicaragua	...	...	...	...	...	...	6.9	...
Total MCCA	**1.5**	**1.0**	**1.0**	**6.6**	**4.0**	**13.8**	**92.1**	**...**
Barbados	...	...		...	...	...	...	...
Guyana	...	...	3.3	...	...	...	3.5	...
Jamaica	...	...	5.6	0.9	...	...	2.1	...
Trinidad y Tabago	1.1	...	42.7	4.1	1.4	5.3	0.1	0.4
Bahamas	0.3	...	22.0	8.1	...	...	4.6	...
Haití	...	...	...	...	...	...	...	...
Panamá	0.3	0.5	...	2.0	0.6	1.1	0.3	0.1
República Dominicana	...	...	6.2	3.7	0.7	...	...	...
Suriname	...	...	3.6	0.1	...	...	...	...
Total Región	**1 779.5**	**441.4**	**2 986.3**	**913.1**	**1 418.0**	**296.6**	**1 223.7**	**643.3**
Mundo	**9 103.0**	**1 004.0**	**21 273.0**	**4 673.0**	**5 778.0**	**2 313.0**	**26 751.0**	**1 032.0**

276. INTRAREGIONAL TRADE IN TOTAL GOODS, 1981

(Based on exports FOB in millions of dollars)

Perú *Peru*	Uruguay	Venezuela	**Total ALADI**	Costa Rica	El Salvador	Guatemala	Destination *Origin*
89.1	128.1	101.7	1 741.6	5.2	0.3	3.7	*Argentina*
31.2	...	3.8	423.5	...	...	...	*Bolivia*
285.0	373.0	408.0	4 208.0	13.0	2.0	15.0	*Brazil*
45.4	2.1	341.2	564.7	4.6	1.7	4.5	*Colombia*
70.3	16.1	72.0	840.8	...	...	...	*Chile*
9.67	100.8	53.0	434.4	1.2	0.4	0.7	*Ecuador*
31.0	6.0	69.0	1 059.0	103.0	77.0	129.0	*Mexico*
0.5	9.12	0.6	148.0	...	...	...	*Paraguay*
-	2.12	45.0	344.9	4.3	1.9	0.5	*Peru*
7.5	-	1.8	313.3	...	...	...	*Uruguay*
28.0	125.0	-	1 835.0	88.0	85.00	103.0	*Venezuela*
597.6	762.3	1 096.1	11 913.2	219.3	168.3	256.4	**Total ALADI**
1.4	0.1	2.3	43.9	-	41.2	68.9	*Costa Rica*
...	...	...	1.4	34.4	-	140.8	*El Salvador*
0.3	...	2.4	71.6	57.5	230.9	-	*Guatemala*
0.1	...	55.9	58.7	14.9	0.3	17.1	*Honduras*
0.3	...	0.2	7.4	30.7	9.3	13.7	*Nicaragua*
2.1	0.1	60.8	183.0	137.5	281.7	240.5	**Total CACM**
...	...	0.1	0.1	...	...	...	*Barbados*
0.4	...	58.9	66.1	...	...	...	*Guyana*
0.1	0.7	34.2	43.6	...	...	0.1	*Jamaica*
0.1	2.7	5.2	63.1	3.1	...	14.0	*Trinidad and Tobago*
0.1	...	1.2	36.3	...	0.2	...	*Bahamas*
0.1	...	0.7	0.8	...	...	0.1	*Haiti*
0.3	0.1	8.2	13.5	11.9	4.3	2.8	*Panama*
...	0.1	71.4	82.1	0.5	...	0.4	*Dominican Republic*
...	...	7.5	11.2	...	...	...	*Suriname*
600.8	766.0	1 344.3	12 413.0	372.3	454.5	514.3	**Total Region**
3 967.0	1 645.0	11 668.0	89 207.0	1 013.0	946.0	1 585.0	*World*

276. COMERCIO INTRARREGIONAL DE BIENES TOTALES, 1981 (conclusión)

(Sobre la base de las exportaciones fob en millones de dólares)

Procedencia \ Destino	Honduras	Nicaragua	Total MCCA CACM	Barbados	Guyana	Jamaica	Trinidad y Tabago Trinidad and Tobago
Argentina	3.0	5.1	17.3	1.3	...	1.7	1.6
Bolivia	...	...	...	...	...	...	...
Brasil	13.0	20.0	63.0	7.0	8.0	16.0	39.0
Colombia	5.2	2.3	18.3	0.4	0.4	0.4	16.7
Chile	...	...	...	...	...	...	...
Ecuador	...	...	2.3	...	...	...	...
México	20.0	86.0	415.0	...	...	88.0	...
Paraguay	...	...	...	...	...	...	...
Perú	0.2	0.6	7.5	...	...	0.2	0.1
Uruguay	...	0.1	0.1	0.2	...	0.7	...
Venezuela	37.0	83.0	396.0	31.0	3.0	171.0	10.0
Total ALADI	**78.4**	**197.1**	**919.5**	**39.9**	**11.4**	**278.0**	**67.4**
Costa Rica	31.8	84.8	226.7	0.4	0.4	0.7	0.5
El Salvador	1.4	30.0	206.6	...	...	...	...
Guatemala	49.7	69.1	407.2	...	...	0.7	1.2
Honduras	-	32.6	64.9	0.5	...	0.2	13.0
Nicaragua	13.2	-	66.9	...	...	...	...
Total MCCA	**96.1**	**216.5**	**972.3**	**0.9**	**0.4**	**1.6**	**14.7**
Barbados	...	...	...	-	1.4	10.8	29.6
Guyana	...	...	...	3.8	-	22.2	24.3
Jamaica	0.1	...	0.2	12.7	3.6	-	30.2
Trinidad y Tabago	46.6	...	63.7	56.9	109.3	68.1	-
Bahamas	...	...	0.2	0.1	1.8	...	0.3
Haití	...	...	0.1	0.2	0.6	0.2	0.1
Panamá	6.7	7.17	32.8	...	1.6	...	0.4
República Dominicana	0.6	0.1	1.6	0.1	...	4.9	1.2
Suriname	...	...	...	0.2	...	0.1	1.2
Total Región	**228.5**	**420.8**	**1 990.4**	**114.8**	**130.1**	**385.9**	**169.4**
Mundo	**793.0**	**727.0**	**5 064.0**	**495.0**	**366.0**	**1 384.0**	**2 506.0**

276. INTRAREGIONAL TRADE IN TOTAL GOODS, 1981 (concluded)

(Based on exports FOB in millions of dollars)

Bahamas	Haití *Haiti*	Panamá *Panama*	República Dominicana *Dominican Republic*	Suriname	Total región *region*	Mundo *World*	Destination *Origin*
0.3	0.3	2.8	0.8	0.1	1 767.8	9 142.9	*Argentina*
...	...	...	...	...	423.5	995.3.2	*Bolivia*
43.0	4.0	40.0	23.0	16.0	4 467.0	23 329.0	*Brazil*
0.5	1.1	61.3	5.8	1.5	671.1	2 956.4	*Colombia*
...	...	11.1	3.1	...	855.0	3 949.3	*Chile*
...	...	17.3	...	...	454.0	2 540.3	*Ecuador*
59.0	12.0	127.0	124.0	...	1 884.0	19 381.0	*Mexico*
...	...	1.2	...	...	149.2	297.2	*Paraguay*
14.1	...	48.7	0.1	...	415.6	3 264.9	*Peru*
0.6	...	0.2	...	...	315.1	1 182.6	*Uruguay*
1.0	...	194.0	267.0	1.0	2 909.0	20 002.0	*Venezuela*
118.5	**17.4**	**503.6**	**423.8**	**18.6**	**14 311.3**	**87 040.9**	**Total ALADI**
0.1	0.7	43.5	3.1	0.5	320.5	966.6	*Costa Rica*
...	...	8.1	0.8	...	216.9	796.5	*El Salvador*
...	0.6	16.9	7.7	...	505.9	1 226.1	*Guatemala*
...	0.1	2.0	2.1	1.1	142.6	826.7	*Honduras*
...	0.4	3.3	...	...	78.0	483.3	*Nicaragua*
0.1	**1.8**	**73.8**	**13.7**	**1.6**	**1 263.9**	**4 299.2**	**Total CACM**
0.6	0.3	...	...	1.4	44.2	194.2	*Barbados*
...	...	...	...	...	116.4	420.5	*Guyana*
1.7	0.9	0.1	2.1	1.7	96.8	975.9	*Jamaica*
1.05	24.1	42.4	22.7	139.5	590.8	3 522.4	*Trinidad and Tobago*
-	0.2	...	0.1	...	39.0	1 715.2	*Bahamas*
0.9	-	0.2	0.5	...	3.6	331.5	*Haiti*
0.5	0.2	-	1.6	0.2	50.8	316.6	*Panama*
...	7.1	0.5	-	2.5	100.0	1 187.1	*Dominican Republic*
...	...	...	0.3	-	13.0	495.9	*Suriname*
123.3	**52.0**	**620.6**	**464.8**	**165.5**	**16 629.8**	**100 499.4**	**Total Region**
4 064.0	**500.0**	**6 180.0**	**1 651.0**	**457.0**	**111 874.0**	...	**World**

VI. COMERCIO EXTERIOR

277. COMERCIO INTRARREGIONAL DE BIENES TOTALES, 1982

(Sobre la base de las exportaciones fob en millones de dólares)

Procedencia / Destino	Argentina	Bolivia	Brasil Brazil	Colombia	Chile	Ecuador	México Mexico	Paraguay
Argentina	-	113.9	567.5	69.6	164.2	19.8	111.8	145.9
Bolivia	399.9	-	19.5	5.9	10.8	0.9	0.2	0.2
Brasil	650.0	80.0	-	272.0	289.0	65.0	324.0	324.0
Colombia	36.4	0.9	3.7	-	11.7	51.9	17.2	0.4
Chile	151.3	11.2	308.2	46.3	-	51.3	22.3	7.5
Ecuador	25.3	0.2	155.8	91.9	29.2	-	2.4	0.1
México	51.0	1.0	715.0	48.0	11.0	22.0	-	...
Paraguay	59.2	0.4	83.4	0.2	6.9	...	0.9	-
Perú [1]	19.4	20.8	68.4	78.1	30.4	9.3	4.5	0.2
Uruguay	109.1	1.0	145.8	3.0	21.8	1.2	3.9	9.9
Venezuela [1]	19.0	...	953.0	280.0	237.0	6.0	3.0	...
Total ALADI	**1 520.6**	**229.4**	**3 020.3**	**895.0**	**812.0**	**227.4**	**490.2**	**488.2**
Costa Rica	0.1	0.2	...	3.4	2.4	1.6	13.5	...
El Salvador	...	...	0.2	...	...	...	0.6	...
Guatemala	1.1	0.1	0.2	4.8	0.4	5.0	35.1	...
Honduras	...	...	...	1.3	...	0.1	4.8	...
Nicaragua	...	...	...	0.2	...	...	14.2	...
Total MCCA	**1.2**	**0.3**	**0.4**	**9.7**	**2.8**	**6.71**	**68.2**	**...**
Barbados [1]	...	...	...	...	...	...	...	...
Guyana [1]	...	...	.	...	...	...	1.4	...
Jamaica	20.6	...	1.0	0.4	...	...	0.2	2.0
Trinidad y Tabago	0.1	...	4.9	37.3	1.6	26.0	0.9	0.6
Bahamas [1]	0.4	...	25.6	6.9	...	...	3.4	...
Haití [1]	...	...	...	...	...	...	...	...
Panamá	...	...	...	3.7	0.3	2.3	0.9	...
República Dominicana	...	...	...	2.3	...	0.1	...	...
Suriname [1]	7.8	...	0.2	0.1	...	...	3.2	...
Total Región	**1 550.7**	**229.7**	**3 052.4**	**955.4**	**816.7**	**262.5**	**568.4**	**490.8**
Mundo	**5 309.0**	**461.0**	**19 822.0**	**5 025.0**	**3 052.0**	**2 036.0**	**17 564.0**	**836.0**

[1] Estimaciones.
[2] Miles de millones.

277. INTRAREGIONAL TRADE IN TOTAL GOODS, 1982

(Based on exports FOB in millions of dollars)

Perú *Peru*	Uruguay	Venezuela	**Total ALADI**	Costa Rica	El Salvador	Guatemala	Destination / Origin
109.8	115.5	97.4	1 515.4	1.6	9.4	...	*Argentina*
23.0	0.4	4.3	465.1	...	...	...	*Bolivia*
222.0	138.0	470.0	2 834.0	10.0	2.0	10.0	*Brazil*
34.0	0.8	366.1	523.1	3.9	1.1	3.3	*Colombia*
49.0	13.1	43.4	703.6	...	...	...	*Chile*
11.3	32.4	54.3	402.9	0.4	0.6	0.3	*Ecuador*
26.0	80.0	61.0	1 015.0	72.0	69.0	107.0	*Mexico*
0.2	4.4	9.3	164.9	...	...	...	*Paraguay*
-	0.9	42.7	274.7	2.0	1.6	0.4	*Peru* [1]
16.6	-	2.1	314.4	...	...	...	*Uruguay*
23.0	83.0	-	1 604.0	80.0	73.0	88.0	*Venezuela* [1]
514.9	**468.5**	**1 150.6**	**9 817.1**	**169.9**	**156.7**	**209.0**	**Total ALADI**
1.4	...	5.6	28.2	-	33.1	64.3	*Costa Rica*
...	...	...	0.8	21.2	-	119.6	*El Salvador*
0.1	...	6.3	53.1	51.6	190.3	-	*Guatemala*
...	0.1	6.0	12.3	10.7	10.5	26.4	*Honduras*
...	...	0.1	14.5	24.8	5.5	14.3	*Nicaragua*
1.5	0.1	18.0	108.9	108.3	239.4	224.6	**Total CACM**
...	...	0.1	0.1	...	...	0.3	*Barbados* [1]
0.3	...	56.0	57.7	...	...	...	*Guyana* [1]
...	0.9	10.5	35.6	...	0.4	0.8	*Jamaica*
6.8	2.2	12.5	92.9	2.3	...	12.7	*Trinidad and Tobago*
0.1	...	1.2	37.6	...	0.2	...	*Bahamas* [1]
...	...	0.7	0.7	...	...	0.1	*Haiti* [1]
0.9	...	12.5	20.6	10.1	3.4	2.5	*Panama*
0.5	0.1	28.2	31.2	3.0	...	0.1	*Dominican Republic*
...	...	7.1	18.4	...	...	...	*Suriname* [1]
525.0	**471.8**	**1 297.4**	**10 220.8**	**293.6**	**400.1**	**450.1**	**Total Region**
3 145.0	1 156.0	11 935.0	70 401.0	797.0	846.0	1 244.0	*World*

[1] *Estimated.*
[2] *Billions.*

277. COMERCIO INTRARREGIONAL DE BIENES TOTALES, 1982 *(conclusión)*

(Sobre la base de las exportaciones fob en millones de dólares)

Procedencia \ Destino	Honduras	Nicaragua	Total MCCA CACM	Barbados	Guyana	Jamaica	Trinidad y Tabago *Trinidad and Tobago*
Argentina	4.3	2.2	17.5	0.9	...	0.2	9.3
Bolivia	...	...	...	...	...	...	...
Brasil	5.0	5.0	32.0	5.0	5.0	18.0	30.0
Colombia	3.2	2.7	14.2	1.2	0.6	0.6	20.4
Chile	...	...	...	...	...	...	...
Ecuador	0.1	...	1.4	...	...	...	...
México	10.0	141.0	399.0	...	...	77.0	1.0
Paraguay	...	...	...	...	...	...	...
Perú [1]	0.1	0.5	4.6	...	...	...	0.6
Uruguay	...	...	...	0.2	...	...	...
Venezuela [1]	31.0	71.0	343.0	11.0	3.0	145.0	9.0
Total ALADI	**53.7**	**222.4**	**811.7**	**18.3**	**8.6**	**240.8**	**70.34**
Costa Rica	23.2	46.6	167.2	0.5	0.1	1.2	1.6
El Salvador	1.2	25.5	167.5	...	...	...	0.1
Guatemala	50.6	44.9	337.4	...	...	0.50	0.2
Honduras	-	8.3	55.9	1.0	...	1.5	14.0
Nicaragua	7.5	-	52.1	...	...	...	...
Total MCCA	**82.5**	**125.3**	**780.1**	**1.5**	**0.1**	**3.2**	**15.9**
Barbados [1]	...	...	0.3	-	0.8	8.6	37.4
Guyana [1]	...	...	...	3.3	-	18.9	27.6
Jamaica	0.1	...	1.3	10.9	3.2	-	54.4
Trinidad y Tabago	95.2	...	110.2	59.8	110.5	47.6	-
Bahamas [1]	...	...	0.2	...	1.6	...	0.2
Haití [1]	...	...	0.1	0.2	0.5	0.2	0.4
Panamá	9.1	2.5	27.6	...	...	0.1	0.1
República Dominicana	0.5	...	3.6	1.2	...	1.3	2.4
Suriname [1]	...	...	...	0.4	...	0.1	1.2
Total Región	**241.1**	**350.2**	**1 735.1**	**95.6**	**125.3**	**320.8**	**209.9**
Mundo	**646.0**	**623.0**	**4 156.0**	**461.0**	**249.0**	**1 312.0**	**2 755.0**

[1] Estimaciones.
[2] Miles de millones.

277. INTRAREGIONAL TRADE IN TOTAL GOODS, 1982 (concluded)

(Based on exports FOB in millions of dollars)

Bahamas	Haití / Haiti	Panamá / Panama	República Dominicana / Dominican Republic	Suriname	Total región / region	Mundo / World	Destination / Origin
0.8	0.3	5.4	1.0	0.1	1 550.9	7 622.6	*Argentina*
...	...	...	...	...	465.1	898.2	*Bolivia*
30.0	4.0	36.0	17.0	15.0	3 026.0	20 168.0	*Brazil*
7.6	0.5	67.9	4.5	2.1	642.7	3 095.0	*Colombia*
...	...	6.8	4.7	...	715.1	3 709.5	*Chile*
...	...	70.1	...	...	474.4	2 139.9	*Ecuador*
14.0	...	150.0	166.0	...	1 822.0	21 580.0	*Mexico*
...	...	2.6	...	...	167.5	329.8	*Paraguay*
13.4	...	3.3	0.1	...	296.7	3 195.7	*Peru* [1]
0.2	...	3.2	...	...	318.0	1 032.3	*Uruguay*
1.0	...	110.0	221.0	1.0	2 448.0	17 047.0	*Venezuela* [1]
67.09	4.8	455.3	414.3	18.2	11 926.4	80 818.0	***Total ALADI***
0.3	1.2	41.4	2.3	0.4	244.4	871.4	*Costa Rica*
...	...	5.3	1.6	...	175.3	879.2	*El Salvador*
...	0.3	21.9	7.2	...	420.6	1 119.8	*Guatemala*
...	...	1.8	2.3	1.7	90.5	667.8	*Honduras*
...	...	1.4	...	...	68.0	390.7	*Nicaragua*
0.3	1.5	71.8	13.4	2.1	998.8	3 928.9	***Total CACM***
0.6	0.2	...	...	1.2	49.2	251.6	*Barbados* [1]
...	...	...	...	...	107.5	388.1	*Guyana* [1]
1.0	0.9	0.5	2.1	1.9	111.8	767.4	*Jamaica*
2.1	24.2	14.7	2.1	109.7	573.8	3 042.3	*Trinidad and Tobago*
-	0.1	...	...	...	39.7	1 530.4	*Bahamas* [1]
0.9	-	0.1	2.4	...	5.5	380.0	*Haiti* [1]
0.1	...	-	0.7	0.2	49.4	308.1	*Panama*
0.3	5.1	0.8	-	0.8	46.7	809.0	*Dominican Republic*
...	...	...	0.6	-	20.7	369.9	*Suriname* [1]
72.32	36.8	543.2	435.6	134.1	13 929.5	92 593.7	***Total Region***
3 185.0	490.0	6 781.0	1 464.0	432.0	91 686.0	1 712.4 [2]	*World*

[1] *Estimated.*
[2] *Billions.*

278. COMERCIO INTRARREGIONAL DE BIENES TOTALES, 1983 [1]

(Sobre la base de las exportaciones fob en millones de dólares)

Procedencia \ Destino	Argentina	Bolivia	Brasil Brazil	Colombia	Chile	Ecuador	México Mexico	Paraguay
Argentina	-	373.6	654.6	43.0	119.3	11.7	37.4	32.1
Bolivia	56.4	-	108.0	1.6	11.0	0.1	0.4	0.4
Brasil	657.0	108.0	-	144.0	192.0	97.0	173.0	234.0
Colombia	59.5	5.4	149.8	-	42.3	158.4	68.3	...
Chile	119.4	11.0	164.3	42.3	-	33.8	1.0	2.4
Ecuador	8.6	...	2.7	133.6	37.0	-	0.3	...
México	37.0	...	635.0	69.0	17.0	25.0	-	...
Paraguay	31.5	...	50.9	...	...	...	...	-
Perú	94.6	21.5	74.8	19.6	39.4	8.3	16.9	2.3
Uruguay	76.8	0.3	104.0	0.4	6.27	0.2	48.7	4.7
Venezuela	58.4	4.0	268.9	117.9	29.7	32.5	32.1	2.9
Total ALADI	**1 199.2**	**523.8**	**2 213.0**	**571.4**	**493.9**	**367.0**	**378.1**	**278.8**
Costa Rica	0.1	0.3	...	3.0	...	1.5	0.1	...
El Salvador	...	...	0.2	0.1	...	...	...	...
Guatemala	0.5	...	6.7	0.2	...	0.6	14.8	...
Honduras	...	...	...	...	...	...	...	...
Nicaragua	...	...	...	0.2	...	0.1	8.4	...
Total MCCA	**0.6**	**0.3**	**6.9**	**3.5**	**...**	**2.2**	**23.3**	**...**
Barbados	...	...	...	...	...	...	...	...
Guyana	...	...	0.5	...	...	...	1.2	...
Jamaica	...	...	7.9	0.1	...	...	0.1	...
Trinidad y Tabago	0.2	...	1.5	1.5	1.6	1.2	...	...
Bahamas	0.4	...	31.7	1.1	...	...	1.2	...
Haití	...	...	...	...	...	...	0.1	...
Panamá	...	...	3.0	4.9	0.2	0.6	49.6	...
República Dominicana	...	...	...	4.8	...	...	1.6	...
Suriname	...	...	0.4	2.2	...	...	...	...
Total Región	**1 200.4**	**524.1**	**2 264.9**	**589.5**	**495.7**	**371.0**	**455.2**	**278.8**
Mundo	**5 272.0**	**378.0**	**15 393.0**	**4 347.0**	**2 547.0**	**1 466.0**	**12 575.0**	**617.0**

[1] Estimaciones.
[2] Miles de millones.

278. INTRAREGIONAL TRADE IN TOTAL GOODS, 1983 [1]

(Based on exports FOB in millions of dollars)

Perú / Peru	Uruguay	Venezuela	Total ALADI	Costa Rica	El Salvador	Guatemala	Destination / Origin
32.0	91.1	0.9	1 395.7	1.5	2.0	1.3	Argentina
13.6	1.8	0.2	193.5	...	...	...	Bolivia
75.0	31.0	270.0	1 981.0	13.0	4.0	6.0	Brazil
79.3	3.6	315.6	882.2	4.8	5.0	3.4	Colombia
39.4	6.2	29.7	449.5	...	...	...	Chile
4.5	0.3	2.0	189.0	0.5	...	...	Ecuador
17.0	49.0	32.0	881.0	68.0	89.0	69.0	Mexico
...	4.4	...	86.8	...	...	...	Paraguay
-	5.0	12.2	294.6	3.1	1.9	0.5	Peru
1.8	-	6.1	249.2	...	...	...	Uruguay
38.5	2.4	-	587.3	60.0	65.0	67.0	Venezuela
301.1	194.8	668.7	7 189.8	150.9	166.9	147.2	**Total ALADI**
1.5	...	5.1	11.6	-	36.4	70.7	Costa Rica
...	...	...	0.3	22.7	-	117.4	El Salvador
13.7	...	0.1	36.6	52.4	163.4	-	Guatemala
...	...	...	...	9.4	14.1	31.3	Honduras
0.3	...	0.2	9.2	18.1	9.2	14.3	Nicaragua
15.5	...	5.4	57.7	102.6	223.1	233.7	**Total CACM**
...	...	0.1	0.1	...	...	0.3	Barbados
0.4	...	50.4	52.5	...	...	...	Guyana
...	...	9.5	17.6	3.4	0.5	0.9	Jamaica
6.3	1.1	2.15	15.5	1.8	...	1.1	Trinidad and Tobago
...	...	1.2	35.6	...	0.2	...	Bahamas
0.1	...	0.6	0.8	0.4	...	0.1	Haiti
3.7	0.9	2.25	65.1	15.5	3.5	2.3	Panama
0.5	0.1	19.5	26.5	5.8	...	0.1	Dominican Republic
...	...	6.4	9.0	...	...	...	Suriname
327.6	196.9	766.1	7 470.2	280.4	394.2	385.7	**Total Region**
2 208.0	707.0	6 104.0	51 614.0	882.0	982.0	995.0	*World*

[1] Estimated.
[2] Billions.

278. COMERCIO INTRARREGIONAL DE BIENES TOTALES, 1983[1] *(conclusión)*

(Sobre la base de las exportaciones fob en millones de dólares)

Procedencia \ Destino	Honduras	Nicaragua	Total MCCA CACM	Barbados	Guyana	Jamaica	Trinidad y Tabago *Trinidad and Tobago*
Argentina	0.5	6.1	11.4	1.6	...	0.6	2.4
Bolivia	...	...	...	...	...	...	...
Brasil	11.0	11.0	45.0	6.0	2.0	12.0	31.0
Colombia	4.4	2.9	20.5	1.1	0.4	1.4	13.5
Chile	...	...	...	...	...	...	...
Ecuador	...	...	0.5	...	...	...	...
México	22.0	154.0	402.0	1.0	...	51.0	6.0
Paraguay	...	...	...	...	...	...	...
Perú	0.1	0.6	6.2	...	...	0.1	0.6
Uruguay	...	...	...	0.3	...	...	0.2
Venezuela	11.0	64.0	267.0	10.0	2.0	162.0	8.0
Total ALADI	**49.0**	**238.6**	**752.6**	**20.0**	**4.4**	**227.1**	**61.7**
Costa Rica	25.5	51.3	183.9	0.5	0.1	1.3	1.0
El Salvador	3.8	29.7	173.6	...	...	...	0.4
Guatemala	31.3	14.8	261.9	...	...	2.8	0.1
Honduras	-	10.0	64.8	...	...	...	15.0
Nicaragua	8.9	-	50.5	...	...	...	...
Total MCCA	**69.5**	**105.8**	**734.7**	**0.5**	**0.1**	**4.1**	**16.5**
Barbados	...	...	0.3	-	0.9	3.4	42.7
Guyana	...	...	...	3.7	-	6.6	23.6
Jamaica	0.1	...	4.9	11.9	3.5	-	51.8
Trinidad y Tabago	29.7	...	32.6	62.9	71.6	33.1	-
Bahamas	...	...	0.2	...	...	...	6.7
Haití	...	...	0.5	0.3	...	0.1	0.2
Panamá	2.1	1.2	24.6	...	...	0.2	3.4
República Dominicana	0.4	...	6.3	0.6	...	0.8	3.0
Suriname	...	...	...	0.4	0.2	...	1.4
Total Región	**150.8**	**345.6**	**1 556.7**	**100.3**	**80.7**	**275.4**	**211.0**
Mundo	**657.0**	**656.0**	**4 172.0**	**505.0**	**171.0**	**1 268.0**	**2 623.0**

[1] Estimaciones.
[2] Miles de millones.

278. *INTRAREGIONAL TRADE IN TOTAL GOODS, 1983* [1] *(concluded)*

(Based on exports FOB in millions of dollars)

Bahamas	Haití *Haiti*	Panamá *Panama*	República Dominicana *Dominican Republic*	Suriname	Total región *region*	Mundo *World*	Destination / Origin
0.6	15.5	6.6	10.8	...	1 445.2	7 019.2	*Argentina*
...	...	...	...	...	193.5	839.0	*Bolivia*
30.0	4.0	40.0	22.0	15.0	2 188.0	21 898.0	*Brazil*
0.5	0.5	67.5	5.7	2.9	996.2	3 080.9	*Colombia*
...	...	3.8	5.1	...	458.4	3 835.5	*Chile*
...	...	216.9	...	...	406.4	2 227.5	*Ecuador*
10.0	...	134.0	150.0	...	1 635.0	21 168.0	*Mexico*
...	...	...	...	...	86.8	251.6	*Paraguay*
12.0	...	4.2	0.2	...	317.9	3 027.0	*Peru*
0.2	...	1.5	...	...	251.4	1 014.5	*Uruguay*
1.0	...	122.0	214.0	1.0	1 374.3	15 636.8	*Venezuela*
54.3	**20.0**	**596.5**	**407.8**	**18.9**	**9 353.1**	**79 998.0**	***Total ALADI***
0.3	1.4	35.6	2.5	0.5	238.7	1 071.9	*Costa Rica*
...	...	5.7	1.7	...	181.7	1 009.8	*El Salvador*
...	0.2	16.1	5.6	...	323.3	1 158.8	*Guatemala*
...	...	...	0.7	...	80.5	680.3	*Honduras*
...	0.4	1.3	0.2	...	61.6	390.6	*Nicaragua*
0.3	**2.0**	**58.7**	**10.7**	**0.5**	**885.8**	**4 311.4**	***Total CACM***
0.6	0.3	...	...	1.4	49.7	328.0	*Barbados*
0.1	...	...	...	0.2	86.75	292.0	*Guyana*
0.9	1.0	1.0	0.8	2.1	95.5	725.5	*Jamaica*
12.7	15.9	7.3	1.4	81.3	334.3	2 343.5	*Trinidad and Tobago*
-	0.1	...	...	...	42.6	1 961.9	*Bahamas*
0.3	-	...	4.1	...	6.3	411.7	*Haiti*
...	...	-	0.9	0.2	94.4	479.6	*Panama*
...	5.4	0.5	-	0.8	43.9	1 006.3	*Dominican Republic*
...	0.2	...	0.7	-	11.9	368.2	*Suriname*
69.2	**44.9**	**664.0**	**426.4**	**105.4**	**11 004.2**	**92 226.1**	***Total Region***
2 771.0	566.0	5 342.0	1 434.0	350.0	70 816.0	1 671.2 [2]	*World*

[1] *Estimated.*
[2] *Billions.*

599

279. INDICES DE VOLUMEN FISICO DE LA PRODUCCION AGROPECUARIA

País	1960	1965	1970		1975		1977
		Base: 1961-1965 = 100			Base: 1969-1971 = 100		Base: 1974-1976 = 100
Argentina	85	96	113	102	109	98	107
Barbados	...	114	103	108	79	95	112
Bolivia	97	108	132	100	134	102	99
Brasil	94	114	128	98	124	100	110
Colombia	93	106	124	100	121	101	111
Costa Rica	102	108	144	98	124	102	110
Cuba	116	112	144	123	97	99	110
Chile	106	103	121	104	106	103	108
Ecuador	80	113	129	102	115	99	104
El Salvador	...	111	113	98	125	104	100
Guatemala	88	113	136	101	129	98	111
Guyana	...	103	108	96	108	101	104
Haití	...	104	110	100	109	100	97
Honduras	92	106	132	97	88	95	113
Jamaica	...	106	105	98	105	97	101
México	91	112	123	100	114	100	110
Nicaragua	...	125	127	98	130	101	107
Panamá	84	109	141	94	116	102	109
Paraguay	86	112	125	102	116	97	120
Perú	93	103	119	102	105	98	102
República Dominicana	114	91	122	100	112	95	106
Trinidad y Tabago	...	109	113	102	104	98	99
Uruguay	88	100	115	106	99	95	92
Venezuela	85	112	148	101	122	107	107
Total	92	107	123	101	116	100	108

1978	1979	1980	1981	1982	1983	Country
		Base year:				
		1974-1976 = 100				
116	121	112	118	127	119	*Argentina*
109	118	133	130	118	116	*Barbados*
100	99	103	108	110	82	*Bolivia*
107	113	121	130	129	133	*Brazil*
114	119	121	128	126	125	*Colombia*
112	114	113	116	109	118	*Costa Rica*
122	131	118	129	130	128	*Cuba*
100	106	106	114	114	112	*Chile*
101	106	113	117	117	109	*Ecuador*
111	116	110	103	98	103	*El Salvador*
113	119	123	123	117	115	*Guatemala*
111	102	102	109	110	102	*Guyana*
102	108	99	102	106	106	*Haiti*
124	124	128	137	139	141	*Honduras*
113	102	102	103	99	101	*Jamaica*
121	116	123	131	124	131	*Mexico*
117	106	77	91	91	98	*Nicaragua*
112	113	116	119	123	122	*Panama*
116	127	129	134	137	143	*Paraguay*
100	103	95	100	103	100	*Peru*
108	109	106	106	114	115	*Dominican Republic*
92	81	76	61	67	71	*Trinidad and Tobago*
91	91	97	111	107	113	*Uruguay*
111	118	112	105	108	116	*Venezuela*
112	115	117	124	123	125	*Total*

280. INDICES DE VOLUMEN FISICO DE CULTIVOS AGRICOLAS

País	1970		1975	1977	1978
	Base: 1969-1971 = 100			Base: 1974-1976 = 100	
Argentina	103	119	97	105	116
Barbados	110	61	93	113	98
Bolivia	100	136	102	95	95
Brasil	97	122	100	110	104
Colombia	101	125	102	110	118
Costa Rica	97	118	103	106	110
Cuba	132	96	100	108	122
Chile	101	103	102	127	107
Ecuador	102	112	100	99	89
El Salvador	97	123	106	95	107
Guatemala	101	135	97	110	112
Guyana	95	100	101	101	111
Haití	100	108	100	96	101
Honduras	97	82	92	116	124
Jamaica	98	99	97	97	115
México	99	104	100	106	119
Nicaragua	96	130	10	100	114
Panamá	92	111	104	109	113
Paraguay	103	125	97	124	117
Perú	103	92	96	100	100
República Dominicana	100	108	94	105	106
Trinidad y Tabago	102	88	92	88	74
Uruguay	104	111	91	83	86
Venezuela	103	106	110	110	101
Total	101	113	100	107	110

1979	1980	1981	1982	1983	Country
		Base year:			
		1974-1976 = 100			
125	111	119	140	131	Argentina
115	133	103	79	74	Barbados
91	93	99	100	60	Bolivia
111	120	131	127	131	Brazil
121	122	127	127	126	Colombia
110	110	115	106	117	Costa Rica
134	112	125	127	120	Cuba
117	108	109	111	110	Chile
94	102	107	104	88	Ecuador
113	106	99	91	97	El Salvador
112	113	111	106	104	Guatemala
99	98	106	106	91	Guyana
108	100	103	107	107	Haiti
131	129	142	136	138	Honduras
97	94	94	87	90	Jamaica
107	114	126	109	124	Mexico
103	77	102	98	108	Nicaragua
116	112	113	115	118	Panama
131	133	139	143	151	Paraguay
105	91	92	94	87	Peru
105	99	100	110	109	Dominican Republic
63	55	27	38	42	Trinidad and Tobago
90	92	106	99	105	Uruguay
109	77	43	45	52	Venezuela
113	113	122	121	122	*Total*

281. INDICES DE VOLUMEN FISICO DE LA PRODUCCION PECUARIA

País	1970	1975		1977	1978
	Base: 1969-1971 = 100			Base: 1974-1976 = 100	
Argentina	102	103	100	110	117
Barbados	98	153	98	111	128
Bolivia	102	130	101	108	112
Brasil	101	129	100	109	112
Colombia	100	115	99	111	109
Costa Rica	100	139	100	118	115
Cuba	101	99	97	113	122
Chile	102	109	104	94	95
Ecuador	103	120	99	115	126
El Salvador	99	129	95	114	125
Guatemala	100	113	100	112	119
Guyana	100	125	100	109	109
Haití	100	120	100	100	111
Honduras	98	110	100	108	123
Jamaica	98	123	98	107	110
México	101	126	100	114	125
Nicaragua	103	129	102	119	121
Panamá	96	122	99	109	112
Paraguay	102	104	98	112	114
Perú	99	126	101	105	101
República Dominicana	100	121	98	111	112
Trinidad y Tabago	103	129	108	114	116
Uruguay	107	94	97	97	95
Venezuela	100	135	105	105	116
Total	101	118	100	110	115

281. QUANTUM INDEXES OF LIVESTOCK PRODUCTION

1979	1980	1981	1982	1983	Country
		Base year:			
		1974-1976 = 100			
115	113	116	109	103	*Argentina*
124	134	174	180	185	*Barbados*
119	127	128	131	133	*Bolivia*
117	123	128	133	137	*Brazil*
117	120	129	124	124	*Colombia*
121	120	120	116	118	*Costa Rica*
125	130	138	138	145	*Cuba*
98	106	118	117	114	*Chile*
130	136	141	145	152	*Ecuador*
127	123	117	123	123	*El Salvador*
143	151	160	149	146	*Guatemala*
108	113	118	121	126	*Guyana*
108	98	95	97	102	*Haiti*
108	124	127	146	148	*Honduras*
112	117	120	122	124	*Jamaica*
127	134	137	141	139	*Mexico*
110	76	72	79	79	*Nicaragua*
109	121	127	132	128	*Panama*
122	124	126	129	131	*Paraguay*
99	103	113	119	120	*Peru*
125	129	128	127	137	*Dominican Republic*
107	104	109	110	112	*Trinidad and Tobago*
91	100	113	112	117	*Uruguay*
122	130	136	141	148	*Venezuela*
118	**122**	**127**	**128**	**128**	*Total*

282. INDICES DE VOLUMEN FISICO DE LA PRODUCCION DE ALIMENTOS

País	1960	1965	1970		1975		1977
		Base: 1961-1965 = 100			Base: 1969-1971 = 100		Base: 1974-1976 = 100
Argentina	85	95	114	101	109	97	106
Barbados	...	114	103	108	79	95	112
Bolivia	97	108	130	101	131	102	100
Brasil	88	115	139	102	129	98	112
Colombia	89	107	125	99	124	100	107
Costa Rica	108	109	149	100	131	103	109
Cuba	117	113	148	124	96	99	111
Chile	106	103	122	104	106	103	108
Ecuador	83	111	130	101	114	100	105
El Salvador	...	107	131	102	124	103	103
Guatemala	88	108	136	101	125	100	109
Guyana	...	103	108	96	108	101	104
Haití	...	104	114	100	108	99	98
Honduras	92	104	137	97	83	93	113
Jamaica	...	106	105	98	105	97	101
México	91	112	133	100	117	102	111
Nicaragua	...	109	141	101	123	103	110
Panamá	84	109	142	94	116	102	109
Paraguay	92	112	128	103	112	98	117
Perú	94	105	127	102	108	98	101
República Dominicana	115	94	126	100	110	95	106
Trinidad y Tabago	...	109	114	104	103	97	99
Uruguay	86	103	121	107	103	95	91
Venezuela	83	112	151	101	122	106	107
Total	91	108	128	102	117	99	109

282. QUANTUM INDEXES OF FOOD PRODUCTION

1978	1979	1980	1981	1982	1983	Country
		Base year:				
		1974-1976 = 100				
116	122	114	122	129	122	Argentina
109	118	133	130	118	116	Barbados
100	99	105	110	113	83	Bolivia
107	113	125	127	134	134	Brazil
113	118	120	126	125	124	Colombia
110	112	108	109	104	109	Costa Rica
124	133	121	130	132	130	Cuba
100	106	106	114	114	112	Chile
101	105	115	118	119	111	Ecuador
117	119	115	108	108	112	El Salvador
111	119	125	128	127	127	Guatemala
111	101	101	109	110	101	Guyana
105	108	101	104	106	107	Haiti
121	117	125	133	138	137	Honduras
113	101	102	103	99	101	Jamaica
123	118	126	135	127	136	Mexico
118	108	83	91	92	97	Nicaragua
112	112	114	118	122	120	Panama
114	128	131	135	141	147	Paraguay
98	100	91	97	103	97	Peru
110	109	105	107	114	120	Dominican Republic
92	81	76	61	68	71	Trinidad and Tobago
91	89	94	110	106	111	Uruguay
112	119	114	106	110	118	Venezuela
112	115	119	124	127	127	*Total*

283. INDICES DE VOLUMEN FISICO DE LA PRODUCCION DE ALIMENTOS POR HABITANTE

País	1960	1965	1970		1975		1977
		Base: 1961-1965 = 100			Base: 1969-1971 = 100		Base: 1974-1976 = 100
Argentina	90	94	104	101	102	97	103
Barbados	...	113	101	108	77	95	109
Bolivia	105	104	111	101	116	102	95
Brasil	103	115	114	102	114	98	106
Colombia	100	99	99	99	111	100	103
Costa Rica	107	100	120	100	115	103	104
Cuba	121	109	129	124	88	99	108
Chile	106	98	106	104	97	103	105
Ecuador	91	104	103	101	98	100	99
El Salvador	...	100	103	102	107	103	98
Guatemala	100	104	111	101	107	100	103
Guyana	...	98	92	96	96	100	99
Haití	...	102	103	100	97	99	93
Honduras	88	97	111	97	71	93	106
Jamaica	...	104	95	98	97	97	98
México	100	106	106	100	100	102	104
Nicaragua	...	105	115	101	105	103	103
Panamá	91	102	116	94	102	102	104
Paraguay	100	106	106	103	96	98	110
Perú	104	99	104	102	94	98	96
República Dominicana	129	87	101	101	95	95	100
Trinidad y Tabago	...	106	106	102	98	97	96
Uruguay	88	100	112	107	102	95	90
Venezuela	91	106	122	101	102	106	100
Total	101	103	106	102	103	99	104

283. QUANTUM INDEXES OF PER CAPITA FOOD
PRODUCTION

1978	1979	1980	1981	1982	1983	Country
		Base year:				
		1974-1976 = 100				
112	116	107	114	118	110	*Argentina*
105	112	124	120	108	105	*Barbados*
92	90	92	94	94	67	*Bolivia*
99	102	111	110	114	111	*Brazil*
106	109	107	111	108	105	*Colombia*
102	102	96	95	88	90	*Costa Rica*
120	128	116	124	125	122	*Cuba*
95	99	97	103	101	98	*Chile*
93	93	99	98	96	87	*Ecuador*
107	106	99	91	88	89	*El Salvador*
101	106	107	107	103	100	*Guatemala*
103	93	91	95	94	85	*Guyana*
97	98	89	90	89	88	*Haiti*
109	101	105	108	108	103	*Honduras*
109	96	95	94	90	90	*Jamaica*
112	104	109	113	103	107	*Mexico*
107	95	70	75	74	75	*Nicaragua*
104	102	102	103	104	100	*Panama*
103	112	111	111	112	114	*Paraguay*
91	89	80	83	85	78	*Peru*
102	98	92	92	95	98	*Dominican Republic*
88	76	70	56	61	63	*Trinidad and Tobago*
89	87	92	106	102	106	*Uruguay*
101	103	95	86	86	89	*Venezuela*
104	104	105	107	107	104	*Total*

284. SUPERFICIE AGROPECUARIA Y SUPERFICIE REGADA

(Miles de hectáreas)

País	1961-1965				1980	
	Tierras arables *Arable land*	Tierras destinadas a cultivos permanentes *Land under permanent crops*	Praderas y pastos perma-nentes *Permanent pasture land*	Superficie regada *Irrigated area*	Tierras arables *Arable land*	Tierras destinadas a cultivos permanentes *Land under permanent crops*
Argentina	19 598	8 500	146 500	1 046	25 150	10 050
Barbados	30	-	4	-	33	-
Bolivia	1 348	1 155	28 353	74	3 250	120
Brasil	22 400	7 854	131 880	546	60 000	11 120
Colombia	3 545	1 506	16 682	231	4 050	1 600
Costa Rica	285	199	969	26	283	315
Cuba	1 616	174	2 349	280	2 525	675
Chile	4 007	199	9 850	1 084	5 332	198
Ecuador	1 709	809	2 200	446	1 755	865
El Salvador	489	166	606	18	560	165
Guatemala	1 125	317	1 039	38	1 270	480
Guyana	350	10	999	100	480	15
Haití	430	270	596	38	545	345
Honduras	1 360	139	2 000	60	1 560	197
Jamaica	187	46	256	23	205	60
México	22 260	1 353	74 499	2 900	21 800	1 530
Nicaragua	1 180	155	3 384	18	1 075	171
Panamá	437	124	910	15	458	116
Paraguay	737	115	13 800	30	1 620	300
Perú	2 171	180	27 977	1 041	3 100	300
República Dominicana	740	280	1 020	113	1 070	350
Trinidad y Tabago	57	82	6	11	70	88
Uruguay	1 726	53	13 769	32	1 403	46
Venezuela	4 580	637	14 229	218	3 080	675
Total	92 367	24 323	493 877	8 388	140 674	29 781

(Thousands of hectares)

1980		1982				
Praderas y pastos permanentes	Superficie regada	Tierras arables	Tierras destinadas a cultivos permanentes	Praderas y pastos permanentes	Superficie regada	Country
Permanent pasture land	Irrigated area	Arable land	Land under permanent crops	Permanent pasture land	Irrigated area	
143 200	1 580	26 000	9 800	143 000	1 620	*Argentina*
4	-	33	-	4	-	*Barbados*
27 050	140	3 250	125	27 000	150	*Bolivia*
161 000	1 800	63 000	11 670	163 000	2 000	*Brazil*
30 000	310	4 050	1 630	30 000	318	*Colombia*
2 010	26	283	352	2 167	26	*Costa Rica*
2 523	962	2 540	675	2 500	1 000	*Cuba*
11 880	1 255	5 330	198	11 920	1 259	*Chile*
2 560	520	1 760	865	3 900	530	*Ecuador*
610	110	560	165	610	110	*El Salvador*
1 334	68	1 300	484	1 334	72	*Guatemala*
1 220	125	480	15	1 220	125	*Guyana*
508	70	550	347	504	70	*Haiti*
3 400	82	1 570	199	3 400	84	*Honduras*
205	33	206	60	205	33	*Jamaica*
74 499	5 100	21 900	1 550	74 499	5 200	*Mexico*
4 880	80	1 085	5 003	4 260	82	*Nicaragua*
1 161	28	462	120	1 161	28	*Panama*
15 600	60	1 640	300	15 600	62	*Paraguay*
27 120	1 180	3 200	315	27 120	1 180	*Peru*
2 092	165	1 100	350	2 092	176	*Dominican Republic*
11	21	70	88	11	21	*Trinidad and Tobago*
13 632	79	1 403	46	13 632	88	*Uruguay*
17 200	315	3 080	675	17 300	317	*Venezuela*
548 699	14 109	144 582	35 032	546 439	14 551	*Total*

285. SUPERFICIE COSECHADA DE ALGODON

(Miles de hectáreas)

País	1960	1965	1970	1975	1977
Argentina	461	534	452	505	518
Bolivia	-	4	8	54	40
Brasil	1 862	2 327	2 873	3 876	4 097
Colombia	150	148	267	281	377
Costa Rica	2	5	-	-	14
Cuba	18	4	4	3	3
Ecuador	17	27	9	32	26
El Salvador	57	111	56	88	79
Guatemala	26	100	74	111	122
Haití	12	8	7	8	9
Honduras	2	14	4	8	10
México	904	793	411	227	420
Nicaragua	61	135	109	178	198
Paraguay	40	57	46	100	200
Perú	252	238	144	97	118
República Dominicana	9	6	4	3	4
Uruguay	1	2	1	1	1
Venezuela	55	55	43	78	52
Total	3 929	4 568	4 512	5 656	6 288

285. SEED COTTON, AREA HARVESTED

(Thousands of hectares)

1978	1979	1980	1981	1982	1983	Country
607	669	568	282	399	343	Argentina
33	34	24	14	8	9	Bolivia
3 951	3 646	3 699	3 511	3 644	2 955	Brazil
328	187	217	149	53	88	Colombia
11	12	7	8	8	8	Costa Rica
4	4	4	4	4	4	Cuba
20	20	19	24	17	23	Ecuador
99	102	85	58	53	49	El Salvador
123	123	123	100	66	50	Guatemala
12	14	10	13	13	13	Haiti
18	11	13	8	6	7	Honduras
350	373	372	355	200	189	Mexico
212	174	45	94	93	95	Nicaragua
285	313	260	324	325	325	Paraguay
116	135	149	132	87	132	Peru
3	4	6	7	7	5	Dominican Republic
1	1	1	1	1	...	Uruguay
47	38	36	21	14	45	Venezuela
6 220	5 860	5 638	5 105	4 998	4 340	Total

286. SUPERFICIE COSECHADA DE ARROZ

(Miles de hectáreas)

País	1960	1965	1970	1975	1977
Argentina	56	68	102	93	91
Bolivia	30	33	55	64	65
Brasil	2 966	4 619	4 979	5 306	5 992
Colombia	227	375	280	372	324
Costa Rica	53	55	43	87	71
Cuba	160	38	187	178	152
Chile	39	27	25	23	35
Ecuador	91	103	87	122	107
El Salvador	12	13	12	17	12
Guatemala	10	8	11	23	12
Guyana	79	119	111	134	136
Haití	36	35	38	43	40
Honduras	13	9	11	21	24
Jamaica	2	2	-	1	1
México	143	138	150	257	180
Nicaragua	21	25	25	30	25
Panamá	89	133	93	115	110
Paraguay	7	8	23	25	34
Perú	87	75	140	122	134
República Dominicana	55	76	83	89	113
Trinidad y Tabago	6	5	4	8	8
Uruguay	14	28	36	46	57
Venezuela	42	105	130	114	166
Total	4 238	6 097	6 587	7 290	7 889

(Thousands of hectares)

1978	1979	1980	1981	1982	1983	Country
95	102	82	82	114	81	Argentina
63	51	66	63	54	43	Bolivia
5 624	5 452	6 243	6 102	6 016	5 112	Brazil
406	442	416	413	446	397	Colombia
76	80	60	80	77	83	Costa Rica
152	147	147	144	150	140	Cuba
33	47	41	31	37	30	Chile
81	111	127	131	132	76	Ecuador
14	15	17	14	11	13	El Salvador
11	13	13	11	8	12	Guatemala
115	89	95	88	93	73	Guyana
52	54	50	50	50	50	Haiti
16	19	20	21	23	24	Honduras
1	1	1	1	1	...	Jamaica
121	150	132	180	175	185	Mexico
28	36	43	42	45	47	Nicaragua
99	99	92	100	95	80	Panama
32	30	38	28	26	34	Paraguay
114	131	96	150	167	190	Peru
103	109	125	111	93	120	Dominican Republic
8	8	10	10	10	10	Trinidad and Tobago
58	68	67	62	69	75	Uruguay
166	197	201	243	223	167	Venezuela
7 468	7 451	8 182	8 157	8 115	7 042	Total

287. SUPERFICIE COSECHADA DE CAFE

(Miles de hectáreas)

País	1960	1965	1970	1975	1977
Bolivia	...	7	13	17	19
Brasil	4 420	3 511	2 403	2 217	1 941
Colombia	893	812	830	830	1 000
Costa Rica	...	86	95	85	81
Cuba	...	50	50	50	50
Ecuador	114	166	215	231	260
El Salvador	125	134	120	147	147
Guatemala	218	237	225	248	248
Guyana	...	1	1	2	2
Haití	...	30	30	30	30
Honduras	100	82	101	110	114
Jamaica	7	6	7	5	5
México	304	350	329	374	389
Nicaragua	83	90	84	84	88
Panamá	17	21	21	22	25
Paraguay	...	9	10	17	17
Perú	69	93	113	121	134
República Dominicana	...	150	75	170	156
Trinidad y Tabago	...	10	10	10	10
Venezuela	...	340	287	275	258
Total	...	6 185	5 019	5 045	4 974

(Thousands of hectares)

1978	1979	1980	1981	1982	1983	Country
20	22	23	24	24	24	Bolivia
2 184	2 406	2 434	2 618	1 857	2 440	Brazil
1 100	1 050	1 084	1 075	1 087	1 080	Colombia
81	82	82	85	85	87	Costa Rica
50	50	50	50	50	50	Cuba
270	262	288	321	322	300	Ecuador
147	170	185	185	161	186	El Salvador
256	248	250	253	257	260	Guatemala
2	2	2	2	2	2	Guyana
25	35	25	27	35	31	Haiti
115	119	119	119	119	126	Honduras
5	5	5	6	6	6	Jamaica
393	404	455	475	533	360	Mexico
95	98	94	88	90	91	Nicaragua
28	27	17	22	24	31	Panama
11	11	11	15	24	18	Paraguay
142	155	143	144	140	140	Peru
157	149	157	157	160	130	Dominican Republic
10	10	10	10	9	10	Trinidad and Tobago
266	256	258	261	259	261	Venezuela
5 357	5 561	5 692	6 037	5 344	5 633	Total

288. SUPERFICIE COSECHADA DE CAÑA DE AZUCAR

(Miles de hectáreas)

País	1960	1965	1970	1975	1977
Argentina	242	250	192	293	350
Barbados	...	21	20	16	16
Bolivia	26	25	39	52	75
Brasil	1 340	1 705	1 725	1 969	2 270
Colombia	294	327	238	252	270
Costa Rica	21	27	38	37	40
Cuba	1 261	979	1 498	1 181	1 137
Ecuador	63	97	83	115	109
El Salvador	13	28	28	42	41
Guatemala	21	33	36	70	91
Guyana	44	43	43	41	51
Haití	100	74	75	75	75
Honduras	34	33	50	50	55
Jamaica	82	60	58	62	51
México	348	461	547	498	464
Nicaragua	22	25	34	35	40
Panamá	20	17	18	30	37
Paraguay	21	27	41	30	31
Perú	52	51	57	65	65
República Dominicana	146	72	143	154	172
Trinidad y Tabago	34	36	35	32	32
Uruguay	4	6	3	8	11
Venezuela	52	62	63	77	84
Total	**4 240**	**4 459**	**5 064**	**5 184**	**5 567**

(Thousands of hectares)

1978	1979	1980	1981	1982	1983	*Country*
343	306	314	320	309	317	*Argentina*
16	16	16	16	16	14	*Barbados*
71	67	66	70	68	67	*Bolivia*
2 391	2 537	2 608	2 826	3 086	3 370	*Brazil*
275	282	292	279	305	310	*Colombia*
43	45	49	51	51	51	*Costa Rica*
1 237	1 313	1 392	1 227	1 281	1 230	*Cuba*
104	103	108	104	92	90	*Ecuador*
41	37	34	27	32	34	*El Salvador*
73	66	79	83	78	90	*Guatemala*
58	56	52	57	52	50	*Guyana*
75	75	80	80	80	80	*Haiti*
68	75	85	90	95	95	*Honduras*
44	47	51	43	44	53	*Jamaica*
537	538	546	522	526	520	*Mexico*
40	40	37	39	44	44	*Nicaragua*
41	44	48	53	50	48	*Panama*
35	35	37	41	36	36	*Paraguay*
63	64	49	39	48	45	*Peru*
174	178	180	185	188	188	*Dominican Republic*
34	39	34	28	25	20	*Trinidad and Tobago*
10	10	9	10	10	10	*Uruguay*
74	69	77	74	77	76	*Venezuela*
5 847	6 042	6 243	6 264	6 593	6 838	*Total*

289. SUPERFICIE COSECHADA DE FRIJOLES SECOS

(Miles de hectáreas)

País	1960	1965	1970	1975	1977
Argentina	28	37	41	137	171
Bolivia	2	9	1	3	3
Brasil	2 560	3 273	3 485	4 146	4 551
Colombia	86	76	66	121	116
Costa Rica	38	58	24	36	24
Cuba	42	35	35	35	35
Chile	81	58	57	68	97
Ecuador	40	55	82	63	59
El Salvador	20	27	36	56	53
Guatemala	58	88	96	93	134
Haití	26	40	41	85	103
Honduras	84	63	72	74	77
México	1 305	2 117	1 747	1 753	1 631
Nicaragua	42	59	61	56	62
Panamá	19	15	18	16	16
Paraguay	22	32	50	63	86
Perú	44	54	77	71	59
República Dominicana	40	35	33	42	42
Uruguay	6	5	4	4	4
Venezuela	149	88	91	89	65
Total	**4 692**	**6 224**	**6 117**	**7 011**	**7 388**

289. DRIED BEANS, AREA HARVESTED

(Thousands of hectares)

1978	1979	1980	1981	1982	1983	Country
136	231	205	211	230	200	Argentina
4	4	4	4	4	4	Bolivia
4 617	4 212	4 643	5 027	5 929	4 077	Brazil
111	112	115	119	112	118	Colombia
29	25	22	24	38	39	Costa Rica
35	35	35	35	35	35	Cuba
112	110	111	118	122	81	Chile
39	44	48	54	51	60	Ecuador
52	55	52	40	56	55	El Salvador
135	100	116	119	97	97	Guatemala
101	90	90	90	90	90	Haiti
81	73	68	76	77	70	Honduras
1 580	1 041	1 763	2 150	1 712	2 103	Mexico
67	53	54	89	68	68	Nicaragua
15	12	7	9	6	6	Panama
81	79	80	85	85	80	Paraguay
64	64	45	50	49	48	Peru
53	46	51	55	55	63	Dominican Republic
5	5	5	5	5	5	Uruguay
70	66	66	59	52	54	Venezuela
7 387	6 457	7 580	8 419	8 873	7 353	Total

290. SUPERFICIE COSECHADA DE MAIZ

(Miles de hectáreas)

País	1960	1965	1970	1975	1977
Argentina	2 415	3 062	4 017	3 070	2 532
Barbados	...	...	1	1	1
Bolivia	200	214	221	230	242
Brasil	6 681	8 771	9 858	10 855	11 797
Colombia	730	869	661	573	581
Costa Rica	55	80	43	65	47
Cuba	189	120	90	82	76
Chile	83	88	74	92	116
Ecuador	209	307	292	274	247
El Salvador	178	193	206	246	245
Guatemala	652	677	662	559	641
Guyana	1	1	1	3	3
Haití	300	300	230	195	210
Honduras	350	294	283	331	469
Jamaica	5	3	3	6	4
México	5 558	7 718	7 440	6 694	7 470
Nicaragua	132	195	259	209	212
Panamá	79	105	65	74	83
Paraguay	110	162	167	223	288
Perú	324	342	382	363	391
República Dominicana	40	25	26	25	35
Trinidad y Tabago	1	1	-	1	1
Uruguay	259	192	227	153	138
Venezuela	398	462	588	506	496
Total	18 949	24 181	25 796	24 830	26 325

290. MAIZE, AREA HARVESTED

(Thousands of hectares)

1978	1979	1980	1981	1982	1983	Country
2 660	2 800	2 490	3 394	3 170	2 970	Argentina
1	1	1	1	1	1	Barbados
259	278	293	313	286	261	Bolivia
11 125	11 319	11 451	11 502	12 601	10 750	Brazil
671	616	614	629	636	598	Colombia
37	44	39	47	54	62	Costa Rica
76	76	77	77	77	77	Cuba
94	130	116	126	115	138	Chile
185	219	226	244	217	180	Ecuador
264	276	292	276	239	280	El Salvador
591	622	655	681	669	925	Guatemala
2	1	1	1	1	1	Guyana
248	234	225	200	185	200	Haiti
474	341	338	338	341	330	Honduras
5	4	3	3	2	2	Jamaica
7 191	5 916	6 955	8 150	5 643	8 408	Mexico
228	168	162	200	164	220	Nicaragua
65	70	52	56	59	70	Panama
276	353	377	400	420	400	Paraguay
351	371	275	316	347	343	Peru
48	33	35	29	21	27	Dominican Republic
1	1	1	1	1	1	Trinidad and Tobago
163	94	132	146	95	100	Uruguay
414	409	394	312	305	251	Venezuela
25 429	24 376	25 204	27 442	25 649	26 595	*Total*

291. SUPERFICIE COSECHADA DE MANDIOCA

(Miles de hectáreas)

País	1960	1965	1970	1975	1977
Argentina	21	23	26	20	21
Bolivia	4	10	18	22	23
Brasil	1 342	1 750	2 025	2 041	2 176
Colombia	120	142	150	257	218
Costa Rica	2	3	3	2	2
Cuba	66	28	33	36	38
Ecuador	25	25	35	35	31
El Salvador	1	1	1	2	1
Guatemala	2	2	2	3	3
Guyana	1	1	1	-	-
Haití	30	30	32	55	57
Honduras	4	4	4	3	3
Jamaica	4	4	2	2	3
México	...	...	2	3	4
Nicaragua	3	3	4	5	6
Panamá	6	2	4	5	5
Paraguay	68	108	103	97	116
Perú	41	41	39	36	37
República Dominicana	16	15	15	19	18
Trinidad y Tabago	-	-	-	-	-
Venezuela	33	25	39	37	38
Total	1 890	2 217	2 536	2 680	2 800

291. CASSAVA, AREA HARVESTED

(Thousands of hectares)

1978	1979	1980	1981	1982	1983	Country
22	21	23	22	24	23	Argentina
15	16	18	18	21	15	Bolivia
2 149	2 111	2 016	2 067	2 133	2 041	Brazil
217	222	208	207	209	210	Colombia
2	2	3	3	3	6	Costa Rica
45	46	47	48	49	50	Cuba
24	20	25	26	20	27	Ecuador
2	2	2	2	2	2	El Salvador
3	3	3	3	4	4	Guatemala
-	-	-	-	...	...	Guyana
58	63	63	63	64	65	Haiti
3	3	2	2	2	2	Honduras
3	3	2	2	2	2	Jamaica
2	2	2	2	2	2	Mexico
6	6	7	7	7	7	Nicaragua
5	5	5	5	5	5	Panama
120	126	136	135	140	145	Paraguay
36	35	33	32	27	31	Peru
19	11	16	18	13	17	Dominican Republic
-	-	-	-	-	-	Trinidad and Tobago
41	43	36	43	30	50	Venezuela
2 772	2 740	2 6547	2 705	2 757	2 704	Total

292. SUPERFICIE COSECHADA DE PAPAS

(Miles de hectáreas)

País	1960	1965	1970	1975	1977
Argentina	215	204	190	111	111
Bolivia	114	115	95	128	125
Brasil	199	202	214	191	196
Colombia	54	67	84	110	130
Costa Rica	2	3	3	2	2
Cuba	9	8	8	9	12
Chile	90	91	72	72	86
Ecuador	30	44	47	39	36
El Salvador	1	1	-	-	-
Guatemala	4	5	7	11	15
Haití	-	-	-	1	1
Honduras	1	1	1	1	1
Jamaica	1	1	1	2	1
México	44	37	48	57	54
Nicaragua	-	-	-	-	-
Panamá	1	1	1	1	1
Paraguay	1	2	1	1	1
Perú	254	251	289	251	247
República Dominicana	-	1	2	4	2
Uruguay	17	26	21	26	23
Venezuela	18	16	14	14	16
Total	1 055	1 076	1 098	1 028	1 060

292. POTATOES, AREA HARVESTED

(Thousands of hectares)

1978	1979	1980	1981	1982	1983	Country
115	110	112	117	102	108	Argentina
157	163	169	177	174	117	Bolivia
211	204	181	171	182	168	Brazil
142	148	142	160	160	160	Colombia
3	3	3	3	3	4	Costa Rica
10	13	14	16	14	13	Cuba
91	81	89	90	77	81	Chile
30	27	30	32	35	31	Ecuador
-	-	-	-	-	-	El Salvador
16	14	10	7	6	6	Guatemala
1	1	1	1	1	1	Haiti
1	1	1	1	1	1	Honduras
1	1	1	1	1	1	Jamaica
69	87	79	68	68	70	Mexico
-	-	-	-	-	-	Nicaragua
1	1	2	1	2	2	Panama
1	1	1	1	1	1	Paraguay
247	242	194	202	217	158	Peru
2	2	1	1	1	2	Dominican Republic
19	21	13	21	21	22	Uruguay
16	17	18	16	17	18	Venezuela
1 133	1 137	1 061	1 086	1 083	964	*Total*

293. SUPERFICIE COSECHADA DE SOYA

(Miles de hectáreas)

País	1960	1965	1970	1975	1977
Argentina	1	16	26	356	660
Bolivia	-	-	1	9	8
Brasil	171	432	1 319	5 824	7 070
Colombia	10	30	67	88	57
Chile	-	-	1	1	1
Ecuador	-	-	1	8	15
El Salvador	-	-	-	-	1
México	4	27	112	344	314
Nicaragua	-	-	-	1	1
Paraguay	1	11	28	150	229
Perú	-	-	-	1	3
Uruguay	-	1	1	10	10
Total	187	517	1 556	6 792	8 368

293. SOYA BEANS, AREA HARVESTED

(Thousands of hectares)

1978	1979	1980	1981	1982	1983	Country
1 150	1 600	2 030	1 880	1 986	2 116	Argentina
19	28	38	35	49	33	Bolivia
7 782	8 256	8 774	8 501	8 202	8 136	Brazil
69	71	78	44	47	60	Colombia
1	2	1	1	1	1	Chile
17	22	25	21	21	20	Ecuador
1	1	1	1	1	1	El Salvador
217	380	155	378	391	451	Mexico
1	1	1	1	1	1	Nicaragua
272	360	475	410	415	445	Paraguay
3	4	6	8	4	1	Peru
22	51	40	34	21	9	Uruguay
9 554	10 776	11 624	11 314	11 149	11 275	Total

VII. RECURSOS NATURALES Y PRODUCCION DE BIENES

294. SUPERFICIE COSECHADA DE SORGO

(Miles de hectáreas)

País	1960	1965	1970	1975	1977
Argentina	610	820	2 111	2 010	2 461
Bolivia	-	-	-	-	1
Brasil	-	1	1	87	178
Colombia	-	30	54	134	190
Costa Rica	3	4	7	11	25
Cuba	24	13	3	1	1
Ecuador	-	-	-	-	1
El Salvador	87	111	124	132	132
Guatemala	23	49	51	38	39
Haití	260	200	215	140	152
Honduras	65	41	36	56	66
México	116	314	971	1 445	1 413
Nicaragua	51	50	57	60	43
Paraguay	3	3	4	6	7
Perú	1	2	4	10	17
República Dominicana	-	2	4	5	5
Uruguay	33	32	32	54	95
Venezuela	-	2	3	44	156
Total	1 276	1 674	3 677	4 233	4 982

(Thousands of hectares)

1978	1979	1980	1981	1982	1983	Country
2 344	2 123	1 341	2 135	2 510	2 520	Argentina
2	3	6	6	4	₁ 1	Bolivia
104	72	78	92	115	110	Brazil
225	221	206	231	291	275	Colombia
24	18	20	21	16	26	Costa Rica
1	1	1	1	1	1	Cuba
-	-	-	-	1	1	Ecuador
137	143	119	115	119	120	El Salvador
43	47	35	41	31	33	Guatemala
166	157	160	163	155	155	Haiti
66	63	62	58	60	50	Honduras
1 399	1 216	1 579	1 767	1 275	1 896	Mexico
51	50	48	56	39	39	Nicaragua
6	7	7	8	8	7	Paraguay
17	16	12	14	12	6	Peru
4	8	4	6	7	14	Dominican Republic
89	39	50	74	57	70	Uruguay
185	241	212	229	220	163	Venezuela
4 863	4 425	3 940	5 017	4 921	5 487	Total

295. SUPERFICIE COSECHADA DE TRIGO

(Miles de hectáreas)

País	1960	1965	1970	1977	1978
Argentina	3 622	4 601	3 701	3 910	4 685
Bolivia	80	63	63	85	88
Brasil	1 141	767	1 895	3 153	2 811
Colombia	160	120	45	34	30
Chile	833	727	740	628	580
Ecuador	70	69	76	41	27
Guatemala	31	29	33	45	52
Honduras	2	1	1	1	1
México	840	774	886	709	760
Paraguay	12	7	45	29	32
Perú	154	153	136	115	104
Uruguay	520	547	337	321	219
Venezuela	2	2	1	1	1
Total	7 467	7 860	7 959	9 072	9 390

(Thousands of hectares)

1979	1980	1981	1982	1983	Country
4 787	5 023	6 400	7 320	6 832	*Argentina*
98	100	96	104	65	*Bolivia*
3 831	3 122	1 920	2 829	1 922	*Brazil*
31	38	39	43	45	*Colombia*
560	546	432	374	471	*Chile*
30	32	31	33	22	*Ecuador*
59	40	41	37	42	*Guatemala*
1	1	1	1	1	*Honduras*
600	739	861	1 013	990	*Mexico*
52	47	49	70	75	*Paraguay*
96	69	102	84	81	*Peru*
320	227	296	234	300	*Uruguay*
1	1	1	1	1	*Venezuela*
10 466	9 985	10 269	12 143	10 847	*Total*

296. PRODUCCION DE ALGODON SIN DESMOTAR

(Miles de toneladas)

País	1959-1961	1965	1970	1975	1977
Argentina	329	457	458	541	522
Bolivia	2	6	15	67	45
Brasil	1 062	1 305	1 950	1 748	1 900
Colombia	200	179	366	401	481
Costa Rica	3	9	4	1	21
Cuba	13	2	3	3	3
Ecuador	8	18	14	30	27
El Salvador	126	222	128	216	182
Guatemala	60	233	159	307	395
Haití	3	4	2	3	4
Honduras	7	33	9	15	20
México	1 146	1 565	862	544	1 197
Nicaragua	126	331	181	368	375
Paraguay	25	42	39	100	227
Perú	342	357	248	173	210
República Dominicana	6	5	4	3	4
Uruguay	1	1	1	1	1
Venezuela	27	41	40	88	58
Total	3 486	4 810	4 483	4 609	5 672

296. SEED COTTON PRODUCTION

(Thousands of tons)

1978	1979	1980	1981	1982	1983	Country
714	573	485	282	491	373	Argentina
52	43	20	18	12	10	Bolivia
1 570	1 636	1 676	1 732	1 935	1 622	Brazil
330	282	353	270	105	160	Colombia
8	11	12	15	15	15	Costa Rica
3	3	3	3	3	3	Cuba
27	25	40	42	25	29	Ecuador
216	203	186	117	113	109	El Salvador
439	491	464	347	208	150	Guatemala
5	6	4	5	5	5	Haiti
32	25	23	19	12	15	Honduras
1 047	1 037	953	961	534	570	Mexico
421	375	62	224	190	242	Nicaragua
284	235	228	330	300	245	Paraguay
265	300	300	259	200	265	Peru
3	4	6	7	6	4	Dominican Republic
1	-	-	-	-	-	Uruguay
57	49	48	25	18	46	Venezuela
5 454	5 298	4 863	4 656	4 172	3 863	*Total*

297. PRODUCCION DE ARROZ

(Miles de toneladas)

País	1960	1965	1970	1975	1977
Argentina	190	268	407	351	320
Bolivia	40	51	73	127	112
Brasil	4 795	7 580	7 553	7 782	8 994
Colombia	450	672	702	1 614	1 307
Costa Rica	56	85	80	196	169
Cuba	307	50	366	447	459
Chile	107	80	76	76	120
Ecuador	132	157	206	364	328
El Salvador	27	35	44	61	33
Guatemala	14	13	23	46	28
Guyana	214	246	210	292	355
Haití	41	72	80	108	90
Honduras	21	11	13	35	29
Jamaica	3	3	1	3	1
México	328	378	405	717	567
Nicaragua	34	54	81	89	76
Panamá	96	151	131	185	186
Paraguay	18	22	45	45	69
Perú	358	291	587	537	587
República Dominicana	114	167	210	219	308
Trinidad y Tabago	124	10	10	20	21
Uruguay	53	90	139	193	228
Venezuela	72	200	226	363	496
Total	7 482	10 686	11 668	13 870	14 892

297. RICE PRODUCTION

(Thousands of tons)

1978	1979	1980	1981	1982	1983	Country
310	312	266	286	413	277	Argentina
89	76	95	101	86	61	Bolivia
7 296	7 595	9 776	8 228	9 716	7 760	Brazil
1 715	1 932	1 798	1 799	2 018	1 780	Colombia
196	208	180	201	142	212	Costa Rica
457	425	478	461	520	490	Cuba
105	181	95	100	131	107	Chile
225	318	381	434	384	222	Ecuador
51	58	61	50	35	43	El Salvador
26	37	42	23	24	46	Guatemala
305	240	282	276	303	220	Guyana
114	122	85	95	105	95	Haiti
27	32	36	37	38	43	Honduras
2	1	2	2	1	1	Jamaica
402	481	456	644	600	655	Mexico
85	115	112	163	162	172	Nicaragua
162	170	171	195	174	169	Panama
58	57	73	64	54	75	Paraguay
468	560	420	712	765	770	Peru
351	377	398	400	447	496	Dominican Republic
21	22	26	27	30	30	Trinidad and Tobago
226	248	288	330	419	332	Uruguay
502	614	619	681	670	509	Venezuela
13 193	14 181	16 140	15 309	17 237	14 565	Total

298. PRODUCCION DE BANANO Y PLATANO

(Miles de toneladas)

País	1959-1961	1965	1970	1975	1977
Argentina	77	37	223	374	220
Barbados	1	-	1	1	1
Bolivia	148	224	311	393	337
Brasil	3 345	4 531	4 806	5 455	6 415
Colombia	1 865	2 037	2 470	2 842	2 894
Costa Rica	456	604	1 201	1 288	1 194
Cuba	107	36	88	182	220
Ecuador	2 773	3 913	3 360	2 950	3 221
El Salvador	115	18	48	61	65
Guatemala	236	152	529	566	598
Guyana	23	28	29	20	25
Haití	242	429	236	445	474
Honduras	918	1 146	1 458	883	1 388
Jamaica	264	343	207	143	162
México	597	960	965	1 195	1 276
Nicaragua	78	64	79	234	237
Panamá	592	649	1 086	1 089	1 130
Paraguay	149	232	242	198	252
Perú	430	586	640	708	755
República Dominicana	816	740	775	799	845
Trinidad y Tabago	6	28	11	8	8
Venezuela	1 106	1 040	1 338	1 230	1 281
Total	14 344	17 797	20 103	21 064	22 998

(Thousands of tons)

1978	1979	1980	1981	1982	1983	Country
129	144	146	77	89	100	Argentina
1	1	1	1	1	1	Barbados
260	267	276	284	285	276	Bolivia
6 240	6 133	6 721	6 710	6 821	6 692	Brazil
2 242	3 276	3 378	3 555	3 764	3 780	Colombia
1 225	1 159	1 187	1 214	1 212	1 091	Costa Rica
248	231	233	261	272	277	Cuba
2 948	2 705	3 020	2 771	2 753	2 770	Ecuador
67	68	67	68	70	70	El Salvador
610	609	702	702	707	728	Guatemala
26	27	29	16	20	23	Guyana
474	511	490	510	510	510	Haiti
1 417	1 589	1 546	1 576	1 393	1 403	Honduras
190	149	125	124	128	126	Jamaica
1 393	1 045	1 501	1 591	1 572	1 624	Mexico
240	240	231	239	240	242	Nicaragua
1 157	1 164	1 112	1 126	1 140	1 183	Panama
254	306	300	305	314	315	Paraguay
755	795	780	423	460	465	Peru
926	825	901	945	920	925	Dominican Republic
8	8	9	8	8	8	Trinidad and Tobago
1 345	1 310	1 308	1 341	1 351	1 399	Venezuela
22 155	22 562	24 063	23 847	24 030	24 008	*Total*

299. PRODUCCION DE CAFE VERDE

(Miles de toneladas)

País	1960	1965	1970	1975	1977
Bolivia	3	3	11	15	17
Brasil	2 085	2 294	755	1 272	975
Colombia	480	492	507	513	639
Costa Rica	58	61	73	80	87
Cuba	42	24	29	20	17
Ecuador	33	66	72	76	83
El Salvador	93	109	129	165	151
Guatemala	99	123	127	139	168
Guyana	-	1	1	1	1
Haití	26	35	33	39	31
Honduras	23	35	39	47	50
Jamaica	2	2	2	1	1
México	126	161	185	228	182
Nicaragua	24	28	39	49	55
Panamá	4	4	4	5	6
Paraguay	2	7	4	8	6
Perú	33	48	65	65	80
República Dominicana	45	43	42	52	60
Trinidad y Tabago	2	4	2	4	3
Venezuela	59	54	61	65	58
Total	3 239	3 594	2 180	2 848	2 670

(Thousands of tons)

1978	1979	1980	1981	1982	1983	Country
13	16	19	17	17	17	Bolivia
1 268	1 333	1 061	2 032	927	1 680	Brazil
683	713	724	808	840	798	Colombia
99	99	109	120	104	126	Costa Rica
15	26	24	22	26	26	Cuba
75	90	69	86	84	63	Ecuador
162	180	165	161	143	155	El Salvador
170	161	163	173	159	154	Guatemala
1	1	2	2	2	2	Guyana
27	40	28	30	39	35	Haiti
60	73	64	75	71	81	Honduras
2	2	2	2	2	2	Jamaica
242	220	222	244	313	240	Mexico
65	56	59	61	64	67	Nicaragua
6	6	7	7	8	9	Panama
7	8	8	13	16	18	Paraguay
88	105	94	96	90	92	Peru
43	60	60	52	63	48	Dominican Republic
3	2	2	2	2	2	Trinidad and Tobago
59	54	58	60	59	61	Venezuela
3 088	3 245	2 940	4 063	3 029	3 676	Total

300. PRODUCCION DE CAÑA DE AZUCAR

(Miles de toneladas)

País	1960	1965	1970	1975	1977
Argentina	10 089	13 100	9 700	15 600	16 000
Barbados	...	1 760	1 456	845	1 045
Bolivia	925	935	1 468	2 367	3 167
Brasil	56 927	75 853	79 753	91 525	120 082
Colombia	13 399	14 312	12 700	20 500	20 500
Costa Rica	919	1 250	1 886	2 324	2 519
Cuba	55 886	36 846	82 900	52 389	60 353
Ecuador	5 000	8 087	6 500	7 723	7 518
El Salvador	764	1 366	1 587	3 166	3 550
Guatemala	965	2 116	2 633	5 093	6 600
Guyana	3 619	3 460	3 754	3 632	3 291
Haití	5 000	3 248	2 705	2 802	2 801
Honduras	804	808	1 363	1 506	1 845
Jamaica	4 438	4 755	4 121	3 580	3 252
México	19 167	30 956	34 651	35 841	29 397
Nicaragua	1 047	1 189	1 862	2 278	2 666
Panamá	660	951	1 185	1 722	2 396
Paraguay	609	992	1 415	1 038	1 160
Perú	7 616	7 772	8 068	8 440	9 293
República Dominicana	8 675	5 544	8 655	9 337	11 091
Trinidad y Tabago	2 518	2 544	2 610	1 737	1 891
Uruguay	133	183	159	376	622
Venezuela	3 001	4 428	5 027	5 486	5 356
Total	202 161	222 495	276 158	279 307	316 395

(*Thousands of tons*)

1978	1979	1980	1981	1982	1983	Country
13 600	14 120	17 200	15 500	15 046	15 794	Argentina
895	1 052	1 205	966	766	705	Barbados
3 431	3 120	3 080	3 103	2 600	2 590	Bolivia
129 145	138 899	148 651	155 924	186 392	208 256	Brazil
22 950	24 700	26 100	25 900	26 800	28 000	Colombia
2 579	2 615	2 516	2 522	2 500	2 500	Costa Rica
69 653	77 311	63 977	66 678	70 500	66 000	Cuba
6 928	6 599	6 615	6 278	5 421	4 800	Ecuador
3 692	3 214	2 207	1 921	2 282	2 609	El Salvador
5 360	4 830	5 409	5 680	6 080	6 624	Guatemala
4 286	3 954	3 658	4 191	3 906	3 600	Guyana
2 844	2 900	3 000	3 000	3 000	3 000	Haiti
2 164	2 600	2 820	3 000	3 100	3 100	Honduras
3 641	2 965	2 816	2 521	2 575	2 655	Jamaica
35 475	34 587	36 480	34 905	34 066	36 000	Mexico
2 734	2 742	2 175	2 459	2 827	3 000	Nicaragua
2 757	2 624	2 386	2 062	2 094	2 590	Panama
1 260	1 287	1 373	1 550	1 350	1 350	Paraguay
8 423	7 506	6 033	5 129	6 725	6 664	Peru
11 094	10 304	9 056	9 629	10 921	11 150	Dominican Republic
1 550	1 600	1 499	1 299	1 201	1 006	Trinidad and Tobago
475	323	448	420	480	495	Uruguay
4 828	4 769	4 987	4 531	4 968	5 132	Venezuela
339 764	354 621	353 691	359 168	395 600	417 620	Total

301. PRODUCCION DE FRIJOLES SECOS

(Miles de toneladas)

País	1960	1965	1970	1975	1977
Argentina	27	38	40	109	155
Bolivia	2	3	1	2	2
Brasil	1 731	2 290	2 211	2 282	2 290
Colombia	40	40	39	90	75
Costa Rica	14	23	10	15	14
Cuba	35	25	22	25	25
Chile	74	59	66	74	112
Ecuador	19	31	41	26	26
El Salvador	10	21	30	40	34
Guatemala	31	57	65	65	67
Haití	17	41	40	44	47
Honduras	36	43	43	32	30
México	528	860	925	1 027	770
Nicaragua	28	49	56	44	41
Panamá	6	4	5	4	3
Paraguay	18	19	32	50	71
Perú	43	48	63	58	56
República Dominicana	27	23	25	36	36
Uruguay	4	4	3	2	3
Venezuela	79	37	33	37	28
Total	2 769	3 715	3 750	4 062	3 885

(Thousands of tons)

1978	1979	1980	1981	1982	1983	Country
133	235	146	224	254	217	Argentina
4	4	4	4	4	4	Bolivia
2 194	2 186	1 968	2 341	2 906	1 592	Brazil
75	75	84	93	73	88	Colombia
14	11	12	12	14	20	Costa Rica
25	26	26	26	27	27	Cuba
112	116	84	138	162	84	Chile
19	23	26	30	29	34	Ecuador
43	47	50	38	38	42	El Salvador
81	85	80	81	84	89	Guatemala
46	52	45	50	50	50	Haiti
42	34	36	42	47	44	Honduras
949	641	971	1 469	1 093	1 427	Mexico
55	29	28	59	47	47	Nicaragua
4	3	2	3	2	2	Panama
65	58	58	68	70	65	Paraguay
54	55	39	44	43	38	Peru
42	50	49	52	58	60	Dominican Republic
3	3	3	3	3	3	Uruguay
34	31	33	33	27	28	Venezuela
3 994	3 764	3 744	4 810	5 0431	3 961	Total

302. PRODUCCION DE MAIZ

(Miles de toneladas)

País	1960	1965	1970	1975	1977
Argentina	4 108	5 140	9 360	7 700	8 300
Barbados	1	1	2	2	2
Bolivia	248	277	286	305	305
Brasil	8 672	12 112	14 216	16 335	19 256
Colombia	866	871	877	723	753
Costa Rica	57	93	47	68	85
Cuba	214	117	85	94	95
Chile	161	270	239	329	355
Ecuador	160	191	256	273	218
El Salvador	178	203	363	439	380
Guatemala	506	646	786	934	842
Guyana	1	1	2	6	3
Haití	227	234	240	180	168
Honduras	262	334	339	358	439
Jamaica	3	4	4	11	9
México	5 420	8 936	8 879	8 449	10 138
Nicaragua	119	171	236	192	181
Panamá	63	86	56	65	80
Paraguay	143	210	220	301	401
Perú	442	557	615	635	734
República Dominicana	52	38	45	46	65
Trinidad y Tabago	2	2	2	5	4
Uruguay	78	63	189	157	121
Venezuela	439	521	710	653	774
Total	22 422	31 078	38 054	38 260	43 708

(Thousands of tons)

1978	1979	1980	1981	1982	1983	Country
9 700	8 700	6 400	12 900	9 600	8 840	Argentina
2	2	2	2	2	2	Barbados
337	378	383	504	450	336	Bolivia
13 569	16 306	20 372	21 117	21 865	18 756	Brazil
862	870	854	880	899	867	Colombia
62	73	65	88	85	113	Costa Rica
95	95	95	95	96	96	Cuba
257	489	405	518	425	512	Chile
176	218	242	281	324	258	Ecuador
507	523	529	500	414	444	El Salvador
906	941	902	997	1 100	1 046	Guatemala
2	2	2	1	2	2	Guyana
161	183	175	185	170	180	Haiti
455	354	387	481	509	470	Honduras
8	6	4	4	3	3	Jamaica
10 930	8 752	12 383	14 766	10 129	13 928	Mexico
254	173	182	198	164	227	Nicaragua
64	64	54	57	63	68	Panama
355	550	585	521	510	600	Paraguay
590	621	453	587	625	583	Peru
66	38	35	41	28	38	Dominican Republic
4	3	3	3	3	3	Trinidad and Tobago
172	71	126	181	97	103	Uruguay
591	612	575	452	501	429	Venezuela
40 125	40 0024	45 213	55 359	48 064	47 904	Total

303. PRODUCCION DE MANDIOCA

(Miles de toneladas)

País	1960	1965	1970	1975	1977
Argentina	277	260	292	300	183
Barbados	...	1	1	1	1
Bolivia	63	150	221	285	294
Brasil	17 613	24 993	29 464	26 118	25 929
Colombia	680	800	1 200	2 021	1 973
Costa Rica	6	10	13	12	14
Cuba	255	200	220	246	262
Ecuador	220	254	371	354	224
El Salvador	8	10	11	17	13
Guatemala	5	5	6	7	8
Guyana	11	10	-	-	-
Haití	110	112	130	235	250
Honduras	14	26	28	10	8
Jamaica	13	9	12	19	28
México	...	...	...	56	66
Nicaragua	11	14	17	22	25
Panamá	45	20	35	40	40
Paraguay	979	1 512	1 580	1 428	1 719
Perú	414	449	498	424	414
República Dominicana	153	152	170	191	185
Trinidad y Tabago	4	3	3	5	5
Venezuela	340	301	317	317	304
Total	21 221	29 291	34 589	32 108	31 945

(Thousands of tons)

1978	1979	1980	1981	1982	1983	Country
182	183	222	200	216	220	Argentina
1	1	1	1	1	1	Barbados
211	201	219	191	271	179	Bolivia
25 459	24 962	23 466	24 515	24 009	22 096	Brazil
2 044	1 909	2 150	2 150	2 174	2 180	Colombia
14	15	18	19	17	28	Costa Rica
312	320	325	330	330	335	Cuba
168	183	229	237	184	240	Ecuador
15	20	20	25	23	24	El Salvador
8	8	8	8	9	9	Guatemala
-	-	-	-	-	-	Guyana
261	254	250	255	260	265	Haiti
8	9	7	7	7	7	Honduras
30	24	23	22	17	18	Jamaica
39	33	20	30	43	43	Mexico
26	24	26	26	27	27	Nicaragua
40	40	34	34	35	35	Panama
1 838	1 888	2 031	2 000	2 100	2 200	Paraguay
410	403	400	327	295	347	Peru
185	119	81	94	68	93	Dominican Republic
5	5	4	4	3	3	Trinidad and Tobago
304	315	312	327	342	365	Venezuela
31 560	30 916	29 846	30 802	30 431	28 715	Total

304. PRODUCCION DE PAPAS

(Miles de toneladas)

País	1960	1965	1970	1975	1977
Argentina	1 860	2 489	2 336	1 349	1 769
Bolivia	605	575	655	834	659
Brasil	1 113	1 246	1 583	1 655	1 896
Colombia	653	762	913	1 320	1 609
Costa Rica	15	25	28	24	25
Cuba	109	83	77	117	137
Chile	700	703	684	738	928
Ecuador	203	396	542	499	417
El Salvador	3	5	3	7	2
Guatemala	12	23	30	46	63
Guyana	...	...	...	-	-
Haití	...	6	7	7	8
Honduras	2	3	4	4	4
Jamaica	10	13	8	14	8
México	294	319	508	693	631
Nicaragua	1	1	1	2	2
Panamá	4	10	6	9	11
Paraguay	4	9	4	4	5
Perú	1 398	1 568	1 896	1 640	1 616
República Dominicana	6	16	23	27	12
Uruguay	59	125	118	121	120
Venezuela	134	136	125	152	179
Total	7 185	8 513	9 532	9 2628	10 101

304. PRODUCTION OF POTATOES

(Thousands of tons)

1978	1979	1980	1981	1982	1983	Country
1 593	1 694	1 568	2 247	1 817	2 013	Argentina
738	730	786	867	900	303	Bolivia
2 014	2 154	1 940	1 912	2 148	1 819	Brazil
1 996	1 966	1 727	2 100	2 000	2 000	Colombia
26	27	27	28	22	35	Costa Rica
198	201	239	273	258	222	Cuba
981	770	903	1 007	842	684	Chile
343	255	323	392	416	394	Ecuador
4	4	6	6	6	6	El Salvador
61	51	33	34	28	30	Guatemala
-	-	-	-	-	-	Guyana
9	10	9	9	9	9	Haiti
6	6	8	8	8	9	Honduras
12	11	7	14	7	8	Jamaica
923	1 053	1 042	861	941	910	Mexico
2	2	2	2	2	2	Nicaragua
9	12	17	20	17	15	Panama
7	9	9	9	9	9	Paraguay
1 695	1 695	1 380	1 705	1 796	1 193	Peru
12	11	7	11	12	18	Dominican Republic
102	135	110	177	149	160	Uruguay
171	191	199	171	217	238	Venezuela
10 902	10 987	10 342	11 853	11 604	10 077	Total

305. PRODUCCION DE SOYA

(Miles de toneladas)

País	1960	1965	1970	1975	1977
Argentina	1	17	27	485	1 400
Bolivia	-	-	2	12	11
Brasil	206	523	1 509	9 893	12 513
Colombia	19	50	132	169	103
Chile	-	-	1	1	1
Ecuador	-	-	1	12	19
El Salvador	-	-	-	-	1
México	5	58	215	599	516
Nicaragua	-	-	-	1	1
Paraguay	2	18	40	220	377
Perú	-	1	-	1	3
Uruguay	-	1	1	17	14
Total	233	668	1 928	11 410	14 959

(Thousands of tons)

1978	1979	1980	1981	1982	1983	Country
2 500	3 700	3 500	3 770	4 150	3 750	Argentina
26	41	48	58	78	52	Bolivia
9 541	10 240	15 156	15 007	12 835	14 582	Brazil
131	146	155	89	100	120	Colombia
1	2	1	1	1	1	Chile
25	30	34	33	37	35	Ecuador
1	1	1	1	1	1	El Salvador
334	702	312	712	672	880	Mexico
1	1	1	1	1	1	Nicaragua
333	549	537	630	690	780	Paraguay
5	7	11	14	80	2	Peru
29	40	49	45	28	12	Uruguay
12 927	15 459	19 805	20 361	18 673	20 216	Total

653

306. PRODUCCION DE SORGO

(Miles de toneladas)

País	1960	1965	1970	1975	1977
Argentina	831	1 059	4 068	4 938	6 730
Brasil	...	2	2	202	435
Colombia	-	70	118	335	406
Costa Rica	5	7	11	20	41
Cuba	32	15	3	1	1
Ecuador	-	-	-	-	1
El Salvador	82	106	147	175	151
Guatemala	14	44	46	62	53
Haití	183	187	210	135	111
Honduras	53	53	46	52	49
México	209	747	2 747	4 126	4 325
Nicaragua	39	46	61	63	43
Paraguay	4	4	5	8	9
Perú	2	4	12	29	55
República Dominicana	...	7	14	17	19
Uruguay	14	16	36	77	162
Venezuela	-	4	7	70	280
Total	1 468	2 371	7 533	10 310	12 871

306. SORGHUM PRODUCTION

(Thousands of tons)

1978	1979	1980	1981	1982	1983	Country
7 360	6 297	3 023	7 603	8 060	8 250	Argentina
228	122	180	213	211	213	Brazil
517	501	431	532	568	579	Colombia
53	34	40	42	28	51	Costa Rica
1	1	1	1	1	1	Cuba
-	-	-	1	3	3	Ecuador
162	160	140	136	124	102	El Salvador
65	76	78	86	77	81	Guatemala
100	123	110	110	110	115	Haiti
48	38	52	58	58	51	Honduras
4 193	3 708	4 812	6 296	4 717	6 367	Mexico
64	63	88	89	84	89	Nicaragua
8	9	9	10	10	10	Paraguay
59	55	35	44	38	15	Peru
12	23	11	19	16	39	Dominican Republic
184	54	84	192	123	106	Uruguay
340	396	353	347	377	280	Venezuela
13 394	11 660	9 447	15 779	14 605	19 352	*Total*

307. PRODUCCION DE TRIGO

(Miles de toneladas)

País	1960	1965	1970	1975	1977
Argentina	4 200	6 079	4 920	8 570	5 300
Bolivia	68	55	44	62	56
Brasil	713	585	1 844	1 788	2 066
Colombia	142	110	54	39	29
Chile	1 044	1 116	1 307	1 003	1 219
Ecuador	58	61	81	65	40
Guatemala	21	27	36	45	56
Honduras	1	1	1	1	1
México	1 190	1 659	2 676	2 798	2 456
Paraguay	9	7	33	18	28
Perú	146	147	125	126	115
Uruguay	420	620	388	456	173
Venezuela	1	1	1	1	1
Total	8 013	10 468	11 510	14 972	11 540

(Thousands of tons)

1978	1979	1980	1981	1982	1983	Country
8 100	8 100	7 780	8 300	15 130	11 700	Argentina
57	68	60	67	66	37	Bolivia
2 691	2 927	2 702	2 209	1 849	2 273	Brazil
38	42	46	62	69	73	Colombia
893	995	966	686	650	800	Chile
29	31	31	41	39	23	Ecuador
60	57	58	55	49	40	Guatemala
1	1	1	1	1	1	Honduras
2 785	2 273	2 785	3 189	4 468	3 697	Mexico
38	58	43	61	70	85	Paraguay
104	102	77	119	101	75	Peru
174	430	307	388	316	450	Uruguay
1	-	-	-	-	-	Venezuela
14 971	15 084	14 856	15 178	22 808	19 254	Total

308. CONSUMO TOTAL DE FERTILIZANTES

(Toneladas)

País	1959-1960	1964-1965	1969-1970	1974-1975	1976-1977
Argentina	12 520	29 500	79 554	75 100	78 229
Barbados	5 511	9 146	4 999	500	4 800
Bolivia	410	1 450	2 912	6 000	32 900
Brasil	164 663	216 948	630 384	1 824 637	2 528 141
Colombia	...	161 243	140 606	263 600	246 079
Costa Rica	...	33 000	54 180	72 500	55 692
Cuba	...	201 000	466 700	302 400	355 600
Chile	38 719	108 419	150 404	170 670	119 730
Ecuador	6 798	10 497	41 397	40 867	81 384
El Salvador	...	50 056	54 000	98 600	102 196
Guatemala	10 345	18 778	32 745	64 607	94 533
Guyana	8 155	7 571	10 809	16 300	10 000
Haití	1 042	100	269	1 616	300
Honduras	7 097	7 800	22 500	18 700	25 400
Jamaica	7 363	21 773	22 800	25 600	13 000
México	187 600	288 158	560 79	864 487	1 120 262
Nicaragua	...	10 400	27 146	35 400	47 894
Panamá	...	11 000	19 300	27 719	22 700
Paraguay	...	1 437	2 900	1 758	1 000
Perú	...	83 177	81 587	142 066	129 000
República Dominicana	8 718	10 000	30 300	98 076	75 800
Trinidad y Tabago	...	6 000	8 200	8 794	7 432
Uruguay	31 120	40 785	59 808	67 900	74 000
Venezuela	11 873	33 000	47 032	128 605	160 997
Total		1 361 238	2 551 330	4 362 502	5 387 069

308. TOTAL CONSUMPTION OF FERTILIZERS

(Tons)

1977-1978	1978-1979	1979-1980	1980-1981	1981-1982	1982-1983	Country
74 305	107 075	130 082	116 000	96 000	113 000	Argentina
3 591	5 400	5 700	5 800	6 000	6 000	Barbados
3 614	4 640	3 255	3 000	7 000	3 000	Bolivia
3 208 894	3 216 018	3 563 000	4 219 000	2 747 000	2 729 000	Brazil
281 700	276 214	294 224	303 500	285 000	306 000	Colombia
66 543	79 880	79 100	73 500	74 000	72 000	Costa Rica
418 000	451 000	464 400	528 900	601 000	555 000	Cuba
98 682	129 442	120 806	132 000	112 000	105 000	Chile
85 938	71 367	79 359	72 579	69 000	73 000	Ecuador
105 606	111 530	74 700	60 000	88 000	60 000	El Salvador
103 428	95 314	100 400	86 000	99 000	89 000	Guatemala
9 695	10 000	11 000	16 000	18 000	8 000	Guyana
3 100	3 600	3 900	400	6 000	5 000	Haiti
27 900	23 400	19 500	29 000	31 000	24 000	Honduras
14 800	15 962	13 341	17 506	19 000	15 000	Jamaica
1 067 732	1 066 615	1 134 400	1 238 000	1 561 000	1 825 000	Mexico
48 358	48 499	22 900	54 200	60 000	23 000	Nicaragua
23 000	23 000	30 000	31 000	30 000	27 000	Panama
1 100	2 800	5 856	6 320	9 000	8 000	Paraguay
139 000	137 000	117 000	118 000	132 000	93 000	Peru
50 000	57 078	71 925	51 800	58 000	51 000	Dominican Republic
6 000	8 000	8 000	8 000	7 000	5 000	Trinidad and Tobago
63 200	58 000	91 760	80 900	64 000	55 000	Uruguay
175 611	196 800	222 083	241 125	146 000	153 000	Venezuela
6 079 797	6 198 634	6 666 691	7 378 130	6 325 000	6 400 000	Total

309. PARQUE DE TRACTORES

(Unidades en servicio)

País	1960	1965	1970	1975	1978
Argentina	110 643	155 000	168 350	188 000	173 000
Barbados	...	350	415	480	530
Bolivia	...	250	350	759	726
Brasil	63 493	108 900	165 870	254 000	300 000
Colombia	23 539	24 800	27 872	24 187	26 500
Costa Rica	...	4 850	5 100	5 650	5 850
Cuba	...	30 000	51 600	54 851	66 349
Chile	...	23 000	21 520	20 800	34 500
Ecuador	1 550	2 000	3 100	5 100	5 564
El Salvador	...	1 800	2 500	2 900	3 150
Guatemala	...	2 550	3 150	3 700	3 900
Guyana	...	3 414	3 650	3 380	3 420
Haití	244	300	360	440	480
Honduras	...	395	1 700	2 900	3 080
Jamaica	...	3 940	1 745	2 500	2 700
México	...	84 000	115 230	130 000	108 259
Nicaragua	...	4 800	500	1 058	1 900
Panamá	...	1 250	2 400	3 700	3 900
Paraguay	...	1 700	2 200	2 700	3 000
Perú	...	8 500	10 976	12 500	13 300
República Dominicana	...	2 800	4 200	2 800	3 000
Trinidad y Tabago	...	1 700	1 850	2 100	2 250
Uruguay	...	24 800	26 677	27 500	27 900
Venezuela	...	15 900	19 200	28 644	35 000
Total	...	506 999	640 515	780 949	888 970

(Units in service)

1979	1980	1981	1982	Country
171 400	166 700	158 900	154 000	Argentina
540	550	560	570	Barbados
750	750	740	750	Bolivia
320 000	330 000	340 000	345 000	Brazil
27 500	28 423	28 500	28 600	Colombia
5 900	5 950	6 000	6 050	Costa Rica
70 374	68 300	64 500	64 700	Cuba
34 550	34 600	34 650	34 700	Chile
5 650	6 198	6 844	7 200	Ecuador
3 250	3 300	3 320	3 340	El Salvador
3 950	4 000	4 020	4 040	Guatemala
3 440	3 460	3 480	3 500	Guyana
500	520	530	540	Haiti
3 160	3 250	3 280	3 300	Honduras
2 750	2 800	2 870	2 900	Jamaica
114 000	115 057	143 078	158 000	Mexico
2 100	2 200	2 250	2 300	Nicaragua
3 950	4 000	4 050	4 100	Panama
3 100	3 200	3 300	3 400	Paraguay
13 600	13 900	14 300	14 600	Peru
3 050	3 150	3 220	3 250	Dominican Republic
2 300	2 350	2 420	2 450	Trinidad and Tobago
28 000	33 878	33 470	33 550	Uruguay
37 000	38 000	39 000	40 000	Venezuela
860 814	873 536	903 282	920 840	*Total*

310. INDICES DE VOLUMEN FISICO DE LA PRODUCCION MINERA

a) Incluido el petróleo
(Año base 1970 = 100)

País	1960	1965	1970	1975	1977
Argentina	48.7	70.0	100.0	98.7	105.3
Bolivia	58.8	72.0	100.0	115.2	118.2
Brasil	37.7	57.7	100.0	191.6	188.7
Colombia	82.0	99.2	100.0	87.1	84.7
Cuba	47.7	81.2	100.0	102.5	100.8
Chile	77.6	88.8	100.0	118.6	147.0
Ecuador	145.0	145.7	100.0	2 575.7	2 972.3
El Salvador	48.7	3.0	100.0	177.8	78.3
Guatemala	42.6	4.4	100.0	58.0	61.9
Guyana	48.5	66.0	100.0	87.9	76.4
Haití	36.2	93.8	100.0	42.2	55.1
Honduras	47.2	74.9	100.0	123.7	110.6
Jamaica	48.5	72.0	100.0	95.6	94.4
México	79.2	85.1	100.0	133.1	165.2
Nicaragua	172.6	242.8	100.0	46.7	37.0
Perú	75.4	84.0	100.0	90.5	131.6
República Dominicana	60.7	78.6	100.0	67.9	50.7
Suriname	57.6	72.7	100.0	78.8	77.7
Trinidad y Tabago	83.0	95.7	100.0	154.0	163.7
Venezuela	77.5	93.1	100.0	65.0	60.4
Total	71.8	86.0	100.0	99.9	110.8

310. QUANTUM INDEXES OF MINING PRODUCTION

a) **Including petroleum**
(Base year 1970 = 100)

1978	1979	1980	1981	1982	1983	Country
109 9	116.2	117.9	119.9	118.6	118.3	Argentina
106.6	95.2	98.6	103.5	93.6	84.9	Bolivia
197.0	215.1	267.7	187.4	206.4	224.4	Brazil
85.2	83.7	95.2	98.1	103.4	105.5	Colombia
96.4	90.1	105.7	111.5	106.1	110.4	Cuba
143.5	149.2	150.4	157.7	176.5	176.1	Chile
3 247.7	3 325.2	3 321.9	3 406.0	3 386.8	3 803.4	Ecuador
132.1	102.6	102.1	96.8	68.3	68.3	El Salvador
15.5	43.2	37.6	35.0	33.6	33.8	Guatemala
79.7	76.5	69.8	55.6	40.9	25.3	Guyana
51.4	45.2	37.3	43.5	30.7	30.9	Haiti
107.4	84.7	67.8	66.2	83.8	87.7	Honduras
96.9	95.0	99.7	95.9	67.4	63.8	Jamaica
186.8	216.4	232.0	277.9	336.2	330.2	Mexico
40.6	36.6	32.6	25.8	24.3	24.0	Nicaragua
146.1	156.2	154.5	149.2	162.9	154.3	Perú
50.0	46.1	44.9	35.7	13.4	13.2	Dominican Republic
87.8	78.7	81.4	66.5	54.4	46.4	Suriname
164.0	153.2	152.0	135.3	126.5	114.2	Trinidad and Tobago
58.5	63.7	58.9	57.4	51.1	57.5	Venezuela
113.9	121.7	125.7	126.1	134.7	136.3	Total

310. **INDICES DE VOLUMEN FISICO DE LA PRODUCCION MINERA** (conclusión)

b) **Excluido el petróleo**
(Año base 1970 = 100)

País	1960	1965	1970	1975	1977
Argentina	72.6	78.6	100.0	86.6	93.2
Bolivia	60.2	74.6	100.0	111.2	116.3
Brasil	33.6	58.2	100.0	225.2	223.8
Colombia	113.6	119.0	100.0	127.1	141.0
Cuba	48.2	81.6	100.0	101.4	99.4
Chile	78.0	88.5	100.0	119.5	148.9
Ecuador	67.8	58.7	100.0	55.4	167.4
El Salvador	11.7	3.0	100.0	177.8	78.3
Guatemala	42.6	4.4	100.0	58.0	61.9
Guyana	48.5	66.0	100.0	87.9	76.4
Haití	36.2	93.8	100.0	42.2	55.1
Honduras	47.2	74.9	100.0	123.7	110.6
Jamaica	48.5	72.0	100.0	95.6	94.4
México	92.0	92.8	100.0	109.9	123.9
Nicaragua	172.6	242.8	100.0	46.7	37.0
Perú	75.5	83.7	100.0	89.7	132.0
República Dominicana	60.7	78.6	100.0	67.9	50.7
Suriname	57.6	72.7	100.0	78.8	77.7
Venezuela	89.8	79.8	100.0	109.1	62.0
Total	71.9	83.4	100.0	117.2	135.3

310. QUANTUM INDEXES OF MINING PRODUCTION (concluded)

b) **Excluding petroleum**
(Base year 1970 = 100)

1978	1979	1980	1981	1982	1983	Country
79.6	92.7	75.5	81.4	82.6	80.5	Argentina
104.4	93.6	98.6	104.4	93.0	84.7	Bolivia
235.3	259.1	327.9	210.0	225.7	234.6	Brazil
150.9	153.3	192.1	193.4	202.7	198.1	Colombia
94.7	88.2	104.3	109.2	101.8	106.1	Cuba
145.4	151.0	151.5	158.5	177.5	177.4	Chile
124.9	156.9	191.0	152.4	99.5	95.4	Ecuador
132.1	102.6	102.1	96.8	68.3	68.3	El Salvador
15.5	43.2	37.6	35.0	33.6	33.8	Guatemala
79.7	76.5	69.8	55.6	40.9	25.2	Guyana
51.4	45.2	37.3	43.5	30.7	30.9	Haiti
107.4	84.7	67.8	66.2	84.0	87.7	Honduras
96.9	95.0	99.7	95.9	67.4	63.8	Jamaica
125.2	133.5	152.9	172.5	173.2	168.4	Mexico
40.6	36.6	32.6	25.8	24.3	24.0	Nicaragua
141.0	147.4	145.3	139.7	154.3	147.6	Peru
50.0	46.1	44.9	35.7	13.4	13.2	Dominican Republic
87.8	78.7	81.4	66.5	54.4	46.4	Suriname
60.5	67.7	71.1	67.8	51.9	41.5	Venezuela
136.3	141.7	151.7	145.0	152.5	150.0	Total

311. PRODUCCION DE BAUXITA [1]

(Miles de toneladas)

País	1960	1965	1970	1975	1977
Brasil	120.8	193.4	480.8	969.0	1 040.2
Guyana	2 141.2	2 918.7	4 417.2	3 829.0	3 344.3
Haití [2]	346.0	428.0	656.8	522.1	685.0
Jamaica	5 872.0	8 721.7	12 105.9	11 570.3	11 433.6
República Dominicana	689.0	893.0	1 086.3	771.6	576.0
Suriname	3 454.9	4 359.9	6 011.0	4 749.0	4 856.0
Total	12 623.9	17 514.7	24 758.0	22 411.0	21 935.1

[1] Mineral.
[2] Exportaciones.

312. PRODUCCION DE CARBON

(Miles de toneladas)

País	1960	1965	1970	1975	1977
Argentina [1]	271.2	373.9	615.5	502.1	533.3
Brasil [2]	1 277.0	2 186.0	2 361.3	2 817.0	3 859.0
Colombia [2][3]	2 600.0	3 072.0	2 500.0	3 175.1	3 800.0
Chile [3]	1 365.0	1 629.0	1 382.4	1 392.4	1 270.9
México [4]	1 771.0	2 005.7	2 959.2	5 193.6	6 594.0
Perú [5]	162.2	128.9	156.1	85.0	85.0
Venezuela	35.3	29.9	40.0	60.1	120.8
Total	7 481.7	9 425.4	10 014.5	13 225.3	16 263.0

[1] Desde 1965 las cifras corresponden a cantidad neta de carbón.
[2] Desde 1970 las cifras se refieren a carbón bituminoso.
[3] Producción neta.
[4] Volumen de mineral "todo uno" (antes de cualquier proceso).
[5] Carbón antracito y bituminoso.

311. BAUXITE PRODUCTION[1]

(Thousands of tons)

1978	1979	1980	1981	1982	1983	Country
1 130.6	1 642.2	4 152.4	4 662.1	4 187.0	5 238.7	*Brazil*
3 479.0	3 354.0	3 052.0	2 395.9	1 783.1	1 087.3	*Guyana*
639.0	560.0	461.0	539.0	377.0	-	*Haiti[2]*
11 735.8	11 505.0	12 064.3	11 606.0	8 158.0	7 725.0	*Jamaica*
568.1	524.1	510.5	405.4	152.3	-	*Dominican Republic*
5 288.0	4 327.6	4 903.1	4 006.0	3 276.3	2 793.0	*Suriname*
22 840.5	21 912.9	25 143.3	23 614.4	17 933.7	16 844.0	*Total*

[1] *Bauxite mined.*
[2] *Exports.*

312. COAL PRODUCTION

(Thousands of tons)

1978	1979	1980	1981	1982	1983	Country
434.0	726.0	389.0	498.0	516.0	492.0	*Argentina[1]*
4 284.0	4 644.0	4 984.6	5 481.0	6 162.1	6 593.2	*Brazil[2]*
4 200.0	4 300.0	...	...	...	...	*Colombia[2][3]*
1 089.8	915.0	995.6	1 147.1	975.1	1 077.8	*Chile[3]*
7 100.0	7 391.0	...	...	...	...	*Mexico[4]*
85.0	85.0	...	...	...	...	*Peru[5]*
80.6	55.6	39.4	48.2	55.2	36.0	*Venezuela*
17 273.4	18 116.6	...	...	...	...	*Total*

[1] *From 1965 onwards, the figures refer to net quantity of coal.*
[2] *From 1970 onwards, the figures refer to bituminous coal.*
[3] *Net production.*
[4] *Volume "run-of-mine" coal (before any kind of processing).*
[5] *Anthracite and bituminous coal.*

667

313. PRODUCCION DE COBRE [1]

(Miles de toneladas)

País	1960	1965	1970	1975	1977
Argentina	0.6	0.5	0.5	0.4	0.2
Bolivia [2]	2.3	4.7	8.8	6.2	3.2
Brasil	1.1	2.0	3.9	1.9	-
Colombia	-	-	0.1	0.1	0.7
Cuba	11.8	6.0	3.0	2.8	2.6
Chile	536.4	605.9	710.7	831.0	1 053.5
Ecuador	0.1	0.1	0.6	0.2	1.0
Haití	0.9	5.9	4.8	-	-
México	60.3	69.2	61.0	78.2	89.7
Nicaragua	4.9	9.9	3.0	0.6	0.3
Perú	184.0	180.3	220.2	176.0	336.4
República Dominicana	-	-	0.4	-	-
Total	802.4	884.5	1 017.0	1 097.4	1 487.6

[1] Contenido metálico.
[2] Exportaciones.

314. PRODUCCION DE ESTAÑO

(Toneladas)

País	1960	1965	1970	1975	1977
Argentina	242.0	1 225.0	1 172.0	538.0	537.0
Bolivia [1]	19 718.0	24 210.0	27 836.0	31 952.0	33 740.0
Brasil	1 581.0	1 219.0	3 610.0	4 550.0	6 400.0
México	371.0	511.0	533.0	378.0	220.0
Perú	6.0	49.9	102.9	274.0	366.0
Total	21 918.0	27 214.9	33 253.9	37 692.0	41 263.0

[1] Se refiere a exportaciones de concentrados de estaño.

313. COPPER PRODUCTION [1]

(Thousands of tons)

1978	1979	1980	1981	1982	1983	Country
0.3	0.1	0.2	0.1	0.1	0.5	Argentina
2.8	1.9	1.9	1.7	2.3	2.0	Bolivia [2]
0.1	-	1.4	13.9	19.2	33.0	Brazil
0.5	1.1	1.4	0.7	0.1	0.2	Colombia
2.8	2.8	3.3	2.9	2.6	2.7	Cuba
1 029.5	1 067.8	1 063.0	1 106.0	1 255.0	1 255.0	Chile
0.8	1.2	0.9	0.8	-	-	Ecuador
-	-	-	-	-	-	Haiti
87.2	107.1	175.4	230.5	239.1	206.1	Mexico
0.1	0.1	-	-	-	-	Nicaragua
376.3	391.7	367.0	327.6	369.0	336.0	Peru
-	-	-	-	-	-	Dominican Republic
1 500.4	**1 573.8**	**1 614.8**	**1 684.2**	**1 887.4**	**1 835.5**	**Total**

[1] Metal content.
[2] Exports.

314. TIN PRODUCTION

(Tons)

1978	1979	1980	1981	1982	1983	Country
362.0	386.0	351.0	413.0	300.0	300.0	Argentina
30 881.0	27 648.0	27 270.0	29 801.0	26 773.0	25 278.0	Bolivia [1]
6 370.0	6 645.0	6 930.0	8 297.0	8 218.0	13 083.0	Brazil
73.0	23.0	60.0	28.0	27.0	50.0	Mexico
736.0	949.0	1 077.0	1 519 0	1 700.0	2 200.0	Peru
38 422.0	**35 651.0**	**35 688.0**	**40 058.0**	**37 018.0**	**40 911.0**	**Total**

[1] It refers to exports of tin concentrates.

VII. RECURSOS NATURALES Y PRODUCCION DE BIENES

315. PRODUCCION DE HIERRO [1]

(Miles de toneladas)

País	1960	1965	1970	1975	1977
Argentina	58.4	54.3	107.3	139.2	543.6
Bolivia [2][3]	-	-	4.2	11.0	4.0
Brasil	6 355.0	13 725.0	24 739.0	73 550.0	68 556.0
Colombia	178.0	350.0	454.0	537.4	459.9
Chile	3 804.3	7 763.0	6 939.9	6 834.1	8 021.4
Guatemala [3]	4.1	8.5	2.0	-	-
México	521.4	1 592.7	2 612.4	3 369.3	3 587.2
Perú	2 818.2	4 038.7	6 249.4	5 067.0	4 107.0
Venezuela	12 473.9	11 206.7	14 080.0	15 359.0	8 483.0
Total	26 213.3	38 739.0	55 188.2	104 867.0	93 762.1

[1] Contenido metálico.
[2] Exportaciones.
[3] Mineral.

316. PRODUCCION DE PETROLEO

(Miles de m[3])

País	1960	1965	1970	1975	1977
Argentina	10 152.9	15 624.7	22 793.2	22 979.5	24 494.3
Barbados	-	-	-	19.5	19.7
Bolivia	568.2	533.7 [1]	1 402.2	2 342.2	2 015.2
Brasil	4 708.5	5 460.3	9 685.6	9 978.9	9 332.0
Colombia	8 865.8	11 637.6	12 725.5	9 102.4	7 983.7
Cuba	14.7	60.0	267.4	238.3	269.8
Chile	1 149.6	2 019.8	1 976.5	1 422.3	1 131.9
Ecuador	438.3	453.1	229.7	9 345.5	10 643.6
México [2]	17 293.0	21 008.0	29 235.0	46 782.0	62 993.0
Perú	3 061.2	3 667.1	4 176.0	4 179.9	5 294.1
Trinidad y Tabago	6 739.0	7 773.3	8 114.3	12 496.6	13 292.0
Venezuela	165 613.4	201 533.0	215 177.0	136 124.4	129.857.8
Total	218 604.6	269 770.6	305 782.4	255 011.5	267 327.1

[1] Desde 1963 incluye la producción de Petróleos Y.P.F.B. y de Bolivian Gulf Oil Co.
[2] Incluye crudos, condensados y líquidos de absorción.

315. IRON PRODUCTION [1]

(Thousands of tons)

1978	1979	1980	1981	1982	1983	Country
483.9	396.0	271.0	247.0	387.0	...	*Argentina*
35.0	16.0	4.0	4.0	5.0	...	*Bolivia*[2][3]
70 649.0	79 901.0	94 991.0	83 444.2	81 559.2	37 503.4	*Brazil*
453.5	377.5	491.3	410.6	445.4	436.1	*Colombia*
7 813.3	8 225.1	8 834.6	8 514.2	6 469.7	5 973.7	*Chile*
-	-	-	-	-	-	*Guatemala*[3]
3 556.1	4 041.0	5 087.4	5 748.7	5 382.2	5 191.4	*Mexico*
4 844.0	5 090.0	5 096.0	5 959.7	5 672.4	4 208.0	*Peru*
8 379.0	9 461.0	9 982.0	9 472.1	7 122.4	5 673.0	*Venezuela*
96 213.8	107 507.6	124 757.3	113 800.5	107 043.2	...	*Total*

[1] *Metal content.*
[2] *Exports.*
[3] *Mineral.*

316. PETROLEUM PRODUCTION

(Thousands of m³)

1978	1979	1980	1981	1982	1983	Country
26 254.0	27 434.0	28 566.0	28 854.2	28 474.6	28 474.6	*Argentina*
43.5	45.1	48.7	46.5	41.1	63.9	*Barbados*
1 882.9	1 617.5	1 383.9	1 286.4	1 417.9	1 215.0	*Bolivia*
9 304.0	9 608.0	10 562.0	12 384.0	15 082.0	19 140.0	*Brazil*
7 589.5	7 201.0	7 303.7	7 766.0	8 229.7	8 831.5	*Colombia*
303.5	303.4	288.0	378.9	581.1	...	*Cuba*
998.5	1 202.0	1 933.1	2 401.4	2 483.3	2 283.7	*Chile*
11 708.9	11 948.6	11 890.3	12 250.5	12 252.1	13 781.2	*Ecuador*
77 154.0	93 890.0	96 846.0	120 203.0	159 476.0	157 312.0	*Mexico* [2]
8 754.6	11 123.5	11 345.4	11 196.3	11 318.1	9 954.0	*Peru*
13 317.4	12 438.8	12 340.9	10 988.7	10 273.6	9 274.6	*Trinidad and Tobago*
125 680.1	136 704.7	125 795.0	122 372.0	109 733.2	125 040.7	*Venezuela*
282 990.9	313 516.6	308 303.0	330 127.9	359 362.7	...	*Total*

[1] *From 1963 onwards, production of YPFB and Bolivian Gulf Oil Company is included.*
[2] *Including crude and condensed petroleum and absorption liquids.*

317. PRODUCCION DE ZINC [1]

(Miles de toneladas)

País	1960	1965	1970	1975	1977
Argentina	35.4	29.7	39.0	37.4	39.2
Bolivia [2]	4.0	13.7	46.5	48.7	63.5
Brasil	0.3	1.0	24.0	31.4	47.0
Colombia	-	-	-	-	-
Chile	1.0	1.4	1.5	3.2	3.9
Ecuador	-	0.3	0.1	0.1	1.9
Honduras	3.5	11.1	16.9	26.0	27.0
México	262.4	224.9	266.4	228.9	265.4
Perú [3]	157.3	254.5	299.1	364.9	446.7
Total	463.9	536.6	693.5	740.6	894.6

[1] Contenido metálico.
[2] Exportaciones.
[3] Peso recuperable en productos mineros y metalúrgicos.

318. PRODUCCION DE FIBRAS SINTETICAS [1]

(Miles de toneladas)

País	1960	1965	1970	1975	1977
Argentina [2]	12.0	34.3	34.5	61.4	54.7
Brasil	45.2 [2]	57.0	92.0	174.8	210.3
Colombia	7.7	13.9	22.0	32.9	42.1
Chile	3.0	7.5	9.0	8.2	10.0
México [2]	21.6	34.7	72.9	180.7	192.0
Perú	1.4	2.5	5.8	21.0	26.1
Venezuela	3.3	6.8	11.8	18.7	20.4
Total	94.2	156.7	248.0	497.7	555.6

[1] Desde 1960, incluye fibras celulósicas y no celulósicas, sean estas continuas o discontinuas.
[2] Excluye las fibras de cristal.

317. ZINC PRODUCTION [1]

(Thousands of tons)

1978	1979	1980	1981	1982	1983	Country
33.6	37.5	33.7	34.9	36.7	33.8	*Argentina*
59.6	44.5	46.7	47.2	45.7	45.1	*Bolivia* [2]
48.0	52.3	67.0	71.0	71.0	73.0	*Brazil*
-	-	1.0	1.0	1.0	-	*Colombia*
1.8	1.8	1.1	1.5	5.7	6.4	*Chile*
1.3	1.0	3.0	1.0	-	-	*Ecuador*
24.0	20.0	16.0	16.2	24.6	24.0	*Honduras*
244.9	245.5	238.2	211.6	231.9	252.2	*Mexico*
403.0	432.0	487.5	498.9	556.0	576.4	*Peru* [3]
816.2	**834.6**	**894.2**	**883.3**	**972.6**	**1 010.9**	***Total***

[1] *Metal content.*
[2] *Exports.*
[3] *Weight recoverable in mining and metallurgical products.*

318. PRODUCTION OF SYNTHETIC FIBRES [1]

(Thousands of tons)

1978	1979	1980	1981	1982	1983	Country
47.7	61.5	38.3	26.1	32.9	...	*Argentina* [2]
226.7	263.8	282.7	248.1	243.1	...	*Brazil*
44.4	40.1	41.5	45.8	39.8	...	*Colombia*
10.0	11.4	11.5	11.5	9.6	...	*Chile*
204.5	217.9	302.9	306.0	279.8	307.8	*Mexico* [2]
27.2	29.3	34.5	32.5	40.8	...	*Peru*
20.0	20.8	20.3	16.3	13.0	...	*Venezuela*
580.5	**644.8**	**731.7**	**686.3**	**659.0**	...	***Total***

[1] *From 1960, including cellulosic and non-cellulosic fibres, both continuous and discontinuous.*
[2] *Excluding glass fibres.*

319. **PRODUCCION DE NEUMATICOS** [1]

(Miles de unidades)

País	1960	1965	1970	1975	1977
Argentina	1 677.5	3 200.8	3 937.4	4 873.1	5 042.4
Brasil	3 525.5	4 128.9	8 455.5	16 481.0	17 802.0
Colombia	856.7	673.1	931.0	1 744.0	2 138.0
Cuba	343.0	197.1	202.0	368.0	172.0
Chile	272.1	506.2	676.4	229.2	852.2
Ecuador	-	70.2	120.0	246.0	345.0
Jamaica	-	-	163.2	222.0	228.0
México	1 242.2	2 003.4	3 369.2	5 386.0	6 096.0
Panamá	-	29.0	35.0	48.0	81.0
Perú	280.0	324.0	609.1	800.4	876.0
Venezuela	752.8	1 225.5	1 576.8	2 669.0	2 934.0
Total	8 949.8	12 358.2	20 075.6	33 066.7	36 566.6

[1] Excluye neumáticos para bicicletas y otros velocípedos sin motor.

320. **PRODUCCION DE PASTA DE PAPEL** [1]

(Miles de toneladas)

País	1960	1965	1970	1975	1977
Argentina	73.0	133.7	205.8	322.4	320.8
Bolivia	0.5	0.4	0.4	1.0	1.0
Brasil	286.4	571.6	884.1	1 304.0	1 737.0
Colombia	8.9	52.1	97.0	136.0	178.0
Chile	104.8	199.0	368.4	405.0	599.0
México	199.0	347.6	422.0	602.0	676.0
Perú	28.0	50.8	57.8	89.0	98.0
Uruguay	3.5	7.2	7.0	19.0	18.0
Venezuela	-	19.0	23.0	30.0	49.0
Total	704.1	1 381.4	2 065.5	2 908.4	3 676.8

[1] Pasta mecánica de madera, pastas químicas, y semiquímicas y otras pastas químicas (bagazo, sisal, paja de trigo, etc.).

319. PRODUCTION OF TYRES [1]

(Thousands of units)

1978	1979	1980	1981	1982	1983	Country
4 556.9	5 756.3	5 591.6	3 925.0	3 783.8	3 312.0	Argentina
19 523.0	20 978.0	22 663.0	17 152.0	18 271.0	18 898.0	Brazil
1 347.0	1 670.0	1 898.2	1 703.6	...	...	Colombia
300.0	301.9	386.7	326.5	218.3	353.7	Cuba
766.5	892.9	878.1	831.6	482.2	595.1	Chile
385.0	507.0	...	...	...	...	Ecuador
257.0	220.0	178.0	232.2	...	...	Jamaica
7 836.0	7 464.0	8 749.0	8 328.0	9 522.0	8 576.0	Mexico
72.0	69.5	...	57.0	...	...	Panama
733.4	716.2	877.4	968.3	809.6	...	Peru
3 089.0	3 445.0	3 483.0	3 680.0	3 590.0	...	Venezuela
38 865.8	42 020.8	...	...	...	...	Total

[1] Excluding tyres for bicycles and other cycles, not motorized.

320. PAPER PULP PRODUCTION [1]

(Thousands of tons)

1978	1979	1980	1981	1982	1983	Country
325.0	423.1	319.6	286.3	349.0	...	Argentina
1.0	1.0	1.0	1.0	...	...	Bolivia
2 084.0	2 604.0	3 488.0	3 488.0	...	...	Brazil
192.0	201.0	207.0	214.0	...	...	Colombia
665.0	700.0	763.0	743.0	...	...	Chile
719.0	696.0	628.6	638.6	449.3	557.1	Mexico
97.0	155.0	155.0	155.0	...	...	Peru
22.0	22.0	24.0	24.0	...	...	Uruguay
52.0	52.0	52.0	52.0	...	...	Venezuela
4 157.0	4 854.1	5 638.2	5 601.9	...	...	Total

[1] Groundwood pulp, chemical and semi-chemical wood pulp, and other chemical pulps (bagasse, sisal, wheat straw, etc.).

321. PRODUCCION DE PAPEL DE PERIODICO

(Miles de toneladas)

País	1960	1965	1970	1975	1977
Argentina	9.3	4.4	3.2	-	15.0
Brasil	65.8	114.9	114.7	124.7	127.6
Chile	51.5	96.6	118.2	117.9	132.5
México	13.7	21.7	49.8	36.9	58.8
Total	140.3	237.6	285.9	279.5	333.9

322. PRODUCCION DE SODA CAUSTICA

(Miles de toneladas)

País	1960	1965	1970	1975	1977
Argentina[1]	35.6	75.6	94.8	112.9	121.4
Brasil	69.0	81.0	131.1	231.6	316.8
Colombia	25.0	35.7	42.1	58.3	36.2
Cuba	-	1.6	3.6	4.0	4.7
Chile	5.7	8.4	2.0	24.0	30.0
México	65.9	122.9	165.8	208.8	211.2
Perú	2.8	16.1	31.0[2]	35.0[3]	...
Venezuela	4.0	10.2	9.7	7.0	10.0
Total	208.0	351.5	480.1	681.6	...

[1] Desde 1960 en adelante se refiere a hidróxido de sodio al 100%.
[2] Soda caústica anhídrida.
[3] Soda caústica al 50%.

321. NEWSPRINT PRODUCTION

(Thousands of tons)

1978	1979	1980	1981	1982	1983	Country
36.0	101.5	98.3	109.3	94.8	124.8	*Argentina*
116.0	109.2	109.2	105.6	105.6	105.6	*Brazil*
132.0	132.0	130.6	129.0	123.1	154.5	*Chile*
61.2	66.0	70.8	69.2	76.6	74.8	*Mexico*
345.2	408.7	408.9	413.1	400.1	459.7	*Total*

322. CAUSTIC SODA PRODUCTION

(Thousands of tons)

1978	1979	1980	1981	1982	1983	Country
101.3	110.1	104.4	105.1	114.0	128.4	*Argentina*[1]
577.0	645.0	691.0	759.6	739.2	...	*Brazil*
32.3	24.0	20.4	18.0	15.6	20.4	*Colombia*
4.9	4.4	3.5	8.0	11.2	16.4	*Cuba*
33.0	43.0	...	...	...	...	*Chile*
188.4	184.8	224.0	296.0	365.0	...	*Mexico*
...	...	...	...	...	...	*Peru*
8.0	8.0	22.0	25.0	30.0	34.0	*Venezuela*
...	...	...	...	...	...	*Total*

[1] *From 1960 onwards, refers to 100% sodium hydroxide.*
[2] *Anhydrous caustic soda.*
[3] *50% caustic soda.*

323. PRODUCCION DE CEMENTO

(Miles de toneladas)

País	1960	1965	1970	1975	1977
Argentina [1]	2 638.9	3 305.5	4 769.6	5 360.6	5 929.9
Bolivia	38.6	60.1	116.2	226.7	267.1
Brasil [2]	4 444.0	5 623.7	9 002.3	16 390.9	20 545.1
Colombia	1 384.9	2 052.9	2 757.0	3 091.0	3 297.5
Costa Rica	-	115.0	187.0	330.0	406.0
Cuba	813.3	801.1	742.0	2 083.0	2 656.0
Chile	835.4	1 187.9	1 349.0	1 206.0	1 140.0
Ecuador	183.0	297.0	458.3	603.7	645.0
El Salvador	86.3	80.7	166.9	335.6	376.0
Guatemala	117.0	231.4	228.0	341.0	491.0
Haití	53.9	42.1	64.9	144.0	268.0
Honduras	36.9	100.9	161.2	271.0	183.9
Jamaica	212.4	316.0	456.7	405.5	333.2
México	3 089.1	4 304.8	7 259.2	11 678.0	13 097.0
Nicaragua	32.3	75.5	98.0	177.0	226.0
Panamá	108.6	166.0	181.0	277.0	271.0
Paraguay	14.0	29.0	62.9	137.7	199.7
Perú	599.7	1 016.8	1 167.0	1 949.0	1 970.0
República Dominicana	169.7	211.8	492.5	555.0	874.9
Trinidad y Tabago	177.2	189.2	266.3	254.9	214.7
Uruguay	405.5	424.7	496.7	632.0	682.5
Venezuela	1 487.0	2 111.8	2 644.0	3 455.0	3 742.0
Total	16 927.7	22 743.9	33 126.7	49 904.6	57 816.5

[1] Incluye cemento Portland (blanco y natural).
[2] Incluye cemento Portland (blanco, alto horno y puzolánico).

(Thousands of tons)

1978	1979	1980	1981	1982	1983	*Country*
6 144.0	6 612.0	6 954.4	6 735.8	5 674.7	5 607.3	*Argentina*[1]
257.2	250.7	318.2	369.5	341.1	327.3	*Bolivia*
22 348.4	23 683.2	27 194.0	26 052.0	25 434.0	20 874.0	*Brazil*[2]
4 152.5	4 256.7	4 355.8	4 459.4	5 032.4	4 825.1	*Colombia*
490.0	528.0	554.0	694.0	750.0	...	*Costa Rica*
2 712.0	2 612.8	2 830.8	3 292.2	3 163.0	3 228.0	*Cuba*
1 203.0	1 357.0	1 583.0	1 862.8	1 131.5	1 255.0	*Chile*
1 057.9	1 075.8	1 070.0	1 380.0	1 800.0	1 530.0	*Ecuador*
520.0	571.0	550.0	500.0	500.0	...	*El Salvador*
515.0	574.0	569.0	568.0	544.0	...	*Guatemala*
253.5	233.6	243.2	240.7	206.0	224.5	*Haiti*
274.3	288.4	283.5	287.0	251.4	...	*Honduras*
293.6	225.4	144.0	168.0	240.0	...	*Jamaica*
13 922.0	15 144.0	16 398.0	18 173.0	19 343.0	17 258.0	*Mexico*
195.0	86.0	154.0	100.0	100.0	...	*Nicaragua*
300.0	510.0	565.0	520.0	526.0	...	*Panama*
166.0	154.5	176.7	156.1	111.2	141.6	*Paraguay*
2 047.1	2 427.5	2 758.0	2 552.0	2 567.0	1 718.0	*Peru*
866.8	886.0	1 014.9	951.9	948.5	1 105.0	*Dominican Republic*
223.5	217.7	186.2	139.3	189.2	389.9	*Trinidad and Tobago*
686.6	702.3	700.5	611.0	551.0	401.7	*Uruguay*
4 107.0	3 973.0	4 843.5	4 876.0	5 432.0	4 151.0	*Venezuela*
62 735.4	66 369.6	73 446.7	74 688.7	74 836.0	...	*Total*

[1] *Including Portland cement (white and natural).*
[2] *Including Portland cement (white, blast turnace and hydraulic).*

679

324. PRODUCCION DE GASOLINA

(Miles de metros cúbicos)

País	1960	1965	1970	1975	1977
Argentina [1]	2 635.3	4 293.7	5 325.3	5 186.1	5 696.0
Barbados	-	-	43.0	48.5	52.1
Bolivia	143.6	187.8	297.1	509.7	678.0
Brasil	3 398.1	5 824.1	9 550.2	15 378.2	13 488.0
Colombia	1 410.3	1 911.0	2 721.5	3 138.4	3 453.9
Chile [2]	707.1	1 015.3 [3]	1 587.2	1 178.9	1 268.3
Ecuador [4]	275.2	342.9	423.9	903.0	785.2
Jamaica	-	136.7	359.1	282.0	299.0
México	4 168.0 [5]	5 525.0 [6]	8 007.0	10 752.0	13 514.0
Paraguay	-	-	72.1	71.4	102.7
Perú	763.6	1 221.3	1 508.6 [7]	2 066.2	1 905.4
Trinidad y Tabago	1 642.3	2 737.7	3 315.9	2 220.6	3 020.3
Uruguay	328.0	372.0 [8]	345.3	368.0	306.8
Venezuela [9]	6 175.1	7 540.4	10 391.0	10 201.2	12 529.5
Total	21 646.6	31 107.9	43 947.3	52 304.2	57 099.2

[1] Motonafta.
[2] Excluye el consumo interno de la Empresa Nacional de Petróleo (ENAP).
[3] Incluye las refinerías de Concón, de Concepción y plantas de gasolina.
[4] Comprende gasolina de 63 y 80 octanos.
[5] Incluye mexolina, supermexolina, gasolmex, gasolina incolora o refinada y gasolmex premium.
[6] Incluye mexolina, supermexolina, gasolmex, gasolmex premium, gasolina incolora y pelmex 100.
[7] Desde 1970 excluye gasolina de aviación.
[8] Incluye gasolina de aviación.
[9] Incluye nafta.

(Thousands of cubic metres)

1978	1979	1980	1981	1982	1983	Country
6 029.5	6 317.6	7 162.0	7 083.3	7 045.9	7 100.0	*Argentina* [1]
52.9	56.4	55.1	58.4	56.4	58.5	*Barbados*
475.8	644.4	548.9	438.4	519.5	452.7	*Bolivia*
14 654.5	13 979.0	11 369.5	11 783.1	11 859.2	10 378.8	*Brazil*
2 750.0	2 630.8	3 870.7	4 300.3	4 379.9	4 379.8	*Colombia*
1 374.3	1 438.6	1 338.0	1 421.3	1 153.6	1 294.4	*Chile* [2]
1 159.5	1 285.1	1 308.6	1 294.0	1 202.4	972.7	*Ecuador* [4]
293.2	277.0	229.7	216.2	...	...	*Jamaica*
14 443.0	16 608.1	20 776.0	22 336.0	24 417.0	...	*Mexico*
127.0	...	...	...	...	...	*Paraguay*
1 764.9	...	...	...	...	...	*Peru*
3 025.4	2 725.8	2 904.5	2 283.0	2 162.3	1 653.2	*Trinidad and Tobago*
350.0	344.6	281.4	251.4	278.4	...	*Uruguay*
12 876.6	12 558.6	11 286.9	12 717.6	13 215.9	...	*Venezuela* [9]
59 376.6	...	...	...	...	...	*Total*

[1] *Motor gasoline.*
[2] *Excluding internal consumption by the National Petroleum Enterprise (ENAP).*
[3] *Including the refineries at Concón and Concepción and gasoline plants.*
[4] *Includes 63- and 80- octane gasoline.*
[5] *Including mexolina, supermexolina, gasoil, unleaded gasoline and premium gasoil.*
[6] *Including mexolina, supermexolina, gasoil, premium gasoil, unleaded gasoline and pelmex 100.*
[7] *From 1970 onwards, excluding aviation gasoline.*
[8] *Including aviation gasoline.*
[9] *Including naphta.*

325. PRODUCCION DE AUTOMOTORES PARA PASAJEROS

(Miles de unidades)

País	1960	1965	1970	1975	1977
Argentina [1] [2]	49.5	141.1	169.0	184.9	168.4
Brasil [2] [3]	57.3	113.5	255.5	550.7	482.2
Colombia [3]	...	0.6	4.8	20.8	28.1
Chile [3]	-	7.1	20.7	4.9	9.9
México [3] [4]	24.8	67.3	136.5	262.2	195.5
Perú [4]	-	-	10.3	21.2	17.6
Trinidad y Tabago [4]	-	-	5.4	6.8	12.0
Venezuela [3] [4]	6.5	41.3	48.0	92.0	99.0
Total	138.1	370.9	650.2	1 143.5	1 012.7

[1] De turismo, rurales y jeeps.
[2] Incluye ensamble de vehículos automotores.
[3] Vehículos automotores con capacidad inferior a nueve personas sentadas.
[4] Ensamble de vehículos automotores.

326. PRODUCCION DE AUTOMOTORES COMERCIALES

(Miles de unidades)

País	1960	1965	1970	1975	1977
Argentina [1]	38.7	54.8	49.6	53.8	67.7
Brasil [1] [2]	75.7	81.8	161.0	370.1	424.1 [3]
Colombia [4] [5]	-	1.1	14.8	8.6	8.9
Chile [4] [5]	2.1	1.4	3.9	2.6	3.2
México [1]	19.7	30.0	54.0	77.3	63.3
Perú [4] [5]	0.2	1.1	4.2	12.9	7.7
Trinidad y Tabago [4] [5]	-	-	0.9	1.2	2.3
Venezuela [4] [5]	3.9	15.4	20.0	52.0	64.0
Total	140.3	185.6	308.4	578.5	641.2

[1] Fabricación y montaje.
[2] Incluye furgones, camionetas, camiones y chasis para camiones, colectivos, omnibuses y otros tipos (coches, ambulancias, remolques, etc.).
[3] Desde 1977, incluye vehículos utilitarios.
[4] Incluye camiones pesados, medianos y livianos, omnibuses y camionetas de carga.
[5] Incluye ensamblaje de vehículos automotores.

325. PRODUCTION OF PASSENGER MOTOR VEHICLES

(Thousands of units)

1978	1979	1980	1981	1982	1983	Country
135.0	199.6	227.5	144.1	110.1	134.4	Argentina [1] [2]
558.8	568.5	651.9	434.1	494.7	576.0	Brazil [2] [3]
31.8	32.7	32.3	24.7	26.7	20.4	Colombia [3]
17.1	17.5	25.2	20.6	7.9	3.0	Chile [3]
249.5	290.3	316.0	369.0	324.1	230.0	Mexico [3] [4]
7.0	5.8	10.7	18.1	15.7	...	Peru [4]
13.8	13.0	10.2	11.0	12.6	...	Trinidad and Tobago [4]
104.0	95.0	94.0	82.0	94.0	90.0	Venezuela [3] [4]
1 117.0	1 222.4	1 367.8	1 103.6	1 085.8	...	Total

[1] Passenger cars, station wagons and jeeps.
[2] Including assembly of motor vehicles.
[3] Motor vehicles with a seating capacity of less than nine.
[4] Assembly of motor vehicles.

326. PRODUCTION OF COMMERCIAL VEHICLES

(Thousands of units)

1978	1979	1980	1981	1982	1983	Country
45.5	53.6	54.3	28.3	22.0	25.5	Argentina [1]
495.6	542.5	516.1	340.7	345.7	320.4	Brazil [1] [2]
12.7	16.0	10.6	10.4	9.1	7.0	Colombia [4] [5]
2.9	2.6	4.1	5.3	2.3	1.5	Chile [4] [5]
92.2	101.1	110.4	119.4	80.4	36.4	Mexico [1]
4.2	4.9	8.0	8.9	6.2	...	Peru [4] [5]
2.4	2.3	1.7	2.6	2.3	...	Trinidad and Tobago [4] [5]
79.0	66.0	61.0	72.0	61.0	22.0	Venezuela [4] [5]
734.5	789.0	766.2	587.6	529.0	...	Total

[1] Manufacture and assembly.
[2] Including vans, pick up trucks, trucks and chassis for trucks, collective taxis, buses and other types (cars, ambulances, trailers, etc.).
[3] Since 1977 including small trucks and vans.
[4] Including heavy, medium and light trucks, buses and pick-up trucks.
[5] Including assembly of motor vehicles.

VII. RECURSOS NATURALES Y PRODUCCION DE BIENES

327. PRODUCCION DE POLIETILENO

(Miles de toneladas)

País	1960	1965	1970	1975	1977
Argentina	-	18.7	30.2	27.3	33.6
Brasil	4.5	17.9	29.8	192.2	253.3
Colombia	-	-	0.8	0.5	0.7
Chile	-	-	10.0	27.2	34.2
México	-	-	25.8	99.3	95.7
Total	4.5	36.6	96.6	346.5	417.5

[1] Sólo polietileno de baja densidad.

328. PRODUCCION DE POLICLORURO DE VINILO

(Toneladas)

País	1960	1965	1970	1975	1977
Argentina	1.9	17.5	32.1	48.0	52.2
Brasil	7.7	19.8	46.5	136.1	160.1
Colombia	-	0.4	7.6	0.7	20.7
Chile	-	-	-	8.5	10.1
México	3.9	13.0	35.2	44.6	55.7
Perú	-	0.4	6.4	...	8.7
Total	13.5	51.1	127.8	...	307.5

327. PRODUCTION OF POLYETHYLENE

(Thousands of tons)

1978	1979	1980	1981	1982	1983	Country
31.9	34.1	34.3	34.2	146.6	...	Argentina
272.2	409.2	436.0	440.7	478.8	...	Brazil
7.0	8.7	14.7	34.0	...	...	Colombia
30.3	37.8	...	...	22.5	32.4	Chile
99.7	154.1	158.3	169.0	171.6	88.3 [1]	Mexico
441.1	643.9	...	...	...	...	Total

[1] Low-density polyethylene only.

328. PRODUCTION OF POLYVINYL CHLORIDE

(Tons)

1978	1979	1980	1981	1982	1983	Country
44.0	58.4	54.2	49.5	64.5	...	Argentina
179.3	196.2	202.2	142.0	165.9	...	Brazil
28.8	31.9	17.3	40.3	...	...	Colombia
9.8	9.2	...	...	...	...	Chile
55.8	55.7	62.5	131.5	142.5	...	Mexico
9.7	9.7	10.0	...	...	...	Peru
327.4	361.1	...	...	...	...	Total

329. PRODUCCION DE FERTILIZANTES [1] [2]

(Miles de toneladas)

País	1959	1964	1969	1974	1976
Argentina	...	7.0	20.9	30.0	28.8
Brasil	48.2	77.5	124.8	514.6	1 126.3
Colombia	...	56.9	57.8	154.9	99.0
Costa Rica	-	30.0	12.0	30.0	31.0
Cuba	...	...	3.1	49.0	79.9
Chile [3]	167.6	219.0	130.1	151.7	123.1
Ecuador	-	-	7.2	2.4	6.9
El Salvador	-	3.0	9.5	8.0	8.3
Guatemala	-	-	-	2.0	12.0
Jamaica	-	-	-	3.0	-
México	...	197.2	477.8	711.8	855.7
Paraguay	-	-	-	-	-
Perú [3]	87.8	70.3	40.5	25.9	57.0
Trinidad y Tabago	...	30.0	75.0	91.1	46.3
Uruguay	3.0	5.0	3.5	10.0	17.4
Venezuela	-	32.0	21.9	67.6	91.7
Total	306.6	727.9	984.1	1 852.0	2 583.4

[1] Los datos se refieren al período comprendido entre julio del año indicado y junio del año siguiente.
[2] Incluye fertilizantes nitrogenados y fosfatados.
[3] Incluye fertilizantes nitrogenados, fosfatados y potásicos.

329. PRODUCTION OF FERTILIZERS [1] [2]

(Thousands of tons)

1977	1978	1979	1980	1981	1982	Country
28.1	28.9	26.3	31.0	25.0	29.0	Argentina
1 353.7	1 403.0	1 541.0	1 967.0	1 536.0	1 536.0	Brazil
121.6	109.7	102.2	87.6	92.0	79.0	Colombia
32.0	33.0	36.0	40.0	42.0	46.0	Costa Rica
60.2	47.8	138.6	117.1	148.0	100.0	Cuba
108.9	100.4	105.0	112.0	100.0	97.0	Chile [3]
5.8	9.0	9.7	9.1	10.0	13.0	Ecuador
16.9	28.4	17.0	-	-	-	El Salvador
12.0	11.0	4.0	17.0	16.0	23.0	Guatemala
-	-	-	-	-	-	Jamaica
893.3	820.4	868.5	940.0	1 114.0	1 320.0	Mexico
-	-	-	-	-	-	Paraguay
70.4	72.1	68.6	78.0	90.0	77.0	Peru [3]
43.0	48.8	44.0	41.0	23.0	29.0	Trinidad and Tobago
23.9	20.4	41.2	30.0	20.0	17.00	Uruguay
93.0	75.7	104.8	168.1	179.0	247.0	Venezuela
2 862.8	2 808.6	3 106.9	3 637.9	3 395.0	3 613.0	Total

[1] The data refer to the period from July of the year indicated to June of the following year.
[2] Including phosphatic and nitrogenous fertilizers.
[3] Including phosphatic, nitrogenous and potassic fertilizers.

330. PRODUCCION DE LAVARROPAS

(Miles de unidades)

País	1960	1965	1970	1975	1977
Argentina	104.1	102.6	156.9	191.6	125.7
Colombia	1.0	12.0	9.0	19.0	22.0
Chile	...	31.7	47.6	47.0	47.0
México	46.0	66.0	197.5	337.9	395.0
Perú	...	...	8.4	23.9	22.5
Total	151.1	212.3	419.4	619.4	612.2

331. PRODUCCION DE REFRIGERADORES

(Miles de unidades)

País	1960	1965	1970	1975	1977
Argentina [1]	205.6	181.8	236.7	260.1	200.3
Brasil	...	260.2	500.9	1 031.0	1 387.0
Colombia	17.0	34.0	50.0	...	120.0
Cuba	-	-	6.0	50.0	46.3
Chile	...	68.9	66.8	27.0	32.0
Ecuador	-	3.0	8.0	51.0	80.0
México	45.0	114.0	241.4	430.9	490.7
Perú	...	...	32.9	16.0	91.0
República Dominicana	...	...	5.0	28.0	33.6
Trinidad y Tabago	-	-	9.0	24.1	23.0
Total	...	...	1 156.7	1 918.1	2 503.9

[1] Heladeras eléctricas a motor (familiares y comerciales) y a absorción (eléctricas, a gas y queroseno).

330. PRODUCTION OF WASHING MACHINES

(Thousands of units)

1978	1979	1980	1981	1982	1983	Country
125.1	141.1	150.1	106.6	109.8	...	Argentina
29.0	40.0	47.5	58.5	43.2	32.8	Colombia
65.0	80.0	104.0	115.0	43.0	...	Chile
425.0	502.0	585.0	620.7	653.7	511.0	Mexico
14.9	21.2	28.9	32.7	...	...	Peru
659.0	784.3	915.5	933.5	...	...	Total

331. PRODUCTION OF REFRIGERATORS

(Thousands of units)

1978	1979	1980	1981	1982	1983	Country
148.2	260.7	260.2	212.3	202.6	...	Argentina [1]
1 555.0	1 719.0	2 026.0	1 757.0	1 725.0	1 676.0	Brazil
175.0	216.0	188.0	179.0	...	...	Colombia
45.6	55.6	26.0	40.6	15.7	13.5	Cuba
43.0	64.0	95.0	86.0	31.7	31.5	Chile
83.0	...	...	...	...	...	Ecuador
491.0	522.4	572.0	642.4	613.4	445.4	Mexico
74.1	75.8	75.9	...	...	...	Peru
41.8	38.1	48.0	35.7	36.7	...	Dominican Republic
25.0	21.1	27.6	14.9	28.7	20.2	Trinidad and Tobago
2 681.7	...	...	...	...	...	Total

[1] Compressor refrigerators (domestic and commercial) and absorption refrigerators (electric, gas and kerosene).

332. PRODUCCION DE TELEVISORES

(Miles de unidades)

País	1960	1965	1970	1975	1977
Argentina	125.0	179.7	193.6	290.2	253.8
Brasil	194.0	308.7	725.7	1 606.6	2 077.4
Colombia	...	11.0	45.0	83.0	102.0
Chile	...	17.0	123.0	168.0	139.0
Ecuador	-	-	2.0	5.0	13.0
El Salvador	-	-	...	23.0	109.0
Jamaica	-	-	9.8	5.5	4.8
México	80.0	212.0	430.6	569.1	699.0
Perú	-	...	34.3	98.4	125.0
Trinidad y Tabago	-	-	7.9	10.8	13.5
Venezuela	...	...	98.0	200.0	...
Total	...	...	1 669.9	3 059.6	...

333. PRODUCCION DE ALAMBRON [1] [2]

(Miles de toneladas)

País	1960	1965	1970	1975	1977
Argentina	175.3	231.2	265.5	300.3	264.6
Brasil	170.3	281.2	509.7	868.8	1 070.0
Colombia	31.5	72.8	60.8	30.0	26.0
Chile	54.8	75.4	48.2	25.8	39.8
Ecuador				-	-
México	110.3	192.5	295.1	417.9	432.0
Panamá	-	-	-	-	-
Paraguay	-	-	2.7	...	...
Perú	1.8	-	7.9	-	23.0
Trinidad y Tabago				-	-
Uruguay				-	-
Venezuela	-	10.2	57.1	60.7	8.0
Total	544.0	863.3	1 247.0	1 703.5	1 863.4

[1] Sólo laminados en caliente.
[2] Comprende barras entregadas en rollos o bobinas, con exclusión de barras para concreto y barras rectas.

332. PRODUCTION OF TELEVISION RECEIVERS

(Thousands of units)

1978	1979	1980	1981	1982	1983	Country
218.9	252.0	454.3	514.8	447.8	...	Argentina
2 422.0	2 747.0	3 254.0	2 517.0	2 353.0	...	Brazil
137.0	100.0	102.6	120.4	...	...	Colombia
70.0	65.0	69.0	74.0	35.0	23.3	Chile
12.0	...	...	...	...	...	Ecuador
76.0	49.0	47.0	74.0	...	...	El Salvador
...	...	...	...	...	...	Jamaica
766.8	850.0	964.0	978.0	781.3	491.4	Mexico
109.2	67.3	75.1	79.3	...	...	Peru
12.0	10.5	12.8	13.3	18.2	21.2	Trinidad and Tobago
...	...	...	...	...	...	Venezuela
...	...	...	...	...	...	**Total**

333. PRODUCTION OF WIRE ROD [1] [2]

(Thousands of tons)

1978	1979	1980	1981	1982	1983	Country
315.8	344.5	291.5	235.8	319.1	406.6	Argentina
1 173.5	1 282.4	1 523.1	1 283.4	1 393.7	1 297.3	Brazil
41.4	38.1	32.6	49.7	64.0	55.7	Colombia
51.6	59.8	62.0	44.1	21.8	47.5	Chile
-	-	-	-	7.0	12.5	Ecuador
537.5	592.8	598.3	645.3	711.0	821.7	Mexico
9.5	-	30.4	6.3	123.4	184.1	Panama
...	...	...	...	...	...	Paraguay
25.4	11.4	31.6	29.1	16.5	17.1	Peru
-	-	-	-	118.2	166.8	Trinidad and Tobago
-	-	-	-	0.5	6.1	Uruguay
37.2	88.2	172.7	153.3	157.6	270.7	Venezuela
2 191.9	2 417.3	2 742.2	2 448.8	2 932.8	3 286.4	**Total**

[1] Hot rolled products only.
[2] Including bars delivered in rolls or coils but excluding construction steel bars and straight bars.

334. PRODUCCION DE ACERO

(Miles de toneladas)

País	1960	1965	1970	1975	1977
Argentina	277.0	1 368.2	1 823.4	2 199.6	2 682.3
Brasil	2 260.1	3 016.8	5 390.4	8 308.0	11 163.8
Colombia	172.3	241.8	238.7	265.6	209.0
Cuba	...	36.0	140.0	307.0	330.5
Chile	450.4	476.5	547.2	457.9	509.3
México	1 473.7	2 454.7	3 881.2	5 272.4	5 601.3
Panamá [1]	-	-	7.9	38.1	61.6
Perú	59.9	93.6	94.4	430.6	379.2
Uruguay	9.7	13.5	16.2	16.2	18.7
Venezuela	46.7	625.0	926.6	1 099.8	854.0
Total	4 749.8	8 326.1	13 066.0	18 395.2	21 809.7

[1] Incluye Centroamérica.

335. PRODUCCION DE ARRABIO

(Miles de toneladas)

País	1960	1965	1970	1975	1977
Argentina	180.7	663.2	801.7	1 044.7	1 100.0
Brasil	1 837.9	2 537.7	4 205.2	7 052.7	9 384.4
Colombia	185.1	199.4	229.3	298.1	222.0
Chile	265.9	308.7	466.0	416.6	426.5
México	669.3	945.9	2 263.0	3 012.0	3 009.0
Perú	38.5	19.9	85.6	286.5	240.8
Venezuela	-	333.6	509.7	534.6	352.3
Total	3 673.7	5 008.4	8 560.5	12 645.2	14 735.0

334. STEEL PRODUCTION

(Thousands of tons)

1978	1979	1980	1981	1982	1983	Country
2 786.4	3 203.1	2 684.9	2 525.8	2 912.7	2 926.7	Argentina
12 107.0	13 891.1	15 337.3	13 226.1	12 995.2	14 659.9	Brazil
390.5	354.4	420.2	402.3	424.8	462.7	Colombia
323.6	327.8	303.8	329.8	301.2	363.7	Cuba
596.9	657.4	703.8	644.3	491.6	611.1	Chile
6 775.4	7 117.3	7 156.1	7 672.7	7 056.0	6 916.8	Mexico
64.3	122.4	138.8	113.3	65.0	45.2	Panama [1]
374.0	378.8	446.7	364.1	272.6	288.4	Peru
6.9	16.1	17.6	15.1	28.0	37.6	Uruguay
858.7	1 475.0	1 975.4	2 029.5	2 225.5	2 320.4	Venezuela
24 283.7	27 543.4	29 184.6	27 323.0	26 772.6	28 632.5	**Total**

[1] Including Central America.

335. PRODUCTION OF PIG IRON

(Thousands of tons)

1978	1979	1980	1981	1982	1983	Country
1 442.0	1 134.9	1 035.4	915.0	1 017.1	922.3	Argentina
10 023.7	11 281.5	12 685.3	10 791.2	10 827.3	12 940.5	Brazil
296.7	240.8	278.7	233.1	207.0	268.1	Colombia
538.7	611.2	648.4	582.2	453.3	539.5	Chile
3 508.5	3 514.0	3 638.7	3 767.0	3 598.0	3 536.1	Mexico
244.1	265.9	261.9	186.9	161.7	112.6	Peru
401.2	497.9	497.4	418.0	201.6	169.0	Venezuela
16 454.9	17 546.2	19 045.8	16 893.4	16 466.0	18 488.1	**Total**

VII. RECURSOS NATURALES Y PRODUCCION DE BIENES

336. PRODUCCION DE LAMINADOS PLANOS [1]

(Miles de toneladas)

País	1960	1965	1970	1975	1977
Argentina	90.5	565.2	933.2	1 504.1	1 479.6
Brasil	709.8	1 073.7	2 062.6	3 114.5	4 473.9
Colombia	-	18.1	47.6	50.4	72.3
Chile	146.4	209.2	250.0	135.1	187.5
México	603.8	1 017.1	1 420.5	2 081.9	2 056.6
Perú	8.0	-	-	106.4	113.5
Venezuela	-	-	-	350.4	434.0
Total	1 558.5	2 883.3	4 713.9	7 342.8	8 817.4

[1] Comprende planchas y láminas y hojalata.

337. PRODUCCION DE LAMINADOS NO PLANOS [1]

(Miles de toneladas)

País	1960	1965	1970	1975	1977
Argentina	698.8	971.5	1 164.0	1 487.8	1 078.1
Brasil	935.4	1 074.0	2 219.8	3 089.9	3 740.9
Colombia	113.4	188.7	265.7	259.7	262.9
Chile	137.8	180.2	186.1	166.0	207.2
Ecuador	-	-	26.9	41.9	74.2
México	632.8	1 021.0	1 444.3	1 952.3	2 025.5
Panamá [2]	-	10.0	38.2	75.5	141.7 [3]
Perú	30.0	73.7	71.7	180.4	180.9
Trinidad y Tabago	-	-	-	-	-
Uruguay	36.5	21.6	20.4	29.2	29.8
Venezuela	50.6	288.3	514.8	518.8	570.2
Total	2 635.3	3 829.0	5 951.9	7 801.5	8 311.4

[1] Comprende barras y perfiles livianos, alambrón, rieles y perfiles pesados.
[2] Incluye Centroamérica.
[3] Incluye a República Dominicana.

336. PRODUCTION OF FLAT ROLLED PRODUCTS [1]

(Thousands of tons)

1978	1979	1980	1981	1982	1983	Country
1 124.8	1 390.1	1 385.9	1 133.1	1 252.1	1 317.1	Argentina
5 116.2	6 001.6	6 910.5	5 684.7	6 153.8	7 153.9	Brazil
86.3	23.4	13.1	9.6	19.7	33.0	Colombia
231.9	216.3	272.5	278.4	128.7	203.7	Chile
2 609.3	2 832.8	2 937.1	2 987.7	2 533.0	2 312.3	Mexico
79.3	88.7	96.0	95.5	59.4	57.7	Peru
516.3	524.9	767.4	719.9	830.9	855.7	Venezuela
9 764.1	11 077.8	12 382.5	10 908.9	10 977.6	11 933.7	Total

[1] Including plates and sheets, and tinplate.

337. PRODUCTION OF NON-FLAT ROLLED PRODUCTS [1]

(Thousands of tons)

1978	1979	1980	1981	1982	1983	Country
1 148.1	1 284.1	1 153.9	1 015.3	1 169.7	1 231.1	Argentina
4 163.3	4 513.9	5 074.4	4 465.7	4 467.2	4 415.2	Brazil
246.8	240.8	306.2	304.7	313.0	345.9	Colombia
180.9	206.0	243.3	216.3	104.5	167.5	Chile
85.3	117.6	115.7	110.3	146.0	150.8	Ecuador
2 327.8	2 663.0	2 932.7	3 079.8	2 902.3	2 962.5	Mexico
182.8	145.4	220.7	174.0	266.8	340.2	Panama [2]
167.3	200.0	192.7	210.2	165.3	155.8	Peru
-	-	-	-	118.2	166.7	Trinidad and Tobago
14.0	27.8	51.2	47.0	36.1	31.8	Uruguay
553.0	581.0	840.6	807.7	800.0	816.7	Venezuela
9 069.3	9 987.5	11 240.5	10 442.7	10 489.1	10 784.2	Total

[1] Including bars and light sections, wire rod, rails and heavy sections.
[2] Including Central America.
[3] Including the Dominican Republic.

338. PRODUCCION DE ENERGIA ELECTRICA

(Millones de kilovatios-hora (GWh))

País	1960	1965	1970	1975	1977
Argentina	10 459	15 383	21 727	29 468	32 477
Barbados	38	75	146	214	264
Bolivia	446	566	787	1 057	1 260
Brasil	22 865	30 128	45 460	78 936	100 804
Colombia	3 750	5 824	8 750	14 025	16 099
Costa Rica	438	660	1 028	1 531	1 760
Cuba	2 981	3 423	4 888	6 583	7 695
Chile	4 592	6 131	7 550	8 732	9 776
Ecuador	387	572	949	1 650	2 260
El Salvador	249	418	671	1 059	1 354
Guatemala	281	449	759	1 167	1 564
Guyana	92	220	323	383	431
Haití	90	96	118	158	215
Honduras	91	175	315	545	701
Jamaica	508	798	1 542	2 331	2 375
México	10 813	17 245	28 707	43 329	50 632
Nicaragua	187	311	627	932	1 188
Panamá	235	510	956	1 447	1 630
Paraguay	96	135	218	598	626
Perú	2 656	3 839	5 529	7 486	8 627
República Dominicana	350	500	1 003	2 556	3 063
Trinidad y Tabago	470	908	1 202	1 207	1 576
Uruguay	1 244	1 744	2 200	2 444	2 834
Venezuela	4 651	8 197	12 708	19 591	23 051
Total	67 969	98 307	148 163	227 429	272 262

338. PRODUCTION OF ELECTRICITY

(Millions of kilowatt-hours (GWH))

1978	1979	1980	1981	1982	Country
33 434	37 640	39 676	39 024	39 804	Argentina
287	300	332	349	336	Barbados
1 354	1 432	1 564	1 677	1 703	Bolivia
112 492	126 079	139 485	142 198	152 089	Brazil
18 108	19 859	22 935	24 195	25 605	Colombia
1 927	1 987	2 226	2 362	2 500	Costa Rica
8 481	9 403	9 896	10 572	10 788	Cuba
10 360	11 133	11 751	11 978	11 871	Chile
2 569	2 665	3 090	3 225	3 350	Ecuador
1 488	1 587	1 543	1 474	1 500	El Salvador
1 726	1 914	1 617	1 614	1 640	Guatemala
409	407	419	430	440	Guyana
246	280	315	325	360	Haiti
777	859	928	1 014	1090	Honduras
2 279	2 268	2 245	2 325	2 350	Jamaica
57 257	62 860	66 954	73 559	80 589	Mexico
1 180	985	1 049	1 086	1 045	Nicaragua
1 564	1 893	2 454	2 530	2 700	Panama
670	772	930	1 014	1 100	Paraguay
8 765	9 252	9 805	10 100	10 400	Peru
3 221	3 113	2 743	2 899	2 965	Dominican Republic
1 675	1 818	2 033	2 169	2 260	Trinidad and Tobago
3 046	2 724	4 559	4 913	6 156	Uruguay
25 625	28 409	35 932	37 542	39 000	Venezuela
298 940	329 639	364 481	378 574	401 641	Total

339. PRODUCCION DE ENERGIA ELECTRICA POR TIPOS DE CENTRAL

(Millones de kilovatios-hora (GWh))

País	Total		Hidroeléctrica *Hydroelectric*		Geotérmica *Geothermal*	
	1981	1982	1981	1982	1981	1982
Argentina	39 024	39 804	14 666	17 586	-	-
Barbados	349	336	-	-	-	-
Bolivia	1 677	1 703	1 155	1 173	-	-
Brasil	142 198	152 089	130 765	141 224	-	-
Colombia	24 195	25 605	17 642	18 553	-	-
Costa Rica	2 362	2 500	2 276	2 430	-	-
Cuba	10 572	10 788	60	100	-	-
Chile	11 978	11 871	7 588	7 871	-	-
Ecuador	3 225	3 350	950	990	-	-
El Salvador	1 474	1 500	763	800	574	600
Guatemala	1 614	1 640	343	350	-	-
Guyana	430	440	5	5	-	-
Haití	325	360	225	250	-	-
Honduras	1 014	1 090	821	870	-	-
Jamaica	2 325	2 350	125	130	-	-
México	73 559	80 589	24 618	22 924	964	1 278
Nicaragua	1 086	1 045	504	510	-	25
Panamá	2 530	2 700	1 651	1 200	-	-
Paraguay	1 016	1 100	890	950	-	-
Perú	10 100	10 400	7 800	8 000	-	-
República Dominicana	2 899	2 965	37	47	-	-
Trinidad y Tabago	2 169	2 260	-	-	-	-
Uruguay	4 913	6 156	3 856	5 009	-	-
Venezuela	37 542	39 000	15 090	15 700	-	-
Total	378 574	401 641	231 830	246 672	1 538	1 903

[1] Proveniente de los derivados del petróleo, del gas natural y del carbón.
[2] Proveniente de los derivados del petróleo solamente.
[3] Proveniente de los derivados del petróleo y del gas natural.

339. PRODUCTION OF ELECTRICITY BY TYPE OF PLANT

(Millions of kilowatt-hours (GWH))

Nuclear		Térmica convencional *Conventional thermal plant*		Country
1981	1982	1981	1982	
2 816	1 870	21 542 [1]	20 348	*Argentina*
-	-	349 [2]	336	*Barbados*
-	-	522 [3]	530	*Bolivia*
-	-	11 433 [1]	10 865	*Brazil*
-	-	6 553 [1]	7 052	*Colombia*
-	-	86 [2]	70	*Costa Rica*
-	-	10 512 [2]	10 688	*Cuba*
-	-	4 390 [1]	4 000	*Chile*
-	-	2 275 [3]	2 360	*Ecuador*
-	-	137 [2]	100	*El Salvador*
-	-	1 271 [2]	1 290	*Guatemala*
-	-	425 [2]	435	*Guyana*
-	-	100 [2]	110	*Haiti*
-	-	193 [2]	220	*Honduras*
-	-	2 200 [2]	2 220	*Jamaica*
-	-	47 977 [1]	56 387	*Mexico*
-	-	582 [2]	510	*Nicaragua*
-	-	879 [2]	1 500	*Panama*
-	-	124 [2]	150	*Paraguay*
-	-	2 300 [3]	2 400	*Peru*
-	-	2 862 [2]	2 918	*Dominican Republic*
-	-	2 169 [3]	2 260	*Trinidad and Tobago*
-	-	1 057 [2]	1 147	*Uruguay*
-	-	22 452 [3]	23 300	*Venezuela*
2 816	1 870	142 390	151 196	*Total*

[1] *Production from petroleum products, natural gas and coal.*
[2] *Production from petroleum products only.*
[3] *Production from petroleum products and natural gas.*

340. POTENCIA INSTALADA

(Miles de kilovatios-hora (MWh))

País	1960	1965	1970	1975	1977
Argentina	3 474	5 432	6 691	9 260	10 073
Barbados	12	21	39	67	101
Bolivia	147	164	267	376	406
Brasil	4 800	7 411	11 233	19 569	22 637
Colombia	911	1 546	2 427	3 504	4 334
Costa Rica	109	161	244	404	440
Cuba	944	976	1 400	1 677	1 858
Chile	1 142	1 454	2 143	2 620	2 905
Ecuador	118	182	304	525	799
El Salvador	74	115	205	314	491
Guatemala	73	118	216	327	504
Guyana	52	98	160	170	180
Haití	28	35	43	89	102
Honduras	33	73	89	159	162
Jamaica	142	205	405	692	705
México	3 048	5 237	7 318	11 328	13 955
Nicaragua	79	135	170	252	361
Panamá	72	110	198	346	529
Paraguay	44	53	112	191	334
Perú	841	1 148	1 677	2 357	2 540
República Dominicana	108	178	327	732	900
Trinidad y Tabago	129	275	334	404	454
Uruguay	406	483	560	705	699
Venezuela	1 353	2 086	3 172	4 570	5 427
Total	18 139	27 696	39 734	60 638	70 896

(Thousands of kilowatt-hours (MWH))

1978	1979	1980	1981	1982	Country
11 187	11 498	11 988	12 220	13 480	Argentina
98	97	94	94	94	Barbados
428	421	489	508	508	Bolivia
26 970	30 272	33 293	36 947	38 904	Brazil
4 600	4 612	5 130	5 500	5 820	Colombia
508	570	646	657	657	Costa Rica
2 288	2 561	2 673	2 704	2 704	Cuba
2 939	2 931	2 940	3 210	3 208	Chile
923	992	1 118	1 160	1 200	Ecuador
495	495	501	499	500	El Salvador
551	566	392	473	473	Guatemala
180	185	162	165	165	Guyana
121	121	121	126	126	Haiti
202	203	234	240	240	Honduras
718	725	725	740	740	Jamaica
16 032	16 380	16 985	19 895	21 574	Mexico
362	358	356	365	400	Nicaragua
525	575	745	744	744	Panama
355	360	338	370	370	Paraguay
2 570	2 913	3 192	3 300	3 400	Peru
930	950	970	960	960	Dominican Republic
575	543	756	760	760	Trinidad and Tobago
700	745	835	944	1 364	Uruguay
6 727	8 356	8 471	9 224	9 312	Venezuela
80 984	88 429	93 154	101 805	107 703	Total

VII. RECURSOS NATURALES Y PRODUCCION DE BIENES /
NATURAL RESOURCES AND PRODUCTION OF GOODS

341. ESTIMACION DEL POTENCIAL HIDROELECTRICO ECONOMICAMENTE APROVECHABLE, EN EL DECENIO DE 1970 [1] / *ESTIMATES OF ECONOMICALLY EXPLOITABLE HYDROELECTRIC POTENTIAL, IN THE 1970s* [1]

(Miles de kilovatios (MW) / *Megawatts*)

Pais / *Country*	A principios del decenio *At beginning of decade*	A fines del decenio *At end of decade*
Argentina	44 800	45 000
Barbados	...	...
Bolivia	20 000	18 000
Brasil / *Brazil*	150 029	213 000
Colombia	50 000	120 000
Costa Rica	8 600	8 900
Cuba	...	...
Chile	17 000	12 000
Ecuador	20 000	22 000
El Salvador	1 350	8 500
Guatemala	4 950	9 900
Guyana	...	...
Haití / *Haiti*	...	...
Honduras	3 800 [2]	2 800
Jamaica	-	...
México / *Mexico*	25 250	25 250
Nicaragua	3 285 [2]	2 950
Panamá / *Panama*	1 890 [2]	2 900
Paraguay	11 015 [3]	17 000 [3]
Perú / *Peru*	30 000	58 000
República Dominicana / *Dominican Republic*	300	...
Trinidad y Tabago / *Trinidad and Tobago*	-	...
Uruguay	2 200	7 000
Venezuela	25 000	36 000
Total	419 460	617 550

[1] Potencial técnicamente aprovechable. Potencial evaluado con una planta de factor 0.5 sobre poder continuo.
[2] Evaluación preliminar.
[3] Correspondiente sólo a las centrales Corpus, Itaipú, Yaciretá y la parte perteneciente al Paraguay de la "Central Presidente Stroessner".

[1] *Technically exploitable potential with a plant of a factor of 0.5 over continuous power.*
[2] *Preliminary estimate.*
[3] *Covering only the Corpus, Itaipú and Yaciretá plants and the portion of the "Presidente Stroessner Plant" belonging to Paraguay.*

342. LONGITUD TOTAL DE LA RED DE CARRETERAS / *TOTAL LENGTH OF THE ROAD NETWORK*

(Kilómetros / *Kilometres*)

País / *Country*	Año *Year*	Total	Porcentaje pavimentadas *Percentage paved*
Argentina	1978	208 087	23
Barbados	1980	1 546	94
Bolivia	1980	39 651	3
Brasil / *Brazil*	1981	1 399 443	6
Colombia	1981	74 735	-
Costa Rica	1981	28 525	9
Cuba	1979	10 847	93
Chile	1981	78 025	12
Ecuador	1980	33 006	13
El Salvador	1981	12 269	14
Guatemala	1980	26 429	11
Guyana	1980	7 630	7
Haití / *Haiti*	1981	3 443	17
Honduras	1981	9 020	27
Jamaica	1978	18 197	69
México / *Mexico*	1981	213 316	45
Nicaragua [1]	1981	6 712	10
Panamá / *Panama*	1980	11 110	37
Paraguay [2]	1979	31 460	-
Perú / *Peru*	1979	56 642	-
República Dominicana / *Dominican Republic*	1981	12 227	83
Trinidad y Tabago / *Trinidad and Tobago*	1981	5 175	-
Uruguay	1980	50 024	14
Venezuela	1981	62 448	38

[1] No incluye carreteras urbanas.
[2] Sólo nacional.

[1] *Excluding urban roads.*
[2] *National roads only.*

343. LONGITUD TOTAL DE LA RED FERROVIARIA

(Kilómetros)

País	1970	1975	1976	1977	1978
Argentina [1]	39 905	39 787	39 779	36 996	34 393
Bolivia	3 284	3 269	3 269	3 373	3 473
Brasil	30 445 [2]	29 788	29 277	28 756	28 972
Colombia	3 436	3 431	3 403	3 403	2 884
Cuba	5 286	5 342	5 342	4 214	4 382
Chile	6 475	6 606	6 378	6 372	6 366
Ecuador	...	1 008	990	990	965
El Salvador	620	161	602	602	602
Guatemala	...	775	775	775	775
Honduras	...	...	...	205	205
México	19 868	19 960	19 441	19 999	20 000
Nicaragua	318	320	320	345	345
Panamá	...	...	...	...	...
Paraguay	441	441	441	441	441
Perú	2 242	1 875	1 875	1 875	1 875
Uruguay	2 975	2 975	2 988	2 988	2 998
Venezuela	226	226	264	284	264
Total	115 521	115 964	115 144	111 618	108 940

[1] Se refiere a la longitud de la red en explotación.
[2] 1969.

343. TOTAL LENGTH OF THE RAILWAY NETWORK

(Kilometres)

1979	1980	1981	1982	Country
34 350	34 077	34 172	34 098	*Argentina* [1]
3 473	3 328	3 628	3 628	*Bolivia*
29 061	28 671	28 310	28 237	*Brazil*
3 403	3 403	3 403	2 710	*Colombia*
4 382	4 382	4 382	4 382	*Cuba*
6 365	6 302	6 300	6 236	*Chile*
965	965	965	966	*Ecuador*
602	602	602	602	*El Salvador*
927	927	927	927	*Guatemala*
205	205	205	205	*Honduras*
20 031	20 058	19 953	19 955	*Mexico*
345	345	345	331	*Nicaragua*
...	118	118	118	*Panama*
441	441	441	441	*Paraguay*
1 882	2 099	2 159	2 159	*Peru*
3 005	3 005	3 005	3 010	*Uruguay*
268	268	268	268	*Venezuela*
109 705	109 496	109 183	108 273	*Total*

[1] *It refers to length of railway being exploited.*
[2] *1969.*

344. TRAFICO FERROVIARIO

a) Toneladas-kilómetros
(Millones)

País	1970	1975	1976	1977	1978
Argentina	13 274.2	10 729.2	11 107.4	11 636.3	9 909.3
Bolivia	455.9	470.1	522.5	594.9	592.2
Brasil	15 494.6	23 669.2	27 743.7	29 587.6	29 706.9
Colombia	1 172.6	1 138.5	1 156.9	1 215.4	1 227.7
Cuba	...	...	...	2 023.6	1 904.4
Chile	2 021.8	1 478.3	1 657.4	1 516.4	1 423.7
Ecuador	...	46.2	34.7	35.1	32.1
El Salvador	...	...	...	56.0	75.6
Guatemala	...	...	...	139.0	139.0
Honduras	...	...	...	33.0	28.8
México	23 083.4	33 400.1	33 666.2	36 374.7	36 713.4
Nicaragua	...	...	...	11.4	11.4
Panamá	...	...	...	...	...
Paraguay [1]	30.6	20.7	12.9	23.7	23.3
Perú	592.0	621.3	621.3	621.3	621.3
Uruguay	300.5	275.9	310.8	285.0	303.0
Venezuela [2]	13.1	14.2	13.7	19.7	20.0
Total	...	...	...	84 173.1	69 732.1

[1] Los datos se refieren solamente al ferrocarril Presidente Carlos A. López.
[2] Excluye el ferrocarril Orinoco Mining Company, cuyo recorrido es de 145 km.

a) Tons-kilometres
(Millions)

1979	1980	1981	1982	Country
10 978.4	9 492.0	9 260.1	11 498.4	*Argentina*
602.4	657.9	631.7	492.9	*Bolivia*
33 641.6	40 602.5	37 980.7	38 979.6	*Brazil*
1 105.4	861.6	624.8	553.1	*Colombia*
1 904.4	1 904.4	1 904.4	1 904.4	*Cuba*
1 344.5	1 444.8	1 299.8	1 327.1	*Chile*
32.1	32.1	32.1	11.9	*Ecuador*
78.1	55.1	30.9	31.5	*El Salvador*
91.0	91.0	91.0	91.0	*Guatemala*
29.0	29.0	28.8	28.8	*Honduras*
37 275.2	41 830.7	43 801.5	38 959.9	*Mexico*
6.4	6.4	6.4	7.5	*Nicaragua*
...	10.3	10.3	10.3	*Panama*
27.5	29.1	23.1	32.8	*Paraguay* [1]
571.2	742.2	687.1	681.7	*Peru*
296.3	253.0	221.0	188.3	*Uruguay*
17.5	20.8	13.5	29.1	*Venezuela* [2]
88 001.0	**98 062.9**	**96 647.2**	**94 828.3**	*Total*

[1] Presidente Carlos A. López railway only.
[2] Excluding the 145 km. Orinoco Mining Company railway.

344. TRAFICO FERROVIARIO

b) Pasajeros-kilómetros
(Millones)

País	1970	1975	1976	1977	1978
Argentina	12 684.2	14 366.7	14 598.3	13 332.6	12 284.3
Bolivia	266.2	309.6	366.8	395.8	397.2
Brasil	12 070.2	10 321.6	11 281.2	11 270.5	12 874.5
Colombia	235.0	522.7	510.8	391.5	344.5
Costa Rica	...	...	...	...	...
Cuba	...	...	...	1 076.0	1 571.4
Chile	2 256.4	2 095.6	2 356.1	2 350.1	2 003.6
Ecuador	...	64.9	69.1	62.8	65.3
El Salvador	...	...	...	30.7	30.8
Guatemala	...	...	...	2.0	2.0
Honduras	...	...	...	7.8	7.9
México	4 534.3	4 122.7	4 058.1	5 040.4	5 326.0
Nicaragua	...	...	...	18.7	18.7
Panamá	...	...	...	...	...
Paraguay [1]	24.0	23.6	16.1	17.6	17.2
Perú	247.6	354.4	354.4	354.4	354.4
Uruguay	473.3	336.6	373.6	388.5	494.0
Venezuela [2]	36.1	39.8	41.9	38.9	40.5
Total	...	...	...	34 778.3	35 832.3

[1] Los datos se refieren solamente al ferrocarril Presidente Carlos A. López.
[2] Excluye el ferrocarril Orinoco Mining Company, cuyo recorrido es de 145 km.

b) Passengers-kilometres
(Millions)

1979	1980	1981	1982	Country
12 893.6	13 510.3	12 025.0	10 873.5	*Argentina*
362.5	528.9	482.2	555.1	*Bolivia*
12 346.9	13 390.0	14 418.9	12 709.1	*Brazil*
322.4	315.2	234.9	157.6	*Colombia*
...	...	...	152.1	*Costa Rica*
1 571.4	1 571.4	1 571.4	1 571.4	*Cuba*
1 727.2	1 420.9	1 558.3	1 502.7	*Chile*
65.3	65.3	65.3	43.3	*Ecuador*
31.0	27.0	14.1	5.9	*El Salvador*
...	...	...	...	*Guatemala*
7.9	7.9	7.9	7.9	*Honduras*
5 252.8	5 296.4	5 286.5	5 2161.1	*Mexico*
14.6	14.6	14.6	25.5	*Nicaragua*
...	37.6	37.6	37.6	*Panama*
20.9	22.3	21.7	20.1	*Paraguay* [1]
401.6	495.8	495.1	491.7	*Peru*
454.8	417.5	338.6	273.7	*Uruguay*
24.6	28.2	9.8	18.7	*Venezuela* [2]
35 497.7	37 149.3	36 581.9	33 707.0	*Total*

[1] *Presidente Carlos A. López railway only.*
[2] *Excluding the 145 km. Orinoco Mining Company railway.*

345. MARINAS MERCANTES, 1982

(Toneladas de registro bruto para barcos de mil toneladas y más)

País	Ultramar / *Overseas*				
	Cargueros *Cargo vessels*	Graneleros *Bulk carriers*	Frigoríficos *Refrigerated vessels*	Buques tanques *Tankers*	Otros *Others*
Argentina	626 554	434 465	43 754	-	-
Bolivia	10 915	-	-	-	-
Brasil	803 638	1 135 788	13 478	2 304 159	-
Colombia	270 123	36 056	-	-	-
Costa Rica	-	5 940	-	-	-
Cuba	463 907	62 576	71 472	3 600	2 333
Chile	99 354	87 853	-	204 434	-
Ecuador	113 964	11 153	81 031	82 613	-
El Salvador	-	-	-	-	-
Guatemala	12 091	3 527	-	-	-
México	125 603	156 826	-	586 049	-
Nicaragua	9 650	2 353	-	-	-
Paraguay	12 714	-	-	-	-
Perú	279 982	201 057	1 544	35 823	-
República Dominicana	18 462	12 002	-	-	-
Uruguay	54 708	13 203	4 172	88 617	-
Venezuela	208 701	56 784	6 682	11 065	-
Total	3 110 366	2 219 583	222 133	3 316 360	2 333

(Gross registered tons for vessels of 1 000 tons and over)

Cabotaje / Coastal				Fluviales y lacustres *Inland waterways*	Country
Cargueros *Cargo vessels*	Frigoríficos *Refrigerated vessels*	Buques tanques *Tankers*	Otros *Others*		
29 454	-	709 847	13 779	172 374	*Argentina*
-	-	-	-	-	*Bolivia*
190 527	-	437 277	178 005	86 256	*Brazil*
1 544	-	25 271	11 234	-	*Colombia*
-	-	-	2 509	-	*Costa Rica*
52 376	-	62 217	21 658	-	*Cuba*
17 693	-	26 966	10 842	-	*Chile*
1 132	-	83 684	3 845	-	*Ecuador*
-	-	-	-	-	*El Salvador*
-	-	-	-	-	*Guatemala*
8 432	4 695	266 082	84 854	-	*Mexico*
-	-	-	-	-	*Nicaragua*
-	-	-	-	17 857	*Paraguay*
-	-	119 184	-	10 955	*Peru*
-	-	-	-	-	*Dominican Republic*
1 110	-	2 516	-	3 749	*Uruguay*
4 896	-	443 666	91 629	1 325	*Venezuela*
307 164	4 695	2 176 710	418 355	292 516	*Total*

346. TRAFICO AEREO

a) Kilómetros volados

(Millones)

País	1960	1965	1970	1975	1977
Argentina	33.1	31.5	47.4	63.7	77.3
Barbados	...	...	...	1.8	1.9
Bolivia	3.8	3.6	3.6	6.0	11.9
Brasil	120.7	77.5	95.4	170.2	201.1
Colombia	38.1	45.0	54.8	48.1	52.7
Costa Rica	3.8	3.1	6.0	6.0	8.6
Cuba	8.5	7.0	7.2	8.4	11.8
Chile	13.5	16.0	20.9	21.6	21.5
Ecuador	5.6	6.5	12.3	10.4	6.6
El Salvador	3.1	2.0	5.8	6.5	10.2
Guatemala	2.1	3.3	4.9	3.8	4.9
Guyana	...	...	0.4	0.5	...
Haití	0.6	0.5	0.5	0.7	...
Honduras	3.1	2.3	6.0	5.7	7.2
Jamaica	...	0.3	5.6	17.3	15.3
México	44.0	43.2	57.7	93.1	103.6
Nicaragua	0.9	1.2	2.2	2.3	...
Panamá	1.4	2.0	5.0	8.7	10.3
Paraguay	0.9	2.1	2.3	2.6	...
Perú	7.2	15.0	20.0	21.8	24.0
República Dominicana	0.8	0.8	3.1	4.5	5.3
Trinidad y Tabago	7.2	7.2	9.9	12.0	14.6
Uruguay	3.2	2.7	2.3	2.7	3.6
Venezuela	23.3	25.1	21.3	37.2	46.5
Total	317.7	297.8	394.6	555.6	...

[1] Cifras parciales.
[2] Se refiere a los primeros nueve meses solamente.
[3] No incluye información sobre aerolíneas SANSA.
[4] Se refiere a los primeros cinco meses solamente.
[5] No cubre las actividades del mes de diciembre de aerolíneas AEROMEXICO.
[6] No incluye información sobre aerolíneas INAIR.
[7] No incluye información sobre los últimos tres meses de aerolíneas VIASA.

a) Aircraft kilometres
(Millions)

1978	1979	1980	1981	1982	1983	Country
80.7	106.6	98.4	93.7	75.9	76.2	Argentina
2.8	3.2	1.2	1.4	1.3	0.7	Barbados
15.0	13.4	13.5	13.0	10.5	9.7	Bolivia
202.0	187.1	203.4	120.1 [1]	203.4	202.7	Brazil
57.9	49.1	44.5	50.7 [1]	70.8	71.3	Colombia
8.9	8.1	7.7 [2]	7.8 [3]	8.4	7.6	Costa Rica
15.1	17.0	7.4 [4]	7.6 [4]	15.6	15.4	Cuba
26.6	24.6	24.6	28.8	26.3	22.5	Chile
8.0	10.5	11.3	...	19.3	19.0	Ecuador
10.4	7.1	6.1	6.3	6.4	4.6	El Salvador
6.7	4.2	3.7	3.5	3.5	2.5	Guatemala
...	...	...	...	2.8	2.5	Guyana
...	...	...	...	0.7	0.7	Haiti
8.2	9.2	9.6	8.3	5.4	5.8	Honduras
16.7	18.1	15.8	11.4	11.9	9.8	Jamaica
95.9	128.1	126.1 [5]	161.4	152.8	163.9	Mexico
...	...	...	...	1.8	1.8	Nicaragua
8.6	8.3	6.9 [6]	7.2	7.4	6.4	Panama
...	...	...	...	7.5	7.4	Paraguay
24.1	24.2	24.7	24.6	27.6	27.3	Peru
5.6	5.5	4.8 [2]	3.2 [2]	5.5	5.1	Dominican Republic
9.4	15.8	16.5	...	13.9	13.3	Trinidad and Tobago
2.7	4.2	1.3 [1]	2.0 [1]	5.5	5.5	Uruguay
55.8	50.0	51.5	43.0 [7]	58.9	57.7	Venezuela
...	...	...	...	743.1	739.4	*Total*

[1] *Partial figures.*
[2] *Refers to first nine months only.*
[3] *Does not include data on SANSA airline.*
[4] *Refers to first five months only.*
[5] *Activities do not cover December for AEROMEXICO airline.*
[6] *Does not include data on INAIR airline.*
[7] *Does not include data on last three months for VIASA airline.*

346. TRAFICO AEREO (continuación 1)

b) Pasajeros transportados
(Miles)

País	1960	1965	1970	1975	1977
Argentina	899	1 042	2 332	3 299	3 923
Barbados	...	...	...	33	46
Bolivia	183	139	244	653	863
Brasil	3 838	2 524	3 340	7 773	9 624
Colombia	1 528	2 445	3 010	3 376	4 125
Costa Rica	155	166	256	372	327
Cuba	321	424	874	711	644
Chile	411	609	575	510	589
Ecuador	135	193	419	448	...
El Salvador	37	110	138	160	215
Guatemala	62	85	113	114	138
Guyana	...	...	18	24	...
Haití	11	10	10	...	...
Honduras	152	135	296	299	329
Jamaica	...	31	279	697	674
México	1 336	1 874	2 967	6 523	8 068
Nicaragua	27	48	107	85	...
Panamá	72	118	307	357	357
Paraguay	14	36	81	65	...
Perú	231	327	391	1 335	1 426
República Dominicana	43	30	129	302	400
Trinidad y Tabago	...	383	361	369	606
Uruguay	275	273	219	334	293
Venezuela	804	885	757	2 355	3 501
Total	10 534	11 887	17 223	30 194	...

[1] Cifras parciales.
[2] Se refiere a los primeros nueve meses solamente.
[3] No incluye información sobre aerolíneas SANSA.
[4] Se refiere a los primeros cinco meses solamente.
[5] No cubre las actividades del mes de diciembre de aerolíneas AEROMEXICO.
[6] No incluye información sobre aerolíneas INAIR.
[7] No incluye información sobre los últimos tres meses de aerolíneas VIASA.

b) Passengers carried
(Thousands)

1978	1979	1980	1981	1982	1983	Country
3 950	5 020	4 398	4 907	4 596	4 400	Argentina
98	133	42	61	44	34	Barbados
1 048	1 249	989	1 240	1 160	1 299	Bolivia
8 639	12 001	13 145	7 975 [1]	13 168	12 606	Brazil
4 775	5 101	4 589	4 598 [1]	6 788	6 701	Colombia
348	383	403 [2]	332 [3]	459	380	Costa Rica
738	879	325 [4]	291 [4]	135	839	Cuba
576	579	670	886	822	652	Chile
...	...	...	...	676	655	Ecuador
231	264	266	243	255	266	El Salvador
136	156	119	124	115	100	Guatemala
...	...	...	...	93	93	Guyana
...	...	...	...	-	-	Haiti
363	418	510	412	377	426	Honduras
833	859	757	705	730	743	Jamaica
8 067	11 229	10 851 [5]	13 719	12 777	13 923	Mexico
...	...	...	...	100	95	Nicaragua
375	395	364 [6]	315	332	323	Panama
...	...	...	...	167	164	Paraguay
1 451	1 688	1 980	1 777	1 740	1 666	Peru
405	402	392 [2]	317 [2]	414	453	Dominican Republic
443	671	890	...	1 381	1 345	Trinidad and Tobago
225	231	89 [1]	179.8 [1]	356	310	Uruguay
4 043	4 775	5 144	4 984 [7]	5 667	5 092	Venezuela
...	...	...	...	52 352	52 565	Total

[1] *Partial figures.*
[2] *Refers to first nine months only.*
[3] *Does not include data on SANSA airline.*
[4] *Refers to first five months only.*
[5] *Activities do not cover December for AEROMEXICO airline.*
[6] *Does not include data on INAIR airline.*
[7] *Does not include data on last three months for VIASA airline.*

346. TRAFICO AEREO (continuación 2)

c) **Pasajeros-kilómetros**
(Millones)

País	1960	1965	1970	1975	1977
Argentina	990	1 128	2 395	4 373	4 905
Barbados	...	...	...	241	314
Bolivia	47	50	109	331	567
Brasil	2 679	2 592	4 385	9 787	11 316
Colombia	777	1 301	2 063	2 778	3 424
Costa Rica	55	89	168	306	359
Cuba	217	281	502	517	807
Chile	414	511	839	1 276	1 444
Ecuador	42	128	256	301	463
El Salvador	55	96	144	185	230
Guatemala	30	60	104	139	143
Guyana	...	...	4	5	...
Haití	1	1	1	...	...
Honduras	44	58	167	240	280
Jamaica	...	3	335	1 438	1 323
México	1 309	1 865	2 939	6 710	8 842
Nicaragua	12	34	77	83	...
Panamá	50	39	134	405	398
Paraguay	10	32	81	76	...
Perú	124	496	789	1 222	1 354
República Dominicana	11	11	68	364	446
Trinidad y Tabago	...	355	511	992	1 233
Uruguay	83	81	63	79	74
Venezuela	386	660	1 033	2 269	3 171
Total	7 336	9 870	17 167	34 117	...

[1] Cifras parciales.
[2] Se refiere a los primeros nueve meses solamente.
[3] No incluye información sobre aerolíneas SANSA.
[4] Se refiere a los primeros cinco meses solamente.
[5] No cubre las actividades del mes de diciembre de aerolíneas AEROMEXICO.
[6] No incluye información sobre los últimos tres meses de aerolíneas VIASA.

c) Passenger-kilometres
(Millions)

1978	1979	1980	1981	1982	1983	Country
5 397	6 947	6 247	7 041	6 099	6 059	Argentina
399	464	303	428	304	149	Barbados
732	889	706	988	787	812	Bolivia
12 872	14 802	15 823	10 932 [1]	17 477	16 874	Brazil
3 842	4 224	4 134	4 322 [1]	5 092	5 062	Colombia
393	468	448 [2]	574 [3]	636	513	Costa Rica
1 161	1 342	515 [4]	545 [4]	1 166	1 366	Cuba
1 540	1 601	1 878	2 220	1 824	1 493	Chile
591	752	861	...	863	896	Ecuador
238	252	290	301	336	282	El Salvador
154	190	159	174	160	156	Guatemala
...	...	...	...	151	149	Guyana
...	...	...	...	-	-	Haiti
327	362	392	344	331	377	Honduras
1 677	1 903	1 646	1 083	1 081	1 201	Jamaica
9 030	12 250	8 048 [5]	14 741	13 585	14 229	Mexico
...	...	...	...	120	120	Nicaragua
403	431	420	380	403	420	Panama
...	...	...	...	479	468	Paraguay
1 461	1 809	1 974	1 755	1 685	1 675	Peru
517	491	449 [2]	272 [2]	481	472	Dominican Republic
737	1 281	1 546	...	1 572	1 523	Trinidad and Tobago
74	169	5 [1]	85 [1]	293	325	Uruguay
3 621	4 178	4 421	3 051 [6]	5 265	3 892	Venezuela
...	...	...	...	60 190	58 513	*Total*

[1] *Partial figures.*
[2] *Refers to first nine months only.*
[3] *Does not include data on SANSA airline.*
[4] *Refers to first five months only.*
[5] *Activities do not cover December for AEROMEXICO airline.*
[6] *Does not include data on last three months for VIASA airline.*

346. TRAFICO AEREO (conclusión)

d) Toneladas-kilómetro de carga
(Millones)

País	1960	1965	1970	1975	1977
Argentina	12.1	8.7	47.9	74.6	119.8
Barbados	...	...	...	-	0.1
Bolivia	5.6	1.1	1.5	2.6	27.6
Brasil	81.4	64.7	164.1	460.5	449.3
Colombia	39.6	51.9	74.7	121.9	172.9
Costa Rica	5.4	6.4	9.3	8.9	18.3
Cuba	10.5	4.7	9.1	13.6	9.4
Chile	8.2	23.4	41.1	57.2	105.2
Ecuador	0.9	2.0	9.3	6.4	5.4
El Salvador	2.7	5.6	11.4	14.0	24.5
Guatemala	2.0	3.0	6.3	4.7	6.7
Guyana	...	...	1.2	0.7	...
Haití	-	-	-	1.9	...
Honduras	3.3	4.2	3.6	3.0	4.2
Jamaica	-	-	2.5	10.9	11.6
México	26.4	30.8	36.7	76.2	92.1
Nicaragua	2.2	0.6	0.8	1.9	...
Panamá	0.7	2.4	4.2	5.4	3.9
Paraguay	0.7	1.1	0.7	1.0	1.4
Perú	6.7	10.2	22.4	22.3	34.8
República Dominicana	0.2	0.4	4.2	1.6	16.9
Trinidad y Tabago	...	2.8	9.7	19.6	25.9
Uruguay	0.3	0.4	0.3	0.1	0.3
Venezuela	10.8	48.6	56.5	71.4	115.5
Total	219.6	273.2	517.6	980.4	...

[1] Cifras parciales.
[2] Se refiere a los primeros nueve meses solamente.
[3] No incluye información sobre aerolíneas SANSA.
[4] Se refiere a los primeros cinco meses solamente.
[5] No cubre las actividades del mes de diciembre de aerolíneas AEROMEXICO.
[6] No incluye información sobre aerolíneas INAIR.
[7] No incluye información sobre los últimos tres meses de aerolíneas VIASA.

d) Ton-kilometres of freight
(Millions)

1978	1979	1980	1981	1982	1983	Country
120.5	136.8	195.4	195.5	170.7	174.3	Argentina
0.9	0.9	0.4	0.3	1.3	-	Barbados
43.1	33.9	37.6	43.7	27.6	17.2	Bolivia
571.3	570.5	588.2	682.5 [1]	734.7	692.1	Brazil
203.4	183.1	146.6	204.0 [1]	307.2	235.3	Colombia
18.9	22.1	17.6 [2]	20.8 [3]	21.5	21.0	Costa Rica
10.4	11.6	6.1 [4]	5.1 [4]	12.7	15.8	Cuba
102.1	85.0	144.9	153.3	141.7	120.3	Chile
8.4	26.4	34.6	...	36.6	37.9	Ecuador
27.3	27.1	17.2	12.8	10.4	7.3	El Salvador
7.1	7.5	6.4	4.9	5.2	6.3	Guatemala
...	...	...	...	2.2	2.2	Guyana
...	...	...	...	2.8	2.8	Haiti
3.4	3.3	3.8	3.0	2.8	2.7	Honduras
13.2	10.7	9.4	9.9	9.7	14.9	Jamaica
90.8	121.5	111.4 [5]	136.8	110.6	109.2	Mexico
...	...	...	...	1.0	1.1	Nicaragua
3.6	5.1	2.7 [6]	15.1	14.4	1.8	Panama
...	...	...	...	2.7	2.7	Paraguay
37.7	35.7	54.8	47.6	83.3	93.9	Peru
20.4	15.7	9.0 [4]	...	9.0	7.4	Dominican Republic
14.6	21.7	17.6	...	4.9	6.7	Trinidad and Tobago
0.2	0.7	...	0.9 [1]	1.0	1.5	Uruguay
110.4	107.5	148.1	106.9 [7]	...	...	Venezuela
...	...	...	...	...	...	*Total*

[1] *Partial figures.*
[2] *Refers to first nine months only.*
[3] *Does not include data on SANSA airline.*
[4] *Refers to first five months only.*
[5] *Activities do not cover December for AEROMEXICO airline.*
[6] *Does not include data on INAIR airline.*
[7] *Does not include data on last three months for VIASA airline.*

347. POBLACION ECONOMICAMENTE ACTIVA[1] /
ECONOMICALLY ACTIVE POPULATION[1]

(Miles de personas / *Thousands of persons*)

País / *Country*	1950	1955	1960	1965	1970	1975	1980
Argentina	6 857	7 342	7 861	8 461	9 107	9 587	10 293
Bolivia	1 384	1 345	1 307	1 358	1 412	1 481	...
Brasil / *Brazil*	17 437	20 020	22 986	26 065	29 557	35 748	43 236
Colombia	3 701	4 260	4 703	5 204	5 759	6 373	...
Costa Rica	279	320	368	439	524	621	736
Cuba	1 945	2 079	2 222	2 423	2 642	3 043	3 506
Chile	2 167	2 279	2 397	2 552	2 717	3 099	3 535
Ecuador	1 239	1 324	1 415	1 603	1 816	2 054	2 324
El Salvador	659	722	792	944	1 124	1 339	...
Guatemala	962	1 082	1 217	1 342	1 479	1 575	1 677
Haití / *Haiti*	1 925	2 001	2 080	2 165	2 254	2 346	...
Honduras	711	637	570	633	703	781	...
México / *Mexico*	8 360	9 261	10 260	11 719	13 386	15 290	...
Nicaragua	358	398	443	481	523	568	...
Panamá / *Panama*	279	316	357	420	493	538	588
Paraguay	453	507	567	642	726	832	954
Perú / *Peru*	2 736	2 901	3 077	3 387	3 728	4 368	5 117
República Dominicana / *Dominican Republic*	726	788	856	1 042	1 267	1 541	...
Uruguay	841	904	971	1 014	1 059	1 106	...
Venezuela	1 732	1 995	2 299	2 641	3 034	3 701	4 515
Total[2]	54 751	60 481	66 748	74 535	83 310	95 991	...

[1] Se refiere a la población de 10 años y más.
[2] Excluye los países de habla inglesa del Caribe.

[1] *Refers to population aged 10 and over.*
[2] *Excludes English-speaking Caribbean countries.*

348. POBLACION ECONOMICAMENTE ACTIVA POR CLASES DE ACTIVIDAD ECONOMICA, 1960[1][2] / ECONOMICALLY ACTIVE POPULATION BY KIND OF ECONOMIC ACTIVITY, 1960[1][2]

(Miles de personas / Thousands of persons)

País / Country	Total	(1)	(2)	(3)	(4)	(5)	(6)	(7)	(8)
Argentina	7 886.5	1 591.5	46.5	2 185.4	493.7	95.4	1 071.0	599.4	1 803.6
Bolivia	1 179.7	752.2	42.8	116.0	35.1	1.3	64.0	28.6	139.7
Brasil / Brazil	23 089.3	12 029.5	161.6	3 163.2	854.3	161.6	1 847.1	1 177.6	3 694.4
Colombia	4 688.6	2 410.0	79.7	609.5	196.9	14.1	361.0	178.1	839.3
Costa Rica	360.8	185.7	1.0	41.6	19.8	3.5	34.2	13.4	61.6
Cuba	2 360.1	864.9	12.0	434.5	106.7	6.7	203.9	136.9	594.5
Chile	2 479.0	743.7	101.6	473.5	146.2	19.8	267.8	128.9	597.5
Ecuador	1 454.3	841.0	4.2	201.8	49.5	4.0	98.3	43.0	212.5
El Salvador	824.5	507.9	0.7	106.4	33.0	1.7	51.1	17.3	106.4
Guatemala	1 229.0	819.8	1.2	129.0	32.0	1.2	75.0	27.0	143.8
Haití / Haiti	1 973.4	1 556.8	0.6	124.4	19.9	1.6	114.7	13.6	141.8
Honduras	609.6	428.0	1.9	48.2	12.2	0.6	27.4	8.4	82.9
México / Mexico	10 704.8	5 898.4	139.2	1 466.6	385.4	42.8	1 006.2	331.8	1 434.4
Nicaragua	483.8	300.7	4.2	55.8	15.0	1.2	31.2	11.5	64.2
Panamá / Panama	349.8	178.1	0.4	30.1	16.4	1.8	34.9	11.6	76.5
Paraguay	598.5	337.0	0.6	91.5	20.4	1.2	42.5	14.9	90.4
Perú / Peru	3 222.6	1 678.1	77.1	442.4	112.7	12.5	302.6	99.6	497.6
República Dominicana/ Dominican Republic	894.8	592.4	2.7	77.0	24.1	3.6	63.5	24.1	107.4
Uruguay	970.0	190.5	3.7	226.6	47.8	19.3	134.5	64.0	283.6
Venezuela	2 353.7	793.2	57.9	306.2	140.0	25.2	313.5	125.3	592.4
Total	67 712.8	32 699.4	739.6	10 329.7	2 761.1	419.1	6 144.4	3 055.0	11 564.5

[1] De acuerdo con la Clasificación Industrial Internacional Uniforme de Todas las Actividades Económicas (CIIU), revisión 1:

    (1) = Agricultura, silvicultura, caza y pesca.
    (2) = Explotación de minas y canteras.
    (3) = Industrias manufactureras.
    (4) = Construcción.
    (5) = Electricidad, gas, agua y servicios sanitarios.
    (6) = Comercio.
    (7) = Transporte, almacenamiento y comunicaciones.
    (8) = Servicios.

[2] Se refiere a la población económicamente activa de 10 años y más, excluidas las personas que buscan trabajo por primera vez.

[1] In accordance with International Standard Industrial Classification of All Economic Activities (ISIC), rev. 1:

    (1) = Agriculture, forestry, hunting and fishing.
    (2) = Mining and quarrying.
    (3) = Manufacturing.
    (4) = Construction.
    (5) = Electricity, gas, water and sanitary services.
    (6) = Commerce.
    (7) = Transport, storage and communications.
    (8) = Services.

[2] Refers to economically active population aged 10 and over, excluding persons seeking employment for the first time.

349. POBLACION ECONOMICAMENTE ACTIVA POR CLASES DE ACTIVIDAD ECONOMICA, 1970[1][2] / ECONOMICALLY ACTIVE POPULATION BY KIND OF ECONOMIC ACTIVITY, 1970[1][2]

(Miles de personas / *Thousands of persons*)

País / Country	Total	(1)	(2)	(3)	(4)	(5)	(6)	(7)	(8)
Argentina	9 054.6	1 485.9	49.8	2 169.5	783.3	107.7	1 335.5	656.4	2 466.5
Bolivia	1 387.2	744.5	53.0	156.3	65.5	1.8	92.7	49.1	224.3
Brasil / Brazil	29 944.1	13 654.5	179.6	4 431.8	1 766.7	299.4	2 784.8	1 287.6	5 539.7
Colombia	6 192.7	2 347.0	61.9	1 071.4	315.8	24.8	767.9	284.9	1 319.0
Costa Rica	511.8	215.0	1.4	70.2	34.1	5.9	55.0	21.8	108.4
Cuba	2 614.8	792.0	13.0	519.3	159.2	5.3	159.2	164.5	802.3
Chile	2 934.9	698.5	91.0	639.8	184.9	26.4	337.5	190.8	766.0
Ecuador	1 803.4	920.3	6.5	281.9	77.2	8.1	157.2	57.9	294.3
El Salvador	1 170.9	656.8	0.1	132.3	31.6	4.7	97.2	35.1	213.1
Guatemala	1 607.9	980.8	3.2	207.4	59.5	3.2	114.2	38.6	201.0
Haití / Haiti	2 297.0	1 641.4	0.9	180.3	38.8	2.6	210.7	28.7	193.6
Honduras	782.9	520.6	2.4	82.2	20.3	2.3	47.8	18.0	89.3
México / Mexico	13 932.8	6 297.6	153.2	2 577.6	613.0	69.7	1 393.3	459.8	2 368.6
Nicaragua	526.8	263.5	2.9	77.0	21.0	4.4	49.7	18.0	90.3
Panamá / Panama	483.5	201.1	1.0	47.9	31.0	4.8	57.0	18.3	122.4
Paraguay	743.4	391.0	0.8	119.0	28.3	2.2	59.4	21.6	121.1
Perú / Peru	3 828.6	1 769.6	65.5	443.8	184.1	9.2	391.3	173.4	791.7
República Dominicana/ Dominican Republic	1 339.1	725.8	1.4	179.4	41.5	2.7	109.8	62.9	215.6
Uruguay	1 082.8	197.3	2.9	249.1	59.5	17.9	149.7	66.1	340.3
Venezuela	3 132.8	803.2	46.4	489.0	191.4	41.1	460.9	150.0	950.8
Total	85 372.0	35 306.4	736.9	14 125.2	4 706.7	644.2	8 830.8	3 803.5	17 218.3

[1] De acuerdo con la Clasificación Industrial Internacional Uniforme de Todas las Actividades Económicas (CIIU), revisión 1:

    (1) = Agricultura, silvicultura, caza y pesca.
    (2) = Explotación de minas y canteras.
    (3) = Industrias manufactureras.
    (4) = Construcción.
    (5) = Electricidad, gas, agua y servicios sanitarios.
    (6) = Comercio.
    (7) = Transporte, almacenamiento y comunicaciones.
    (8) = Servicios.

[2] Se refiere a la población económicamente activa de 10 años y más, excluidas las personas que buscan trabajo por primera vez.

[1] In accordance with International Standard Industrial Classification of All Economic Activities (ISIC), rev. 1:

    (1) = Agriculture, forestry, hunting and fishing.
    (2) = Mining and quarrying.
    (3) = Manufacturing.
    (4) = Construction.
    (5) = Electricity, gas, water and sanitary services.
    (6) = Commerce.
    (7) = Transport, storage and communications.
    (8) = Services.

[2] Refers to economically active population aged 10 and over, excluding persons seeking employment for the first time.

350. POBLACION ECONOMICAMENTE ACTIVA POR CLASES DE ACTIVIDAD ECONOMICA, 1980[1][2] / ECONOMICALLY ACTIVE POPULATION BY KIND OF ECONOMIC ACTIVITY, 1980[1][2]

(Miles de personas / Thousands of persons)

País / Country	Total	(1)	(2)	(3)	(4)	(5)	(6)	(7)	(8)	(9)
Argentina	10 068.4	1 314.1	50.8	2 147.8	111.1	1 080.0	1 842.8	495.7	425.9	2 620.0
Brasil / Brazil	42 801.2	12 991.5	256.1	7 670.3	418.7	3 231.7	5 140.4	1 985.4	1 021.6	10 085.6
Costa Rica	764.9	219.3	1.5	123.5	9.4	55.9	115.4	33.5	20.0	186.3
Chile	3 580.9	582.5	81.0	596.1	27.1	188.3	641.6	231.9	108.1	1124.3
Ecuador[3]	2 341.5	814.3	7.2	292.5	14.9	162.4	273.8	106.2	39.4	630.8
Guatemala[4]	1 638.8	945.6	2.4	186.7	8.0	89.7	155.4	45.1	22.3	228.6
Panamá / Panama	554.8	174.5	1.0	57.7	8.4	33.1	72.9	30.9	20.3	156.1
Paraguay[3]	1 018.7	458.0	1.1	125.3	2.6	67.3	86.1	26.4	17.1	234.8
Perú[4] / Peru[4]	5 126.4	2 029.2	101.1	597.4	19.0	204.6	692.1	220.1	131.1	1 131.8

[1] De acuerdo con la Clasificación Industrial Internacional Uniforme de Todas las Actividades Económicas (CIIU), revisión 2:
  (1) = Agricultura, caza, silvicultura y pesca.
  (2) = Explotación de minas y canteras.
  (3) = Industrias manufactureras.
  (4) = Electricidad, gas y agua.
  (5) = Construcción.
  (6) = Comercio al por mayor y al por menor y restaurantes y hoteles.
  (7) = Transporte, almacenamiento y comunicaciones.
  (8) = Establecimientos financieros, seguros, bienes inmuebles y servicios prestados a las empresas.
  (9) = Servicios comunales, sociales y personales.
[2] Se refiere a la población económicamente activa de 10 años y más, excluidas las personas que buscan trabajo por primera vez.
[3] Corresponde a 1982.
[4] Corresponde a 1981.

[1] In accordance with International Standard Industrial Classification of All Economic Activities (ISIC), rev. 2:
  (1) = Agriculture, hunting, forestry and fishing.
  (2) = Mining and quarrying.
  (3) = Manufacturing.
  (4) = Electricity, gas and water.
  (5) = Construction.
  (6) = Wholesale and retail trade and restaurants and hotels.
  (7) = Transport, storage and communications.
  (8) = Finance, insurance, real estate and business services.
  (9) = Community, social and personal services.
[2] Refers to economically active population aged 10 and over, excluding persons seeking employment for the first time.
[3] Corresponds to 1982.
[4] Corresponds to 1981.

IX. EMPLEO

351. POBLACION ECONOMICAMENTE ACTIVA POR OCUPACIONES

a) De acuerdo con la Clasificación internacional uniforme de ocupaciones de la OIT [1]
(Miles de personas)

País	Año de referencia *Reference year*	Edad en años [2] *Age in years* [2]	Ocupaciones [3]			
			Total	0/1	2	3
Argentina	1970	10	9 011.5	677.5	137.9	1 025.4
Argentina	1980[4]	14	9 989.2	995.8	51.4	1 454.7
Brasil	1970[5]	10	29 557.2	1 397.1	349.2	1 510.6
Colombia	1973	10	5 971.0	269.7	39.3	355.2
Cuba	1970	10	2 633.3	220.3	112.7	136.2
Ecuador	1974	12	1 890.4	94.1	15.2	67.4
México	1970	12	12 955.1	733.2	319.8	977.2
Perú	1972	14	3 871.6	288.0	16.1	223.0
Perú	1980[7]	15	4 926.1	392.6	24.3	514.4
República Dominicana	1970	10	1 241.0	34.1	3.8	81.2

[1] Edición revisada, 1968.
[2] Límite inferior de edad.
[3] Principales grupos ocupacionales:
  0/1 - Profesionales, técnicos y trabajadores asimilados.
  2 - Directores y funcionarios públicos superiores.
  3 - Personal administrativo y trabajadores asimilados.
  4 - Comerciantes y vendedores.
  5 - Trabajadores de los servicios.
  6 - Trabajadores agrícolas y forestales, pescadores y cazadores.
  7/8/9 - Obreros no agrícolas, conductores de máquinas y vehículos de transporte y trabajadores asirnilados.
  X - Trabajadores que no pueden ser clasificados según la ocupación.
[4] Excluye personas que buscan trabajo por primera vez.
[5] Utiliza una clasificación nacional que fue adaptada a la Clasificación internacional uniforme de ocupaciones, revisada en 1968.
[6] Incluye personas sin ocupación.
[7] Población ocupada.

351. ECONOMICALLY ACTIVE POPULATION, BY OCCUPATION

a) According to the International standard classification of occupations of the ILO [1]

(Thousands of persons)

Occupations [3]					Country
4	5	6	7/8/9	X	
1 072.8	1 136.6	1 296.1	3 091.4	573.9	*Argentina*
1 338.9	1 222.4	1 123.6	3 513.9	288.5	*Argentina*
2 193.7	2 297.1	13 109.1	5 689.8	3 010.6	*Brazil*
443.1	597.5	1 600.4	1 229.4	1 440.4[6]	*Colombia*
............564.4		708.2	857.1	34.4	*Cuba*
142.3	128.8	878.2	427.2	137.2	*Ecuador*
967.3	1 560.6	4 972.2	2 768.8	676.0	*Mexico*
323.9	336.0	1 570.3	879.5	234.8	*Peru*
523.9	375.8	1 817.4	992.7	285.0	*Peru*
61.7	63.2	551.6	241.5	203.9	*Dominican Republic*

[1] *Revised edition 1968.*
[2] *Minimun age.*
[3] *Major occupational groups:*
    0/1 - Professional, technical and related workers.
    2 - Administrative and managerial workers.
    3 - Clerical and related workers.
    4 - Sales workers.
    5 - Service workers.
    6 - Agriculture, animal husbandry and forestry workers, fishermen and hunters.
  7/8/9 - Production and related workers, transport equipment operators and labourers.
    X - Workers not classifiable by occupation.
[4] *Excludes persons seeking employment for the first time.*
[5] *Uses a national classification which was adapted to the International standard classification of occupations, revised edition, 1968.*
[6] *Including unemployed persons.*
[7] *Employed population.*

351. POBLACION ECONOMICAMENTE ACTIVA POR OCUPACIONES

b) De acuerdo con la Clasificación Ocupacional de COTA-1970 del IASI
(Miles de personas)

País	Año de referencia *Reference year*	Edad en años [1] *Age in years* [1]	Ocupaciones [2]					
			Total	0	1	2	3	4
Barbados	1970	10	84.0	7.8	1.2	7.5	7.5	13.0
Bolivia	1976	7	1 510.6	88.4	29.0	60.3	78.1	682.9
Costa Rica	1973	12	585.3	46.6	9.7	33.6	45.5	207.7
Chile	1970	12	2 607.4	185.0	49.9	249.0	213.7	549.9
El Salvador	1971	10	1 314.9	39.3	2.2	42.2	77.3	610.7
Guatemala	1973	10	1 547.3	48.5	24.3	41.8	89.1	874.3
Honduras [3]	1974	10	755.6	31.0	7.0	31.8	43.9	453.1
Jamaica	1970	14	566.4	31.3	3.4	31.5	35.9	138.1
Nicaragua	1971	10	504.2	26.0	4.8	21.1	35.9	235.1
Panamá	1970	10	488.3	27.6	12.9	38.6	30.3	181.7
Panamá	1980	10 [4]	503.5	55.1	24.2	51.5	33.8	139.4
Paraguay	1972	12	728.3	31.3	4.6	27.4	50.2	367.6
Uruguay [3]	1975	12	1 077.3	79.2	16.0	114.3	100.0	170.3
Venezuela	1971	15	3 014.7	233.7	76.0	245.6	306.9	611.8

[1] Límite inferior de edad.
[2] Principales grupos ocupacionales:
  0 - Profesionales, técnicos y personas en ocupaciones afines.
  1 - Gerentes, administradores y funcionarios de categoría directiva.
  2 - Empleados de oficina y personas en ocupaciones afines.
  3 - Vendedores y personas en ocupaciones afines.
  4 - Agricultores, pescadores y personas en ocupaciones afines.
  5 - Conductores de medios de transporte y personas en ocupaciones afines.
  6 - Artesanos y operarios.
  7 - Otros artesanos y operarios, mineros y canteros y personas en ocupaciones
    afines.
  8 - Obreros y jornaleros no clasificados en otro grupo (n.c.e.o.g.).
  9 - Trabajadores en servicios personales y ocupaciones afines.
  X - Personas en ocupaciones no identificables o no declaradas y otras personas n.c.e.o.g.
    (incluye miembros de las fuerzas armadas).
[3] Excluye personas que buscan trabajo por primera vez.
[4] Excluye la población de los corregimientos de Cristóbal, Ancón y áreas indígenas.

351. ECONOMICALLY ACTIVE POPULATION, BY OCCUPATION

b) According to the IASI COTA-1970 Employment Classification.

(Thousands of persons)

5	6	7	8	9	X	Country
1.2	············· 23.5 ············		3.9	16.1	2.3	Barbados
41.4	217.1	68.5	51.8	128.4	64.7	Bolivia
17.4	···················· 67.7 ····················			68.1	89.0	Costa Rica
103.6	425.7	138.2	203.4	303.7	185.3	Chile
································ 190.6 ································				93.6	259.0	El Salvador
38.5	···················· 283.4 ····················			124.3	23.1	Guatemala
6.5	61.0	39.2	24.7	49.7	7.7	Honduras [3]
5.0	119.6	32.9	1.4	67.6	99.7	Jamaica
16.2	61.4	18.6	14.2	55.1	15.8	Nicaragua
18.4	55.4	10.0	20.2	71.4	21.8	Panama
24.2	63.6	12.4	17.6	73.5	8.3	Panama
15.9	131.2	-	14.3	72.1	13.7	Paraguay
29.5	182.3	75.7	41.2	148.0	120.8	Uruguay [3]
································ 777.4 ································				361.9	401.4	Venezuela

Occupations [2]

[1] Minimun age.
[2] Major occupational groups:
    0 - Professional, technical and related workers.
    1 - Managers administrators and officials.
    2 - Clerical office and other workers in related occupations.
    3 - Sales workers and persons in related occupations.
    4 - Farmers, fishermen and persons in related occupations.
    5 - Workers operating vehicles and persons in related occupations.
    6 - Craftsmen and operatives.
    7 - Other craftsmen and operatives, miners, quarrymen and persons in related
       occupations.
    8 - Workers and labourers not elsewhere classified (n.e.c.).
    9 - Personal service and related workers.
    X - Workers in unidentifiable or unspecified occupations and other workers, n.e.c.
       (including members of the armed forces).
[3] Excluding persons seeking employment for the first time.
[4] Excluding population of administrative areas of Cristóbal and Ancón and indigenous areas.

352. POBLACION ECONOMICAMENTE ACTIVA POR CATEGORIA DE EMPLEO

(Miles de personas)

País	Año de referencia *Reference year*	Edad en años [1] *Age in years* [1]
Argentina	1970	14
Argentina	1980	14
Bolivia	1976	10 [2]
Brasil	1970	10
Brasil	1980	10
Colombia	1970	12
Costa Rica	1973	12
Cuba	1970	14
Cuba	1981	15
Chile	1970	12
Ecuador	1974	12
El Salvador	1971	10
Guatemala	1973	10
Haití	1975	5
Honduras	1974	10
México	1970	12
Nicaragua	1971	15
Panamá	1970	10 [2]
Panamá	1980	10 [5]
Paraguay	1972	12
Perú	1972	6
Perú	1980	15 [2]
República Dominicana	1970	10
Uruguay	1975	12
Venezuela	1971	15

[1] Límite inferior de edad.
[2] Población ocupada.
[3] Incluye 230 700 personas cuya categoría de empleo es "miembros de cooperativas de producción".
[4] Incluye cooperativistas, pequeños agricultores y trabajadores por cuenta propia.
[5] Excluye la población de los corregimientos de Cristóbal, Ancón y áreas indígenas.

352. ECONOMICALLY ACTIVE POPULATION BY CATEGORY OF EMPLOYMENT

(Thousands of persons)

Categoría del empleo / *Category of employment*			Familiares no remunerados *Unremunerated family members*	Country
Total	Asalariados *Wage earners*	Autoempleados *Self-employed*		
8 807.0	6 506.7	2 010.3	290.0	*Argentina*
9 989.2	7 147.3	2 515.4	326.5	*Argentina*
1 448.3	576.7	697.8	173.8	*Bolivia*
29 338.4	16 049.6	10 408.2	2 880.6	*Brazil*
42 271.5	27 141.8	12 879.9	2 249.8	*Brazil*
6 046.8	3 573.7	2 006.7	466.4	*Colombia*
564.9	430.1	100.1	34.6	*Costa Rica*
2 627.5	2 334.4 [3]	30.3	32.1	*Cuba*
3 540.7	3 331.6 [4]	202.1	7.0	*Cuba*
2 662.0	2 016.6	582.9	62.5	*Chile*
1 940.6	1 004.1	763.3	173.3	*Ecuador*
1 146.8	717.4	306.6	122.9	*El Salvador*
1 535.6	746.6	616.0	173.0	*Guatemala*
2 091.8	380.3	1 040.6	670.9	*Haiti*
756.1	349.1	304.3	102.7	*Honduras*
12 955.1	8 054.8	4 054.1	846.2	*Mexico*
474.8	291.4	152.9	30.5	*Nicaragua*
424.6	230.3	171.2	23.1	*Panama*
503.5	352.3	131.2	20.0	*Panama*
746.0	308.8	346.4	90.8	*Paraguay*
3 800.1	1 933.2	1 635.2	231.7	*Peru*
4 926.1	2 476.0	2 178.4	271.7	*Peru*
1 211.7	629.2	495.9	86.6	*Dominican Republic*
1 082.8	787.6	270.7	24.5	*Uruguay*
2 978.2	1 918.9	1 017.1	42.2	*Venezuela*

[1] *Minimum age.*
[2] *Employed population.*
[3] *Including 230 700 persons classified as "members of production co-operatives".*
[4] *Including members of co-operatives, small farmers and own-account workers.*
[5] *Excluding population of administrative areas of Cristóbal and Ancón and indigenous areas.*

353. CAMAS DE HOSPITAL

(Número de camas)

País	1960	1965	1970	1975	1977
Argentina	130 958	141 888	133 847	...	...
Barbados	1 368	1 629	2 445	2 161	2 146
Belice	...	...	...	...	665
Bolivia	6 184	9 381	9 674	10 722	9 193
Brasil	233 905	290 298	354 373	425 413	454 764
Colombia	43 416	46 591	47 318	44 642	45 143
Costa Rica	5 610	6 226	7 008	7 549	7 163
Cuba	30 500	48 669	57 653	51 244	51 192
Chile	27 954	35 956	35 932	38 645	37 758
Dominica	...	...	...	...	...
Ecuador	8 304	12 034	14 024	13 464	13 950
El Salvador	5 629	5 552	7 027	6 022	5 918
Granada	...	...	...	...	...
Guatemala	10 427	11 053	12 304	11 403	10 898
Guyana	3 172	3 962	3 377	3 969	...
Haití	2 316	2 389	3 545 [1]	4 104	4 514 [1]
Honduras	3 118	3 324	4 376	4 602	4 653
Jamaica	6 753	7 023	7 672	7 780	7 717
México	62 964	86 151	71 318	82 141	81 802
Nicaragua	3 328	3 652	4 841	4 840	5 052
Panamá	4 251	4 434 [2]	4 974 [2]	6 324 [2]	6 842 [2]
Paraguay	4 401	4 304	3 829	3 332	3 015
Perú	23 948	28 284	28 666	33 359	29 934
República Dominicana	7 524	10 425	11 674	12 618	...
Suriname	...	...	...	...	...
Trinidad y Tabago	4 712	4 247	4 800	4 815	...
Uruguay	13 989	13 743	16 603	11 812	...
Venezuela	26 029	28 348	32 877	35 867	39 687

[1] Se refiere al número de camas en establecimientos del gobierno solamente.
[2] Incluye camas para recién nacidos.

(Number of beds)

1978	1979	1980	1981	1982	1983	Country
142 975	...	151 568	...	...	...	Argentina
...	...	2 129	2 144	2 151	...	Barbados
...	...	...	...	...	...	Belize
9 353	9 947	10 135	...	...	...	Bolivia
475 382	488 323	509 104	...	...	...	Brazil
45 003	44 853	...	...	...	...	Colombia
7 358	7 505	7 570	...	...	...	Costa Rica
51 595	52 676	53 417	56 492	58 271	...	Cuba
37 871	38 856	37 967	37 547	...	...	Chile
...	...	...	...	...	...	Dominica
14 294	14 316	...	...	...	...	Ecuador
5 921	5 909	5 987	6 177	6 202	...	El Salvador
639	...	...	...	...	...	Grenada
11 198	12 401	12 595	11 356	...	...	Guatemala
3 906	...	...	...	...	...	Guyana
4 591 [1]	...	...	5 250 [1]	...	...	Haiti
4 619	5 025	4 980	5 033	...	...	Honduras
7 644	...	...	...	...	...	Jamaica
81 059	81 478	82 717	...	...	...	Mexico
4 427	4 813	4 677	4 729	4 765	4 897	Nicaragua
6 954 [2]	7 042 [2]	7 345 [2]	7 398 [2]	7 482 [2]	...	Panama
2 900	3 207	3 305	3 273	...	...	Paraguay
...	29 341	28 708	...	29 991	...	Peru
...	...	...	...	...	...	Dominican Republic
2 073	...	...	...	...	...	Suriname
...	...	...	...	...	...	Trinidad and Tobago
...	...	17 441	...	...	...	Uruguay
41 386	40 575	41 296	43 546	43 546	...	Venezuela

[1] *Beds in government establishments only.*
[2] *Including beds for newborn.*

354. MEDICOS

(Número de médicos)

País	1960	1965	1970	1975	1977
Argentina	30 295 [1]	...	45 340	48 695	...
Barbados	77	94 [2]	...	166	181
Belice	...	...	...	...	46
Bolivia	657 [3]	...	2 143	1 445 [3]	2 878
Brasil	32 795	34 251 [2]	46 051 [4]	...	76 615 [4]
Colombia	5 970	7 310	9 299	11 491	12 720
Costa Rica	458	725	1 067	...	...
Cuba	6 609	6 238 [3]	6 152 [3]	9 328 [3]	13 908 [3]
Chile	4 621 [3]	4 842 [2 3]	4 401 [3]	4 414 [3]	6 516 [5]
Dominica	...	...	...	...	...
Ecuador	1 656 [4]	1 698 [4]	2 082 [4]	3 281 [4]	4 660
El Salvador	483	652	851	1 007	717
Granada	...	...	...	...	...
Guatemala	...	1 112	1 435	2 437	3 124
Guyana	145	...	...	120 [6]	...
Haití	...	314	...	428	...
Honduras	154 [3]	350	658	926	1 007
Jamaica	...	854 [2]	710 [6]	...	361 [3]
México	20 227	21 165	33 981	48 939	59 204
Nicaragua	524	779	961	1 233	1 319
Panamá	401	586	857	1 251	1 383
Paraguay	493 [1]	1 180 [2]	2 567	2 225 [6]	...
Perú	5 061 [1]	5 262 [2]	...	9 229	10 514
República Dominicana	442 [3]	2 153 [2]	...	1 052	1 229
Suriname	...	...	...	...	...
Trinidad y Tabago	352	255	...	550	...
Uruguay	1 164 [3]	3 051 [2]	3 070	3 983	...
Venezuela	5 045	6 584 [2]	9 471	13 608	14 565

[1] Número de médicos registrados; no todos son residentes o trabajan en el país.
[2] 1964.
[3] Ministerio de Salud solamente.
[4] Médicos que trabajan en establecimientos de salud.
[5] Médicos inscritos en el Colegio Médico y que trabajan en el país.
[6] Cobertura desconocida.

(Number of physicians)

1978	1979	1980	1981	1982	1983	Country
74 098	...	72 762	...	...	...	Argentina
192	201	212	218	221	...	Barbados
...	...	...	...	...	...	Belize
3 410	2 725	2 853	...	...	...	Bolivia
83 515 [4]	86 114 [4]	94 921 [4]	...	...	...	Brazil
12 915	13 446	14 546	15 261	...	...	Colombia
1 358	...	...	...	2 009	...	Costa Rica
14 338 [3]	15 038 [3]	15 247 [3]	16 210 [3]	17 026 [3]	...	Cuba
5 248 [3]	6 972 [5]	9 748 [5]	4 128 [3]	...	...	Chile
10	...	...	...	...	...	Dominica
...	...	...	...	...	...	Ecuador
1 323	1 383	1 582	1 603	1 607	...	El Salvador
25	...	...	...	...	...	Grenada
3 474	3 901	...	...	...	...	Guatemala
...	85 [3]	...	...	...	...	Guyana
...	...	...	482 [3]	...	...	Haiti
1 083	1 141	1 212	1 323	1 429	1 618	Honduras
365 [3]	759	...	...	...	...	Jamaica
49 068	62 713	66 378	...	...	...	Mexico
1 311	1 345	1 212	1 541	1 951	2 060	Nicaragua
1 550	1 686	1 821	1 975	2 044	...	Panama
...	...	...	...	2 077	...	Paraguay
...	...	12 432	13 542	14 751	...	Peru
...	...	...	...	...	...	Dominican Republic
214	...	...	...	...	...	Suriname
780	...	786	...	...	...	Trinidad and Tobago
...	5 400	...	5 480	...	...	Uruguay
14 771	15 359	16 242	17 425	19 204	...	Venezuela

[1] Number of doctors registered; not all live or work in the country.
[2] 1964.
[3] Ministry of Health only.
[4] Doctors working in health institutions.
[5] Doctors enrolled in the Medical Association and working in the country.
[6] Extent of coverage unknown.

355. AUXILIARES MEDICOS [1]

(Número de auxiliares médicos)

País	1960	1965	1970	1975	1977
Argentina	...	30 332[2]	38 181[3]	...	40 811[4]
Barbados	449	813[2][5]	...	796	1 058
Belice	...	...	...	...	326[4]
Bolivia	822	1 559[2]	1 806[4]	1 784[4][6]	4 363[4][6]
Brasil	...	...	34 864[4]	...	59 619[4]
Colombia	...	12 077	9 640	16 298	19 971
Costa Rica	1 575[4][5]	2 166	3 436	...	...
Cuba	...	9 637	11 803	21 193	24 900
Chile	10 282	15 040[4]	19 364[4][5]	24 215[4][5]	...
Dominica	...	...	...	...	...
Ecuador	...	2 213	3 711	6 844	9 322
El Salvador	1 293[5]	2 829	2 426	3 183	3 631
Granada	...	...	...	...	...
Guatemala	...	2 780	4 246	...	...
Guyana	325[5][8]	...	...	...	...
Haití	...	347[4]	...	1 548[5]	...
Honduras	624	1 328	1 767	3 035[4]	4 166[4]
Jamaica	...	...	1 088[5][9]	...	3 450[4]
México	4 610	48 252	36 850	63 790[4]	74 719[4]
Nicaragua	421	1 601	2 558	2 596	3 506
Panamá	1 447	1 921	2 683	3 957	3 903
Paraguay	...	1 605	1 275[10]	1 682[10]	...
Perú	2 736[9]	9 383	...	7 573[8]	19 706
República Dominicana	994[5]	1 938	...	...	3 484
Suríname	...	...	...	...	...
Trinidad y Tabago	1 254[8]	1 583	2 097[3]	2 576	...
Uruguay	...	4 252[2]	...	...	...
Venezuela	...	...	24 604	31 419	35 637

[1] Incluye enfermeras graduadas y auxiliares de enfermería.
[2] 1964.
[3] 1969.
[4] Incluye matronas.
[5] Sólo funcionarios del Ministerio de Salud.
[6] Incluye laboratoristas, técnicos y otros.
[7] Sólo auxiliares de enfermería.
[8] Sólo enfermeras graduadas.
[9] No especifica si se trata de enfermeras graduadas, auxiliares de enfermería o de ambos tipos.
[10] Cobertura desconocida.
[11] Sólo matronas.

355. MEDICAL ASSISTANTS [1]

(Number of medical assistants)

1978	1979	1980	1981	1982	1983	Country
69 577[4]	...	71 997[4]	...	...	...	Argentina
997	1 205	1 192	1 189	1 183	...	Barbados
...	...	...	...	...	...	Belize
...	4 958	5 610	...	...	...	Bolivia
65 500[4]	70 297[4]	76 547[4]	...	...	...	Brazil
21 780	22 833	24 639	25 653	26 415	...	Colombia
3 140	...	...	...	7 687	...	Costa Rica
26 249	26 457	27 193	29 399	31 855	...	Cuba
23 259[57]	23 248[57]	24 975[57]	24 975[57]	...		Chile
136[4]	...	...	...	...	...	Dominica
...	...	12 200	...	...	...	Ecuador
3 964	3 935	4 049	4 095	4 069	...	El Salvador
144[4]	...	...	...	...	...	Grenada
...	...	4 759	...	5 396	...	Guatemala
...	1 427[4 5]	1 850[4]	...	...	...	Guyana
...	3 911[4 5]	1 899[4]	1 384[5]	...	...	Haiti
5 448[4]	7 108[4]	7 819[4]	9 151[4]	10 141[4]	848[8]	Honduras
2 595[4]	3 915[4 5]	...	...	...	...	Jamaica
77 824[4]	83 731[4]	98 066[4]	...	...	...	Mexico
2 252	640[8]	4 687	4 862	4 790	5 377	Nicaragua
4 184	4 314	4 415	4 885	5 036	...	Panama
...	...	12 232[4 8]	13 064[4 8]	...	...	Paraguay
...	18 843[4]	...	...	...	...	Peru
...	...	4 481	...	...	...	Dominican Republic
1 123[4]	...	...	...	...	...	Suriname
...	...	2 837	...	...	...	Trinidad and Tobago
...	...	...	373[11]	...	...	Uruguay
38 061	43 848	43 848	46 028	...	...	Venezuela

[1] *Including graduate nurses and nursing auxiliaries.*
[2] *1964.*
[3] *1969.*
[4] *Including midwives.*
[5] *Ministry of Health staff only.*
[6] *Including laboratory workers, technicians and others.*
[7] *Nursing auxiliaries only.*
[8] *Only graduate nurses.*
[9] *It is not specified whether these are graduate nurses, nursing auxiliaries or both.*
[10] *Extent of coverage unknown.*
[11] *Midwives only.*

356. MATRICULA EN LA ENSEÑANZA DE PRIMER NIVEL

(Número de matriculados)

País	1960	1965	1970	1975	1977
Argentina	2 849 071	3 124 870	3 648 057	3 802 299	3 884 025
Barbados	37 401	39 615 [1]	37 866 [1]	32 884	34 324
Belice	...	...	31 629	33 444	...
Bolivia	397 934	542 564	679 123	879 826	718 794
Brasil	8 368 285	11 568 503	15 904 627	19 549 249	20 566 760
Colombia	1 690 361	2 274 014	3 286 052	3 911 244	4 160 257
Costa Rica	198 049	283 210	356 696	370 115	374 622
Cuba	1 136 277	1 242 256	1 530 376	1 795 752	1 693 942
Chile	1 257 106	1 636 017	2 040 071	2 298 998	2 242 111
Dominica	...	...	17 808	17 166	17 402
Ecuador	569 019 [3]	800 507 [3]	1 016 483 [3]	1 216 233	1 307 158
El Salvador	339 372 [3]	387 249	531 309	640 315	690 140
Granada	...	...	30 355	21 195 [4]	19 618 [4]
Guatemala	277 816	424 526	523 095	619 834	673 026
Guyana	106 086 [1]	131 247 [1]	130 484 [1]	130 240 [1]	138 144 [1]
Haití	238 982	283 799	315 704	451 140	510 720 [5]
Honduras	205 113	283 606	381 685	460 744	493 223
Jamaica	194 667 [6]	262 920 [6]	354 486	371 876	350 816 [2]
México	4 884 988	6 916 204	9 248 290	11 395 258	13 220 187
Nicaragua	162 330	206 241	285 285	350 519	378 943
Panamá	161 800	203 429	255 287	342 043	357 753
Paraguay	301 711 [3]	356 998 [3]	431 743 [3]	452 249 [3]	477 237 [3]
Perú	1 408 365 [3]	1 900 617	2 341 068	2 840 625	3 019 624
República Dominicana	505 046	556 694	764 085	903 440	946 869
Suriname	...	...	91 834	80 171	85 250
Trinidad y Tabago	126 550 [1]	151 319 [1]	166 108 [1]	199 033 [1]	181 863 [1]
Uruguay	319 904	335 089	354 096	322 602	324 361
Venezuela	1 222 978	1 453 310	1 769 680	2 108 413	2 309 173

[1] Escuelas públicas y subvencionadas solamente.
[2] Enseñanza pública solamente.
[3] Incluye escuelas nocturnas.
[4] A partir del año 1975, las "forms I, II y III" clasificadas anteriormente en la enseñanza de primer nivel han sido incluidas en la enseñanza general de segundo nivel.
[5] A partir del año 1976 la duración de la enseñanza de primer nivel disminuyó de siete a seis años.
[6] Hasta 1969 se estimó la enseñanza privada en un 11% del total en primer nivel.
[7] Cambio en el número de años de escolaridad en Nicaragua a partir de 1980.

356. ENROLMENT IN PRIMARY LEVEL

(Number of students enrolled)

1978	1979	1980	1981	1982	1983	Country
3 937 135	4 003 670	4 110 821	4 217 992	4 382 351	4 511 122	Argentina
38 536	37 434	37 422	37 270	36 496	34 848	Barbados
...	...	...	...	...	...	Belize
817 662	846 849	863 927	1 022 624	...	...	Bolivia
21 473 100	21 886 805	22 148 809	...	...	...	Brazil
4 265 598	4 337 607	4 168 200	4 217 800	...	...	Colombia
357 057 [2]	361 025	354 789	354 318	...	...	Costa Rica
1 626 386	1 550 323	1 468 538	1 409 765	1 363 078	...	Cuba
2 232 990	2 235 861	2 413 232	2 354 958	2 306 817	...	Chile
16 540	...	...	...	...	...	Dominica
1 367 205	1 427 627 [3]	...	...	...	...	Ecuador
830 323 [3]	873 710 [3]	868 600	709 567	...	...	El Salvador
19 114 [4]	18 720 [4]	18 076 [4]	...	...	...	Grenada
739 839	739 636	826 613	...	...	...	Guatemala
137 315 [1]	132 075	130 832	...	...	...	Guyana
517 723 [5]	528 611 [5]	580 127 [5]	642 391 [5]	658 102 [5]	...	Haiti
524 720	575 152	601 337	613 633	671 786	...	Honduras
370 516	363 420	359 488	...	...	...	Jamaica
13 536 265	14 126 414	14 666 257	14 981 028	...	...	Mexico
378 640	449 157	172 267 [7]	203 669 [7]	213 500 [7]	202 290 [7]	Nicaragua
368 738	372 823	337 522	335 239	336 740	...	Panama
493 231	504 377	518 968	530 083	...	...	Paraguay
3 093 017	3 117 055	3 161 375	3 215 322	3 343 631	3 393 086	Peru
1 032 508	1 069 117	1 105 730	1 149 805	...	...	Dominican Republic
85 060	...	...	...	...	...	Suriname
...	...	...	...	...	...	Trinidad and Tobago
324 615	327 009	331 247	335 600	343 957	...	Uruguay
2 378 601	2 456 815	2 530 263	2 591 051	2 660 440	...	Venezuela

[1] *State-run and State-subsidized schools only.*
[2] *Public education only.*
[3] *Including night schools.*
[4] *As from 1975, forms I, II and III, previously classified under primary education, have been included under general secundary education.*
[5] *As from 1976, duration of primary education was reduced from seven to six years.*
[6] *Up to 1969 private education was estimated to be 11 per cent of total primary education.*
[7] *As from 1980, there has been a change in the number of years of schooling in Nicaragua.*

357. MAESTROS EN LA ENSEÑANZA DE PRIMER NIVEL

(Número de maestros)

País	1960	1965	1970	1975	1977
Argentina	129 732	153 685	193 996	216 865	217 865
Barbados	811 [1]	...	1 293	1 419	1 453
Belice	...	...	1 150	1 207 [2]	...
Bolivia	13 895	17 773	25 509	38 737	...
Brasil	226 059	351 466	654 395 [3]	896 652 [3]	897 163 [3]
Colombia	44 910	63 250	86 005	121 957	128 494
Costa Rica	7 632	6 963	11 984	12 429	12 500 [1]
Cuba	29 924 [4]	42 632 [4]	60 592	81 830	77 541
Chile	...	29 162 [1]	40 823 [1]	65 817	70 561
Dominica	...	...	...	674 [5]	...
Ecuador	15 344 [6]	21 418 [6]	26 609 [6]	32 279 [6]	36 783 [6]
El Salvador	8 681 [6]	12 185	14 193	14 256 [1][6]	15 133 [1]
Granada	...	...	800	...	610 [7]
Guatemala	9 735	12 251	14 486	17 862	19 295
Guyana	3 181 [1]	5 021 [1]	4 485 [1]	4 052	4 460
Haití	5 566	6 210	7 770	11 320	12 953 [8]
Honduras	6 451	9 862	10 816	13 045	14 464
Jamaica	4 540	5 643 [1]	8 053 [1]	11 531	7 092 [1]
México	111 134	148 273	201 453	253 939	325 807
Nicaragua	4 605 [4]	5 577 [4]	7 645 [4]	8 817 [4]	9 729 [4]
Panamá	5 672	6 391	9 431	12 459	14 633
Paraguay	10 719 [6]	11 796 [6]	13 392 [6]	15 938	16 869
Perú	41 900 [6]	53 116	65 965	72 641	75 491
República Dominicana	8 758 [6]	10 466	13 796	17 932	...
Suriname	...	...	2 487	2 552	3 077
Trinidad y Tabago	5 444 [9]	6 312 [9]	6 548 [2]	6 471 [2]	6 363 [2]
Uruguay	9 738 [4]	10 800	12 009	13 572	13 685
Venezuela	34 700	42 623	50 822	69 466	79 899

[1] Enseñanza pública solamente.
[2] Escuelas públicas y subvencionadas solamente.
[3] A partir del año 1971, la duración de la enseñanza de primer nivel aumentó de cuatro a ocho años; en el presente cuadro se modificó desde el año 1970 en adelante.
[4] Incluida la enseñanza anterior al primer nivel.
[5] Incluye la enseñanza general de segundo nivel.
[6] Incluidas las escuelas nocturnas.
[7] A partir del año 1975, las "forms I, II y III" clasificadas anteriormente en la enseñanza de primer nivel, han sido incluidas en la enseñanza general de segundo nivel.
[8] A partir del año 1976, la duración de la enseñanza de primer nivel disminuyó de siete a seis años.
[9] Escuelas públicas y subvencionadas solamente e incluye las secciones intermedias de las escuelas secundarias.

357. PRIMARY LEVEL TEACHERS

(Number of teachers)

1978	1979	1980	1981	1982	1983	Country
207 878	224 673	216 627	218 294	225 212	233 426	*Argentina*
1 496	1 472	1 469	1 483	1 492	1 379	*Barbados*
...	...	...	...	...	...	*Belize*
...	...	48 894	45 024	...	...	*Bolivia*
854 813 [3]	863 335 [3]	883 029 [3]	...	...	...	*Brazil*
131 214	139 277	136 381	137 721	...	...	*Colombia*
...	14 924	14 073	13 896	...	...	*Costa Rica*
77 605	77 063	73 884	72 045	71 251	...	*Cuba*
71 846	66 354	...	...	...	...	*Chile*
887 [5]	...	...	...	...	...	*Dominica*
37 665	39 825 [6]	...	...	...	...	*Ecuador*
...	17 411	17 364	17 441	...	...	*El Salvador*
608 [7]	587 [7]	...	...	...	...	*Grenada*
21 041	22 210 [6]	24 242	...	...	...	*Guatemala*
4 215	4 310	3 909	...	...	...	*Guyana*
12 554 [8]	12 751 [8]	13 401 [8]	14 581 [8]	15 113 [8]	...	*Haiti*
14 479	13 305	16 385	15 724	17 930	...	*Honduras*
...	8 783 [1]	8 676 [1]	...	...	...	*Jamaica*
319 418	347 104	375 220	400 417	...	...	*Mexico*
9 986 [4]	12 535 [4]	14 113 [4]	14 713	14 711	17 302	*Nicaragua*
15 276	16 044	14 479	15 144	15 065	...	*Panama*
17 525	18 038	18 948	19 748	20 746	...	*Paraguay*
78 429	80 331	84 360	86 249	89 370	92 473	*Peru*
...	...	...	...	...	...	*Dominican Republic*
3 068	...	...	...	...	...	*Suriname*
...	...	...	...	...	...	*Trinidad and Tobago*
13 728	14 542	15 676	15 676	16 821	...	*Uruguay*
82 226	88 493	92 551	97 045	100 681	...	*Venezuela*

[1] *State education only.*
[2] *State-run and State-subsidized schools only.*
[3] *As from 1971, duration of primary education was increased from for to eight years; in this table, change was reflected from 1970 anwords.*
[4] *Including pre-primary education.*
[5] *Includes general secundary education.*
[6] *Including night schools.*
[7] *As from 1975 forms I, II and III, previously classified under primary education, have been included under general secundary education.*
[8] *As from 1976, duration of primary education was reduced from seven to six years.*
[9] *State-run and State-subsidized schools only; also includes "intermediate" schools.*

358. MATRICULA EN LA ENSEÑANZA DE SEGUNDO NIVEL [1]

(Número de matriculados)

País	1960	1965	1970	1975	1977
Argentina	578 481	789 077	980 558	1 247 683	1 286 368
Barbados	14 722 [2]	21 613 [2]	20 451 [3 4]	29 025 [3 4]	30 021 [3]
Bolivia	27 951	48 223	89 574	130 029	143 072
Brasil	267 144	509 110	1 003 475	1 935 903	2 437 701
Colombia	253 786	434 171	750 055	1 370 567	1 616 111
Costa Rica	27 202	41 118	76 573 [4]	134 862 [4]	150 840
Cuba	122 897	231 807	272 526	629 197	953 872 [6]
Chile	145 190	240 184	312 064	448 911	487 264
Dominica	...	...	...	6 487	6 342
Ecuador	67 028	117 268	216 727 [7]	383 624 [7]	469 968 [7]
El Salvador	16 106	51 452	86 853	128 603	140 374
Granada	...	...	4 081	...	...
Guatemala	30 172 [7]	47 831	74 549	122 324	145 770
Guyana	35 066 [8]	47 025 [8]	60 412 [8]	71 327 [8]	...
Haití	19 453	26 391	31 772	52 402	55 816
Honduras	15 186	23 132	39 839 [9]	51 896	89 863 [9]
Jamaica	101 163 [10]	130 018 [10]	136 539 [4]	216 248 [4]	...
México	512 216	1 002 610	1 584 342	2 827 470	3 402 727
Nicaragua	11 372	26 577	51 383	80 202	105 429
Panamá	38 874	54 906	78 466	125 745	137 185
Paraguay	24 582	35 402	55 777	75 424	92 437
Perú	198 259 [7]	328 104	546 183 [4]	813 489 [4]	969 129
República Dominicana	28 137	65 323	119 653	206 985	249 409
Suriname	...	...	23 504	30 603	34 121
Trinidad y Tabago	24 208	46 116	52 639 [4]	67 872 [4]	...
Uruguay	93 127	122 665	174 300	186 556	184 371
Venezuela	162 677	267 240	425 146	669 138	751 430

[1] Incluye enseñanza general, normal y otra.
[2] Se estimó que la enseñanza privada constituía el 25% del total de matriculados y se agregó esa estimación a la cifra de enseñanza pública.
[3] Escuelas públicas y subvencionadas solamente.
[4] Excluye la enseñanza normal.
[5] Enseñanza pública, incluidas las escuelas nocturnas.
[6] A partir del año 1977, la duración de la enseñanza general de segundo nivel disminuyó de siete a seis años.
[7] Incluye escuelas nocturnas.
[8] Escuelas públicas y subvencionadas solamente. Excluye las secciones superiores de las "escuelas completas".
[9] Incluye los alumnos de jornadas parcial.
[10] Hasta 1970, la enseñanza privada ha sido estimada en alrededor de 3% del total de la enseñanza de segundo nivel.
[11] A partir de 1980, la duración de la enseñanza general de segundo nivel disminuyó de seis a cinco años.

358. ENROLMENT IN SECONDARY EDUCATION [1]

(Number of students enrolled)

1978	1979	1980	1981	1982	1983	Country
1 299 439	1 295 815	1 326 680	1 366 444	1 425 648	1 466 424	Argentina
29 446 [4]	26 717 [4]	26 190 [4]	26 189 [4]	25 737	26 552	Barbados
...	...	170 710	166 325	...	...	Bolivia
2 519 122	2 658 078	2 823 544	...	...	...	Brazil
1 751 980	1 879 118	1 811 003	1 891 530	...	...	Colombia
147 444 [5]	168 019 [4]	173 176 [4]	169 967 [4]	...	...	Costa Rica
1 062 166	1 127 591	1 146 414	1 158 151	1 116 930	...	Cuba
510 471	536 428	628 757	640 659	643 405	...	Chile
6 779	...	...	...	...	...	Dominica
487 306	535 445 [7]	...	...	...	...	Ecuador
...	78 107	73 030	64 702	...	...	El Salvador
...	...	...	...	...	...	Grenada
159 040	156 345	171 903	...	...	...	Guatemala
...	...	...	...	...	...	Guyana
72 651	80 860	87 680	96 596	95 600	...	Haiti
102 964 [9]	114 564	127 293	...	148 508	...	Honduras
242 272 [4]	255 231 [4]	248 001 [4]	...	...	...	Jamaica
3 838 084	4 268 002	4 791 262	5 332 131	...	...	Mexico
98 874	110 726	73 874 [11]	94 062	109 028	112 302	Nicaragua
139 323	137 816	171 273	174 078	174 791	...	Panama
101 126	110 095	117 779	124 481	135 829	...	Paraguay
1 050 566 [4]	1 151 748 [4]	1 203 116 [4]	1 212 499	1 249 293	1 312 820	Peru
318 905	337 511	356 091	379 377	...	...	Dominican Republic
34 372	...	...	...	...	...	Suriname
...	...	...	...	...	...	Trinidad and Tobago
180 029	176 950	171 502	174 069	183 010	...	Uruguay
787 032	820 660	850 470	884 233	939 678	...	Venezuela

[1] Including general, teacher-training and other types of education.
[2] Private education was estimated at 25% of total enrolment, and this amount was added to figure for public education.
[3] State-run and State-subsidized schools only.
[4] Excluding teacher-training.
[5] State-run education, including night schools.
[6] As from 1977, duration of general secondary education was reduced from seven to six years.
[7] Including night schools.
[8] State-run and State-subsidized schools only. Excludes higher divisions of "comprehensive schools".
[9] Including part-time pupils.
[10] Up to 1970, private education was estimated to be about 3% of total secondary education.
[11] As from 1980, duration of general secondary education was reduced from six to five years.

359. MAESTROS EN LA ENSEÑANZA DE SEGUNDO NIVEL [1]

(Número de maestros)

País	1960	1965	1970	1975	1977
Argentina	78 007	110 476	135 991	151 347	173 714
Barbados	511[2]	875[2]	1 050[2]	1 421[2]	1 517[2]
Bolivia	4 018	5 495	5 825	7 143	...
Brasil	94 136	144 943	112 243	133 070	163 366
Colombia	22 366	32 620	43 695	70 451	79 742
Costa Rica	1 619	2 133	3 326	4 929	7 737
Cuba	6 934	14 294	21 828	43 780	68 010[3]
Chile	16 900[4]	21 325	18 060	29 567	28 460
Ecuador	5 912	9 230	15 699[5]	23 446[5]	28 817[5]
El Salvador	2 290	3 124	2 849	2 869	...
Granada	...	...	161	...	...
Guatemala	4 002	6 291	5 473	7 342	8 275
Guyana	745[2]	1 600[2] [6]	2 364[2]	3 081[2]	...
Haití	1 529	1 642	2 093	3 236	3 324
Honduras	1 567	1 884	2 727	3 132	3 366
Jamaica	1 103	1 731[2]	2 782[2]	6 473[7]	...
México	39 169	74 300	109 470	161 885	206 859
Nicaragua	904	1 701	1 979	2 455	2 954
Panamá	1 695	2 638	3 784	5 670	5 882
Paraguay	3 239	4 500	5 938	7 512	7 951
Perú	16 100[5]	22 272	31 587	34 136	35 183
República Dominicana	3 067	2 347[6]	4 668	8 450	...
Suriname	...	...	1 367	1 793	1 785
Trinidad y Tabago	838[2] [4]	1 884[2]	1 996[2]	2 373	...
Uruguay	7 400	10 200	15 316	15 863	...
Venezuela	9 623[5]	14 564[5]	22 893[5]	39 876[5]	47 137[5]

[1] Incluye educación general, normal y otra de segundo nivel (técnica y profesional).
[2] Escuelas públicas y subvencionadas solamente. En Trinidad y Tabago excluye las secciones intermedias.
[3] A partir de 1977, la duración de la enseñanza general de segundo nivel, disminuyó de siete a seis años.
[4] Excluye la enseñanza normal.
[5] Incluye escuelas nocturnas.
[6] Excluye la enseñanza técnica.
[7] En la enseñanza general de segundo nivel, excluye las secciones superiores de las "escuelas completas".
[8] A partir de 1980, la duración de la enseñanza general de segundo nivel disminuyó de seis a cinco años.

359. TEACHERS IN SECONDARY EDUCATION [1]

(Number of teachers)

1978	1979	1980	1981	1982	1983	Country
173 779	178 681	181 884	191 096	191 729	193 551	Argentina
1 453 [2]	1 326 [2]	1 353 [2]	1 121 [2]	1 317	1 141	Barbados
...	...	...	...	...	...	Bolivia
180 782	183 352	198 276	...	...	...	Brazil
84 258	85 938	88 905	88 103	...	...	Colombia
...	11 080	10 660	10 656	...	...	Costa Rica
78 031	81 821	85 134	88 821	91 408	...	Cuba
28 803	27 207	...	...	...	...	Chile
30 169	31 489 [5]	...	...	...	...	Ecuador
...	3 118	3 080	...	...	...	El Salvador
...	...	...	...	...	...	Grenada
8 604	9 025 [5]	9 613	...	...	...	Guatemala
...	...	...	...	...	...	Guyana
3 833	3 849	3 637	4 034	4 239	...	Haiti
3 491	4 355	4 489	5 090	5 227	...	Honduras
...	...	...	...	...	...	Jamaica
219 054	244 395	271 174	301 939	...	...	Mexico
2 720	3 532	4 221 [8]	4 221	4 103	4 132	Nicaragua
5 975	6 202	8 138	8 610	8 928	...	Panama
...	...	...	...	...	...	Paraguay
37 757	...	45 209	47 106	50 075	53 509	Peru
...	...	...	...	...	...	Dominican Republic
1 867	...	...	...	...	...	Suriname
...	...	...	...	...	...	Trinidad and Tobago
...	...	...	...	...	...	Uruguay
47 496 [5]	49 930 [5]	53 253 [5]	60 897 [5]	84 341 [5]	...	Venezuela

[1] Including general, teacher-training and other secondary level education (technical and professional).
[2] State-run and State-subsidized schools only. In Trinidad and Tobago, excludes intermediate sections.
[3] As from 1977, duration of general secondary education was reduced from seven to six years.
[4] Excluding teacher-training.
[5] Including night schools.
[6] Excluding technical education.
[7] In general secondary education, excludes upper classes of comprehensives schools.
[8] As from 1980, duration of general secondary education was reduced from six to five years.

X. CONDICIONES SOCIALES

360. MATRICULA EN LA ENSEÑANZA DE TERCER NIVEL [1]

(Número de matriculados)

País	1960	1965	1970	1975	1977
Argentina	173 935	246 680	293 302	572 045	536 450
Barbados	121	407	763	1 065 [2]	4 824
Belice	...	...	113	...	...
Bolivia	12 055	16 912	35 250	49 850	41 408
Brasil	95 691	155 781	430 473	1 089 808	1 182 411
Colombia	23 013	44 403	85 560	186 635	237 477
Costa Rica	4 703	5 824	12 913	32 794	38 629
Cuba	25 295	26 162	35 137	84 750	122 456
Chile	26 027	43 608	78 430	149 647	131 793
Dominica	...	...	...	...	...
Ecuador	9 361	14 038	38 692	170 173	...
El Salvador	2 320	3 918	9 071	26 909	27 997
Granada	...	...	...	...	...
Guatemala	5 229	7 673	16 572	27 690	36 084
Guyana	-	319	1 112	2 852	...
Haití	1 361	1 607	1 538	2 373	2 653
Honduras	1 680	2 112	4 847	11 907	20 205
Jamaica	2 093	4 305	6 892	3 963 [4]	...
México	78 599	133 374	247 637	543 057	609 070
Nicaragua	1 435	3 233	9 385	9 092	10 799
Panamá	4 030	8 883	8 947	26 219	35 144
Paraguay	3 425	5 833	8 001	17 153	20 032
Perú	30 247	64 676	109 230	...	246 147
República Dominicana	3 448	6 716	23 546	28 628 [5]	44 725
Suriname	...	...	292	465	900
Trinidad y Tabago	513	1 594	2 375	2 940	2 477 [2]
Uruguay	15 320	16 975	21 200	32 627	39 402
Venezuela	26 477	46 325	100 767	221 581	265 671

[1] Incluye enseñanza en universidades, establecimientos equivalentes, enseñanza normal no universitaria y otros establecimientos no universitarios.
[2] Universidades y establecimientos equivalentes.
[3] Excluye las cifras de la Universidad Nacional, que cerró sus puertas.
[4] Universidad de "West Indies" solamente.
[5] Universidad "Autónoma de Santo Domingo" solamente.

360. ENROLMENT IN TERTIARY LEVEL [1]

(Number of students enrolled)

1978	1979	1980	1981	1982	1983	Country
477 725	475 799	491 473	525 688	550 556	580 626	Argentina
5 228	5 374	5 402	5 680	3 556	...	Barbados
...	...	...	...	...	...	Belize
44 946	...	...	...	56 632	...	Bolivia
1 251 116	1 340 662	1 409 243	...	...	...	Brazil
274 893	271 302	279 194	318 293	...	...	Colombia
38 889	40 611	54 734	60 508	...	...	Costa Rica
133 014	146 240	151 733	165 496	173 403	...	Cuba
130 982	127 349	119 008	118 669	119 462	...	Chile
...	...	284	...	...	...	Dominica
235 274	251 660	264 136	258 054	...	...	Ecuador
23 142	29 891	8 820 [3]	...	...	...	El Salvador
153	614	...	...	...	...	Grenada
42 931	47 540	50 890	...	...	...	Guatemala
2 604	2 491	1 681 [2]	1 995 [2]	...	...	Guyana
2 926	3 081	3 801	4 099	3 597	...	Haiti
20 635	23 989	26 824	30 149	33 249	...	Honduras
4 496 [4]	4 574 [4]	13 999	...	...	...	Jamaica
740 073	848 875	935 789	1 007 123	...	...	Mexico
11 940	12 192	57 381	60 397	73 332	91 065	Nicaragua
34 966	37 885	40 446	42 816	46 189	...	Panama
20 496	22 291	25 333	27 041	29 677	...	Paraguay
256 052	...	311 851	353 167	375 079	409 885	Peru
42 412	...	...	...	...	...	Dominican Republic
...	...	...	...	...	...	Suriname
4 659	2 458 [4]	2 503 [4]	...	...	...	Trinidad and Tobago
32 229	36 459	34 044	36 458	48 234	...	Uruguay
282 074	298 884	307 998	330 986	348 803	...	Venezuela

[1] *Including education in universities, equivalent institutions, non-university teacher-training and other non-university institutions.*
[2] *Universities and equivalent institutions.*
[3] *Excluding figures for the National University, which has now been closed.*
[4] *University of West Indies only.*
[5] *Autonomous University of Santo Domingo only.*

361. MAESTROS EN LA ENSEÑANZA DE TERCER NIVEL [1]

(Número de maestros)

País	1960	1965	1970	1975	1977
Argentina	8 619	15 401	24 061	...	42 500
Barbados	26	...	...	...	...
Belice	...	...	15	...	...
Bolivia	1 680	2 331	...	...	...
Brasil	21 912	33 126	54 389	83 386	90 557
Colombia	4 782 [2]	6 489	10 295	21 153	24 960
Costa Rica	438	617	...	...	...
Cuba	986	3 032	4 415	6 326	8 827
Chile	6 397	8 835	...	11 419 [5]	...
Dominica	...	...	...	...	...
Ecuador	1 135	1 756	2 867	...	...
El Salvador	485	609	751	2 137	1 809
Granada	...	...	...	...	...
Guatemala	471 [7]	576 [7]	1 314	1 411 [7]	...
Guyana	9	61 [4]	...	...	...
Haití	226	215	...	408	482
Honduras	...	...	...	817	1 136
Jamaica	218	...	567	...	...
México	...	17 170	...	47 529	52 140
Nicaragua	...	430	604	1 066	1 236
Panamá	144 [4]	361	489	1 022	1 508
Paraguay	479 [4]	783	702	1 741	1 756
Perú	3 544	7 125	7 736	...	14 236
República Dominicana	145	422	...	1 435 [4]	...
Suriname	...	...	...	...	118
Trinidad y Tabago	...	225	412	...	...
Uruguay	...	...	...	2 332	3 263
Venezuela	3 093	4 762	8 155	15 792	21 534

[1] Incluye universidades y establecimientos equivalentes, enseñanza normal no universitaria y otros establecimientos no universitarios.
[2] Excluye la enseñanza normal de tercer nivel.
[3] Los datos se refieren a los puestos de enseñanza y no al personal docente.
[4] Universidad solamente.
[5] Profesores de jornada completa solamente.
[6] Excluye las cifras de la Universidad Nacional, que cerró sus puertas.
[7] Universidad de San Carlos solamente.

361. TEACHERS IN TERTIARY LEVEL [1]

(Number of teachers)

1978	1979	1980	1981	1982	1983	Country
42 377	45 089	46 267	54 039	53 166	56 089	*Argentina*
...	...	317	...	...	...	*Barbados*
...	...	...	...	...	...	*Belize*
...	...	...	...	...	...	*Bolivia*
98 172	102 588	109 788	...	...	...	*Brazil*
25 708	...	27 985	34 844 [3]	...	...	*Colombia*
...	...	4 380 [4]	...	...	...	*Costa Rica*
10 139	10 736	10 680	12 068	12 222	...	*Cuba*
...	...	...	9 086	10 372	...	*Chile*
...	...	59	...	...	...	*Dominica*
10 706	...	11 326 [4]	11 679 [4]	...	...	*Ecuador*
2 556	2 757	893 [6]	...	...	...	*El Salvador*
23	77	...	...	...	...	*Grenada*
2 845 [7]	...	...	...	...	...	*Guatemala*
496	...	...	...	...	...	*Guyana*
493	420	569	559	598	...	*Haiti*
1 495	1 530	1 693	1 895	...	...	*Honduras*
...	...	...	...	...	...	*Jamaica*
62 334	69 494	73 789	74 944	...	...	*Mexico*
...	1 299	...	935	1 079	1 207	*Nicaragua*
1 727	1 679	1 935	2 192	2 548	...	*Panama*
1 945	2 004	1 893	2 014	...	...	*Paraguay*
16 228	17 223	17 895	21 147	22 149	23 139	*Peru*
...	...	...	...	...	...	*Dominican Republic*
...	...	...	...	...	...	*Suriname*
...	...	...	...	...	...	*Trinidad and Tobago*
...	3 635	3 847	4 149	...	...	*Uruguay*
23 451	26 633	28 031	28 039	29 071	...	*Venezuela*

[1] *Including universities and equivalent institutions, non-university teacher-training and other non-university establishments.*
[2] *Excluding tertiary-level teacher-training.*
[3] *Data refer to teaching posts and not to number of teachers.*
[4] *University only.*
[5] *Full-time teachers only.*
[6] *Excluding figures for the National University, which has now been closed.*
[7] *University of San Carlos only.*

362. ENSEÑANZA DE TERCER NIVEL: DIPLOMADOS SEGUN SECTORES DE ESTUDIO

(Número de diplomados) [1]

País	Año Year	Total	Sectores de estudio [2]								
			1	2	3	4	5	6	7	8	9
Barbados [3]	1980	681	137	48	17	-	-	142	-	-	230
Bolivia [4]	1978	1 542	3	35	2	172	187	61	3	-	-
Brasil	1978	198 716	77 143	3 872	2 162	16 574	13 230	25 011	5 468	221	913
Colombia [5]	1981	28 573	6 672	306	569	2 029	1 333	6 999	...	...	...
Costa Rica [6]	1978	4 146	1 273	383	71	112	541	214	42	-	-
Cuba [7]	1980	25 898	13 691	533	152	650	383	2 422	237	-	-
Chile	1981	20 037	9 147	423	308	272	180	1552	75	178	30
Dominica	1980	15	3	-	-	2	-	-	1	-	-
Ecuador [7]	1981	15 441	6 892	179	86	858	1 445	991	93	61	-
El Salvador	1978	1 487	150	1	-	46	28	30	17	-	18
Granada	1979	152	41	-	-	-	-	-	-	-	-
Guatemala [8]	1979	1 340	425	23	-	74	19	161	-	-	-
Guyana	1981	511	103	46	-	7	53	69	20	-	-
Haití [9]	1978	344	11	7	-	-	10	13	-	-	-
Honduras	1980	918	14	11	-	131	164	106	-	1	-
Jamaica	1980	4 266	1 887	278	91	31	289	327	19	48	-
México	1981	78 644	626	757	570	6 877	6 208	12 228	1 639	-	698
Nicaragua	1980	4 173	54	243	-	63	751	1 020	69	87	-
Panamá	1981	2 900	935	37	58	117	158	487	15	2	-
Perú	1980	18 530	3 034	16	19	685	547	5 656	351	228	27
República Dominicana [4]	1978	2 452	523	13	28	79	86	122	12	11	61
Trinidad y Tabago [9]	1977	585	67	123	-	24	104	74	-	124	69
Uruguay	1981	2 932	1	44	3	827	66	316	22	-	-
Venezuela	1980	15 819	3 582	217	-	1 197	1 589	1 652	234	-	147

[1] Incluye las tres clases de niveles de títulos o diplomas, a saber: Nivel 5. Diplomas y certificados no equivalentes a un primer título universitario concedido al final de unos estudios superiores de breve duración (en general menos de tres años). Comprenden, por ejemplo, los certificados concedidos a ciertos tipos de técnicos, los diplomas de enfermeras o enfermero, los *associate degrees*, los certificados de competencia jurídica, etc. Nivel 6. Primeros títulos universitarios o diplomas equivalentes que sancionan unos estudios superiores de duración normal (en general de tres a cinco años, y a veces siete). Son los más frecuentes y comprenden no solamente títulos tan conocidos como la Licenciatura, el grado de Bachiller, etc., sino también títulos de carácter profesional, como ciertos doctorados que se pueden obtener en algunos países al final de los estudios de Medicina, Ingeniería, Derecho, etc. Nivel 7. Títulos universitarios superiores o diplomas equivalentes que pueden obtener continuando sus estudios quienes ya tienen un primer título universitario (o un diploma equivalente). Por ejemplo, los diversos diplomas obtenidos después de la preparación de un primer título universitario (diploma de postgraduados), el grado de Magister, los diversos tipos de doctorado, etc.

[2] Sectores de estudio según la Clasificación Internacional Normalizada de la Educación (CINE) de la UNESCO, 1976:
1. Ciencias de la educación y Formación de Personal Docente; 2. Humanidades, Religión y Teología 3. Bellas Artes y Artes Aplicadas; 4. Derecho; 5. Ciencias Sociales y del Comportamiento; 6. Enseñanza Comercial y de Administración de Empresas; 7. Documentación y Comunicación Social; 8. Economía Doméstica (Enseñanza del Hogar); 9. Formación para el Sector de los Servicios; 10. Ciencias Naturales; 11. Matemáticas e Informática; 12. Ciencias Médicas, Sanidad e Higiene; 13. Ingeniería y Tecnología; 14. Arquitectura y Urbanismo; 15. Artes y Oficios Industriales; 16. Transportes y Comunicaciones; 17. Enseñanza Agronómica, Dasonómica y Pesquera; 18. Otros Programas.

[3] Los datos excluyen la Universidad de "West Indies".
[4] Universidades y establecimientos equivalentes solamente.
[5] Ciencias Sociales y del Comportamiento incluyen Documentación y Comunicación Social. Enseñanza Comercial y de Administración de Empresas comprende Economía Doméstica y Formación para el Sector de los Servicios. Ciencias Naturales incluyen Matemática e Informática. Ingeniería y Tecnología incluyen Artes y Oficios Industriales y Transportes y Comunicaciones.
[6] Universidad de Costa Rica solamente.
[7] Ingeniería y Tecnología incluyen Artes y Oficios Industriales.
[8] Universidad de San Carlos solamente.
[9] Universidades solamente.

362. THIRD LEVEL EDUCATION: GRADUATES, BY FIELDS OF STUDY

(Number of graduates) [1]

Fields of study [2]									Country
10	11	12	13	14	15	16	17	18	
--------50--------		48	9	-	-	-	-	-	Barbados [3]
24	305	505	107	57	35	-	46	-	Bolivia [4]
2 740	971	19 380	18 140	2 183	809	209	5 931	3 759	Brazil
450	...	3 825	4 627	895	...	...	868	-	Colombia [5]
154	85	699	234	161	-		177	-	Costa Rica [6]
623	104	1 409	2 905	345	...	274	1 739	431	Cuba [7]
373	152	3 043	2 912	278	158	46	536	374	Chile
-	-	7	-	1	-	-	1	-	Dominica
-	-	2 077	1 074	397	...	-	1 252	36	Ecuador [7]
12	10	164	691	49	50	16	205	-	El Salvador
-	-	48	-	-	-	-	63	-	Grenada
29	3	354	142	14	-	-	71	25	Guatemala [8]
32	8	53	85	6	-	-	5	24	Guyana
31	-	151	83	-	-	-	38	-	Haiti [9]
14	20	132	146	-	-	-	167	12	Honduras
159	1	816	157	97	-	-	66	-	Jamaica
1 925	1 033	20 744	15 032	2 341	-	57	7 688	221	Mexico
201	63	496	682	195	113	-	52	84	Nicaragua
101	13	310	433	56	-	-	178	-	Panama
153	182	2 340	1 943	186	1 474	-	1 077	612	Peru
118	27	823	406	67	-	-	76	-	Dominican Republic [4]
-	-	-	--------------------124--------------------				69	-	Trinidad and Tobago [9]
113	40	901	127	62	118	-	224	68	Uruguay
315	437	2 307	2 787	401	127	-	827	-	Venezuela

[1] Includes the three types of levels of degrees or diplomas, namely: Level 5. Diplomas and certificates, not equivalent to a first university degree, granted after higher studies of short duration (generally less than three years). Examples are certificates given to certain types of technicians, diplomas granted to nurses, associate degrees, legal certificates of competence, etc.; Level 6. First university degrees or equivalent diplomas attesting to higher studies of normal duration (generally three to five years or sometimes even seven). These form the most frequent type of degree and include not only such well-known qualifications as bachelors' degrees, etc., but also professional qualifications such as certain doctorates which can be obtained in some countries on completion of studies in medicine, engineering, law, etc.; Level 7. Higher university degrees or equivalent diplomas which can be obtained after further study by those who already have a first university degree or equivalent diploma. Examples are the various diplomas obtainable after receipt of a first university degree (postgraduate diplomas), Masters' degrees, various types of doctorates, etc.

[2] Fields of study by International Standard Classification of Education (ISCED) (UNESCO 1976): 1. Education Science and Teacher Training; 2. Humanities, Religion and Theology; 3. Fine and Applied Arts; 4. Law; 5. Social and Behavioural Science; 6. Commercial and Business Administration; 7. Mass Communication and Documentation; 8. Home Economics and Domestic Science; 9. Service Trades; 10. Natural Science; 11. Mathematics and Computer Science; 12. Medical and Health-Related Sciences; 13. Engineering; 14. Architecture and Town Planning; 15. Trade, Craft and Industrial Programmes; 16. Transport and Communications; 17. Agriculture, Forestry and Fishery; 18. Other programmes.

[3] Data excluded University of West Indies.

[4] Universities and equivalent institutions only.

[5] Social and Behavioural Science includes Mass Communication and Documentation. Commercial and Business Administration includes Home Economics and Domestic Science and Service Trades. Natural Science includes Mathematics and Computer Science. Engineering includes Trade, Craft and Industrial Programmes and Transport and Communications.

[6] University of Costa Rica only.

[7] Engineering includes Trade, Craft and Industrial Programmes.

[8] University of San Carlos only.

[9] Universities only.

363. POBLACION ECONOMICAMENTE ACTIVA POR NIVEL DE INSTRUCCION, ALREDEDOR DE 1970 / *ECONOMICALLY ACTIVE POPULATION BY LEVEL OF EDUCATION, AROUND 1970*

(Miles de personas / *Thousands of persons*)

País / *Country*	Total	Número de años de estudio aprobados/*Number of years of schooling completed*						
		Ninguno / *None*	1 a 3 / *1 to 3*	4 a 6 / *4 to 6*	7 a 9 / *7 to 9*	10 a 12 / *10 to 12*	13 y más / *13 and over*	No declarado / *Not declared*
Argentina	9 011 450	-	1 424 700	1 830 250	3 303 600	1 177 800	527 150	747 950
Bolivia	1 492 337	467 549	323 837	301 452	203 107	97 599	46 561	52 232
Brasil / *Brazil*	29 557 224	10 637 714	8 155 530	6 780 913	1 812 833	1 439 408	690 184	40 642
Colombia	5 136 375	1 109 450	1 597 425	1 427 900	513 650	287 625	143 825	56 500
Costa Rica	616 090	66 540	150 140	270 090	50 340	62 470	16 140	370
Chile	2 608 960	213 940	403 080	824 440	339 680	351 940	104 100	371 780
Ecuador	1 964 628	446 632	427 858[1]	708 675	137 685	117 823	72 353	29 602
El Salvador	1 313 560	595 960	323 520	273 880	54 260	40 320	10 780	14 840
Guatemala	1 597 000	806 800	394 620	257 920	42 640	54 140	22 040	18 840
Honduras	762 795	324 520	205 898	166 870	17 825	35 446	9 197	3 039
México / *Mexico*	12 922 600	3 502 000	3 910 400	3 835 400	765 000	476 900	431 600	1 300
Nicaragua	504 240	241 280	93 330	100 040	22 540	17 250	11 400	18 400
Panamá/*Panama*	490 760	84 165	79 845	192 670	55 310	52 855	25 520	395
Paraguay	740 130	76 310	259 640	273 550	57 360	40 120	19 470	13 680
Perú / *Peru*	3 847 060	743 260	1 049 100	1 079 100	302 380	362 000	186 200	125 020
República Dominicana/ *Dominican Republic*	1 200 581	437 978	249 237	223 666	98 206	54 029	13 688	123 777

[1] Incluye "alfabetizados".   [1] *Including those who have completed a literacy programme.*

364. POBLACION TOTAL Y POBLACION ECONOMICAMENTE ACTIVA (PEA)
CUBIERTA POR LA SEGURIDAD SOCIAL, ALREDEDOR DE 1980 /
*TOTAL POPULATION AND ECONOMICALLY ACTIVE POPULATION (EAP)
COVERED INSURED BY SOCIAL SECURITY, AROUND 1980*

(Porcentajes / *Percentages*)

País /*Country*	Año *Year*	Asegurados sobre la población total *Insured population as a percentage of total population*	Activos asegurados sobre la población económicamente activa *Insured economically active population as a percentage of total economically active population*
Argentina	1980	78.9	69.1
Bolivia	1980	25.4	18.5
Brasil / *Brazil*	1980	96.3	95.6
Colombia	1979[1]	11.6	22.4
Costa Rica	1980	76.0	68.3
Cuba	1981	99.3[2]	93.0[2]
Chile	1980	67.2	61.7
Ecuador	1980	7.8	23.2
El Salvador	1980	6.3	11.6
Guatemala	1981	15.0	33.1
Haití / *Haiti*	1980	0.8	1.6
Honduras	1982	7.3	13.3
México / *Mexico*	1980	53.4	42.0
Nicaragua	1980	9.1	18.9
Panamá / *Panama*	1980	50.4	45.5
Paraguay	1980[1]	18.2	14.0
Perú / *Peru*	1980	17.4	37.5
República Dominicana / *Dominican Republic*	1980	7.9	14.0
Uruguay	1980	73.3	91.3
Venezuela	1980[1]	45.2	49.8
Total	...	61.4	61.3

[1] Excluye a varios grupos de asegurados.
[2] Debido a la falta de datos estadísticos se hizo una estimación basada en la cobertura legal.

[1] *Excluding various groups of persons covered insured by social security.*
[2] *Due to lack of statistical data, an estimate was made on the basis of legal coverage.*

751

X. CONDICIONES SOCIALES

365. TELEVISORES [1] / *TELEVISION RECEIVERS* [1]

(Miles de unidades / *Thousands of units*)

País / Country	1960	1965	1970	1975	1977	1978	1979	1980	1981
Argentina	450	1 600	3 500	4 500	4 600	4 600	4 715	5 140	5 540
Barbados	-	6	16	40	50	50	50	50	53
Bolivia	-	...	...	43.5	49	50	100	300	341
Brasil / Brazil	1 200	2 400	6 100	10 680	11 000	12 000	15 000	15 000	15 500
Colombia	150	350	810	1 600	1 850	...	2 000	2 250	2 500
Costa Rica	3	50	100	150	160	160	161	162	164
Cuba	500	552	582	600	800	975	1 114	1 273	1 500
Chile	0.5	52	500	700	...	1 210	1 225	1 225	1 250
Ecuador	2	42	150	252	340	360	400	500	530
El Salvador	20	35	92	135	148	180	276	300	310
Guatemala	32	55	72	110	150	150	160	175	180
Guyana	...	...	...	...	...	...	...	...	...
Haití / Haiti	1.8	7	11	13.2	14	14	15	16	17
Honduras	1.3	2.2	22	47	48	48	49	49	49
Jamaica	-	25	70	110	120	120	167	167	180
México / Mexico	650	1 218	2 993	...	5 480	5 600	5 700	7 500	7 900
Nicaragua	5	16	55	83	100	120	150	175	185
Panamá / Panama	11	70	142	185	206	206	220	220	233
Paraguay	-	...	34	54	55	56	57	68	75
Perú / Peru	33	210	395	500	825	...	850	850	900
República Dominicana / Dominican Republic	...	50	100	158	...	250	300	385	396
Suriname	...	7	28	34	...	...	40	40	41
Trinidad y Tabago / Trinidad and Tobago	0.02	20	60	105	125	140	150	210	265
Uruguay	25	200	258	351	360	361	362	363	366
Venezuela	250	650	794	1 284	1 530	...	1 710	1 710	1 800

[1] Estimaciones sobre número de receptores en funcionamiento

[1] *Estimated number of functioning receivers.*

366. TITULOS DE LIBROS PUBLICADOS[1] / *NUMBER OF BOOK TITLES PUBLISHED*[1]

(Unidades / *Units*)

País / *Country*	1965	1970	1975	1977	1978	1979	1980	1981	1982
Argentina	3 539	4 627	5 141	5 285	4 627	4 451	4 698	4 251	...
Barbados	...	...	87	173[2]	216	...	...	...	...
Bolivia	...	104	339	...	...	596	...	...	...
Brasil / *Brazil*	...	...	13 333	17 994	18 103	20 808	...	...	...
Colombia	709	...	1 272	...	...	...	5 492	...	...
Costa Rica	...	...	186	78	24	...	...	71[34]	...
Cuba	724	647	734	942	1 003	1 095	1 031	1 319	1 387
Chile	1 497	1 370	628[2]	387	432	273	1 055	741	1 489
El Salvador	...	...	14	...	144	...	...	...	...
Granada /*Grenada*	...	...	...	...	...	10[2]	...	...	...
Guatemala	335	...	...	...	...	41[3]	...	574	...
Guyana	...	...	...	107	97	...	110[2]	80	...
Haití / *Haiti*	25	...	...	...	...	...	...	...	...
Jamaica	40	159[2]	...	13[2]	143	18[5]	...	...	...
México / *Mexico*	4 851	4 812	5 822	...	...	...	1 629[3]	2 954[3]	...
Panamá / *Panama*	...	132	226	84[6]	126	130	...	171	...
Perú / *Peru*	927	885	1 090	910	968	857	766	767	...
República Dominicana / *Dominican Republic*	...	...	...	...	...	...	2 219	...	...
Trinidad y Tabago / *Trinidad and Tobago*	...	...	7	...	186	...	...	...	...
Uruguay	141	...	481	...	...	1 012	857	837	...
Venezuela	...	...	...	257	257	...	5 201	4 200	...

[1] Se refiere a número de títulos de primeras ediciones y reediciones de obras originales y de traducciones.
[2] Primeras ediciones solamente.
[3] No incluye los folletos.
[4] Los datos se refieren a las primeras ediciones de los manuales escolares (70) y los libros para niños (1).
[5] Folletos solamente.
[6] Excluye tesis universitarias.

[1] *Refers to number of titles of first editions and re-editions of original works and translation.*
[2] *First editions only.*
[3] *Not including pamphlets.*
[4] *Data refer to first editions of school books (70) and children's books (1).*
[5] *Pamphlets only.*
[6] *Excluding university theses.*

367. UNIDADES DE VIVIENDA OCUPADAS SEGUN TIPO DE TENENCIA, EN ZONAS URBANAS Y RURALES

(Número de unidades de vivienda)

País	Año[1] Year[1]	Total Total	Propietario Owner	Inquilino Tenant	Otras formas[2] Other[2]	Urbana / Urban Total	Propietario Owner
Argentina	1970	6 056 100	3 553 250	1 380 950	1 121 900	...	...
Barbados	1970	59 391	43 626	12 066[3]	3 699[3]	26 345	...
Bolivia	1976	1 040 704	724 696	155 494	160 514	421 188	198 096
Brasil[4]	1970	17 628 699	10 631 603	3 356 051	3 641 045	10 276 340	6 157 744
Brasil	1980	25 210 639	15 546 151	5 682 173	3 982 315	...	...
Colombia[5]	1973	3 471 834	1 858 344	1 066 564	546 926	2 249 342[6]	1 105 469
Costa Rica	1973	330 857	199 372	75 907	55 578	143 837	76 707
Cuba	1970	1 907 923	...	...	...	1 241 293	...
Chile[8]	1970	1 689 840	890 440	767 440	31 960	1 312 860	720 960
Ecuador	1974	1 193 940	755 837	280 696	157 407	486 534	198 909
El Salvador	1971	654 539	315 039	166 732[9]	172 768	270 726	97 698
Guatemala	1973	997 768	565 236	127 906	304 626	368 462	191 449
Guyana	1970	129 722	73 621	53 234	2 867	...	...
Haití	1971	863 605	...	...	...	123 885	...
Honduras	1974	463 004	332 616	76 346	54 042	146 409	72 135
Jamaica	1970	420 008	218 957	196 031	5 020	188 671	55 632
México[10]	1970	8 286 369	5 471 412	........2 814 957		4 864 160	2 638 023
Nicaragua[10]	1971	302 544	194 908	61 357	46 279	148 428	78 123
Panamá[11]	1970	285 321	179 592	79 433	26 296	141 761	54 933
Panamá	1980	364 325	254 905	76 590	32 545	199 750	111 710
Paraguay	1972	428 111	350 081	37 454	40 576	172 127	126 986
Perú[12]	1972	2 686 471	1 757 230	555 316[9]	373 925	1 530 335	798 011
República Dominicana	1970	752 550	...	...	...	...	...
Trinidad y Tabago	1970	193 186	117 511	70 595	5 080	...	...
Uruguay	1975	794 501	...	...	...	...	...
Venezuela	1971	1 827 140	1 286 407	372 056	168 677	...	...

[1] Año de la última información disponible.
[2] Incluye formas de tenencia no declaradas.
[3] Incluye arrendatarios y subarrendatarios.
[4] Resultados obtenidos de una muestra aproximada del 1.3% de las unidades de vivienda. Corresponde a viviendas particulares construidas para fines residenciales; no incluye viviendas improvisadas.
[5] Hogares particulares.
[6] Cabeceras municipales.
[7] Resto del país.
[8] Resultados obtenidos de una muestra del 5% de los hogares, y que corresponde al número de hogares en las unidades de habitación.
[9] Incluye "arrendatarios con promesa de venta".
[10] Viviendas.
[11] Excluye la población indígena agrupada en tribus.
[12] Viviendas particulares cuyos ocupantes estaban presentes en el momento del censo.

367. OCCUPIED DWELLING UNITS, BY TYPE OF OCCUPATION, IN URBAN AND RURAL AREAS

(Number of dwelling units)

Urbana / *Urban*		Rural				
Inqui-lino *Tenant*	Otras formas[2] *Other*[2]	Total	Propie-tario *Owner*	Inqui-lino *Tenant*	Otras formas[2] *Other*[2]	*Country*
...	...	...	...	...	...	*Argentina*
...	...	33 046	...	...	...	*Barbados*
130 502	92 590	619 516	526 600	24 992	67 924	*Bolivia*
3 146 399	972 197	7 352 359	4 473 859	209 652	2 668 848	*Brazil*[4]
...	...	...	...	...	...	*Brazil*
...	57 639	1 222 492[7]	752 875	135 761	333 876	*Colombia*[5]
57 546	9 584	187 020	122 665	18 361	45 994	*Costa Rica*
...	...	666 630	...	...	...	*Cuba*
573 520	18 380	376 980	169 480	193 920	13 580	*Chile*[8]
239 232	48 393	707 406	556 928	41 464	109 014	*Ecuador*
142 075[9]	30 953	383 813	217 341	24 657[9]	141 815	*El Salvador*
115 212	61 801	629 306	373 787	12 694	242 825	*Guatemala*
...	...	...	...	...	...	*Guyana*
...	...	739 720	...	...	...	*Haiti*
63 528	10 746	316 595	260 481	12 818	43 296	*Honduras*
130 077	2 962	231 337	163 325	65 954	2 058	*Jamaica*
...2 226 137...		3 422 209	2 833 389	...588 820...		*Mexico*[10]
58 650	11 655	154 116	116 785	2 707	34 624	*Nicaragua*[10]
74 565	12 263	143 560	124 659	4 868	14 033	*Panama*[11]
70 215	17 665	164 575	143 195	6 375	14 880	*Panama*
31 262	13 879	255 984	223 095	6 192	26 697	*Paraguay*
532 742[9]	199 582	1 156 136	959 219	22 574[9]	174 343	*Peru*[12]
...	...	...	...	...	...	*Dominican Republic*
...	...	...	...	...	...	*Trinidad and Tobago*
...	...	...	...	...	...	*Uruguay*
...	...	...	...	...	...	*Venezuela*

[1] *Year of latest information available.*
[2] *Including undeclared forms of occupation.*
[3] *Including tenants and subtenants.*
[4] *Results obtained from an approximate sample of 1.3% of dwelling units. Covers private permanent dwellings constructed for residential purposes, excluding improvised dwellings.*
[5] *Private households.*
[6] *Municipal Capitals.*
[7] *Rest of Country.*
[8] *Results obtained from a sample of 5% of households. Represents the number of households in the dwelling units.*
[9] *Includes dwellings rented with an option to buy.*
[10] *Dwellings.*
[11] *Excluding indigenous population grouped in tribes.*
[12] *Occupied private dwellings with occupants present at the time of the census.*

368. UNIDADES DE VIVIENDA OCUPADAS, SEGUN NUMERO DE CUARTOS

(Número de unidades de vivienda)

País	Año [1] Year [1]	Total	1	2	3
Argentina	1970	6 056 100	...	...	...
Barbados	1970	59 391 [2]	1 456 [2]	8 832 [2]	11 400 [2]
Bolivia	1976	1 040 704	395 336	303 536	163 591
Brasil [3]	1970	17 628 699	498 641	1 697 186	2 941 854
Brasil	1980	25 210 639	764 786	1 986 380	3 415 262
Colombia	1973	3 028 051 [4]	463 777 [4]	805 910 [4]	597 281 [4]
Costa Rica	1973	330 857	14 567	32 977	61 719
Cuba	1970	1 900 657	185 784	280 160	395 415
Cuba	1981	2 290 176	111 727	262 293	422 117
Chile	1970	1 689 840	184 280	347 560	363 380
Ecuador	1974	1 193 940	406 291	378 679	184 392
El Salvador	1971	654 539	399 032	154 475	48 261
Guatemala	1973	997 768	300 300	409 928	143 522
Guyana	1970	129 722	...	...	...
Haití	1971	863 605	...	...	...
Honduras	1974	463 004	91 840	202 160	90 854
Jamaica	1970	420 008	137 512	110 365	67 614
México	1970	8 286 369	3 326 520	2 395 916	1 144 121
Nicaragua	1971	302 544	116 633	94 034	50 253
Panamá	1970	285 321	109 012	83 800	45 270
Panamá	1980	364 325	98 020	93 625	81 980
Paraguay	1972	428 111	179 116	121 197	57 611
Perú	1972	2 686 471	883 399	791 528	409 898
República Dominicana	1970	752 550	...	...	...
Trinidad y Tabago	1970	193 186	22 478	49 577	58 435
Uruguay	1975	794 501	74 517	146 541	248 595
Venezuela	1971	1 827 140	545 789	609 876	418 284

[1] Año de la última información disponible.
[2] Número de cuartos por cada hogar.
[3] Excluye viviendas improvisadas.
[4] Viviendas cuyos ocupantes estaban presentes en el momento del censo.

368. OCCUPIED DWELLING UNITS, BY NUMBER OF ROOMS

(Number of dwelling units)

4	5	6 y más 6 and over	No declarado Not declared	Country
...	...	...	...	*Argentina*
22 495 [2]	9 429 [2]	5 779 [2]	-	*Barbados*
92 184	40 773	45 284	-	*Bolivia*
3 868 246	3 412 341	5 210 431	-	*Brazil* [3]
4 733 736	5 022 369	9 206 138	81 968	*Brazil*
·········· 720 947 [4] ··········		440 136 [4]		*Colombia*
77 952	········· 143 642 ·········		-	*Costa Rica*
447 511	353 285	230 933	7 569	*Cuba*
608 583	505 809	379 647	-	*Cuba*
352 600	175 780	266 240	-	*Chile*
104 897	49 644	70 037	-	*Ecuador*
24 184	12 176	16 411	-	*El Salvador*
61 456	33 480	48 961	121	*Guatemala*
...	...	...	...	*Guyana*
...	...	...	...	*Haiti*
35 438	········· 42 712 ·········		-	*Honduras*
35 627	22 385	22 504	24 001	*Jamaica*
657 459	312 065	450 288	-	*Mexico*
20 770	········· 20 854 ·········		-	*Nicaragua*
27 700	11 185	8 354	-	*Panama*
52 405	········· 33 960 ·········		4 335	*Panama*
32 163	17 126	20 898	-	*Paraguay*
271 979	········· 286 488 ·········		43 179	*Peru*
...	...	...	...	*Dominican Republic*
36 488	10 529	5 935	9 744	*Trinidad and Tobago*
147 496	100 387	76 726	239	*Uruguay*
145 202	46 051	34 902	27 036	*Venezuela*

[1] *Year of latest information available.*
[2] *Number of rooms per household.*
[3] *Excluding improvised dwellings.*
[4] *Dwellings with occupants present at the time of the census.*

369. UNIDADES DE VIVIENDA OCUPADAS, SEGUN NUMERO DE OCUPANTES

(Número de unidades de vivienda)

País	Año [1] Year [1]	Total	1	2	3	4
Argentina	1970	6 056 100	615 900	1 125 250	1 230 600	1 255 000
Argentina	1980 [2]	7 103 853	729 616	1 354 405	1 330 635	1 438 472
Barbados	1970	59 391	12 709	10 704	8 149	6 968
Bolivia	1976	1 040 704	122 850	142 957	161 697	161 578
Brasil	1970	17 628 699	911 966	2 127 132	2 620 362	2 762 113
Brasil	1980	25 210 639	1 540 888	3 436 568	4 304 593	4 482 823
Colombia	1973 [2]	3 471 834	201 027	318 062	.... 860 544	
Costa Rica	1973	330 857	15 647	31 751	42 639	46 719
Cuba	1970	1 907 923	173 430	261 078	318 628	349 576
Cuba	1981	2 290 176	194 294	321 650	425 421	477 389
Chile	1970 [3]	1 689 840	93 720	187 420	235 220	266 700
Ecuador	1974 [2]	1 193 940	84 134	122 307	.... 308 294	
El Salvador	1971	654 539	55 072	55 916	.... 162 713	
Guatemala	1973 [4]	934 954	39 199	79 517	118 135	138 296
Guyana	1970	129 722	13 859	15 037	14 394	14 393
Haití	1971 [2]	863 605	...	...	...	....
Honduras	1974	463 004	19 442	36 715	....	
Jamaica	1970 [2]	420 008	79 939	65 439	.... 107 130	
México	1970	9 851 042	769 693	1 421 459	1 415 471	1 324 243
Nicaragua	1971	314 297	...	...	...	...
Panamá	1970 [5]	285 321	32 912	34 819	.... 73 194	
Panamá	1980 [5]	364 325	42 610	45 710	50 910	55 445
Paraguay	1972 [4]	428 111	26 743	42 544	53 277	57 562
Perú	1972 [6]	2 771 553	290 047	324 854	369 552	394 994
República Dominicana	1970	722 550	61 030	86 250	93 210	97 335
Trinidad y Tabago	1970 [2]	193 186	28 152	26 527	23 791	22 914
Uruguay	1975	794 501	116 211	179 345	165 106	146 346
Venezuela	1971 [2]	1 827 140	122 650	159 010	.... 436 841	

[1] Año de la última información disponible.
[2] Hogar.
[3] Resultados obtenidos de un muestra del 5% de las boletas censales.
[4] Viviendas particulares ocupadas.
[5] Excluye la población indígena agrupada en tribus.
[6] Excluye la población indígena selvática estimada en 39 800 personas en 1972. Se refiere a hogares en viviendas particulares cuyos ocupantes estaban presentes en el momento del censo.

369. OCCUPIED DWELLING UNITS, BY NUMBER OF OCCUPANTS

(Number of dwelling units)

5	6	7	8	9 y más 9 and over	Country
818 550	443 250	276 750	121 450	169 350	*Argentina*
977 870	560 703	345 526	·········· 366 626 ··········		*Argentina*
5 778	4 602	3 522	2 444	4 515	*Barbados*
145 344	116 202	79 223	·········· 110 853 ··········		*Bolivia*
2 504 218	1 960 171	1 505 933	1 115 278	2 121 526	*Brazil*
3 691 913	2 583 643	1 889 337	1 231 216	2 049 658	*Brazil*
·········· 1 487 047 ··········				605 154	*Colombia*
43 657	38 090	31 465	24 943	55 946	*Costa Rica*
271 056	188 153	129 386	80 416	136 200	*Cuba*
341 351	213 954	130 563	75 542	110 012	*Cuba*
252 140	204 740	151 320	109 200	189 380	*Chile*
·········· 502 947 ··········				176 258	*Ecuador*
·········· 288 935 ··········				91 903	*El Salvador*
139 707	126 758	99 738	73 826	119 778	*Guatemala*
14 253	13 285	11 965	10 088	22 448	*Guyana*
...	...	...	...	...	*Haiti*
·········· 334 721 ··········				72 126	*Honduras*
·········· 128 544 ··········				38 956	*Jamaica*
1 205 538	1 079 480	850 659	659 096	1 125 403	*Mexico*
...	...	...	...	...	*Nicaragua*
·········· 111 130 ··········				33 266	*Panama*
50 550	40 305	31 320	17 740	29 735	*Panama*
56 060	51 405	41 697	33 596	65 227	*Paraguay*
373 879	330 969	291 822	150 470	244 966	*Peru*
95 570	95 480	60 140	51 875	111 660	*Dominican Republic*
21 186	18 494	15 276	12 012	24 834	*Trinidad and Tobago*
87 029	48 945	23 330	12 563	15 626	*Uruguay*
·········· 773 563 ··········				335 076	*Venezuela*

[1] *Year of latest information available.*
[2] *Household.*
[3] *Results obtained from a sample of 5% of census forms.*
[4] *Occupied private dwellings.*
[5] *Excluding indigenous population grouped in tribes.*
[6] *Excluding indigenous population in jungle, estimated at 39 800 persons in 1972. Refers to households in private dwellings with occupants present when the census was taken.*

370. UNIDADES DE VIVIENDA OCUPADAS, SEGUN TIPO Y DISPONIBILIDAD DE SERVICIOS EN ZONAS URBANAS Y RURALES

(Número de unidades de vivienda)

País	Año[1] Year[1]	Total	Agua por tubería[2] Piped water[2]		Inodoros (retretes de agua) Water closets	
			Urbana Urban	Rural	Urbana Urban	Rural
Argentina	1970	6 056 100	...	...	...	...
Barbados	1970	59 391[4]	25 806[4]	32 222[4]	7 917[4][5]	7 878[4][5]
Bolivia	1976	1 040 704	354 495	54 467	197 848	26 593
Brasil	1970	17 628 699[6]	5 592 606[6]	191 662[6]	4 539 340[6]	145 137[6]
Brasil	1980	25 210 639	13 523 338	319 407	...	...
Colombia	1973	3 471 834[7]	2 000 066[7][8]	352 526[7][9]	1 848 978[7][8]	150 681[7][9]
Costa Rica	1973	330 857	·········· 258 849 ··········		·········· 146 430 ··········	
Cuba	1970	1 904 810	1 092 631	178 187	793 913	40 266
Cuba	1981	2 290 176	1 453 190	244 714	1 542 499	542 454
Chile	1970	1 689 840[10]	1 200 980[10]	124 020[10]	836 100[10]	27 620[10]
Ecuador	1974	1 193 940	405 765	106 509	354 054	43 741
El Salvador	1971	654 539	237 713	71 095	140 143	6 388
Guatemala	1973	997 768	303 374	118 947	167 488	11 559
Guyana	1970	129 722	...	...	...	...
Haití	1971	863 605	22 236	2 180	7 754	760
Honduras	1974	463 004	132 521	67 234	69 607	10 972
Jamaica	1970	420 008	179 448	128 111	187 160	219 208
México	1970	8 286 369	3 899 607	1 156 560	...	...
Nicaragua	1971	302 544	107 845	9 153	56 276	1 998
Panamá	1970	285 321	129 831[11]	19 072[11]	104 844	9 534
Panamá	1980	364 325	191 065	83 730	141 075	17 890
Paraguay	1972	428 111	47 446	73	57 889	3 428
Perú	1972	2 686 471	781 380	14 948	615 301	9 139
República Dominicana	1970	752 550	...	...	...	...
Trinidad y Tabago	1970	193 186	·········· 180 253 ··········		·········· 189 815[12] ··········	
Uruguay	1975	794 501	...	...	...	...
Venezuela	1971	1 827 140	·········· 1 322 479 ··········		·········· 977 470 ··········	

[1] Año de la última información disponible.
[2] Agua por tubería incluye agua dentro de la vivienda, fuera de la vivienda pero dentro del edificio, y fuera del edificio.
[3] Por sistema de alcantarillado.
[4] La parte urbana se refiere a la Parroquia de Saint Michael solamente.
[5] Conectado a un sistema de eliminación de excretas.
[6] Se refiere a viviendas particulares permanentes.
[7] Se refiere a hogares particulares.
[8] Se refiere a cabeceras municipales.
[9] Se refiere al resto de los municipios.
[10] Datos obtenidos de una muestra del 5% de los hogares.
[11] Incluye 3 258 unidades de habitación cuyo abastecimiento de agua se realiza por acueducto particular, (1 256 urbanas y 2 002 rurales).
[12] Incluye unidades de habitación con un tipo de retrete distinto del inodoro (letrina, pozo ciego, pozo negro, excusado lavable y de hoyo, etc.).

370. OCCUPIED DWELLING UNITS, BY TYPE OF SERVICES AVAILABLE, IN URBAN AND RURAL AREAS

(Number of dwelling units)

Sistemas de eliminación de excretas[3] / Sewage disposal systems[3]		Instalación de baño Bathroom		Alumbrado eléctrico Electric lighting		Country
Urbana Urban	Rural	Urbana Urban	Rural	Urbana Urban	Rural	
...	...	...	...	...	...	Argentina
...	...	...	...	18 411[4]	16 693[4]	Barbados
126 748	2 262	72 133	5 599	321 017	35 855	Bolivia
...	...	...	...	7 768 721[6]	615 273[6]	Brazil
6 885 018	104 898	...	...	15 674 731	1 594 744	Brazil
1 702 394[78]	82 685[79]	...	...	2 006 099[78]	167 247[79]	Colombia
49 044		...	...	219 277		Costa Rica
...	...	812 533	75 659	1 215 570	130 408	Cuba
...	...	...	...	1 587 000	310 867	Cuba
633 000[10]	10 120[10]	...	...	...	...	Chile
313 513	22 257	...	...	410 041	82 118	Ecuador
105 448	-	164 945	17 708	196 194	25 983	El Salvador
...	...	...	...	249 908	34 123	Guatemala
...	...	...	...	...	...	Guyana
...	...	...	...	33 426	1 560	Haiti
56 574	3 725	...	...	98 248	17 518	Honduras
-	-	...	...	...	...	Jamaica
...	...	2 269 807	367 245	3 926 753	949 792	Mexico
46 046	289	109 259	10 990	114 208	10 697	Nicaragua
88 203	2 094	123 531	26 113	125 387	22 731	Panama
116 350	4 535	180 900	59 175	181 190	54 805	Panama
...	...	114 902	50 390	71 707	3 065	Paraguay
587 251	5 849	611 441	13 552	830 660	31 347	Peru
...	...	...	...	...	...	Dominican Republic
23 569		...	...	...	...	Trinidad and Tobago
...	...	...	...	...	...	Uruguay
736 717		1 069 962		1 402 819		Venezuela

[1] Year of latest information available.
[2] Piped water includes water supplied within the dwelling, outside the dwelling but inside the building, and outside the building.
[3] By sewer.
[4] Urban portion refers to Saint Michael parish only.
[5] Connected to a sewerage system.
[6] Permanent private dwellings.
[7] Private households.
[8] Municipal Capitals.
[9] Rest of Municipalities.
[10] Data obtained from a sample of 5% of households.
[12] Including 3 258 dwelling units whose water is supplied by private pipeline (1 256 urban and 2 002 rural).
[12] Including dwelling units with other types of facilities than flush toilets, (latrine, cesspool, cesspit, outhouse with or without water).

Publicaciones de la CEPAL

COMISION ECONOMICA PARA AMERICA LATINA Y EL CARIBE

Casilla 179-D   Santiago de Chile

NACIONES UNIDAS

PUBLICACIONES PERIODICAS

Revista de la CEPAL

La **Revista** se inició en 1976 como parte del Programa de Publicaciones de la Comisión Económica para América Latina y el Caribe, con el propósito de contribuir al examen de los problemas del desarrollo socioeconómico de la región. Preparada por la Secretaría de la CEPAL, la **Revista** es dirigida por el Dr. Raúl Prebisch. Las opiniones expresadas en los artículos firmados, incluidas las colaboraciones de los funcionarios de la Secretaría, son las de los autores y, por lo tanto, no reflejan necesariamente los puntos de vista de la Organización.

La **Revista de la CEPAL** se publica en español e inglés tres veces por año —en abril, agosto y diciembre.

Libros de la C E P A L

Agua, desarrollo y medio ambiente, 1980, 443 pp.

Los bancos transnacionales y el financiamiento externo de América Latina. La experiencia del Perú. 1965-1976, por Robert Devlin, 1980, 265 pp.

Transnational banks and the external finance of Latin America: the experience of Peru, 1985, 342 pp.

América Latina en el umbral de los ochenta, 1979, 2ª ed. 1980, 203 pp.

La dimensión ambiental en los estilos de desarrollo de América Latina, por Osvaldo Sunkel, 1981, 2ª ed. 1984, 136 pp.

Manual de Proyectos de Desarrollo Económico, 1958, 5ª ed. 1980, 264 pp.

Manual on economic development projects, 1958, 2nd. ed. 1972, 242 pp.

¿Se puede superar la pobreza? Realidad y perspectivas en América Latina, 1980, 286 pp.

La mujer y el desarrollo: guía para la planificación de programas y proyectos, 1984, 115 pp.

Women and development: guidelines for programme and project planning, 1982, 2nd. ed. 1983, 123 pp.

Africa y América Latina: perspectivas de la cooperación interregional, 1983, 286 pp.

Sobrevivencia campesina en ecosistemas de altura, vols. I y II, 1983, 720 pp.

La mujer en el sector popular urbano. América Latina y el Caribe, 1984, 349 pp.

Cuadernos Estadísticos de la C E P A L

1   América Latina: relación de precios del intercambio, 1976, 2ª ed., 1984, 66 pp.
2   Indicadores del desarrollo económico y social en América Latina, 1976, 2ª ed. 1984, 178 pp.
3   Series históricas del crecimiento en América Latina, 1976, 2ª ed. 1984, 206 pp.
4   Estadísticas sobre la estructura del gasto de consumo de los hogares según finalidad del gasto, por grupos de ingreso, 1978, 110 pp. (Agotado, reemplazado por Nº 8)
5   El balance de pagos de América Latina, 1950-1977, 1979, 2ª ed. 1984, 164 pp.
6   Distribución regional del producto interno bruto sectorial en los países de América Latina, 1981, 2ª ed. 1985, 68 pp.
7   Tablas de insumo-producto en América Latina, 1983, 383 pp.
8   Estructura del gasto de consumo de los hogares según finalidad del gasto, por grupos de ingreso, 1984, 146 pp.

Estudios e Informes de la C E P A L

1   Nicaragua: el impacto de la mutación política, 1981, 2ª ed. 1982, 126 pp.
2   Perú 1968-1977: la política económica en un proceso de cambio global, por Aníbal Pinto y Héctor Assael, 1981, 2ª ed. 1982, 166 pp.
3   La industrialización de América Latina y la cooperación internacional, 1981, 170 pp. (Agotado, no será reimpreso.)
4   Estilos de desarrollo, modernización y medio ambiente en la agricultura latinoamericana, por Nicolo Gligo, 1981, 4ª ed. 1985, 138 pp.
5   El desarrollo de América Latina en los años ochenta, 1981, 2ª ed. 1982, 153 pp.
5   Latin American development in the 1980s, 1981, 2ª ed. 1982, 134 pp.
6   Proyecciones del desarrollo latinoamericano en los años ochenta, 1981, 3ª ed. 1985, 96 pp.
6   Latin American development projections for the 1980s, 1982, 2nd. ed. 1983, 89 pp.
7   Las relaciones económicas externas de América Latina en los años ochenta, 1981, 2ª ed. 1982, 180 pp.
8   Integración y cooperación regionales en los años ochenta, 1982, 174 pp.
9   Estrategias de desarrollo sectorial para los años ochenta: industria y agricultura, 1981, 2ª ed. 1982, 100 pp.
10 Dinámica del subempleo en América Latina, 1981, 2ª ed. 1985, 101 pp.
11 Estilos de desarrollo de la industria manufacturera y medio ambiente en América Latina, 1982, 2ª ed. 1984, 178 pp.
12 Relaciones económicas de América Latina con los países miembros del Consejo de Asistencia Mutua Económica (CAME), 1982, 154 pp.
13 Campesinado y desarrollo agrícola en Bolivia, 1982, 175 pp.
14 El sector externo: indicadores y análisis de sus fluctuaciones. El caso argentino, 1982, 2ª ed. 1985, 216 pp.
15 Ingeniería y consultoría en Brasil y el Grupo Andino, 1982, 320 pp.
16 Cinco estudios sobre la situación de la mujer en América Latina, 1982, 2ª ed. 1985, 178 pp.
16 Five studies on the situation of women in Latin America, 1983, 2nd. ed. 1984, 188 pp.
17 Cuentas nacionales y producto material en América Latina, 1982, 129 pp.
18 La financiación a las exportaciones en América Latina, 1983, 212 pp.
19 Medición del empleo y de los ingresos rurales, 1982, 2ª ed. 1983, 173 pp.
19 Measurement of employment and income in rural areas, 1983, 184 pp.
20 Efectos macroeconómicos de cambios en las barreras al comercio y al movimiento de capitales: un modelo de simulación, 1982, 79 pp.
21 La empresa pública en la economía: la experiencia argentina, 1982, 2ª ed. 1985, 134 pp.

22 Las empresas transnacionales en la economía de Chile, 1974-1980, 1983, 178 pp.
23 La gestión y la informática en las empresas ferroviarias de América Latina y España, 1983, 195 pp.
24 Establecimiento de empresas de reparación y mantención de contenedores en América Latina y el Caribe, 1983, 314 pp.
24 Establishing container repair and maintenance enterprises in Latin America and the Caribbean, 1983, 236 pp.
25 Agua potable y saneamiento ambiental en América Latina, 1981-1990/Drinking water supply and sanitation in Latin America, 1981-1990 (bilingüe), 1983, 140 pp.
26 Los bancos transnacionales, el estado y el endeudamiento externo en Bolivia, 1983, 282 pp.
27 Política económica y procesos de desarrollo. La experiencia argentina entre 1976 y 1981, 1983, 157 pp.
28 Estilos de desarrollo, energía y medio ambiente: un estudio de caso exploratorio, 1983, 129 pp.
29 Empresas transnacionales en la industria de alimentos. El caso argentino: cereales y carne, 1983, 93 pp.
30 Características principales del proceso y de la política de industrialización de Centro América, 1960-1980, 1983, 168 pp.
31 Dos estudios sobre empresas transnacionales en Brasil, 1983, 2ª ed. 1983, 141 pp.
32 La crisis económica internacional y su repercusión en América Latina, 1983, 81 pp.
33 La agricultura campesina en sus relaciones con la industria, 1984, 120 pp.
34 Cooperación económica entre Brasil y el Grupo Andino: el caso de los minerales y metales no ferrosos, 1983, 148 pp.
35 La agricultura campesina y el mercado de alimentos: la dependencia externa y sus efectos en una economía abierta, 1984, 201 pp.
36 El capital extranjero en la economía peruana, 1984, 178 pp.
37 Dos estudios sobre política arancelaria, 1984, 96 pp.
38 Estabilización y liberalización económica en el Cono Sur, 1984, 193 pp.
39 La agricultura campesina y el mercado de alimentos: el caso de Haití y el de la República Dominicana, 1984, 255 pp.
40 La industria siderúrgica latinoamericana: tendencias y potencial, 1984, 280 pp.
41 La presencia de las empresas transnacionales en la economía ecuatoriana, 1984, 78 pp.
42 Precios, salarios y empleo en la Argentina: estadísticas económicas de corto plazo, 1984, 378 pp.
43 El desarrollo de la seguridad social en América Latina, 1985, 348 pp.
44 Market structure, firm size and Brazilian exports, 1985, 104 pp.
45 La planificación del transporte en países de América Latina, 1985, 248 pp.
46 La crisis en América Latina: su evaluación y perspectivas, 1985, 118 pp.
47 La juventud en América Latina y el Caribe, 1985, 181 pp.
48 Desarrollo de los recursos mineros de América Latina, 1985, 144 pp.
49 Las relaciones económicas internacionales de América Latina y la cooperación regional, 1985, 224 pp.
50 América Latina y la economía mundial del algodón, 1985, 122 pp.
51 Comercio y cooperación entre países de América Latina y países miembros del CAME, 1985, 89 pp.

SERIES DE PUBLICACIONES

Cuadernos de la C E P A L

1 América Latina: el nuevo escenario regional y mundial/ Latin America: the new regional and world setting, (bilingüe), 1975, 2ª ed. 1985, 120 pp.
2 Las evoluciones regionales de la estrategia internacional del desarrollo, 1975, 2ª ed. 1984, 71 pp.
2 Regional appraisals of the international development strategy, 1975, 2nd. ed. 1985, 82 pp.

3 Desarrollo humano, cambio social y crecimiento en América Latina, 1975, 2ª ed. 1984, 103 pp.
4 Relaciones comerciales, crisis monetaria e integración económica en América Latina, 1975, 85 pp.
5 Síntesis de la segunda evaluación regional de la estrategia internacional del desarrollo, 1975, 72 pp.
6 Dinero de valor constante. Concepto, problemas y experiencias, por Jorge Rose, 1975, 2ª ed. 1984, 43 pp.
7 La coyuntura internacional y el sector externo, 1975, 2ª ed. 1983, 117 pp.
8 La industrialización latinoamericana en los años setenta, 1975, 2ª ed. 1984, 118 pp.
9 Dos estudios sobre inflación. La inflación en los países centrales. América Latina y la inflación importada, 1975, 2ª ed. 1984, 57 pp.
10 Reactivación del mercado común centroamericano, 1976, 2ª ed. 1984, 145 pp.
11 Integración y cooperación entre países en desarrollo en el ámbito agrícola, por Germánico Salgado, 1976, 2ª ed. 1985, 66 pp.
12 Temas del nuevo orden económico internacional, 1976, 2ª ed. 1984, 84 pp.
13 En torno a las ideas de la CEPAL: desarrollo, industrialización y comercio exterior, 1977, 54 pp.
14 En torno a las ideas de la CEPAL: problemas de la industrialización en América Latina, 1977, 2ª ed. 1984, 48 pp.
15 Los recursos hidráulicos de América Latina, 1977, 60 pp.
15 The water resources of Latin America, 1977, 2nd. ed. 1985, 80 pp.
16 Desarrollo y cambio social en América Latina, 1977, 2ª ed. 1984, 62 pp.
17 Estrategia internacional de desarrollo y establecimiento de un nuevo orden económico internacional, 1977, 3ª ed. 1984, 61 pp.
17 International development strategy and establishment of a new international economic order, 1977, 3rd. ed. 1985, 95 pp.
18 Raíces históricas de las estructuras distributivas de América Latina, por A. di Filippo, 1977, 2ª ed. 1983, 67 pp.
19 Dos estudios sobre endeudamiento externo, por C. Massad y R. Zahler, 1979, 2ª ed. 1978, 63 pp.
20 Tendencias y proyecciones a largo plazo del desarrollo económico de América Latina, 1978, 3ª ed. 1985, 134 pp.
21 25 años en la agricultura de América Latina. Rasgos principales 1950-1975, 1978, 2ª ed. 1983, 128 pp.
22 Notas sobre la familia como unidad socioeconómica, por Carlos A. Borsotti, 1978, 2ª ed. 1984, 60 pp.
23 La organización de la información para la evaluación del desarrollo, por Juan Sourrouille, 1978, 2ª ed. 1984, 66 pp.
24 Contabilidad nacional a precios constantes en América Latina, por Alberto Fracchia, 1978, 2ª ed. 1983, 69 pp.
25 Ecuador: desafíos y logros de la política económica en la fase de la expansión petrolera, 1979, 2ª ed. 1984, 158 pp.
26 Las transformaciones rurales en América Latina: ¿Desarrollo social o marginación?, 1979, 2ª ed. 1984, 165 pp.
27 La dimensión de la pobreza en América Latina, por Oscar Altimir, 1979, 2ª ed. 1983, 95 pp.
28 Organización institucional para el control y manejo de la deuda externa — El caso chileno, por Rodolfo Hoffman, 1979, 41 pp.
29 La política monetaria y el ajuste de la balanza de pagos: tres estudios, 1979, 2ª ed. 1984, 67 pp.
29 Monetary policy and balance of payments adjustment: three studies, 1979, 60 pp.
30 América Latina: las evaluaciones regionales de la estrategia internacional del desarrollo en los años setenta, 1979, 2ª ed. 1982, 243 pp.
31 Educación, imágenes y estilos de desarrollo, por G. Rama, 1979, 2ª ed. 1982, 77 pp.
32 Movimientos internacionales de capitales, 1979, 2ª ed. 1984, 90 pp.
33 Informes sobre las inversiones directas extranjeras en América Latina, por A. E. Calcagno, 1980, 2ª ed. 1982, 114 pp.

34 *Las fluctuaciones de la industria manufacturera argentina, 1950-1978,* por Daniel Heymann, 1980, 2ª ed. 1984, 240 pp.

35 *Perspectivas de reajuste industrial: la Comunidad Económica Europea y los países en desarrollo,* por Ben Evers, Gerard de Groot y Willy Wagenmans, 1980, 2ª ed. 1984, 69 pp.

36 *Un análisis sobre la posibilidad de evaluar la solvencia crediticia de los países en desarrollo,* por Alvaro Saieh, 1980, 2ª ed. 1984, 82 pp.

37 *Hacia los censos latinoamericanos de los años ochenta,* 1981, 152 pp.

38 *Desarrollo regional argentino: la agricultura,* por Juan Martin, 1981, 2ª ed. 1984, 119 pp.

39 *Estratificación y movilidad ocupacional en América Latina,* por C. Filgueira y C. Geneletti, 1981, 2ª ed. 1985, 162 pp.

40 *Programa de acción regional para América Latina en los años ochenta,* 1981, 2ª ed. 1984, 69 pp.

40 *Regional programme of action for Latin America in the 1980s,* 1981, 2nd. ed. 1984, 66 pp.

41 *El desarrollo de América Latina y sus repercusiones en la educación. Alfabetismo y escolaridad básica,* 1982, 254 pp.

42 *América Latina y la economía mundial del café,* 1982, 104 pp.

43 *El ciclo ganadero y la economía argentina,* 1983, 168 pp.

44 *Las encuestas de hogares en América Latina,* 1983, 130 pp.

45 *Las cuentas nacionales en América Latina y el Caribe,* 1983, 109 pp.

45 *National accounts in Latin America and the Caribbean,* 1983, 97 pp.

46 *Demanda de equipos para generación, transmisión y transformación eléctrica en América Latina,* 1983, 201 pp.

47 *La economía de América Latina en 1982: evolución general, política cambiaria y renegociación de la deuda externa,* 1984, 113 pp.

48 *Políticas de ajuste y renegociación de la deuda externa en América Latina,* 1984, 114 pp.

49 *La economía de América Latina y el Caribe en 1983: evolución general, crisis y procesos de ajuste,* 1985, 106 pp.

49 *The economy of Latin America and the Caribbean in 1983: main trends, the impact of the crisis and the adjustment processes,* 1985, 108 pp.

— *Canada and the foreign firm,* D. Pollock, 1976, 43 pp.

— *United States — Latin American Trade and Financial Relations: Some Policy Recommendations,* S. Weintraub, 1977, 44 pp.

— *Energy in Latin America: The Historical Record,* J. Mullen, 1978, 66 pp.

— *The Economic Relations of Latin America with Europe,* 1980, 2nd. ed. 1983, 156 pp.

Las publicaciones de la Comisión Económica para América Latina se pueden adquirir a los
distribuidores locales o directamente a través de:

Publicaciones de las Naciones Unidas
Sección de Ventas — DC-2-866
Nueva York, NY, 10017
Estados Unidos de América

Publicaciones de las Naciones Unidas
Sección de Ventas
Palais des Nations
1211 Ginebra 10, Suiza

Unidad de Distribución
CEPAL — Casilla 179-D
Santiago
Chile

Publications of the Economic Commission for Latin America can be ordered from your local
distributor or directly through:

United Nations Publications
Sales Section, — DC-2-866
New York, NY 10017, USA

United Nations Publications
Sales Section
Palais des Nations
1211 Geneve 10, Switzerland

Distribution Unit
CEPAL — Casilla 179-D
Santiago, Chile

◁ As your climbs get steeper your strength needs to be developed to enable you to hang on for longer.

▷ A combination of technique and strength in equal proportions makes a good climber.

◁ Bouldering outside in a perfect sun and sea setting. What better way to train for longer climbs?

Finding rests on a route

The ability to find resting positions while in the most unlikely climbing situations pays enormous dividends. On easier climbs there are frequently large ledges to accommodate the whole foot, the rock angle lays back and all the weight can be taken over the feet. On steeper ground it may not be possible to stand in a position where you can take both hands off to rest. You might find yourself standing on a tiny foothold with the edge of one shoe and very little for the other foot. Handholds might be smaller than you would like and the aura of the situation might be very intimidating. By using your imagination, it is usually possible to find a rest of sorts.

KEEPING CLOSE INTO THE ROCK

On steep rock you must keep your body pushed up against the rock surface and the body weight directly over the feet. To achieve this a fine positioning of the body may be required and the difference of a few centimetres one way or the other can often make a significant difference. To stand efficiently on tiny toeholds, you'll need to use the inside edge of your rock shoe. The reasons for this are simple enough – you need to glean as much support as you can from the shoe and the lateral rigidity offers more than the longitudinal rigidity. It is also possible to stand on the outside edge of the shoe but it is less effective for upward movement unless you are making moves across the rock face. As an aid to resting, however, you'll find it very useful for relieving pressure and tension from cramped feet.

RESTING YOUR ARMS

Try not to hang on too tightly with the hands and arms. Concentrate wholly on placing as much weight as possible over the feet and if your feet tire change position occasionally. The ideal resting handhold is a side-pull or under-cut. The reasons for this are simple enough – the arm is in a fairly low position where blood can flow freely to the muscles. If you are hanging on to a hold above your head, the blood will drain from your arms and the muscles will not be replenished with oxygen.

◁ *Resting between difficult sections of a climb is vitally important and every opportunity should be taken.*

△ *By varying the holds that you use, arms and fingers are less likely to cramp up.*

△ *Arms can be rested most effectively by dangling them at full stretch to allow the blood to flow back into the fingers. Alternate arms for effective rests.*

If you are forced to hang on holds above your head, you must try to rest each arm by alternately dangling each down below waist level and shaking the hand loosely to assist blood flow. This is called "shaking out". Try not to rush the process. If you are very tired, it takes a good 5 minutes or more to rest adequately and recover sufficient energy to continue. By moving on before you are properly rested, you'll find that strength wanes very rapidly to the extent that you might not have enough power to complete a sequence. If you have to, don't be afraid to back down to a "no-hands" resting-place, even though it might mean down-climbing a fair distance. It is all about maximizing the remaining power to achieve the next rest or the end of the difficulties.

◁ *Sometimes a full rest can be found by climbing down a few feet to a ledge. This is the best possible rest you can have.*

Saving your arms

Rests where you are able to use under-cut holds or side-pulls are generally more efficient. You only use strength to hold body weight in to the rock surface rather than hang on. Of course, holds such as these are not always available and some imagination may be required to find the most effective resting position. If you have to hang on to large holds above your head, it's worth trying to open up the hand as much as possible. Big jugs or flat holds can be held with the palm where the wrist is bent over at 90 degrees like a hook – rest with a straight arm to save the precious energy in your muscles. Again, try to alternate hands so that you get a good rest for each arm.

△ A combination of heel-hook with the foot wedged in the crack adds security while also being effective for saving strength.

Crack climbing can be extraordinarily trying and tiring. Feet and hands become cramped from continually being wedged into the crack. If the crack is wide enough, it might be possible to get a hands-off rest by wedging your knee into the crack and levering your foot against one side. This is called a knee-bar. Knee-bars may also be found anywhere where there is a suitable feature and can sometimes even be effected on open features such as below overlaps or overhangs.

The heel-hook is another good way to save energy and it is used to surmount overhangs. It is exactly what it sounds like – by hanging underneath an overhang by your hands, the foot is brought up to the same level and hooked on to a suitable protrusion or ledge. You can take a surprisingly large proportion of the strain from your arms by using the foot and the

△ A large jug or ledge can be held in a hook grip for greater comfort.

◁ Experiment with different body positions to find the most comfortable rest.

leg as a lever. The drawback with this is that you do need to be rather gymnastic and flexible, for it is a powerful manoeuvre.

In a similar vein is the toe-hook. Whilst not used as a powerful movement, it is a useful way to maintain balance or equilibrium. Take one example – on a layback sequence you find it difficult to prevent the opposing forces, of feet pushing while hands pull, causing you to swing outwards. This rather alarming effect is known as "barn-dooring" and once it comes into effect it is a struggle to prevent the inevitable flying fall. If you can hook the toe of one boot into a crack or behind a rib of rock, it is possible to use it to hold your body stable while you try to move into a position of more security. Toe-hooks can sometimes be used to help gain a rest in an otherwise seemingly impossible situation.

▷ *A toe-hook in a large hole provides leverage for the move up as well as helping to gain a useful rest.*

▽ *The arms will not tire so quickly if they are used at full stretch or fully bent.*

Energy-saving techniques

By far the most efficient and energy-saving way to climb is to use the technique of bridging. This was, of course, a technique that we introduced right at the very beginning when we took our first steps on rock and it is something that we can apply, with some imagination, to many situations encountered on more difficult climbs. It is possible, for example, to use a bridging technique on a steep, open wall where none of the more recognizable features of grooves and corners are apparent. You might find yourself taking all your weight on the very tip of the inside of the toe of your shoe. This is an incredibly tiring position for the foot to be in for any protracted period of time, but if you are able to reach out and push sideways with the other foot it is possible to alleviate much of the strain.

An "Egyptian" or "drop knee" is a useful technique to conserve energy on very steep rock. It is a comfortable position that allows you to keep the torso very close in to the rock surface and more weight on the feet and legs than would normally be possible. As the illustration (right) shows, however, it is an advantage to be able to contort the body and to retain flexibility. It is such an unconventional technique to employ that many climbers forget its usefulness. Milder forms and shapes than that shown can be achieved in a great many climbing scenarios – all it requires is some imagination.

MORE DYNOS!

Dyno is a shortened term for dynamic motion. A dyno move is one in which the climber utilizes momentum to their advantage. Take

◁ Any feature that can be straddled by bridging across it is likely to be less tiring.

▷ The same feature climbed using the technique of back-and-footing, which is most commonly associated with chimney climbing.

△ On steep, open climbs it is often difficult to engineer a rest position. You will be reliant on good footwork and stamina to get you through.

◁ Here the toe is hooked to a hold to help secure the body in close, thus permitting weight to be borne by the foot and directly below the handgrips. This is sometimes called an Egyptian or "drop knee".

the example of a scenario in which you can see an excellent handhold that is just out of arm's reach or that you can touch but not get enough grip on to pull up your body weight. A little momentum from a small push up from the feet will allow you to make the extra distance needed to curl your hand over the good hold and heave up. An extreme form of dyno is where one might leap for a hold neither knowing whether it is good, bad or indifferent – discovering it to be usable is the only justification for such a technique to be deemed to make life easier for yourself!

"Flagging" is a term applied to describe a technique that is a perfectly natural movement of the body in motion, retaining balance. It is simple enough to use in a huge number of climbing scenarios at any grade – except perhaps the easiest, where it may be frowned upon as unnecessary and energy-wasting. It is often interpreted as a thrashing or leg-kicking movement – the fact that it is useful seems to be overlooked. The leg is used in one of two ways in flagging, either as a counterbalance to maintain equilibrium or as a pendulum action to assist in dynamic motion.

More energy-saving tips

There are other things not directly associated with body movement or holds that will help you conserve energy on steeper climbs. These include the efficiency with which you are able to place protection on the lead and also how you carry or "rack" your gear. There are several ways in which you can do this and every climber will, over time, learn which is the most suitable for their preferences. This does require experimentation and a mind open to change.

Considerable energy can be wasted trying to fiddle a nut into a crack that it clearly will not fit. Sometimes you look at a crack and be so convinced that a particular-sized nut will fit in that you become blind to other possibilities,

▷ *Whenever you place runners on steep rock, try to find good holds and a comfortable position from which to operate.*

whether of size of nut or even a different part of the crack! You will gain considerable advantage if you carry nuts of a similar size on individual karabiners, say large on one, medium on another and small on a third. If one nut doesn't fit the crack, there will almost certainly be another on the karabiner that will.

PREPARING PROTECTION

Many climbers, when faced with a difficult or crucial nut placement, will prepare themselves while in a comfortable position. If you know, or are fairly positive, that one particular-sized nut is likely to fit into the crack, you could remove it from the rack and if necessary clip in a quickdraw, and then move up to the placement with it held in your teeth. Once you reach the right spot all you need to do is to place it! Obviously you must be certain of the size, because if you're not you will needlessly waste valuable energy.

Some harness manufacturers have developed a special plastic clip for connecting a karabiner to; using the karabiner becomes simply a matter of pulling it rather than unclipping from the gear loop. It is helpful to rack gear in a particular order that you become familiar with. This, too, will save precious energy. Quickdraws, any nuts on rope slings and camming devices also need to be carefully positioned so that they are accessible almost by feel alone. Many items of protection equipment are colour-coded by the manufacturer – long winter evenings can be whiled away learning all the codes for your personal rack. No single method can be said to be categorically the best, so it is important to experiment and adapt a method to suit your needs. You may even find that you come to favour particular pieces of protection. Keep them to hand.

△ **1** *A runner gripped between the teeth ready for placement will save valuable energy on steep rock.*

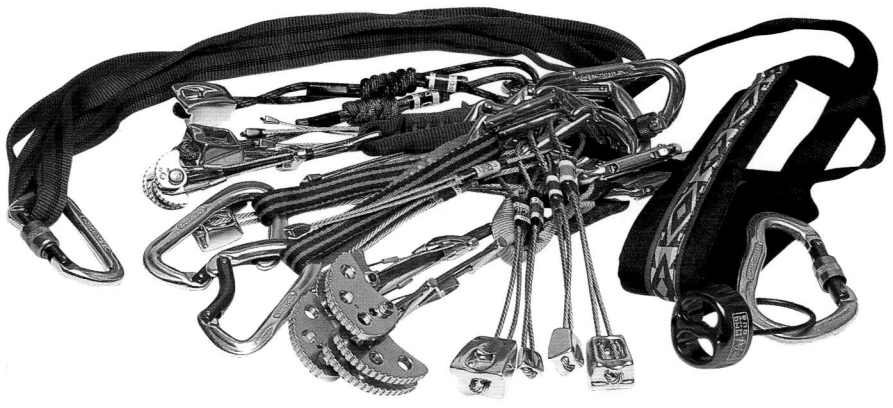

△ *When you rack your gear, make sure you work with a system that you are happy and familiar with.*

▽ *The climber checks out the way ahead. In doing this, he may save precious energy once on the climb.*

△ **2** *You just have to hope it's the right size!*

Clipping the rope

Efficient clipping of the rope has two main benefits: you save energy the quicker you can perform the task, and there are ways to clip that increase your safety in the event of a fall.

The method by which you clip the rope into protection can also make a tremendous difference to the energy you expend. It is difficult to comprehend perhaps, but a fumbled clip could conceivably lead to dire consequences such as a long fall on the sharp end of the rope.

There are any number of ways to clip the rope into a runner efficiently. Like racking, it is as well to experiment with several before latching on to a method that suits your preferences and dexterity. Regardless of the method adopted, there are two important aspects to remember. Firstly, the gate of the karabiner

◁ On sustained and steep climbs, energy conservation is crucial to success.

▽ Practise clipping the rope into running belays until you can do it blindfold!

△ A quickdraw clipped correctly with the straight-gate karabiner clipped to the bolt, and the rope running through the bent-gate karabiner.

● GETTING IT WRONG

In this situation, the bent-gate karabiner has been clipped to the bolt. This will make it harder to clip the rope. The quickdraw should basically be the other way round (see far left).

◁ It is not so easy to clip the rope into a straight-gate karabiner.

into which you are clipping the rope should face away from the immediate direction you are going to be climbing in. This is to ensure that, in the event of a fall, the rope does not unclip itself. Secondly, you must ensure that the quickdraw is not twisted in any way once the rope is clipped in. A twist in the sling of the quickdraw can in rare cases also allow the rope to become unclipped in the event of a fall. It is a simple enough matter of adopting good habits in ensuring both aspects are observed.

One suggested method of clipping the rope into a quickdraw is illustrated. If you are clipping the rope into a runner that is way above your head you might have to pull a short length of rope up, grip it in your teeth and then pull up more so that you have enough slack rope to reach up and make the clip. Once the rope is in the karabiner, you can release the teeth grip and continue climbing. Holding the rope momentarily in the teeth means that you don't have to heave with all your might on the rope to pull it up to make the clip, and thus saves valuable energy resources. If, for whatever reason, you think you might fall off while you are

attempting the clip, don't forget to drop the rope from your teeth as you fall – only circus performers can hold someone in their teeth on the end of a trapeze!

◁ A well-placed nut, with the quickdraw clipped to it.

Falling off

Though falling is something that every climber must come to terms with, there are those to whom the idea is complete anathema and there are others to whom it is par for the course. To achieve the utmost purity of style, you should always try to climb without falling. This is called an "on-sight" ascent. Not so many years ago there was a saying amongst climbers that the "leader never falls". In times past this was a good adage to work to because there was little, if any, protection on a pitch. Today the situation has changed significantly. Leading climbs has become less of a risky business as equipment for arranging crack protection has developed and improved. There are still climbs on which it is impossible to arrange adequate protection, but they are fewer in number.

MODERN ATTITUDES

Purity of style and ambition to climb hard are not always good bed partners. Ambition can become headstrong and ignore purity entirely. More commonly, ambition will bring purity around to its way of thinking and a compromise is reached that is acceptable to both. Many climbers will push themselves beyond their "on-sight" grade, knowing full well that they will probably fall off at the crux and may do so several times before successfully completing the sequence. This ethic or compromise approach is better conducted on bolted or "sport" climbs where you know full well that the runners on to which you are falling will be capable of absorbing the shock of repeated falls. Traditional routes, where one places one's own protection, are not always so

△ *The old adage, "the leader never falls", was sound advice in the days when climbers tied the rope directly around their waists.*

▷ *While the modern-day climber with all the safety trappings is more secure, it is still purer to climb without falling. You may find an acute lack of protection on some climbs!*

◁ *A steep bolt-protected climb is an ideal place to practise falling off!*

▷ *Make sure that you push yourself clear of the rock and look down to see where you're heading to.*

reliable. It is an accepted method of climbing, but it may not be entirely satisfactory to all climbers. Knowing that it is relatively safe to fall off helps you to keep your composure. At the extreme end of the scale there are climbs of high technical difficulty where the prospect of falling will mean certain death – if you attain those levels one would assume that you have advanced far beyond the scope of this book.

FALLING TECHNIQUE

Taking a fall will come to most leaders at some time. This may be on to bolts at the wall or on a sport climb, or it may be on to gear that the leader has placed. It is important to understand that it is not the act of falling that puts the climber in danger of injury – it is the impact with the rock face, wall, ledge or even the ground itself. Falling into space may be frightening, but provided that is all it is there should be no problem. It will be evident from this that, provided the protection is good and holds, falling off overhanging hard climbs is safer than falling off an easy slab. Falling off a slab means that the climber will come into contact with rock. There some tips for falling more safely. For example, you can push your-

◁ *It is easier to attempt climbs that are beyond your current ability on an indoor wall – here falling off is much less serious.*

self away from the wall or rock, rather than clinging on and scraping down the surface, doing untold damage. However, this takes a lot of experience and courage to do. The natural instinct is to cling!

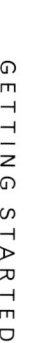

Tips for seconding

When discussing techniques and ways to conserve energy, it is easy to forget that seconding a climb can sometimes be as tiring as leading. It may not be as mentally stressful (the fear factor should not be as great as that involved in lead-ing a climb), but stress levels could easily be equal in terms of frustration. Climbing tech-niques apply in the same way, but when it comes to taking out protection, energy loss can be outrageously high.

MENTAL ATTITUDE

Seconding a climb, if you are more used to leading, is generally approached in a rather lackadaisical manner and with the attitude that it'll be a lot easier on the blunt end of the rope. Climbers who set off to follow a pitch in this frame of mind will quite commonly get caught out and surprised by the awkwardness of the climbing. If at the same time they expe-rience difficulties removing runners that the leader has placed, the whole experience could prove quite harrowing.

REMOVING RUNNERS

Sometimes, particularly on the crux of a climb or on sections where it is preferable to keep going, the second might well decide to remove the runners from the crack but leave them on the rope rather than waste valuable energy unclipping them and clipping them on to the harness. When you arrive at a more comfort-able place to rest, the runners can be removed from the rope and placed on the harness. If a piece of protection proves difficult to remove and it is clear that you are going to waste a lot of strength getting it out, it may be better to ask the leader for a tight rope to take your full body weight while you fiddle the offending piece out. It is always a good excuse for a rest!

◁ On serious climbs of great difficulty the role of the second is vital. Having confidence in the second allows the leader to concentrate on the all-absorbing task of leading.

△ *Sometimes you'll find it more difficult to second climbs than you would if you were leading – it's an odd fact of life!*

▷ *Traverses, particularly difficult ones, can be intimidating and very serious for the second.*

● TRAVERSING AND DOWN-CLIMBING

There are certain situations in which seconding a climb can be as risky as leading it. An unprotected traverse is one such situation. Here, if a seconding climber comes off, he or she will swing down and out. If this happens on one of the numerous sea-cliff traverses that can be found around the world, the situation could be particularly exciting! A knowledge of prussiking will come in useful (see Chapters 3 and 5).

Another tricky situation for the second involves down-climbing. If the moves are not protected from above, a fall could be a long one. In these situations, the second needs to be as confident and capable as the leader.

ROPEWORK

Ropework is a fundamental part of modern rock climbing. It is worth practising the techniques described until they become second nature. There are usually several ways of doing things, but the methods shown here are simple and quick to learn. Ropework can be daunting, but taking things one step at a time will help. Do not try to remember everything at once. When learning new skills, it is important to remember the principles behind the instruction. By doing this, it should be easier to remember the steps as progress is made. This step-by-step approach to the ropework required for climbing should provide the tool kit needed to cope with most situations. It is up to the climber to dip into that tool kit and find the necessary tools required.

Opposite: *An exposed, hard route. Although the climbing is relatively straightforward, good judgement, a thorough knowledge of modern ropework and a cool head are necessary for a safe ascent.*

Fitting the harness

Many different designs of harness are available. Most are manufactured in one piece – the leg loops are an integral part of the harness. Some harnesses are "one size fits all", while others are produced in small, medium and large sizes. Some have adjustable leg loops which allow you to wear the harness over several layers of clothing if needed. Those harnesses without adjustable leg loops will require a little more judgement to ensure a good fit.

DOING THE HARNESS UP

Almost all harnesses rely on a double-back system on the buckle. The waistbelt has to be threaded though both parts of the buckle and back through one. This will hide half the buckle and form a "C" for closed and not "O" for open. If the buckle is not doubled back, it can come undone. There are several harness manufactures using different designs, so it must be stressed that in all cases the manufacturer's instructions must be followed to the letter.

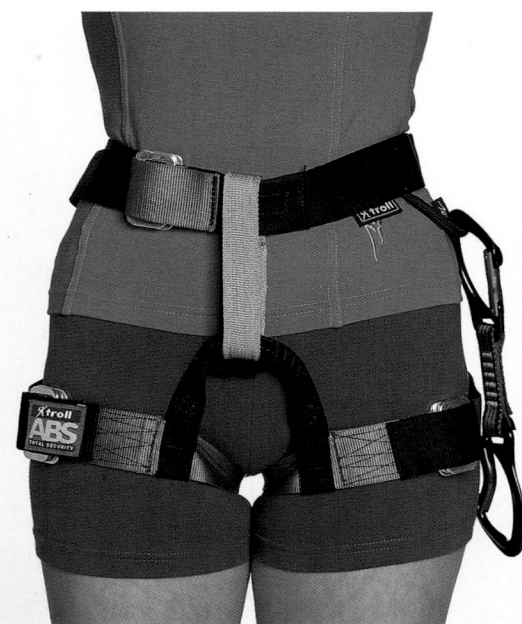

△ This is a simple harness designed specifically for beginners. The waist belt cannot be undone completely so a "step-in" system is used. There is minimal provision for equipment-carrying, which makes this this harness more suitable for indoor venues.

◁ Here a climber is being lowered off a modern sport route. The consequences of an uncomfortable or incorrectly fastened harness need only be imagined.

Leg loops may be padded, to a greater or lesser extent, on the inside for comfort. Leg loop buckles should be doubled back like the waist belt, and should be on the outside of the leg. When putting a harness on, ensure the waist belt goes around the waist and not over the hips, and that the leg loops are positioned comfortably at the top of the leg and base of the buttocks.

If the harness has adjustable leg loops, adjust the waist belt part of the harness first and then the leg loops. This should ensure the correct fit. If the leg loops are tightened first, there will be a tendency not to position the waist belt correctly, leaving it too low on the hips. This is particularly important on harnesses that are designed to be put on without having to step into the leg loops, often referred to as a "nappy system" harness.

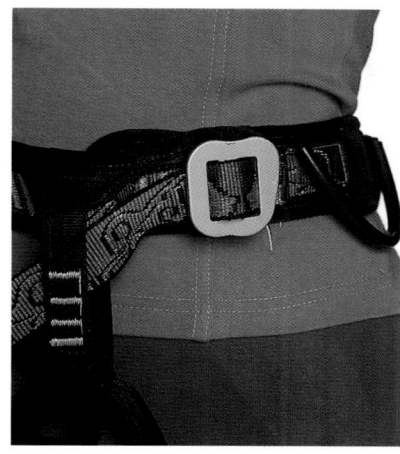

△ The buckle system is vitally important. Here the strap has not been doubled back, making the harness extremely dangerous because only a small amount of force will be necessary to release the buckle.

△ Here the "C" for closed is clearly visible and although not all harnesses employ the same fastening system, most are very similar. Take the time to look for an obvious way of checking your own and other people's harnesses easily.

● GETTING IT WRONG

There are a number of problems that may occur fitting a harness. The main ones are:

① Not getting the right position around the waist
② Not doing the buckle correctly
③ Getting a twist in the harness or leg loop

There have been many instances where expensive harnesses have been put on incorrectly in the enthusiasm to get on with the climb, but it must be stressed a little care and attention to detail is important at this stage. Spend a couple of minutes doing this job correctly. It is vitally important! Before you climb, make one last check.

△ The leg loops are too tight and the harness is positioned over the hips, making the centre of gravity too low. In the event of a slip, the climber could turn upside down.

△ This picture illustrates how easy it is to see an incorrectly fastened harness when clothing is tucked into the harness – however much or little clothing you happen to be wearing.

△ This is a comedy of errors! The support straps for the leg loops are crossed and the right leg loop is twisted, putting unnecessary strain on the stitching.

Attaching the rope

Although there are many different designs of harness on the market, the method of tying the rope shown here is almost universal. The rope loop formed around the harness is not only important for the climber but forms an essential part of rope work outdoors, so it is important to get this right from the start.

TYING THE FIGURE-OF-EIGHT KNOT
It is vitally important to do this correctly. The harness and rope are both incredibly strong, but both are useless if they are not joined correctly. Most people use what is called a figure-of-eight knot, although some climbers prefer the bowline. Harnesses will have slight variations on where the rope is threaded and you must refer to the manufacturer's instructions and follow them implicitly.

△ **1** *To tie a figure-of-eight knot, form a loop of rope a little over 1 m (3 ft) from the end of the rope.*

△ **2** *Now twist the loop and pick up the end of the rope. Push this through the loop to form a figure-of-eight knot in the rope.*

△ **3** *The end of the rope goes through the harness (see also the manufacturer's instructions) and then is re-threaded through the figure-of-eight knot.*

△ **4** *To do this, simply follow the rope back through the figure-of-eight knot, starting with the part of the knot that is nearest the harness.*

△ **5** *When the knot is completed there should be a spare tail of about 30 cm (12 in). The rope loop now formed should be fist size and the spare tail tied to form a stopper knot.*

● MAKING MISTAKES WITH THE FIGURE-OF-EIGHT KNOT

There are several mistakes which are often seen on indoor walls. Although many are not dangerous in themselves, they can lead to situations that can be either painful or dangerous, or both! These include clipping on to the main loop of the harness (if it has one) with a screwgate (locking) karabiner. Although this is still safe (providing it is a screwgate karabiner which is locked), any solid metal object next to the abdomen can cause bruising in the event of a slip. Using a screwgate karabiner also introduces an extra link to the system, which is unnecessary.

Another mistake is tying directly into the belay loop of the harness. Although probably still safe, it is not best practice. The main problem with doing either of the above is the tendency for the karabiner and figure-of-eight to get in the way and not keep everything neat and tidy. If everything is neat and tidy, you can see immediately when things are not right.

△ Tying into the rope using a screwgate (locking) karabiner attached to the belay loop of the harness.

THE STOPPER KNOT

The stopper knot is an important part of the tying-on procedure, ensuring the figure-of-eight cannot come undone while at the same time tidying up any loose ends of rope. Take the spare tail twice around the main rope and then back through itself. The trick is to get the tail the right length in the first place, about 30 cm (12 in), so that when the knot is finished there are no long ends to get in the way. This is not just for cosmetic reasons but for safety reasons also. A long trailing end of rope dangling down by the feet can be a real problem, especially if it is lying exactly where you don't want it, such as on a hold you are trying to use.

△ To tie the stopper knot, take two turns around the main rope, then pass the tail back through the turns. Finally, tighten the knot.

△ The completed "stopper knot" should be tight against the figure-of-eight, and there should still be a short "tail" of about 18–20 cm (7–8 in).

● MAKING MISTAKES WITH THE STOPPER KNOT

If the length of the tail of rope is judged correctly in the first place, there should be few problems. If, however, the tail is too long after the stopper is tied, it will not only look untidy but also get in the way and the climber may step on it if it's dangling by the feet. If it is too short, it will not form an effective knot. The only way this will affect security is if the figure-of-eight is allowed to work loose. This is unlikely in an indoor situation because you are only tied on and actually climbing for short periods at a time. The big difference comes when you move outdoors. Here you will use the same system, but in a different environment in which you may stay tied into the harness for hours on end. Therefore it's worth taking trouble to get it right! Always ask yourself, what happens if?

△ Doing it wrong: too much rope has been used, and the stopper knot is not snug up against the figure-of-eight knot.

Belaying and belay devices

Until a few years ago climbers were still using the old method of "waist belays". This is where the rope is taken around the waist of the belayer and "paid out" or "taken in" round the waist and through the hands. The traditional waist belay still has a place in the greater game of mountaineering. However, today there are a multitude of belay devices on the market.

USING FRICTION

Although there is a vast range of belay devices on the market, most work on the same principle – that of friction generated by the rope being used to arrest a falling climber. There

are, however, some differences which you will need to be aware of. The original metal belay device that uses friction was the sticht plate, which was developed in the early 1970s. There have been many developments in design with this type of belay device, and today there are lots to choose from. These include the Air Traffic Controller (ATC), the Sherriff, Tuba and Bug.

TOO LITTLE FRICTION

Some devices require a particular type of karabiner to give a smooth operation (you should refer to the manufacturer's instructions when purchasing a belay device); but, above all, it

◁ **1** *Here the rope is being "taken in" – the right hand is pulling the rope towards the belay plate while the left hand is pulling through the plate. Note the attention of the belayer to the climber above.*

▷ **2** *The rope is now in the "locked" position ready for the belayer to change hands and be ready for the next time that the climber moves (see also page 94).*

must be a screwgate (locking) karabiner! Devices which are easy and quick to pay the rope through to a lead climber are often referred to as "slick" and require an alert and attentive belayer at all times. This is because in the event of a fall, the rope will start to move very quickly through the belay device. The belayer will need to lock off, and effectively stop the rope running out, as quickly as possible. The slicker the device, the more difficult this will become if you do not act immediately.

PINCHING BELAY DEVICES

There are also devices that operate by pinching the rope to stop a fall. These work automatically – the belayer does not have to actively lock off. Because of this, they have found favour on many climbing walls. An inattentive belayer should, in theory at least, still be able to hold a falling climber. They also allow greater control when the climber is being lowered. However, it is very bad practice to get in the habit of being inattentive. It is a belayer's responsibilty to look after the lead climber, and this should not be taken lightly.

The belayer should always operate the device by keeping both hands on the rope and paying attention to the climber at all times.

Belay devices differ in their operation, but all come supplied with specific instructions, which must be adhered to.

● USING A GRI-GRI

The Gri-Gri has been designed for use at indoor climbing walls and on sport routes that are well equipped with bolts. Because they are less "dynamic" than most other belay devices, they should not be used on traditionally protected climbs – they will put too much force on the protection.

They are deceptively easy to use, but the instructions that come with them must be read and fully understood first. It is, for example, possible to thread the rope incorrectly through the mechanism. Also, when lowering a climber, the brake handle should not be used as a means of controlling speed.

△ The Gri-Gri will give a bigger jolt to the belayer should the climber fall off because it will stop or lock more quickly.

Bottom roping (indoors)

△ *This climber is being belayed from below.*

The most difficult job when starting out is learning how to operate an effective belay system. It is vitally important, because if you can't do this you will soon run out of climbing partners! Many climbing walls will have a section where ropes are permanently anchored at the top using a pulley system. The two ends of the rope will trail down the wall, enabling a climber to tie on to one end, while being protected by the belayer holding the other end. This is called bottom roping, because the belayer is operating from the bottom of the climb.

TAKING IN AND PAYING OUT

A belayer takes in and pays out the rope while the climber goes to the top of the wall and then lowers them back down again. The technique the belayer uses is called belaying and must be done correctly to ensure safety at all times, otherwise all the expensive equipment is of little use. There is a "live", or active, end of rope and a "dead" rope. The active rope goes from the climber to the belay plate via the top anchor, while the dead rope is that which is on the lower side of or below the belay plate. There is therefore a "live hand" and a "dead hand", which can be the left or right hand as occasion and position demands.

Belaying correctly from the start will develop a good technique for any climbing situation. It is important to keep one hand on the dead rope at all times, and in the locked position unless actually taking in, whichever belay device is used. Learn good belay habits from the start and follow the same procedure at all times. Also, remember to practise with your weaker hand.

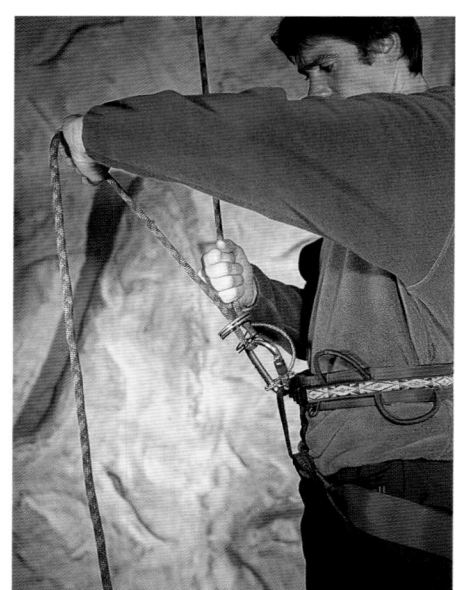

△ **1** *Take the rope in with the "live" hand and pull through the plate with the "dead" hand. This requires good co-ordination.*

△ **2** *Lock the rope behind the plate with the dead hand and hold it by the hip to leave enough space for the live hand to move on to the dead rope.*

△ **3** *Take over the locking position on the rope with the live hand. You can then take the dead hand off the rope, move it up to take in the rope and repeat the same procedure.*

LOWERING A CLIMBER

When the climber reaches the top of the wall, control their descent with both hands behind the belay device on the dead rope, creating as much friction as possible, and then ease the hands forward as necessary. When lowering a very light climber, it may be necessary to bring the dead rope forward slightly and decrease the friction. Devices like the Gri-Gri and Single Rope Controller (SRC) will need to be released before anyone can be lowered, but keep the hand in the locked position while the brake is released to ensure a controlled descent. You must refer to the manufacturer's instructions before trying out any type of device.

USING BOTTOM ANCHORS

Many walls now provide additional anchors or in situ belays at the bottom of the wall for the belayer to clip on to. This is particularly useful where there may be a big weight difference between the belayer and the climber. In this case, either belay direct from the anchor or clip a sling from the anchor to the main load-bearing loop of your harness to stop you flying into the air in the event of your heavier leader falling off – it does happen!

△ *The climber is being lowered under control. The belayer is watching closely from a good braced position against the wall, with both hands controlling the descent on the dead rope.*

● GETTING IT WRONG

Common mistakes include loading the rope incorrectly in the belay device, making it impossible to get the "S" shape through the plate. This generates little friction on the belay device. Another mistake often seen is someone holding the "live" and "dead" ropes together in front of the plate. This will also result in little or no friction being generated by the device.

▷ *The belay device is clipped to the equipment-carrying loop and will probably rip out in the event of a fall or when lowering.*

Learning to lead (indoors)

The natural progression after doing some bottom roping is to lead a route from the bottom of the wall, clipping the bolts (running belays) and the top anchor, and then being lowered back to the ground. Most climbers who are ready to lead will by this time have experienced a good deal of bottom roping.

THAT FIRST LEAD

The first lead should be completed on a climb that you are familiar with. The grade of the climb should be well within your capacity –

you don't want to frighten yourself too much on your first lead! There will be a continuous line of bolts (those running belays) placed every few feet on the route to clip as the climber gains height. Each bolt will have a short sling and metal snaplink karabiner on the end which the rope can be clipped in to. If your chosen route does not have these quickdraws already in place, make sure that you carry your own. You will have to place these as you lead the route, so make sure you take enough for each of the bolts. You should ensure that there are no twists in the rope or

△▷ *Clipping the rope into the quickdraw can be done with either hand. Here the climber demonstrates, using his thumb to hold the karabiner and fingers to work the rope (above, right hand); and fingers to hold the karabiner and thumb to work the rope (right, left hand).*

quickdraws as you make the clip, which can cause unnecessary friction or tangles. The best way to avoid tangles is to take one hand off the rock, staying in balance as you do so. Lift the rope from your waist and clip the protection by holding the karabiner steady with the third finger and twisting the rope in with the index finger and thumb. Always warn your belayer (they should be watching anyway) that you require some slack rope to reach up and clip the protection.

THE ORDER OF EVENTS

After checking your harness and the tie-in knot, climb up and clip the first karabiner. With the protection clipped, simply continue up and clip the next bolt with a quickdraw through it, until you reach the top. The belayer pays out the rope to the climber as they gain height and should be alert to their demands, especially when they need to clip a high bolt which requires the belayer to pay the rope out, take in as the climber passes the bolt, and then pay out again! Belay devices that lock automatically (such as the Gri-Gri or SRC) are not so easy to use to pay the rope out, so more warning must be given to the belayer. Lowering with a Gri-Gri employs exactly the same technique as all belay devices, but don't try and control the lower with the handle. The first few leads should be well within the capabilities of the climber, allowing them to familiarize themselves with the technicalities of ropework, rather than be near their technical climbing limit and unable to clip the protection.

Holding a falling leader will create much more of a shock on the belayer and may well lift them off the ground. In this situation you learn the value of using a ground anchor. This may take the form of a metal bolt in the floor or wall, or you may find a belay bag – a heavy bag to which the belayer can attach themselves. When the climber has reached the top, or they fall off (whichever comes first!), take the rope back in to the braking position, hold and control their descent with both hands and release the brake.

△ The climber has tied the figure-of-eight correctly, but the stopper knot is incorrect and will have to be adjusted before they are ready to lead the climb.

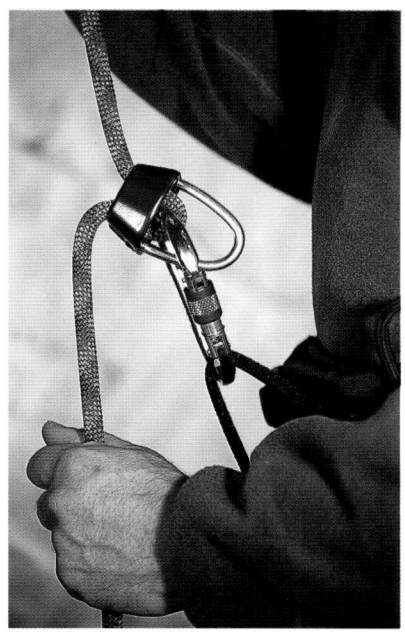

△ This is a "slick" device and it is therefore very easy and quick to pay the rope out to a leader, but will be a little more difficult to hold someone. In all indoor situations, the belay device is clipped to the main load-bearing loop of the harness with a karabiner.

△ This is similar to the original design of the belay plate. It is simple, relatively inexpensive and very effective. A fairly high degree of friction will be generated with this device so holding falls should be easier.

Using the climbing wall

There is no need to frighten yourself by jumping into leading when you first start climbing. Use the bottom roping system to get used to ropes, harnesses and belay devices. In this situation, provided the person at the other end of the rope is alert, the rope is positioned correctly and properly attached to your harness, there is very little that should go wrong. As soon as you reach the top of the wall, simply sit back on the rope while your partner lowers you to the ground. Falling off is no problem, because the rope goes from your harness, through the top anchor and down to your anchor person (belayer). You are able to climb in complete safety and this is a very good way to improve your technique, by pushing yourself with minimal risk. Finally, it is important to communicate with your partner. Keep the climbing calls to a minimum. Indoors you should require nothing more than the words "slack" (I want more rope) or "tight" (I want less rope). When the wall is busy it may be important to add your partner's name to avoid confusion. However, a full list of calls is included here with an explanation of what the call means (see opposite). The climbing calls are useful at the indoor wall. However, they become a vital part of the safety system when climbing multipitch routes outside. Communication is essential in this situation, but it is useful to become familiar with the calls early in your climbing career.

CLIMBING WALL PROCEDURES

When you are on a leading wall you will need your own rope, unlike in most bottom roping situations, where the ropes will be in place and it is normal practice to use those. All indoor walls will have their own system for monitoring and checking the ropes periodically. What you must do is establish what the procedures are when you go to an indoor wall, as circumstances will vary enormously. Something else that may vary considerably is the top anchor from which you will lower off. In most cases there will be a screwgate (locking) karabiner which can easily be clipped (and screwed up) before commencing your descent. Other walls may have a system similar to the lower-off points shown on page 104. This should present no problem as long as you are prepared, otherwise things may come as a shock, particularly at the top of your first lead!

▽ *The first bolt is often the most difficult to clip but is also the most important. It will stop you hitting the ground in the event of a fall.*

● THE CLIMBING CALLS

The call (UK)	The call (US)	Its meaning
Safe!	*Off belay!*	Leader's call to inform belayer (second) that leader is safe.
Taking in!	*Taking in!*	Leader's call to second that leader is taking excess rope in.
That's me!	*That's me!*	Second's call to leader, rope is tight on second.
Climb when ready!	*Climb when ready!*	Leader's call to second after putting rope through belay plate.
Climbing!	*Climbing!*	Second informing leader they are ready to climb.
OK!	*Climb on!*	Leader's affirmative to second, second starts climbing.
Slack!	*Slack!*	Pay out more rope.
Tight! (Tight rope!)	*Take!*	Take in any slack rope
Watch me!	*Watch me!*	Leader's call to belayer to pay attention during sequence of hard moves.

● LIVING DANGEROUSLY

Because of the friendly atmosphere of many indoor climbing venues, and climbers in the main being sociable animals, there is a tendency to be lulled into a false sense of security and to be a little casual. This has to be fought against at all times. One lapse could lead to an accident. Here are some common dangerous situations seen at climbing walls:

• Standing too far away from the wall when belaying. This is especially dangerous if the climber is heavier than the belayer, because it is possible for them to be pulled off their feet and into the wall, letting go of the belay device in the process.

• Allowing the elbow of the "dead" or locking hand to become trapped by standing with it too close to the wall. This could make it very difficult to lock off properly if your climber falls. You need to give your locking-off hand plenty of room to move.

• Talking to people standing around you while you are belaying. This is dangerous because it means you are not concentrating on what your climber is doing.

▷ *These belayers are standing too far away from the wall and are not concentrating on their climbing partners.*

Safety outdoors

Although the techniques used climbing indoors can be used outside on real rock, there are many differences that the novice climber should be aware of. These are not always obvious. Safety and self-reliance become very important in this wider environment, as do considerations such as conservation, first aid, navigation, weather and appropriate clothing and equipment.

● USING A GUIDEBOOK

It is important to have access to a guidebook. This will enable you to find the routes you want. Starting up the wrong route could quickly lead you into trouble if the route is harder than you expected! Remember that guidebooks have different conventions.

▷Guidebooks often have maps, topographical guides and photographs to help locate your chosen route.

THINKING OF THE ENVIRONMENT

Before looking in detail at climbing outdoors, and particularly the ropework involved, it must be stressed that the natural environment is fragile and easily damaged. All climbers have a responsibility regarding the countryside they enjoy and must ensure a minimal impact and help to preserve it for future generations. Follow the Climbers' Code and be considerate to landowners, property as well as others enjoying the outdoors. As climbers you will come into contact with hikers, backpackers and those just out for a Sunday afternoon stroll.

PERSONAL SAFETY

Even if you are just going bouldering, consider telling someone where you're going and, more important, when you expect to be back. There is a great deal of difference in climbing real rock away from the chalk-laden atmosphere of the indoor wall and many more things to consider, not least of which may be the weather! Remember that rock is a natural material and subject to weathering which will occasionally result in loose hand or footholds; it may be slippery and covered in moss and lichen, so take care, especially in wet conditions. The advice of an experienced person can be invaluable in these situations. The climbing calls are much more important outside, especially on busy crags and on windy days on long pitches. A list of the calls and an explanation of what they mean is given on page 99. Stick to the list to avoid confusion and use your partner's name if the crag is crowded.

◁This is an example of human erosion, caused by the passage of thousands of feet. It is a serious problem in some areas.

Single-pitch climbs

Ropework in the outdoors follows exactly the same principles as indoors – it's just the environment that's changed! On traditional climbs, anchors must be created using wires, slings, hexes and spring-loaded camming devices (SLCDs) (see pages 108–109), rather than just clipping the bolts, as you would indoors or on sport crags. If the crag is situated at the top of a steep hillside, belays will have to be constructed before starting the climb. The leader will place protection (the wires, hexes, and so on) as they climb, create belays at the top, anchor themselves securely, then take the rope in and belay the second climber. All anchor points and belays require a sound judgement as to how safe or marginal they are. Sport climbs normally have all belays and anchors in place, which makes life much simpler. The following pages deal exclusively with climbs that have only one section of climbing from the bottom to the top. These are called single-pitch climbs. Routes that have two or more pitches are referred to as multipitch routes, and are dealt with later in this chapter (see pages 128–143).

△ *A popular single-pitch climbing venue, offering superb routes at every grade. The rock is gritstone, which provides tremendous friction for the feet.*

● CLIMBERS' CODE

- A climbing party of two is minimum
- Always leave word of where you have gone
- Take care with all rope work and anchors and put the rope on as soon as necessary
- Test each hold, wherever possible, before trusting any weight to it
- Keep the party together at all times
- Don't let desire overrule judgement; never regret a retreat
- Don't climb beyond the limit of your ability and knowledge
- Always carry a first aid kit, whistle and sufficient food and clothing if you intend climbing on outdoor crags
- Check the weather forecast if venturing into the hills

△ *Belaying at the top of a single-pitch climb. But how safe is a belay using snaplink karabiners?*

Sport routes

There are many climbing areas throughout the world consisting entirely of sport climbs. All the anchors will (or should) be in place and fixed lower-off points will be found situated at the top of the climb. This makes life relatively simple for the climber, and certainly cuts down on the amount of climbing equipment that will be needed to deal with a route. You will need your harness, a rope, some slings, and as many quickdraws as there are bolts to clip on the route. You will also need your partner, belay device and some screwgate (locking) karabiners. The clothing you wear (see pages 20–21 and 156–160) will depend upon the weather and your preference. As you are on single pitch climbs, being caught out by the weather may not be as bad as being caught out on a much longer multipitch route. These routes offer an easy transition from indoor climbing.

▷ *This is a typical rack required for modern sport, or bolted, routes. It is well worth taking an extra couple of quickdraws and a spare screwgate (locking) karabiner.*

▽ *Many limestone crags are bolted because they are often difficult to protect in the traditional way. Limestone usually offers steep, exhilarating and gymnastic climbing.*

PREPARATION

Before starting, the rope should be run through the hands and laid loosely on the ground. The leader then ties on to the end of rope that is on top of the pile. This is important as it will reduce the risk of unnecessary tangles. If the leader ties on to the end of rope at the bottom of the pile, the rope will run out through the entire length of itself and may at some point create an unwanted knot or tangle. Now check each other's harness and knots. Climbing is about teamwork, and this is where it starts. The leader shoud clean and dry their shoes before starting the climb to remove all traces of dust or dampness – slipping off on the first two or three moves frightens you and doesn't impress your belayer! Do not forget to use the climbing calls either (see page 99).

THE CLIMB

The leader clips the bolts exactly the same as with indoor climbing. This will ensure that, in the event of a fall, they will not hit the ground! The belayer should remain alert at all times, paying out the rope when needed and taking it in when necessary. The bolts are clipped using a short sling, the quickdraw, which has a karabiner on each end. One karabiner is for clipping the bolt and the other is for clipping the rope. It should be possible to count from the ground the number of quickdraws needed, eliminating the need to carry excess equipment (although it's good practice to allow for one or two more quickdraws than seem necessary – there's the chance of one bolt being hidden from view, or you may drop a quickdraw in your excitement!). Karabiners with a bent gate should always be used on the rope and not directly clipped to the bolt. This is because there is a possibility of them becoming unclipped in the event of a fall.

△ This is a sport route. The next piece of protection is visible above and to the left of the climber. To reach that point the climber will rely almost exclusively on the superb frictional quality of the rock.

◁ Climbing calls may seem a little pedantic for single-pitch venues, but they are important on windy days and multipitch routes, so develop good habits early in your climbing career.

A fixed lower-off

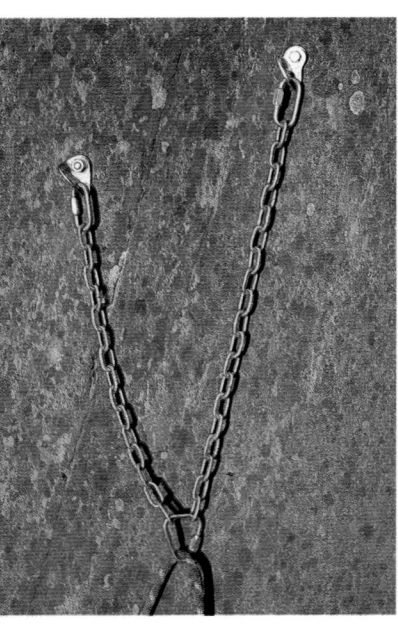

There should be fixed lower-off anchors in place at the top of sport routes. These will take the form of bolts or rings through which the rope can be threaded. You should always follow a strict procedure when using them, as any mistake could be fatal. You should also keep your belayer informed as to what you are doing, making sure that they know when you want them to start lowering.

◁ *These two anchor points are equally and independently loaded so if one should fail, which is highly unlikely, the other will not be shock-loaded. Having two separate anchors also gives some lateral stability to the system.*

THE STAGES

The stages you should take are as follows. Clip yourself to the lower-off anchor points using the main load-bearing loop of the harness with a quickdraw or sling. Now pull some rope in (you will have to warn the belayer) and thread this through the lower-off anchors. Next, tie a figure-of-eight knot in the rope which is through the lower-off and attach with a screwgate (locking) karabiner to the main load-bearing loop of the harness. The original figure-of-eight knot that you tied to your harness before you started to climb can now be untied. Now remove the quickdraw or sling that you used to attach yourself to the lower-off anchors. Inform your belayer that they can now take in

△ **1** *Clip a quickdraw between the anchor and main load-bearing loop of the harness, pull some rope up from the belayer and pass this through the "lower-off".*

△ **2** *Now tie a figure-of-eight on the length of rope you have passed through the lower-off. Clip this with a screwgate (locking) karabiner into the main load-bearing loop of the harness.*

△ **3** *The original figure-of-eight tied in to the harness can now be untied and taken off, the quickdraw removed and the climber lowered down.*

the slack rope and then lower you back down the route in safety. Quickdraws can be retrieved from the bolts on the way down and the rope can be pulled down through the lower-off ready for the next climb. Alternatively, the rope can be left in place and your belayer can bottom rope the route should they decide not to lead it. This is a fairly simple procedure, but must be adhered to step by step. Do not be tempted to take any shortcuts. Good communications should be maintained between the climber and belayer and shouldn't be too complicated. If, however, there are problems in communication (due to a high wind, long pitch or whatever), then you can resort to some form of hand signals or sharp tugs on the rope. It is as well to discuss these other forms of communication before you leave the ground, making sure that both of you know precisely what each gesture or tug will stand for. This goes back to the overall importance of communication when climbing outside.

● SORTING OUT PROBLEMS

Problems can occur when either the sequence of events you should follow to safely carry out a lower-off is forgotten or you don't have a spare quickdraw with which to make yourself safe when you arrive at the lower-off anchors. You can try and retrieve a quickdraw from lower down the climb to use, though this may prove difficult and time-consuming. The important point is clipping the figure-of-eight knot into the main load-bearing loop of the harness. If you were to clip it to the rope loop formed by the original figure-of-eight knot which goes through the harness, you would not be able to untie this original knot, which would at the very least be embarrassing. This is why the quickdraw is used to back the system up in the first place.

The other difficulty occurs when the route is longer than half of the length of the rope (say, over 20 m/65 ft in length), making lowering-off impossible. This is solved by belaying at the top of the route rather than at the bottom. This is called top roping, and is explained in detail on pages 114–127. Take care to keep a good belay directly in line between the anchor and the climber below. If there is a descent route it may be worth taking a pair of shoes suitable for scrambling down steep, slippery paths. Modern rock shoes are wonderful things but useless on wet ground! Alternatively, you could use two ropes to double the length of any lower-off that is required, though this requires a lot of ropework skill and thought.

△ *If the climb is longer than half the length of the rope, the true top roping method must be used: that is where the belayer is at the top of the pitch, which is identical to belaying at the top of the first pitch in multipitch routes.*

ROPEWORK

105

Traditional routes

Traditional climbs do not have any fixed gear in them (in general) to protect the lead climber as they ascend the route. This is why the Victorian climbers had the dictum that the lead climber should never fall. The consequences were too high a price to pay. This may well have restricted many lead climbers of the day to leading routes well within the grade at which they could comfortably climb – although climbing outdoors on traditional routes can, and will, throw up surprises. The picture has changed considerably with the advent of modern leader-placed protection – nuts on wire and spectra, hexes and camming devices. This gear is placed into cracks or pockets by the leader and is removed by the second when they go up the route. What this does mean is that planning a traditional route in terms of the equipment needed is far more complicated than that needed for a bolted sport route.

GETTING TO YOUR ROUTE

Having selected the crag you want to climb on from the guidebook and decided on what route to do, you will need to get to it. This will

△ *A traditional mountain rock climbing venue, where the leader places all the protection they need. The second removes it from the rock as they climb up.*

▷ *This crag is very obvious and only 20 minutes from the road. The difficulty arises when it comes to finding the route.*

involve finding the crag on a map and walking to it (life is a little more adventurous outside!). This may take 2 minutes or 2 hours, but you will need the skills to be able to locate your crag and then the start of your route (see pages 178–191).

ON A TRAD ROUTE

The time has come to get the rope out and uncoil it carefully, leaving the leader's end on top. Put your harness and rock shoes on. Tying on is exactly the same as with indoor or sport routes outside. However, a big difference is that the belay plate is operated from the rope loop formed by the figure-of-eight knot on the harness, and not the main load-bearing loop of the harness. This is particularly important at the top of the pitch where considerably more strain will be applied to the anchor and belayer because the force is directly on to them and not absorbed by any other equipment. On traditional climbs both climbers should tie on to the rope before the leader starts, and if necessary select a good anchor if there is steep and exposed ground below the crag. Although this is not strictly necessary on some single-pitch venues, it will be on others; so if in doubt, follow this procedure.

SORTING OUT A RACK

The leader will need to arrange the rack of hardware on their harness or bandolier (gear sling) so they know where everything is very quickly. Placing protection on traditional climbs can be a precarious and time-consuming operation at the best of times. The last thing a leader will want, when strength and confidence are waning on an overhanging crack, is to be fumbling around searching for the one nut that will fit the crack and provide them with much-needed protection and restore composure! So, the trick here is to become familiar with your lead rack and know where everything is by touch and feel. Stick to the same order of racking each time you come to lead. This will save moments of blind panic when, as your strength fades, you become desperate to place a piece of protection.

◁ The ground here is safe, so it is not strictly necessary to construct an anchor before leaving. The belayer is in a good position and able to watch the leader closely.

△ Here the belayer is still able to watch the leader but is standing in an exposed position and creating slack in the belay. The sideways pull could easily lift the chock out.

△ This is a much better position for any exposed belays. The belayer is tight on the anchors and sitting down. Note also the position of the belay plate in the rope loop around the harness.

Constructing anchors

Protecting yourself and your friends on traditional climbs is an art that requires a creative mind and lots of skill and judgement based on experience. Everything that a rock face or ridge has to offer may be used. This will include cracks and pockets for gear, spikes of rock around which to put the rope or a sling, a thread, a tree (though there are environmental considerations here) and even the friction of the rope running over a rock surface. It is important that you learn the art of protecting a climb and creating safe anchors from which to belay. There are few short cuts to learning this art.

◁ *This is an excellent bollard, on which a full-weight sling sits comfortably. It will take a downwards or sideways pull.*

SPIKES AND BOLLARDS

Tying on to a large spike or bollard of rock was the original way the early climbers anchored themselves to the rock to provide some security for themselves and their colleagues. Spikes are still used but, as with all anchors, any spike should be thoroughly tested to make sure it's part of the crag. If it wobbles like a bad tooth, it should be rejected and something else tried. To test a spike, check it visually for cracks around the base and hit it with one hand whilst keeping the other hand on the spike. Any movement or vibration should be felt instantly. Alternatively, tap the spike with a karabiner and listen to the sound made. It will be obvious to what is good and what isn't. Any spike which produces a hollow sound should be treated with suspicion.

△ *Although this projecting flake is separated from the surrounding rock, it is still an excellent anchor because it is solidly jammed.*

● GETTING IT WRONG

△ *This anchor is poor because the sling is precariously balanced over a poor spike and any lateral movement could lift it off completely.*

△ *This anchor is poor because the sling is too tight around the spike. This will considerably weaken the sling. If a larger sling was used, the anchor would be good.*

△ *Spike belays are always very "directional". In this situation the slightest change in the direction of pull could result in the total failure of the belay.*

HOW TO USE A SPIKE

There are several ways to use a spike:

① Place a sling over the spike and clip the screwgate (locking) karabiner directly to the rope loop of the harness.

② Take the rope from your waist and tie a clove hitch to the screwgate karabiner.

③ If the spike is out of reach, take the rope from your waist, through the screwgate karabiner and clove hitch back to your waist. Alternatively the rope can be taken right around the spike and then clove hitched direct to your rope loop.

It goes without saying that all karabiners on belays should be screwgates (locking). Choose where you want to stand with care directly "in line" between the climber and the anchor. The clove hitch allows easy adjustment, so whenever a belay is constructed keep the rope tight between the anchor and belayer on all occasions, and adopt a good braced position, feet apart and knees bent. Most spike belays

are very "directional", which means they are excellent for a downward pull but can be lifted off easily with an upward pull. Bearing this in mind, they may be much more useful at the top of the crag (downward pull) rather than at the bottom (upward pull) if the leader falls off above some protection (running belay).

THREAD BELAYS

This is where tape slings are threaded in around two immovable objects, either a large boulder which is jammed into a crack or where two large boulders are touching so slings are easily threaded around. As with all belays, check the surrounding rock carefully because the slings are very thin and a boulder will only have to move a couple of millimetres to render the anchor useless. Thread belays do, however, have one great advantage over all others and that is the fact that they are multi-directional so they can be used in any situation irrespective of the pull. When the sling is fixed around the thread, clip the rope into the karabiner and tie in as before, either straight into the rope loop or using one of the methods with the clove hitch. The most important point is the position of the stance (how the belayer stands) and a tight rope between belayer and anchor.

▽ *The sling is taken through a small natural thread and both ends are then clipped together. The result is a belay that will take a "multi-directional" pull.*

● GETTING IT WRONG

◁ *This is a poor thread belay. The boulder is poorly wedged and a good heave on the sling will pull it straight out.*

Using lead-placed protection

Nuts on wires or spectra, camming devices and hexentrics (commonly called "hexes") make up the majority of gear used by climbers around the world to protect themselves on traditional routes. They come in a variety of sizes. There are several names given to some of these items (for example, nuts are sometimes called chocks, rocks or stoppers!). Leader-placed protection is usually placed in cracks. It makes excellent anchors for main belays as well as protection (running belays) for the leader while they are climbing. The function is similar to bolts on indoor walls or sport crags, the big difference being that the leader is using their own judgement about whether the protection is good, marginal or very poor.

PLACING PROTECTION

Each nut or hex (camming devices are dealt with on page 112) is specially designed to provide several options on which way it can be placed. They are also designed to give maximum holding power (using wedged shapes in the case of nuts and an asymmetric shape for hexes). Try and get as much of the metal of the nut or hex as possible in contact with the rock when you are placing it. This comes down to the correct selection of the size of the piece of protection. A general rule is to use the largest size that will fit the crack. Give a sharp down-

△ Slings, wires, quickdraws, cams and karabiners: collectively this equipment makes up a leader's rack.

▷ This is an excellent wired nut: well placed and with a lot of metal-to-rock contact for stability. The placement will even allow a good lateral strain to be applied with no fear of the wire failing.

● GETTING IT WRONG

△ Even though there is a lot of metal to rock contact, this nut is wedged against a loose rock and will take little strain.

△ This is a really poor placement. There is little of the nut in contact with the rock and it is simply resting on minute crystals.

▷ This large hexentric will offer a range of three different fittings depending on which way it is placed.

▷▷ This is an excellent placement and any strain will "cam" this hexentric into the rock.

▷ Extend wires with a quickdraw to keep the rope running more freely, particularly where wires are placed under an overhang. This will help prevent rope drag.

● GETTING IT WRONG

◁ This is a poor placement because there is little metal-to-rock contact – the corner of the hex can be seen clearly resting against the rock.

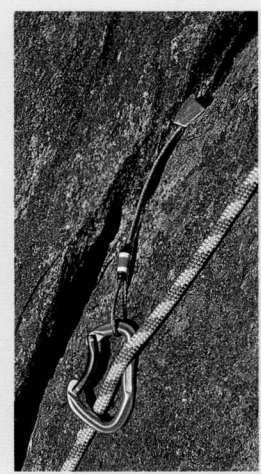

◁ Don't have wires clipped directly to the rope. This increases friction and may put a lateral strain on the protection and lift it out.

ward tug to jam or settle the piece of protection into place. Test each one in this manner and be sure to keep a good handhold when doing so, just in case the piece pulls out! Some placements will not be as good as others, but are the best available in the circumstances. As the leader, you will have to be able to cope mentally with this. The best solution is to find another placement as soon as possible that you feel is more reliable – this will calm those nerves and beating heart!

EXTENDING RUNNERS

All wired nuts and hexes must be extended using a quickdraw, otherwise they could be pulled out where any lateral strain is applied. This also applies to any gear placed under an overhang or in a way that the rope is moved out of line with the climb, creating friction in the system.

● RETRIEVING GEAR

The second retrieves all protection when it is their turn to climb. This can be difficult unless you have a nut key – a short steel bar with a hooked end which is used to lever or bash nuts and hexes out of their cracks. There is an art to understanding how best to get gear out, which only comes with time and practice.

▷ The natural constriction in which this hex is placed makes it extremely secure, so much so that it can take time to remove.

Camming devices

▷ *A selection of camming devices that are designed to work in either parallel-sided or flared cracks where conventional chocks are difficult to use.*

△ *Place camming devices in the direction they are likely to finish in in the event of a sudden strain being put on them.*

▽ *This is a large camming device perfectly placed in a parallel-sided crack.*

Over the last few years these have made a tremendous difference to the sport, particularly where any cracks are either very wide or parallel-sided and there are few natural constrictions to facilitate the placement of wires or chocks. There are various designs on the market and a variety of names. All have three or four cams that are depressed by pulling the triggers and then placed in a crack. They work well in cracks with parallel sides where conventional chocks would be extremely difficult to place. Some have solid stems and therefore work best in vertical cracks, but care must be taken in horizontal cracks unless the cam is placed with the end of the stem flush with the edge of the crack (see illustrations for more details). Others have flexible stems so they can be placed in either vertical or horizontal cracks with confidence. Try to find a placement where the cams are biting about mid-point, which is the best locking position for the cam. The geometry and direction of pull down the stem should ensure the harder the pull, the stronger the device. The closer the cams are to either fully open or fully closed the less likely they are to hold.

PROBLEMS WITH CAMS

There are several problems with camming devices, working on the principle of the more technical the equipment, the more problems there are, or at least likely to be! Beware of "over" or "under" camming. The former can create a problem for your second when trying to remove the cam; the latter can be unsafe. If the rope is clipped directly to any camming device, the action of the rope moving backwards and forwards will "walk" the device deep into a crack, much to the annoyance of anyone trying to retrieve it.

● **GETTING IT WRONG**

◁ *The camming device shown here is very poor because only a few of the cams are actually working against the rock. The front cam is almost fully open and little force would need to be applied to make it come out. Cams used in "flared" cracks can be good or almost useless, but if there is no other option, they will have to do.*

The main belay

For a main belay use at least two pieces of gear which are equally loaded and independently tied off. There are several ways of doing this. Either use a sling to link the two anchors together creating a single point or use the following procedure: clip the rope through both karabiners and then back to a clove hitch on the rope loop of your harness – now clip the other (live) rope into the same karabiner with a second clove hitch. Use a pear shaped (HMS) karabiner in the rope loop to accommodate both clove hitches and snaplink karabiners back-to-back on main belays if no screwgates are available.

Try never to use poor placements for a main belay. It needs to be able to take a potentially large force from a falling climber. Bolts at the wall or sport crag provide relatively reliable and frequent runners. A fall should not be huge. On traditional crags protection may not be so frequent so longer falls, which exert a greater force on the belayer, are often encountered.

△ This detail of a clove hitch clearly shows the "lay" of the rope (see page 121).

◁ There are many cases where it's not possible to rely just on one anchor, particularly if the anchor is a hex or wire. The answer is to link all the anchors to a single point.

▷ If your anchor is a single point, take the rope, create a clove hitch and fasten the gate.

▷ Any pull on anchors placed at the bottom of a route could be an upward one and is one of the major considerations when selecting an anchor.

• GETTING IT WRONG

◁ The belayer is not tight on the anchor. If a sudden force is applied to the rope, the belayer will be pulled forward and may let go of the rope or may shock-load the anchor.

The system

Climbs at this popular venue will be top roped, bottom roped or led from the ground in what many would argue is a purer style of climbing.

Arranging top or bottom ropes on outdoor crags has become very popular over the last few years, particularly where several people want to climb together. One reason could be that no one in the group is prepared to take responsibility or is competent enough to lead. Top and bottom ropes require less equipment and follow many techniques discussed in the previous chapter. If there are two or three ropes and two or three competent belayers within the group, it is the ideal way to allow beginners to "have a go" and try rock climbing. The downside to this is that arranging two or three ropes in one area could monopolize the crag and discourage others from attempting the routes. It is important to consider those waiting to climb the routes where the rope is arranged and it costs nothing to push the ropes to one side for a few minutes and allow others their fun, especially if they want to lead the climb. Top or bottom roping can be a little controversial and the complete picture is not here – this is just an insight!

THE TERMINOLOGY

There is often confusion among climbers as to the difference between a top rope and bottom rope, so here is an explanation of the terminology. If the belayer stands at the bottom of the crag or wall, they are bottom roping. They may or may not be attached to a

◁ *This is bottom roping and, because of the relative safety, requires nothing other than the belayer to stand close in to the bottom of the crag.*

▽ *This is top roping where the belayer stands at the top of the climb in a direct line between the anchor and climber, and tight on the anchor. It can be much more difficult to hold someone when top roping.*

belay, depending on the exposure of the ground they are standing on and the likelihood of being lifted off their feet in the event of the climber falling. If the belayer is standing or sitting at the top of a climb, they are top roping. Because they are always exposed to being pulled off the crag, they must be anchored to a main belay. Climbs that can be bottom roped must be no higher than half the length of the rope – the rope must go from the climber up to the anchor and back to the belayer, who stands on the ground. If this is not possible, then top roping must be used.

In short, any climb of less than about 20 m (65 ft) should be possible to bottom rope; anything more than that will make it necessary for the belayer to anchor themselves at the top of the climb to belay.

Bottom ropes

We will start by looking at bottom roping, which to add to the confusion relies heavily on the top anchor! In fact the terminology, top and bottom ropes, doesn't relate to the ropes, as we have seen, but to where the belayer is positioned. The belayer is below the climb when bottom roping and above the climb when top roping. These terms only apply for single-pitch, not multipitch, climbs.

TOP ANCHORS

The ideal bottom rope should be established on a route suitable for everyone concerned. The rope goes from the climber's harness, tied on in the usual way, up through the top anchor and down to the belayer in exactly the same way as for indoor climbing. The only difference being the need to create a top belay. If

there is easy access to the top of the crag, creating a belay should be relatively safe but do take care if it's slippery or exposed to strong winds. And always warn others before you throw the ropes down. The usual call is a good loud shout of "below" or "rope below". Bottom belays at the base of the crag will also be desirable, especially if the crag is at the top of a steep slope. Failing this, stand close in to the base of the crag just as you would indoors.

SPORT CRAGS

Many sport crags will have two bolts at the top of the routes so it's simply a question of linking these with slings and screwgate (locking) karabiners so the strain is equally divided and each bolt independently tied off. In some cases the bolts will already be linked by a small chain to a central ring and this could not be simpler. Clip a screwgate karabiner to the central point and clip in the middle of the rope. Always ensure any karabiners have the gate away from the rock and the opening end of the gate pointing down. This will ensure any vibration or movement will keep the gate closed. If the bolts are over the top of the crag, extend them with slings to just over the edge to avoid rope abrasion or erosion of the crag. Finally, double-check all screwgate karabiners are securely fastened. The other major consideration to remember is that a failure of the top anchor in any bottom roping situation could be catastrophic. The climbers' weight will also test the anchor when they are lowered so it must be absolutely secure.

◁ *This climber is carefully checking out the top of a single-pitch climb, with a view to setting up a secure anchor for either top or bottom roping.*

CREATING A BELAY

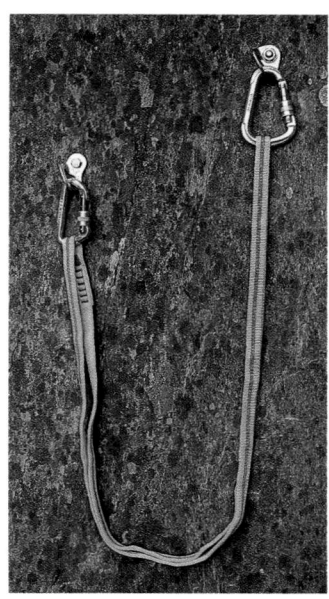

◁ **1** *To create a belay from two bolts is really quite simple. The two ends of a sling are clipped into the bolts with screwgate (locking) karabiners.*

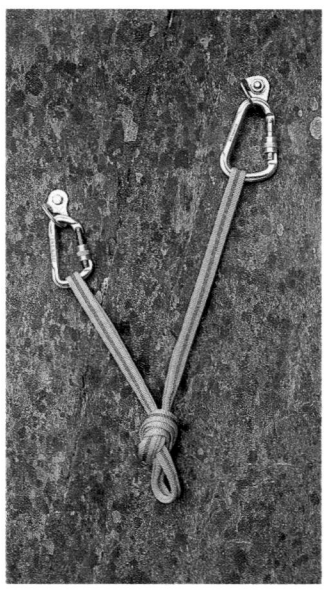

◁ **2** *Gather the sling and tie a simple overhand knot. Keep the double-stitched part of the sling away from the overhand.*

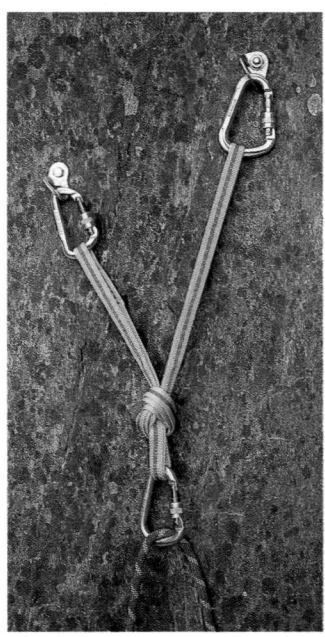

◁ **3** *All the screwgate karabiners should be attached with the gates downwards. Clip the middle of the climbing rope into the bottom karabiner. This method keeps to the principle of equally loaded and independently tied off anchors.*

● POINTS TO REMEMBER

Many crags have "in situ" anchors and bolts, iron stakes or pegs (pitons), which are specially designed steel spikes that can be driven into cracks. If this "in situ" gear looks fairly new and well maintained, it should be okay. There are occasions, though, where some of this equipment may be old and in a poor state of repair, especially on sea cliffs where the salty atmosphere will have affected the metal. Always check carefully and don't trust this equipment implicitly. You don't know how long it's been there, who put it in or how far it goes into the rock. Treat all equipment you find in place on the crag as suspect until it's been thoroughly checked. Finally, if you are bottom roping ensure that the rope is long enough to reach the top of the crag doubled; some ropes have a colour change at the mid-point to assist with this.

◁ *The metal stake here is being used correctly, with a sling wrapped round the bottom next to the ground. This reduces leverage to a minimum.*

● GETTING IT WRONG

△ *In this example, excessive strain will be put on the stake because the sling is well above ground level.*

△ *This sling has not been secured around the stake. This may lead to excessive movement of the sling and consequent wear and tear.*

Using traditional gear

Creating anchors at traditional crags using traditional gear takes sound judgement concerning good placements of nuts, hexes and camming devices. Boulders, spikes and threads are often used as anchors and these too must be checked and deemed to be 100 per cent soundproof before being committed to use. Remember, the anchor you create in this system acts as a pulley and therefore takes around twice the weight of the climber using it. Creating anchors using slings, nuts, hexes and camming devices can be difficult to construct at first because of the inevitable lack of knowledge about what is safe and what is not. Because there will be a considerable strain on the anchor, it's vitally important to make sure it is safe.

USING SLINGS

Slings are used in a variety of ways. For example, they can be placed over spikes, threaded between two immovable boulders or around natural chockstones that are firmly wedged in a crack. They can also be placed around a convenient tree, but this should be discouraged as excessive use will eventually cause severe

◁ *Here a sling has been placed over a large spike. The belay would have been improved if the sling had been clipped to the belayer's harness and the belay operated from there.*

ANCHOR SELECTION

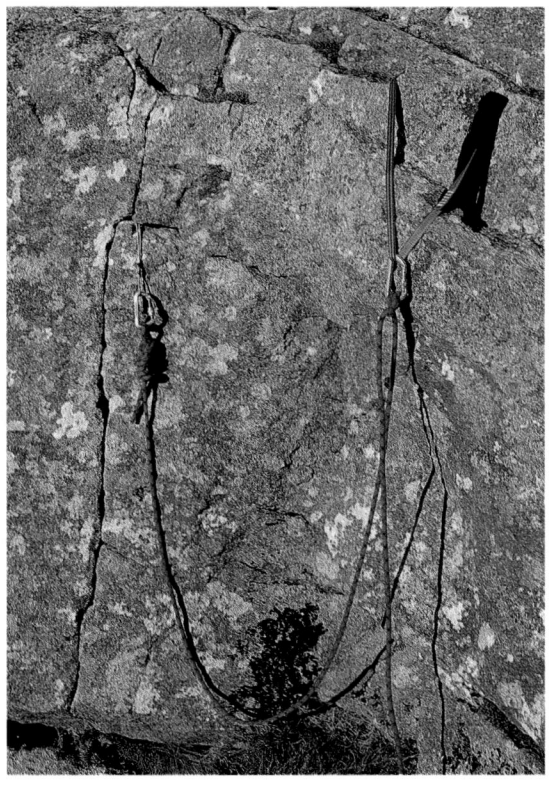

◁ **1** *An anchor has been created using a nut and a spike.*

▷ **2** *The rope has been attached to the nut with a figure-of-eight and to the spike with a clove hitch. The anchors have been equalized using a figure-of-eight on the bight.*

damage to the tree. If a tree has to be used, place a rucksack under the sling to protect it. Where two anchors are used, slings may be needed to link them to create a central point.

LINKING THE ANCHORS

Nuts and hexes can be placed in cracks and wedged to create an anchor. First look for natural constrictions within the crack and choose a chock or wire of an appropriate size. The trick is to get as much metal to rock contact as possible and settle in with a sharp tug. Never use one nut or hex as a main anchor – two or even three are always preferable. Link the two nuts with a sling (or the rope – see photographs above), gather the middle of the sling together and tie with an overhand knot. This is the simplest knot in the world – just form a loop and pass the end through the loop. Again, the trick here is to "equalize" the sling before tying the overhand. Using this method means that both chocks are equally loaded and independently tied off; in other words, the failure of one will not affect the other. With SLCDs find a placement with the trigger half depressed and the cams at about mid-point

and the direction of pull straight down the stem. Avoid if possible any lateral strain across the stem, although this is not important with "flexible" stems. Another point worth bearing in mind with SLCDs is that they have a tendency to "walk" deeper into cracks if there is any movement in the rope system, so extend them with a quickdraw to minimize the risk of this happening.

◁ *The overhand knot is the simplest knot in the world. Take a section of rope, form a loop and pass the end through the loop. Here it is tied on the bight – a doubled section of rope.*

Constructing a top anchor

There are some special considerations to bear in mind when constructing anchors at the top of a crag. Some of these relate to the fact that if the belayer is at the bottom of the crag, the motion of taking in and paying out rope will inevitably create some friction around the anchor at the top of the crag.

▽ *Always pad any sharp edges to prevent abrasion on the rope. Use purpose-made rope protectors or empty plastic bottles, thoroughly cleaned, with the top and bottom removed.*

EXTENDING THE ANCHOR

All belays should be extended just below the top of the crag to avoid abrasion to the rope from constant rubbing as it is taken in or payed out. This action can also create erosion at the top of the crag, especially in the softer types of rock like sandstone. Where anchors are away from the edge of the crag, a spare rope can be used to extend everything to create a belay just over the top. To do this, tie a

△ *Allow enough rope to tie a figure-of-eight below the top anchor. This will reduce abrasion and make for easier rope handling.*

● GETTING IT WRONG

◁ *Here, one of the anchors is not taking any strain of the bottom rope. All the weight is on one anchor. It is vitally important to equally load two anchors and tie them off independently. In addition, the belay is not far enough over the edge, and there is a danger that the rope will become jammed in the crack.*

TYING AND TIGHTENING A CLOVE HITCH

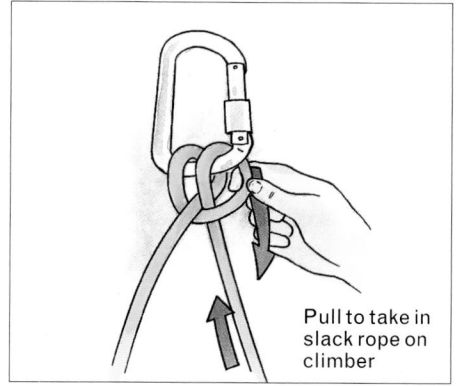

Pull to take in slack rope on climber

△ **1** To tie a clove hitch, form two identical loops in the rope and pass one in front of the other. Clip on to a karabiner.

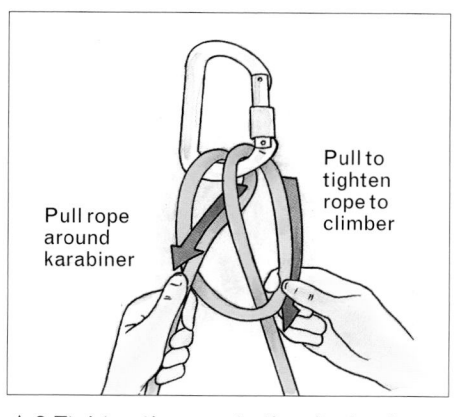

Pull rope around karabiner

Pull to tighten rope to climber

△ **2** Tighten the rope to the climber by loosening the knot in the karabiner. Pull on the rope as shown.

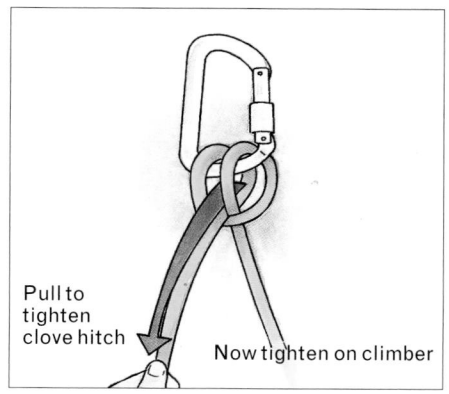

Pull to tighten clove hitch

Now tighten on climber

△ **3** Once you have the rope tight on the climber, you can pull on the section of rope to tighten the knot safely.

figure-of-eight knot on the bight. Allow a 1 m (3 ft) loop to drape over the edge and tie a clove hitch into the second anchor. To do this, form two loops in the rope, right over left and right over left, and slide the second loop behind the first. Place both loops over the karabiner. The rope loop hanging down the crag is then tied in a figure-of-eight. After the rope protector is put in place, a karabiner is attached to the figure-of-eight and the middle of the climbing rope clipped in the usual way. Check all screwgate (locking) karabiners are locked before descending to the bottom of the climb. The angle formed in the rope leading to each anchor should ideally be between 45 and 60 degrees, but should never exceed 120 degrees as this will increase rather than decrease the strain on each anchor.

● THE COW'S TAIL

Take a long sling and thread it through your harness and then back through itself. Clip a screwgate (locking) karabiner to the end of the sling and attach it to any anchor when you are in an exposed position. This might be at the top of a climb when arranging belays, for example. This method of attaching a sling to a harness (called a lark's foot) is perfectly acceptable for a personal back-up system. It must not be used where a severe strain may be applied.

△ The cow's tail attached to the harness with a lark's foot knot. The karabiner can be used to secure the climber to a belay.

● TYING A FIGURE-OF-EIGHT KNOT ON THE BIGHT

The figure-of-eight knot tied on the bight is a useful knot to know. It is used for securing a climber to the anchors of a belay and for creating a loop in which to put a karabiner on a bottom rope anchor.

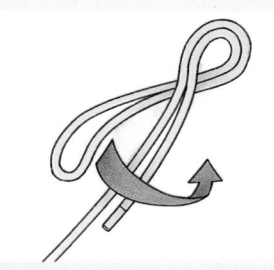

△ **1** Take a 1 m (3 ft) loop or bight of rope, and double it back on itself.

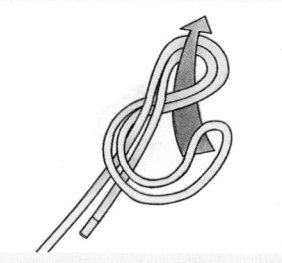

△ **2** Take the loop behind the rope, bring it round to the front and pass it through "eye" in the loop.

△ **3** The figure-of-eight knot can now be made more secure by finishing with a stopper knot (see page 91).

Creating bottom anchors

Although anchors at the base of the crag are not always necessary or possible to construct, they are worth considering. This is particularly so where the climber is heavier than the belayer, or where there is steep ground beneath the crag and the belayer is not secure. Indeed, in this latter scenario, an anchor of some sort becomes essential.

CREATING THE ANCHOR

Anchors at the base of the crag are created in exactly the same way as they are at the top – using slings, nuts, hexes and camming

▷ *In this situation the selection of a good anchor at the bottom of the climb is absolutely essential. Although the anchors here will not take an upward pull, they are the best available.*

devices. Remember that the direction of pull from a falling climber in a bottom roping situation will always be upwards and not down. The anchor you make will therefore have to take an upward pulling force. A thread is ideal – it will take a pull in any direction. A spike, which is good for downward-pulling falls, may be useless for an upward pull where a sling might be simply lifted off. Trees also make good anchors, but there is growing evidence that they can be damaged excessively and will eventually die when all the bark is stripped off.

If the ground anchor is not 100 per cent trustworthy, add your own body weight by clipping to the anchor itself and belaying off the main load-bearing loop of your harness. In this way you are doing the best you can to improve the anchor, although you should still question whether it is good enough or not. If unsure, look again and apply some lateral thinking. It is really important to consider what you are trying to achieve when making your anchor. No two situations are ever the same, which makes it difficult to give textbook answers. Look around and get the best anchors you can and use them in the best way you can. If there are no good anchors, either belay from your main load-bearing loop on your harness or abandon the attempt and go elsewhere to create your belay, maybe doing a different route instead.

USING A DIRECT BELAY

If the anchor is absolutely secure, the ideal belaying system to use in this situation is a direct one. Simply attach the belay device to the anchor itself, using a screwgate (locking) karabiner, rather than to your harness. You have remember to keep behind the belay plate, so that you can lock it off successfully in

◁ *When the ground anchors are absolutely secure it is common practice to belay "direct" from the anchor.*

▷ *One problem with bottom anchors is that when standing in front of the belay plate the belayer will have no chance to take the rope into the braking position. There should also be padding between the sling and the tree.*

the event of a fall. Alternatively an Italian (or Munter) hitch can be used in the place of a belay device. It is less critical where the dead rope is held when using this. It is also very easy for a more experienced person to "back up" the system by just keeping a hand on the dead rope, thus allowing a beginner to learn how to belay. The Italian (or Munter) hitch is ideal for bottom roping situations, especially if novices are involved.

● TYING THE ITALIAN HITCH

To tie an Italian hitch, form two loops exactly like a clove hitch: right over left, right over left. Fold the loops together and clip both ropes into a HMS (pear-shaped) karabiner. The hitch is fully reversible and ideal for taking in or paying out rope. The friction is increased by taking the dead rope forwards and not backwards. Therefore the locking-off action involves taking the hand holding the dead rope forwards (not backwards, as with a normal belay device). This makes it an ideal knot to use with ground anchors, in that the belayer does not have to

stand behind the anchor – they can stand in front, which is usually an easier position to adopt. Never use a twist lock karabiner when belaying with the Italian hitch – the action of the rope can open this type of

karabiner. Use a screwgate (locking) karabiner.

▷ *The Italian (or Munter) hitch can be used in a variety of situations for either belaying or abseiling (rappelling).*

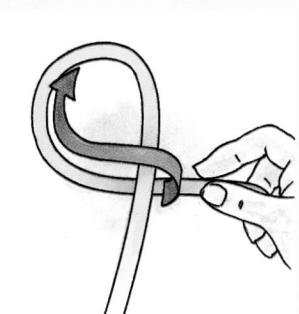

△ **1** *To tie the Italian hitch, form two loops in the rope and fold them on top of each other ...*

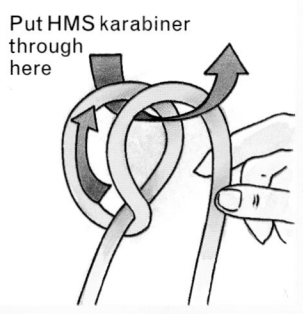

Put HMS karabiner through here

△ **2** *... as shown here. Attach the knot to a HMS or "pear-shaped" karabiner.*

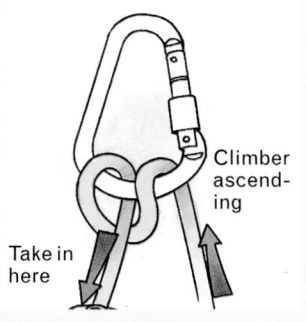

Climber ascending

Take in here

△ **3** *The Italian hitch in action. The pear-shaped karabiner is essential, as it allows the knot to reverse.*

Belaying from the top

There are many situations where it will be necessary to belay from the top of the crag. For example, if the climb is over half the length of the rope you will not be able to belay from the bottom. Instead you will have to create an anchor at the top of the crag and use a top rope.

EXTRA STRAIN

When belaying from above, you should be aware that a top rope will create considerably more strain on you, the belayer, should you have to hold the climber who is coming up from below in the event of a fall. There are two reasons for this:

① There is less energy-absorbing rope in the system.

② The rope does not run through an anchor (where some helpful friction is created) before coming on to the belayer, as it does in a bottom roping situation.

Any force applied will pull directly on the anchor and belayer, so it's vitally important to make sure the belayer is in a direct line between the anchor and the climber. The belay needs to be about 1 m (3 ft) back from the edge of the crag. In situations where there are bolt belays at the top, life is much simpler. Link the two bolts as described earlier (see page 117) and clip into the main load-bearing loop on the harness with a screwgate (locking) karabiner and lock the gate. The belay device or Italian hitch can be operated from the main load-bearing loop in the normal way but be warned: any force will be taken directly through the harness and on to you. This is a major consideration if the climber is heavy! Alternatively you can belay direct from the bolts and consider the use of a cow's tail for your personal safety (see page 121). Either of these methods will work in any situation where the anchors are near, or where you are within a few feet of the top of the climb and the anchors are 100 per cent secure.

If the anchors are 2–3 m (6–10 ft) back from the edge, use the system of clipping a figure-of-eight knot into the main anchor and clove hitching to the second anchor, leaving the loop 1 m (3 ft) back from the edge. The subtle difference here is that a figure-of-eight knot on the bight is now tied by tying a normal figure-of-eight knot, then pushing the end back through and over itself. If done correctly this forms two loops, one to belay off and one for personal safety. In this way the belayer is

keeping in position and belaying direct, and if the climber falls off the strain is put on the belay system and not the belayer's waist. Use a belay plate or Italian (Munter) hitch and the climber can either be lowered back down or finish at the top of the crag.

△ When creating a top anchor to belay from, try to find something of a suitable height above waist height. Sitting on the stance, as shown here, can help this situation.

△ It is vital that the belayer is correctly positioned. They should be in a direct line between the climber and the anchor.

◁ A popular single-pitch venue. There are literally hundreds of climbs at different grades. The rock is gritstone, which is a sedimentary rock similar to, but much coarser than, sandstone. It has excellent frictional qualities and good protection.

Looking at alternatives

There is very rarely a single correct way to make safe anchors. There are usually lots of ways to make unsafe anchors! The trick is to be able to judge between safe and unsafe anchors. You must always ask yourself what would happen to your overall anchor if one of the pieces of gear failed. Would a big shock-load come on to the remaining anchors? Would the entire anchor fail? In any situation, however you have made your belay, keep asking yourself these "what if?" questions.

THE TOOL BOX APPROACH

If you have understood the basic ideas behind building sound anchors and belays, you should be able to cope with most situations that the crags and mountains will throw at you.

◁ *This is an alternative method of creating a single-point belay from separate anchors. The overhand knot is used exclusively to link all the points.*

Remember that the skills you learned have to be adapted to these real-life situations. You will have to be inventive in your use of your own personal tool box of acquired skills to cope with the thousands of permutations of anchor creation.

TOP ANCHORS

In situations where several anchor points are needed to create a top belay, the overhand knot can be used in the system. Start as before with a figure-of-eight knot tied on the first anchor. Make sure you create the first loop just over the edge of the crag and then take the rope back through the next anchor, then back to the loop. When all the anchors have been included, tie an overhand knot in all the loops and clove hitch the rope on each anchor point. This will take a little practice to judge the right amount of rope required, but it is very effective and creates several anchor points to work from if necessary.

◁ *The system here is very similar but utilizes overhand knots and clove hitches. As long as all the anchor points are independently tied off and equally loaded, there will be little cause for concern.*

● USING A RIGGING ROPE

▷ *Here is a good example of how to set up a bottom rope. A spare – or rigging – rope has been utilized to bring the main load-bearing point over the edge to reduce friction, erosion of the crag and wear and tear on the rope. The anchors are equally loaded and independently tied off so any force applied to the belay will be shared equally between the anchor points. A plastic bottle has also been used to protect the rope from any sharp edges there may be on the crag.*

● COILING AND CARRYING THE ROPE

Many ropes are sold with a rope bag which incorporates a sheet on which the rope is laid at the foot of the route and folded around the rope at the end of the day. This is by far the best method not only of storing the rope but also carrying it to the crag. Another good method is to double the rope and feed two arm spans of the doubled ends through the hands.

Now take an arm span at a time and lay each one across one hand. Still holding the rope with one hand, take the two ends and whip them round the main body of coils. Finally a loop can be pulled over the coils and down on to the whipping. The two ends can be used to carry the rope rather like a rucksack, providing the ends are not too short.

△ **1** *Feed the doubled rope in coils over the hand.*

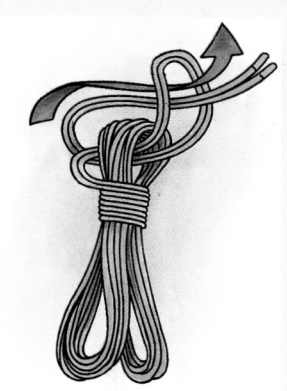

△ **2** *Leave some rope at the top to secure the coils.*

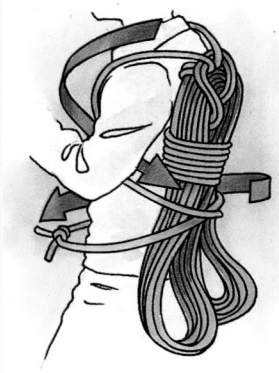

△ **3** *Feed a bight of rope through the top coil and loop through to secure.*

△ **4** *Sling the rope over the back and tie across the chest and around the waist.*

● THE OVERCROWDED CRAGS

There is evidence that a growing number of large groups are visiting the crags, and the rope systems described here are used extensively by beginners and groups. The main problem is that of monopolizing the crags. The popular areas are under extreme pressure and large, noisy groups can ruin someone else's enjoyment of a peaceful afternoon on the crags. Apart from all the technicalities, tolerance, an appreciation of your surroundings and consideration of others are important to bear in mind when visiting popular areas in a group.

△ *A popular climbing venue on a Sunday afternoon during the summer.*

Is this mountaineering?

Multipitch climbing takes us into the mountain or big crag environment. A multipitch route, as the name implies, indicates several rope lengths of climbing at least. All your rope skills and belay judgement, as well as climbing technique, will be called upon to overcome a multipitch route. The rewards are great – you have arrived at one of the culminations of enjoyment that the game of climbing can offer. You will be called upon to lead pitches, create a sound belay on a stance, bring up the second climber and then belay them when their turn to lead comes around. The seriousness of the situation should be stressed. If anything goes wrong high up on a climb, a long way from the road, you will have to draw on your self-reliance.

COMMITMENT

The number of pitches can have little bearing on the difficulty of a particular route, just the commitment required and different skills that will be needed to succeed. The longest rock climbs in the world are often situated in remote areas which could take 2 or 3 weeks just for the approach and several weeks to complete. These require a great deal of commitment, effort and self-reliance because in many cases there would be little chance of rescue if things went wrong. Some of the most difficult climbs, however, will only have a little actual climbing and take only a few minutes to complete but still require hours of preparation and training. These climbs generally have easy access. A good comparison is the difference between a marathon and a 100-metre sprint.

◁ *This climb is steep, exposed and demands a bold approach.*

△ *High mountain crags such as the one shown here can be very serious places. They may have loose and damp lichenous rock and often provide difficult routes.*

▷ *This is the other end of the spectrum – a few minutes' stroll from the car and within easy reach of sun, sea and sand. Who said that rock climbing didn't cater for all tastes?*

● OUT FOR ADVENTURE

The ultimate ambition for many is to lead their own multipitch climbs and enter the world of mountaineering, and perhaps more important, mountain safety, which a subject in its own right. The old saying, don't try and run before you can walk, is very appropriate, so take time and learn the basic techniques first. Inevitably accidents will occur on the crags, but remember the basic essentials of first aid, airway, breathing and circulation and know how to send for help. Six blasts on a whistle or six flashes on a torch, repeated after 1 minute, should summon help if you can't get to a phone.

△ *Many mountain routes will demand a full day to complete, starting with a walk of 2–3 hours with a heavy rucksack.*

Carrying the gear

The problem of how to carry the gear, or "rack", will have become evident on single pitch routes. The problem is particularly obvious when preparing to climb a traditional route, where the amount of gear carried is far greater than that carried on a sport route. On multipitch routes this is more important, particularly if two climbers are alternating leads. Obviously if some of that gear is dropped, it could have serious consequences, not only for the climbers concerned, but others who happen to be below them.

HARNESS OR BANDOLIER (GEAR SLING)

The two choices available are to rack the gear around the harness, which should have adequate facilities, or to use a "bandolier" which is a specially designed padded loop that goes around the shoulders. On steeper routes the bandolier system works very well, and you can simply swap bandoliers at the end of each pitch (at which point it's possible to drop the whole rack). On easier-angled routes, there is a tendency for the bandolier to swing round to the front, making it difficult to see your feet. Using the gear loops on the harness is probably a better option in this situation, and although this may slow you down on the change-overs at the end of each pitch, at least you won't drop the whole rack.

Whichever way, keep the rack organized so everything is in order and always in the same place. Gear will then be quick to retrieve when you're on a long, lonely "run out".

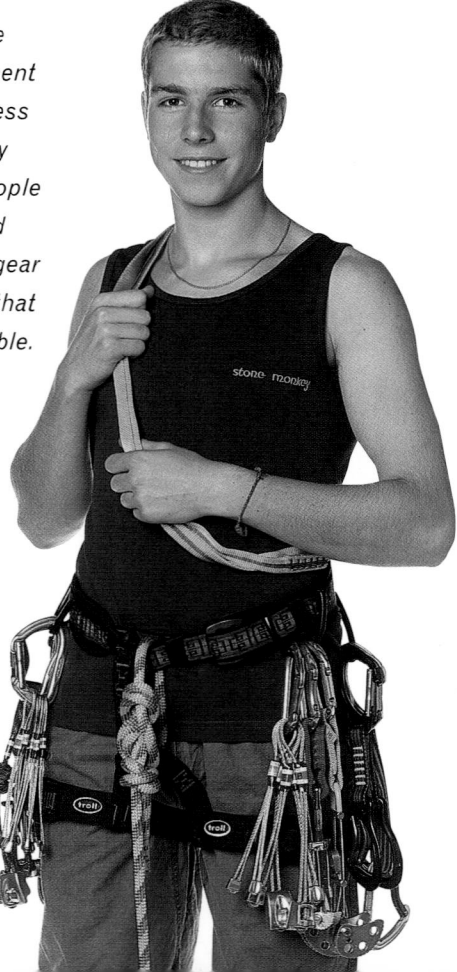

▷ *The system here shows the equipment loops on the harness being used to carry the gear. Many people prefer this method because it allows gear to be arranged so that it is easily accessible.*

▷ *Using a bandolier is a quick and efficient way of carrying gear, especially if two climbers are alternating leads (leading through).*

Problems at the stance

Climbing multipitch routes poses many more questions as to what to do and when to do it. If the chosen climb is in an exposed position above a steep slope, a suitable anchor (belay) will be required. Consider the implications of the leader slipping off the first few moves: if they were to land at your feet it shouldn't be a problem. If, however, they were to fall past you and continue down the steep ground, they could pull you after them. This could, at the least, be an inauspicious start to a day's climbing or at worst lead to a very short climbing partnership! Starting a climb from a steep and exposed position is therefore a much more serious situation, so be aware of potential problems.

If your climb starts from a safe position, it may be okay to stand or sit close to the bottom. There is, however, one complication. If the leader falls, with protection placed, they will create a "pulley" effect, lifting the belayer off the ground and possibly into a protruding spike. An upward-pulling anchor, mentioned earlier, becomes much more important here and the biggest problem is making the initial judgement to use one, and then a second judgement as to whether it's good enough! A poor anchor may be worse than no anchor because at least you are aware that there is no belay, whereas if you have one that fails – who knows what will happen? Another way around the problem is to place some good protection (running belay) as soon as possible.

△ Any multipitch climb is complicated if one climber is leading all the pitches. Care is needed at the stances and the rope will have to be run through so that the leader's end is on top of the pile.

▷ Holding a leader fall can be difficult on a multipitch traditional route. The climber (faller) will be climbing past any protection and a fall may result in a greater force being applied to the belayer.

The safety chain

The safety chain includes everything a climber has in terms of equipment and what to do with it. The harness and rope are probably the most important, but the belay device, nuts, hexes, camming devices, slings and karabiners all play their part. The old adage about a chain only being as strong as its weakest link holds good for climbing, too. Always try to be aware of where the weak links in your safety chain might be. The safety chain is present in single pitch climbing (top or bottom roping and leading), but it is at its most complicated and interesting in multipitch climbing situations.

RUNNING BELAYS

The ultimate challenge is perhaps leading your own multipitch route on natural gear (using nuts, hexes and so on) or on bolted protection. When leading, the question of greatest importance for most climbers is, what is the protection (running belays) going to be like?

△ *Clipping that all-important running belay. This may have to be done in a physically tiring position.*

◁ *To get good protection for a leader on traditional routes relies on good nuts, cams or slings being placed and, as ever, an alert second as belayer.*

This is a big question and assumes a greater importance on adventure or traditional routes than on a sport route. Protection on traditional routes relies on the placement of nuts, hexes and camming devices, and the leader may find their position precarious while they fiddle a tiny wire behind a small flake of doubtful security. This is a far cry from sport routes where the protection relies on bolts which are usually bombproof and take only seconds to clip. Another consideration is the steeper the route the safer it is (provided your protection does not fail) because it's not the falling off that damages climbers, it's what they hit on their way down, especially if it happens to be the ground which can be pretty unforgiving. If a route is very steep with lots of protection the climber will bounce gently to a stop in mid-air, with the elasticity of the rope absorbing most of the shock. If, on the other hand, the climber slithers down a granite slab, they will feel sore, at the very least. Always get in what you can, when you can; but remember, the more "runners" you place, the more drag you'll get on the rope and more lateral strain, possibly lifting them out.

DYNAMIC ROPES

By the time any climber is contemplating multipitch routes, it should be fairly evident to them that there is a good deal of stretch in any climbing rope and this is a very important factor. Basically this means that any force or shock in the system is absorbed slowly and with less shock to the climber's body or the belay system. If these forces were stopped with a static, or low-stretch rope, there would be considerably more force, not only on the climbers but also on the belay system, with the distinct possibility of failure of part of that system. This is because of the greater force involved or, put more correctly, same amount of force but over a shorter period of time. Apart from the energy absorbed by the rope, energy is also absorbed by the belay plate, the belayer being lifted off the ground, the knots tightening up or, more drastically, a runner failing. Not to be recommended if it's the only

△ **1** On a sport route clip the bolt with the bent-gate karabiner down and away from you. Now reach down and take the rope between your first and second finger.

△ **2** By hooking the thumb and third finger through the karabiner it will be held steady while the index finger twists the rope into position.

● GETTING IT WRONG

◁ This rope has been clipped the wrong way through the karabiner. If the climber falls there is a distinct possibility that the rope will be taken across the gate and out of the karabiner altogether. Always look ahead to see which way the route is going and clip the quickdraws from behind the gate in the karabiner, with that gate facing away from the direction in which you intend to climb.

one you have got in! The whole safety chain is therefore vital and it is only as strong as its weakest link. However, remember that upward-pulling anchors could, if they are too tight, prevent the belayer from being lifted off the ground, which would possibly weaken the belay. So always, always consider the implications and ask your self, "What happens if ...?"

Using a single rope

▽ In the situation here there will be so much friction created that either the running belays will pull out or the leader will have great difficulty in making further progress.

You have the choice of climbing on one full rope or two half ropes (see page 25 for an explanation of full and half ropes). Once you have progressed to leading and multipitch routes, you should be aware of the pros and cons of using either. Only in understanding these things can you form your own opinion and come to a decision about what to use on any given route.

△ *Here, the rope is running in a straighter line than in the photograph left. However, the protection could have been extended further with a longer sling.*

ROPE DRAG

In many situations climbers use a single rope and this is adequate on either single pitch or easier multipitch routes. There are, however, some limiting factors, which means that in some situations a compromise must be found to deal with a potential problem. Using a single rope on a complicated traditional route can create a lot of friction as the rope passes through the runners. This is called rope drag. On sport routes the bolts are usually in a straight line, so it isn't generally a problem. On traditional routes the protection has to be placed where it occurs and this presents a problem if the rope zigzags from side to side. If the first piece of protection is to the left of the climber

and the second to the right there will be a great deal of friction on the rope, making it difficult to move and causing a severe lateral strain on the runners which could pull them out. Often it's the amount of friction engendered near the top of a pitch rather than at the start that causes the problem, so there is a need to look carefully which way the route goes and extend any runners that are off to one side. The longer the extender, the more likely it is to stay in place. The other answer may be to place the first two runners, then climb down to remove the first one. The other limiting factors with a single rope are the length of abseil (rappel) possible and the difficulty of arranging suitable protection for the second climber on a traverse.

● THE FALL FACTOR

The fall factor refers to the severity of the forces involved in any fall. These forces vary in severity depending on a number of factors. The fall factor is usually expressed as a number, which is arrived at by dividing the length of the fall by the amount of rope that is involved. The numerical values normally run between 0.1 and 2, with 2 creating the greatest impact of force on climber and belayer. For example, if on the third pitch up a multipitch route a leader climbs 3 m (10 ft) above the belay with no runners in between and falls off, they will fall a total of just over 6 m (20 ft) – they will fall below the belay itself. This is a factor 2 fall. The leader has fallen 6 m (20 ft) with 3 m (10 ft) of rope paid out ($6 \div 3 = 2$; $20 \div 10 = 2$). If the same leader falls off at 30 m (100 ft) above the stance with a runner at 27 m (90 ft), they still fall 6 m (20 ft) but the elasticity of a climbing rope and the dynamic factors of the safety chain will absorb most of the force. In this situation the belayer may hardly notice the fall. The fall factor in this situation would only be 0.2, although the actual distance fallen is identical. The moral of this is, get a running belay in as soon as you can after leaving the stance.

△ *Multipitch climbing and the fall factor.*
A: Fall factor of 2; B: Fall factor of 1; C: Fall factor of 0.5

Using double ropes

Double ropes are thinner (usually 9 mm) and lighter than single full ropes. This makes them easier to distribute amongst the climbing party and carry to the crag, mountain or sea cliff. If used properly, they will help reduce or entirely cut out any rope drag. If tied together and used double, they give the potential of a full 50 m (165 ft) abseil (rappel) which can still be retrieved. These advantages are looked at below, and in the following section on abseiling.

TYING ON

This is an easy operation. Simply tie each rope into your harness using the normal figure-of-eight knot re-threaded. It is essential to use two different coloured ropes. This makes life easy when clipping runners. You can let your belayer know that you want slack on red or green or whatever. You should both tie on in the same way and make sure that you have the same coloured rope on the same side (left or right) before setting off on the route. This will help prevent twists in the ropes. Your belayer will thread both ropes through the slots in their belay device. Practice will be needed in paying out separate ropes.

△ It is important to communicate with your belayer when clipping runners to keep them informed as to which rope you need slack on. Keep the instructions short and simple.

ADVANTAGES

Using double ropes can be a tremendous advantage on either harder single pitch or multipitch climbs where the route weaves an intricate path up the crag. Running belays can be clipped either alternately or the ropes can be separated out, one to the left and one to the right. This not only reduces the friction but makes it much easier to arrange protection for the leader and second. Any traverse can be protected for the leader with one rope while the other can be left free to protect the second from directly above. There is also a huge difference in the length of any abseils that can be

▷ *Some practice will be needed to overcome the difficulties of handling double ropes, but on longer routes they can be a tremendous advantage.*

made. A further point is the ease of tying on to two anchor points at the top of the pitch. Simply take one rope to each anchor, tie on with a clove hitch and adjust each independently so both anchors are equally loaded.

TWIN ROPES

Although not particularly popular, this method of ropework has its devotees, particularly where longer multipitch routes are common. The twin rope method uses both ropes as a single rope when climbing. This means putting both ropes through each point of protection, thereby working on the principle that two are better than one. However, long abseils can be made similar to double ropes, so an effective and rapid retreat can be made if necessary. Because of the different thicknesses of all the various ropes involved in climbing, it is essential that they are used only for the purpose they were designed for and that double or twin ropes are not used singly, even for top roping.

◁ *Protecting a climb that has running belays to the left and right of the actual climb is so much easier when double ropes are used, and there is less friction to hinder the leader (see page 134).*

△ *With doubled ropes, any abseil (rappel) can be increased from half the length of the rope to the full length, in most cases from 25 m – 50 m (80 ft – 160 ft).*

△ *Using doubled ropes in this situation is a real advantage. The leader can arrange better protection for both leader and second.*

● GETTING IT WRONG

◁ *Although doubled ropes are being used here, it is not to any great advantage. Both ropes are taken in to the corner, which is going to increase friction and give little support to the second climber in the case of a fall.*

Multi-point anchors

▽ *Sea cliffs around many coastal areas offer an exciting venue, but the different environment means that specific skills and techniques must be learnt to deal with the hazards of tidal approaches.*

On a multipitch route, there are many things to consider when constructing each belay. These will include: the soundness of the anchors; the direction of fall (don't forget that if you are leading through your second will become your leader and will go from climbing below you to climbing above you); your position on the stance; where you will flake the rope (will it be safe from snagging if it simply runs down the rock face?); and how

you will exchange gear when your second arrives at the stance. You will need both hands, so how will you make your second safe while you do this?

DOUBLE ROPES AND ANCHORS

If you are using double ropes, your life is made easier. Where the anchor is a single point and within reach of the belayer, treat both ropes together and tie a clove hitch to the screwgate (locking) karabiner. If there are two anchors, both out of reach, take one rope to each anchor and back to a pear-shaped (HMS) karabiner in the rope loop of the harness and tie with a clove hitch.

By using any of the belay systems described here, any force is transmitted through the belayer and back to the belay, which is a very important point when it comes to dealing with any problems. Any belay anchor or stance will be greatly improved by a good runner being

△ *The perfect position, high on a route with steep rock which is warm, dry and comforting.*

placed immediately on leaving the stance by the leader (see fall factors, page 135). Of particular importance in multipitch climbing is the need to consider whether to belay left- or right-handed. Any belay device should be on the same side as the belay ropes so that it is much easier to bring the arm back into the locking position; a good deal of dexterity will be required. If the locking hand is on the opposite side of the body to belay it will be much more difficult to create the "s" shape through the belay device because the arm cannot be brought back fast enough. This is important on any rock climb but becomes more of a problem when dealing with a tight, constricted or even hanging stance, where there is little or nothing to stand on. All the belayer can do (after tying on of course) is sit back in their harness.

Any multipitch climbing situation is further complicated if one climber is leading all the pitches. In this situation, great care will have to be taken at the change-overs. The ropes will need to be run back through at each stance so that the leader's end is back on top of the pile when they start on the next pitch. If the climbers are leading through this will be unnecessary because each leader's end of rope will be naturally on top of the pile at each stance. On very small or hanging stances the belayer should drape the rope either across the belay ropes or around their feet to make sure it doesn't hang down the rock face and either get jammed in a crack or annoy other climbers. The belayer should always be able to reach the rope to sort any problems out.

● SAFETY CHECKLIST

A good belay will have all of the following:

① Tight ropes leading to two or three strong anchors.
② Equal tension on each rope.
③ The stance will be stable and adjustable from where the belayer stands.
④ Screwgate (locking) karabiners or snaplinks back-to-back on all the anchors.

USING MULTI-POINT ANCHORS WITH A ROPE

△ **1** *Take the rope from your harness to each anchor and back to the harness or rope loop.*

△ **2** *Tie a large overhand knot or a clove hitch to a pear-shaped (HMS) karabiner and clip to your harness.*

USING MULTI-POINT ANCHORS WITH SLINGS

△ **1** *To link two nuts or cams to create a single-point anchor, clip a sling to the karabiner and tie an overhand knot loosely in the sling.*

△ **2** *Clip the other end of the sling to the other karabiner. Adjust the overhand knot to a point where the load is equalized and tighten.*

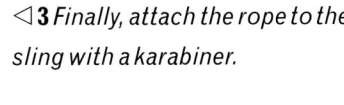

◁ **3** *Finally, attach the rope to the sling with a karabiner.*

Further knots (1)

The concept of the tool box has been mentioned earlier. This implies that as you progress in your climbing, you come to have a lot of alternative techniques that you can use as and when required. You must be clear about when such alternatives might be used and why. Using knots is a good example. When is it preferable to use the figure-of-eight knot rather than the clove hitch in creating a belay? Which knot is best to use when tying two ropes together to abseil (rappel) off and why?

TYING A BOWLINE KNOT

▷ **1** *Pass a length of rope through the climbing harness, making sure that the manufacturer's instructions are followed closely.*

PROBLEMS WITH THE BOWLINE KNOT

The bowline is commonly used amongst climbers as an alternative method of tying the rope on to a harness and is perfectly acceptable. However, there are two main considerations which are worth bearing in **mind. It is** easier to tie the bowline incorrectly **than the** figure-of-eight. If tied incorrectly, it is dangerous as it converts into a slip knot very easily!

△ **2** *Create a loop in the rope with the main rope on the underside of the loop. Hold firmly with the finger and thumb. Pass the short end of rope through this.*

△ **3** *Then go behind the main rope and back through the loop. Remember, the rope loop should be about fist size when completed.*

△ **4** *Finish with the stopper knot (see page 91). The stopper knot is even more important with the bowline than the re-threaded figure-of-eight.*

It is also more difficult to see if the bowline has been correctly tied than the figure-of-eight. This makes it more difficult to check both your own knot simply by casting an eye over it and that of your climbing partner's.

TYING THE BOWLINE

However, it is useful to know how to tie it. Form a loop in the rope about 1 m (3 ft) from the end with the loop to your right (as you look at it) with the main rope underneath the loop. Thread the end of the rope through the harness and then take the end up through the loop, around the main rope and back down through the loop. This has often been quoted as the "rabbit coming out of his burrow, round the tree and back down again". It is vitally important to make sure the end of the rope is on the inside of the knot and finished securely with a "stopper knot" in exactly the same way as the figure-of-eight knot.

ROPE TRICKS

The clove hitch can be tied using only one hand. This may be useful for the leader on arriving at a hanging stance. Having placed a good piece of gear or clipped a bolt, the clove hitch can be tied one-handed, while the other hand keeps you on the rock. The sequence for tying the knot one-handed is shown here.

• KNOTABILITY

The width and construction of your rope will affect how easy (or hard) it will be for you to tie knots in it. Thin ropes tend to be easier to tie knots into than thicker ones. Some ropes are softer and suppler than others, and these qualities also make them easier to handle. Also, a wet and frozen rope might be nearly impossible to tie.

Some rope manufacturers will supply a knotability ratio, designed to give climbers some idea as to how well the rope will handle in this respect. These qualities will also affect how well tied each knot will be.

The Italian hitch can also be tied one-handed using the same technique. However, you take one less twist in the rope before clipping it into the screwgate (locking) karabiner. Double check!

• TYING THE CLOVE HITCH ONE-HANDED

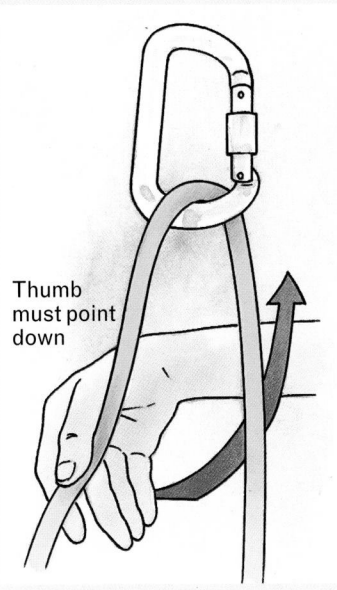

Thumb must point down

△ **1** Clip a karabiner into the belay with the gate towards you and the opening end down. Now take the left-hand rope between finger and thumb.

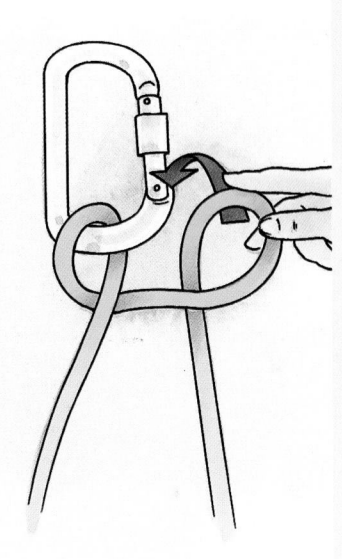

△ **2** Pull the rope back towards you, twisting the palm of your hand down to form a loop in the rope.

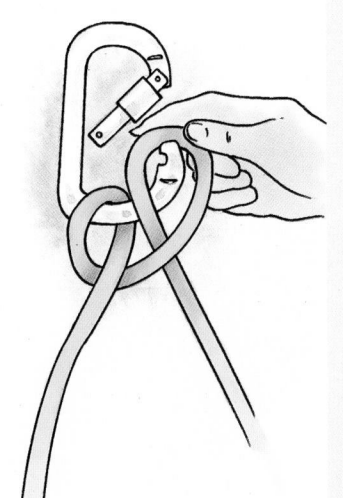

△ **3** Keep the karabiner unlocked up to this stage and complete the hitch by pushing the loop into the karabiner.

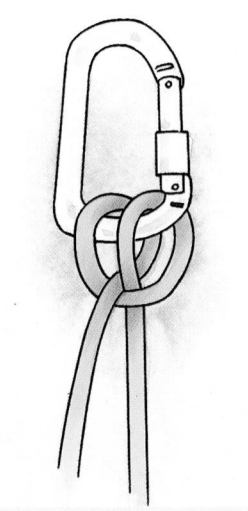

△ **4** Finally check the hitch and lock the screwgate (locking) karabiner.

Further knots (2)

Up to now only the minimum number of knots have been described to allow you to get on with the fun and enjoyment of climbing. The time has come, however, to look at some further knots to add to the armoury, because getting into the world of multipitch routes also takes you into the area of learning a little self-reliance and knowing how to deal with everyday problems that may occur.

△ *This chock is threaded on a short length of cord which is then tied with a double fisherman's knot. This is the traditional method of joining two ropes of equal thickness.*

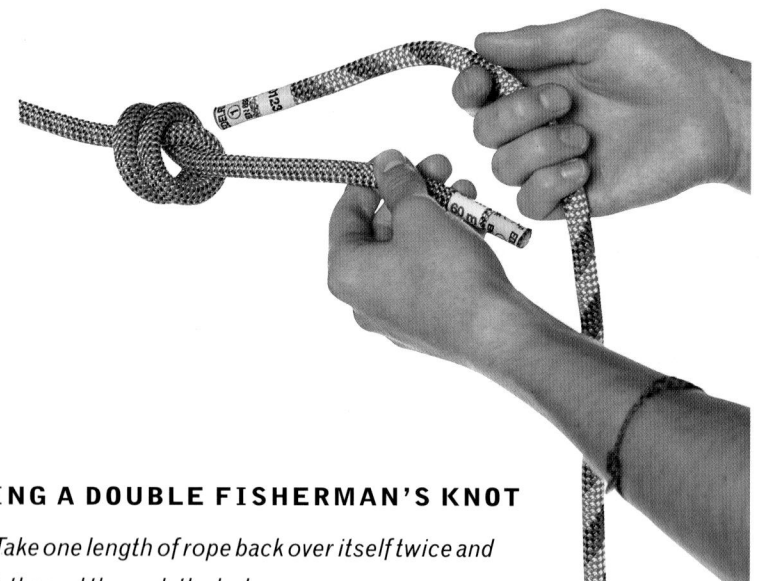

TYING A DOUBLE FISHERMAN'S KNOT

△ **1** *Take one length of rope back over itself twice and push the end through the hole.*

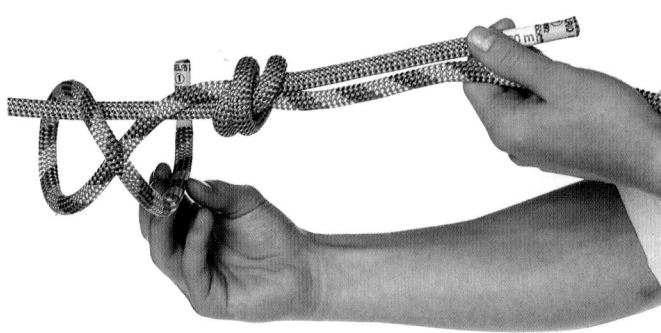

△ **2** *Now push the other length of rope through the same hole, but from the opposite direction. Now do exactly what you did with the first length of rope, that is twice round and back through itself.*

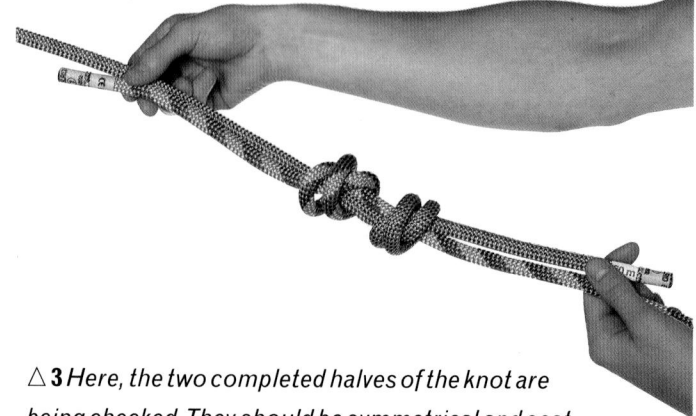

△ **3** *Here, the two completed halves of the knot are being checked. They should be symmetrical and seat well together. If they don't, then try again.*

DOUBLE FISHERMAN'S KNOT

The double fisherman's knot has traditionally been used over the years to join two ropes together, often for use in abseiling (rappelling). Although this has now to a certain extent been superseded by the overhand knot, it is still worthwhile knowing how to tie it. The most common use of the double fisherman's knot today is to join the two ends of a short length of rope after threading through nuts and hexes. Take one end of the rope and wrap it twice around itself and then through the hole it has formed. Now push the other end through the loop and wrap this twice around itself and the other rope but in the opposite direction. The two halves of the knot should then slide together and lie side by side. They should look symmetrical. If they are not, then try again. The single fisherman's knot is very similar, almost as strong and uses much less rope. Either will do for joining any two ropes if they are of equal thickness, but be sure to leave adequate lengths of rope after the knot has been tied. The over-hand knot has being described already but in a different context; here it is used to tie two ropes together so that a longer abseil can be contemplated. The reasons will be discussed in greater detail on pages 144–153. Take the two ends of rope together and tie the simplest knot in the world, always allow 1 m (3 ft) of rope at least on the two trailing ends.

TYING THE FRENCH PRUSSIK (AUTOBLOCK)

The step-by-step sequence below shows how to tie the French prussik and how to rig it for use as a safety back-up to an abseil (rappel). The French prussik is used in other situations as well, mostly for emergency techniques, such as performing assisted and unassisted hoists and escaping from the belay system (see Chapter 5 for further details).

Advantages: Released under load – amount of friction dependent on turns.

Disadvantages: Can slip without warning. Must be tied with a short sling. Doesn't work with tape (spectra).

TYING THE FRENCH PRUSSIK

 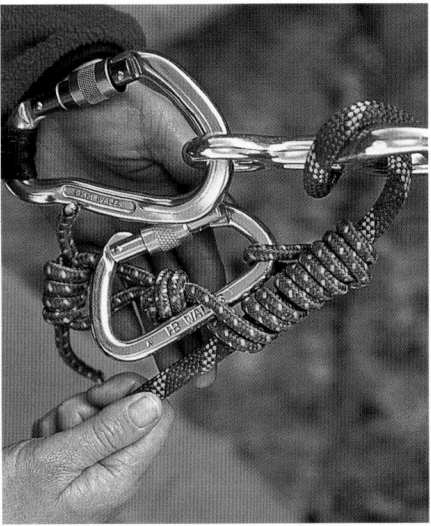 

△ **1** *The best way of giving protection on any abseil (rappel) if you are the first to go down is to use a French prussik. This is a short loop of 6 mm (¼ in) cord wound four or five times round the abseil rope and attached to the leg loop on the harness. This is slid down the rope with your "bottom" hand as you abseil and should "lock" in an emergency.*

△ **2** *The completed French prussik is shown here.*

△ **3** *The French prussik attached to the leg loop of the harness. This prussik has many more uses (see Chapter 5).*

What is abseiling (rappelling)?

▽ Having completed a route, this climber is abseiling (rappelling) back to the ground.

Abseiling (rappelling) is the technique used for descending steep rock either after the climb has been completed, or in certain cases where there is difficult access to the start of the climb. The rope is attached to a safe anchor at the top and a friction device, either a figure-of-eight descender or belay device, placed on the rope and attached to the load-bearing loop of the harness with a screwgate (locking) karabiner. By applying slight pressure with the lower hand below the device, a safe and controlled descent is easily accomplished. Some crags will have abseil descents from the top or in some cases, particularly sea cliffs, an abseil approach. In other situations, such as the onset of bad weather or misjudgement of the difficulty of the route, an abseil may be the only way of getting back down. In the early days of rock climbing, many primitive forms of abseiling were developed. On smaller traditional cliffs it is usually possible to scramble down the easy way. In alpine countries this is not always the case and abseiling is a necessity, particularly on the longer routes. The development of modern equipment makes abseiling far easier than it was but it is important to remember that any abseil is only as safe as the anchor, and that cannot be truly tested until you test it for real.

The perfect position

The perfect position for abseiling is easily achieved on a smooth slab with few ledges or obstructions and it's possible to see all the way down. A high anchor will make life much easier when starting the abseil. This is ideal for a beginner, but with more experience steeper, or even overhanging rock can be descended easily. The anchor must be 100 per cent bombproof. If it isn't, don't abseil! Just as in belaying, there is a live or active hand which is used below the abseil device to control the descent and a dead hand which is usually above the descender, although some beginners will want to use both hands below the device to control their descent at first. Keep the feet shoulder-width

▽ *The perfect abseil (rappel) stance*

Upper hand guiding the rope

Plenty of space between descender and back-up

French prussik or safety rope as a back-up

Looking where going

Body turned towards the leading hand

Lower hand maintaining friction on the dead rope and controlling the descent

Knees slightly flexed, acting as shock absorbers

Feet flat against the rock for a firm stance and shoulder-width apart

△ *This smooth slab is ideal for practising abseiling (rappelling). There are no obstructions or cracks where a boot could get jammed. The ropes can be clearly seen reaching the ground.*

apart and turn slightly to the right if right-handed or to the left if left-handed. By turning sideways it becomes much easier to see where you are going and gives more freedom of movement to operate the controlling hand on the descender. The difficult part is committing yourself and going over the edge to start the abseil, but once that is done just feed the rope out and walk backwards down the crag. The feet should be flat against the rock and the closer you are to the horizontal, the less likely your feet are to slip. Flex the knees and control the rope with your bottom hand. There should also be a separate safety rope for beginners or a French prussik (see page 143) as a safety back-up for the more experienced.

◁ *When beginners practise abseiling (rappelling), there should always be an extra rope used as a safety back-up.*

ROPEWORK

145

Abseil (rappel) devices

There are several devices that have been developed especially with abseiling (rappelling) in mind. They give a smooth descent and tend to dissipate the heat generated through friction very well. However, it is worth bearing in mind that most devices designed for belaying can be used for abseiling as well. It is a good idea to test a new device in a safe environment (on a short abseil or at the wall) before using it in a more adventurous situation!

THE FIGURE-OF-EIGHT DESCENDER

The figure-of-eight descender is undoubtedly the best device for the job and specifically designed for the purpose, giving a controlled and safe descent. Harnesses which have a central load-bearing loop should present no problems; however, some harnesses require a karabiner to hold the leg loops up or clip the two parts of the harness together. In some cases this can "hold" the karabiner in place and possibly create loading against the gate.

The problem with this type of harness, sometimes referred to as a "Bod" system, is easily overcome by using a "mallion" (designed specifically to take a multi-directional pull) to connect the two parts of the harness together and thus create a central load-bearing loop. It is important to load the rope down through the eye so that it is on top of the descender when it goes over the back bar. If the rope goes up through the "eye" and under the back bar it could catch on a sharp edge of rock and "lock off" around the eye, thus preventing any further descent. (see Chapter 5).

OTHER ALTERNATIVES

As mentioned, most belay devices offer reasonable options for abseiling and a varying degree of friction on either double or single ropes. The biggest problem with most (Tuber excepted) is a relatively small surface area which doesn't dissipate the heat caused by the friction during the abseil. In a series of long multiple abseils it is important to remove the

▽ *This is a figure-of-eight descender loaded correctly with the rope over the connecting bar. Get into the habit of doing this automatically and always use a screwgate (locking) karabiner.*

▷ *With a "diaper" harness system, it is necessary to connect the two halves of the harness together with a "mallion". This is designed to take a three-way pull – karabiners, even screwgates, are not.*

△ This is a belay device which works very well as an abseil device. In a learning or practice situation it is possible to abseil on a single rope.

device quickly at the end of each abseil (rappel). Whichever device is used, it is important to always use either a safety rope or French prussik and clip this to the leg loop below the device with a screwgate (locking) karabiner. This is slid down the rope by the control (lower) hand and if this is removed (for whatever reason) the prussik should automatically lock. Where multiple abseils are involved have a "cow's tail" attachment from your harness to clip the anchor on arrival at the next stance before unclipping from the rope.

△ Tie a knot in the end of the rope before setting off. This may prevent you sliding off the end!

● GETTING IT WRONG

It is very easy to make mistakes setting up your abseil (rappel). To guard against this, make sure that you check your harness, abseil device and screwgate (locking) karabiner. A common mistake is to feed the rope up through the main hole of the figure-of-eight descender. If the rope is underneath the main bar of the descender it may turn in to a "lark's foot" if it catches an edge on the way down. This will lock the descender solid and necessitate a rescue, especially if you are on a free abseil and can't reach the rock.

△ A dangerous situation: the abseil (rappel) device is connected to the harness with a snaplink karabiner.

△ The common mistake of allowing clothing to get caught in the descender.

ROPEWORK

147

Joining the rope

Traditionally the double fisherman's knot or reef knot with a double fisherman's knot either side have been used to join two ropes, which allows a longer abseil (rappel). A much better method which is becoming common practice is a simple overhand knot. This allows the rope to "roll" outwards away from the rock when it's being retrieved and reduce the chance of the knot jamming on the way down. Always leave a long "tail" (1 m or 3 ft) and use a second overhand to prevent clipping the device in to the "tails". The second overhand can be removed just before leaving the stance after checking everything (twice). Even when using this method of joining two ropes, it is important to check the position of the knot carefully and make certain that it will run clear of any cracks. When the first climber has abseiled, get them to try pulling the ropes a little to check whether they will run. If not try and reposition them. Finally, clip a quickdraw on to the rope that needs to be pulled – just as a reminder.

ABANDONING EQUIPMENT

This is something which no self-respecting climbers like to do, but in serious situations there may be no option. After all equipment, although it's expensive, can be replaced unlike a life. There are, however, some tricks of the trade which may be of value in the situation where there is a doubtful anchor but with a perfectly reasonable second anchor nearby. Use the doubtful anchor as the main abseil

▽ *The overhand knot has recently found favour as a way of joining two ropes. The knot will "roll" away from the rock when the end is pulled and is therefore less likely to jam in a crack.*

△ *This abseil (rappel) has been rigged so that the rope can be retrieved, but not the karabiner and sling. The karabiner is a snaplink, so it may have been better to thread the rope directly into the sling.*

▷ *A popular way to get down off a crag – but the tree at the top is suffering.*

point and put all the load on to that anchor. Now put a good back-up into the second anchor with a few centimetres (inches) of slack in the system and send the heaviest climber first! If the doubtful anchor holds for the heaviest person, in theory the secondary anchor can be retrieved before the second (lighter) person abseils! If nothing else, this should provoke a few arguments among the party as to who is the lightest! It must be stressed that this is for really serious situations only – in particular where equipment is at a premium and may be needed further down the mountain. In 30 years of mountaineering and rock climbing the author has only used the technique three or four times and anyone who tries this must ask themselves what price is equipment anyway.

RETRIEVABLE ABSEILING (RAPPELLING)

Do you leave a sling in place to ensure that the rope can be retrieved or do you risk it? In truth there is often no easy solution, unless one person goes down and tries to pull the rope through a few centimetres (inches) first. If at that stage it doesn't run round the anchor, the second person would have to rearrange the rope and try again. As a general rule, if there is any doubt leave a sling. On long multipitch routes many leaders carry a few metres (feet) of cord or tape specifically for rigging abseils and leaving behind, and a penknife for cutting to the required length. It is worth being particularly careful when dealing with a rounded spike – there is a tendency for rope to "roll" off when the rope is loaded. In this situation, a short length of tape would be much less likely to roll.

△ The ropes have been joined using an overhand knot and placed over a large flake. There will be some friction when the rope is pulled through once the climber is down.

△ The rope has been threaded which may create far too much friction for the rope to be retrieved.

◁ The perfect retrievable abseil (rappel). However, the screwgate (locking) karabiner and sling will be left behind. The climber has a French prussik for safety and has clipped a quickdraw to the rope that will need to be pulled through once down.

● ABSEILING (RAPPELLING) IN SAFETY – TOP TIPS

- Make sure your ropes reach the ground, or at least to another stance.
- Get a sound anchor, at any price.
- Practise and become familiar with the technique.
- Use a French prussik from your leg loop, and of the right length. This is usually a 1.25 m (4 ft) length of 6 mm (¼ in) cord joined with a double fisherman's knot.
- Keep your anchor as high as possible in relation to the take-off point.
- Don't use trees unless you really have to, and then leave a sling or length of tape.
- Back the anchor up if in doubt.
- Buy yourself a mallion if your harness requires "holding" together at the front, for example a "Bod" system.

The anchor point

On sport crags, the anchor points are invariably good, although don't trust bolts implicitly, especially some of the ancient relics from a bygone age and always abseil (rappel) with care. The steadier you go down, the less strain there will be on the anchor, ropes and harnesses. On traditional climbing areas it can be much more difficult and the perfect anchor, one which allows the rope to be retrieved, is often elusive. In some cases it may be necessary to abandon a sling and abseil off this rather than risk getting the rope jammed in a crack. Trees often make excellent anchors but this causes serious damage when ropes are pulled down. However, if it is absolutely necessary, leave a sling in place and abseil off this rather than placing the rope directly round the tree. Many

trees have been killed over the years by continual use, particularly by people abseiling at many climbing venues throughout the world. This is bad enough, but further damage will be caused to the crag when the root systems die, so use them only as a last resort. Choose a high anchor point, at least above waist-height. Having a low anchor not only increases the risk of the rope slipping off but increases strain on the anchor because of the outward directional pull on it. Finally a low anchor will make life difficult, and therefore dangerous, when you are going over the edge. Last but by no means least, choose the place to abseil with care, making sure that no one is climbing up and giving a good warning shout of "rope below" when throwing the ropes down just in case.

◁ Where there are several pieces of equipment to abseil (rappel) off, try and link all the anchors to ensure all are equally loaded and independently tied off.

▷ A well-placed nut will save the situation should the anchor fail. Note that the nut is not loaded – it is a back-up. If all has gone well, the last person to abseil (rappel) may risk removing it.

• GETTING IT WRONG

A very poor site has been chosen, especially for someone who is just learning. The abseiler will be unable to see if the ropes reach the bottom because of the extremely steep take-off point and low anchor. This will create difficulties as they go over the edge. They could turn upside down because of the direction of pull on the anchor. There have been a few cases where a hole has been punched in the karabiner gate, causing the system to fail. This is much more likely if an anchor point which is lower than the take-off point has been chosen, allowing the descender to flick over and pull across the gate.

△ *Choice of anchors for an abseil (rappel) is crucial for success. Here the anchors are too low.*

△ *A high anchor point makes life easy at the start of an abseil (rappel). The anchor is above the belay device and allows the abseiler to get the correct position before going over the edge.*

The popularity of abseiling as the normal means of descent from many crags is due to the dislike of slithering down muddy paths in expensive footwear that is totally unsuited for the purpose. Abseiling is an essential (and inherently dangerous) technique to be learnt. There are many shiny gadgets on the market which are designed to make life easier, but none are of the slightest use unless the anchor point is chosen with care and due regard for the consequences of the abseil. Once you have leant back and weighted the rope and anchor, there is no turning back. The anchor must not fail! When abseiling, all climbers trust the rope without question, but remember the rope is only as good as the anchor.

◁ *Never abseil (rappel) above a climber who may be leading a route. The last thing a leader wants is for someone to dislodge stones on to their head.*

Security

There are several ways in which you can make abseiling (rappelling) a safer activity. You can even abseil if you drop your belay device – using the Italian hitch!

THE ITALIAN HITCH

Although the Italian hitch is not ideal for abseiling it can be used in a situation where no other device is available, although in double ropes extensive twisting will occur. If the rope is used singly (that is, tied off at one end) the Italian hitch is much easier to use, although it still may twist alarmingly. It is essential to use a large pear-shaped (HMS) screwgate (locking) karabiner (not a twistlock type) to ensure the rope runs smoothly and to increase the heat dissipation. To create an Italian hitch, form two loops, right over left, right over left, fold the loops together and clip the two ropes into the karabiner. The use of a French prussik as a "back-up" will make it possible to untangle the ropes. In spite of the problems, this method can be used in any situation where the abseil device has been dropped or forgotten. If using this method, ensure that the Italian hitch is operating against the back bar of the karabiner and not anywhere near the gate.

USING A PRUSSIK

This is a length of 6 mm (¼ in) cord about 1.5 m (4½ ft) long. Tie the ends together with a double fisherman's knot to form a loop; the loop should run from the thumb to a point level with the elbow. This is wound at least four or five times round the ropes, taking care to include both ropes if double ropes are being used.

Keep the French prussik short and snug and do not use any other prussik knots in this situation as they are not easily released once they are loaded.

Consider also how each device will be effected if the prussik is too long. In some cases the prussik will simply be released and in others it may be dragged into the abseil device.

△ **1** *If you want to stop mid-descent (to retrieve some gear left on a route, for example), you can use the following method to free your hands.*

△ **2** *Take a length of rope around your leg for three or four turns. Make sure you keep hold of the controlling rope.*

△ **3** *Now carefully let go of the controlling rope. The wraps around your thigh should stop your descent. Your hands are now free.*

Either way it could be disastrous and best not to find out, so keep those prussiks short and snug. There are of course some devices which are designed to lock automatically so a French prussik may be unnecessary, unless of course a malfunction (grit, dirt or inexperience) causes a problem in any way. In that case you'll look foolish if you haven't used one. An alternative way of providing safety back-up once the first person is down (or there is a responsible person already at the bottom) is to get them to pull gently on the bottom end of the rope. This should have the effect of locking off the abseil device and will not only give confidence to beginners but could save a good deal of time if multiple abseils are involved.

● SECURITY FROM BELOW

Today this is the standard way of helping beginners to gain confidence when learning to abseil (rappel). Good communication is important for both parties. Surprisingly little tension is required on the rope and with a little practice the person at the bottom can lower the abseiler (rappeller) a few centimetres (inches) and then lock off again. The same technique can also be used in a situation where a series of abseils is needed to get off a major climb. The first climber should go down protecting themselves with a French prussik and the second climber protected by the first in exactly the same way. This will speed the whole process up for both parties. If the abseil is an emergency one where the Italian hitch is used, the technique will still work although in some cases there will be a little less friction on the rope so more tension will be needed. The amount of tension needed will depend on the amount of friction, and this will depend upon several factors: the thickness of the ropes, whether you are using single or double ropes, the type of belay device, the weight of the abseiler, and so on.

△ **1** *An alternative method of providing security for the abseiler (rappeller): the first abseiler down simply holds the abseil rope lightly.*

△ **2** *Should they need to stop the next abseiler from descending any further, they simply pull on the rope, applying tension to the system. This will lock the abseil device.*

4

INTO THE HILLS

Days out on the crags are not always sunny and warm affairs – life would be much less interesting if we didn't get a good soaking from time to time. We have already looked at the basic requirements for rock climbing, which are enough to get you going. By now, though, you'll be hooked and it's time to delve a little deeper into the wallet for that extra equipment you'll need to adventure farther afield in greater safety – but we'll not get too carried away. It is important to think carefully about your equipment in terms of staying warm and dry in the mountains. Any fool can be uncomfortable, after all! It takes careful thought and planning to be able to cope with whatever nature throws at you.

Opposite: *The full outdoor experience – wilderness, solitude and a sense of self-reliance. Rock climbing in this environment requires more skill and judgement than that required on a roadside crag or indoor climbing wall.*

Further equipment

▽ *There are a number of waterproof and breathable fabrics available. All do their job efficiently.*

If you plan to venture farther than your local climbing wall or roadside crag, then careful consideration must be given to your clothing. Even in summer, wind and wet can create life-threatening conditions, if you are not equipped to meet them. The contents of your rucksack will make all the difference.

SHELL CLOTHING

The most important addition to the wardrobe is a waterproof suit of some kind. For the mountains we need something a good deal more serious. This outer layer is more often referred to as shell clothing (not to be confused with shell-suits). Fabrics and styles are varied and most climbers will opt for a waterproof and breathable fabric. The most famous of these is probably Gore-Tex™ but there are others of a similar ilk that will perform in exactly the same way. The most significant advantage this type of fabric has to offer is its ability to prevent moisture penetration from the outside but to allow moisture out from the inside, leaving the wearer warm and dry.

DESIGN FEATURES

When choosing a jacket try as many different styles on as you can. The two important aspects to consider are the overall fit and the hood. Fit is tested easily by doing up the front opening of the garment and lifting your hands above your head and stretching them out in front of you. A well-fitting jacket should not ride up over the hips nor should it stretch tightly across the back. The hood must be spacious, easy to close and, most important, should turn with the head from side to side so that your vision is not restricted.

Pockets on a jacket are entirely dependent on personal preference. If you need a jacket to wear when you are climbing it is pointless having pockets at waist level or below because they will interfere with the harness. Chest pockets on a diagonal slash are probably the best. Some people like an integral map pocket inside the jacket at chest level, but unless the pockets are big enough to accommodate a map

◁ *Make sure the hood of your chosen jacket will fit over the top of a helmet.*

inside a case they are useless.

TROUSERS

Shell pants are a must for wilder climates. Considerable heat is lost through the thigh muscles, so they should be protected. Here again, fit is very important. The most obvious aspect is that you should be able to sit in a squatting position without the pants becoming too tight and restrictive. Some people prefer a bib-and-brace type pant, while others opt for a more traditional trouser style. The bib or high-waist pant does help to keep the midriff warm, particularly in windy, snowy conditions.

▷ *All closures, particularly cuffs, should be effective and easy to use.*

◁ *Waterproof legwear is as important as a jacket, though many climbers overlook this fact.*

● HOW BREATHABLE FABRICS FUNCTION

wind

perspiration

rain

face fabric

membrane

inner lining

base layer

◁ *Waterproof and breathable fabrics are expensive but perform well in wet, windy weather. The special membrane contains millions of micro-pores that allow sweat to pass through, but prevent larger raindrops from entering.*

The layer system

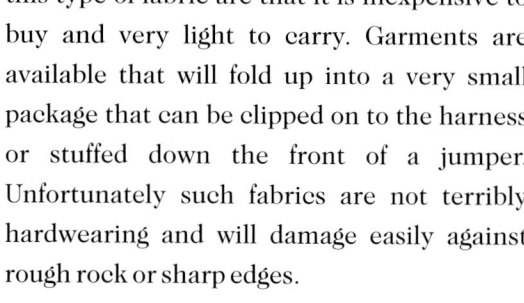

The shell clothing that you choose forms the outer part of the layering system. This begins with a warm comfortable layer next to the skin followed by other thicker and warmer layers on top. The number of layers is entirely dependent on the outside temperature. Regardless of the number of layers you wear, try to ensure that you do not parcel yourself up too tightly for this will only limit the range of movement that you are capable of. Fortunately, modern fabrics perform extremely well and even seemingly thin layers offer effective insulation.

WINDPROOF CLOTHING

Light showerproof and windproof clothing is also worth considering. The advantages with this type of fabric are that it is inexpensive to buy and very light to carry. Garments are available that will fold up into a very small package that can be clipped on to the harness or stuffed down the front of a jumper. Unfortunately such fabrics are not terribly hardwearing and will damage easily against rough rock or sharp edges.

GLOVES AND HATS

Gloves and hat are important additions to the safety gear you'll need to carry in the mountains. Here again, weight and a combination of functionality and good design is important. You may need to wear a hat with a helmet on top. Clearly, Granny's home-knitted hat is unsuitable for this purpose. Some manufacturers offer hats that are

◁ Make sure that the layers of clothing you choose do not restrict movement, and that by adding subsequent outer layers you combine insulation with wind and water repellency.

▷ A basic layering system might begin with thermals and then light fleece or hardwearing fabric on top. A lightweight shell top and leggings would complete the outfit.

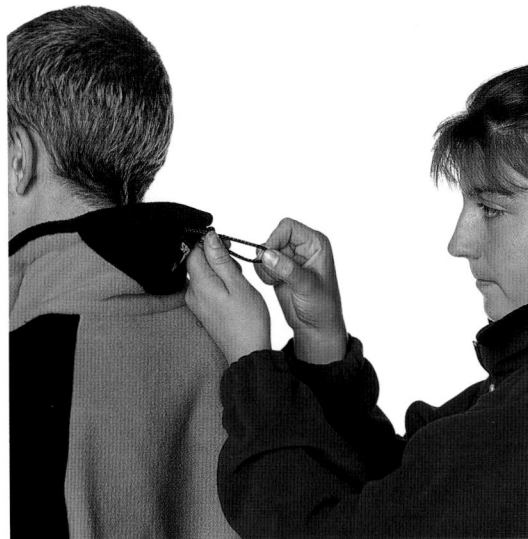

△ *The collar of this jacket features a neck warmer that can be adjusted to a snug fit, thus retaining valuable body heat.*

▷ *These jackets are reversible. On one side they have a windproof material, and on the other a warm fleece layer.*

close fitting and specifically designed to fit under a helmet while there are many others that will suffice. Style, colour and fashion are all influences over the choice of hat for personal use, though fleece is possibly the most practical fabric.

Gloves merit closer scrutiny. Light fleece gloves made from a fabric such as Wind-bloc™ or Windstopper™ are worth consideration. Unfortunately fleece is not terribly hardwearing, and for the occasions where you might actually want to climb with gloved hands you'll be better off having gloves with leather fingers. Though such products will be more expensive, the fact that they will last longer is a strong enough reason to sway your choice in that direction. For climbing you'll benefit from finger gloves rather than mittens. Handling gear with mittens is awkward, to say the least.

◁ *A light and effective pair of gloves made with leather palms for better grip and windproof and warm fleece.*

● FIRST AID KIT

Finally, but certainly not of least importance, is a first aid kit. Wherever you venture, be it 500 m (1600 ft) from the road or 50 km (30 miles) into the mountains, a first aid kit is essential. Having cobbled one together, it is the sort of thing that can remain in the bottom of your pack until it's required. A suitable pack need not be heavy or widely comprehensive – a few plasters, wound dressings and a triangular bandage are all that's needed. Make sure that the pack is kept tightly sealed in a waterproof bag so that nothing is likely to become sodden and ruined and periodically check the condition of the packages. It is also worth putting in a lightweight foil survival blanket and a whistle for dire emergencies.

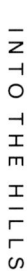

Footwear

I t is important to consider what you want your mountain footwear for – approaching a climb where it will be taken off and exchanged for rock shoes or wearing on an easy long route or scramble?

THE APPROACH SHOE

A simple approach walk to the crag might be undertaken in a pair of ordinary training shoes. In fact climbers have adopted this type of footwear for many years, and in response to this fact manufacturers now produce a range of footwear categorized as "approach shoes" or cross- functional footwear. There are considerable advantages in travelling to the crag in lightweight footwear, not simply because it is more comfortable. Many climbs finish high on a mountainside from which the descent might be a either a moderate walk or a difficult scramble. Clearly, rock shoes are impractical, uncomfortable and potentially lethal on such descents. A lightweight pair of shoes can be clipped on to the back of the harness where they will be barely noticed during the climb but greatly appreciated for the descent.

THE MOUNTAIN BOOT

There was a time, and not so long ago, that fully stiffened rock climbing boots were used quite widely. Whilst the demand for this type of boot has waned considerably, there are occasions where the benefits of a stiffer-soled boot might be advantageous. Examples of such situations include long techni- cally easy climbs or mountain- eering routes that might include the occasional

△ *Approach walks to the crags might be hot and sweaty affairs or you may feel the need to be warmer.*

◁ *Approach shoes.*

patch of snow or ice to cross. Despite the demise of the fully rigid rock climbing boot, there is still a wide range of boots available that will fulfil these requirements and in recent years one or two manufacturers have re-intro- duced the specialist stiffened rock boot.

IMPORTANT CRITERIA

The important criteria to consider after comfort are the rigidity and type of sole unit. Boots that are totally rigid are uncomfortable to walk in but excellent for climbing. On the other hand a boot with considerable flex will be comfy to walk in but horrendous for rock climbing. The compromise is one that you can stand on the very tiptoe of and that offers some support to the foot. When trying a boot on in the shop, stand on the toe on a small edge for a couple of minutes without moving. If the boot is sufficiently rigid, your foot will not tire or cramp up during this test. Boots in this cate- gory do not include plastic boots or any boot of double construction. They are usually full leather or soft Nubuck.

△ *Full-blown mountain wear for those days when you encounter a bit of everything.*

Rucksacks

A simple rucksack of rudimentary design is more than adequate for carrying gear for a short distance to the foot of a climb and back home again. However, if you intend to go farther afield, and particularly if you think you might need to carry a pack on your back while climbing, you are certain to need something much more sophisticated.

THE CLIMBING PACK

A pack that will be comfortable for climbing should conform to one or two basic design principles. Firstly it shouldn't be too large for your needs. Avoid the temptation to go for a larger pack in the belief that it will squash down to a smaller size if it isn't full. A pack with a capacity of around 30–40 litres (7–9 gallons) should be large enough for most needs on a daily basis – after all, you only need to carry a little food and water, a light shell and maybe a spare fleece.

The pack should have no internal frame other than a padded back. It should be quite narrow so as not to restrict movement of the arms from side to side and it should be fairly short so that head movement remains unrestricted, particularly when tilting the head backwards. A teardrop-shaped pack with zip closure at the top seems to be the preferred style of day pack for rock climbing. It is also useful to have a large strong loop at the top of the pack, which is used both as a handle and to clip the pack to the belay when it is not being carried.

▷ A frameless rucksack of between 30–40 litres (7–9 gallons) and a rope bag. In addition to rope, the rope bag can be used to carry any extra bits of gear, as necessary.

△ A good pack will barely be noticed on the back. Make sure that you are not over-burdened.

Climbing among mountains

Rock climbing amongst the mountains is the main reason for climbing for many people. Here, it is not necessarily the technical difficulty of the climb that is important (though many mountain routes are as extreme as they come) but the special atmosphere, the solitude, the self-reliance and the companionship of a few other souls.

ADVENTURE IN THE HILLS

A sweeping sun-touched arete, crisp mountain air, snow-clad hills all around, early morning and already five pitches up. Cragging in a mountain setting is hard to beat. Rock climbing grew out of the alpinism of the Victorian era and soon developed into an entity in its own right. Until the 1960s most climbers felt that rock climbing anywhere but in a mountain setting was a cop-out or a compromise to be made if the weather was bad or you could not get to the mountains because of work or some other diversion. Roadside crags, sun-drenched sea-cliffs and quarries were ok, but it

△ *Beinn Shuas in the Scottish Highlands, a long walk in, isolation and big rewards.*

▷ *The bolt – providing sanitized and safe climbing?*

◁ *A true mountain setting. Self-reliance and all your mountaineering skills will be needed here.*

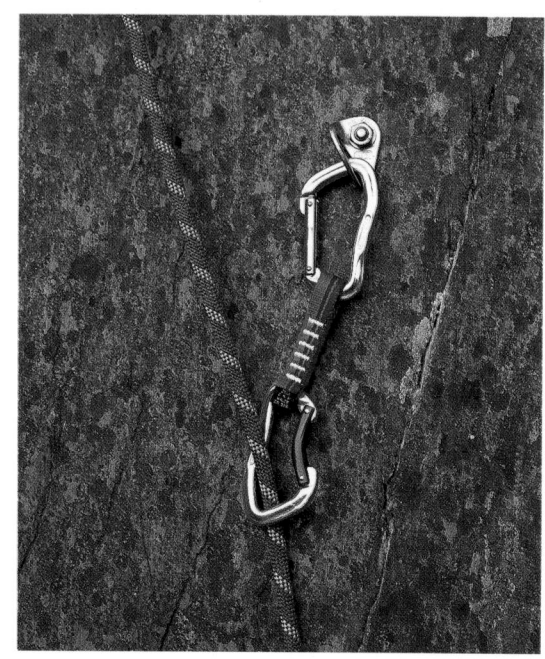

was the real thing they hankered after. The thought of hurling yourself from bolt to bolt or up and down a bit of artificial rock in a dust-filled shed was definitely beyond the comprehension of the hardy mountaineering types. The arrival of the "rock jock" was still some way off. The idea that rock climbing should be safe, warm and comfortable was beyond the grasp of climbers who had been through one, and in some cases two, world wars. Climbing was dominated by tough characters who enjoyed pitting their mental and physical wits against the mist-shrouded crags. Rain, snow, wind, falling rocks and darkness were all seen as challenges that added to the heroics and the mystique of this eccentric pastime.

SANITIZED CLIMBING?

At some stage climbers realized that it was possible to climb on solid rock using pre-placed equipment that was guaranteed to keep you safe, but most were too embarrassed to let on. It was not until sometime in the early 1980s that some of the old die-hards faltered under the influence of the "new wave" and admitted that climbing didn't have to be cold, wet, miserable and dangerous. It all made so much sense, but climbing had changed forever. It had been sanitized and made to fit in with the changing ideas of the latter part of the twentieth century.

ADVENTURE CLIMBING

What some of today's climbers now want is adrenalin rushes without the risk. Sadly, throughout the mountains of the world climbers are bringing the mountains down to them rather than rising up to meet them. Happily though, adventure climbing still exists and its advocates guard it jealously. The challenge of adventure climbing on big mountain crags or committing sea-cliffs utilizes every physical and psychological skill a climber can cobble together, and as a result provides a level of retrospective satisfaction that can make your toes wriggle with joy for months afterwards. The technical skill may be less (though not always) but the overall experience far greater than that found on a sport climb.

◁ A bolted sport climb will often be desperately hard but relatively safe due to the nature of the protection used.

▽ The climbing may be easier, but the agenda is bigger. Placing your own protection requires planning, strength and mental coolness.

Finding your crag

Big, serious crags do not give of their pleasures easily and can give you a humbling cuff under the ear with the greatest of ease! To sample the pleasures and to avoid the chastisement requires plenty of research, foresight and a combination of boldness and commitment that must be learnt but cannot really be taught.

MAPS AND GUIDEBOOKS

Much of the fun associated with adventure climbing lies in the anticipation and dreaming, which is bolstered by endless reading of guidebooks and climbing literature prior to setting off for the crag. Most writers hype up the accounts of climbs, so your job is to filter out the important information from the

△ *Time spent ensuring that you are on the right route and your starting point is correct is time well spent. Study the guidebook well.*

◁ *Finding your crag and finding the start of your route are often the biggest challenges in the mountains.*

▷ *Navigating accurately to your chosen mountain crag can be complex and confusing even with good weather and visibility.*

embellishment. Having settled on your crag and route, the next thing to wrestle with are the mysteries of the map. This will ensure you have a good picture of how best to get to and from the crag and what type of terrain you can expect to encounter. Interpreting maps and spotting the problems before you lurch off is an important skill. Climbers are notorious for being poor navigators but it doesn't have to be like this.

WEATHER – FRIEND AND FOE OF THE CLIMBER

On a committing crag you should always be armed with as much knowledge and information as possible, the more up-to-date the better. Rain can turn the delightful finishing groove into an unclimbable grade III rapid, an electrical storm can fry you on the spot, and nil visibility can turn the gentle descent from the crag into an epic return to the wrong valley or a night out clad only in your rock shoes and T-shirt. Conversely, you can easily spoil a perfect day by running off with your tail between your legs in the early morning cloud and drizzle, only to discover it is an inversion which burns off with the arrival of the sun to give a perfect anti-cyclonic day.

ESCAPING

If you are about to buy a one-way ticket to hell, it is best if you know this and are prepared for the consequences. Having a workable escape plan tucked up your sleeve to deal with exhaustion, changing terrain, time and weather is essential on a big crag. As you become more experienced, this can almost become sub-conscious; but in your early sorties it needs to be a reasonably formal exercise. Be aware that on many big routes you cannot abseil (rappel) off and your escape plan can only be to keep climbing to the top of the route.

▷ *Success is at hand, but what about getting back to the safety of the ground and rucksack?*

Adventure climbing

△ Loose rock, poor gear and no climbing down – total commitment!

▷ Can you get a hand off to get the gear in? The jugs usually appear when the protection is clipped.

It is the potential danger and total commitment of adventure climbing that attracts some and drives others into hiding. Which of these camps you fall into is very dependent on whether you are a risk-taker and thrive on retrospective enjoyment.

RISK ASSESSMENT

There is a big difference between making a bold dash for the glinting bolt and guaranteed safety, with the potential of retreat, and setting off up the rock ahead not knowing whether any protection exists, or if it does, whether any of your diminishing rack will fit. The prospect of the perfect crack viewed from below turning out to be blind and flared, and the jug reducing to a sloper, awaits the adventure climber. Staying under control both physically and mentally in this setting is the key to successful ascents. Physical strength is

△ Under control, with time to think and to get the protection right.

obviously a great attribute in a situation like this, but counts for little if it is not bolstered by clear foresight and a cool mind. You will notice that the placement of a good runner suddenly makes the foot holds bigger and allows you to find the obvious jug around the corner — the whole thing suddenly becomes two grades easier. The trick is to create the same effect next time when the runner isn't there!

MOTIVATION

In climbing we often hear about people being "naturals". This is a nice idea, but most successful climbers emerge as a result of experience punctuated by failure, fright and constant learning. Anyone can develop the skills if they are determined enough. If there is no motivation however, forget it. To succeed as a climber on committing crags you need to be a strange combination, selfish on one hand and a team worker on the other. The skill is to disguise the selfishness enough to avoid alienating your partner – not an easy task. It is hard to define the complex feelings that may course through your mind and body as you wind up to take on a big route. The most interesting feeling is the overpowering sense of inevitability: this climb is definitely going to happen. This should be countered by a healthy dollop of nervousness and a touch of self-doubt to balance the whole affair. Once you have set off up the rock, a sense of determination must take over. At this point the strangest things start to happen, depending on the day. They could range from one extreme to another – feeling as though you have never climbed before through to feeling as though you are on the easiest climb of your life.

SUCCESS AND RETREAT

It is important to respond to how you feel, but on a big climb you need to be able to push through the bad patches in the hope that a good one is on the way. Sometimes this just doesn't happen, so you have to either rely on your trusty partner or pack it in and go home. Backing off is an important skill for the adventure climber to develop. In Victorian times, armed with ropes that broke and no technical gear, the advice to the leader was to never climb anything that could not be reversed. Today we are blessed with equipment that allows us to abandon this approach, but we still need to be sure that the reading of the route and our forward planning allows us to bail out if need be or face the consequences. The real skill is in avoiding going through the point of no return without spotting it. There is a delicate and frustrating balance between recklessly hurling yourself at a problem and confidently and boldly climbing something right on the edge of your ability. If we always got it right however, there would no adventure in adventure climbing.

▷ *Desperate moves and sustained climbing wait for you on mountain crags as well as on sport routes and roadside crags.*

▽ *Big, bold and desperate. Isolation as well as beauty in Ireland's Mountains of Mourne. The climb is Divided Years, possibly the hardest traditional mountain route in the world.*

Sea-cliff climbing

The crashing sea adds a very special and satisfying dimension to climbing. It provides a dynamic aspect to what is often a very static pastime. Sea cliffs are serious places. They are often big, under-cut, tidal and intimidating. Your option often is to climb or swim, unless you are prepared to face the embarrassment of the arrival of the lifeboat.

A SPECIAL PLACE WITH SPECIAL PROBLEMS

Never underestimate the sheer power and unpredictability of the sea. The fact that the tide tables are called tidal predictions should provide a good warning. Swell and wave patterns are often influenced by factors thousands of miles away, so the perfect weather and calm sea as you approach your route can be misleading. Tides rush in and take little account of the fact that you are finding the crux unclimbable. As you abseil (rappel) off, you may find that the sun-drenched beach you set off from is now deep ocean. Sea cliffs are not only the home of climbers; most have populations of sea birds in residence during the breeding season. Climbing through their nests can be very disturbing for the birds, but the birds can be very disturbing to you as well. Their defensive skills range from knocking you off your minute holds by dive bombing, through to regurgitating evil-smelling semi-digested fish all over your colourful climbing clothes. The breeding season usually lasts for about six months of the year, leaving plenty of time for you to climb in peace.

VARIABLE ROCK

The rock on sea cliffs varies dramatically from the wave-cleansed lower sections, a joy to behold, to overhanging, shattered blocks covered in lichen and interspersed with grass and mud, guarding your escape at the top. Belays can often be delightfully problematical or non-existent. All this adds to the excitement and satisfaction when you eventually complete your ascent.

◁ *Hard climbing in a very serious setting.*
A long abseil (rappel) to the start of the route and only one way out.

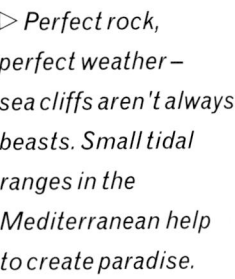

△ *Abseiling (rappelling) down sea cliffs can lead to a difficult escape. It pays to leave a rope in place just in case.*

▷ *Perfect rock, perfect weather – sea cliffs aren't always beasts. Small tidal ranges in the Mediterranean help to create paradise.*

▽ *A classic sea cliff scene. Not far left to go, but has the climber made other plans for escape should he not be able to make it to the top?*

● ESCAPING FROM TROUBLE

If you have to abseil (rappel) down a sea cliff to the start of your intended route, consider carefully the consequences of not being able to finish your climb. Is there an easier route by which you could escape? Is your partner a better climber and able to take over? Is there an easy scramble out of danger? What effect will the tide have on your plan? Is there a problem leaving your belayer on a low stance if you take longer to lead the first pitch? Might they get wet feet – or worse?

Always consider leaving an abseil rope in place, so that you can, as a last resort, prussik back up the cliff.

A question of access

The restriction of access to crags will probably be the biggest threat to climbing in the twenty-first century. Climbers can be a selfish and self-righteous lot, who historically have cared little for who owned the mountains and crags so long as they could climb on them. This attitude may have to change if access is to remain open.

WHO OWNS THE LAND?

It should be remembered that all land is owned by someone and, with the massive increase in climbing and other outdoor sports, we can no longer expect the tolerance of the owners. It is your responsibility as a climber to know whether you are permitted to climb on a particular crag and to be aware of any special requirements associated with access. These special agreements range from those designed to preserve bird and plant life to military restrictions and safety considerations to protect tourists. Climbers are often their own worst enemies. Through their ill-considered behaviour, some crags have been closed to climbing after years of free access. This type of occurrence should be a warning to us all that we must consider our behaviour carefully and respect the rights and wishes of the owners of our play areas.

Climbers have no special rights beyond those of any other citizen, although to read some of our climbing magazines you may get a very different impression. If you climb in many different countries you would do well to familiarize yourself with any aspects of criminal or civil law that may affect you. In keeping with the anarchic facade we like to cultivate, most climbers are pleasantly ignorant of their legal responsibilities. This is a delightfully relaxing approach until something goes wrong.

CONSERVATION – THE BALANCE

Climbers want clean rock and clean cracks to climb and nice wide, dry paths leading to the crags. They want to walk along the tops of the crags and mill about the bottom to watch their friends. They want their dogs to watch them climb and their dog is never the one that chases

◁ *Climbing bans range from the flippant to the serious. Know your rights, but more importantly know your responsibilities.*

sheep. They want handy trees to belay on and to abseil (rappel) off. They want to climb all year round and they want to drive to and park as near to the crag as possible. They also want to conserve the pristine wilderness. Unfortunately, the balance does not hang level. All our "normal" behaviour has a dramatic effect on the country we climb on. It kills the ground cover and the trees, it chases off the birds and it jams the roads and clutters the verges. Small numbers of climbers do little harm; large numbers cause huge amounts of damage. It is always the other people who cause the damage and make up the crowds. This may sound cynical but it is very hard to pretend that climbing is good for the wilderness. We can't stop the damage but we can do a lot to minimize it through sensible, considered behaviour. The main thing to remember is that crowds are made up of individuals and your individual behaviour will contribute dramatically to a positive or negative outcome. So we must all try to bear in mind our own impact on the very environment we love to operate in.

◁ *Climbing can never be good for the wilderness. Dead trees caused by compacted earth and ring barking from abseil (rappel) ropes are commonly seen on crags.*

▽ *Footpath erosion is inevitable as the outdoors become more crowded. Repairs cost a fortune. Are we prepared to pay?*

Emergency procedures

The mountains are neither for nor against a climbing team, so they are not out to get you. From time to time however, climbers' interaction with the mountain can lead to an accident or injury. This can be caused by you hitting the mountain, by some of the mountain hitting you, or by the weather turning against you. If this happens, you can load the odds in your favour by knowing how to deal with an incident and how to preserve life.

First Aid

In the event of an accident, stop, think – think again. Then act decisively. This is more easily said than done. A lot will depend on your own experience with first aid. It is strongly recommended that you attend one of the many first aid courses to acquaint yourself with some of the basic knowledge for dealing with an accident victim.

△ Carefree and fun but let's hope your friends can cope if the holds run out.

◁ A good knowledge of how to deal with emergencies is vital in wild, isolated country.

● THE FIRST PRINCIPLES AND AIMS OF FIRST AID

① Your own safety is paramount – you are not only useless if you become a victim as well, you will also complicate the situation and put everyone at greater risk.

② Leave the patient no worse off than when you began. Only move an injured person if it is absolutely essential. Often the best first aid is to do nothing.

③ Reassure the patient. This will contribute to a feeling of well-being and will help fight medical shock.

④ Keep the patient warm. A major job in a mountain setting.

The aims of first aid:
• preserve life
• prevent deterioration
• promote recovery

You should arrange for help to be mobilized, and continue with the aims of first aid until the arrival of medical aid, which will most commonly be in the form of the Mountain Rescue team.

● VITAL SIGNS

Before you can tell whether someone is injured or ill, you must know the vital signs of a normal, healthy adult.

• Breathing – 10 to 15 breaths per minute. This will obviously be increased if they have just run up a hill or fallen off the crux of a climb.

• Pulse – 60 to 80 beats per minute. Again, this may be much higher if they have been through a traumatic experience or heavy exertion.

• Level of consciousness:
  Alert – capable of initiating a coherent conversation
  Vocal – may speak if spoken to, but incoherently

Responsive – responding to pain
Unresponsive – not responding to pain

The important thing for the first aider is to monitor whether the patient is remaining stable or becoming more or less conscious. Do this by recording breathing and pulse rate and level of response, every 10 minutes.

Colour – pink and oxygenated. The inside of the lips is the best place to check this, as it avoids confusion due to outside factors and difference in skin colour.

Temperature – core temperature of 37.5°C (98.6°F). Difficult to determine in the mountains with no equipment.

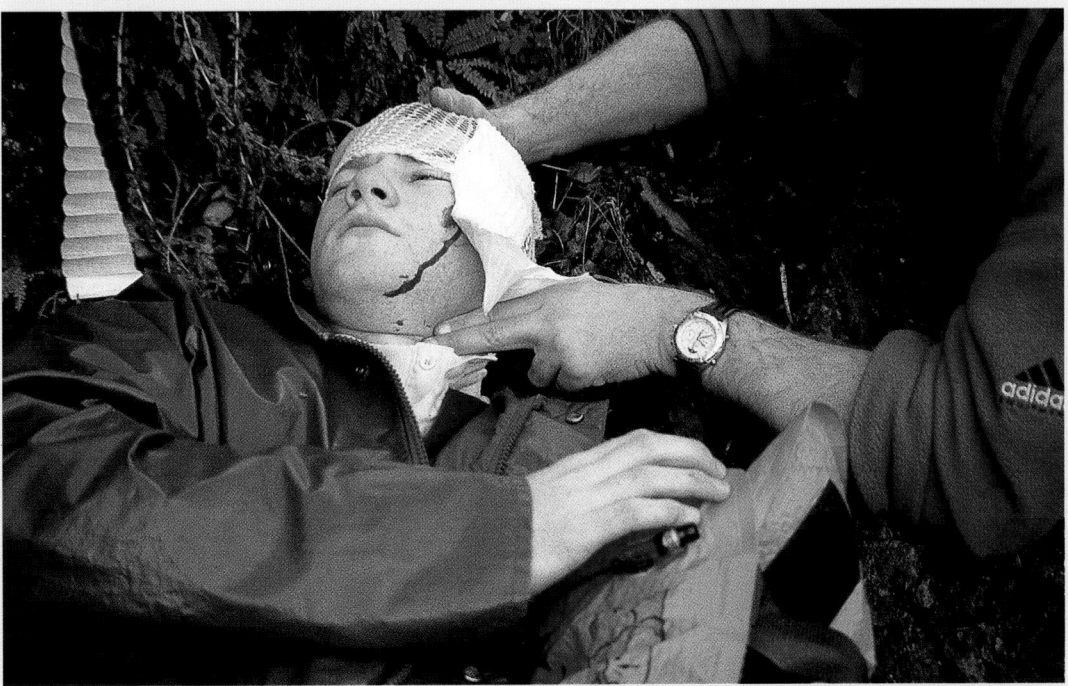

◁ *Monitoring an injured person's vital signs is one of the main responsibilities of the first aider once you have stabilized the situation.*

Dealing with an accident

An accident in a crag setting will unnerve you, so you must be sure to assess the situation accurately before acting. Establish whether the victim is conscious by introducing yourself and if necessary by gently squeezing the shoulders. Then carry out the A B C of survival:

A – AIRWAY. Check they have an airway that is open; if not open it. If someone is speaking or screaming their airway is open.

B – BREATHING. Check by looking, feeling and listening.

C – CIRCULATION. Do they have a pulse? Check the neck pulse for 15 seconds. Check for severe bleeding.

UNCONSCIOUSNESS

A person is unconscious if they cannot instigate a coherent conversation. One in four unconscious persons will die if they are left lying on their backs. They must be placed in the recovery (safe airway) position and monitored for A B C.

△ Dealing with bleeding – use direct pressure, elevation and then good padding and bandaging.

SHOCK

Medical shock is the reaction of the body to insufficient oxygen reaching the vital organs due to a drop in the effective circulating blood volume. The signs of shock are:

- a rapid weak pulse
- rapid breathing
- cold, pale, clammy skin and a feeling of anxiety

You are dealing with a life-threatening condition. Treat the injuries. Reassure the casualty. Raise the legs and keep the patient warm. Keep reassuring the casualty throughout this procedure. The psychological benefits of this are immeasurable.

△ Head low, legs elevated, then warmth and reassurance all help a person suffering from medical shock.

◁ *To help stop bleeding, raise the injured limb. This will reduce the flow of blood to the wound.*

▷ *Bandage the wound, having put a pad on to the wound itself. Do not overtighten, or this will cut off the blood supply to the limb.*

SEVERE BLEEDING

Severe bleeding is controlled by direct pressure to the wound site, elevation of the wound above the heart, if possible, and then padding and firm bandaging. If the initial bandaging does not stop the bleeding, leave it in place and put further bandaging on top.

HYPOTHERMIA

The human body reacts badly if the core temperature (that of the vital organs) drops below 37.5°C (98.6°F). A 2°C (3.5°F) drop is a medical emergency, a 5°C (9°F) drop can kill. We lose heat in the mountains through convection, conduction, radiation and evaporation.

COMBATING THE ELEMENTS

WIND, WET and COLD together are the worst combination, often with a relatively high air temperature. Prevention is far more effective than having to treat someone in a mountain setting. The signs of hypothermia mirror drunkenness: stumbling, confusion, erratic behaviour and slurred speech. Below 32°C (90°F) unconsciousness will occur. Often the best you can achieve in a mountain setting is to prevent further cooling. Any re-warming undertaken must be *slow* and *gentle*. The availability of a nylon emergency shelter will dramatically improve the chances of saving a

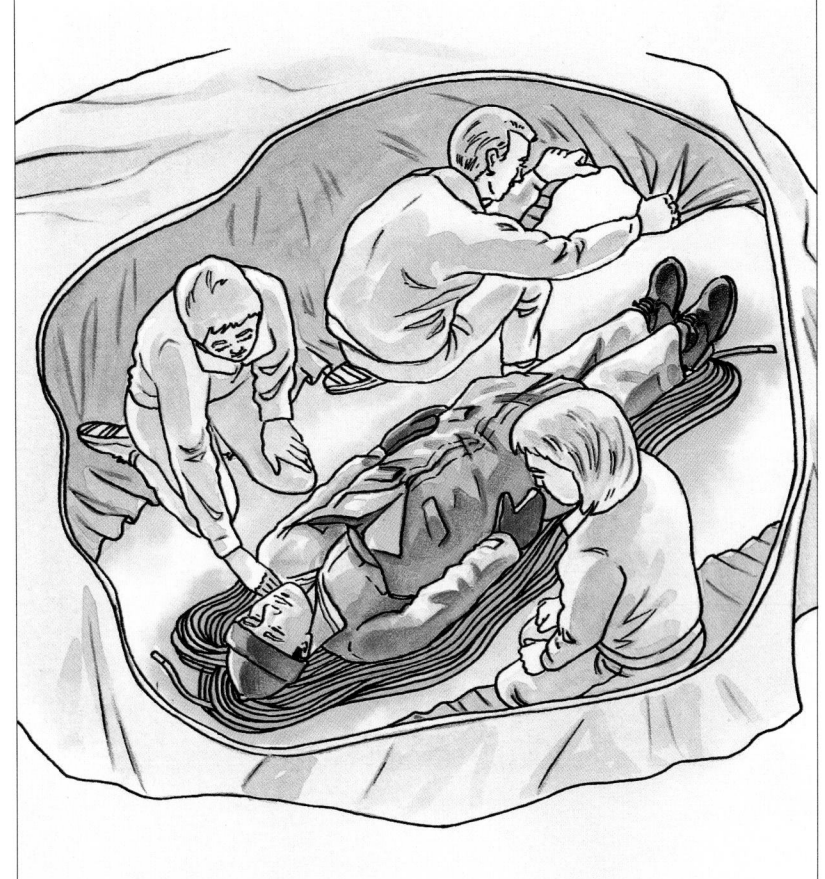

victim of hypothermia by providing instant shelter as well as keeping a party in a contained setting that contributes greatly to communication and morale. Several people inside one of these shelters will raise the temperature considerably.

△ *Hat and gloves, good insulation from the cold ground and a group shelter will keep an injured person warm.*

Maintaining life

The most important thing to attempt to do is stabilize the situation. This may be done by arranging shelter and insulation for the casualty. It is very important to give reassurance and warmth. You should encourage other members of the party to help you with this. The morale of the victim can be crucial. You should also keep a constant monitoring of vital signs, such as heart rate, breathing, skin colour, consciousness and alertness, and response. Should their condition start to deteriorate, shown up in one or more of these vital signs, immediate appropri-

ate first aid action should be taken. This appropriate treatment will ensure a victim's best chance of survival.

HELICOPTERS

In many parts of the world, mountain rescues are primarily carried out by helicopter. In all cases the most important thing to do if a helicopter arrives on the scene is to make yourself visible, secure all loose or light equipment, and do nothing unless specifically directed by the pilot or crew. Never approach an aircraft on the ground unless a clear sign has been given

▽ *Salvation from the air. When a helicopter arrives, make yourself visible, stay still and wait until you receive clear directions about what to do.*

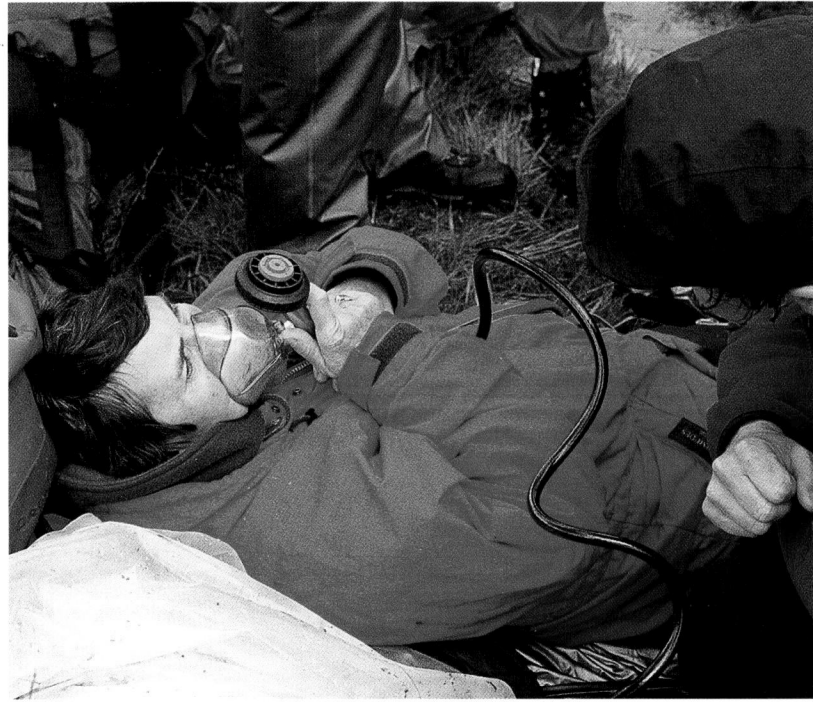

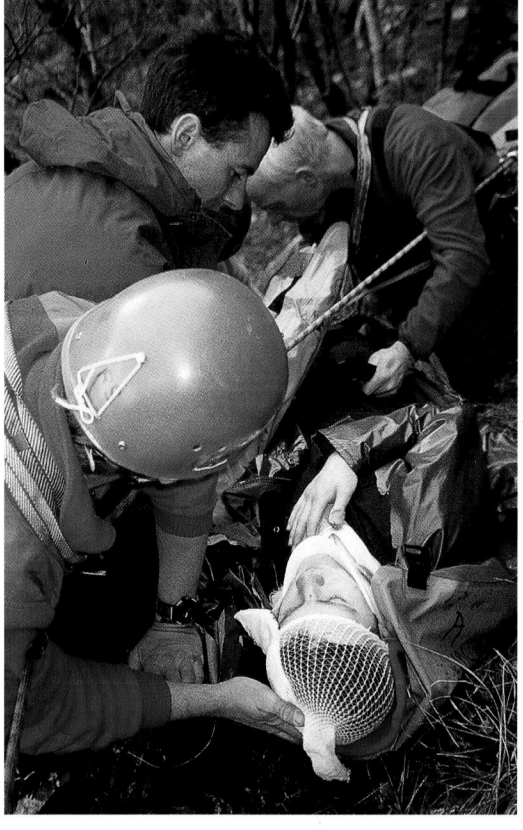

△▷ *With the arrival of experienced medical help, you will be asked to pass on all the information you have about the accident and the casualty's immediate and present condition.*

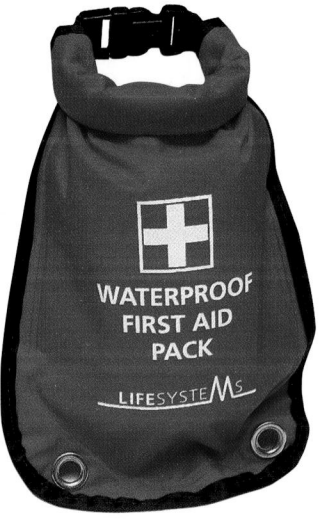

△ *A small but well-planned first-aid kit and some basic skills are all that is needed to save lives.*

to do so, then approach only in sight of the pilot and always from the front and downhill side of the aircraft.

EMERGENCY EQUIPMENT

When climbing on isolated mountain and sea cliffs you should always carry or at least leave at the bottom of the route an emergency shelter, first aid equipment suitable for controlling severe bleeding, warm clothes and head torches. This will ensure you are capable of stabilizing the situation in the event of an accident and of going for help in darkness, if this is the best course of action. Do you go for help or stay with the victim? The big dilemma. Textbook solutions are rarely of any help in making the right decision. The choice hinges around whether anyone knows where you are and if they are expecting you back at a particular time. If they are then the choice is easy; if not you must do a mental "profit and loss"

account before making your decision. Start with the fact that if the victim is unconscious, then the justification for leaving them alone must be overwhelming. Finally, you are the only one who can decide, so disregard what judgements might be made by others after the event and keep a clear mind.

▽ *A group shelter. These are light and cheap, and make all the difference in terms of warmth, shelter and morale when things go wrong.*

First principles

Everyone navigates continuously and at a very sophisticated level, far more complex and sophisticated than mountain navigation. We are not taught to navigate around our homes, workplaces, or our cities; we learn it instinctively. Drop us into the mountains however, and many of us panic and promptly abandon all the skills we have used for years. Navigation is mainly science with a touch of flair and art in the closing stages. To navigate successfully you need to know and monitor the following.

▽ Navigating along ridges is easy when the visibility is good. In poor conditions it is very easy to end up on the wrong spur.

YOUR DIRECTION OF TRAVEL

This is determined by following a line feature, such as a valley or a ridge for example, by using a distant object such as a peak as a goal, or by creating an imaginary line feature by following a compass bearing (a compass bearing is an angle made up of a line between two points and a line to the North Pole). The good old Boy Scout idea of using the sun should be treated with caution. You are unlikely to make it to the sun and it moves all the time! Clouds may also blot it out at a crucial moment.

● TAKING A COMPASS BEARING

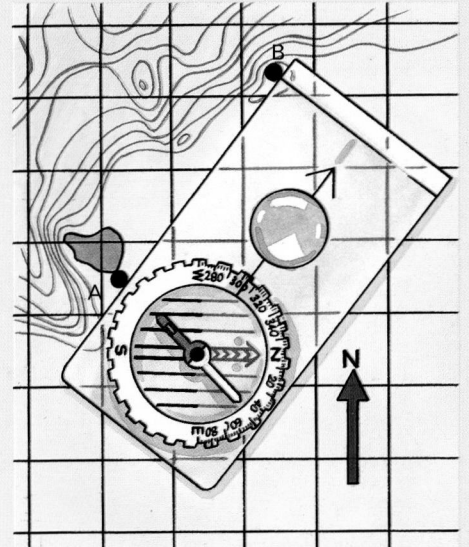

△ To get a bearing on the ground, simply point your direction of travel arrow on the compass at the feature you want to walk to. Then turn the compass housing until the compass needle lines up with the North sign. You will now have a bearing that you can read from the numbers around the outside of the compass housing. You will also have an imaginary line along which you can travel. Should the mist come down, you will still have a route to your goal. (See pages 184–7.)

● GETTING IT WRONG

You may well think that you know where you are when visibility is good, or you may not be worried about being too precise. This is fine – as long as the weather remains so also. But don't forget in your desire to get to your mountain crag that weather is fickle. It changes quickly. Do not get caught out if the mist does come down. If you notice the weather deteriorating, establish precisely where you are so that you can use the map and compass to navigate from the point when the mist really does set in.

△ Cloud forms very quickly in the mountains and can turn a simple journey into a complex navigational problem. Here a compass is not much use as the rocks contain spectacular concentrations of magnetic iron.

● MAKING THE LANDSCAPE FIT

Unless you have accidentally fallen out of the back of an aircraft at night, you will know where you are starting from and hopefully where you are going. However, a common mistake among mountaineers is that of making the landscape fit the conception of where they think they are on the map. For example, they may well be standing by a bridge over a stream in a deep valley, which fits with the map, but are prepared to overlook the fact that the stream is running the wrong way. This clue should tell them that it is the wrong bridge and stream! Neither map nor compass get things wrong (mostly, at least!). The trap of making what you see around you fit with where you think you are is convenient but may well be wrong. You must be rigorous with your navigation, especially when lost. Do not let clues as to your real whereabouts go unnoticed.

◁ Poring over the map won't help if you are determined to make the wrong landscape fit.

Time and distance

There are several principal methods of keeping track of distance travelled in the mountains. If you are working with reliable maps in country with obvious features then you can read the map and tick off the features as you pass them. This will enable you to know where you are all the time without necessarily knowing how far you have travelled. If you spend lots of time in the hills, you can build up a good picture of how far you travel over various terrain. Keep a mental track of distance during the day, filing the information in your head so you can recall it later in the day should it become necessary.

TIMING – NAISMITH'S RULE

To give you somewhere to start, there was a Scottish walking machine named Naismith who worked out he could pound through the hills at 5 km (3 miles) per hour plus 30 minutes for every 300 m (1000 ft) of ascent. Your job is to work out your own figures. If you have plenty of money, you can buy a reliable altimeter and when used correctly this can turn every contour line into a "tick off" point. All will be revealed later.

PACING

Another skill which is useful over short distances in poor visibility or darkness is pacing. You need to determine how many double paces (that is how many times one leg or the other touches the ground) you do in 100 m (330 ft). Do this over different types of terrain – a flat easy path, gentle incline, steep hill, rough broken ground and steeply down

▽ *A perfect mountain scene, but it can all change very quickly. Keep track of where you are even in good visibility.*

△ *Wild conditions with zero visibility and snow can occur in the mountains at any time of the year. Being ready for it is the key.*

△ *When things fall apart, change gear and accept that the journey home needs care and discipline. The more meticulous you are, the quicker you will reach safety.*

hill. Try to memorize your double paces for each of these, having tested them lots of times until you trust the figures and your ability to judge the terrain implicity. You can then count as you walk to measure the distance you have travelled. You will need to concentrate hard. This technique is not ideal if you have a mind that wanders!

THE PSYCHOLOGY

People fail to navigate accurately or get lost for two reasons, laziness or panic. Concentration, discipline and being meticulous overcome the first, and learning to be self-confident and developing the art of justified reassurance solve the second. Navigating in poor conditions is a lonely job if you are on your own with no one to bounce ideas off, or if you are the only member of a party who knows what to do. It is particularly testing if you are in a party surrounded by "doubting Thomases". An analytical and logical approach works wonders in helping you cope.

one double pace

shorter pace

one double pace

PACING

◁ **1** *Make sure you know how many double paces you take to every 100 m (330 ft) of travel. This way, you can accurately determine your location over short distances if visibility is very poor.*

◁ **2** *Bear in mind that your paces will be shorter going steeply up (and down) a hill. Therefore you will use more double paces for every 100 m (330 ft) covered.*

The map

Wye Valley
& Forest of Dean
KOMPASS
Gower

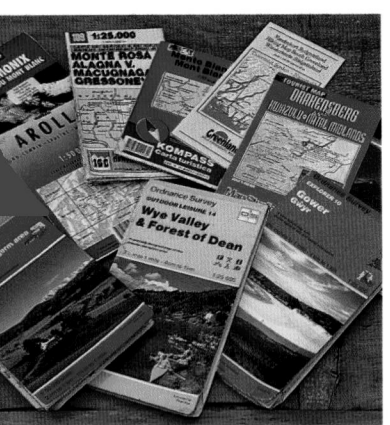

△ *Maps vary the world over but have a reassuring similarity in most cases. Take care to become familiar with the map before you need it in difficult conditions.*

Most navigation hinges around a map, which may range from a rough sketch map in a rock climbing guidebook through to a near-perfect national map series epitomized by the Swiss Carte Nationale or the British Ordnance Survey. You should familiarize yourself with all aspects of the maps that cover the areas in which you plan to climb. This will include magnetic variation (see page 187), the legend, contour intervals and scale.

A PICTURE OF THE LANDSCAPE

A map is a picture of the land. The good ones are brought alive by contour lines and clear, easily understood symbols. Most maps point roughly towards the North Pole; the only reason for this is that the early cartographers lived in the Northern Hemisphere. There is no up and down in space. It is important to grasp a few vital pieces of information from a map you are not familiar with before you start navigating.

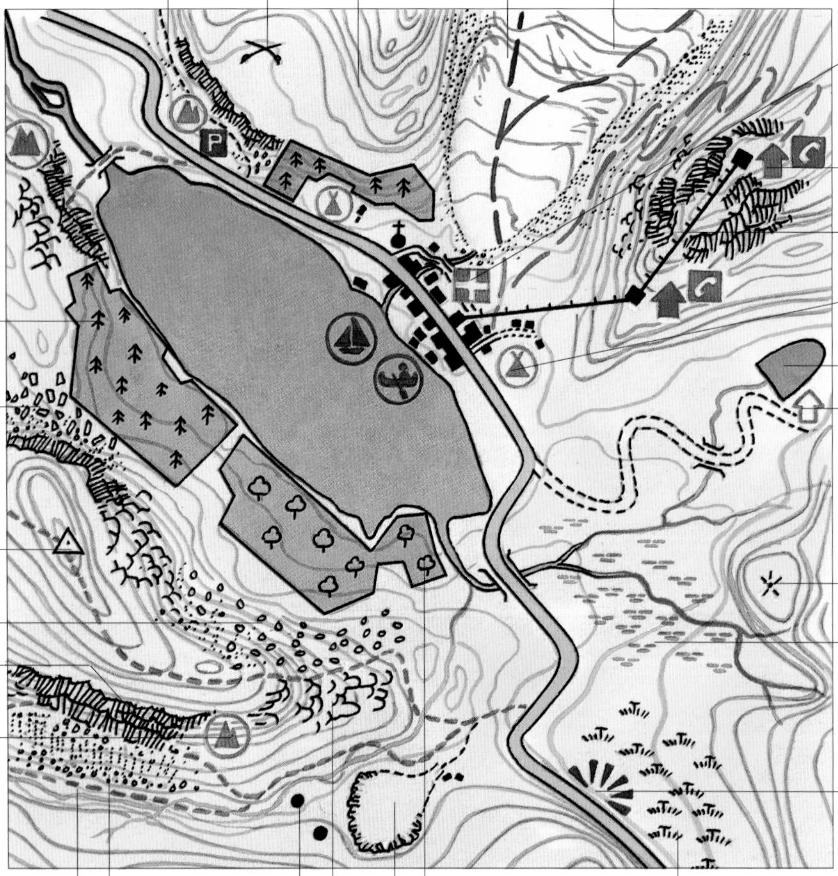
permissible footpath
site of battle
contour lines
ski route
glacier
first aid post
refuge-hut with keeper
téléphérique
camp site
dam
refuge-hut
cairn
marsh, reeds
viewpoint
coniferous trees
loose rock
triangulation pillars
boulders
cliff
climbing facilities
scree
mine shaft
outcrop
footpath
quarry
deciduous trees
rough grassland, bracken

SCALE

The first is the scale. This varies dramatically but the typical scale for mountain use is 1:50,000. This means that one unit of measurement on the map equals 50,000 of them on the ground. In practical terms, if using a metric scale, 2 cm on the map equals 1 km on the ground. The important thing is to be sure you know the scale and what that means to you.

CONTOURS AND GRIDS

Contour interval (lines of equal altitude) also varies a lot and can create embarrassing problems if you confuse it. Typically they are at 10 or 20 m (30 or 60 ft) intervals, get it wrong and your calculations will be 100 per cent out. Many maps have some form of grid or co-ordinate system which is unique to the country of origin. The good news is that in general they are made up of 1 km squares and the lines run pretty well north, south, east and west. The grid system is handy for estimating rough distances and makes taking a compass bearing easier and more accurate, but it is primarily used to positively identify a position that has a unique number reference that cannot be confused with any other.

Familiarity with the map and its symbols is vital and the more time you can spend pouring over it prior to going into the mountains the better. Trying to understand the map on a windblown col just as the unseasonable blizzard hits you is not the way forward.

● **SCALES OF MAPS AND THEIR USES**

Scale	Meaning	Use
1:15,000	1 cm=150 m	Orienteering
1:25,000	1 cm=250 m	Ideal for walking (very detailed)
1:40,000	1 cm=400 m	Mountain and orienteering maps
1:50,000	1 cm=500 m	Most common mountaineering map
1:100,000	1 cm=1,000 m	Cycling, holidays
1:250,000	1 cm=2,500 m	Motoring
1:1,000,000	1 cm=10 km	Map of country

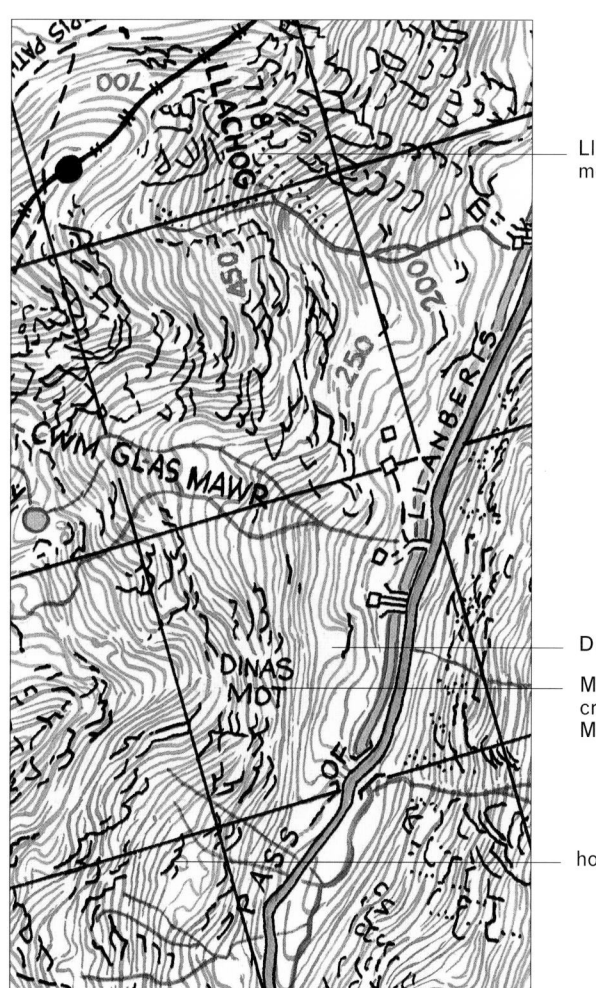

Llachog mountain top

Dinas Bach

Main climbing crag – Dinas Mot

house platform

◁ △ *The map represents the landscape in two dimensions. Contour lines are designed to give an accurate interpretation of the shape and height of the land. You can see this clearly in the map and accompanying photograph.*

The compass

After the map, the compass is the most important tool the mountain navigator has. Knowing how to use it is essential for accurate movement around the hills and mountains in poor visibility. This is not an easy skill to acquire. It is important to practise in a safe environment until you are thoroughly conversant with all the techniques involved with its correct use.

MANY TOOLS IN ONE

The modern compass used by mountain navigators is made up of several different components. There is the floating needle which points to magnetic north, a protractor, a ruler and the flat plate that holds the rest together. From early childhood we have been told that the compass points north. In reality an unmodified compass needle will point through the earth at a spot in northern Canada, and worse than that, this point

moves all the time, albeit very slowly indeed. Fortunately people with more skill than us keep it all under control by making the compass needle sit up and swing and by publishing the magnetic variation so that with an incredibly simple adjustment to the compass we can pretend it is pointing to the North Pole.

USES OF THE COMPASS

The compass can be used for many useful navigational tasks. These are as follows:

① taking bearings directly from the ground
② taking bearings from the map and applying them to the ground
③ measuring distances on your map
④ finding north (using the magnetic variation)
⑤ setting the map to the landscape
⑥ working out grid references

▽ *The compass is a versatile tool: protractor, navigator and distance measurer all in one.*

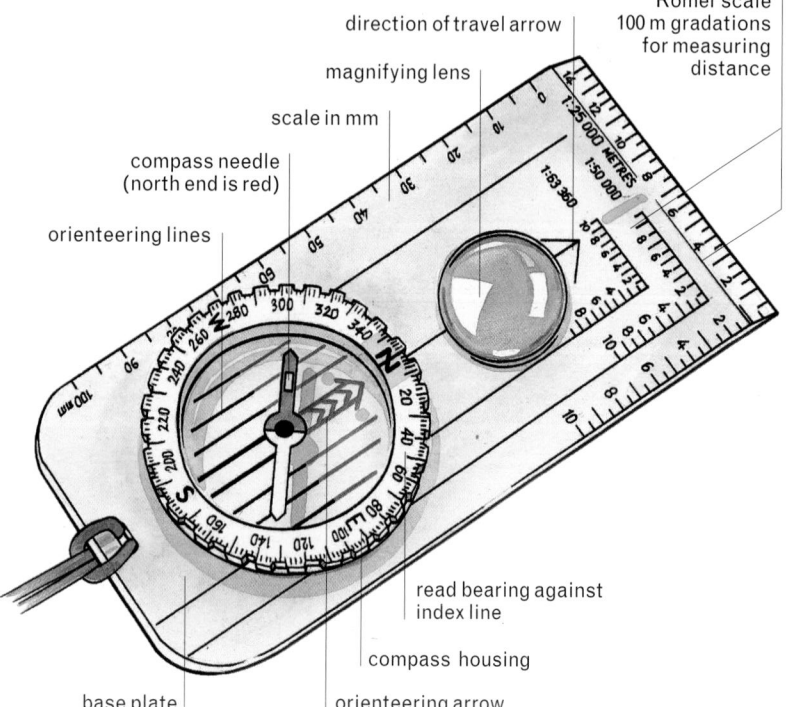

direction of travel arrow
magnifying lens
scale in mm
compass needle (north end is red)
orienteering lines
Romer scale 100 m gradations for measuring distance
read bearing against index line
compass housing
base plate
orienteering arrow

△ *A direct bearing can be taken from the ground in the absence of a map, or the bearing can be applied back on to the map.*

◁ *Most commonly in mountain navigation we take a bearing from the map (using grid north) and apply it to the ground (converting to magnetic north).*

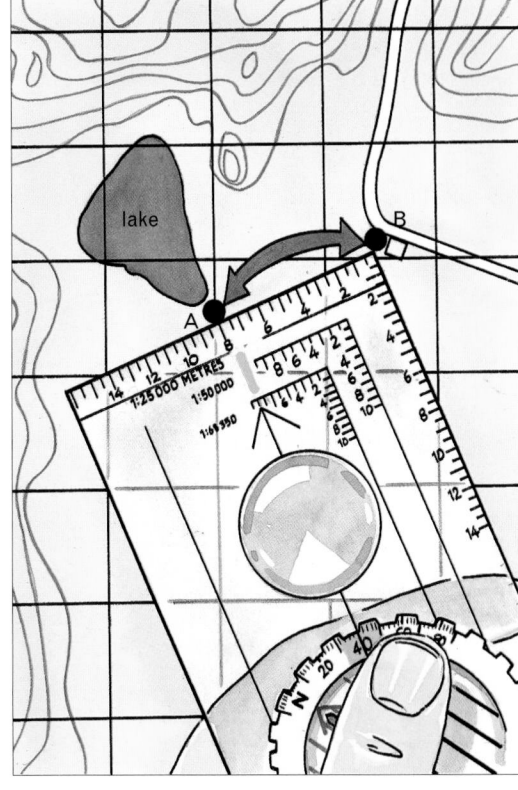

▷ *Make sure you are using the right scale on the compass when you are measuring distances off the map.*

BEWARE DISTRACTIONS

Tiredness and stress will work against you being able to work effectively in close navigation. Make sure that you give it all your attention when necessary. This may mean cutting yourself off from the rest of the party while taking your bearing and working out your timing and pacing.

● USING YOUR EYES, EARS AND BRAIN

These are almost certainly the most important tools in navigation. Things are not always as they seem, particularly when they are distorted by mist or darkness. So always look, listen and think. If you are trying to find a stream in the dark, then listening for the stream is obviously more important than looking for it.

● GETTING IT WRONG

One of the most common mistakes in navigation is to get your compass bearing 180 degrees out. This means that you will be heading off in exactly the opposite direction to that in which you want (or need) to go. It is the easiest thing in the world to place the compass wrongly on the map, in effect getting the map upside down. Try to guard against this by double-checking the bearing before setting off. You might also take a quick note of the landscape and special features from the map that you should see when turning to face your bearing – if you can see anything at all, that is!

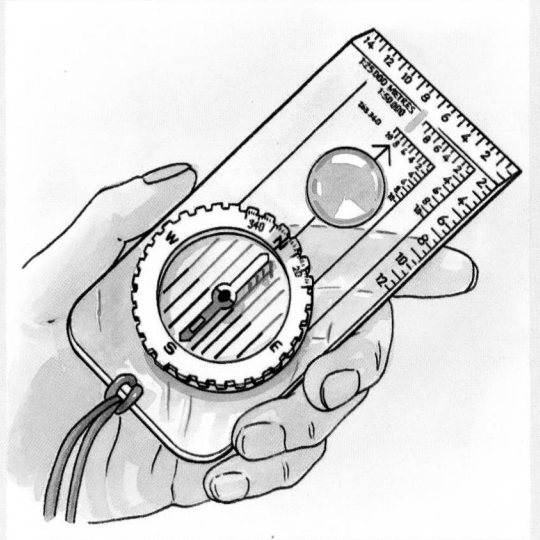

◁ *This compass is 180 degrees out – the red north-pointing arrow has been aligned to the south. This is a common mistake.*

The science

Is navigation a science or an art? It is probably a bit of both. It is certainly one of those skills that can be practised at home or other safe environment until you feel confident enough to trust your life to it.

THE MAP

Taking information of your route accurately from the map is the basis of good navigation. What direction do I need to travel in, how far do I need to travel, and what am I expecting to happen are the three questions you must ask.

The last is perhaps the most important, as this will reassure you that what you are doing is right or alert you to the fact that things are going wrong. You need to interpret the map to know whether you are about to go steeply downhill or that after a kilometre you will run into a very steep slope, at which point you must turn left. This is map-to-ground interpretation and in its most sophisticated form can be used alone to navigate extremely accurately. When combined with other techniques as well, your navigation will become bombproof.

▽ *A featureless plateau can lead to massive cliffs, a big danger if your navigation is poor.*

△ *Keep your map safe and handy for reference. It is not much good to you at the bottom of your rucksack – worse still if it blows away.*

◁ *The top of this mountain ends in massive cliffs, a danger to any climber on a poor-visibility day.*

THE COMPASS

Compass bearings become important in navigation if visibility is poor or you think it may become poor shortly. The most common bearing is taken off the map and then applied to the ground. Imagine you are at a stream junction having walked up a valley heading for your crag. The mist is down and the crag is nowhere to be seen.

Place the edge of the compass plate on the stream junction on the map and then on the crag. Make sure the direction of travel arrow is pointing from the junction to the crag otherwise your bearing will be 180° wrong.

Turn the compass housing around until the lines on the base of it are parallel with the grid lines or the vertical edge of the map. Make sure that the orienteering arrow on the base of the housing is pointing north.

You now have a grid bearing which must be adjusted to magnetic before you apply it to the ground. Magnetic variation is different depending on where you are on the globe, so you must look on the map to find what it is. It will be either east or west of grid north and it will be increasing or decreasing annually. In most cases the map will be dated and the annual change will be recorded. Having established the variation, adjust your grid bearing accordingly.

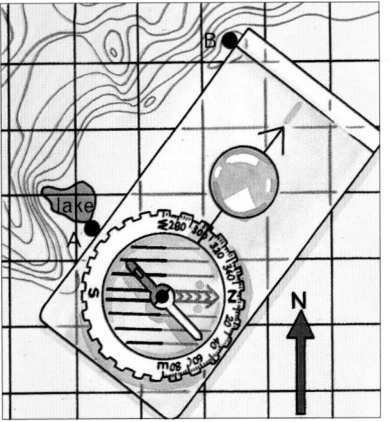

△ **1** *Place the edge of the compass on the point where you are (A) and the point you wish to reach (B). Make sure the direction-of-travel arrow is pointing to your destination.*

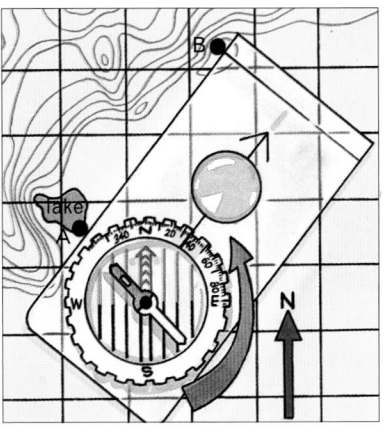

△ **2** *Turn the housing of the compass around until the lines on its base are in line with the grid lines on the map. Make sure the orienteering arrow is pointing to north on the map.*

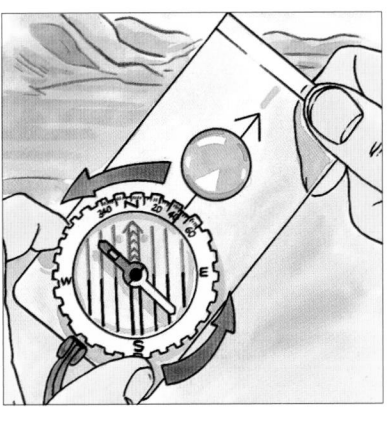

△ **3** *Add or subtract the magnetic variation (this will depend on which part of the world you are in).*

△ **4** *You now have a magnetic bearing to march on. Turn the compass until the north needle lines up.*

● MAGNETIC VARIATION

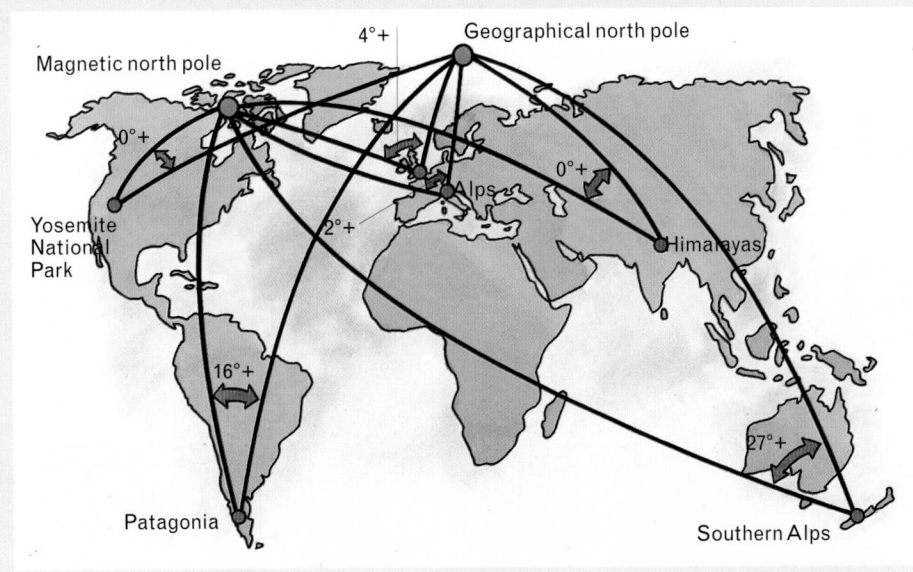

◁ *Magnetic variation is hard to visualize because we are dealing with a sphere – the earth. The important thing is to read your map to find the appropriate magnetic variation figure and the rate of annual change.*

Using an altimeter

Like most pieces of specialist equipment, the altimeter certainly has a place in the armoury of the modern climber. But it is as well to know when and where to use it.

THE ALTIMETER

An altimeter measures the change in air pressure, so if you remain in one place it acts as a barometer and lets you know if the atmospheric pressure is changing as weather systems pass over you. If you climb up or down, it tells you how far you have ascended or descended. However, if the atmospheric pressure is changing dramatically as you are moving up or down, it will act as a barometer and an altimeter at the same time and will therefore be very inaccurate. Properly used and with a knowledge of the problems outlined above, an altimeter is an invaluable navigational tool. Altimeters use an aneroid or vacuum vessel which expands or compresses

1000 m outer ring

km window

adjustment for 1000 m ring

△ Good-quality altimeters are expensive but very accurate if used properly.

▷ How much farther to the top of the climb? An altimeter will solve the problem.

as the surrounding air pressure varies. This movement is then transferred either mechanically or electronically to an analogue needle or an LED display which is calibrated to read in metres.

With the arrival of watch-based altimeters, the cost of owning one has dropped dramatically, but do remember that you tend to get what you pay for. Altimeters work best if they are used over short periods of time and can be regularly re-set at known altitudes. They are most useful for identifying obscure turn-off points in ascent or descent, so can be used for short periods using more obvious features as starting points. It is worth noting that every 1 milli-bar of atmospheric pressure change represents 8 m of altitude. Maintaining time and distance calculations in descent is notoriously difficult so this is really where they come into their own. They can be used either by setting them on a known altitude or they can be zeroed and then used in an absolute mode for however many vertical metres you wish to travel. This is often the best method in bad conditions as calculations are easier and less open to mistakes. Altimeters will never be a substitute for accurate navigation using more traditional methods, but as an extra tool to reassure and double-check in bad conditions they are invaluable.

◁ *Watch altimeters can be cheap and convenient but they are not always accurate. You get what you pay for.*

▽ *When the conditions are like this on the way home, an altimeter can make all the difference for safe and efficient navigation.*

The art

▽ *Getting to the top of the climb is sometimes the easy bit. Now you have to get home again! This is often where the navigation starts.*

To be a successful navigator you will need to be confident in your own skills. You will need to be able to juggle with lots of competing data, to sift through it and to prioritize it. You will also need to be flexible in your approach. No two situations are ever the same. Get in the habit of choosing your main skills that you will use for the situation you are in and call upon other data to back you up. For instance, you may choose to pace a short leg, walking on a bearing. But you might also work out how long it should take to reach your destination (probably only a matter of minutes in this instance), and use your watch to back up your pacing. This is where the flair and imagination comes in.

KEEP YOUR LEGS SHORT!

Navigation at this level will always be an inexact game but it is designed to keep the level of accumulated error to a manageable scale. Obviously, the shorter the navigational legs you undertake the smaller any error will be and you can relocate after each leg. So cut the journey up into small bits using the most obvious targets as way points.

USE COMMONSENSE

Keep a sense of scale. If what you are looking for is 500 m (550 yd) away from you to start with, then there is no point in crashing on looking for it for 2 km (2,000 yd). If when you have travelled the correct distance on the correct bearing and you can't find what you are looking for, stop and have a think about where it might be. There will be many things to think through. If you are walking up a stream looking for a junction and have not seen one when your distance calculation is up, then it is most likely it will be in front of you a short distance. Continue on for a further 10 per cent of the original distance and you should arrive at it. If

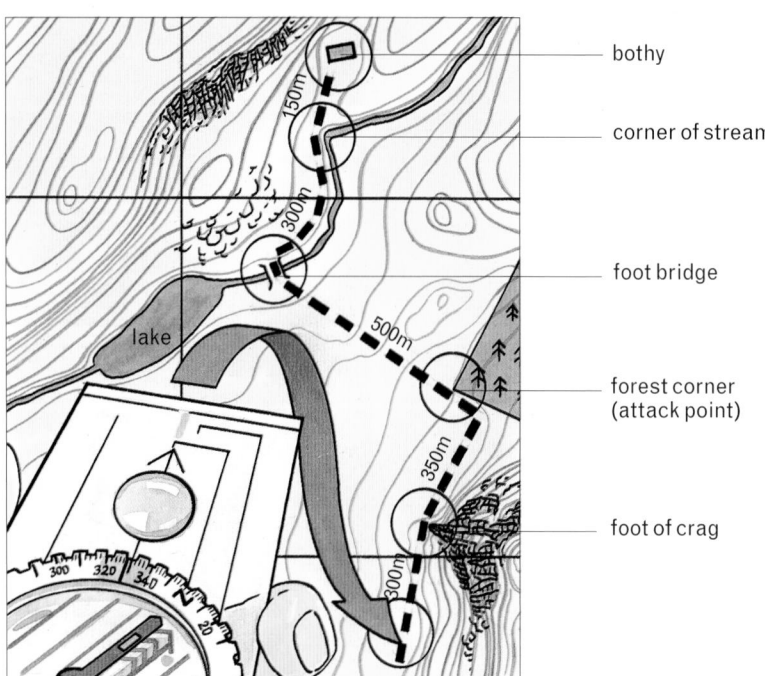

bothy

corner of stream

foot bridge

forest corner (attack point)

foot of crag

lake

◁ *Navigating via short legs in bad conditions reduces accumulative errors. Divide your journey up so that you find each point – foot of crag, edge of forest, foot bridge, stream and bothy – in turn.*

you find a stream junction too early then you have more of a dilemma. It may be the wrong junction if it is very early or you may just be travelling faster than you thought. Check the angle at which it joins the main stream: does it fit? It would still pay to carry on to see if there is another junction, but again have a definite distance in mind.

There is an old saying in navigation, "The tent will not come to you no matter how long you wait for it." You must find it, it will not find you. So you must be quite aggressive when you have navigated yourself near to your target, but make sure your search is logical and controlled; running around like the proverbial headless chicken is of no value to anyone.

◁ *Taking a bearing in wet, cold and windy conditions can be very testing. It is often hard to achieve the accuracy you need in difficult conditions.*

● **SEARCHES**

In very poor visibility, it is essential to be totally accurate in pinpointing each stage of your navigation legs. You must find what you set out to arrive at. It is no good saying that the crag foot must be somewhere near, and then trying to continue on to the forest corner. Small errors at each leg may mean that you miss the bothy by hundreds of metres (yards), which in a storm could mean the difference between life and death. So, if you cannot find the foot of the crag after your pacing on a bearing, and timing, then organize a search to find it. You must assume that you are in the vicinity. Here are three examples of the type of search you might choose to use: the star search, sweep search and box search. Always make sure you know your way back to your starting point.

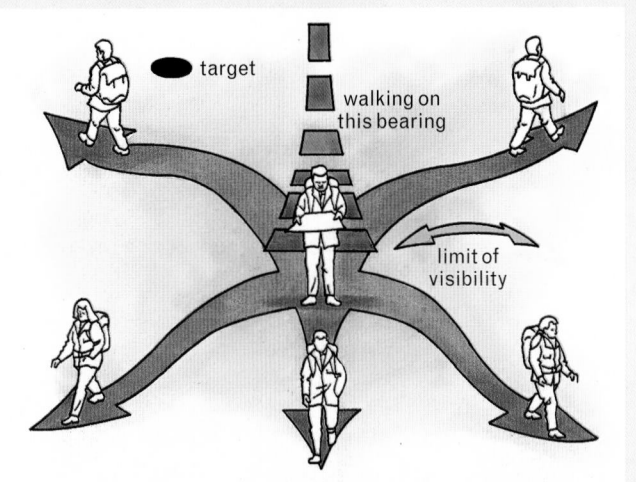

△ *You can adopt the star pattern with several people or alone, providing you return each time to your original spot.*

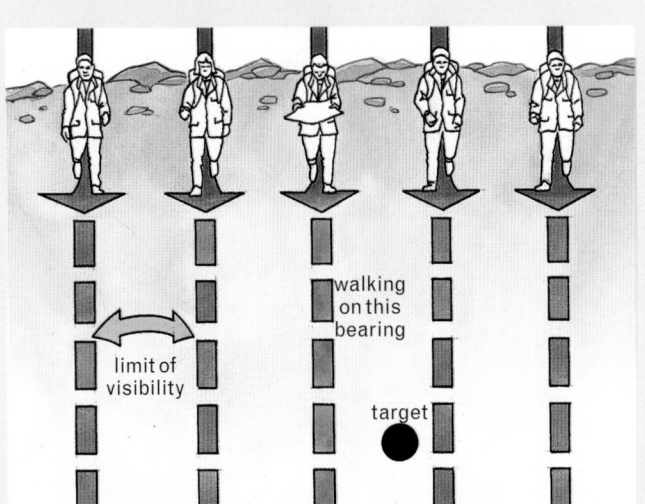

△ *Sweep search – useful for finding your tent or an injured person if you are travelling with several people.*

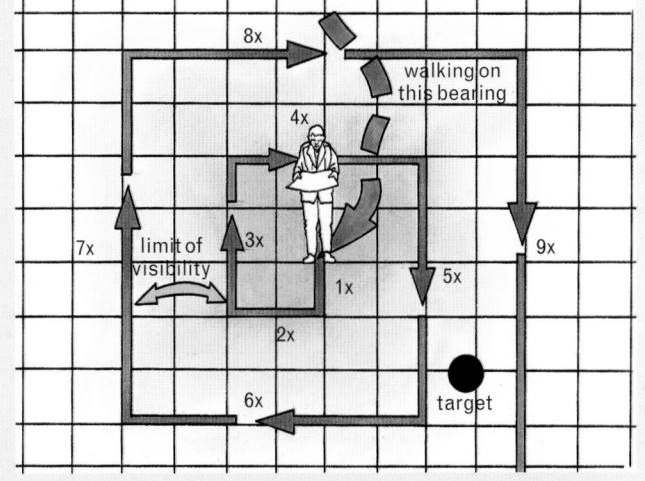

△ *Using the box search is a sure way of eventually finding your goal but it is tedious and very time-consuming.*

What do we mean by weather?

Weather is generally taken to mean the day-to-day effects of the humidity, precipitation, temperature, wind speed and direction, cloud cover and visibility at a specific place on earth. This is different to climate, which indicates the average conditions that weather produces over long periods of time in a specific place. It is the weather that we as climbers will be interested in – what is it going to do today?

Like navigation, weather forecasting is a mixture of science and art. It is important for climbers who venture farther afield to be able, through whatever means, to be able to make their own judgements about it.

A CHANGEABLE MEDIUM

Weather by its very definition is changeable – in some places at certain times this may be a constant factor, almost hourly; in other places the weather may be more stable and predictable. With the development of modern physics

theory, Seligman's statement appears to be more accurate than he imagined. This does little to reassure the humble rock climber wrestling with a weather forecast prior to committing themselves to a towering mountain route. However, despite the seeming chaos of the atmosphere, there is a lot we can do to up our odds against the weather. Armed with the best and most up-to-date forecast, a little knowledge, good observation and common sense, it is possible to win most of the time.

At various times all these can be good or bad for the rock climber, depending on circumstances. There is nothing like a bit of rain to allow you to rest!

THE GLOBAL PICTURE

The world's weather is driven by the sun. Because the earth is a sphere, various areas of it receive more or less radiation than others, creating dramatically differing temperatures, hot at the equator and cold at the poles. Hot air

▷ *A fine day in early summer and all is well in the mountains ...*

rises at the equator and descends at the poles, creating an area of low pressure at the equator and an area of high pressure over the Arctic and Antarctic. If only it was that simple. As the warm air flows towards the poles, it gets obstructed by the stable high pressure and some of it descends in the subtropical regions to create a band of subtropical high pressure. The semi-permanent Azores High that creates the wonderful climate of the Mediterranean is part of this system. Mid-latitudes are dominated by low pressure, which explains to some extent the climate of Northern Europe and Patagonia. To complete the circulation, air flows back from the poles to the equator, spreading over the earth's surface. As a result of the spinning of the earth, this air is deflected. The direction in which it is deflected is determined by which direction it is flowing and whether it is in the Northern or Southern Hemisphere.

△ ... until minutes later a summer snow shower has raced through, changing the situation dramatically.

● GLOBAL CIRCULATION

▽ The weather is a complex machine driven by the sun. It is complicated by the tilt and spin of the earth.

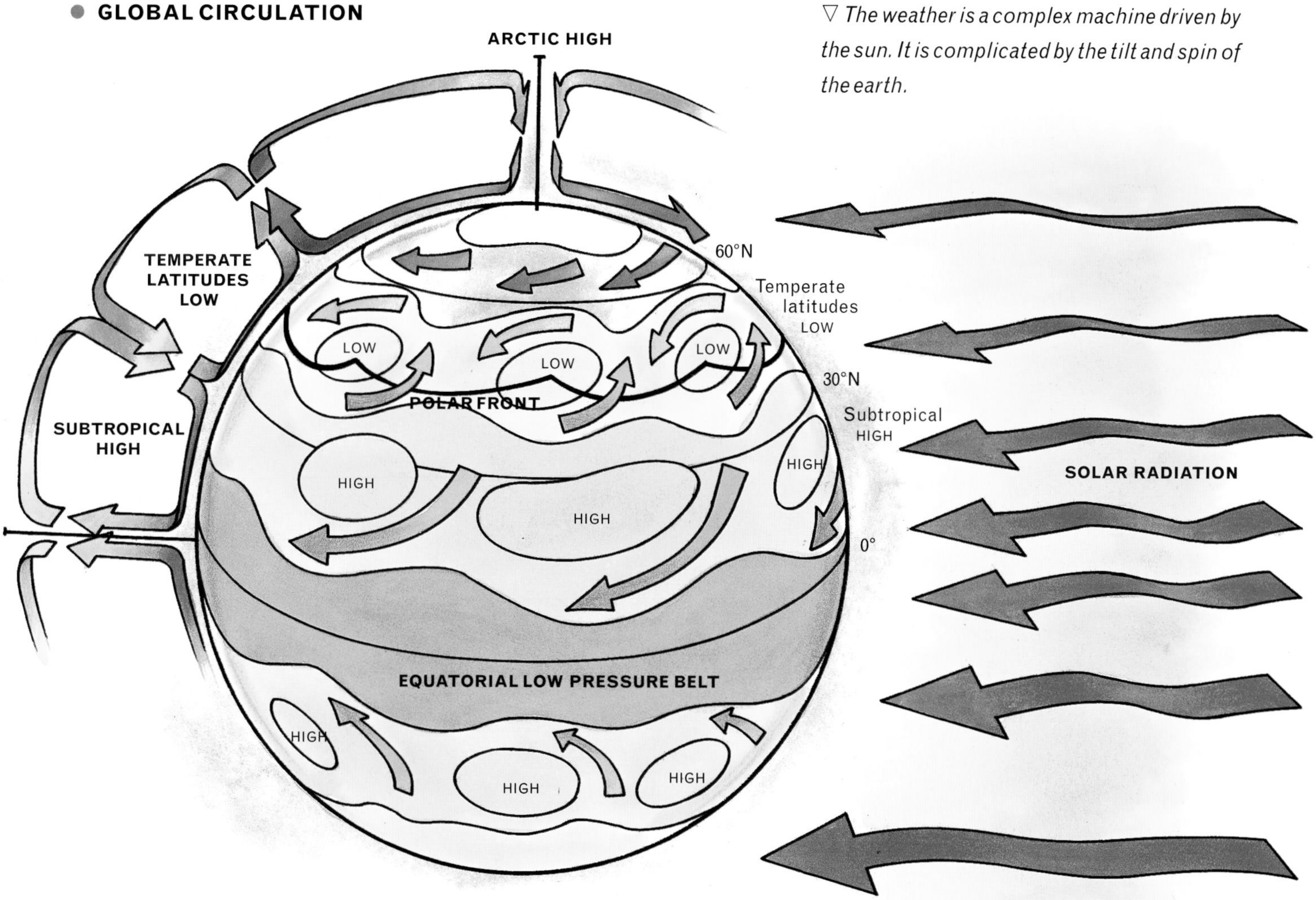

ARCTIC HIGH

TEMPERATE LATITUDES LOW

60°N

Temperate latitudes LOW

LOW

LOW

LOW

POLAR FRONT

30°N

SUBTROPICAL HIGH

Subtropical HIGH

HIGH

SOLAR RADIATION

HIGH

HIGH

0°

EQUATORIAL LOW PRESSURE BELT

HIGH

HIGH

HIGH

Major weather systems

Major prevailing weather systems provide clues to weather patterns in most parts of the world. These should be studied and absorbed for the place in which you plan to climb. These weather systems will contain air masses coming from particular directions, having travelled over certain landscapes or seascapes.

AIR MASSES

An air mass is a body of air in which the horizontal temperature and humidity gradients are relatively slight. Air masses develop the characteristics of the terrain they are in contact with or are travelling over. So, if a mass of air is travelling over a large area of warm sea it will warm up and become very moist; a mass of air that is stationary over very cold land will become very cold and dry. If two air masses of different temperatures run into each other, one will either bulldoze under or will ski-jump over the other, causing air to rise.

ANTICYCLONES

An anticyclone is an air mass where air is converging at high levels and descending. It is an area of high pressure relative to its surroundings. Because the air is descending it is compressing, warming and can therefore hold a higher percentage of water vapour, so cloud will be limited and precipitation unlikely. Winds blow clockwise around an anticyclone in the Northern Hemisphere and anticlockwise in the Southern Hemisphere, and are generally light.

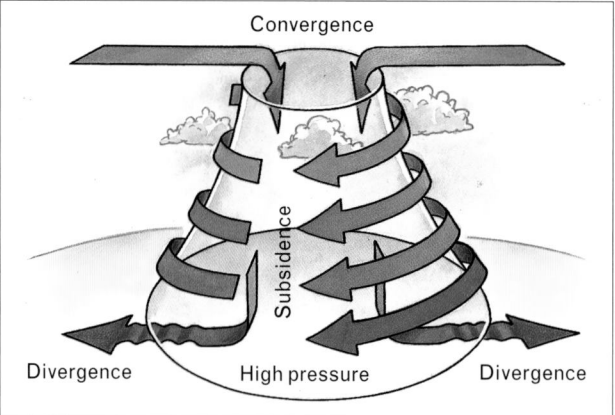

△ The air in an anticyclone is descending, compressing and warming. Cloud will tend to evaporate and winds will be generally light.

DEPRESSIONS (CYCLONES)

These are highly mobile air masses with divergence at high levels. Air rushes in the bottom and flows out of the top. This creates low pressure. The air is rising, expanding and cooling, therefore it can hold less water vapour so condensation results in cloud formation and precipitation in the form of rain or snow. Winds blow anticlockwise around a depression in the Northern Hemisphere and clockwise in the Southern Hemisphere.

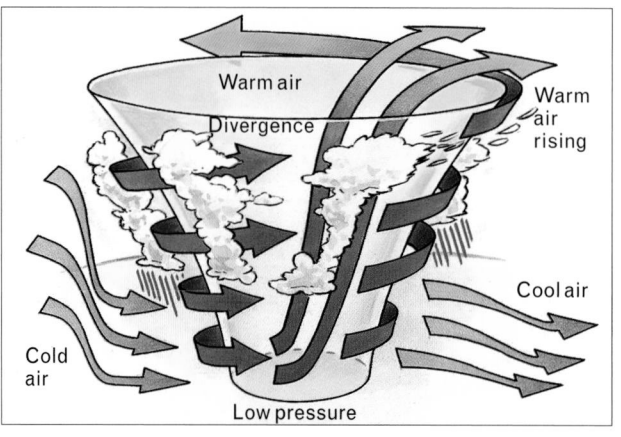

△ In a depression the air is rising, expanding and cooling. Water vapour will condense forming large amounts of cloud and shortly rain or snow will fall.

△ Sunny skies are associated with high pressure, but the wind is blowing hard. Low pressure is somewhere near, causing a steep pressure gradient.

FRONTS

These are the "battle areas" between diverse air masses. The name "front" was actually assigned to them in 1918 during World War I. They bring the wildest, wettest and most unsettled periods of bad weather.

COLD FRONT

A cold front occurs when a cold air mass runs into a warm air mass. The cold air moves along the ground surface pushing the warm air up. The rapid movement and steep slope of the leading edge causes strong lifting of the warm air, usually resulting in cloud formation, and precipitation associated with a cold front is usually confined to a narrow band of high intensity.

WARM FRONT

A warm front occurs when a warm air mass runs into a cooler air mass. A warm front usually moves more slowly than a cold front and the slope of the overriding front is very shallow. This ski-jump effect again creates cloud and precipitation which is spread over a broad area but is usually less intense than a cold front.

OCCLUDED FRONT

An occluded front develops when a rapidly moving cold front overruns a slower-moving warm front. The warmer air is lifted out of contact with the ground surface, cooling as it lifts. Cloud and precipitation result if there is sufficient moisture. The formation of an occluded front represents a breakdown of a frontal system. The weather associated with an occluded front may vary considerably in its intensity.

▷ *An occluded front.*

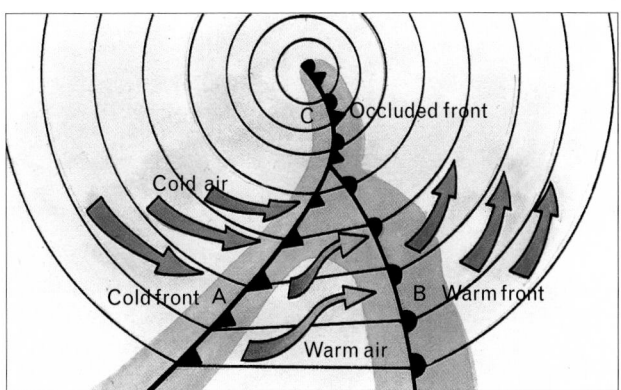

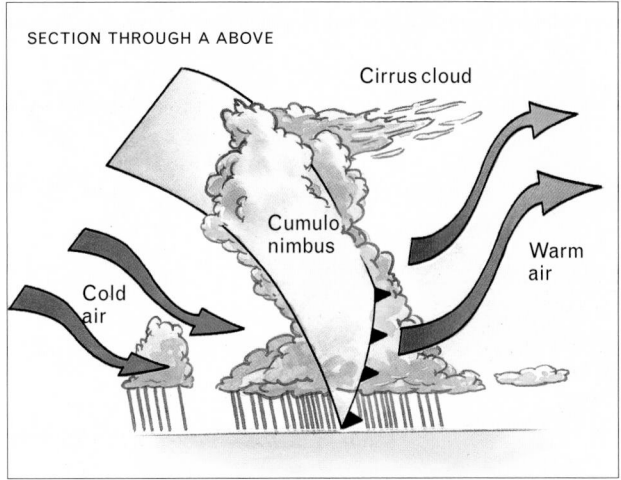

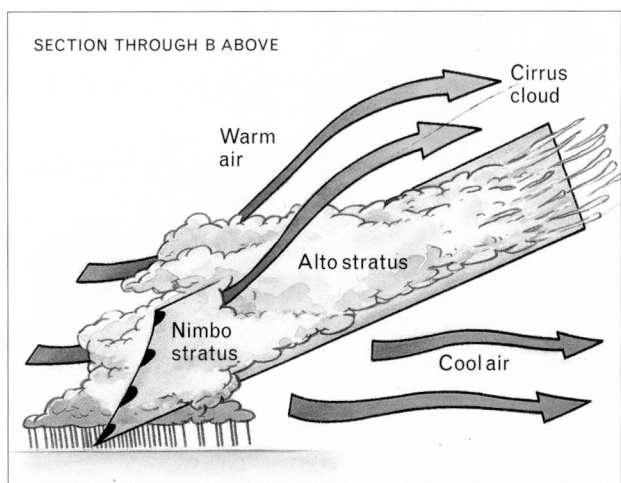

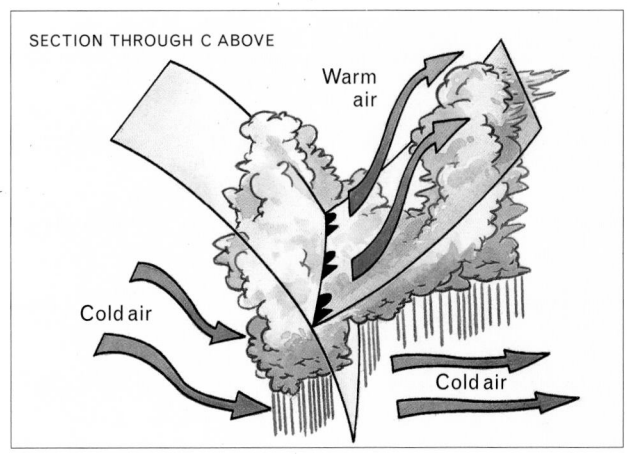

◁ *A representation of a typical Northern Hemisphere mid-latitude depression.*

◁ *A cold front.*

◁ *A warm front.*

▽ *Racing cirrus clouds give warning of a warm front on its way. It is time to think about descent.*

Interpreting weather charts

▽ *Learn to read, understand and interpret weather charts. They are the key to good forecasting and medium-term planning in the mountains.*

The weather charts we see in newspapers, on television, or coming out of fax machines are two-dimensional pictures of the atmospheric conditions at certain times. The chart is corrected to show sea level pressure despite the altitude of the terrain it covers. There are two types of chart commonly published for use by the general public. A synoptic chart is a picture of the actual weather situation at the place named on the chart. This is an exact statement of where each weather system was at the given time. The second type of chart is a forecast chart and is how the forecasters imagine the weather systems will look at a stated time in the future. If you cast back to Seligman at the start of the chapter you can see that these will be open to considerable error and therefore will require careful interpretation and conservative use. The newer the forecast chart or the more up-to-date the information you have to apply to it, the better.

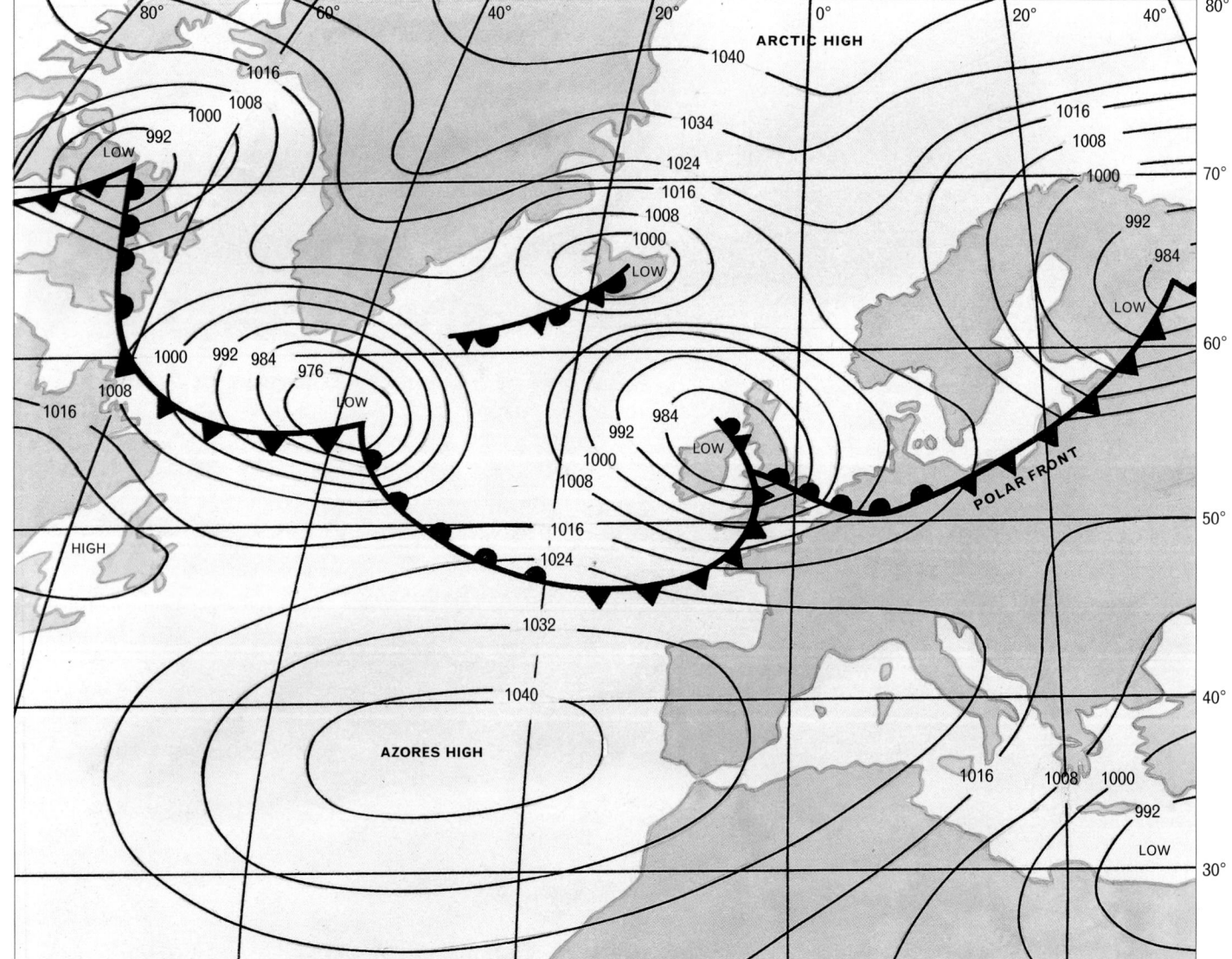

INTO THE HILLS

ISOBARS

The chart is dominated by isobars – lines of equal pressure. These define areas of high and low pressure, the wind direction and, depending on how close together they are, the wind speed. The other major piece of information on the chart is the position and type of front associated with the various weather systems. A single chart is of limited use to us unless it is accompanied by information as to how fast and in what direction the various systems are moving, and whether they are intensifying or decaying. A series of updated forecast charts will help bring the situation alive for you. The other piece of knowledge that is vital is where each weather system has come from and the nature of the terrain it has travelled over before it gets to you. This varies dramatically from season to season.

● GETTING TO KNOW THE WEATHER CHARTS

To make your own assessment of the weather, you will need to become familiar with these charts and the weather systems that they indicate. You will also need to know where you can get hold of accurate information in the area in which you plan to operate. This may not always be easy. You will need to be able to understand the symbols and other data, and be able to make a reasonable guess as to what this may mean for you over the next 10 hours, or whatever your timescale is. Be prepared to change your plans if foul weather comes in sooner than predicted and try not to get caught out high up on a multipitch route when the rain and wind drive in!

▽ *Climbing big walls in the Greenland summer. Here it is important to get a view on what the weather may be doing before setting off to climb.*

The effects of mountains

△ *Cold temperatures high in the mountains mean snow will lie right through the summer, particularly on shaded slopes.*

▷ This diagram shows the main effects that mountains have on weather in general. You can see how warm, moist air is forced to rise over the mountain barrier, causing it to cool and clouds to form. This may lead to rain or snow on the tops. Wind increases in speed and intensity as well.

Most weather forecasts are produced for the lowlands and to let people know if they should take an umbrella to work or not. Your job is to transfer this information into a mountain setting and to appreciate the differences. It will usually be colder and wetter, the wind will be stronger and there will be more cloud; or it may even be sunnier than the weather in the lowlands, in the instance of a temperature inversion.

TEMPERATURE

As you gain altitude the air becomes colder. This is because the pressure is less and so the air is less compressed. On a clear day the temperature will usually decrease by 1°C per 100 m (110 yd). If cloud is forming, this lapse rate is reduced to around 0.5°C as a result of heat being released into the atmosphere by the process of condensation.

TEMPERATURE INVERSION

This usually occurs after a beautiful clear night when the mountain tops have become very cold. This cools the air in contact with them. The air is now heavy and it rolls down the mountain side to pool in the valley floor, forcing the lighter, warmer air back up the mountain.

CLOUD AND PRECIPITATION

Mountains are cloudier and wetter than lowlands, because they force warm, moist air to rise, where it expands, cools and water vapour condenses.

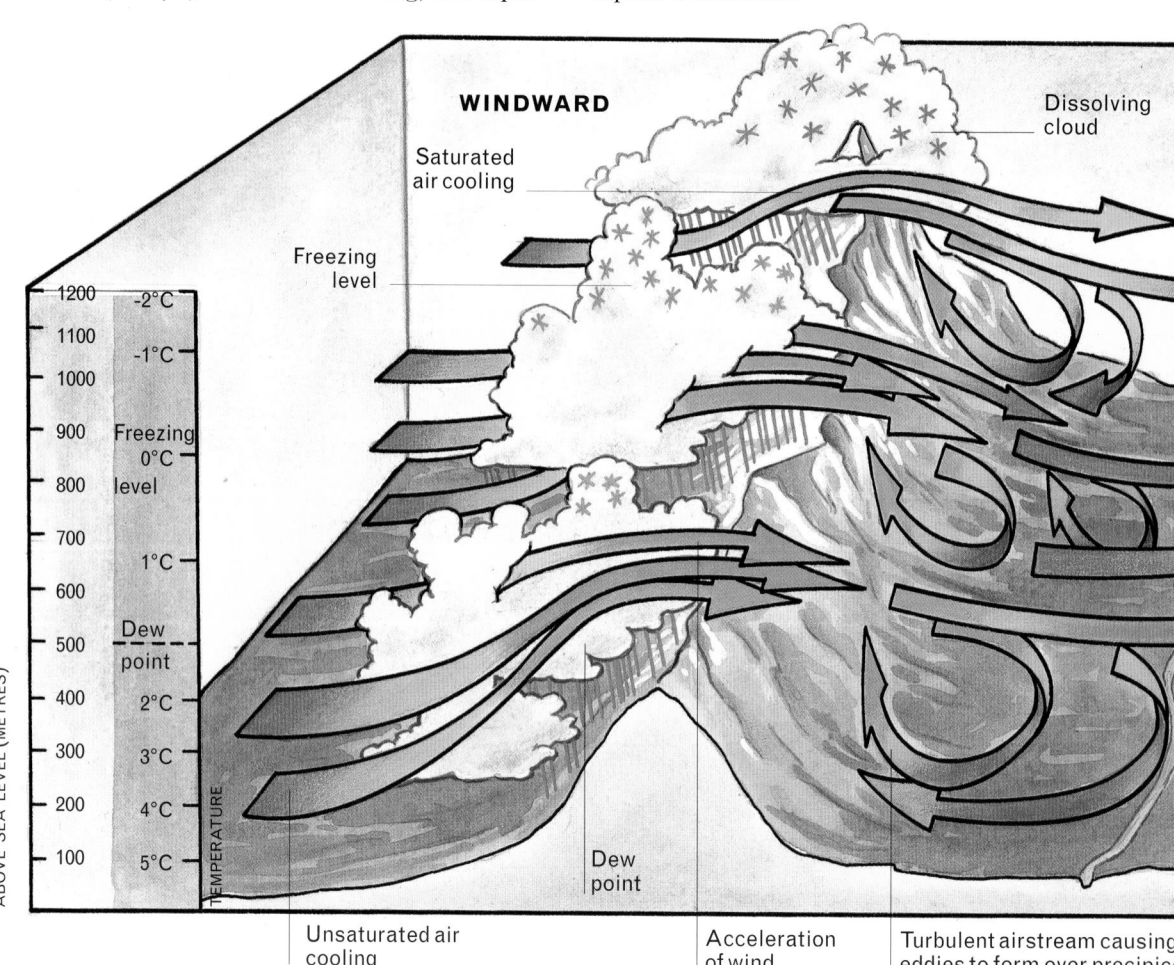

WINDWARD

Saturated air cooling

Freezing level

Dissolving cloud

1200 — -2°C
1100 — -1°C
1000
900 — Freezing 0°C level
800
700 — 1°C
600
500 — Dew point
400 — 2°C
300 — 3°C
200 — 4°C
100 — 5°C

ABOVE SEA LEVEL (METRES)

TEMPERATURE

Unsaturated air cooling

Dew point

Acceleration of wind

Turbulent airstream causing eddies to form over precipices

● WIND CHILL

Wind will have a dramatic effect on how warm or cold you feel. Even if the air temperature is a comfortable 10°C (50°F), a wind blowing at 32 kph (20 mph) will make it feel more like freezing or below. Any flesh exposed to this wind will go numb quickly. In the climbing context, this usually means your fingers.

WIND SPEED KPH/MPH						
64/40	-3/26	-12/10	-20/-5	-30/-22	-38/-36	-48/-54
56/35	-3/27	-11/11	-20/-4	-31/-20	-37/-35	-47/-52
48/30	-2/28	-10/13	-19/-2	-28/-18	-36/-33	-45/-49
40/25	-1/30	-9/16	-18/0	-26/-15	-34/-29	-43/-45
32/20	0/32	-8/18	-16/3	-23/-9	-31/-24	-40/-40
23/15	2/36	-5/22	-12/11	-21/-6	-28/-18	-36/-33
16/10	5/40	-2/28	-9/16	-17/2	-23/-9	-30/-22
	10°/50°	5°/40°	-1°/30°	-7°/20°	-12°/10°	-18°/0°

AIR TEMPERATURE °C/°F

△ Orographic cloud forming due to moist air rising, expanding and cooling, causing the water vapour to condense. As the air descends down the lee side the water vapour re-evaporates.

△ Perfect climbing weather above the low cloud and drizzle associated with a temperature inversion.

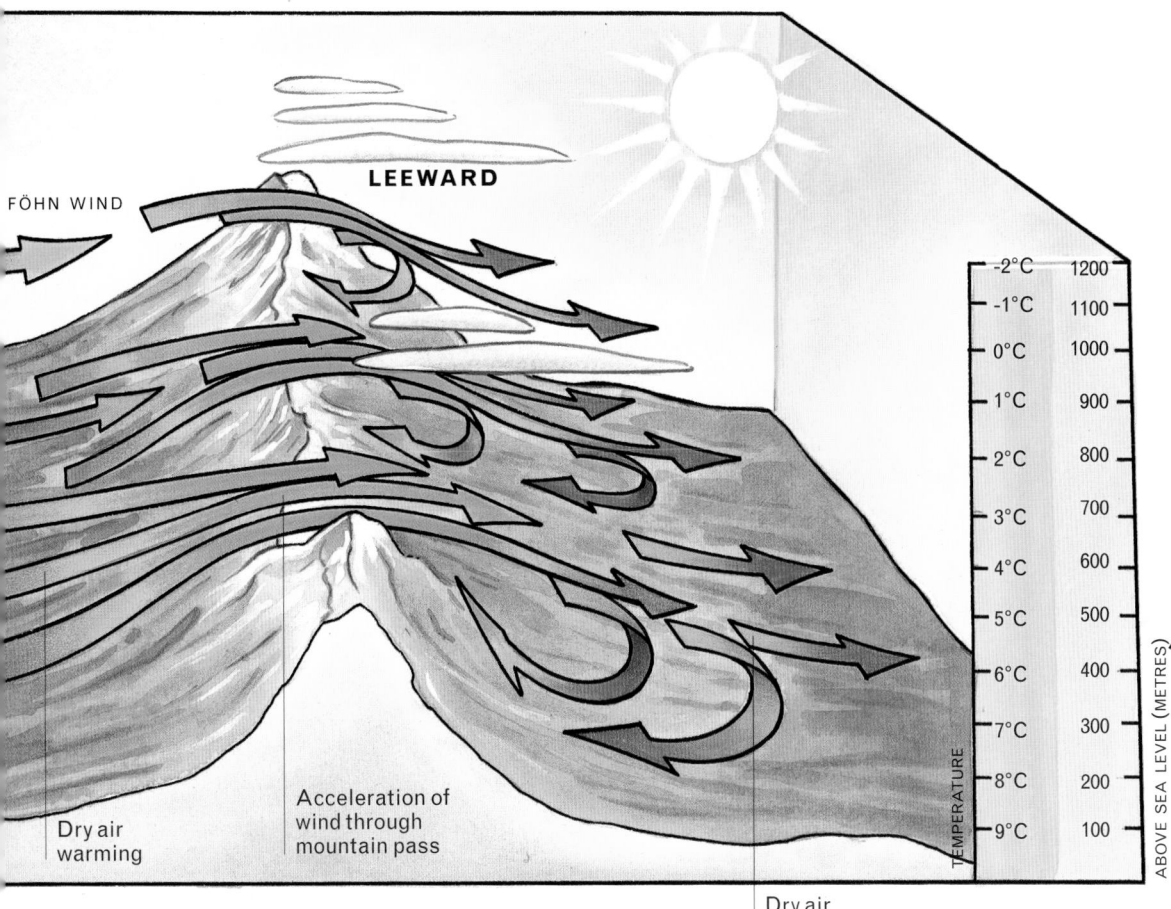

FÖHN WIND

LEEWARD

Dry air warming

Acceleration of wind through mountain pass

Dry air warming

TEMPERATURE	ABOVE SEA LEVEL (METRES)
-2°C	1200
-1°C	1100
0°C	1000
1°C	900
2°C	800
3°C	700
4°C	600
5°C	500
6°C	400
7°C	300
8°C	200
9°C	100

△ The wind on top of mountains may be two or three times stronger than that felt 1,000 m (3,000 ft) lower down.

Special considerations

Certain conditions that might be experienced in the mountains can at first appear puzzling or perhaps so obvious as to pass unnoticed. However, they may become significant as the day wears on – such as the effect of sunshine over a period of time.

WIND TURBULANCE

As the wind blows over the land and sea, it is slowed to a greater or lesser extent by friction when it comes into contact with the features on the surface of the earth. An exposed mountain top will therefore be in the stronger air flow. There are no rules to determine how much windier it will be as we gain altitude, as there are so many variables, but you should always assume it is going to be windier as you gain height or approach an exposed ridge. The mountains act like boulders in a river and create unseen rapids in the air. This causes spectacular turbulence that can lead to gusts far in excess of the actual wind speed. Not nice if you are teetering up a delicate runnerless pitch!

△ *Clear skies can seem perfect, but hot sun brings disadvantages such as sunburn, dehydration and heat exhaustion.*

SUNSHINE

High in the mountains the air is free of the dust, dirt and pollution that we experience at lower altitudes, so the effect of the sun is much stronger. This can greatly increase the problems of sunburn and dehydration.

ELECTRICAL STORMS

The complex mechanisms of thunderstorms are still not fully understood, but the dangers of them are very obvious. They are caused by extreme instability in the atmosphere either as a result of heat or very active cold fronts. Apart from the obvious danger of being struck by lightning, thunderstorms also produce very heavy rain and spectacular hail that can turn a

▷ *Wind in the mountains can dangerously cool you and can also be strong enough to knock you off your feet or blow you off your climb.*

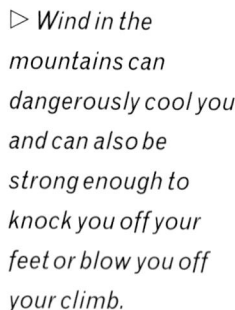

pleasant, sunny rock climb into a survival nightmare in minutes. Good planning and finishing your route as early in the day as possible will reduce the risk of being zapped. Storms triggered by the heat tend to hit in the late afternoon or early evening. If you are caught, then try and avoid high points, exposed ridges, caves and chimneys. If you are going to sit it out then the place to be is 100–200 m (330–650 ft) down the side of a ridge or face.

◁ *The ominous cumulo-nimbus and anvil cloud associated with electrical storms. Beware if you are downwind of it – it is coming your way!*

● ANABATIC AND KATABATIC WINDS

Air that comes into contact with the ground is heated or cooled depending upon the temperature of the ground. When it is warmed, the surface air will move uphill. This is known as an anabatic wind. The reverse is true when the surface cools the air in contact with it. Wind will tumble down off the hillsides into the valleys, causing frost hollows and belts of fog. This wind is known as a katabatic wind, and it reaches high speeds around high mountains.

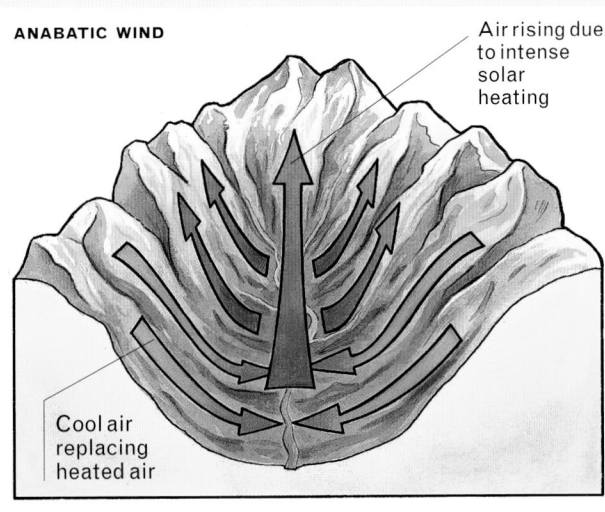

ANABATIC WIND

Air rising due to intense solar heating

Cool air replacing heated air

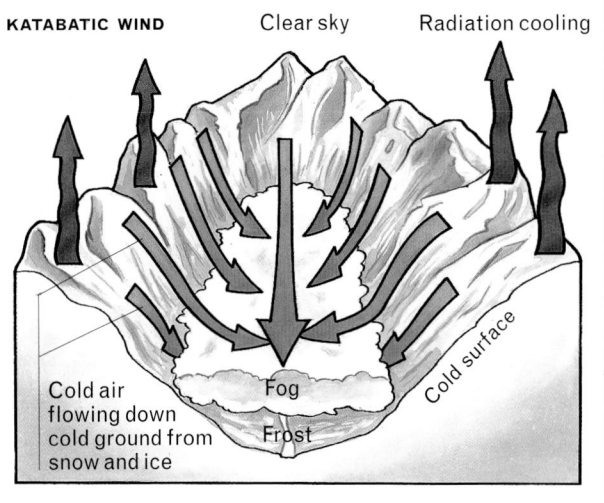

KATABATIC WIND — Clear sky — Radiation cooling

Cold air flowing down cold ground from snow and ice

Fog
Frost
Cold surface

Weather forecasts

There is no end to the availability of weather forecasts in this age of information. We can get them in newspapers, on radio and T.V., by fax and phone, on the Internet and by talking to the forecasters themselves in their offices and towers. Despite all this, we still spend most of our time moaning about how wrong they got it. You must remember that it is a forecast of what might happen and not a statement of fact. Armed with the forecast, you must put quite a bit of work into interpreting it and applying it to the exact location you are in. Thought is also needed regarding the possible changes in the atmosphere that might have occurred since the forecast was issued.

THE ATMOSPHERE

An important thing to bear in mind is if the atmosphere is stable then forecasting is going to be very accurate; if it is unstable then the accuracy will be greatly reduced and the chance of local variability greatly enhanced. Unfortunately, it is when things are unstable that we need good forecasts most. Such is life.

UP-TO-DATE FORECASTS

To stay on top you need as recent a forecast as possible for as small an area as possible, and if you can get hold of several from different sources you will get a much broader picture of what is going on. Most forecasts are general in nature and you will have to apply some of the information above to get a picture of what is happening in the mountains. However, in many areas of the world where climbing is a major sport, specialist mountain forecasts are produced and are extremely useful. In most countries a 12-hour forecast will be broadly accurate to around 85 per cent, but this accuracy drops off dramatically as you extend the time scale. A 4-day forecast will drop to around 50 per cent. Watch the development – the key to your own short-term forecasting.

FORECASTS IN THE FIELD

In order to accurately forecast changes in the weather we need to be fed new information. This is not normally possible when you are on a climb, so we need to observe continuously and make our decisions on what we see. You

▽ *Perfect climbing weather associated with the semi-permanent high pressure which establishes itself over the Mediterranean in summer.*

◁ *Wild wave clouds provide a timely warning as a front approaches the Southern Alps of New Zealand. You have a few hours to finish your climb and find shelter.*

▽ *Thickening high cloud follows cirrus clouds as the front gets nearer.*

need to decide on a time-scale based on the seriousness of the situation. If you are on an easy rock climb with a straightforward descent, then it probably doesn't matter whether it rains or not. A very different situation would be if you are already ten pitches up and about to traverse three pitches across into an inescapable gully system that will turn into a cascade if it rains. In this situation, before you commit yourself, you need to look back to the start of the climb and decide if the weather has remained the same or has deteriorated in any way and if so how much. Has the wind increased, decreased or changed direction? Has the cloud built up or has it dissolved, and more importantly are the clouds growing vertically or all dying at a particular height? Clouds growing vertically indicate an unstable atmosphere with a lot of lift. This will often lead to storms and rain. Has the temperature risen or fallen? If there have been significant changes, then you must decide if you are happy to push on or not.

▷ *Turbulence in the mountains can be severe. Ridges act like boulders in a river and cause acceleration and eddy effects in the air.*

EMERGENCY ROPEWORK

The art of getting out of trouble is not to get into it in the first place. All experienced rock climbers would agree, but it is easier said than done! Even the best-laid plans can go wrong and problems have a nasty habit of appearing when they are least expected. Incidents will inevitably happen and the trick is to anticipate the incident and change plans if necessary to make sure it doesn't become an accident. In other words, have an awareness of what's going on around you. All climbers have a responsibility to themselves and others on the crag so a certain level of self-reliance, knowledge and skill must be reached to deal with a problem situation effectively.

Opposite: *High on a mountain crag, where problems can quickly accumulate and become serious. Do you know how to deal with them when they occur?*

Getting out of trouble

By following the standard procedures that have been taught throughout this book, many potentially dangerous situations can be easily solved. The ropework and belay methods has been taught for the very good reason that, should any problem arise, there will be a simple answer to deal with it. All the different skills involved in rescue can be learnt individually and then used as needed. Treat each situation as the occasion demands – look at the problem, don't rush and, above all, think clearly and decide what to do and when. If in doubt, get help.

LOCKING OFF A BELAY DEVICE

Locking off a belay device under load is the action to take in most incidents. It allows a breathing space and ensures nothing else can go wrong. Moreover, it leaves the belayer with both hands free. The belayer can either lower the casualty or hoist them to the stance, whichever is most appropriate. Always make sure that the rope is tied off against the back bar of the karabiner and not the gate.

△ **1** *Keeping the rope in the "locked" position – take a bight of rope through the karabiner.*

△ **2** *Take a second loop through the first loop and pull the rope tight.*

△ **3** *Now tie a couple of half-hitches back around the karabiner.*

● GETTING IT WRONG

◁ *In this picture the rope has been locked off against the gate. Always lock off against the back bar of the karabiner.*

△ **4** *The belay device is now locked off and you can take both hands off the rope.*

△ **5** *To release the load take the half-hitches out and pull the tail, keeping the hand against the rope and the belay device.*

Prussik knots

Prussik knots consist of a 6 mm (¼ in) cord which is wound several times round the main climbing rope, tied and then locked off. All prussik knots have slightly different properties and it is important to be aware of them. For example, the French prussik (see page 143) can release under load. Therefore there are situations where the French prussik can be dangerous when climbing (prussiking) up a rope. If the French prussik is grabbed in the heat of the moment it could let you down.

THE ORIGINAL PRUSSIK
Advantages: Quick, easy to tie one-handed. Number of turns can be increased when using thicker ropes or to increase the amount of friction.
Disadvantages: Tendency to jam solid especially on wet ropes. Not recommended with tape/spectra – cannot be released under load.

△ **1** *Take the prussik loop two or three times around the main rope and push the end through itself. Pull tight.*

△ **2** *The completed knot. It should be neat and tidy if it is to work efficiently on the rope.*

THE KLEMHEIST
Advantages: Any thickness of rope can be used – the number of turns is variable. It can be tied either with tape or spectra.
Disadvantages – Cannot be released easily when it is loaded.

△ **1** *Take the prussik loop three or four times around the main rope and push the lower end through the top end.*

△ **2** *The completed Klemheist. It can now be clipped directly on to the waist harness with a screwgate (locking) karabiner.*

French prussik (see page 143)

● SPECIALIZED EQUIPMENT

Mechanical devices can be used instead of prussik knots; they do the job more efficiently but are relatively expensive. If rock climbing is to be attempted in serious situations, either in sea cliff or high mountain locations, their use may be worth considering. Ascenders, metal clamps which attach to the rope, come in a variety of guises, with or without handles and will slide one way (preferably upwards) and by means of a cam lock on the rope when downward pressure is applied. All are supplied with manufacturer's instructions which must be followed to the letter.

△ *The handled ascender (left) and ropeman have almost rendered prussik loops obsolete but are relatively expensive pieces of equipment for occasional use.*

Hoisting

There are situations in which you may need to help your second over a difficult move by giving them a quick hoist on the rope. Or you may need to help a climber knocked unconscious by a falling stone. These are but two of the many, though hopefully rare, situations in which you may need to set up a hoist. There are two basic kinds of hoist.

ASSISTED HOIST

This is a relatively simple method of giving someone a quick pull over a difficult move. Even so, it should only be tried when all other efforts have failed. The stages are:

① Lock off the belay device as described on page 206.

② Attach a French prussik or auto-block, (see page 143) to the rope immediately below the belay device and clip with a screwgate (locking) karabiner to the rope loop around the harness, making sure there are a few centimetres (inches) of slack in the prussik. If there is more the hoist will be inefficient.

③ Throw a loop of rope down to the second instructing them to clip it to the main load-bearing loop of their harness with a screwgate karabiner. The rope now goes from their harness, through the French prussik and belay device, back down to their harness and back up to you. Untie the belay device carefully, making sure the French prussik is gripping the main rope.

④ Get the second to pull on the rope running down to them while you pull on the rope coming back up.

△ **1** If your second is tiring and is faced with a difficult move, you can perform an assisted hoist. First, lock off the belay plate.

△ **2** Attach a French prussik below the plate and around the main climbing rope. Clip with a screwgate (locking) karabiner to the rope loop in your harness.

△ **3** Throw a loop of rope to your second so they can clip it to a load-bearing part of the harness with a screwgate. Untie the locked-off belay device and check that the French prussik is holding.

△ **4** Your second can then pull on the loop running down to them while you pull on the rope coming back up. Keep an eye on the French prussik; they can let you down.

MECHANICAL ADVANTAGE

In technical terms the assisted hoist gives a 3:1 mechanical advantage, and the advantage of both climbers pulling on the ropes. The French prussik gives a one-way braking system, so the leader and second can take a rest. Watch the prussik closely. If it is too tight it will jam in the system and if it is too loose it won't grip the main rope. In theory, the assisted hoist can be used where the second is less than 15 m (50 ft) below the leader, although in practice it can be difficult to get the rope in position and communicate effectively at this distance. When the system is established there are three lengths of rope between both climbers – and there is generally only 50 m (165 ft) available. If the climbers are more than 15 m (50 ft) apart, can't communicate or have difficulty in getting the rope in position, the unassisted hoist must be used.

UNASSISTED HOIST

The unassisted hoist would be used if you did not have enough rope to send down to the climber who needs a hoist. It would also be used if the climber in question could not assist you in any way (they are unconscious or have received an injury to the arm, for example). Be warned: this is a very tiring exercise to undertake, and you may find it easier to lower rather than to hoist.

① Lock off the belay device and attach the French prussik (or auto-block) as in the assisted hoist.
② Tie a further prussik on the main rope. Attach the loop of rope (which in the assisted hoist would have gone to the second climber) via two snaplink (back-to-back) or screwgate (locking) karabiners. This will give a greater radius for the rope to run round and reduce the friction.
③ Slide the second prussik down the rope as far as possible with the foot. Now untie the locked-off belay plate, again ensuring the prussik is working effectively and pull on the tail.

The Z system, or 3:1 ratio, is exactly the same as before but over a much shorter distance, so the autoblock (brake) will be needed after each pull while the lower prussik is pushed down ready for the next hoist. Always keep hold of the "tail" of the loop and keep a watchful eye on both prussiks.

△ **1** *Lock off the delay device and attach the French prussik (or autoblock) to the rope loop around the harness.*

△ **2** *Place the second prussik around the main climbing rope and clip in a loop with either a screwgate (locking) karabiner or two snaplinks to increase the radius and decrease the friction.*

△ **3** *Slide the second prussik down the rope with your foot until you can make an effective pull. The procedure may have to be repeated several times because the casualty can only be moved a short distance at a time.*

Escaping the system

You may need to get out of the belay and free yourself from the rope to go and get help in the event of an accident or abseil (rappel) down to your partner to render first aid. This is a serious situation, especially if the injured climber is hanging by their harness in free space and is unconscious. This is a worst case scenario, for in this situation you will have to act very quickly to prevent them from suffocating as they hang backwards.

ANCHOR WITHIN REACH

The use of the Italian hitch in this situation should allow you to either lower the casulty or set up a 3:1 hoist to pull them up to the stance, once their injuries have been dealt with. When you have escaped the system, you can either abseil (rappel) or prussik to your casualty, or get help.

△ **1** *If you decide that you need to escape the system, first stabilize the weight of the climber on the end of the rope.*

△ **2** *Lock off the belay plate and confirm that you can reach the anchor by touching it.*

△ **3** *Now put a French prussik just below the belay device and attach this to the anchor with a sling and screwgate (locking) karabiners, and weight this.*

△ **4** *Take the main rope, released from tension by the prussik and sling, and attach this to the anchor via an Italian hitch that is tied off to a screwgate (locking) karabiner.*

△ **5** *Release the French prussik and remove it. The weight will now be off your harness. Retrieve any gear not needed. Protect yourself with a cow's tail and escape from the system.*

ANCHOR OUT OF REACH

If the anchor point is out of reach, proceed as with the anchor in reach, but taking several extra steps as shown in the sequence here. If you are working with a single anchor point, it should be possible to transfer everything to the main anchor point and retrieve the rope. Otherwise, with one end of rope trapped in the system, you may have to prussik down the loaded rope to reach the casualty – unless, of course, you have some spare rope with you.

▷ **1** *Lock off the belay device and tie a French prussik on the load rope. Tie a Klemheist prussik with a tape sling around the main belay rope. Attach a screwgate (locking) karabiner and connect the two prussiks with a sling.*

△ **2** *Create an Italian hitch and clip this to the Klemheist with a separate screwgate karabiner. Release the belay plate (gently) and pull the spare rope through the Italian hitch.*

△ **3** *Lock off the Italian hitch in the Klemheist and make yourself safe with a cow's tail. You can now untie and escape the system. Leave a knot in the end of the rope, just in front of the Klemheist.*

△ **4** *Take the rope back to the main anchor and use a tied-off Italian hitch to secure it. Don't hesitate to back up the main anchor if there is any doubt.*

△ **5** *Both prussiks can now be released so the load is transferred to the Italian hitch on the main anchor. Where there are several belay points, tie a Klemheist around all the ropes.*

Accompanied abseil (rappel)

▽ *An accompanied abseil (rappel) in action. This can be a particularly useful technique where either minor injuries are concerned or the casualty is nervous of abseiling.*

This is not as difficult as it sounds and can be used to introduce beginners who are simply nervous of abseiling or situations where there is an injured person to assist down the crag. Accompanied abseils can be done on either single or double ropes but due consideration must be given to the combined weight of two people on the abseil device and extra friction may be required.

HOW TO GO ABOUT IT

Tie an overhand knot in the middle of a long 2.5 m (8 ft) sling and clip the abseil (rappel) device via a screwgate (locking) karabiner into both halves of the sling. One end of the sling is for each abseiler and the control rope is taken by the person in charge of the abseil. A French prussik on the leg loop is essential and if extra friction is required use an Italian hitch on the load-bearing loop of the harness. The position of the casualty can be adjusted by changing the position of the overhand knot in the sling. If the knot is in the middle they will be alongside. If the knot is moved 50–70 mm (2–2¾ in) one way with the controller on the longer end the casualty will be above (across the lap) of the controller. On steeper ground it should be possible to straddle the casualty and put them face outwards, which is particularly useful if they have sustained a lower leg injury. A quickdraw clipped between the load-bearing loops on the harnesses should ensure the casualty's back is clear of the rock. It is worth noting that a close eye can be kept on the casualty when using this method, which is a distinct advantage.

ABSEILING (RAPPELLING) PAST A KNOT

If it is known there is a knot or damaged area within the rope, attach a French prussik above the abseil device, ensuring that it stays within reach (you can use a quickdraw). Three handwidths above the knot, lock the French prussik off and apply a second abseil device or Italian hitch to the harness and lock off before removing the first one. By releasing the French prussik it should be possible to continue with the abseil. Before you do so, make sure that you reposition the French prussik on the leg loop.

LOWERING PAST THE KNOT

For whatever reason you need to lower your partner off a crag, you can combine the length of two ropes tied together to get maximum distance. It will entail lowering past a knot. Equally, if your rope has been damaged and you want to lower someone, you will have a knot to pass. Tie a simple overhand knot at the damaged area, thus eliminating it. Lower the casualty until the knot is three hand-widths from the lowering device and apply a French prussik with a 1.2 m (4 ft) sling to the anchor. Thread a second lowering device or Italian hitch, locked off above the knot. Remove the first lowering device and release the French prussik temporarily to allow the knot to pass through. Then continue lowering.

△ **1** *Join the ropes with either a double fisherman's or an overhand knot. Lower the casualty down until the second rope, which is already tied on, appears.*

△ **2** *Apply a French prussik, using a 1.2 m (4 ft) sling to allow sufficient freedom of movement and lock the lowering device off.*

△ **3** *Thread a second lowering device or Italian hitch on to the second rope above the knot and lock this off.*

△ **4** *The first device can now be removed. This will introduce a little slack into the system but if the French prussik is released slowly the weight will eventually come on the second device.*

△ **5** *Remove the French prussik temporarily to allow the knot to go through the system and continue lowering as before.*

Dealing with traverses

Traverses present the leader with a variety of problems. They not only have to protect themselves, but they should also be thinking about how best to protect their second when they come to climb the pitch. If something goes wrong while the second is on the traverse, then these problems become considerable. For example, if a second is unable to make the moves on a straight up and down pitch, or is injured, then the leader can arrange to hoist them over the difficult move (see page 208) or right up to their stance if necessary. But in the case of a traverse the leader's belay is not directly above the second. A hoist becomes much more problematic. However, there are solutions.

● THE STAGES OF TRAVERSE RESCUE

These diagrams clearly show the main stages in performing a traverse rescue.

A– Leader's harness

B– Anchors

C–Clove hitch

D–Second's harness

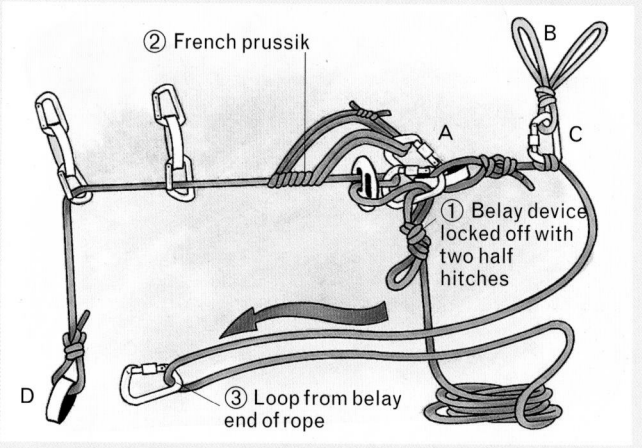

△ **1** Tie the belay plate off and apply a French prussik to the load rope. Now take a loop of rope from the belay end, that is direct from the anchor, and throw it to the casualty.

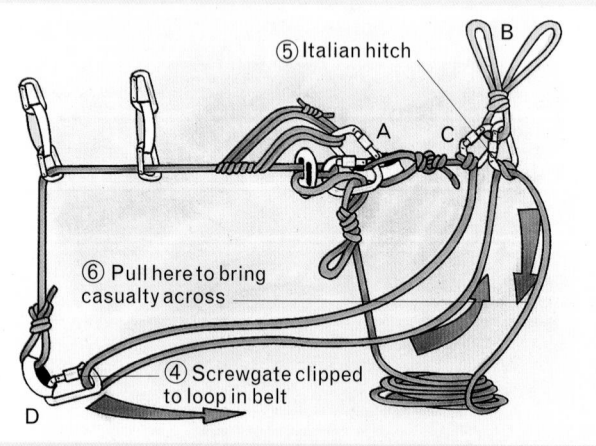

△ **2** Instruct the casualty to clip this to the main load-bearing loop of the harness with a screwgate (locking) karabiner. The other end goes to an Italian hitch on the main anchor.

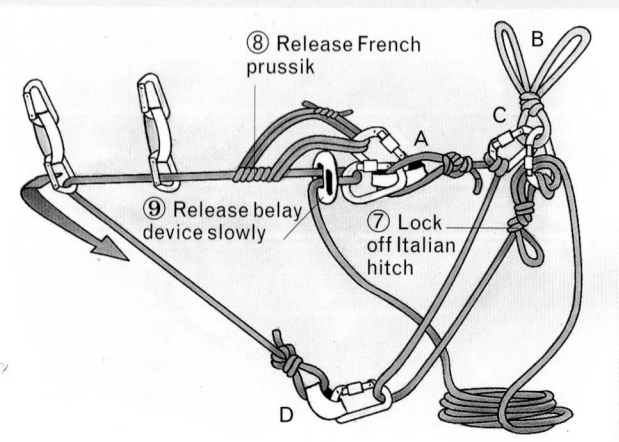

△ **3** Pull the loop as far as possible then lock off the Italian hitch. Now release the French prussik, allowing the tension in the rope loop to swing the casualty across.

EMERGENCY ROPEWORK

their harness. Do not use the rope loop on the harness in this case. Create an Italian hitch in the rope that is running back to the belay and attach to the main anchor. The casualty can pull on the loop going towards them while the belayer pulls on the loop and ties off the Italian hitch when no more of the loop can be pulled in. The next step is to release the French prussik on the belay plate slowly so the tension in the loop swings the casualty towards the belayer. Lock off the belay plate and repeat the procedure, pulling on the loop, to bring the casualty to a point alongside or just below the belay.

IN EXTREMIS

In extreme cases where a loop will not reach the casualty, it may be necessary to escape the system and throw the end of rope to them and then proceed. A lateral strain will be applied to any running belays and, if they fail, the casualty could pendulum rapidly towards the anchor. Once the casualty is pulled in, the original end to which they were attached can be untied, the rope retrieved and an abseil (rappel) retreat undertaken.

△ *Any route that contains a traverse can present both the leader and second with a problem. If a climber falls off while either above or below their partner it can be fairly easy to sort things out. If however the climber falls off on a traverse the situation will require a little more cunning.*

THE STAGES

Lock off the belay plate and apply a French prussik immediately behind the plate. If the casualty is relatively close, a couple of slings tied together is the answer. Simply throw one end and pull them aboard. It may be necessary to release the belay device a little and give enough slack rope for them to reach the stance. If the casualty is 7–10 m (20–30 ft) away, lock the plate off and apply a French prussik as above, and throw them a loop from the belay end of rope so the rope is going from the anchor to the casualty and back to the belayer. Make sure there are no twists in this loop and get them to clip this to the load-bearing loop on

PRUSSIKING UP A ROPE

△ **1** *Two prussiks are used to ascend the rope, one tied above the other. You can use Klemheist or original prussiks. The top one is connected to the harness and the bottom one, via a sling, to the foot.*

△ **2** *Sit back in your harness and weight the prussik connected to your waist. Move the foot prussik up the rope.*

△ **3** *Now weight the foot prussik by standing in it. Move the freed waist prussik up the rope and weight that in turn. Repeat the procedure to the top.*

6

ADVANCED TRAINING

Rock climbing is being swept away by training hysteria. You only have to listen to a conversation at your local climbing wall or open one of the many climbing magazines to see just how much technical jargon and hype surrounds this controversial and fashionable subject. Gone are the days of pints of beer and pull-ups; today's climber speaks of plyometrics, intervals and super-compensation. To the average climber who aspires to improve their performance, the amount of conflicting views and information on training can prove overwhelming and, indeed, most climbers will use this as an excuse simply not to bother and to continue climbing in the same manner. This chapter seeks to clarify matters.

Opposite: *Rock climbing can be a serious business. Hard training and hard moves are the order of the day.*

Putting more in

The majority of climbers will experience a steady and satisfying rate of progress through the lower grades and up into the middle grades, simply by putting the time in on the crags and then using the wall on a fairly random basis during the winter season. However, regardless of our own individual base level of talent, we will all eventually reach a point where it simply is not possible to improve our performance any further without adopting a slightly more organized and self-analytical approach. Training does not mean taking the enjoyment away from climbing; it enables you to get more out as a result of putting more in.

A SYSTEMATIC APPROACH

Climbing is a complex, multi-faceted sport consisting of many subcomponents which contribute to overall performance. In your new systematic approach, you must think of climbing performance as a chain whose weakest links will hinder you far more than the stronger links will assist you. For example, it is

△ *Steep bouldering develops strength and power and refines technique.*

▷ *For gaining mental control and crag skills, there's no substitute for sharp-end experience.*

irrelevant how strong your arms are if your fingers are too weak to connect you to the rock. It is equally irrelevant how good you are at bouldering indoors when it comes to completing a long, arduous, multipitch route on a remote mountain crag.

PRIORITIZE YOUR GOALS

Having examined your strengths and weaknesses, you must then offset them against your overall aims in climbing. It may be that you have no desire to be good at slabs and are content to dangle on overhangs from your marsupial-like arms for the rest of your climbing career – in which case, so be it, but never lose sight of the fact that the gaps in your performance will only widen as you hone in on your strengths and ignore your weak points.

PLAN TO BE FLEXIBLE

Fitting climbing and training in with all the other factors in your life can be a difficult task at times. Having determined what you want to achieve, both in the short, mid and long term, you must then identify the key areas of training and practise what you will need to focus on in order to achieve those goals. Your approach should then prioritize those areas on an overall basis but not concentrate on them exclusively. For example, if your aim is to improve your ability to do long routes by training stamina and focusing on your on-sighting technique, don't become so channelled that you miss out on that long weekend's bouldering holiday with your friends. A balanced approach to climbing should accommodate minor day-to-day variations and changes of plan. After all it is unlikely that these deviations will disrupt the overall momentum of your program. If you are forced to take a week off right in the middle of an intensive training phase, either through work or illness, worry not – it is incredible how often an unexpected break can motivate you to put that much more effort into the final part of the phase.

▷ *Your ability to remain relaxed on long, sustained routes can be significantly enhanced by specific endurance training.*

Periodized training

Those who wish to obtain maximum benefit from systematic training may wish to organize their climbing year into a periodized cycle. Periodized training is the term given to the use of a series of planned training phases (or microcycles) to provide momentum and emphasis towards a final peak. These microcycles may be anything between 3 and 12 weeks in length and they may show a specific bias towards a particular area of climbing fitness. For example, a so-called "strength phase" may consist of three sessions (or units) per week of bouldering and one unit per week of stamina training. The idea is that strength is emphasized and improved while endurance is simply maintained. If the endurance sessions were to be excluded then losses in fitness could be expected. Similarly a year's training (which

can be regarded as a macrocycle) may be organized to achieve a particular degree of training emphasis, just over a longer time period. If your aim is to achieve a "balanced" performance peak (with equal emphasis on strength and endurance) then your yearly macrocycle could consist of consist of four strength microcycles and four endurance microcycles. Alternatively, if your aim is to focus more on your strength and bouldering ability during the climbing year, then you may choose to conduct six strength microcycles and two endurance microcycles in order to prioritize the overall macrocycle towards a strength peak. Again, this may sound far too rigid and organized to those who are used to adopting a carefree, random approach to climbing, but remember that it does still allow you to simply go climbing and have fun!

◁ *A balanced climbing program could combine short power problems at the crag . . .*

▷ *. . . with longer endurance circuits on the indoor wall.*

Physical training principles

Climbing is not like weightlifting, and stored strength or endurance are useless unless you have the technical ability to utilize them. Gymnasts always incorporate a high skill element into their physical training and climbers are well advised to do the same. The age-old cliché that "the best training for climbing is climbing" still holds true up to a point.

PROGRESSIVE OVERLOAD

It is always tempting to start a new training phase by launching straight in and pulling as hard as you can on your hardest routes or boulder problems. Yet every prolonged period of training should start with a light foundation of easier climbing to prepare your body for the more intensive sessions that are to follow and to help you avoid injury. By increasing the overload (the term used to describe the level of healthy training stress) gradually and progressively, you will also avoid burning out prematurely and be able to stay at a peak for longer when the phase is complete.

UNDER-RESTING

Over-training has become a less popular term with sports coaches as it can act as a deterrent from hard training. The secret is to train hard but rest well. Ensure that you allow your body enough rest between training sessions; in doing this you must take into account not only the intensity of training but the type of climbing from which you are recovering (most climbers need to rest longer after strength training than endurance training). You must also take sufficient rest between longer training phases to allow complete mental and physical rejuvenation. A week of complete rest or light activity every two to four months will usually suffice.

◁ *Stay hydrated and energized both before and during climbing. Sports energy drinks and bars are a convenient solution.*

● LEVEL 4 SYSTEM

This system ranks training sessions according to their level of intensity or severity, level 1 being the easiest and level 4 being the hardest. A level 1 session barely allows you to break sweat and actually helps the body to recover by encouraging blood flow and gentle excitation of the muscles. A level 4 session would be an all-out fight, involving hours of gruelling training and climbing. The idea is that you use these rankings to assess what type of session you should have the next day, and in turn, how much recovery you need. You can also use this system to prevent yourself from going too hard in the early stages, and to allow you to attempt progressively harder sessions with correspondingly less recovery time as the phase progresses and you gain the fitness to cope. This process is known as progressive heightening.

Sample use of the level 4 system to achieve progressive heightening of a training phase (r = rest):

Week	Monday	Tuesday	Wednesday	Thursday	Friday	Saturday	Sunday	
Week 1	3	1	2	r	3	2	r	
Week 2	3	2	r	3	1	3	r	TRAINING LEVEL
Week 3	4	r	2	3	1	3	1	
Week 4	4	1	3	2	1	4	r	

Structuring your training

▷ *Dynamic moves on steep ground require a potent combination of arm power and finger strength.*

Another important training principle for climbing is to try as far as possible to structure your various different types of climbing workout in the correct chronological order so as to maximize their respective training benefits. For example, many climbers feel that it is both possible and worthwhile to have a quality stamina training session after a relatively hard bouldering session (whether it is in the same day or the following day), whereas to attempt to boulder after getting completely pumped on longer routes would be a waste of time and energy. The rule of thumb is to precede longer, less intense climbing with shorter, more intense climbing although you will need to experiment to see if this works for you.

PHYSICAL TRAINING
In this section of the chapter we will presume, hypothetically, that we have all developed perfect climbing technique and supreme mental control. The reality could not be more different, yet if this were the case then further improvements in our performance could only come from training our body's relevant energy systems which provide us with specific local muscular strength and endurance for climbing. That is to say, we will be focusing purely on gaining stronger and fitter muscles and tendons for climbing, with less regard to how we should actually use them most efficiently.

STRENGTH AND POWER TRAINING
Strength and power are the physical components of climbing performance which are required to execute short, hard crux moves or boulder problems. The predominant muscle and tendon groups affected are those of the fingers, forearms, upper arms, shoulders,

● PHYSICAL SUBCOMPONENTS OF CLIMBING PERFORMANCE

SUBCOMPONENT	VARIABLES
Finger strength	Finger angles / hold type
	Contact strength / hanging
Arm strength	Arm position / move type
	Isometric (static) or Isotonic (dynamic)
Anaerobic endurance	Move type / rock angle
Specific aerobic endurance	Move type / rock angle
	Rest availability

△ In a campus board move, the arms work isotonically and the fingers work isometrically (see pages 226-7).

◁ Use strength and power training to help you tackle those hard crux moves.

▽ Finger strength is the most important aspect of overall climbing strength.

upper back and, to varying extents, the lower torso. Although leg strength is of great importance for climbing on low-angled rock, most climbers find that their legs are sufficiently strong to attempt the majority of climbs in comparison to their fingers and upper body.

CLIMBING STRENGTH DEFINED

There are two main types of strength in climbing. Crudely defined these are: isotonic strength, which is the ability to make controlled movements against high resistance forces (for example when pulling up), and isometric strength, which is the ability to hold static positions (for example, in the fingers when holding a hold, or in the arms when "locking off"). It must be made clear that finger strength is by far the most desirable type of climbing strength; after all, the fingers are the last connective link in the chain through which all other forms of bodily strength are channelled.

CLIMBING POWER DEFINED

Power in climbing is simply the ability to perform extreme dynamic moves at high speed when required. In these situations, sufficient upward momentum must be generated not only to gain sufficient height to reach the next hold, but in order to create a state of "split-second weightlessness" within which to latch on to it. This technique is sometimes known as deadpointing.

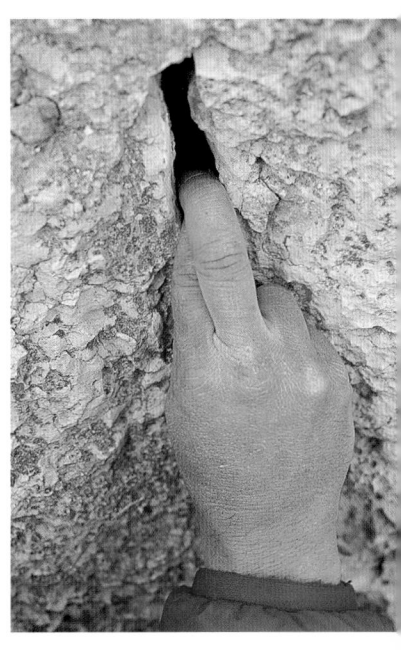

Strength and power (1)

Having outlined the basic definitions and concepts of strength and power for climbing, the rest of this section will deal with the most popular methods that are used by climbers to improve this vital aspect of physical performance.

BOULDERING

Bouldering is by far the climber's greatest weapon for developing strength and power in combination with climbing technique.

▽ *Variety is the spice of bouldering! Train at different angles and experiment with different holds and moves.*

However, to obtain maximum benefit from your boulder problems it is vital to be aware of the great number of training variables that can be incorporated. For example, if your aim is to improve finger strength then don't climb on a wall that is so steep that it only enables you to use huge jug handholds. Conversely, if your aim is to work your arms then make sure you use large but well-spaced handholds and the smallest possible footholds. The most important principle of bouldering is to use different training facilities with different types of holds and surface angles and to vary the types of problems that you try.

This can be achieved according to the following guidelines:

① **Vary the handholds**
Full crimp, half crimp, hang (open hand), sloper, pinch

② **Vary the type of moves**
Pull-down, undercut, side-pull, reverse side-pull

③ **Vary the number of moves**
2–4 moves – for maximum strength and muscle fibre recruitment
4–8 moves – for core mid-range strength work
8–16 moves – for the link between strength and anaerobic endurance

You can use a pyramidal structure with your bouldering, starting first with the shorter problems with harder moves and finishing with longer problems with easier moves in order to train in the correct order for optimum physiological adaptation. The most important thing is to take rests between attempts to maximize the quality of work.

SYSTEM TRAINING

Developed by legendary British training guru Matt "Smythe" Smith, system training is an advanced concept which enables you to apply systematic training principles to bouldering. It requires a specialized purpose-built training facility with the holds laid out in a uniform grid or ladder plan.

The idea is to be able to create boulder problems that enable you to repeat a series of identical moves in such a way that taxes a set sequence of climbing muscles repeatedly and to the point of absolute failure.

ISOLATION EXERCISES

For those climbers who find that they have a major deficit in either finger or arm strength, it may be worth performing some additional specific exercises that enable you to target your weak areas much more specifically than is possible with general bouldering. Note that these exercises should be used as a supplement (as opposed to a substitute) for bouldering.

① Finger isolation exercises

Deadhanging – This is simply a straight-armed static hang, performed most conveniently on a fingerboard with one or both arms (subject to ability) for a time duration of between 2–12 seconds. Select a hold that you can only hang from for 2–4 seconds and then work with it until you can hang from it for 8–12 seconds. When you have achieved this then move on to a poorer hold. It is important to experiment with different types of holds but beware of those that exert damaging "tweaks" on your joints or tendons.

② Arm isolation exercises

Pull-ups on a bar – The most basic exercise for building specific arm strength for climbing performed with one or two arms (and with additional weight if required) for between two and fourteen repetitions.

Travelling pull-ups – Perform as above, but move from one side to the other at the top of each pull-up.

△ Footless bouldering is a superb high-intensity exercise for building specific strength and power.

Bachar ladders – With this classic armblasting exercise, an overhanging rope ladder is tensioned off and climbed (with a foot for assistance, foot free or with additional weight subject to ability) for anything between two and fourteen repetitions

Isometric locks – To train your ability to lock your arms statically, simply use a bar with one or two arms (and extra weight if required) and experiment by holding three positions (fully locked, 90 degrees and 140 degrees) using the same time guidelines as for deadhanging.

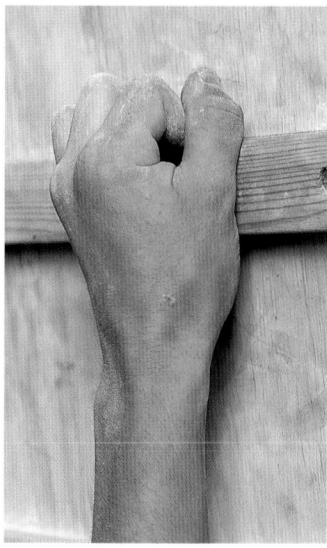

△ A full crimp.

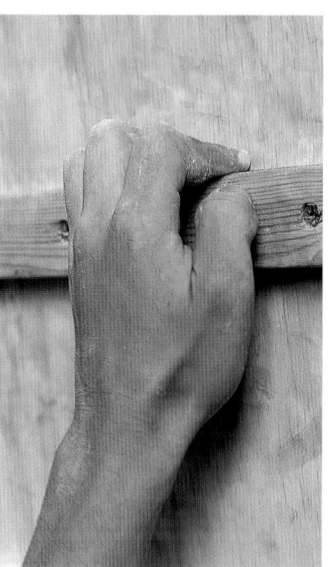

△ A half crimp.

△ An open-handed hang.

Strength and power (2)

Note that those with a major overall weakness in upper body strength may benefit from a more general strengthening program. However it is important to seek appropriate advice and to avoid exercises or repetition structures which may cause you to gain excessive and unwanted muscle bulk.

ABDOMINAL AND LOWER BACK TRAINING

Climbing on steep rock requires a great deal of strength from the abdominal muscles, especially when attempting to lift your feet up to get them on to the rock. Certain extreme moves where you are stretched out a long way from your footholds also require what climbers sometimes refer to as body tension. This is the ability to keep your torso stable by using a combination of the abdominal and

lower back muscles. Of course, this type of strength will be developed simply by climbing on steep rock but those who consider that they have a major weakness in this area may wish to perform the following additional exercises.

Abdominals

Crunch sit-ups – Lie flat on your back with knees bent and then curl your torso up to your knees.

Hanging knee raise – Hang from a bar and lift your knees up to your chest, keeping your legs bent.

Lower back

Hyper extensions – Lie flat on your stomach, hands behind head, and arch your spine upwards taking great care not to overstrain.

△ *A laddering sequence on the campus board.*

◁ *A plyometrics sequence on the campus board.*

ADVANCED HIGH-INTENSITY STRENGTH AND POWER TRAINING

For those who have already gained a good base level of strength and power, the following exercises can be used occasionally and cautiously to help you gain higher levels of strength and power than are possible with conventional bouldering. But be warned, it is vital to warm up thoroughly and to treat these exercises with extreme caution.

Footless bouldering

The first and most obvious high-intensity exercise is simply to climb boulder problems on a steep wall without using your feet. This is a superb way to hone your strength, power and neuromuscular co-ordination for hard climbing.

Campus boarding

The campus board is a gently overhanging wooden board which is climbed footless using fingertip rungs that are spaced at uniform intervals. Developed by the late legendary German climber Wolfgang Gullich, Campus boards are perhaps the most advanced and highly intensive training facilities that have been used to date for developing extreme finger strength and upper body power. There are three main exercises:

① *Ladder climbs*

Simply start footless and climb to the top of the board, using the widest possible rung spacings and without matching hands on each rung.

② *Touches*

Start from the bottom rung, pull up as fast as possible, touch a high rung, drop back down and catch yourself on the low rung again. Repeat, leading with alternate arms until failure.

③ *Plyometrics (double dynos)*

A highly advanced and specialized exercise which was converted from training principles used for sprinting to develop the elastic response in relevant muscles to negative climbing movements. Start with both hands on a high rung, drop with both hands simultaneously and catch yourself on a lower rung (absorbing as much energy as possible with your whole body) and then explode back up again to catch yourself on the high rung with both hands.

Endurance training

Controlling and reducing the dreaded forearm pump is the cornerstone of climbing long sustained routes. You may well have the strength and technical ability to do hard bouldery moves, but if your arms are so full of lactic acid by the time you reach the crux that you can barely hold on to a huge jug then your skills will be entirely wasted. Developing endurance for climbing is as much an aspect of technique as physical fitness. Learning to spot rests and use them effectively is a learned skill, and sometimes even the fittest climbers are caught out by those who have a better eye for a place or a position in which to recover.

Most climbers find it useful for training purposes to split the broad category of "Endurance" into two distinct areas.

△ Endurance training can be developed at the wall by performing traversing circuits.

ANAEROBIC ENDURANCE

This applies to so called "middle-distance" routes which are sustained in difficulty and which are between approximately 15 and 30 moves in length. A typical anaerobic endurance route will have hard moves which will be less than your maximum bouldering capability but far too difficult to allow you to hang around and rest. Typically when you fail on an anaerobic endurance route you will not feel completely pumped with lactic acid; it is more likely that the sensation will be a combination of "pumping out" and "powering out"! Most routes at the average indoor climbing wall of 10–15 m (30–50 ft) in height will fall into this category.

△ Learning to rest takes skill as well as fitness.

△ Steep, sustained, middle-distance climbs demand high levels of anaerobic endurance.

STAMINA AND AEROBIC ENDURANCE

This is the type of fitness that will be required on long (20–60 m or 65–200 ft) single pitch or multipitch climbs with individual moves that are of a relatively low standard. By definition, it is important that it is possible for you to rest and recover intermittently on stamina climbs as the effort required must be sustained over a long time duration, that is anything in excess of 3–4 minutes. During an ascent of a stamina route you must consciously attempt to "shake out" and flush the accumulating lactic acid out of your forearms. This may be done mid-move with a quick flick of the arm or alternatively by stopping on a rest or good hold for as long as it takes for you to feel more recovered.

▷ *Longer climbs, in excess of 15 m (50 ft), require aerobic endurance – especially if traditional protection has to be arranged.*

● ANAEROBIC AND AEROBIC THRESHOLDS DEFINED

The terms "anaerobic" and "aerobic" refer to the ability of the body's energy systems to make use of oxygen to enable activity to be sustained during prolonged exercise. On longer stamina climbs, the body uses oxygen to take lactic acid (which is the bi-product of the energy production process) from the working muscles and transfer it into the blood stream in order for activity to be sustained. On the shorter, middle-distance climbs, the level of activity is too intense for this same system to be effective and energy must now be provided by a different, non-sustainable system which works in the absence of oxygen. In a process known as anaerobic glycolysis, a chemical called ATP is used and resynthesized within the muscles until such a point where lactic acid bi-products prevent the cycle from continuing. The inevitable result of this is that we fall off.

Anaerobic endurance

The best way to develop anaerobic endurance for climbing is simply to use routes or bouldering circuits of the appropriate length and difficulty in accordance with the criteria given above. However, it is important to gauge the difficulty of the routes so that you are able to complete them as opposed to burning out and falling off on every attempt. You must also allow yourself sufficient rest between climbs in order for you to complete a sufficient volume of quality work successfully.

TRAINING TO FAIL IS FAILING TO TRAIN

Forget the old and outdated cliché, "no pain, no gain". When it comes to anaerobic endurance training for any sport, there is an optimum level of training which must be sustained in order to tax and therefore extend your anaerobic threshold. If you climb until your fingers uncurl on every route, you will overtax your body and burn out before you are able to complete a sufficient volume of work. It is a simple equation: if the routes are too intense then you won't achieve sufficient volume; too much volume and the intensity is compromised.

INTERVAL TRAINING FOR ULTIMATE ANAEROBIC ENDURANCE

Achieving this balance between volume and intensity of climbing would be a nearly impossible task if it were left up to chance or guesswork. It is fortunate for us climbers that this

▽ *This classic 8a route requires anaerobic endurance.*

complex issue is well and truly understood in the more advanced world of mainstream sport. The French competition climbers were the first to realize that anaerobic endurance training can be summarized with one word: intervals. With interval training, you decide on a set route or grade of route, a set number of work intervals, a set recovery time (or rest interval) and then aim to compete all the work, but only just! – or perhaps to burn out only on the very last one. By definition, this means that the first few work intervals will feel relatively easy; but as the session progresses, you will start to feel under increasing pressure, until at the end it will be all you can do to squeeze out that final interval. Hence there is progression within the session and, ultimately an intensity climax.

GUIDELINES FOR INTERVAL TRAINING FOR CLIMBING

The table below shows a sample interval training structure for combining the length and intensity of climbing work with the appropriate rest times for anaerobic endurance. The idea is to start by using the higher values for rest times and the lower values for the number of intervals, and to achieve the lower and higher values respectively as you gain fitness over time. Remember also to vary the types of routes you use and to use the crag for training as well as indoor routes and bouldering walls.

△ *Anaerobic endurance also comes in handy for sustained sequences between rests on traditional climbs.*

● INTERVAL TRAINING

Suggested interval training layout for the development of anaerobic endurance:

Work time	40 seconds	60 seconds	90 seconds	2 minutes
Approx. no. of moves	10	18	26	34
Rest time	1–2 minutes	3–5 minutes	4–10 minutes	5–15 minutes
No. per session	6–16	5–15	4–12	4–10

Adapted from D.R. Lamb, *Physiology of Exercise*, 1984

Aerobic stamina

W hen it comes to developing endurance for much longer climbs with easier moves, the process which must be simulated in training is that of flushing out the burning cramp that is induced in fatiguing muscles by lactic acid. In this type of training you must maximize the volume of work at all costs, by using routes of a sufficiently low intensity to enable you to hang in there for as long as it takes. If you make the mistake of training on a route that is too diffi-cult and which requires near-maximum effort, the local muscles are forced to contract so hard that the surrounding capillary network is literally squeezed shut and, hence, blood flow is temporarily restricted. The result is that the process of lactic acid uptake and transfer is hindered rather than encouraged. Stamina climbing is all about the ability to recover on easier ground. So by training at a reduced intensity for an increased duration we can actually increase the density of the capillary network that supplies the local climbing muscles, the result being more efficient use of oxygen and dispersal of lactic acid, a process known as capilliarity improvement.

▽ No situation will test stamina more than a long arduous and committing pitch on a mountain crag . . .

△ . . . except perhaps a long arduous and committing pitch on a sea cliff.

ADVANCED TRAINING

● RECOVERY

As said before, the ability to rest and recover on strenuous ground should be regarded as a technique in its own right. Any of the techniques given previously should be employed to reduce the strain on the arms when attempting to "shake out", though particular attention should be paid to making shifts in body positioning as you recover each arm. For example, if you have two evenly spaced footholds at shoulder-width and two equivalent high handholds, when you take your left hand off to shake it you should shift your body to the right to align your centre of gravity directly beneath your right arm. This will enable you to hang straight-armed beneath it and thus use less muscular force to hold on. You should then shift to the left when you change arms. Breathe slowly and deeply and hang your resting arm down as low as possible. It is vital not to shake the resting arm too vigorously in your attempts to get the blood back into it as this will only cause instability in your body and a resultant strain on the active arm. A gentle and relaxed flicking motion will more than suffice.

▷ *"Shaking out" on a steep sport climb.*

GUIDELINES FOR STAMINA TRAINING

With stamina training you should aim to climb for between 15 and 45 minutes at a time, on terrain which makes you feel moderately taxed, but in complete control. To make this possible, the climbing must be no harder than between approximately 30–50 per cent of your limit. For gauging intensity, a good rule of thumb is that you should be able to stop, chalk up and shake comfortably and hold a conversation at almost any point. You can also experiment by attempting some routes or circuits that have a fairly constant level of difficulty and others that have particular crux sections interspersed with good rests. Always aim to finish in a relatively well-recovered state, almost as if you could have kept going for an hour or two if boredom thresholds had allowed. With the shorter stamina routes or circuits that take between 15 and 25 minutes to complete, you may wish to repeat the efforts between four and ten times subject to your level of fitness or how hard you desire to train on that day. With the longer (25–45 minute) bursts, two to five repetitions will usually suffice. Note that one to three very light 15–20 minute stamina climbs can make an ideal active rest day to help you flush the toxins from your muscles and recover from previous hard sessions.

● STICK TRAINING

This popular method can be used when training stamina on a bouldering wall to help you simulate the effect of climbing on-sight on a route. The idea is for a partner to use a stick to point to the next hold or sequence of holds and for you to work out the most efficient way to climb between them. Obviously this requires good knowledge of your training partner's ability so you can set them a circuit of the appropriate standard.

7

ROCK AROUND THE WORLD

Rock climbing today is a world-wide passport to adventure. Low-cost air travel has made it easier than ever to be part of the international climbing scene. The experience of visiting far-flung and exotic destinations to climb can be as much, if not more, of an adventure than the sport itself. Exposed to new sights and sounds that threaten to overwhelm your senses, the climbing at times can almost seem like an excuse to be there. What follows is a brief tour around some of the world's most popular climbing playgrounds.

Opposite: *Rock climbing in Thailand – pure delight in a sun-drenched environment above a sparkling sea.*

Britain

▽ Lundy is a small island in the Bristol Channel. Around its granite coastline, it offers brilliant sea-cliff climbing of all grades. The island is approached only by boat or helicopter.

Although small in area Britain has a complex geology that offers a great variety of rock types and climbing venues, requiring a traditionally adventurous style of climbing using natural protection. Bolts are only used on a few crags, mainly featureless limestone. The unreliable weather is as much a feature of climbing in Britain as the wide choice and high quality of the routes.

THE SOUTH-WEST

Devon and Cornwall are home to marvellous sea-cliff climbing. Sennen and Bosigran are impeccable granite crags; the Culm coast offers plenty of excitement on less than perfect metamorphosed shale cliffs; and at Berry Head there are impressive limestone cliffs. Even with ideal tidal conditions, exercise caution if a heavy swell is running on any sea cliff. Most sea cliffs come into best condition from March through to autumn. Inland, Devon has granite climbing on the Dewerstone near Plymouth and the Dartmoor Tors, together with limestone at Chudleigh Rocks, a short distance from Exeter.

THE LAKE DISTICT

In the north-west of England is the Lake District National Park, where it is claimed rock climbing began as a sport in its own right with the ascent of Napes Needle in 1886. There are plenty of roadside crags in the accessible green valleys of Langdale, Borrowdale and Buttermere. Even the high mountain routes on Scafell, Great Gable and Bowfell take little more than an hour to reach from the road. Being a mountainous area, it is one of the wettest regions of England.

THE PEAK DISTRICT

Farther east, close to the cities of Manchester and Sheffield, is the Peak District – Britain's busiest national park. Climbing here is mostly on outcrops although some climbs reach 60 m (200 ft). Limestone crags can be found in sheltered dales and exposed gritstone edges stand stark against the otherwise featureless moorland. Gritstone gives the ultimate intense outcrop outing; jamming, balancy slabs and rounded breaks are all features of a day on grit.

NORTH WALES

North Wales has a variety of superb crags all within a short distance of one another, from rocky mountain bastions steeped in history to modern sport crags such as Pen Trwyn with desperately hard climbing. Gogarth is a world-famous sea cliff in the north-west corner of Holy Island just off Anglesey. Many of the routes are affected by the tide and since some parts are colonized by sea birds during the nesting season, a voluntary access restriction applies during this period. The weather on the island is substantially better than in the mountains of nearby Snowdonia. Clogwyn du'r Arddu on the flank of Snowdon is one of the great testing grounds. An outing to "The Black Cliff" is akin to a pilgrimage for some climbers. Its dark gothic grandeur is definitely best sampled in the summer. The Llanberis Pass and Ogwen Valley have classic, naturally protected routes of all grades with easy access.

SCOTLAND

There are plenty of mountain crags offering idyllic seclusion, such as Creag an Dubh Loch, 300 m (1,000 ft) high in the southern Cairngorms, which requires a 2½ hour walk-in. Carn Dearg on Ben Nevis, the highest mountain in Britain, the Shelter Stone Crag above lonely Loch Avon and the tiered sandstone of Torridon's Beinn Eighe will all give memorable outings. Glencoe in western Scotland and Buachaille Etive Mor standing at the entrance to the valley are popular Highland venues. Skye is a beautiful mountainous island out to the west with climbing on rough gabbro. To the north-east of Scotland lie the Orkney Islands and the famous 140 m (460 ft) sandstone sea stack known as The Old Man of Hoy. The sea cliffs around the Isle of Lewis in the Outer Hebrides have recently seen a great deal of climbing development. The best conditions for climbing are found in May and June; any earlier and snow may still be present.

△ Strong natural lines on the imposing bulwark of Carn Dearg, Ben Nevis, are an obvious challenge to climbers.

Europe

Continental Europe has some of the best climbing venues in the world. Most areas get warm, sunny summers that last for six months or more, so there is plenty of opportunity to spend long days on hot rock!

SPAIN

Think of climbing in Spain and sun-drenched bolted limestone comes to mind. There is no shortage of areas to choose from: Costa Blanca near Alicante and Benidorm with its holiday atmosphere; Costa Daurada, close to Barcelona; the atmospheric gorge of El Chorro, near Malaga; and the islands of Majorca and Tenerife are all popular destinations. Long adventurous limestone routes can be found in the Picos de Europa. For a radically different experience, try pulling on the pebbles protruding from the conglomerate walls and towers of Montserrat or yarding up the "vertical potatoes" of Riglos.

▽ The Sierra Bernia in the Costa Blanca region of Spain is a Mecca for climbers who enjoy hot rock.

FRANCE

France is the home of "clip and go" climbing. Although it may lack a variety of rock types, there is something for everyone on its endless, mostly limestone crags. The Verdon Gorge in Haute-Provence is one of Europe's premier climbing areas. Its immaculate white walls are set in a position of mind-blowing exposure, a fact you become immediately aware of since the approach to most routes is by abseiling from the rim hundreds of metres above the river that winds along the gorge floor. Routes vary in length from one pitch to over 300 m (1,000 ft). It can be very hot in July and August and too cold for climbing from December to March.

Buoux and Ceuse are also found in this south-east corner of France: two top-quality sport climbing cliffs that provide steep modern test-pieces. Further south, between Marseilles and Cassis, Les Calanques offers year-round sea-cliff adventures or cragging. The wooded sandstone area surrounding Fontainebleau, near Paris, is a Mecca for bouldering. Scattered throughout the beautiful forest are groups of fine grained sandstone boulders. Each area has individually numbered problems and colour-coded circuits representing certain levels of difficulty that lead you from one problem to the next on a grand tour.

ITALY

The Dolomites, a group of limestone mountains in north-east Italy, provide classic and modern routes on an alpine scale but with straightforward access. A unique feature of this region are the Via Ferratas – exposed walkways and ladders protected by cables. Arco, close to Lake Garda, has better weather than the neighbouring Dolomites and offers plenty of roadside crags.

△ The mountainous Mediterranean island of Corsica is a spectacular climbing get-away. Strangely shaped granite crags, such as Roccapina on the coast, are a stark contrast to the cliffs of its rugged interior.

◁ La Chapelle is a good medium-grade route in the Mont Blanc, Chamonix region of France.

Between Aosta and Turin, the Val Dell'Orco in the Gran Paradiso National Park gives excellent granite climbing. It can, however, suffer from mountain weather, which can restrict access. The Val di Mello in the rain shadow of the Bregaglia Alps is another granite venue and is best known for its poorly protected slabs. July, August and September are the best months to visit these two areas. The Mediterranean limestone of Finale di Ligura, less than 2 hours drive from Nice, allows climbing throughout the year.

SWITZERLAND

Switzerland has many big limestone and granite cliffs set against dramatic mountain backdrops. A high concentration of routes are based around the Furka, Grimsel and Susten Passes. As with the other alpine countries, a lot of excellent rock climbing is to be found that involves glacial approaches. Many of the routes to be found here offer both bolt and natural protection.

● ESOTERIC GEMS

The compact limestone of the Frankenjura, north of Nuremberg in Germany, gives mostly difficult but well-protected climbing. In stark contrast is the excitement guaranteed on the sandstone spires and walls found in the Elbesandstein and Rheinpfalz (below) regions of eastern Germany. Knotted slings are the only protection allowed between occasional widely spaced bolts. The Czech Republic's most well-developed area lies 110 km (70 miles) from Prague. The conglomerate cliffs of Meteora in Greece, with its perched monasteries, are a spectacular setting for climbing. Sport and traditional routes, up to 14 pitches long, can be found. Spring and autumn are the times to visit.

The United States

I t is difficult to grasp the scale and diversity of climbing in the United States. There is somewhere for every season and something to suit all tastes, from sport climbing at Wild Iris in Wyoming to big wall multi-day ascents in California.

YOSEMITE VALLEY

Yosemite Valley in California is the altar stone of American climbing and one of the world's best-known destinations. Famed for its big walls, it also offers good-quality cragging and bouldering. Walkers and tourists arrive in droves to view the glacier-carved features, such as the unlikely split mountain, Half Dome, together with the impressive 1,000 m (3,000 ft) sweep of granite known as El Capitan. This shield of rock has a mixture of

aid and difficult free climbs, inspiring climbers from both disciplines. Sometimes the speed of ascent is the most important consideration. In spring and autumn it is normal to see queues on the classic routes, such as The Nose and Salathé. To escape the heat and crowds, Tuolumne Meadows, less than 2 hours from Yosemite, provides a relaxing and scenic venue for shorter routes on granite domes dotted amongst pine forests, with views to the snowy Sierra Nevada.

In mid-summer the West Coast climbing areas provide cooler havens. Tahquitz, in the San Jacinto mountains, has a mixture of crack and face climbs on granite cliffs ranging between 60 m (200 ft) and 300 m (1,000 ft) in height. Neighbouring Suicide is a south-facing 120 m (390 ft) crag, ideal at the beginning or

▽ *Half Dome in the Yosemite Valley is one of the most popular big-wall climbing venues in the world.*

by the tree from which it takes its name. There are over 3,500 traditional and sport climbs on coarse granitic boulders between 6 m (20 ft) and 60 m (200 ft) high.

SMITH ROCK

Smith Rock in Central Oregon is a desert area with an unusual geology of soft volcanic tuff, forming complex multi-coloured towers and cliffs. It is best known for its single-pitch sport climbs. The mixture of crack, corners and face routes up to six pitches long rise above low-growing juniper scrub and sage brush. On the horizon, the snow-clad Cascade Mountain peaks can be seen. This venue is best visited in the spring and autumn.

◁ *Superb hard crack climbing can be found in the Yosemite Valley. This route is Outer Limits.*

▽ *Fantastic climbing in a great setting – Smith Rock in Oregon.*

end of summer. Set among coniferous forests in the southern Sierra Nevada, The Needles are a quiet summer venue. The climbing is focused on ten semi-independent summits. The characteristic bright yellow-green lichen-covered granite has routes on all aspects between three and twelve pitches long, giving some of California's finest crack climbing.

The steep airy granite of Lover's Leap near Lake Tahoe has a range of routes from moderate cracks to overhanging sport climbs up to 180 m (590 ft) high. Protruding quartz and feldspar dykes band the cliff forming small fingerholds to large ledges. Its north-west aspect offers welcome midsummer shade.

As Yosemite cools off at the end of autumn, many climbers head farther south to Joshua Tree National Monument in the Mojave Desert, where it is possible to boulder and climb through the winter and into spring. Many are attracted by its unique setting, characterized

△ Granite climbing at the City of Rocks National Reserve in Idaho.

RED ROCKS

Red Rocks in Nevada is a West Coast sandstone venue and is a complicated arrangement of crags and canyons cut into a 900 m (3,000 ft) escarpment rising out of the desert. The climbing ranges from short clip-ups to long free routes. The rock can be friable and some descents are complicated. Only a short distance from the gambling showtown of Las Vegas, Red Rocks is highly accessible and most popular in spring and autumn.

On the edge of the Sawtooth Mountains, the City of Rocks National Reserve is Idaho's number one climbing area. A multitude of granite domes and pinnacles give mostly one-pitch sport and traditional routes. At an elevation of around 2,300 m (7,500 ft) it is a place to visit in the summer.

BOULDER, COLORADO

Since the city of Boulder in Colorado has so much nearby rock to climb, it has unsurprisingly attracted a large climbing community. The solid sandstone of the 300 m (1,000 ft) Flatirons, Eldorado Canyon and the granite Boulder Canyon are all within an easy drive. An hour to the north lies Estes Park on the outskirts of the Rocky Mountain National Park. Bordering this runs Lumpy Ridge with its string of accessible granite crags for short excursions.

Within the National Park, mountain routes with long but straightforward marked trail approaches give a remote feel to the climbing here. Some bolted routes exist but most require a full rack of natural gear, route-finding skills and an awareness of mountain hazards. Although not glaciated, snow patches linger into the early summer and violent afternoon electrical storms are common. Much of the climbing is on an alpine scale at an elevation between 3,000 m (9,600 ft) and 4,000 m (12,800 ft), so acclimatization is necessary.

June to September are the best months for a memorable experience on the quality routes of Spearhead, Petit Grepon and the area's centre-piece, the impeccable granite of The Diamond on Long's Peak. Also accessible from Boulder are the long serious routes in the Black Canyon

of Gunnison. The harsh Utah desert is home to the sandstone towers of the Canyonlands and Zion National Parks, revered among climbers for their sustained crack climbs in some of the world's most incredible scenery.

△ *Unique climbing on a unique geological feature – Devil's Tower, Wyoming.*

EAST COAST

The north-east United States has a landscape of gentle slopes with crags set among dense forests, the most popular being the Shawangunks. They can be reached in a ½ hour drive north from New York City. The quartzite escarpment boasts over a thousand one-and two-pitch routes. Mostly naturally protected, they are characterized by steep juggy walls and roofs. Often hot and humid in summer, the Gunks are busiest during spring but perhaps best seen during the dramatic colours of autumn.

Recently very popular with East Coast climbers is the New River Gorge in West Virginia. Along the 24 km (15 mile) sandstone escarpment there is a mixture of more than a thousand single-pitch traditional and sport outings. Spring and autumn are the best seasons to visit.

▷ *Climbing near Boulder, Colorado – an area that has attracted a large climbing community.*

Australia

Australia is the flattest continent on earth. It also holds some of the best climbing crags to be found anywhere. Unlike many northern hemisphere venues, heat can be a major problem.

ARAPILES

Australia is home to one of the world's best-known climbing venues: Mt Arapiles in Victoria. Only a half day's drive from Melbourne, a line of brightly coloured quartzite-hard sandstone bluffs above a group of pine trees that shelter the campsite gives classic climbs at all grades. With easy access, good weather and plenty of routes to choose from, it is a deservedly popular destination on the international circuit. The climbs rely mostly on traditional gear with the odd bolt for protection. Spring and autumn are the most popular seasons while shade from the searing summer sun can be found on the walls rising out of the numerous gullies.

In recent years, the Arapiles has had to share the limelight with a group of newly developed crags close by known as the Grampians, offering a variety of climbing styles and settings. The rock is again sandstone although unlike the Arapiles extensive bouldering can be found here and the weather tends to be cooler.

Mt Buffalo Gorge about 300 km (185 miles) north-east of Melbourne in the Victoria Alps is an altogether different experience on coarse granite. The style of climbing can vary from big walls to run-out slabs and flesh-tearing cracks. At an altitude of 1,500 m (4,800 ft), it is an ideal summer cliff.

THE BLUE MOUNTAINS

The Blue Mountains on Sydney's doorstep is a fantastic national park! In the midst of eucalyptus forest a multitude of sandstone canyons and escarpments offer dozens of crags mainly known for their short sport climbs. If only a limited time is available in the "Blueys", then Cosmic County and Mount Piddington are an ideal introduction to the vast amount of high-quality rock to be found. It can be wet and cold here in the winter so best avoided; spring and autumn give the most pleasant conditions.

Australia's premier sport climbing venue is close to the town of Nowra. It is an ideal place in winter when you are feeling strong and the Blue Mountains are too cold. Short and steep, it has a high concentration of hard routes.

▽ Hanging out down under on one of the Arapiles best known routes, Kachoong, offering big holds and plenty of exposure.

Over the state border in Queensland, Girraween National Park is an idyllic venue and well worth a short visit. Set in prime bush-whacking country, the routes are mostly single-pitch with bolt protection on granite domes and curiously balanced huge blocks. At an altitude of 800 m (2,500 ft) the temperature can be below freezing at night.

About 1½ hours west of Brisbane is Frog Buttress, the ideal place to perfect your jamming and bridging techniques. Composed of rhyolitic columns up to 50 m (160 ft) tall, the crag is best-known for its continuous cracks and smooth grooves. There is very little fixed gear as most of the routes follow natural lines. Almost tropical in climate, it is definitely best to visit in the winter (June–September).

South Australia's finest climbing destination is Moonarie, about 400 km (250 miles) north of Adelaide, in the heart of the Flinders Range National Park. Situated on the crater rim of Wilpena Pound in an inspirational wilderness setting are routes of all grades up to 140 m (450 ft) long. Spring and autumn bring favourable conditions for climbing.

△ *Mount Rosea in the Grampians offers long climbs high above lush eucalyptus forest.*

◁ *Cosmic County crag is one of the many sandstone cliffs and canyons found in the "Blueys".*

Asia and the Middle East

As well as being home to the highest mountains on earth, Asia offers great diversity to rock climbers, from the desert of the Middle East to the seaside crags of Thailand.

THAILAND

Thailand, the ancient kingdom of Siam, offers a paradise for climbers in which pocketed limestone walls draped with stalactites drop into the turquoise Andaman Sea. The main

▽ *Routes on the Ao-Nang tower, Thailand, can only be accessed by boat.*

△ *The aptly named Groove Tube is a gentle introduction to climbing on the Phra Nang peninsula, Thailand.*

destination for climbers is the Phra Nang peninsula, with around 300 sport routes within easy reach. Although the Phi Phi islands, a 1½ hour boat ride from Phra Nang, was the first area to be developed for climbing, the fixed protection has not been maintained and the poor condition of the bolts has meant a decrease in their popularity. Phra Nang's beaches can only be reached by boat, usually from Krabi or Ao Nang. Krabi is a 15 hour overland journey south from Bangkok or a 3 hour bus ride from Phuket. The peninsula has accommodation in bungalows across a wide price range; the cheapest bungalows can be found at Ton Sai Bay. In general the climate is a humid tropical one. Mid-November to the end of February is the best period for climbing. It can get very busy over Christmas and New Year.

▷ *In Hampi, India, there is a saying that every stone has a story to tell. For the climber it is like reading it in Braille.*

INDIA

Hampi, a holy village on the bare granite Deccan plateau of southern India, is one of the world's most unusual bouldering venues. It is an extraordinary landscape. Eroded into fantastic shapes, a confusion of huge stones sit piled up and precariously balanced in every direction you look. Many of them are strewn among the ruins that were once the capital of the Vijayanagar Hindu empire, destroyed in 1565. A sense of discovery and exploration still exists for the visiting climber.

CHINA

In southern China the area of limestone towers that rise out of the rice paddies around the town of Yangshuo have been tipped to become an important new climbing destination. A stunning limestone archway called Moon Hill is the main attraction for both climbers and tourists alike. At present the outcrop has 16 one- and two-pitch bolted lines. The middle of October to the end of February is the time to plan a climbing trip here.

JORDAN

The grandeur of the Wadi Rum desert in southern Jordan was first brought to the world's attention by Lawrence of Arabia. Prior to exploration beginning in 1984 to assess its potential for rock climbing, the region and its mountains were largely only familiar to the local bedouin. There are now some 300 routes of all grades on sandstone of variable quality. Original pioneers adopted a policy of using a minimum of fixed gear for protection to preserve the spirit of adventure. Recent excessive bolting has been seen as out of place in a wilderness area that has a timeless tranquillity about it.

▷ *Climbing the Vanishing Pillar in Jordan with the Wadi Rum Desert in the background.*

Africa

It is only recently that rock climbing in Africa has been brought to the attention of international climbers. South Africa and Morocco are already popular destinations; others are still awaiting discovery.

MALI

The Massif des Aiguilles de Garmi, in the Sahel region bordering the southern Sahara, has emerged as the biggest attraction for visiting climbers. This striking collection of five sandstone spires includes the formation known as The Hand of Fatima. The great West African classic, The North Pillar, follows the pinnacled edge of the east face of the tallest tower Kaga Tondo in around 15 pitches. Descents generally involve abseiling (rappelling) and are equipped for 60 m (200 ft) ropes. An incongruous strip of immaculate tarmac passes through the arid plain just below the cliffs, making access easy. Camping is literally just off the road among boulders up to 15 m (50 ft) high, sporting numerous bolted lines. Hombori, the closest town, is 12 km (7½ miles) away dominated by the squat mass of Hombori Tondo, the highest point in Mali (1,155 m/3,789 ft). Some 140 routes have now been recorded. Many cliffs are under the stewardship of the local village and permission to climb should first be negotiated with the village chief. The Sahel can be ferociously hot so the best months to visit are December and January.

MOROCCO

Between the mountains of the High Atlas and the Sahara Desert in North Africa lies the Todra Gorge, a stunning natural feature of orange limestone standing some 300 m (1,000 ft) high and 30 km (20 miles) long. At its narrowest point it is only 10 m (32 ft) across. The gorge has hundreds of bolted single and multipitch routes with in situ belays. There is a regular bus service from Marrakech via Ouarzazate to Tinerhir (about 7 hours) and then a taxi from here covers the remaining 14 km (9 miles) to Todra. Two hotels close to the gorge entrance not only provide cheap rooms and dormitory-style accommodation but also details of routes. The best times to visit Todra are March to April and September through November. Further superb limestone climbing can be found in the Taghia Canyons of the Central Atlas, with climbs of all grades up to 700 m (2,250 ft) long.

NAMIBIA

The dramatic 600 m (2,000 ft) granite plug of Spitzkoppe is Namibia's big attraction for climbers. This national monument rises out of the Namib-Naukluft Desert to a 10 m (32 ft) wide summit with vast views. The classic route

▽ Base camp below The Hand of Fatima; taking advantage of what little shade is on offer.

▷ *The huge granite dome of Spitzkoppe in Namibia is a national monument and a big draw to climbers.*

begins with a meandering line and even a spot of caving before six pitches of mid-grade climbing takes you to the top in about 6 hours. It can be reached by car with a bit of off-road driving and camping is allowed at designated sites, for which a fee is paid to the local community. Bring your own water.

SOUTH AFRICA

Since the end of apartheid a steadily increasing number of climbers have visited South Africa, bringing back reports of world-class climbing on sun-hardened sandstone. Table Mountain with its cableway to the summit dominates the skyline above Cape Town and is home to some great mid-grade lines up to six pitches long. A half-day's drive from there, Rocklands in the Cederberg Nature Preserve has incredible rock formations with sport routes in an exquisite setting and superb bouldering. A couple of

hours drive south from here brings you to the overwhelming rock walls of Wolfberg and Tafelberg. The main face of Wolfberg, about an hour's walk from the campsite, is nearly 200 m (650 ft) high with many multipitch traditional routes on perfect orange rock.

◁ *The spectacular Todra Gorge in the Atlas Mountains of Morocco.*

▷ *South African climbing at its best – Rocklands in the Cederberg Nature Reserve.*

Glossary

Abseil – a method of descending the rope using friction from a belay device or a figure-of-eight descender. The word is of German origin and often shortened to "ab". The French word rappel, "rap", is more common in the USA.

Anchor – A secure point of attachment between the climber and the rock. This could be a wire, sling, nut, thread or cramming device with a karabiner to which the rope is attached.

Altimeter – An instrument used for measuring height above sea level. It works using the differences in atmospheric pressure as height is gained.

Bandolier (gear sling) – A rope or tape shoulder sling (often padded) to which climbing equipment can be attached and easily transferred between leader and second.

Bearing – The direction in which to walk to reach a certain point when navigating.

Belay – To belay: to hold the rope of the person climbing to prevent them going the full length of the rope should they fall. The belay: the location at which belaying takes place. A "good belay" denotes secure anchors for attaching the climber, a "poor belay" less so (see also Stance).

Belayer – The person belaying. The "inactive" climber acts as belayer for the "active" climber.

Belay device – A friction device fitted to the rope and used by the belayer. The device allows the belayer to control the energy generated by a falling climber and arrest their fall.

Bolt – A fixed metal eye through which a karabiner can be clipped for protection when leading, or as a secure anchor for belaying, bottom roping or abseiling. The eye is attached to a rod, which is glued or hammered into a hole specially drilled in the rock.

Bottom roping – A roped system in which the belayer stands at the bottom of the climb.

Bouldering – A general term for climbing without ropes on small boulders or pieces of rock a few metres (feet) off the ground.

Camming device – A mechanical device that can be placed in a crack for protection when leading, or as a secure anchor for belaying, top or bottom roping or abseiling.

Clove hitch – A special knot that is easy to tie and tightens when loaded, but is easily adjusted and untied.

Chock – An old collective word to describe wires and nuts. It comes from the word chockstone, which is a stone or boulder jammed in a crack or gully. A chock is a piece of protection.

Dynamic or dyno – A dynamic or dyno move will involve a directed lunge or jump for a hold. Climbing ropes are dynamic in their nature, absorbing the energy created by a falling climber by stretching.

Edging hold – A positive foothold on which the edge of the rock shoe can get purchase and support, no matter how slight.

Figure-of-eight descender – A friction device used for abseiling.

Figure-of-eight knot – The most commonly used and strongest knot for tying a climber to a belay anchor. However, the knot is difficult to adjust and can be difficult to undo after heavy loading.

Grade – A degree of relative difficulty given to a route. Grading systems vary around the world, but the principle remains the same: that of providing a means to compare difficulty between one climb and another.

Harness – Specially constructed and padded waist belt and leg loops worn by the climber and into which the climbing rope is tied. Massively strong, the harness helps to absorb the energy generated in a fall.

Hold – Anything which can be used by the feet, hands or any other part of the body to aid upward progress.

Jamming – A method of climbing in which any part of the body can be securely jammed into a crack or hole in the rock to aid upward progress. The most common jamming involves the hands and feet.

Karabiner – An aluminium alloy snaplink with a sprung gate most often used to connect the rope with protection when leading and with anchors when belaying. With screwgate (locking) karabiners a special sleeve covers the gate to lock it closed.

Lapse rate – The rate of change in temperature in terms of height above sea level. In most conditions, temperature drops as you walk or climb higher up a mountain. This rate of change will vary depending on weather conditions at the time.

Leading – The process of climbing whereby the first "active" climber on the rope places protection if traditional climbing, or clips bolts if sport climbing, while the second "inactive" climber belays.

Legs – In navigation, a leg is an intermediate stage in reaching an overall destination. For example, in trying to reach your campsite 8 km (5 miles) away, you may, in bad weather, break your journey down into eight legs, each of around a kilometre, going from specific points spotted on your map to the next until you reach your tents and safety.

Lower-off – Most sport climbs have bolts and chains at the top from which the lead climber can be lowered by the belayer.

Magnetic variation – The difference in degrees between magnetic north and grid north, as shown on most maps. This variation will change depending on where you are in the world.

Multipitch – A climb that is longer than one rope length. This implies creating belays as the climb is negotiated, with the leader moving up to the next belay until the top is finally reached.

Nut – A collective word to describe wires and roped nuts. A nut is a piece of protection.

Overhand knot – A knot formed by making a loop and then drawing one end through. It is frequently used to tie off spare rope.

Pacing – In navigation, a means of keeping in touch with how far you are walking when weather conditions provide little or no visibility. Pacing is only used over short distances, up to about 500 m (¼ mile).

Peg – A metal spike with an eye, a peg can be hammered into a crack and the eye clipped for protection when leading, or as a secure anchor for belaying, top roping or abseiling. In the UK pegs are rarely placed when rock climbing, although many remain in place. Corrosion is a problem and they should be carefully inspected before use. Also known as a piton.

Pitch – Climbs that are longer than the climbing rope have to be climbed in stages. Climbers call these stages "pitches".

Piton – See Peg.

Protection – A collective name to describe a bolt, peg, wire, sling, nut, thread or camming device that the leader can clip to the climbing rope for "protection". On traditional climbs protection has to be placed by the leader and removed by the second. On sport climbs the protection is fixed in place.

Prussik – A special knot used for ascending the rope. The knot jams when loaded, but can be moved up the rope when the load is released. They are usually used for self-rescue. Three types of prussik are described in this book: standard, French (autoblock) and Klemheist.

Quickdraw – A loop of nylon tape with a karabiner at each end, it is used for clipping the rope to protection and to facilitate easy movement of the rope through protection when climbing.

Rack – All the protection equipment necessary for two climbers on an average climb.

Rappel – See Abseil.

Rope drag – Unwanted friction created by the rope running over rock and through protection. This usually happens towards the end of a long pitch and can be quite alarming, as the effect is to pull the climber backwards and downwards.

Runner – Short for running belay, which is a technical term for any piece of protection clipped to the rope by the leader.

Seconding – When the leader is securely tied to the belay anchors he or she can belay the second up the climb. Seconding includes belaying the leader, climbing the route second and removing the protection placed by the leader so that it can be used on the next pitch or climb.

Searches – In navigation, a means by which an area of ground can be systematically covered when looking for a specific point or object. Searches are also used when looking for avalanche victims.

Shake out – With exertion, lactic acid builds up, especially in the arm muscles. Hanging each arm in turn and giving it a shake helps to restore blood flow and aids the removal of lactic acid. Anywhere this is possible is called a "shake out".

Shock-load – A sudden unwanted shock exerted on the anchors of a belay or abseil. Shock-loading can cause anchors to fail, which is why it is important to avoid it happening.

Single pitch – A climb that is less than a rope length. In other words, the top of the climb can be reached in one go, without the need to make intermediary belays.

Slack – Slack rope between the climber and belayer is to be avoided as it generates greater shock loads should a fall take place, as well as increasing the distance fallen. However, slack may be needed by the second to remove protection, or by the leader when clippping overhead protection. In this case shout "Slack!".

Sling – A loop of nylon tape, usually factory sewn but sometimes hand-knotted. Slings can be hung over spikes or threaded through holes in the rock and used as protection when leading, or as a secure anchor for belaying, top roping or abseiling.

Smearing – A method of using the foot to maximize friction between rubber and foothold when the hold isn't good enough to give positive edging support. You might also need to smear your hand on a sloper.

Sport climbing – Sport climbs originated in Europe and generally have fixed bolt protection. They have a different ethos and style of climbing than traditional climbs.

Stance – At the end of a pitch the belay may have a good stance or a poor one, regardless of how good the belay anchors are. There may be

excellent anchors, but the stance is a single foothold to stand on, or the anchors may be very poor, but the stance is an excellent, roomy ledge. Most often it is something between the two.

Tape – This is another term for nylon webbing used for quickdrawers, harnesses and slings. Zinc oxide tape is used by many climbers for securing sore finger tendons and for wrapping around the hands to prevent cuts when climbing, especially jamming.

Thread – A situation where a tape sling can be threaded through a feature in the rock and the two loops joined and used as protection when leading, or as a secure anchor for belaying, top roping or abseiling.

Top roping – A climbing system whereby the "active" climber is secured by a rope from above. The belayer may either be below or above the climber.

Traditional climbing – The form of climbing where protection is placed by the lead climber and removed by the second.

Traversing – Any situation where a climber moves horizontally or diagonally to the right or left for a number of moves, or even a full pitch.

Wire – Any aluminium wedge threaded on a wire. In general they are too small for threading on rope or tape. They are used as protection when leading, or as a secure anchor for belaying, top roping or abseiling. Also called nuts and chocks.

Contact Addresses

UNITED KINGDOM
British Mountaineering Council
177–179 Burton Road, West Didsbury,
Manchester M20 2BB

Association of Mountaineering Instructors
c/o MLTB, Capel Curig, Gwynedd LL24 0ET

British Mountain Guides
Capel Curig, Gwynedd LL24 0ET

AUSTRALIA
Australian School of Mountaineering
166B Katoomba Street, Katoomba, NSW 2780

Australian Sports Climbing Federation
GPO Box 3786, Sydney, NSW

CANADA
Alpine Club
PO Box 2040, Indian Flats Road, Canmore,
Alberta T0L 0N0

UNITED STATES
American Alpine Club
710 Tenth Street, Suite 100, Golden, CO 80401

Acknowledgements

No book would be complete without a strong team of writers who not only understand their subjects inside out, but have made decisions in everyday climbing and mountaineering situations based on that knowledge. To that end, the author has been extremely fortunate in having Nigel Shepherd, Nick Banks, Neil Gresham and Ray Wood as co-writers for this book. Thanks also go to Libby Peter for giving technical advice on many of the photographic shoots.

I would also like to thank all those who have either allowed me to trawl through their precious photographic libraries or assisted in providing specially commissioned photographs. These are Ray Wood, Mark Duncalf, Alex Gillespie, Nigel Shepherd, Chris Craggs, Tony Howard, Simon Carter, Graham Parkes, Nick White, David Simmonite and Nick Banks.

George Manley's clear and explicit diagrams have reached the parts that even these excellent photographers cannot reach.

I am grateful to the models Libby Peter, Sam Oliver, Edward Cartwright, Paul Houghoughi, Debbie Birch, Caroline and Simon Hale, Patrick (Patch) Hammond, W Perrin and Gavin Foster; and to Neil Adam and Roger Jones of Bethesda for the loan of historic climbing gear.

Finally, this section would not be complete without a word of thanks to Judith Simons at Anness Publishing and Neil Champion, who had the unenviable task of trying to tie up all the loose ends and deal with a crowd of itinerant climbers who insisted in disappearing to the four corners of the world at the drop of a hat!

The authors and publisher would like to thank the following companies and organizations for their generous help in providing clothing, equipment and facilities:

Troll
Spring Mill, Uppermill, Oldham,
Lancs OL3 6AA (for their harnesses)

Edelrid Safety Products
Shap Road, Industrial Estate, Kendal,
Cumbria LA9 6NZ (for their ropes)

DMM International Ltd
Y Glyn, Llanberis, Gwynedd LL55 4EL
(for their slings, karabiners, chocks, belay devices and rock shoes)

HB Climbing Equipment
24, Llandegai Industrial Estate, Bangor,
Gwynedd LL57 4YH (for their slings, karabiners, chocks and belay devices)

High Places
Globe Centre, Penistone Rd, Sheffield,
Yorks S6 3AE (for their T-shirts and sun hats)

Jagged Globe
45 Mowbray St, Sheffield, Yorks S3 8EN
(for their sweatshirts)

Regatta Ltd
Risol House, Mercury Way, Dumplington,
Urmston, Manchester M41 7RR
(for their fleece jackets and walking trousers)

Royal Robbins UK
16a Mill St, Oakham, Rutland LE15 6EA
(for their clothing)

Schoffel UK
16a Mill St, Oakham, Rutland LE15 6EA
(for their windshell and other waterproof garments)

Sprayway Ltd
16 Chester St, Manchester M1 5GE
(for their windshells, fleece jackets and other clothing)

Stone Monkey
Y Glyn, Llanberis, Gwynedd,LL55 4EL
(for their clothing)

Salomon Taylor Made Ltd
Annecy House, The Lodden Centre, Wade Rd,
Basingstoke, Hants RG248FL
(for their approach shoes)

Plas y Brenin
National Mountain Centre, Capel Currig,
Gwynedd LL24 0ET (for the use of their climbing wall and other facilities)

Index

INDEX

Photo credits

© Simon Carter: pages 244 and 245 t b.
© Chris Craggs: pages 238, 239 b, 240,
241 t b, 242 and 253 t.
© Malc Creasey: pages 5, 11 tl tr, 82 t,
114, 127 and 239.
© Alex Gillespie: pages 10, 100 b, 129 tl,
155, 160 br, 162 t bl, 164 l, 165 t, 171 b,
172 b, 173, 174, 177 tl tr, 179 t, 181 tl tr,
186 tl bl, 189 b, 190, 191, 198, 199 tr and
237 b.
© Neil Gresham: pages 15 tl, 28, 225 tl,
230 and 232 l r.
© Nomad: page 248 b.
© Graham Parkes: page 243 b.
© Nigel Shepherd: pages 11 bl, bc, br, 38 l,
51 l r, 52 t, 53 b, 131 b, 138 r, 156, 157 bl,
165 b, 170, 176, 177 b, 178, 179 b, 180,
182 tl, 184, 185, 186 r, 189, 192, 193,
194 b, 195, 197, 199 tl b, 200 bl, 201,
203 t c b, 236 and 249 t bl br.
© David Simmonite: pages 17 t b, 101 b,
167 b, 168, 219 and 231.
© Paul Twomey: page 16 t.
© Ray Wood: front jacket tl and br;
pages 2 tl cl bl, 3, 4 t, 7, 9, 12, 13 tl tr b,
14 br, 16 b, 20 bl, 23 tr cr, 35 b, 36 b, 38 r,
39 tl, 43 t, 54, 59 r, 64 l r, 66 br, 67 tl tc tr,
68 l c, 69 tl tc tr bl bc br, 71 tr b, 77 l r, 78,
80 l, 83 tl tr, 84, 85 r, 88 l, 103 t, 106 b,
112 tl, 116, 129 br, 132 l r, 134 r, 137 tr,
138 l, 144, 161 t, 163 t, 166 tl tr, 167 t,
169 tr b, 172 t, 188, 200 t, 202, 217, 218 l,
223 tl, 224, 235, 237 t, 239 tr, 246 bl tr,
247 t and 248.